CROSSING A GREAT FRONTIER

ESSAYS ON GEORGE MACDONALD'S PHANTASTES

EDITED BY
JOHN PENNINGTON

Crossing a Great Frontier
Essays on George MacDonald's Phantastes

John Pennington, Editor

Copyright © 2018 John Pennington

Winged Lion Press
Hamden, CT

All rights reserved. Except in the case of quotations embodied in critical articles or reviews, no part of this book may be reproduced or transmitted in any form or by any means, electronic or mechanical, including photocopying, recording, or by any information storage or retrieval system, without written permission of the publisher. For information, contact Winged Lion Press: www.WingedLionPress.com

Cover Design
Thanks to Joyce O'Dell for the cover design based on artwork from 19th century covers for a paired set of Lewis Carroll's books *Alice's Adventures in Wonderland* and *Through the Looking-Glass*

ISBN-13 978-1-935688-16-7

Dedication

To my parents Doris and Elmer Pennington,
who lived in Amberg, Wisconsin,
a sort of fairyland for me growing up.

Acknowledgements

A special thanks goes to a variety of people at St. Norbert College, who provided support in numerous ways. First, to the college for funding my sabbatical project, which you are holding in your hands right now. I would also like to thank Jeff Frick, Dean of the College and Vice President for Academic Affairs, and Paul Johnson, Associate Dean of Humanities, who provided additional monetary support for the editing of this text. In particular, I would like to extol the virtues of Mary Paplham, a graduate of St. Norbert, and one of the best editors I could imagine. Gideon Dobson-Repinski was eager to help with various editing tasks. Natasha Igl, the English assistant was a wonderful proofreader, as was Erika Ditzman, the editorial assistant for *North Wind: A Journal of George MacDonald Studies.* And I would be remiss if I did not thank Lois Velicer, Office Manager of Humanities at St. Norbert, and Kelly Krummel, Administrative Secretary of Humanities at St. Norbert, who provided needed technology support—but, more important, who provided moral support by offering large doses of humor!

Finally, I would like to thank Robert Trexler, of Winged Lion Press, for believing in this project (and for coming up with the title for the volume *and* the cover design); Colin Manlove for reviewing the text, and Roderick McGillis, my co-editor of the annotated edition of *Phantastes* (also by Winged Lion), which complements *Crossing a Great Frontier.* Or is it the other way around!

A Note on the Texts

The articles in *Crossing a Great Frontier* come from a variety of sources—books, articles, and other collections of critical essays. For consistency, this volume uses endnotes for the articles, even when the original used footnotes, though I abide by the documentation style used in each publication, which can vary widely. When an excerpt of an article or book chapter is used, I took the liberty of reordering endnotes. In a few cases, in the spirit of conciseness, I eliminated short block quotations and integrated them as quotations in the text. In a few instances I broke paragraphs into component paragraphs for readability. Finally, I silently corrected any obvious editorial or factual errors in the original manuscripts, which were few.

TABLE OF CONTENTS

Introduction   1
John Pennington

***Phantastes*: Full-Length Adult Fantasies**   15
Richard Reis

Death's Ecstasies: Transformation and Rebirth in George MacDonald's *Phantastes*   23
Joseph Sigman

The Quest for "The Truth": A Reading of George MacDonald's *Phantastes*   53
Keith Wilson

Wells and Cisterns: *Phantastes*   69
Rolland Hein

Circularity in Fantasy: George MacDonald   95
Colin Manlove

The Psychology of the Self in MacDonald's *Phantastes*   121
Max Keith Sutton

Phantastes* and *Lilith   145
David S. Robb

From *Bildungsroman* to Death-Romance: *Phantastes*, *Lilith*, and German Romanticism   169
Stephen Prickett

The Sources of *Phantastes*   195
John Docherty

The Community of the Centre: Structure and Theme in *Phantastes*   207
Roderick McGillis

Meta-*Phantastes*: A Self-Referential Faerie 223
Romance for Men and Women
   Graeme A. Muirhead

The Multiple Realms of George 241
MacDonald's *Phantastes*
   Adrian Gunther

George MacDonald, Julia Kristeva, 261
and the Black Sun
   William Gray

From Fact to Fantasy in Victorian Fiction: 279
Dickens's *Hard Times* and MacDonald's *Phantastes*
   John Pennington

George MacDonald's *Phantastes*: 289
The Spiral Journey to the Goddess
   Bonnie Gaarden

The Angel in the Cosmos: *Phantastes's* 313
Recasting of the New Gentleman
   Kelly Searsmith

Mirrors in MacDonald's *Phantastes*: 335
A Reflexive Structure
   Fernando Soto

Allegory and Aestheticism in the 365
Fantasies of George MacDonald
   Yuri Cowan

Riddled with Evil: Fantasy as Theodicy 387
in George MacDonald's *Phantastes* and *Lilith*
   Courtney Salvey

The Shadow of Anodos: 407
Alchemical Symbolism in *Phantastes*
   Aren Roukema

The Fairy Palace: Sabbath Restoration and Twilight Vision Daniel Gabelman	425
Select Bibliography	439
Contributors	447
Permissions	453
Index	457
Other Books of Interest	468

Introduction
John Pennington

At the end of *Lilith* (1895), George MacDonald's last fantasy novel, Mr. Vane returns from "the region of the seven dimensions" (30) to find himself back in his library. When he gazes upon his books, "they seem to waver as if a wind rippled their solid mass, and another world were about to break through" (358). And that is precisely what fiction does—it transports us to another dimension, providing a vicarious experience that is somehow connected, yet not connected, to the lived world of the reader. To the Victorians, novel reading accomplished (or could accomplish) such transportation. And novels, most especially "realistic" novels, were quickly becoming the most popular form for readers.

But what exactly is a novel? "The truth is that the novel is a genre which resists exact definition," writes Terry Eagleton in *The English Novel: An Introduction*. "The point about the novel, however," continues Eagleton, "is not just that it eludes definitions, but that it actively undermines them" (1).

Charles Dickens sensed this problem of defining an evolving literary form long before Eagleton's claim, as demonstrated in Dickens's Preface to *Bleak House* (1853). "I mention here that everything set forth in these pages concerning the Court of Chancery is substantially true, and within the truth" (5), writes Dickens forcefully. Yet Dickens feels compelled to justify his use of spontaneous combustion as a major—and sensational—plot device, responding to George Henry Lewes's complaint that such a thing "could not possibly be" (6). Dickens defends his choice by presenting numerous cases of such combustion throughout history, though he concludes with an admission: "In Bleak House, I have purposely dwelt upon the romantic side of familiar things" (7). Dickens captures a central moment in the evolution of the novel: what is the obligation of the novel to mirror reality?

In America, Nathaniel Hawthorne knew that defining the kind of novel he was writing was important. He takes pains to describe the legitimacy of his romance *The Scarlet Letter* (1850), which he knew would strain the credibility of what is considered realistic. Hawthorne argues in "The Custom House" (a long introduction to the novel) that a romance hovers in a "neutral territory, somewhere between the real world and fairy-land . . ." (111). Dickens's Preface to *Bleak House* seems a mini-"Custom House" statement. Unlike Hawthorne, who is proud to announce his romantic—dare we say fantastic?—enterprise, Dickens somewhat undermines his own attempt at verisimilitude in the novel, simultaneously arguing for truth in representation *and* for romantic or fantastical trappings. Of course, the romance has always had affinities to the realistic novel, often working in consort, as Hawthorne and Dickens demonstrate. Terry Eagleton notes that Sir Walter Scott excelled in such a combination: "Romance trades in the marvelous, and realism in the mundane; so that by blending these two narrative forms into one, Scott hoped to forge a literary style true to both the revolutionary drama and the everyday experience of his age" (103).

Within this climate of speculation of what a novel should do, George MacDonald published *Phantastes* (1858). It boldly claims to be a *Faerie Romance for Men and Women* and was an oddity compared to the wealth of novels published at this time. During that same year, George Eliot (Mary Ann Evans) published *Scenes of Clerical Life*, three stories that centered on religious tensions in England over a 50-year period—and certainly a work founded in realism, not in romance. Lewes, the critic of Dickens's spontaneous combustion, eventually became a life-partner of Eliot and defended the importance of truth in literary representation (what Eliot was pursuing in her work). In a review of German fiction, Lewes argues that *realism* should be the dominant literary genre and complains that "German novels are, for the most part, dreary inflictions . . . because they have so little realism that they resemble nothing on earth or under it" (287). That Dickens published *A Tale of Two Cities* in 1859, a historical novel about the French Revolution, suggests that Dickens believed novels might best convey truth in a more realistic setting, though his novels continued to flirt with the "romantic side of familiar things": *Hard Times* (1854) is a satire on fact-based Utilitarian education and uses fairy-tale motifs to counter Coketown's lack of imagination, and *Little Dorrit* (1857) includes an interpolated fairy tale that is in keeping with the spirit of *Phantastes*. The major novels of the 1850s, including the above by Dickens, tend to bear out such a generalization about the emphasis on the real in fiction: William Makepeace Thackeray's *Pendennis* (1850), *Henry Esmond* (1852), *The Newcomers* (1855), and *The Virginians* (1859); Elizabeth Gaskell's *Cranford* (1853) and *North and South* (1855); Charlotte Brontë's *Vilette* (1853); Anthony Trollope's *The Warden* (1855) and *Barchester Towers* (1857); and George Eliot's *Adam Bede* (1859).

Essays on George MacDonald's *Phantastes*

Imagine when *Phantastes: A Faerie Romance for Men and Women* appeared by a writer, who had published just one major work, a poetic drama *Within or Without* (1855). In this period of prized realism, MacDonald chose to write an unabashed fantasy. *Phantastes*, now seen as a foundational book in the rise of modern fantasy practiced by J. R. R. Tolkien and C. S. Lewis, is a remarkable work in its own right. But its connections to the rise of the more realistic novels of the nineteenth century suggests an originality that eluded many readers of MacDonald's day. The faerie romance made manifest Dickens's "romantic side of familiar things," except that MacDonald made familiar the invented world of *faerie*. *Phantastes* was a radical and subversive novel that challenged literary conventions, mirroring other genre-bending works such as Thomas Moore's *Lalla Rookh* (1817), Thomas Carlyle's *Sartor Resartus* (1836), Sara Coleridge's *Phantasmion* (1837), and George Meredith's *The Shaving of Shagpat* (1856).

To understand how the realistic novel defined the nineteenth century is to better understand the subversive quality of *Phantastes*. George Levine in *The Realistic Imagination: English Fiction from Frankenstein to Lady Chatterley* ferrets out the nuances of this entity called the realistic novel of the nineteenth century. "Realism, as a literary method," writes Levine,

> can ... be defined as a self-conscious effort, usually in the name of some moral enterprise of truth and extending the limits of human sympathy, to make literature appear to be describing directly not some other language but reality itself (whatever that may be taken to be); in this effort, the writer must self-contradictorily dismiss previous conventions of representation while, in effect, establishing new ones. (617)

Realism, furthers Levine, "is a mode that depends heavily on our commonsense expectation that there are direct connections between word and thing" (618).

One is reminded of Humpty Dumpty's claim to Alice in *Through the Looking-Glass* (1872): "When *I* use a word ... it means just what I choose it to mean—neither more nor less." Alice retorts: "The question is ... whether you *can* make words mean so many different things" (161). Humpty Dumpty responds to Alice by displaying his theory of language by interpreting "Jabberwocky," ultimately proving that words do not necessarily have a direct connection to something recognizable. Humpty Dumpty promotes nonsense. MacDonald is acutely aware that words cannot reflect reality, and in *Phantastes* he flaunts the entire enterprise of realism. Yet MacDonald is not interested in nonsense for nonsense's sake—there is an underlying meaning to MacDonald's fantastical method. In chapter IV Anodos admits: "But it is no use trying to account for things in Fairy Land; and one who travels there soon learns to forget the very idea of doing so, and takes everything as it comes; like a child, who being in a chronic condition of wonder, is surprised at nothing" (24). A few paragraphs later, Anodos, in his attempt to describe the horrific hand of the Ash-tree, says, "I can only try to describe something that is not it, but seems somewhat parallel to it; or at least is suggested by it" (27).

MacDonald was hoping that readers—and critics—would agree with his notions of what is "real." His idea of the real was more cemented in German Romanticism and Christian Mysticism than in the popular realistic and social novels that pervaded the 1850s. As might be expected, when *Phantastes* was published in 1858, the work confounded critics, for good or ill. The most famous review, the one that generated the ire of MacDonald, was from the *Athenæum*, which called *Phantastes* an "allegory" that was "a riddle that will not be read." The critic lamented that while the best of allegory "shows us life moving with its shadow," MacDonald had given the reader "the shadow without the life which should cause it to him, and account for it to us" (580). Thus the *Athenæum* concluded that the work was a "confusedly furnished second-hand symbol-shop" (580) and hoped that MacDonald's "mistake" would not be repeated again. Another review in the *Spectator*, while chastising MacDonald for his inconsistent weaving of classical and fairy mythologies into the novel, does conclude that it "is a very remarkable book": "There is in it an extraordinary fertility of invention and considerable powers of fancy" (1286). Maybe the most astute reading of *Phantastes* comes from an appraisal in the *British Quarterly Review* (1859) that found MacDonald's "glimpse into the tempting land of Faerie" intoxicating, yet concludes: "Not a few will spend a charmed hour over the mystic fascinations of this volume; whilst others, we venture to predict, will incontinently return against its hero—perchance against its author too—a verdict of 'determination of nonsense to the brain'" (297).

Phantastes confused and confounded its readers. Compared to the popular realistic novels of the day, this fantasy seemed nonsense. Critics today still confront the "hesitant" acceptance of *Phantastes*. Ironically, the hesitance is not for its importance to the development of modern fantasy, but for its importance in the canon of the great realistic novels of the nineteenth century. *Crossing a Great Frontier: Essays on George MacDonald's* Phantastes is a monument to the evolving critical discussion of this fantasy novel as an important mid-Victorian work and as one foundational to fantasy literature.

When MacDonald died in 1905, he was seen as a marginal novelist at best. On the centenary of MacDonald's birth in 1924, two works appeared that spurred the reassessment of *Phantastes* specifically and MacDonald generally. H. J. C. Grierson in "George MacDonald," for *The Aberdeen University Review*, admits that "neither his novels of everyday life nor his more popular fairy tales can stand quite on their own legs as stories . . . ," yet he posits that *Phantastes* "has proved itself a delightful fairy tale pure and simple, to readers young and old, no one can re-read it without feeling how instinct it is with MacDonald's deepest thoughts about life and death" (9). Early in his review, Grierson muses over MacDonald's literary legacy:

> Is George MacDonald read to-day? I cannot say. I have not read him myself for many years or met readers, except children—lovers of some of his fairy tales. I asked a young man of letters, whose father had known George MacDonald, and he could only tell me that in preparing a new edition of a biographical dictionary he had cut out most of the article on the poet to make room for the Prime Minister. Which will have the largest space in 2024? . . . . (2)

In 2018, MacDonald is still read by a devoted audience. In another seven years, a magical span in fairy tales, will we finally be able to answer Grierson's question more definitively? The answer is a resounding, "Yes." *Phantastes* has never been out of print, though it remains a hidden gem without the popularity of Carroll's *Alice* books (1865; 1872) or even Charles Kingsley's *The Water-Babies* (1863). Yet, *Phantastes*'s reach is great. Fantasy reigns supreme today. It reigns in popular culture, including literature and film. J. K. Rowling and Philip Pullman, maybe the two most influential fantasy writers practicing now, are indebted to C. S. Lewis and J. R. R. Tolkien (whose popularity show no signs of waning). All these authors write under the shadow of MacDonald.

Greville MacDonald, son of George, was also concerned about his father's literary legacy, and he channels Grierson's concern. In 1924, the year of Grierson's reassessment of George, Greville published *George MacDonald and His Wife*, a biographical work that has become foundational to MacDonald studies. Greville's rehabilitation of his father and his work, however, actually began in 1905, the year of MacDonald's death, and focused on *Phantastes*. Greville produced a special edition of *Phantastes*, with illustrations by George's long-time collaborator, Arthur Hughes. In the Preface to that edition, Greville provides a rationale for the newly illustrated edition: first, Greville desires to provide illustrations to replace those of John Bell, who illustrated an unauthorized edition of *Phantastes*—the MacDonald family generally disliked the images to his fantasy—and to secure copyright, which was still a major concern of writers. Second, Greville wants "to pay a small tribute" to his father and remind readers of this early fantasy novel that "rings with the dominant chord of his life's purpose and work" so "that wider knowledge and love of the book should be made possible." Finally, Greville wishes readers to experience Arthur Hughes's illustrations, thereby giving readers "some perception of the brotherhood between George MacDonald and Arthur Hughes" (vii).

To help with this rehabilitation project in *George MacDonald and His Wife*, Greville commissioned G. K. Chesterton to write a critical introduction to the biography. Chesterton was a well-respected writer, penning a biography of Dickens (1906), the fantasy *The Man Who Was Thursday* (1908), and the exceedingly popular Father Brown mystery stories (51 in all) that included one mystery called "The Fairy Tale of Father Brown." In the Introduction, Chesterton ignites the critical debate on MacDonald, writing: "I can testify to a book that has made a difference to my whole existence, which helped me to see things which even so real a revolution as a change of religious allegiance has substantially only crowned and confirmed." That book is *The Princess and the Goblin* (1872), which, to Chesterton, "remains the most real, the most realistic, in the exact sense of the phrase, the most like life" (9). Chesterton proceeds to place MacDonald in a literary historical context, particularly comparing him to Thomas Carlyle. Chesterton's focus, however, centers on MacDonald's religious significance, not on his literary stature, admitting that

> in noting that he may well have this place in history in the sense of religious and of national history, I make no attempt here to fix his place in literature. He is in any case one of the kind that it is most difficult to fix. He wrote nothing empty; but he wrote much that is rather too full, and of which the appreciation depends rather on a sympathy with the substance than on the first sight of the form. (15)

As early (or late) as 1924, the jury was out on the greatness of MacDonald's work. Chesterton pinpoints a central MacDonald tension: the tension over his importance as a writer of the sacred—that was made most manifest in his more realistic novels—and his limitations as a novelist.

Another later critic picked up where Chesterton left off, articulating MacDonald's legacy as a writer of the fantastic. That person is C. S. Lewis. Lewis has done more than any writer to popularize MacDonald—*and* to question his artistic legacy. In *The Allegory of Love: A Study in Medieval Tradition* (1936), a seminal work in literary criticism, Lewis examines the medieval emphasis on allegory as "the Dominant Form." Lewis contends that such a dominant form often leads to "monotony," for

> a dominant form tends to attract to itself writers whose talents would have fitted them much better for work of some other kind. Thus the retired Cowper writes satire in the eighteenth century; or in the nineteenth a mystic and natural symbolist like George Macdonald is seduced into writing novels. (232)

For Lewis, the critic should be able to discern good writing from the bad—"between the poetic use and the fashionable abuse" (233). Lewis focuses on MacDonald's choice to conform to the conventions of the day that dictated novels (realistic novels, specifically) be the dominant form. Lewis implies that MacDonald's true genius lies elsewhere—in fantastical works.

The most important statement by Lewis on MacDonald can be found in his 1947 anthology *George MacDonald: 365 Readings*. His Preface has taken on a life of its own. First, the Preface appeared in the dual edition of *Phantastes and Lilith* in 1962 by Victor Gollancz and then by Eerdmans in their dual edition first published in 1964. Eerdmans continues to reprint the Preface in the single edition of *Phantastes* (beginning in 1981 and updated in 2000), as well as in its edition of *Lilith* (same dates). Lewis's Preface defines MacDonald for many readers today. Lewis begins by stating that his concern with MacDonald is "not as a writer but as a Christian teacher" (xxv), thus emphasizing the religious dimension of MacDonald that attracts readers today. All one has to do is log onto The George MacDonald Society Facebook page to follow the MacDonald devotees.

Lewis admits that at the time of first reading *Phantastes*, his world-view did not really include Christianity. Yet he claims that upon reading MacDonald's fantasy he "had crossed a great frontier" and that *Phantastes* performed a kind of religious conversion to him: "What it actually did to me was to convert, even to baptize . . . my imagination . . ." (xxxiii) into "the real universe, the divine, magical, terrifying, and ecstatic reality in which we all live. I should have been shocked in my teens if anyone had told me that what I learned to love in *Phantastes* was goodness" (xxxiv). Lewis's reach is so extensive that he has even inspired the name to this volume of essays on *Phantastes*!

That goodness did not necessarily extend to the quality of MacDonald's writing. Lewis bluntly states: "If we define Literature as an art whose medium is words, then certainly MacDonald has no place in its first rank." Not the kindest of praise. But Lewis adds a punctuation "dash" and continues "—perhaps not even in its second" (xxvi). A critical dagger! Lewis is more concerned about the "goodness" of MacDonald as a religious writer, reflected in the majority of passages included in the anthology. Yet Lewis feels compelled to justify MacDonald's fantasy writing to readers since that is where MacDonald excelled. Lewis is caught in a double-bind, a catch 22. Lewis argues that "fantasy that hovers between the allegorical and mythopoeic," the kind MacDonald excels in, is a lesser form of literature, thus creating a divide between serious literature with an "L" and the popular fictions, fantasy included: "The critical problem with which we are confronted is whether this art—the art of myth-making—is a species of the literary art" (xxvi). "No," seems to be Lewis's conclusion. But why? To Lewis, mythopoeic fantasy goes beyond words since "the mere pattern of events is all that matters. Any means of communication whatever which succeeds in lodging those events in our imagination has, as we say 'done the trick.' After that you can throw the means of communication away" (xxvi). Thus Lewis, while extolling the virtues of MacDonald, simultaneously undercuts MacDonald and the literariness of fantasy.

In effect, much criticism on MacDonald has pegged him as a mythopoeic writer, a writer of a genre that appears less serious as legitimate literature. The countless critical books on fantasy as a genre or mode, from Todorov's *The Fantastic*, Rosemary Jackson's *Fantasy: A Literature of Subversion*, Kathryn Hume's *Fantasy and Mimesis*, to Lucie Armitt's *Theorizing the Fantastic*, have as their charge an implicit defense of fantasy, which seems a shadow fiction compared to the more prestigious realism of "literary art," to use Lewis's phrase. In fact, Ann Swinfen's important study is called *In Defense of Fantasy*. *Phantastes* was published between Dickens's *Little Dorrit* (1857) and *A Tale of Two Cities* (1859), two towering novels of the mid-Victorian age. That fact alone appears to support Lewis's apology for the inferior literariness of fantasy fiction.

As you might suspect, Lewis is a mixed-blessing for MacDonald's reputation as a writer. The same holds true for the first full-length critical analysis of MacDonald's work, Robert Lee Wolff's *The Golden*

Essays on George MacDonald's *Phantastes*

Key: A Study of the Fiction of George MacDonald (1961). Wolff boldly claims that MacDonald's *Phantastes* and *Lilith* "form almost a new literary genre in themselves" (4). This is high praise certainly, until we encounter a somewhat dismissive statement that begins Wolff's Preface: "George MacDonald's fiction has certain features that give it a compelling interest of its own: to students of comparative literature, of theology, of psychology, and of the Victorian Age; and even to the reader who is a student of nothing at all" (vii). Prefaces have not been entirely kind to MacDonald.

Wolff's first sentence in his Preface is followed by a long quotation from, you might guess, Lewis. In fact, Wolff provides an excerpt from *The Personal Heresy. A Controversy* (1939) by E. M. W. Tillyard and C. S. Lewis. In that work, Lewis defines two kinds of poetry: "the greatest" that captures "'just representation of general nature'" and a lesser form (like MacDonald's writing) that "give[s] [one] a new and nameless sensation" (vii). Thus from the start of *The Golden Key*, Wolff, following in the footsteps of Lewis, seems driven by the belief that MacDonald is more an interesting curiosity than a bona-fide first-rate writer.

Wolff also popularized a critical approach to MacDonald that many critics have embraced—Freudian psychoanalysis. Wolff argues that all of MacDonald's work reflects his desire for a lost mother: "Of George MacDonald we know that all his life he preserved the record of his weaning as his most precious and secret possession. He longed for a mother, and repressed the longing. He felt rebellion against his father, whom he also loved dearly, and this gave him deep feelings of guilt" (372) that reflected "so much hatred for mankind" (374). An early work such as *Phantastes* "reflects MacDonald's own personal sorrows, and his own outlook on life and death" (46) and finds Anodos searching for his sexual awakening as he quests after a mother-figure, further leading to guilt and shame. *Phantastes* is a narrative of loss. Wolff finds a darker story of loss in *Lilith* and suggests that "MacDonald was not Job but God tried him as hard," finally concluding about *Phantastes* and *Lilith*: "And despite their Victorian conventionality in form, their often shoddy style, their interminable sermonizing, their lack of invention, their clumsiness, and frequent absurdity in plotting, MacDonald's novels strike one as off-key and somehow memorable" (379). Faint praise, indeed.

Lewis and Wolff unintentionally define many of the parameters that frame the literary criticism on MacDonald. Those parameters can be seen in the various essays in *Crossing a Great Frontier*. First, Lewis's use of the verb *baptize* (the Eerdmans's editions use *baptise*) to describe his sensation reading *Phantastes* plays into the notion that MacDonald is a religious writer. Second, Lewis's argument that MacDonald is a "mythopoeic" writer places him in the lineage of other myth-based fantasists that include the Inklings—Lewis, J. R. R. Tolkien, and Charles Williams. Maybe as important, Lewis's contention that MacDonald's brand of mythmaking may not be the highest order of literary achievement since such stories do not demand a sensitivity to language—"you can throw the means of communication away" (xxvii)—tempts critics to justify or to apologize for MacDonald's "lack" as a major writer. Thus Lewis has done more than anyone to popularize MacDonald *and* to marginalize MacDonald in literary history. Third, Wolff in *The Golden Key* suggests that psychoanalysis is the golden key for interpreting MacDonald. Critics either challenge Wolff's more vulgar Freudian reading, or push for a more complex Freudian theory via poststructural appropriations of Freud by Donald Winnicott, Melanie Klein, Jacques Lacan, or Julia Kristeva. In addition, many of the anti-Freud critics push a Jungian reading, some arguing that a Jungian reading complements the kind of mythopoetic fantasy that MacDonald creates. Following Lewis, Wolff also hints at the "lesser quality" of MacDonald's literary creations, and his tepid reading of *Phantastes* has prompted critics to respond to Wolff's censure.

Crossing a Great Frontier is a collection of critical essays tracing the critical enterprise that cements the reputation of *Phantastes* as a vital novel in the Victorian canon *and* as a foundational one in the development of modern fantasy. In addition, the collection grapples with the anxiety of critical influence created by Lewis and Wolff.

The organization of this volume is straightforward: the essays are arranged chronologically, which provides an intriguing look into the evolution of criticism on *Phantastes*. In *Toward an Aesthetic of Reception*, Hans Robert Jauss claims that "the historical life of a literary work is unthinkable without the active participation of its addressees. For it is only through the process of its mediation that the work enters into the changing horizon-of-experience of a continuity in which the perpetual inversion occurs from simple reception to critical understanding, from passive to active reception, from recognized aesthetic norms to a new production that surpasses them" (19). Jauss's "aesthetics of reception" (19) situates a writer's critical reputation over time as readers' (and critics') needs and expectations change. "The coherence of literature as an event," writes Jauss, "is primarily mediated in the horizon of expectations of the literary experience of contemporary and later readers, critics, and authors" (22). Jauss's "literary evolution" (34) suggests that a work's aesthetic response transforms—positively or negatively—according to the readers' views over time. Current MacDonald scholarship, consequently, is directly related to past criticism, and contemporary attitudes toward MacDonald will influence MacDonald studies for the future. *Crossing a Great Frontier* traces the horizon of expectations that has defined MacDonald scholarship on *Phantastes* historically, and may suggest to readers the future direction or directions for MacDonald studies.

The essays that follow can be classified in ways that tend to address the anxiety of critical interpretation raised by Lewis and Wolff. One major category critics explore is MacDonald as primarily a *religious writer*, *Phantastes* reflecting that perspective (Hein, Wilson, Robb, Salvey, and Gabelman are key examples). Another category can be seen as a *structural and thematic* cluster, whereby critics defend or describe—or apologize—for *Phantastes*'s seemingly plotless work (here we could place Reis, Manlove, McGillis, Gunther, Soto, and Roukema). Many of the essays in this collection also confront the *psychological approach*—Freudian, Jungian, or post-structural Lacanian and Kristevan readings (Sigman, Sutton, Gaarden, and Gray). Finally, critics focus on MacDonald as a Victorian writer, examining his work in light of its *cultural context or genre exploration* (Prickett, Docherty, Searsmith, Muirhead, Pennington, and Cowan).

Crossing a Great Frontier is the first collection of critical essays devoted solely to MacDonald's first fantasy novel. This collection is a companion to *Behind the Back of the North Wind: Critical Essays on George MacDonald's Classic Children's Book* (Winged Lion, 2011), edited by John Pennington and Roderick McGillis, which focused on *At the Back of the North Wind* (Broadview, 2011). There are excellent volumes of collected essays on MacDonald—*For the Childlike*, *The Gold Thread*, *A Noble Unrest*, *George MacDonald: Literary Heritage and Heirs*, *Rethinking George MacDonald: Contexts and Contemporaries*—but none of these collections focus on a single work. The recent collection, *Lilith in a New Light*, is an exception, concentrating on MacDonald's last fantasy novel. The essays in that volume focus around a central question crucial to *Lilith*—what to make of the fantasy's structure and ending, again leading critics to defend or critique MacDonald's storytelling prowess.

The collection of essays that you will soon begin reading is an omnibus of some of the most significant and influential interpretations of *Phantastes* over time.

Speaking of time. *Phantastes* begins as Anodos celebrates his 21st birthday and ends with his return from Fairy Land, which, he claims, took 21 days, yet feels like 21 years. To keep to the spirit of Anodos's—and MacDonald's—fascination with the number 21, *Crossing a Great Frontier* contains 21 essays canvassing a large swath of criticism on *Phantastes*. Anodos ends his narrative with a simple, "And so, *Farewell*." And this Introduction will follow suit: "And so, *Read well*."

Works Cited

Carroll, Lewis. *Alice in Wonderland*. 3rd ed. Ed. Donald Gray. Norton, 2013.

Chesterton, G. K. Introduction. *George MacDonald and His Wife*. 1924. By Greville MacDonald. Johannesen, 1998. 9-15.

Dickens, Charles. Preface. *Bleak House*. Ed. Nicola Bradbury. Penguin, 2003. 5-7.

Eagleton, Terry. *The English Novel: An Introduction*. Blackwell, 2005.

Grierson, H. J. C. "George MacDonald." *The Aberdeen University Review*, vol. 12, no. 35, Nov. 1924. 1-13.

Harriman, Lucas H. *Lilith in a New Light: Essays on the George MacDonald Fantasy Novel*. McFarland, 2008.

Hawthorne, Nathaniel. "The Custom House." *The Scarlet Letter*. 1850. Riverside ed. Ed. Rita K. Gollin. Houghton Mifflin, 2002. 87-117.

Jauss, Hans Robert. *Toward an Aesthetic of Reception*. U of Minnesota P, 1982.

Levine, George. *The Realistic Imagination: English Fiction from Frankenstein to Lady Chatterley*. U of Chicago P, 1981.

Lewes, George Henry. "Realism in Art: Recent German Fiction." *Westminster Review*, October 1858. 271-87.

Lewis, C. S. *The Allegory of Love*. Oxford UP, 1936.

—, ed. Preface. *George MacDonald: 365 Readings*. 1947. Collier, 1986.

MacDonald, George. *Phantastes*. 1858. Ed. Roderick McGillis and John Pennington. Winged Lion, 2017.

—. *Lilith*. 1895. Johannesen, 2001.

MacDonald, Greville. *George MacDonald and His Wife*. 1924. Johannesen, 1998.

—. Preface. *Phantastes*. 1905. By George MacDonald. Dover, 2005. vii.

McGillis, Roderick, ed. *For the Childlike: George MacDonald's Fantasies for Children*. Children's Literature Association and Scarecrow Press, 1992.

—. *George MacDonald: Literary Heritage and Heirs*. Zossima Press, 2008.

MacLachlan, Christopher, and John Patrick Pazdziora and Ginger Stelle, eds. *Rethinking George MacDonald: Contexts and Contemporaries*. Scottish Literature International, 2013.

Pennington, John, and Roderick McGillis, ed. *Behind the Back of the North Wind: Critical Essays on George MacDonald's Classic Children's Book*. Winged Lion, 2011.

Raeper, William, ed. *The Gold Thread: Essays on George MacDonald*. Edinburgh UP, 1990.

Rev. of *Phantastes*. *Athenæum*, no. 1619, Nov. 6, 1858. 580.

Rev. of *Phantastes*. *Spectator*, Dec. 1858. 1286.

Rev. of *Phantastes*. *British Quarterly Review*, vol. 29, 1859. 296-97.

Webb, Jean, ed. *A Noble Unrest: Contemporary Essays on George MacDonald*. Cambridge Scholars Publishing, 2007.

Phantastes: Full-length Adult Fantasies
Richard Reis
From *George MacDonald's Fiction*

MacDonald's masterpieces are the two full-length, thoroughly symbolic fantasies for adults, *Phantastes* and *Lilith*. In these books, as in *The Princess and the Goblin*, *The Princess and Curdie*, *At the Back of the North Wind*, "The Light Princess," and "The Golden Key," his symbolic techniques reach their fullest realization. And, since MacDonald wrote these two works with adult readers in mind, he includes in them an admixture of terror and evil which he largely omitted from the works for children, presumably for fear of frightening his readers. Both *Phantastes* and *Lilith* are serious, exciting, richly textured, and crammed with astounding imaginative strokes. Because of their excellence, I draw most heavily upon these two works for examples of the typical devices found throughout MacDonald's imaginative fiction. Yet the two stories are in some respects very unlike each other, as might be expected from the fact that *Phantastes* was published in 1858 and *Lilith* in 1895. *Lilith* is darker and less triumphant, *Phantastes* more in the tradition of the heroic Romance whose hero succeeds in the end. They are even more different in plot: *Phantastes* is looser, less integrated, like "The Golden Key"; *Lilith* is more tightly constructed, like "The Light Princess."

(A) *Phantastes*. The word "Phantastes" is taken from the name of a character in Phineas Fletcher's early seventeenthcentury Spenserian pastiche, *The Purple Island* (1633), but I have been able to discover no particular resemblance between Fletcher's work and MacDonald's. What seems to be significant is that Edmund Spenser and his imitators "founded" the symbolic fantasy for adults, at least in English, although they wrote in verse. MacDonald's *Phantastes* is the earliest such work in English prose, so far as I know. Professor Wolff is no doubt correct, however, in tracing the major influence upon MacDonald, not to Spenser and the Spenserians, but to the German Romantic prose works of such writers as Novalis, Jean Paul Richter, and E. T. A. Hoffmann; Wolff does an admirable job of tracing such influences. The question of the literary ancestry of the genre is of some importance, especially because of the important twentieth-century works in the form by such writers as Franz Kafka, C. S. Lewis, J. R. R. Tolkien, and Mervyn Peake. Lin Carter, who edits the Adult Fantasy Series published by Ballantine Books, argues that William

Crossing a Great Frontier

Morris's *The Wood Beyond the World* (1895) is the first English prose fantasy for adults; but there is reason to believe that Carter came to Morris first and learned about MacDonald only later. Primacy, insofar as it is important, clearly belongs to MacDonald's *Phantastes*.

The protagonist and narrator of *Phantastes* is named Anodos, a Greek word usually interpreted as meaning "a way back." Wolff, however, states in *The Golden Key* that it means "pathless" (47); either significance seems to fit the story, in that Anodos is a young man who does not know where he is going, and in that the story indicates his unknown goal as finding "a way back" to the guiltlessness of childhood. I personally suspect that MacDonald had "a way back" in mind, since that phrase occurs a couple of times in the text.

On the day after his twenty-first birthday, Anodos is assigned by his family the bedroom which had belonged to his dead father (his mother is also dead), where he explores his father's old desk. While he is searching for relics, Anodos comes upon a tiny, lovely creature who identifies herself as his "fairy grandmother," a variation upon the traditional "fairy godmother" also used in *The Princess and the Goblin*. When Anodos moves as if to kiss the apparition, she warns him that one may not make love to one's grandmother. Wolff, who cites this passage as evidence of an Oedipal syndrome, points out that MacDonald kept in a secret drawer of his own desk a letter from his mother to his father, expressing sorrow at the infant George's difficulties in being weaned. The psychoanalysis is interesting and even almost convincing, but the Oedipal interpretation is quite irrelevant to the appreciation of *Phantastes* as literature. It may at least be argued that MacDonald was no more of an Oedipus than most of us and that, as in "The Light Princess," he was perfectly aware of what he was doing: dramatizing and symbolizing a universal psychic phenomenon, not because it was unconsciously repressed in himself, but because he knew it to be everywhere.

The "grandmother" informs Anodos that he is about to visit fairyland, and he goes to sleep in apprehension. The next morning, he awakens to the second of his adventures:

> I suddenly, as one who wakes to the consciousness that the sea has been moaning about him for hours, or that the storm has been howling around his window all night, became aware of the sound of running water near me; and, looking out of bed, I saw that a large green marble basin, in which I was wont to wash, . . . was overflowing like a spring; and that a stream of clear water was running over the carpet. . .

> My dressing-table was an old-fashioned piece of furniture of black oak, . . . elaborately carved in foliage, of which ivy formed the chief part. The nearer end of this table remained just as it had been, but on the further end a singular change had commenced. I happened to fix my eyes on a little cluster of ivy leaves. The first of these was evidently the work of the carver; the next looked curious; the third was unmistakably ivy; and just beyond it a tendril of clematis had twined itself about the gilt handle of one of my drawers. . . . I thought it high time to get up; and, springing from my bed, my bare feet alighted upon a cool green sward; and although I dressed in all haste, I found myself completing my toilet under the boughs of a great tree.[1]

This passage is an example of what Auden calls "dream-realism." Things do, after all, happen this way in our dreams; the elaborateness of details is characteristic not of dreams themselves, which are vague, but rather of the way we rationalize and make coherent the uncanny changes of a dream when we try to tell someone about it. MacDonald is putting into practice his own critical theory about the invention of other worlds with their own laws, consistent in themselves but quite unlike the laws of this world, and partaking of the nature of that dream world which is our deepest insight into what the afterlife may be like. It may be noted also that the hero's casual, offhand, unastonished acceptance of this strange wakening is just the way we react to the odd events of dreams when we are still dreaming; it is not until we awaken that the strangeness of dream-events strikes us as impossible. Auden calls the phenomenon "dream-realism" because, as in realistic fiction, the plain "truth" is reported matter-of-factly.

Anodos is now in fairyland, where he undergoes a great many equally dreamlike experiences. What may be called the "shape" of the plot is remarkably unstructured: episodes succeed one another without apparent causal relationship or interconnection (except insofar as they all happen to the same protagonist). The reader feels that the order of Anodos's adventures might often be shuffled without loss of coherence. The protagonist is generally traveling eastward, but a spatial as well as temporal rearrangement of his encounters would not be disturbing; we feel that he is not so much making progress in his spiritual education as simply adding to the number of his experiences. Along the way he stops overnight at a succession of houses, huts, cottages, and palaces which he conveniently arrives at just as the sun is setting. Many of these buildings are inhabited by middle-aged and old women who give Anodos advice and explain the nature of fairyland to him; he usually fails to heed or understand what they tell him, and then departs the next morning, none the wiser. *Phantastes* is what Auden calls a "chain adventure story," full of events which are strung out like beads on a string (the string being the central character, who alone connects the episodes) rather than interconnected into a tight network with every event and character connected by causality and relationship to every other. In this, the plot of *Phantastes* resembles what is called the picaresque novel, a Renaissance genre in which the rogue-hero goes from one place to another when a locality "gets too hot for him" because of his pranks and seductions; or it resembles a tale of knight-errantry ("errant" means "wandering"), in which the hero, after each conquest, moves on to whatever adventure awaits him next. Spenser's *The Faerie Queene* and many long sections of Malory's *Morte Darthur* have this kind of plot-structure.

Despite its loose organization, the plot of *Phantastes* does have a certain degree of coherence, provided by several devices. For one thing, it may be read as an allegorical representation of the first twenty-one years of Anodos's life. The story begins just after his twenty-first birthday, and at the end Anodos makes a significant remark upon returning to the real world and to his family: "I had been gone, they told me, twenty-one days. To me it seemed twenty-one years."[2] Presumably, therefore, we are to read *Phantastes* as if each of its episodes corresponds to a childhood or youthful experience of its narrator—but this is not easy to do, since we have little information about the first twenty-one years of Anodos's life to compare with his possibly corresponding adventures in fairyland. Furthermore, as Professor Wolff insists, the story may possibly be read not merely as an analogical biography of Anodos but as an autobiography of MacDonald himself. Wolff's chief suggestion toward this kind of interpretation is the Oedipal motif already mentioned, but I can think of at least one other. At one point, Anodos forms an alliance with two other young men, sons of a local king, who "adopt" Anodos as a third brother. The three enter into a pact to rid the countryside of three giants who have been harassing the kingdom. Each kills a giant in the ensuing battle, but Anodos survives while the other two die as the giants do. This otherwise detached episode is, to anyone who has read the biography of George MacDonald, clearly an allegorical representation of the fact that George and his brothers Alec and John all contracted tuberculosis in their youth, and only George survived it. As always, it is the moral lesson of the adventure that is important, for MacDonald's reader could hardly be expected to know about the family's troubles with consumption. After the battle, Anodos delivers a dungeonful of prisoners who had been captured by the giants and becomes the hero of the hour. But he is uneasy in his triumph: "I was almost ashamed that I was alive, while they, the true-hearted, were no more . . . I released the prisoners, knights and ladies, all in sad condition from the cruelties and neglects of the giants. It humbled me to see them crowding round me with thanks, when in truth the glorious brothers, lying dead by their lonely tower, were those to whom the thanks belonged."[3] But reading *Phantastes* as an autobiographical allegory throughout would no doubt be unwise. MacDonald frequently expressed his distrust of mere allegory as sterile equation-mongering, and he could hardly have had an emotional experience precisely equivalent to each adventure of Anodos. And even if he did, we lack knowledge of the details of MacDonald's childhood which we would have to know in order to establish a one-to-one correspondence; further, it would not be worth doing for the appreciation of *Phantastes*, for the work's merits as literature must extend beyond mere autobiographical allegory. Nevertheless, the allegorical-autobiography aspect of the story does provide a suggestion of unity in a plot otherwise rather incoherent.

Another unifying aspect of the plot lies in the fact that several characters do reappear in different episodes, although most are met only once. The two most important of these are Sir Percivale, taken from the late medieval Arthurian Romances, and a young woman whom Anodos awakens into life and falls in love with. Percivale first appears in rusty armor, the stain having been caused by his having been seduced (we gather) by a fairyland inhabitant called the Aldermaiden (she is a tree spirit, and a sinister one, as is the Ash; Oak, Elm, and Beech are benevolent, while Birch is flighty and undependable). Percivale reappears from time to time, rescuing Anodos from danger on several occasions and, in the process of doing noble deeds, gradually gets rid of the rust on his armor. As for the woman, who also is recurrent, she is at first sung into life by Anodos, who finds her statue embedded in a block of alabaster but awakens her as Pygmalion awakened Galatea. Anodos falls in love with this girl and meets her several times; but she eventually becomes Percivale's wife, and Anodos admits that she has mated with the better man. Other than these two characters and Anodos himself, almost none of the people whom Anodos meets in fairyland reappear after the episode in which they are first encountered. Still, the presence in the story of Percivale and the alabaster maiden does serve, to some extent, to unify the story.

A third unifying factor is a rather frightening being called the

Shadow. When visiting one of the many cottages inhabited by old women Anodos is warned not to open the door of a mysterious-looking closet, but he neglects the warning. At once the Shadow engulfs him, and thereafter becomes a constant, sinister companion, blackening his view of the world. In *The Golden Key* (65-68), Robert Lee Wolff equates it with the *Doppelgänger* of German folklore and traces several parallels in German Romantic literature. Whatever its origin, the Shadow becomes a symbol of great and sometimes rather confusing complexity, as it seems to acquire different meanings in different contexts. The manner of its acquisition, for instance, suggests that the Shadow represents stubborn willfulness, in that Anodos fails to heed the old woman's wise advice. But the first two incidents in which it affects the story suggest a quite different meaning. Anodos meets a little boy whom he regards as quite lovely and who is carrying two magical instruments used by poets (although their significance is not made explicit, I daresay that MacDonald meant them to represent Fancy and Imagination). But when the Shadow falls on the child, he is transformed into a commonplace urchin carrying nothing more remarkable than a kaleidoscope and a telescope. The second incident is similar: Anodos meets a little girl carrying a shimmering and wondrous sphere, but when the Shadow touches it the sphere shatters, to the girl's dismay. This second incident has sexual implications, suggesting loss of virginity and of childhood innocence. Anodos is at first horrified at what his companion does to things that had appeared lovely, but eventually he feels a perverse satisfaction in being "realistic" enough not to see beauty where it is not, in seeing things "as they really are," even as ugly. As Wolff remarks (67), this aspect of the Shadow represents not willfulness but "pessimistic and cynical disillusionment, the worldly wiseness that destroys beauty, childish and naive pleasures, the delights of friendship and love; it is the foe of innocence, of openness, of optimism, of the imagination." Wolff suggests that the Shadow's acquisition by Anodos has been caused, not by neglecting the old woman's warning, but by his having been seduced by the Alder-maiden—the same way that Percivale acquired the rust on his armor. The seduction incident, if it is that, is strikingly similar to what happens in Keats's "La Belle Dame Sans Merci." Wolff's sexual interpretation seems quite feasible in connecting the loss of virginity with the acquisition of a sour and cynical outlook.

But in still other incidents, the meaning of the Shadow seems to change. After the deaths of the two brothers in the battle with the giants, Anodos feels guilty at having survived; and the Shadow immediately gets blacker because he should not feel such guilt. Later, his mood changes to pride in having killed his own giant and rescued the prisoners; now the Shadow fades and almost disappears, suggesting that pride rather than guilt is the "correct" feeling. At other points in the story, the Shadow blackens when Anodos feels smug pride which is, unlike that which he felt regarding having killed his giant, not justified, but mere vanity. At the very end of *Phantastes*, Anodos finally succeeds in getting rid of the Shadow because he has heroically sacrificed himself in killing a vicious wolf at a pagan initiation rite which had impressed Percivale but whose evil Anodos had seen. But at an earlier incident, Anodos had met a fierce knight which looked like himself (the *Doppelgänger* motif again) and had shrunk from doing combat with this representative of his own darker side: The Shadow had immediately grown blacker. Taken together, these incidents suggest that the Shadow represents the guilt which comes from not doing one's duty, and it reminds us of MacDonald's precept to the effect that doing the duty that lies nearest us, rather than avoiding it, is the path to wisdom. In this context, then, the Shadow seems to be connected with cowardice and its removal with courage in action. The suggestion is parallel to the way Percivale loses the rustiness of his armor—by doing righteous deeds. Thus, although its symbolic meanings are multifold, there is a subtle unity among the significances of the Shadow; it comes to represent the complex relationships between guilt and innocence, humility and pride, courage and cowardice, living life and fleeing from it. Yet, since it is really a part of Anodos's self, the Shadow imparts only a minor unity to *Phantastes*, complementary to that provided by the fact that all the adventures happen to the same central character.

The loose, episodic plot of *Phantastes*, then, is not really tied together very well by the reappearance of characters like Percivale and the alabaster maiden, or of the symbolic Shadow. In many episodes, MacDonald appears to "forget" these unifying factors—even the Shadow—and seems to have included some incidents for the sake of mere excitement. I have mentioned several adventures which have considerable suggestiveness, imaginativeness, and symbolic resonance; but I have not mentioned many others which lack these qualities. The looseness and unevenness of *Phantastes* must be counted as defects, though in most respects the work is surely an excellent one. . . .

ENDNOTES

1. *Phantastes*, 9-11 (Ch. II).
2. *Phantastes*, 320 (Ch. XXV).
3. *Phantastes*, 271-72 (Ch. XXI).

WORKS CITED

MacDonald, George. *The Visionary Novels of George MacDonald*. Ed. Anne Freemantle. Intro. W. H. Auden. Noonday, 1954.

Wolff, Robert Lee. *The Golden Key: A Study of George MacDonald's Fiction*. Yale UP, 1961.

Death's Ecstasies: Transformation and Rebirth in George MacDonald's *Phantastes*

Joseph Sigman

From *English Studies in Canada*

George MacDonald, one of the most hauntingly imaginative of Victorian writers, published *Phantastes, A Faerie Romance For Men and* Women in 1858. His first prose work, it seems to have attracted little attention except for a review in the *Athenæum*, which dismissed it as a "second-hand symbol shop" whose author had "lost all hold on reality." However the fact that MacDonald's fantasy has never been long out of print indicates that through the years it has cast its spell over more than a few readers. Four further editions of *Phantastes* appeared in the nineteenth century and two more in the early twentieth. In 1915 it became a title in Everyman's Library, and in recent years two paperback editions have been available. In spite of this limited but enduring popularity and, perhaps, some literary influence as well,[1] this strange and complex work has attracted little critical attention. The only serious study of it is a chapter in Robert Lee Wolff's *The Golden Key*, a book that surveys all of MacDonald's fiction.[2] In Wolff's judgment *Phantastes* is an "entirely episodic" work, whose only structure is provided by recurring Oedipal fantasies and by some allegorizations of events in MacDonald's life.[3] In this essay I shall take issue with this concept of *Phantastes* and argue instead that its unity and coherence become apparent if it is seen as a depiction of a psychological crisis and the resulting process of transformation and rebirth. As the basis for this discussion I shall use the work of C.G. Jung and his disciple Erich Neumann, a choice governed by pragmatic rather than ideological considerations. The case simply seems to be that Jungian ideas "fit" MacDonald's fantasy. One possible reason for this may be that the roots of Jung's work, like those of MacDonald's, lie deep in German Romanticism.

The psychology of MacDonald's young narrator (who, for reasons that will be explained shortly, is called "Anodos") is described through curiously illogical metaphors of inheritance and family history. The basic situation is this: Anodos's parents are dead, and he seems oddly uninformed about them and about his family's history generally. To begin with, his father's "personal history" is "unknown" to him,[4] and he appears to be unable to remember anything about his mother, who died when he was a baby. This is clear enough and not necessarily unbelievable, but when MacDonald turns from the parents to the more distant ancestors, he does a strange and significant thing. Instead of discussing them in terms of different family lines, as would be most natural, he simply categorizes them according to whether they are male or female. This tends to assimilate the mother and father into a general division between male and female predecessors, and we find that Anodos has the same relative lack of knowledge about these two groups as he does about his parents. His male ancestors, he tells us, are "strange men" about whom he knows "little or nothing" (16), but we later learn that, in fact, he knows more about these male ancestors, his "great-grandfathers," than he does about his female ancestors, his "great-grandmothers on either side" (18). One important thing he does not know about his great-grandmothers is that they came from Fairy Land (23). Because of these fairy great-grandmothers the two groups—the male ancestors and the female ancestors—are very different, and Anodos appears to have received a different inheritance from each of them. The patriarchal inheritance consists of "lands and moneys" (16), and Anodos seems to take little interest in it. The matriarchal inheritance, however, is much less prosaic, for it is "fairy blood" (22). Anodos takes an intense interest in this inheritance, even though he does not yet know of its existence. MacDonald sketches this initial situation in such a rapid and fragmentary fashion that some of its details must remain conjectural, but its general significance seems clear. The father and the mother, the male and the female ancestors, and the two inheritances (one external, visible, practical, and male; the other internal, invisible, mystical, and female) are images of Anodos's dualistic composition. They describe the objective and subjective aspects of his psyche: the conscious and the unconscious. The fact that Anodos is ignorant of the female inheritance and disinterested towards the male strongly suggests a psychological situation often discussed by Jung.[5] Anodos's conscious personality has become closed off and isolated from his unconscious. This, it would appear, is largely because of an environment that has forgotten the great-grandmothers and Fairy Land. In any case, because one entire side of his psyche cannot find expression, a complex of suppressed material, centring on the female figures who naturally symbolize those elements excluded from the conscious male personality, has formed in the unconscious and has become so emotionally charged that it has drawn energy away from the consciousness, leaving the ego empty and unable to relate meaningfully to society. In Jung's view the ego is poised between the external world and the unconscious. It must relate to both, and this can be done only through the balanced interaction of the conscious and the unconscious. If such a fruitful relation is prevented by the suppression or neglect of the inner life, Jungian theory holds that the psyche will naturally strive to restore its lost equilibrium through "dreams, phantasies, and even neurotic symptoms," which Jung sees as "compensatory, aiming at a better balance within the psyche."[6] In the case of Anodos it seems clear from his longings for Fairy Land (18 and 38) and from the manner in which he has decorated his bedroom (19 and 76) that hidden powers are seeking to find expression in him. If the conflict between these powers and the one-sided structure of his personality becomes severe enough, the result will be a psychological crisis in which the structure of the personality will be overturned by the eruption into consciousness of the dammed-up unconscious material.[7]

What MacDonald's first chapter describes is precisely such a crisis. On his twenty-first birthday Anodos receives the keys to the secretary in which his father's private papers are kept, and he immediately sets out to examine them. The fact that it is his twenty-first birthday suggests that it is time for him to take his father's place in the active world. His search of the secretary in the hope of discovering something of his father's personal history is, therefore, an act of introversion, a turning inward of psychic energy which rejects adult duties and responsibilities. At its core would seem to be a secret wish to discover something of the father's relation with the mother and ultimately of the mother herself. It is, in other words, an instinctive attempt to bring into consciousness the female complex which has constellated in his unconscious and which symbolizes all those undeveloped aspects of his male personality. MacDonald, therefore, describes the simple act of searching the secretary as a penetration into darkness, the past, a mystery, a labyrinthine fortress, a subterranean world, and a realm of the dead. According to Jung such a turning inward of psychic energy will activate unconscious materials and bring them into consciousness.[8] This is what now occurs, and the emerging unconscious materials are naturally symbolized by a female figure: the mysterious Fairy Woman. At first Anodos's ego-consciousness rationalistically resists her, but it soon loses control and deeper forces take command of his life. As we have seen, the goal of these forces is the establishment of a new and more healthful psychic balance. The fact that Anodos will be in Fairy Land twenty-one days that will seem like twenty-one years (181) identifies this new balance with true and not merely chronological maturity. The chief characteristic of this maturity will be a more harmonious integration of the different aspects of the psyche, which will make it possible for the ego to relate meaningfully both to the inner world and the active, external world.

The essence of what is happening to MacDonald's narrator is contained in the strange name, "Anodos," twice bestowed on him in the first chapter. This name is given first at a critical moment and is hardly intended to be taken as the narrator's ordinary name. Rather, it is title describing the adventure he is fated to experience. Wolff says that "the hero's name is presumably Greek, meaning 'pathless'";[9] however, he oddly neglects to note that ανοδος can have other meanings and should, therefore, be properly seen as a pun. In Greek οδος means a "road" or "way," while ανοδος can mean "having no way," a "journey inland," and the "way up." Initially Anodos is without a path in the sense that his life is static and his development halted. This situation is altered when the Fairy Woman appears and reveals what MacDonald variously calls the "way," "road" (18), or "path" (20) into Fairy Land. Following this path might be seen as a "journey inland," an inward journey into the unconscious. But, more important, the path is a "way up," for it will lead Anodos to a transcendence of his original condition and to the achievement of a deeper and richer mode of life. This is in keeping with the fact that in philosophical texts ανοδος, can describe the ascent of the soul to spiritual realms and in Christian texts the ascension of Christ. Anodos begins to follow the path that will lead him upward when he discovers "faint traces of a footpath" (20) beside the bed in his metamorphosized bedroom. Later in *Phantastes* the reader is periodically reminded that Anodos continues to journey along this path (e.g., 42, 61,121).

It is in the nature of things, however, that before this path can lead Anodos to the shining heights, it must first lead him into the depths to confront the dangers that wait in the darkness.[10] Early in *Phantastes* these depths are hinted at when the voice of the Fairy Woman causes Anodos to experience a sensation of "twilight, and reedy river banks, and a low wind" (17). He stands, as it were, at the threshold of night and of watery depths, typical symbols of the unconscious, and the movement of the spirit (πνευμα, *spiritus*) begins. The mention of water at this point is a prelude to the development in the first three chapters of an elaborate image of Fairy Land as an underwater realm (see 17, 18, 19, 20, 21). This realm is associated with light and dark, sun and moon, birth and death, mother and grave, for it is a place of both opportunity and peril. Anodos's turning away from external life to such an inner world is technically a regressive act and in one sense, therefore, evidence of weakness and inferiority. But since it offers the possibility of rebirth and deeper insight, there is a sense in which such regression may be evidence of potential superiority. Jung tells us that it may be "precisely the strongest and best men, the heroes, who give way to their regressive longing and purposely expose themselves to the danger of being devoured by the monster of the maternal abyss."[11] But Anodos will only be a hero if he conquers the "monster" of the unconscious and returns to society with the treasure of rebirth that the monster guards. If Anodos allows himself to be overwhelmed by the unconscious contents that erupt into his consciousness, the result will be a psychosis or a permanent crippling of his life. According to Jung, what is necessary if a psychological crisis is to lead to a higher state of integration is the "understanding" and the "assimilating" into consciousness of the unconscious contents.[12] The reader of *Phantastes* should never forget that the unconscious threatens the individual with destruction as well as offering him the possibility of rebirth. It is MacDonald's awareness of this that gives his fantasy much of its uniqueness. In general, *Phantastes* is the same sort of tale of transformation and rebirth as such German Romantic works as E.T.A. Hoffmann's *The Golden Pot* and Novalis's *Heinrich van Ofterdingen*. Like *Phantastes*, they open with descriptions of the unconscious breaking into the consciousness of the hero, but *Phantastes* differs from them by placing its emphasis less on belief, wonder, and imagination than on the challenge offered by the unconscious, on the dangers it holds for consciousness. It might not, in fact, be too extreme to characterize *Phantastes* as a book pervaded by a sense of the horror and fascination of the unconscious as well as its wonder and power.

Because Fairy Land consists of those elements excluded from Anodos's conscious male personality, it is a largely female realm. But any analysis of MacDonald's female characters will necessarily be complex, and it will perhaps be best, therefore, to establish some general principles first about MacDonald's portrayal of them and second about the Jungian conception of the archetypal feminine before going on to consider the significance of specific female characters. Three things about MacDonald's portrayal of his female characters are particularly noticeable. First, he introduces a very large female cast. Second, in various ways he blurs the lines of demarcation between different female characters. Third, he describes several of these characters as though they were both Anodos's beloved and his mother. In these ways MacDonald creates an odd effect, which a brief survey of his female characters and their relations to each other will make apparent. To begin with, the Fairy Woman of chapter 1 seems to identify herself as Anodos's grandmother, but she emerges from a secret compartment in his father's secretary, and her eyes cause Anodos to remember the death of his mother. However, since Anodos appears immediately to fall in love with her, and later to think of her as "the lady" (23), she is the beloved as well as the mother. Her white garments and the description of her as a "Greek statuette" (16) associate the Fairy Woman with the Marble Lady of chapter 5, with whom Anodos also falls in love, and who, in turn, is almost explicitly identified with Anodos's mother through the quotation from *The Winter's Tale* that opens chapter 14. On the other hand, the Marble Lady also seems identified in chapter 19 with a woman who died prior to the beginning of the book and with whom Anodos had evidently also been in love. The Wise Woman in chapter 19 is linked to Anodos's mother (and, therefore, at one remove, to the Marble Lady) through her maternal characteristics, which also associate her with the motherly women of the cottages in chapters 3 and 7, while her union of youth and age links her to the Fairy Woman of chapter 1 as well. In the final chapter the Wise Woman's voice is heard in the leaves of a beech tree, an event which identifies her with the Beech Tree of chapter 4 who says she loves Anodos, but who also possesses strong maternal characteristics. The little girl of chapter 9 is similar to the other little girls of chapters 3 and 7, but she later reappears as a young woman in chapter 22, where her song soothes Anodos "like a mother's voice and hand" (162). The song particularly links her to the Wise Woman, while the sun-like "radiance" with which she gleams as she enters the forest (164) is very like the "intenser radiance" (48) with which the sun falls on the Marble Lady as she vanishes into the forest earlier in the book. It is, I think, clear from this survey that by dealing with a series of female characters in this way MacDonald tends to cause them to coalesce. It is difficult for the reader to respond to them as individuals. Rather he is given the impression of a generalized female principle which is more than any single woman, which cannot be defined in terms of any one female role, and which manifests itself in almost all of the book's events.

 The presence of such a generalized female power indicates that one of the unconscious contents activated by the psychological crisis with which the book opened is what Jungian psychology calls the archetype of the feminine. In a general way this collective image symbolizes nature and the unconscious. Since it is understandably complex, we are fortunate to have a structural analysis of it in Erich Neumann's book, *The Great Mother*, which will provide us with a useful classification of the female characters of *Phantastes*.[13] According to Neumann, the female archetype has two fundamental aspects, both of which have a positive and a negative side. The first of these, the maternal or elementary aspect, centres on the image of the uterus and its enclosing and containing function. It is, therefore, the feminine as both womb and grave, as the principle that gives and withdraws life, protects and imprisons, nourishes and starves, entraps and releases. In general, this aspect of the female archetype finds expression in the mythological figure of the Great Mother, who embodies both the creative and the destructive sides of nature and the unconscious, and who is associated with images of water, caves, darkness, depth, and enclosures of all sorts. The second aspect of the archetypal feminine is the virginal or transformative aspect. It centres on the beauty of the female and is, therefore, that aspect of the feminine that sets in motion, impels, and provokes. This aspect of the archetype appears in its purest form in what Jung calls the "anima": the personification of a man's inner life, his ideals, longings, dreams, and desires. Like the maternal figure, the anima can be either negative or positive, thereby embodying both the creative and destructive sides of a man's desires. She can inspire and poison, guide and deceive, attract to achievement and lure to destruction. In general, these varied attributes of the feminine find expression in four archetypal female figures: the good mother, the terrible mother, the muse, and the temptress. Simple examples of such figures are the Virgin Mary, the goddess Kali, Dante's Beatrice, and Homer's Circe. In MacDonald's Fairy Land these four appear in the persons of the Fairy Woman (and later the Wise Woman), the Ogress, the Marble Lady, and the Alder Maid. Because the Marble Lady is so central to Anodos's adventures, we will now turn to her.

Anodos discovers the Marble Lady on his second day in Fairy Land. Seeking shelter from the sun, he enters an opening in a rock almost concealed "with shrubs and creeping plants, some of them in full and splendid blossom" (43) and finds first a well of clear water, then a bas-relief illustrating the legend of Pygmalion, and finally a block of alabaster in which the form of a woman is visible. With the story of "Orpheus and the following stones" (45) in mind, Anodos frees the woman from the alabaster through song, only to see her flee from him and vanish into the forest. The cave, the vegetation, the well, and the rather sexual description of the cave entrance all suggest the mother archetype. But these images are secondary to the later association of Anodos with Pygmalion and Orpheus, both traditional types of the artist, and the identification of the Lady with a marble statue, an odd image that appears occasionally in the nineteenth century as a means of describing a woman as a representative of ideal beauty. It is found, for example, in poems like Poe's "To Helen" and Thomas Stoddard's "Her, a Statue." The Marble Lady is, therefore, an anima figure, and the scene of her discovery seems to derive from similar scenes of an artist's vision of his ideal in the work of Shelley and Novalis. The setting recalls the bower of "odorous plants" beneath "hollow rocks" in *Alastor* where Shelley's Poet dreams of the "veiled maid," as well as the cave Novalis's Heinrich enters prior to his vision of the blue flower and also the cave containing a marble statue of a woman which Heinrich's father saw in a dream.[14] Anodos's description of the Marble Lady's face as "the face that had been born with me in my soul" echoes Shelley's assertion that the voice of the maid is to the Poet "like the voice of his own soul," and Anodos's curious experience of a "harmonious tumult" (43) of sounds and colours and forms rushing through his mind has its source, perhaps, in Heinrich's feeling that "countless thoughts strove to mingle within him" and that "new images never seen before arose and interfused and became visible beings around him."[15] In all three of these works the hero loses his ideal beloved, for it is in the nature of things that she cannot be fully possessed in this life. If the hero did unite with her, it would be an assertion that the ideal had been attained and that reality had turned into dream. For Shelley's Poet this loss is fatal, leading him into isolation and death. Heinrich, on the other hand, retains and treasures the memory of his beloved as the inspiration for an active and creative life. The fact that MacDonald not only echoes *Alastor* and *Heinrich von Ofterdingen* in the key scene in the Marble Lady's cave, but also quotes from *Alastor* at the beginning of the first chapter and from Heinrich at the beginning of the second, strongly suggests that he considers Heinrich and Shelley's Poet as emblems of the two possible courses of action open to Anodos. Either he can destroy himself in a search for the Marble Lady or else he can learn to accept the inevitable alienation from his ideal that earthly life requires. The significance of this proposition will become increasingly evident if we analyze Anodos's relationship with the Marble Lady.

In the Marble Lady's cave Anodos is associated with Pygmalion and Orpheus, and the Marble Lady is described both as a statue and as dead. The block of alabaster in which she is enclosed is an "alabaster tomb," a "pale coffin," an "antenatal tomb" (45), and a "stony shroud" (47), while her sleep is a "death of dreams"; and in order to awaken her Anodos must struggle with "primal Death" (46). In other words, as well as Pygmalion's statue, she is Eurydice. The motif of the dead beloved is widespread in Romanticism. Its probable sources are Petrarch's sonnets and Dante's *La Vita Nuova*, which describe, respectively, the deaths of Laura and Beatrice. Major Romantic examples of this motif can be found in the work of Goethe, Novalis, Byron, Poe, and Nerval. It has already been observed that the ideal cannot be possessed in this life. As an anima figure associated with ideals, vision, and inspiration, the dead beloved images a world from which all that the hero loves and desires is absent. On the other hand, the rescue of Eurydice by Orpheus is an apocalyptic image signifying the realization of the ideal and the transformation of reality. What, however, are we to make of the Marble Lady's behaviour? The scene somewhat recalls Ovid's description of Orpheus closing his arms on empty air as Eurydice vanishes,[16] but the Marble Lady seems to flee Anodos rather than to be withdrawn against her will. Perhaps an indication of the significance of this flight can be found later in *Phantastes* in the violent image of Orphic failure that appears in the story of Sir Aglovaile and his ghostly lady (131ff). In this story the knight attempts to embrace the ghost of his mistress and finds a corpse in his arms. In relation to Anodos's quest for the Marble Lady this would seem to imply that any attempt actually to possess one's ideal will destroy it. One sense in which this may be true is based on the simple fact that the ideal cannot be made real without distorting it, but a more profound sense becomes apparent when the significance of Anodos's association with Pygmalion is examined.

Pygmalion's desire to have his statue come to life is obviously another image of the desire to make the ideal real. In the original legend the wish is granted, but the story takes a strangely sinister turn in MacDonald's hands. The version he refers to at the opening of chapter 5 is the particularly Romantic one of Thomas Lovell Beddoes, which, like Rousseau's *Pygmalion, scene lyrique*, distorts the legend in a morbidly erotic fashion. In it the statue draws her life from the sculptor with the result that he nears death as she nears life. Apparently his death is their union. It is not surprising, therefore, that the bas-relief in MacDonald's cave shows the sculptor "more rigid" than his statue (43), and that Anodos's song contains these words:

> Or art thou Death, O woman? for since I
> Have set me singing by thy side,
> Life hath forsook the upper sky,

> And all the outer world hath died.
>
> Yea, I am dead; for thou hast drawn
> My life all downward unto thee. (47)

In *Phantastes*, as in Beddoes's poem, the love of the ideal is the love of death. Like a vampire the beloved draws the life from the artist. A variant on this theme lurks in another line of Anodos's song in which he makes clear his wishes if it proves impossible to wake the Lady, if, that is, the ideal cannot be made real:

> Or, if still thou choosest rather
> Marble, be its spell on me;
> Let thy slumber round me gather,
> Let another dream with thee! (47)

This amounts to a total inversion of the Pygmalion legend. The statue now becomes a kind of Medusa, and the sculptor is himself turned to stone. It appears, therefore, that the Marble Lady has the potential to become a negative anima figure, a temptress who uses Anodos's deepest desires and dreams to lure him to his destruction. This, then, is a second sense in which the quest for the ideal destroys the ideal. It does so by using the ideal in the wrong way and thereby turning it into its exact opposite. A clue to the fuller meaning of these strange images of a quest that destroys both the questor and his ideal can perhaps be found in the fact, noticed earlier, that the Marble Lady's cave combines imagery of the mother archetype with that of the anima.

Anodos's attempt to awaken and embrace his ideal woman is characterized from the start by a curious ambiguity, for, as we have seen, the Marble Lady is closely associated with the mother. Anodos's desire to possess her would seem, therefore, in some sense incestuous. Already in the first chapter a suggestion of incestuous longings on the part of Anodos is introduced when he reaches out to the Fairy Woman, only to have her step back and say, "Foolish boy, if you could touch me, I should hurt you. Besides, I was two hundred and thirty-seven years old, last Midsummer eve; and a man must not fall in love with his grandmother, you know" (17-18). The Marble Lady's flight and the Fairy Woman's backward step seem parallel acts, and a similar parallel exists between the first chapter and the later scene in which Anodos rediscovers the Marble Lady in the hall of statues in the Fairy Palace (110 ff). The suggestion of incest is very much heightened in this scene because this is the chapter which opens with the quotation from *The Winter's Tale* that all but explicitly identifies the Marble Lady with the mother. In this scene the Fairy Woman's warning, "if you could touch me, I should hurt you," is twice echoed, first by the words "TOUCH NOT!" which appear in the hall and second by the Marble Lady's cry as she is embraced by Anodos: "You should not have touched me!" (119-20). One of the ways in which MacDonald builds his meanings is with such parallels, and there is another very sinister one between this scene and the story of Sir Aglovaile, in which the dead lady says: "Come, if thou darest, and sit by my side; / But do not touch me, or woe will betide" (133). The Marble Lady is, therefore, both the mother and the dead beloved, and Anodos's relation with her threatens both incest and the absolute loss of the Lady. Jungian psychology can, perhaps, help us to understand the significance of this. Anodos's relationship with the Marble Lady turns on a blurring of the roles of lover and child. In other words, Anodos seems unable to distinguish between the elementary and the transformative aspects of the archetypal feminine, between, that is, the maternal archetype and the anima. Jungian theory holds that the degree to which an individual makes clear distinctions between archetypes is a measure of the strength of that individual's ego-consciousness.[17] If this is so, then Anodos's blurred and confused relation to the archetype of the feminine that has burst into his consciousness indicates that his ego-consciousness is in a position of weakness in relation to the unconscious. In other words, Anodos is not exercising "the critical understanding" of unconscious contents that Jung held was essential if a crisis were to lead to a higher state of development. Instead, he is being dominated by the unconscious. This can be seen in the odd oceanic moods that characterize the first part of *Phantastes*. Anodos floats in diffuse emotions. The world is permeated with an undefined sense of femininity. Will and discrimination are seldom exercised.

Both Jung and Neumann see unconsciousness as the natural and original state and hold that consciousness is maintained only with effort. The unconscious exerts a continual gravitational pull on consciousness, and if ego-consciousness is not well developed, it will succumb to this powerful drag. In such a situation the individual experiences an unconscious desire to lapse back into the darkness of the unconscious and to cease to exist. Since the unconscious is the source, the mother, such a lapsing back is symbolized in dreams and myths as incest. It is a wish to escape the tensions of conscious life and to return to an infantile state where there are no cares or responsibilities and where no effort is required. This death wish is described by Neumann in this way: "a desire to be dissolved and absorbed; passively one lets oneself be taken, sinks into the pleroma, melts away in an ocean of pleasure

—a *Liebestod*. The Great Mother takes the little child back into herself, and always over uroboric incest there stand the insignia of death, signifying final dissolution in union with the Mother."[18] For Jung, too, the desire for the Great Mother is an aspect of "human fate": "in the morning of life the son tears himself loose from the mother, from the domestic hearth, to rise through battle to his destined heights. Always he imagines his worst enemy in front of him, yet he carries the enemy within himself—a deadly longing for the abyss, a longing to drown in his own source, to be sucked down to the realm of the Mothers. His life is a constant struggle against extinction, a violent yet fleeting deliverance from ever-lurking night. This death is no external enemy, it is his own inner longing for the stillness and profound peace of all-knowing non-existence, for all-seeing sleep in the ocean of coming-to-be and passing away."[19] Anodos's confusion between the anima and the mother suggests that his desire for the ideal is essentially such a longing for nonexistence and sleep. The conflict between the true ideal and the false ideal of escape from life is the moral centre of *Phantastes*, while the longing for nothingness is its great theme. It is this theme that is the basis of the profound link between MacDonald's work and that of Novalis. The German poet had long fascinated MacDonald, whose first published work was a translation of Novalis's *Geistliche Lieder*. We have already spoken of the links between *Phantastes* and *Heinrich von Ofterdingen*, but now the more relevant work by Novalis is one MacDonald never mentions: the famed *Hymns to the Night*. These strange mixtures of prose and verse given an intense portrayal of the poet's desire to join his lost beloved in death. "*Welche Wollust, welchen Genuss bietet dein Leben, die aufwögen des Todes Entzückungen?*" ("What bliss, what sensual delight does thy life provide which would outweigh Death's ecstasies?"), Novalis's speaker cries.[20] The same question lies at the heart of *Phantastes*.

It is now clear why Anodos's quest for his ideal woman is pictured as a destruction of both ideal and quester. In his case the desire for the ideal is essentially a desire for nothingness. Because of this both the ideal and the unconscious are turned into negative principles. The ideal does not inspire to creativity; it lures to destruction. The unconscious does not beckon because it offers the possibility of rebirth; it beckons because it offers the possibility of cessation. This shift in polarity caused by Anodos's attitude is presented by MacDonald as a movement from the sphere of the Marble Lady and the Fairy Woman to that of the Alder Maid and the Ogress. In them we have MacDonald's portrayal of the negative side of the archetypal feminine: the temptress (or negative anima figure) and the terrible mother. We have already seen that the Marble Lady possesses the potential to become a vampire and a Medusa. In the Alder Maid this dark potential is fully manifested. The uncertainty of her relation to the Marble Lady is MacDonald's indication that they are two sides of the same principle. The Maid's coffin-like hollowness was probably derived from contemporary books on folklore,[21] while Joseph von Eichendorff's *Das Marmorbild* may have suggested something of the mood of the encounter. Shelley's *Epipsychidion* may also be in the background, for in it the hero falls prey to a demonic female whom he imagines to resemble an ideally beautiful woman seen in a vision: "One, whose voice was venomed melody / Sate by a well, under blue nightshade bowers: / The breath of her false mouth was like faint flowers, / Her touch was as electric poison" (256-59; also see 291ff). As a negative anima figure the Maid symbolizes Anodos's own deepest longings and dreams that have now become destructive. Like Sir Aglovaile, Anodos attempts to embrace her, and finds he has embraced a corpse. The image is an all but explicit statement that his true love is death. The Ogress, on the other hand, is MacDonald's image of the mythological terrible and devouring mother. Whereas the Fairy Woman symbolized the unconscious as a mother who grants wishes and offers a renewal of life, the Ogress symbolizes it as a dark and destructive womb in which life is extinguished. In her "Church of Darkness" (75) one worships the gravitational attraction that unconsciousness exerts on consciousness and the inertia that operates against life. From her ancient book she reads a passage evidently intended to recall the discourse of Goethe's Mephistopheles on Mother Night (*Faust*, 1349 ff). Her vision, like that of Mephistopheles, emphasizes the hopelessness of human progress and the cyclic pointlessness of existence. Her "long, white, shining teeth" (64) and her association with the "mighty sea" (63) of darkness identify her with the engulfing and swallowing aspects of nature and the unconscious.

The two other monsters that Anodos encounters, the Ash Tree and the Shadow, require special comment because they are male, not female. The most important thing about the Ash is that he introduces the image of the father into Fairy Land. Once more Neumann offers us considerable assistance, for in his classification the Ash is the mythological terrible father and is, therefore, the male equivalent of the Ogress. Since the father is society and consciousness, not nature and unconsciousness, the terrible father often symbolizes the harsh and unjust laws of a repressive society which restrict the energies of the son. However the stage of Anodos's development at which the Ash is encountered is so introverted and so under the power of the unconscious that the father figure appears in a much more primitive form. The Ash is the father as he is found in the domain of the Great Mother. In myth the original state which precedes the emergence of consciousness is commonly symbolized by the world parents slumbering in their original embrace, for the dualities that characterize conscious experience are not yet separated. The male, therefore, is still part of the state of primal unconsciousness and can symbolize it in the same fashion as the mother.[22] The Greek Titan, Cronus, is such a primal, child-devouring father. The Ash is a dream image of a condition that is still very close to the original state. His characteristics are wholly chthonic and ultimately identical, therefore, with those of the Ogress. His hollowness suggests the uterine cavity as a tomb. He hunts by night, is linked with the moon and bestiality, and he buries his victims in his roots. The Shadow, on the other hand, as his name implies, is an image of Anodos himself rather than a parental image. In Jungian psychology the "shadow" is the personification of the evil side of an individual that goes unrecognized by him. MacDonald defines his Shadow in much the same way when, in the quotation at the opening of chapter 8, he parallels this figure with Goethe's Mephistopheles, who externalizes the negative elements in Faust's personality: his cynicism, indifference, and selfishness. Anodos acquires the Shadow in the Ogress's Church of Darkness because his own longing for nothingness has brought him so far into the gravitational field of the unconscious as terrible mother that his psychic buoyancy and imaginative energy have drained away. As a result he can no longer perceive life as beautiful and meaningful. The quotations from Coleridge at the beginning of chapter 9 identify this inability as a specifically imaginative failure. If, in the imagery of the Coleridge quotations, the imagination is a light that issues forth from the soul, bringing nature to life, the Shadow is a darkness that similarly issues forth, killing nature. These images are part of the larger structure of light and dark imagery in *Phantastes* and are parallel in significance to the repeated movements from light to dark (e.g., 20, 4.3, 50, 80) which image Anodos's wish for death.

At this point it is essential to observe that Anodos's encounters with the monsters we have just considered have not been without positive results. The monsters force Anodos to realize that there is horror as well as beauty in Fairy Land, and his terrified recoil from them indicates a basic soundness in his character. He begins to discriminate between his experiences when he recognizes that the Alder is "another kind altogether" (56) from the Marble Lady and when his Shadow causes him to feel "loathing and distrust" (68). At such moments Anodos exercises something akin to the "critical understanding" that Jung held necessary to the successful outcome of a crisis. As a result Anodos undergoes a partial and somewhat ambiguous experience of rebirth and renewal (71-72) and moves into a new stage of his development. This new stage centres on his residence in the palace of Fairy Land and introduces the myth of Narcissus, a myth which shifts away to some degree from the implications of the earlier myths of Orpheus and Pygmalion. The Narcissistic imagery of reflections and mirrors first emerges dearly as Anodos drifts down a river to the palace. The moon is reflected in the water, and he wonders, "Why are all reflections lovelier than what we call the reality?" (72). The stories read by Anodos in the palace library also contain Narcissistic imagery, and this is particularly important because they are so obviously analogues to his spiritual state. The first story describes a strange planet where sex as it exists on earth is unknown and where the egg-shaped sky "reflects everything beneath it, as if it were built of water" (86). In the second story Cosmo von Wehrstahl sees a vision of his ideal woman in a magic mirror and, forsaking normal life, becomes intent only on possessing her. In these stories, as in Anodos's residence in the palace generally, themes of isolation, solipsism, and obsession mingle. But if the "egg-shape" of the other planet's sky suggests an undeveloped and prenatal existence, it also looks forward to a possible breaking of the shell and an emergence into a new existence. Anodos's earlier adventures had indicated that his ego-consciousness was feeble in relation to the power of the unconscious. The story of Narcissus, on the other hand, suggests precisely an increase in self-consciousness. This ego-centrism is, of course, adulterated with illusion and weakness, but this does not lessen its significance. Like Pygmalion and Orpheus, Narcissus is a type of the artist,[23] and Anodos's lonely residence in the palace recalls Tennyson's picture of the artist in "The Lady of Shalott" and "The Palace of Art." Such an existence leaves Anodos incomplete and partially developed like the women of the other planet, and yet MacDonald seems to judge it superior to his previous condition. The female monsters cannot enter the Palace; the Marble Lady rather than the Alder Maid appears there; and the Shadow temporarily ceases to torment Anodos. When Anodos does succumb once more to the beauty of the Marble Lady, embraces her, and is plunged into an underworld clearly symbolic of the devouring and imprisoning aspects of the terrible mother, his ability to understand and to judge his situation critically is further increased. As a result, when goblins taunt him that the Marble Lady belongs to a better man, Anodos replies, "Well, if he is a better man, let him have her" (123). The tone of resignation and stoicism in this statement is new to the book. Later, when he encounters a female demon, he is no longer deceived and seduced. This increased ability to understand and to cope with his situation makes possible Anodos's first true experience of transformation and rebirth.

 Chapter 18, the pivotal point of *Phantastes*, is prepared for by the earlier introduction of the myth of Narcissus. Since the first chapter water in the form of stream, well, river, and fountain had been a pervading image, and the appearance of Narcissus gave this image renewed force. The symbolic logic of *Phantastes* demands that the version of the legend operative in the book is not that of Ovid, but the other version, which seems to have been first told by Plotinus and which is the one found in Shakespeare and Marlowe.[24] In this version Narcissus does not expire by the side of the pool but rather hurls himself into it. If this version is assumed, the Narcissistic imagery can be seen to culminate in chapter 18 when Anodos, aware now that he can never possess the Marble Lady and despairing at the barrenness of his life, plunges into the sea. Earlier, this would have marked his final surrender to the unconscious. Now, however, Anodos has accepted the loss of the Marble Lady and resisted the female demon. His plunge into the sea is an act of rebellion against death. "I will not be tortured to death," he cries, "I will meet it half-way. The life within me is yet enough to bear me up to the face of Death, and then I die unconquered" (127). In terms of the traditional hero myth Anodos has reached the nadir of his quest in the underworld and the ocean depths, and he has slain the monster of the unconscious. By overcoming the terrible mother he has released the nourishing and fruitful aspects of the feminine principle. Because he has changed his attitude to the unconscious, it has become a giver of life. As he sinks into the sea, therefore, it is the good mother that he finds there: "a blessing, like the kiss of a mother, seemed to alight on my soul" (128). The polarity of Anodos's desires has been reversed. The death wish is no longer a desire for nothingness and rest; rather it is a desire for the death of the old self and the end to one's old way of life.

 Similarly the image of incest no longer signifies a desire to re-enter the mother in order to escape life; instead, it signifies a desire to re-enter the mother in order to be reborn. Anodos emerges, therefore, from what are now the waters of life as a new child. All the emphasis is placed on the activity of the unconscious: "The waters of themselves lifted me, as with loving arms, to the surface" (128). A fish-like boat appears and, moved by ocean currents, carries him to the island of the Wise Woman.[25] She is MacDonald's most profound image of the archetypal good mother, who, as the creative, nourishing, and sustaining power of the unconscious and of nature is the precisely opposite pole to the ogress. The escape from the underworld, the arrival at a southern island, and the bathing of the face with dew (144) have Dantesque overtones, but it is more important that the Wise Woman is associated with the earth itself and that she acts to reconcile Anodos to life. One aspect of this process of healing and reconciliation is the necessity for Anodos to come to terms with the guilt and sorrow of his life. In a scene that parallels the earlier scene on the river leading to the Fairy Palace Anodos looks over the side of the fish-boat as he is carried to the island of the Wise Woman and sees the stars reflected in the water. But the scene is not Narcissistic, for he looks beneath the reflections (into, that is, the self) and sees that he is floating over his "whole Past" (128). Barriers and defences within his personality have crumbled, and memories (presumably suppressed earlier) flood into his consciousness in a fashion that powerfully contrasts the strange emptiness and lack of information that characterized Anodos when the book opened. This process is continued in the cottage of the Wise Woman, where his passages through the four doors are basically encounters with the deaths of loved ones and with the necessity to leave the paradise of the unconscious and to endure individual existence in the desert of experience. These are precisely the necessities of human life that Anodos has tried to flee.

Anodos's separation from the Wise Woman as her island, like Atlantis,[26] sinks into the sea at the end of chapter 19 begins a whole new phase of his development. If the Wise Woman is the good mother who symbolizes nature and unconsciousness, the departure from her island re-enacts a key moment in Romantic myth: the primal loss of union with the unconscious and instinctive processes of nature and the fall into separate conscious existence. This is the start of what M.H. Abrams has called "the circuitous journey," which is the educational pilgrimage by which man, alienated from his original unity, finds his way back to his home.[27] If Anodos is to survive in the world of experience and eventually transcend it, he must develop a mature and independent masculine ego able to resist the regressive temptations of unconsciousness. This new concern is signalled by the quotations from Fletcher and Spenser that open chapter 20. They describe Renaissance concepts of virtue and nobility and mark a highly significant shift in the tone of *Phantastes*. The mood they establish is immediately reinforced when Anodos sees "a lonely tower" and hears "the clang of an anvil" (146). The first nineteen chapters of *Phantastes* centred in the realm of the mother and concerned Anodos's relation to the inner world. The basic issue was whether or not he could achieve psychological renewal by opening his consciousness to the deeper forces in his psyche without being overwhelmed by these internal powers. In the final six chapters we are in the realm of the father. At issue is the consolidation of ego-consciousness and the orientation of the personality towards the external world. The father is the key to this process because he serves as a model upon which to base an active masculine personality. A series of contrasts between the two parts of *Phantastes* defines this shift of focus. The caves of the first part are replaced by the towers of the second, the palace of the Fairy Queen by that of the old King, the wisdom of the Wise Woman by the simple and practical philosophy of the Knight. In general, a largely female cast is replaced by a largely male one. The emphasis is no longer on Anodos's relationships of love and dependence with various females, but on his fellowship with other men in the performance of their duties. Also there is the sudden appearance of a city and a public ceremony after the earlier rural scenes in which only a few characters took part. Because of the movement from a matriarchal to a patriarchal context Anodos is no longer described as a child and lover; now he must learn to become a warrior, working with metal, practising arms, and striking blows. His songs no longer conjure up the ideal; they hearten others for battle. There are monsters in this part as well—the three giants, the dragon, and the wolf—but Anodos no longer flees them and in fact kills two of them himself. Finally the danger now is not that the ego will be submerged in the unconscious, but rather than the ego will become too sharply defined and exaggerate its own importance. This occurs when Anodos imagines his achievements to be equal to those of Sir Galahad (159). As a result he imprisons himself in the dark tower of the ego.[28] Masculinity and consciousness have now become over-emphasized and have lost touch again with the unconscious. Another rebirth sequence is necessary, therefore, to right the balance. The catalyst is, of course, another female figure, but now a sister figure around whom no erotic or infantile emotions gather. She is an anima figure in the sense of a spiritual helper, and her song of "the mother Earth" and her children recalls Anodos from the isolation of exclusive ego-consciousness back "into the house, so high and wide" (162-63).

The model for this new condition of selfhood which combines

an active life with sensitivity to the inner world is the Marble Lady's Knight. He is the archetypal good father and, therefore, the opponent of the Ash. If the chthonic, bestial, and devouring Ash is the masculine aspect of the primal unconscious, the Knight, from the moment he first rides down "the rays of the setting sun" which flow "like a stream" from the west (48), symbolizes, in Neumann's terms, the "solar" or "higher" masculinity of consciousness and individuality. He is the hero who acts to order the world and to introduce human justice into nature. The union of sun and water images in the sun-stream makes it clear that he is not merely the defender of a barren and legalistic order, but the representative of creative consciousness vitally linked to the unconscious. It is also clear that the Knight has had to actively win his masculine independence. Early in *Phantastes* he is associated with Malory's Perceval through a book, written in a style imitative of Malory that Anodos reads in the first cottage he visits. As Perceval in book xiv of *Morte Darthur* falls prey to a demon lady, MacDonald's Knight falls to the Alder Maid. In remorse Perceval "rooff hymselff thorow the thygh" (xiv.10.29), while the Knight cleans his rusted armour through pure acts of service. The armor rusted, presumably, because he removed it like Malory's Perceval and Spenser's Redcrosse (*The Faerie Queene* 1. vii.2). This is also the case with Spenser's Verdant:

> His warlike Armes, the ydle instruments
> Of sleeping praise, were hong upon a tree;
> And his brave shield, full of old momiments,
> Was fowly ras't, that none the signes might see:
> Ne for them ne for honour cared hee. (ii.xii.80)

The rusted armor, therefore, is part of a complex of heroic motifs going back to Homer and Virgil. In this tradition the hero, who symbolizes duty, order, selfhood, and civilization, must resist the female temptresses, who offer pleasure, passivity, loss of identity, and disorder. Surrender to the female principle was commonly associated with the donning of effeminate garments. For example, in the *Aeneid*, Virgil describes Aeneus at Carthage in this way:

> A purple scarf, with gold embroidered o'er
> (Queen Dido's gift) about his waist he wore;
> A sword, with glittering gems diversified,
> For ornament, not use, hung idly by his side.
> (Iv, 384-87; Dryden's translation)

Chastity, on the other hand, was the symbol of a mature and individualized masculine ego-consciousness able to resist nature and the unconscious.²⁹ Traditional heroic images of this sort define the later stages of Anodos's development. As this material comes to dominate MacDonald's narrative, it forces a reevaluation of Anodos's earlier adventures in the matriarchal realm from a stern patriarchal point of view. Anodos as a poet and a dreamer now appears to have been a fallen and effeminate knight who had betrayed his public duty. His acceptance of a room in the Fairy Palace labelled "The Chamber of Sir Anodos" was, therefore, an ironic indication of his inadequacy and unworthiness. The Alder Maid now appears to have played a role very similar to that of Malory's demon lady and Spenser's Duessa and his false Florimell. On the other hand, in this context, the Marble Lady is akin to Spenser's Una, as a type of the beloved to whom the knight owes pure service, and to Milton's Lady in *Comus*, who is threatened by Circe's son in this way: "if I but wave this wand, / Your nerves are all chain'd up in Alabaster" (659-60).

But there is yet another element at work here. The fact that Malory's Perceval was one of the chaste knights who accomplished the grail quest necessarily introduces the motif of the grail into *Phantastes*. Furthermore, within this context of Christian legend, it should be remembered that the words of the Marble Lady, "You should not have touched me!" are very close to Christ's words to Mary Magdalene at the tomb: "Touch me not" (John 20:17). The association of the dead beloved with Christ is not as eccentric as it might at first seem. Dante in section 24 of *La Vita Nuova* associated Beatrice with Christ, for, after all, Christ can also be thought of as a dead beloved, a point certainly not lost upon Novalis in the *Hymns to the Night*. But what precisely is the significance of this for MacDonald's tale? For one thing, the goal of Anodos's quest is now given a more definitely religious connotation, and chastity, in the sense of resistance to the desire for rest and unconsciousness, is defined as the prerequisite for the quest. On the other hand, the simple introduction of the Christological motif seems to associate Anodos with the archetype and to suggest that the imitation of Christ, in the sense of self-sacrifice, is the means to the completion of the quest. As we shall see, Anodos ends his adventures in Fairy Land by sacrificing himself, dying, and being reborn.

The significance of these images will, perhaps, become clearer if we turn to the sinister ceremony Anodos and the Knight come upon in the forest. The seemingly religious nature of the ceremony deceives the Knight, who responds reverently to it. Anodos, however, perceives that it is evil and succeeds in exposing it even though he is killed in the process. The scene seems inspired in part by Spenser's description of the idol set up by the tyrant Gerioneo (*The Faerie Queene*, v.xi.19-20), while the rotting wood of the idol (cf 57), the grave-like pit, and the vicious wolf recall the monsters, associated with the devouring and destructive aspects of the unconscious, who earlier threatened Anodos. But what is the meaning of these images in the patriarchal context of Anodos's later development? And what is the significance of Anodos's second experience of death and rebirth? In order to understand the role of these elements in Anodos's development, one should recall that psychologically and mythically the mothers symbolize nature, the unconscious, and instinct, while the fathers symbolize culture, consciousness, and law. Therefore, the realm of the mothers is universal and permanent, but that of the fathers is relative and historical. In order to attain a creative, integrated, and individualized self the hero must conquer the negative aspects of both the mother and the father. In other words, he must free himself from both the devouring aspect of the unconscious and the static and obsolete aspect of the cultural order. Both are forms of cessation, passivity, and death.[30] The relevance of the archetype of Christ at this point in the narrative is, therefore, obvious. Christ is a clear example of a hero who rejected the old law of the letter and replaced it by the new law of the spirit. Since the officiators at the forest ceremony are male, they can be taken to represent a fossilized and humanly destructive order from which Anodos, in the manner of Christ, must free himself if he is to achieve full individuality and creativity. It is especially significant that the Knight, although the archetypal good father and the model for Anodos's mature male personality, is deceived. It is an inherent part of the patriarchal realm that the son must go beyond the father, although MacDonald rather disguises this fact and takes care in no way to criticize the Knight. This makes it probable that it was the anxiety involved in the rejection of the old law that caused MacDonald to identify Anodos with Christ and to stress that the rejection was simultaneously an act of self-sacrifice. However the fact that this death comes in combat makes its role in the crystalization of a male ego-consciousness clear.

Anodos's experience of death and rebirth in the patriarchal realm completes and balances his earlier experience in the matriarchal realm. Although death is again imaged as a re-entry into the mother, the paternal element is also present in this sequence. As Anodos had earlier risen from the sea a new child, he now rises from the grave a flower—a child of mother earth which recalls the myths of Narcissus and Hyacinthus. However, whereas the fish-boat had carried him to the island of the Wise Woman where he listened to her songs, a cloud now carries him to a city where he hears the sounds of human suffering. The cloud, perhaps, suggests a rising above nature. Clearly the focus is less on contact with the unconscious and with memories than with social realities. Given this theme, it is highly significant that both the Knight and the Marble Lady appear at the side of Anodos's grave. They seem his parents, and since the father was totally absent from the earlier rebirth sequence, the presence of both father and mother at the grave seems a symbol of psychic wholeness achieved through the death of the ego. This wholeness is open to the beating of the heart of mother earth (178) and to the cries from the city (179). It is the "something deeper and stronger" that the death of the ego causes to emerge from "the unknown abysses of the soul" (165). In Jungian psychology it is known as the "self": the new psychic centre that comes into existence between the conscious and the unconscious as the result of the individuation process. It is interesting to speculate that some such concept may lie behind MacDonald's title. The relation between the passage in Phineas Fletcher's *Purple Island*, from which MacDonald derives the title *Phantastes*, and his book itself has long been felt to be a problem. Even Greville MacDonald, in his introduction to the Everyman edition of his father's work, admitted that the title was "a little puzzling."[31] Similarly Richard Reis has recently remarked that he has "been able to discover no particular resemblance between Fletcher's work and MacDonald's."[32] However Northrop Frye has usefully suggested that MacDonald used Fletcher's Phantastes and not the Phantastes of Spenser (*The Faerie Queene*, 11.ix.49-52), on whom Fletcher based his figure, because Spenser's did not represent "the seat of poetic imagination" whereas Fletcher's Phantastes was "the source of art."[33] If Phantastes did suggest to MacDonald the Romantic concept of the imagination, which Coleridge defined as a "synthetic and magical power" that brings about "the balance or reconciliation of opposite or discordant qualities,"[34] the fact that Fletcher's Phantastes "Oft dreams of fire and water" (*Purple Island*, v1.xlvii) may suggest, perhaps, that MacDonald's "Faerie Romance" is an imaginative effort to embody (to "dight" in "habiliments") an experience of psychic wholeness and the process by which it was achieved.

The final chapter, which describes Anodos after his return from Fairy Land, extends MacDonald's perspective beyond this life. On the most basic level its description of Anodos labouring with his reapers in the sun indicates that he has now taken his father's place in the active world. But his anxiety about the stability of his new position suggests that his adaptation to the patriarchal world of consciousness, individuality, and labour is far from total. Any effort to understand the significance of this must base itself on the two quotations that open the final chapter. One is drawn from Chaucer: "And on the ground, which is my modres gate, / I knocke with my staf, erlich and late, / And say to hire, Leve mother, let me in." The words of the life-weary old man in the Pardoner's Tale come as something of a shock. A wish for rest and non-existence linked to the image of re-entry into the mother seemed to have been left behind at an earlier stage of Anodos's development, but now it suddenly reappears in all its primitive force. In the chapter itself Anodos confesses that he often feels like a ghost—not really a part of life at all. This state is very similar to the final condition of Novalis's heroes. The speaker in the Hymns to the Night eagerly, looks forward to joining his dead beloved and addresses the light of day in this fashion: "*Gern will ich die fleissigen Hände rühren, überall umschaun, wo du mich brauchst . . . Aber getreu der Nacht bleibt mein geheimes Herz*" ("Gladly will I bestir my industrious hands, cast my gaze wherever thou hast need of me . . . But faithful unto the Night will my private heart remain").[35] However Anodos's ideal beloved is the mother. The Marble Lady is married to the Knight, and in the final chapter Anodos's thoughts are focused on the Wise Woman's cottage rather than on a betrothed. Incest remains, therefore, a key theme. What Anodos looks for beyond the grave is that union with the mother which is either impossible or forbidden in this life. But what precisely is the significance of this wish that makes Anodos's relation to life so tenuous? For one thing, it should be carefully noted that none of the negative imagery and sinister emotions earlier associated with incest appear in the final chapter. Only in the quotation from Chaucer are they felt, and there they seem an expression of Anodos's anxiety rather than a definition of his psychology. Since Anodos is reconciled to his duty and no longer tries to escape life, the fact that the goal that lies beyond the grave is imaged as the mother rather than the betrothed gives an ethereal and spiritualized quality to his desires. In other words, union with the mother after death is a symbol of rebirth and transformation which, rather like Faust's pursuit of the "*Ewig-Weibliche*" into the infinite at the end of Goethe's great tragedy (*Faust* 12110), points to stages of spiritual evolution beyond earthly life. Something of this kind has been hinted at a number of times earlier in the book. For example, on the strange planet of which Anodos read there is no union of lovers. But the hope is held out that after they die they may be reborn on the higher plane of earthly existence and then consummate the formerly impossible union (87; also see 38).

The biblical imagery of the final chapter makes it clearer that this is MacDonald's meaning.

At this point the other quotation at the beginning of the final chapter should be noted. It is from Novalis: "Our life is no dream; but it ought to become one, and perhaps will." The apocalyptic nature of this aphorism strongly suggests that Anodos's labour with his reapers should be seen in the context of the harvest imagery of the Bible (e.g., is 5:1-7; Matt 13; Rev 14:14-20). This labour is, therefore, not simply farming, but the preparation for what Blake calls "the Great Harvest and Vintage of the Nations" (*Milton*, plate 43). Similarly the curious description of the Wise Woman as "the ancient woman in the cottage that was four-square" (182) can only by an attempt to link the Wise Woman with Christ and her cottage with the New Jerusalem of Revelation, which is described in this way: "the city lieth foursquare, and the length is as large as the breadth" (Rev 21:16). Such a fantastic parallel is profoundly typical of MacDonald's re-imagining of Christianity. The union with the mother after death is, therefore, his equivalent to the apocalyptic marriage of the Lamb celebrated in the heavenly city (Rev 21:16). Novalis employs a similarly radical image at the end of Klingshor's *märchen* in *Heinrich van Ofterdingen*: "the king embraced his blushing beloved, and the people followed the example of the king and caressed one another. One heard nothing but words of endearment and a whisper of kisses."[36] At the end of *The Golden Pot* Hoffmann unites his hero, Anselmus, with his beloved in Atlantis while all existing things rejoice. Probably one should see these apocalyptic marriages in Romantic literature as symbolizations of the ultimate union of man with nature. Abrams has pointed out that most Romantic philosophies of history have the form of a cyclic myth similar to that in the Bible. Mankind originally lives an instinctive life as a part of unconscious nature. With the emergence of consciousness man falls from this unity into separate existence and is fated to endure the difficult educational pilgrimage that is history. Through the historical process mankind will eventually "win its way back to a higher mode of the original unity."[37] This state will be higher than the original one because it will unite nature and consciousness, instinct and reason. Often, as Abrams has also pointed out, this final union is symbolized by the Romantics as an apocalyptic marriage.[38] In terms of the symbolism of *Phantastes* the mother is nature and unconsciousness and her son is consciousness and individuality. Their union is a new stage of cosmic history. This, then, is the meaning of the words that the leaves of the beech tree whisper to Anodos: "A great good is coming—is coming—is coming to thee, Anodos" (182).

It must be observed, however, that from the naturalistic point of view of Jungian psychology Anodos's final relationship to the mother cannot be considered a satisfactory outcome of the crisis. Anodos remains alienated from life and more than half in love with death. The anxiety he feels about a possible regression to his earlier condition suggests that the terrible mother has not, in fact, been fully defeated. In the structure of images found in *Phantastes* her survival expresses itself in the lack of a bride for Anodos in this life. According to Neumann the hero myth must include the slaying of the dragon, the rescue of the captive, the marriage with her, and the founding of a kingdom. If all of these are not present, it means that the psychological process has not gone far enough:

> All redeemer and savior figures whose victory stops short without rescuing the captive, without sacramentally uniting themselves with her, and therefore with out having founded a kingdom, have something dubious about them from the psychological point of view. Their manifest lack of feminine relationship is compensated by an excessively strong unconscious tie to the Great Mother. The nonliberation of the captive expresses itself in the continued dominance of the Great Mother under her deadly aspect, and the final result is alienation from the body and from the earth, hatred of life, and world negation.[39]

Not all of this is applicable to Anodos, but enough of it is to raise questions. One of these concerns MacDonald himself. If, as seems probable, *Phantastes* has its source in the psychological difficulties of MacDonald's youth and early manhood, to what extent can Neumann's analysis be applied to him? Does such a powerful tie to the unconscious in tension with a commitment to a highly, moralistic patriarchal value system explain many of the weaknesses and disbalances in MacDonald's work as well as its psychological and animistic power? Whatever the answer, the important thing at the moment is that MacDonald's psychological problems brought him into contact with what Jungians would call collective or trans-personal images. MacDonald responded to these dream images with profound anxiety and awe. In *Phantastes* he interpreted them and gave them form in terms of the materials made available to him by his culture. Over the years his fantasy has succeeded in conveying to a good many readers something of the numinosity and power of these images.

Crossing a Great Frontier

Endnotes

1. For MacDonald as one of the "household gods" of the Oxford group of C.S. Lewis, Charles Williams, and J.R.R. Tolkien, see John Wain, *Sprightly Running* (London 1962), p 182.

2. Robert Lee Wolff, *The Golden Key: A Study of the Fiction of George MacDonald* (New Haven 1961). Richard H. Reis's brief treatment in his volume in the Twayne's English Authors series, *George MacDonald* (New York 1972), adds little to Wolff's chapter.

3. Wolff, p 50. Reis is disturbed by this lack of unity and emphasizes the autobiographical element, but he agrees with Wolff that the plot is essentially "loose" and "episodic"; see Reis, p 93.

4. George MacDonald, *Phantastes and Lilith* (Grand Rapids, Mich. 1964), p 16. All reference to *Phantastes* will be to this paperback edition published by W.B. Eerdmans. Hereafter they will simply be incorporated in the text.

5. See, for example, C.G. Jung, *The Structure and Dynamics of the Psyche* (Princeton 1969), paras 139, 204, and 255; *Alchemical Studies* (Princeton 1968), paras 14 and 15; and *The Practice of Psychotherapy* (Princeton 1966), paras 59, 125, and 257. All references to Jung are to the volumes in the *Collected Works* published by the Boliden Foundation and edited by Sir Herbert Read, Michael Fordham, and Gerhard Adler. As is conventional, the references will be to paragraphs rather than pages. There is a discussion of the complex in Jolande Jacobi's excellent book, *Complex, Archetype, and Symbol in The Psychology of C.G. Jung* (Princeton 1959).

6. Anthony Storr, *Jung* (London 1973), p 67. Storr's lucid little book in the Fontana Modern Masters series contains a good discussion of the concept of the "self-regulating" psyche.

7. See C.G. Jung, *Two Essays in Analytical Psychology* (Princeton 1966), paras 252 and 253.

8. Ibid, para 252.

9. Wolff, p 47. Reis's remark that "Anodos" is "a Greek word

usually interpreted as meaning 'a way back'" (see p 87) is not supported by the Liddell and Scott Lexicon. Presumably he bases it on the sense of "journey inland, esp. into Central Asia," but it is difficult to see how this can be interpreted as implying, as Reis feels it does, a way back to childhood. For MacDonald's knowledge of Greek, see Greville MacDonald, *George MacDonald and His Wife* (London 1924), p 118.

10. See C.G. Jung, *The Archetypes of The Collective Unconscious* (Princeton 1968), para 40.

11. See Jung, *Two Essays*, para 261.

12. Ibid, paras 253 and 254. Also see C.G. Jung, *Symbols of Transformation* (Princeton 1967), para 468.

13. Erich Neumann, *The Great Mother* (Princeton 1963). Neumann's interpretation of the archetype is, of course, based on Jung. See, for example, *Archetypes of the Collective Unconscious*, para 158.

14. Novalis, *Henry von Ofterdingen*, trans Palmer Hilty (New York 1964), pp 16 and 21.

15. Ibid, p 17.

16. Ovid, *Metamorphoses*, x, lviiiff. Also related to Ovid's scene are Anodos's two attempts to embrace a beloved woman (17 and 119). Cf the similar attempts by Goethe's Faust to embrace Helen (*Faust* 6561) and by Byron's Manfred to embrace Astarte (*Manfred*, 1.i.199).

17. See Neumann, *The Great Mother*, pp 12-13; and *The Origins and History of Consciousness* (New York 1962), p 198.

18. *Origins*, p 17. On the death-wish in German Romanticism, see *Origins*, pp 379-80 and *The Great Mother*, 34n.

19. Jung, *Symbols of Transformation*, pp 355-56.

20. Novalis, hymn no 4, English version from *Hymns to the Night and Other Selected Writings*, trans Charles E. Passage (New York 1960), p 6.

21. Such works contain a number of references to dangerous elf women and "forest wives" who are hollow behind. See Benjamin Thorpe, *Northern Mythology* (London

1851), I, 26-27n, and II, 74 and 136. Also Thomas Keightly, *The Fairy Mythology* (London 1828), r, 87-88, 141-54, 241-44, and, 34-35. One of MacDonald's early poems, "My Room," contains a casual reference to "the goblin hollow woman"; see *Poems* (London 1857), p 272.

22. See Neumann, *Origins*, pp 13, 18, and 170.

23. In a famed aphorism A.W. Schlegel identified all poets with Narcissus: "*Dichter sind doch immer Narcisse.*" See Louise Vinge, *The Narcissus Theme in Western European Literature up to The Early 19th Century* (Lund 1967), p 305.

24. Ibid, pp 37 and 171-72.

25. The figure of the Ancient Wise Woman plays a central part in MacDonald's imaginative world. Perhaps the fairy godmothers of Perrault and the story of "Frau Holle" in the Grimms' *Kinder und Hausmärchen* helped to shape MacDonald's conception. Tacitus' *Germania* (40) describes Nerthus, an Earth Mother (*Terrum matrem*), inhabiting an island (*est in insula Oceani castum nemus*). This passage is quoted in the first volume of the Grimms' *Deutsche Sagen* under the title "*Der heilige Seeder Hertha.*" The figure of the Wise Woman is rare in Romantic literature, but in La Motte Fouqué's *Der Zauberring*, from which MacDonald quotes at the beginning of chapter 6, Frau Minnetrost, the "*fromme Drude,*" uses her magical powers to aid various of the characters and eventually proves to be the mother of the young hero.

26. Atlantis has been made a familiar image of the lost original state by Blake, but it is also found in Novalis's *Heinrich von Ofterdingen* and Hoffmann's *The Golden Pot*.

27. M. H. Abrams, *Natural Supernaturalism: Tradition and Revolution in Romantic Literature* (New York 1971), pp 169ff.

28. Wolff mentions various examples of the double in Romantic literature; see pp 65-66. But he neglects the

scene in La Motte Fouqué's *Der Zauberring* that is the closest parallel: "*Es war sein eignes Gesicht . . . das ihm unter dem fremden Helme hervor im eben aufgehenden Vollmondslichte wie aus einem Spiegel sichtbar war . . .*" See *Ausgewiihlte Werke von Friedrich Baron de la Motte Fouqué, II* (Halle 1841), 95.

29. See Neumann on chastity as a psychological symbol, *Origins*, p 92.

30. See Neumann, *Origins*, pp 173ff.

31. Greville MacDonald, "Introduction," *Phantastes, A Faerie Romance* (London 1923), p viii.

32. Reis, p 87.

33. Northrop Frye, "The Structure of Imagery in *the Faerie Queene*," *Fables of Identity* (New York 1963), p 81.

34. Coleridge, *Biographia Literaria*, ed J. Shawcross (Oxford 1907), II, 12.

35. Novalis, hymn no 4, English translation by Passage in *Hymns to the Night*, p 6. Near the end of *Heinrich van Ofterdingen* Heinrich (like Anodos) hears the voice of his dead beloved speaking from a tree: "you still have a while to stay on earth, but the girl will comfort you until you die too and enter in to our joys" *Ofterdingen* (p 155).

36. *Henry von Ofterdingen*, p 148.

37. Abrams, p 191. A good example of such a cyclic myth is found in F.W.J. Schelling: "With consciousness innocence and reconciliation with nature were lost; voluntary surrender to it became necessary. From the ensuing struggle freedom emerged as both the conquered and the conqueror. Conscious reconciliation with nature, which has supplanted unconscious identity with it and conflict with fate and which restores unity on a higher plane, is expressed in the idea of Providence. It was Christianity that introduced the period of Providence as well as its dominant view of the universe as history and as world ruled by Providence"; *On University Studies*, trans E.S. Morgan (Athens, Ohio 1966), pp 86-87.

38. Abrams, p 194.
39. Neumann, *Origins*, p 206.

The Quest for "The Truth":
A Reading of George MacDonald's *Phantastes*
Keith Wilson
From *Études Anglaises*

George MacDonald was born at Huntly in Aberdeenshire in 1824 and died in 1905. During this substantial lifetime, his literary output was prolific and varied, classified by his son Ronald into twenty-five novels, three prose fantasies, eight children's tales, five sermons, three collections of short stories and five volumes of verse.[1] He achieved a recognition that went beyond the mere whims of mass popularity, though popular he certainly was, especially in America where "we find as many as three different publishers in different towns issuing a novel of his in the same year."[2] In the biography of his father,[3] Greville MacDonald gives a list of the family friends which is at the same time a list of the intellectual leaders of Victorian England. The close friends include Ruskin, Carroll, Kingsley, F.D. Maurice, A.J. Scott and Lady Byron; the acquaintances number Tennyson, Burne-Jones, Matthew Arnold, Octavia Hill, George Henry Lewes, Leslie Stephen, Leigh Hunt and William Morris. The biography contains a montage showing MacDonald with Dickens, Thackeray, Wilkie Collins, Trollope, BulwerLytton, Carlyle, Froude and Macaulay. Tennyson wrote to congratulate MacDonald on his first volume of poetry, Dickens praised *Phantastes*, Twain praised *At the Back of the North Wind*, and Ruskin cited *Diary of an Old Soul* "as a proof that Faith and Poetry were still united—'quaint, full of devotion, high in tone, the best example of the survival of faith in this sceptical age.'"[4]

Despite the appeal to both populace and literati, MacDonald's reputation was already beginning to suffer an eclipse during his own life and by the time of his death, and notwithstanding such eulogies as G.K. Chesterton's claim that he was "one of the three or four greatest men of the nineteenth century,"[5] obituary notices can carry the following qualifications:

> It has been said that some of his books are now unreadable because of their excess of theological argument; that "young ladies do not nowadays sit beside young men on sofas and ask for proofs of the existence of the Deity." But even this part of MacDonald's writing was in its day almost dramatic in its intensity, because it voiced the terrible struggle against formalism and rigid-creed interpretation of a man afire with

deep and genuine religious fervor, a nature instinct with spirituality.[6]

However, it is not "this part of MacDonald's writing," of which much of the novels is comprised, that has survived. The works of his that are still known and read, in part because of their influence on C.S. Lewis and the circle of his Oxford friends that included Tolkien and Charles Williams and became known as the Inklings, are the children's stories and the two adult prose fantasies, *Phantastes* (1858) and *Lilith* (1895). All have been reissued with greater or lesser regularity throughout this century and all have benefitted from the recent resurgence of interest in fantasy in the wake of the astonishing Tolkien cult.[7]

Recent work on that most apocalyptic of Victorian fantasists, George MacDonald, has at last begun to reveal the extent to which his imaginative work is an extension of the religious insights that so imperatively demanded expression. Admittedly, Ronald MacDonald stated the fact not long after his father's death, citing MacDonald's admission that "having begun to do his work as a Congregational minister, and having been driven. . . . into giving up that professional pulpit, he was no less impelled than compelled to use unceasingly the new platform whence he had found that his voice could carry so far."[8] But only recently have commentators begun to confront the fact that the myth that inspires *Phantastes*, *Lilith* and many of the children's stories "is a modern literary variation of the old Christian concept of *via negationis*: the discovery of God or reality by the Progressive stripping away of the veils of illusion."[9] That isn't to say that MacDonald's *viae* can't appear a little overgrown, taking his protagonists and readers through terrain that can seem as arbitrary as the inspired mazes created by his friend, Lewis Carroll. But, unlike Carroll, MacDonald does provide his reader with a map that clarifies considerably the direction of the journey that his protagonists take.

The map consists of the three volumes of *Unspoken Sermons*, published in 1867, 1885, and 1889. In passages from these sermons one finds, in their extra-literary form, the truths of the message that MacDonald felt himself compelled to preach. To read his fantasy works in conjunction with the sermons is to find apparent arbitrariness of event suddenly shaped into logical continuity. It is the purpose of this article to trace one of these suggestive strands, and to discuss the moral direction in which *Phantastes* (1858) points in the light of MacDonald's speculations in the sermon entitled "The Truth" from the third series of *Unspoken Sermons*.

MacDonald provides in this sermon his own very specific

definition of a natural object's "truth":

> The truth of a *thing*, then, is the blossom of it, the thing it is made for, the topmost stone set on with rejoicing; truth in a man's imagination is the power to recognize this truth of a thing; and wherever, in anything that God has made . . . we see the glory of God, there a true imagination is beholding a truth of God.[10]

Man's first move towards fulfilling his own "truth" is just such an imaginative act; the individual perceives anew the natural world, a world which tacitly proclaims the glory of God, and thereby is himself made closer to the Almighty:

> When the truth, the heart, the summit, the crown of a thing, is perceived by man, he approaches the fountain of truth whence the thing came, and perceiving God by understanding what is, becomes more of a man, more of the being he was meant to be. (*Unspoken Sermons*, p. 70)

The understanding is not a scientific process of murder by dissection but a joyous acceptance of the finished article, the completed "idea" that God created; MacDonald uses the example of a flower:

> Ask a man of mere science, what is the truth of a flower: he will pull it to pieces, show you its parts, explain how they operate, how they minister each to the life of the flower; he will tell you what changes are wrought in it by scientific cultivation; where it lives originally, where it can live; the effects upon it of another climate; what part the insects bear in its varieties—and doubtless many more facts about it. Ask the poet what is the truth of the flower, and he will answer: "Why, the flower itself, the perfect flower, and what it cannot help saying to him who has ears to hear it." The truth of the flower is, not the facts about it, be they correct as ideal science itself, but the shining, glowing, gladdening, patient thing throned on its stalk—the compeller of smile and tear from child and prophet . . . The idea of God is the flower: His idea is not the botany of the flower. (*Unspoken Sermons*, pp. 63-64, 65)

The effect on man of the revelation to him of one of God's completed "ideas" is made more explicit elsewhere:

> Let a man go to the hillside and let the brook sing to him till he loves it, and he will find himself far nearer the fountains of truth than the triumphal car of the chemist will ever lead the shouting crew of his halfcomprehending followers. He will draw from the brook the water of joyous tears, "and

> worship him that made heaven, and earth, and the sea, and the fountains of waters." (*Unspoken Sermons*, p. 69)

The distinction between imaginative vision and scientific analysis, between nature as manifestation of God and nature as devitalized scientific fact, is primary to MacDonald's thought. The imaginative vision is, as we shall see, the first possession that the hero Anodos must acquire in the quest on which *Phantastes* takes him.

The power to "recognize this truth of a thing," and thereby its revelation of God, is the passive acquirement in the movement of the individual towards his own "truth." The active stage centres upon the fulfilment of "duty." The initial advance is made with Carlylian moderation and practicality; when a man has perceived "the crown of a thing," "he has relations with the universe undeveloped in him till then. But far higher will the doing of the least, the most insignificant duty raise him. He begins thereby to be a true man" (*Unspoken Sermons*, p. 70). The duties make themselves apparent by being part of a logically ascending succession. When in MacDonald's *Robert Falconer*, the hero is asked "what is one's duty" the reply he gives is "The thing that lies next you, of course." The sermons reveal that once that has been established, the process is an organic unfolding:

> Man is man only in the doing of the truth, perfect man only in the doing of the highest truth, which is the fulfilling of his relations to his origin. But he has relations with his fellow man, closer infinitely than with any of the things around him, and to many a man far plainer than his relations with God. Now the nearer is plainer that he may step on it, and rise to the higher, till then the less plain. These relations are a large part of his being, are essential to his very existence, and spring from the very facts of the origination of his being. They are the relation of thought to thought, of being to being, of duty to duty. (*Unspoken Sermons*, pp. 71-72)[11]

Thus a man is only a man to the extent that he acknowledges his relationship with forces around him—with the natural world, with his fellow man, and ultimately with his God—and fulfils the duties that are implicit in the relationship. The duties may at first be irksome; man

> is so constituted as to understand them at first more than he can love them, with the resulting advantage of having thereby the opportunity of choosing them purely because they are true; so doing he chooses to love them, and is enabled to love them in the doing, which alone can truly reveal them to him, and make the loving of them possible. Then they cease to show

> themselves in the form of duties, and appear as they more truly are, absolute truths, essential realities, and eternal delights. The man is a true man who chooses duty; he is a perfect man who at length never thinks of duty, who forgets the name of it. . . . relations, truths, duties are shown to the man away beyond him, that he may choose them, and be a child of God, choosing righteousness like him. (*Unspoken Sermons*, pp. 72-73)

Duty thus becomes, ideally, progressively less onerous in proportion to its fulfilment. And however completely a man fulfils his duty to his fellow men, unless he comes to a realization of his relation with God he remains incomplete. When that relationship is fulfilled, he becomes what God has intended that he should be, he has fulfilled the "divine idea." For

> The highest truth to the intellect. . . . is the relation in which man stands to the source of his being . . . when the soul, or heart, or spirit, or what you please to call that which is the man himself and not his body, sooner or later becomes aware that he needs someone above him, whom to obey, in whom to rest, from whom to seek deliverance from what in himself is despicable, disappointing, unworthy even of his own interest. . . . then indeed is the man in the region of truth, and beginning to come true in himself. (*Unspoken Sermons*, pp. 76-77)

Once he has come to an awareness of "someone above him, whom to obey" his final step is to submit himself to this power. The end of the process then, the point at which a man expresses the "truth" of himself and, like the flower, blossoms as a complete "idea" of God, comes in the free submission of the man to the divine power of which he has been made aware: "To be right with God is to be right with the universe; one with the power, the love, the will of the mighty Father, the cherisher of joy, the lord of laughter" (*Unspoken Sermons*, p. 82).

The process outlined here is exactly the process that the sometimes baffling experiences of Anodos, the hero of *Phantastes*, take him through. When Anodos makes his frequent faulty decisions during his journey through Fairy Land, he makes them as a result of either ignoring or misinterpreting his duty, sometimes as a result of wilfulness and sometimes merely as a result of inexperience. By the end of *Phantastes* his imagination has been educated to the point at which he can recognize the correct course and the divine intention and fulfil them instinctively. To pick up MacDonald's words, he comes to the point where duties "appear as they more truly are, absolute truths, essential realities, and eternal delights." The process which he undergoes is a peeling of the eyes and the mind, so that he may come to recognize "the truth, the heart, the summit, the crown of a thing." His adventures fall roughly into two unequal parts. The first leads up to his beguilement by the spirit of the alder tree and the second explores his attempts, sometimes unconscious and often misguided, to rid himself of the burden of failure that this initial susceptibility has placed upon him. His final success in ridding himself of this burden comes after his imaginative powers have been refined and he develops the capacity to bestow love altruistically, an inevitable result of coming to perform (first unwittingly, then deliberately and at last instinctively) "the truth."

Almost as soon as Anodos enters Fairy Land he receives advice about the moral divisions of an anthropomorphic Nature; he meets a country maiden who warns him to trust the Oak, the Elm and the Beech, to beware of the Birch, and to shun the Ash and the Alder. When he comes to the cottage owned by the maiden's mother, he receives a further warning, reading in an ancient volume about Sir Percival, who has himself been betrayed by the maid of the Alder-tree and is wandering through Fairy Land attempting to expiate his sins. After pursuit through the wood by the Ash, and rescue from him by the Beech, Anodos duly mistakes the Alder for a "white lady" he has previously rescued from her prison of alabaster, and this despite a third warning from Sir Percival himself. Directly after the warning, and directly before his fall, Anodos is guilty of a statement of self-sufficiency and pride which is itself ample justification for his downfall: "Yet . . . I have now been often warned; surely l shall be well on my guard; and I am fully resolved I shall not be ensnared by any beauty, however beautiful. Doubtless, some one man may escape, and I shall be he."[12] The woman immediately appears, Anodos immediately falls victim to her, and is rescued from delivery to the Ash only by the intercession of Sir Percival, whose action is a further stage in his own process of redemption. After his rescue, the power which he has succumbed to is explained to him by the farmer's wife in whose cottage he takes shelter:

> ". . . the chief thing that makes her beautiful is this; that although she loves no man, she loves the love of any man; and when she finds one in her power, her desire to bewitch him and gain his love . . . makes her very lovely—with a self-destructive beauty though; for it is that which is constantly wearing her away within, till, at last, the decay will reach her face, and her whole front, when all the lovely mask of nothing will fall to

pieces, and she be vanished forever." (*Phantastes*, pp. 56-57)

The maiden of the Alder-tree is the quintessence of self-referential love, the idealization of outer rather than inner form. At the moment of his betrayal to the Ash, Anodos had seen the Alder maiden as she really was:

> The damsel had disappeared; but in the shrubbery, at the mouth of the cave, stood a strange horrible object. It looked like an open coffin set up on one end; only that the part for the head and neck was defined from the shoulder-part. In fact, it was a rough representation of the human frame, as if made of decaying bark torn from a tree. (*Phantastes*, pp. 53-54)

Her essential quality is her hollowness. Percival and Anodos have both in their turn been unable to distinguish the true from the false and the failure brings with it for both men the necessity to redeem themselves in action, by performance of the correct duty, and to come to recognize true worth.

For both of them the fall expresses itself in sexual terms, their susceptibility to and betrayal by a female principle that is slowly being eaten away from within by its own self love in a kind of fantasy parody, at least in the way that the farmer's wife describes it, of the effects of venereal disease. But in the fall from innocence to experience Anodos suffers a loss more reminiscent of that loss of imaginative wonder that so many Romantic and early Victorian poets saw overtaking the maturing child. Given the centrality of an emotional responsiveness to nature in MacDonald's discussion of the way to "The Truth," Anodos's loss of wonder is a clear indication that he has taken the wrong path. At his first entry into Fairy Land, Anodos had been made aware of a closer communion with nature than was customary in the "real" world. Consequent upon his failure, and as a preliminary to the actual purgative part of his journey, he loses the sense of communion. Having challenged, like the maturing child, the prohibitions and warnings of Fairy Land, having allowed the intercession of his own wilfulness and pride, Anodos experiences his own dark night of the soul, losing any sense of relationship with the surrounding natural world: "I took my way I knew not whither, but still towards the sunrise. The birds were singing; but not for me. All the creatures spoke a language of their own, with which I had nothing to do, and to which I cared not to find the key any more" (*Phantastes*, p. 55).

Anodos continues his wanderings and finds himself in the hut of an ogress against whom he has been warned by the farmer's wife. Despite his past experiences, he is again disobedient, opening a forbidden door which unites him with his "shadow." The ogress makes it clear that the shadow is not only a result of this disobedience but a further consequence of his subjection to the Alder maiden. Its immediate effect is to destroy in Anodos all power of imagination and joy, to shackle him to the mundane. In the context of MacDonald's sermon, the significance could not be clearer. If the shadow is the foe of all delight in the natural, it is also the foe of God; by deadening Anodos's sensibilities it is moving him farther away from communion with the power which is the source of all beauty. It also leads to self-satisfaction in the power that it seems to give Anodos to strip away illusion and arrive at what he mistakenly imagines to be "reality." As a direct result of his wilfulness, Anodos is completely alienated from his surroundings and takes with him wherever he journeys a fetidness which destroys everything with which he comes into contact, a fetidness akin to the destruction of a flower by the "man of mere science" in an attempt to arrive at its illusory reality. Whether he knows it or not, indeed whether MacDonald consciously knew it or not, the path that Anodos is walking is the path that took the nineteenth century from a Romantic sacramental view of nature to a post-Darwinian determinism, and ultimately that other waste land that might conceivably be saved by advice—Datta. Dayadhvam. Damyata. / Give. Sympathize. Control.— not that far removed from that which MacDonald had to offer.

The lost sense of communion with nature is rediscovered by Anodos when he comes upon, and drinks from, a small spring which gradually opens up into a full, fast-flowing, river—the associations with *The Waste Land* are again of passing interest. In the wider context of MacDonald's writings the implications of this are clear, and one thinks especially of his paean of praise for water in "The Truth." There he speaks of the man who lets "the brook sing to him till he loves it . . . He will draw from the brook the water of joyous tears, 'and worship him that made heaven, and earth, and the sea, and the fountains of Waters.'" The appearance of the stream to Anodos is the first step back towards the ultimate realization of a "great good," just as the brook on the hillside is the first stage for the imaginative man to an awareness of God. The discovery is followed by a reawakening of Anodos's receptivity to the wonders of Fairy Land:

> As I sat, a gush of joy sprang forth in my heart, and overflowed at my eyes. Through my tears, the whole landscape glimmered in such bewitching loveliness, that I felt as if I were entering

> Fairy Land for the first time, and some loving hand were waiting to cool my head, and a loving word to warm my heart. (*Phantastes*, p. 71)

When Anodos travels down the river he arrives at a palace which is to provide the surroundings for the full re-awakening of his imagination. The palace is a literal rendering of what for the nineteenth century was a very familiar metaphor—the Palace of Art.

At the centre of the palace is a library, and it is here that Anodos spends much of his time. Whatever he reads, he seems himself to be taking a part in, and it is in one of these stories, the story of Cosmo von Wehrstahl, that we find the implied explanation of Anodos's experience in the palace. The story is, significantly, about selflessness and self-sacrifice in love—a theme which Anodos will have cause to remember—and it centres upon a magical mirror that transforms the mundane into the exotic: Cosmo speculates

> What a strange thing a mirror is! and what a wondrous affinity exists between it and a man's imagination! For this room of mine, as I behold it in the glass, is the same, and yet not the same. It is not the mere representation of the room I live in. . . . All its commonness has disappeared. The mirror has lifted it out of the region of fact into the realm of art; and the very representing of it to me has clothed with interest that which was otherwise hard and bare. . . . But is it not rather that art rescues nature from the weary and sated regards of our senses . . . and, appealing to the imagination . . . reveals Nature in some degree as she really is, and as she represents herself to the eye of the child, whose everyday life, fearless and unambitious, meets the true import of the wonder-teeming world around him, and rejoices therein without questioning. (*Phantastes*, p. 94)

The Wordsworthian echoes are instructive. For MacDonald as for Wordsworth the child is father of the man, his mind having been less sullied by what Coleridge referred to as "the lethargy of custom" for both, the path to the transcendent (however different the absolutes they would have understood by this) lay through a heightened sense of the wonders of the natural, innate in the child who comes "trailing clouds of glory . . . / From God, who is our home" but something that the adult has to work at.

It is in the relationship between the palace of art and the heightening of the responsiveness to a natural world that so many of MacDonald's intuitions, at times apparently contradictory, coalesce.

Crossing a Great Frontier

Whenever MacDonald speaks of the "truth," as evidenced in *Unspoken Sermons*, he is speaking of a truth revealed to the imagination rather than to the intellect, to the artist rather than to the scientist. It is perhaps for this reason that his children's stories are among his most successful works for, given that he is also a propagandist for a framework of belief, he can assume with audience of children as ready an acceptance at the most basic level of the truths of the imagination as of those of the intellect. This is also why the religious intuitions are expressible so much more successfully in the fantasy works than in such nominally realistic novels as *David Elginbrod* and *Robert Falconer*. In the fantasies the faculty that gave birth to the intuitions, the type of imagination that is not restricted to the verifiable and to realistic representation, is allowed greater play. When MacDonald looks at the world, he is looking at it as if in a mirror; it has for him a constant freshness, akin to that incandescence that Hopkins catches so well in such poems as "Pied Beauty" and "Hurrahing in Harvest" and that makes him both a supreme "nature" poet and a supreme "religious" poet. MacDonald's religious view and his imaginative faculty are inextricably intertwined. The first step towards God is an exercise of the imagination, and this is the step Anodos takes in the Fairy Palace. The room which has been specially prepared for Anodos in the Palace, and has his own name on the door, is an exact replica of the room in his own house. The only distinction is that his receptivity to it is heightened; with his newly stimulated imaginative faculty, he sees it freshly.

If the awakening of the imagination is essential, it is also only part of the process. Anodos must come to realize his own truth as a man and, as we have seen, this is accomplished by action. When Anodos's imaginative powers are revivified and, accompanying himself on a harp, he summons by song the white lady he has rescued and for whom he has been searching, he again defies the fairy law, urged on by an instinct of which he is not fully in control, and touches her. When she runs from him and he follows her out of the palace, her final words are a clear indication of the imaginative preserves of the Palace, preserves which Anodos has attempted to extend: "You should not have touched me . . . Ah! you should have sung to me; you should have sung to me!" (*Phantastes*, pp. 119-120). By a fantasy variant of the fortunate fall, Anodos is forced out of his Eden of the imagination to exercise the results of his imaginative refinement in the world of action and duty. The sojourn in the Palace has obviously been beneficial. Anodos rapidly vanquishes the goblins who taunt him with the white lady's love for Sir Percival, the "better man," and does so by altruistically crying "Let him have her." This act of spontaneous, self-sacrificing generosity is followed by his making the first correct choice since his arrival in Fairy Land; he resists the wiles of the old woman who plays upon his solitude to tempt him and turns herself into a young girl. His love is now of an altruistic kind that allows him resign his claim to a woman who is clearly not intended for him; his perception is now of a kind to allow him to distinguish between true beauty and false temptation. He is well on the path to understanding, and performing, his "duty."

Anodos comes to another place of refuge and rest, the cottage of the old woman, the omniscient and all-loving woman who is present in one form or another in nearly all MacDonald's fantasy works. It is from his experiences in passing through the doors of the woman's cottage that Anodos learns most completely the value of love and the proximity of the next world, which is instrumental in giving him the courage that results from the banishing of the fear of death. The experience offered by the second door is perhaps the most telling. It reveals to him the truth of the relationship between the white lady and Sir Percival and forces him to accept the second place in her affections that he has spontaneously declared to the goblins his willingness to accept. This experience not only allows him to express a generosity of which he has only recently become capable; it also indicates to him the limitations of his spiritual progress and the sphere of action in which he must still involve himself before he becomes a complete man. Percival is discussing Anodos with the white lady: "There was something noble in him but it was a nobleness of thought, and not of deed. He may yet perish of vile fear" (*Phantastes*, p. 139). The power of the imagination has not yet expressed itself in the active life. As we have seen from the *Unspoken Sermons*, the imaginative power of the poet to see the truth of the universe is but the starting point; such a man "has relations with the universe undeveloped in him till then. But far higher will the doing of the least . . . duty raise him. He begins thereby to be a true man." Anodos is at last ready to move into "the torrent of mighty deeds."

Anodos's self-sufficient pride is allowed a final fling. When he fails to meet his death after the successful killing of the giants which is his first "mighty deed," he again falls victim to self-satisfaction and again suffers a fall; he is vanquished by a knight identical to himself and imprisoned, with his reappeared shadow, in a tower. From this imprisonment in and by self, he is rescued by a singing girl who has herself—after earlier losing joy by falling under the baleful influence of Anodos's shadow—been educated in the power of the imagination by the Fairy Queen. The girl's song invites Anodos to come from his house of pride and be united with the Spirit of the Earth; he must lose the overweening sense of self and submit himself to a benevolent cosmic force, something akin to MacDonald's benevolent God. It is from this experience that Anodos fully grasps what he has already learned in the old woman's cottage; she is indeed ultimately in control of everything, and pride in self is a denial of the source from which the ability to perform a deed comes. One remembers from *Unspoken Sermons* MacDonald's avowal of the necessity of duty: "The man is a true man who chooses duty; he is a perfect man who at length never thinks of duty, who forgets the name of it . . . relation truths, duties are shown to a man away beyond him, that he may choose them and be a child of God, choosing righteousness like him" (*Unspoken Sermons*, pp. 72-73). To choose the correct duty is to prove oneself a man; but this is to be no source of empty pride, since to fail in the choice is to be less than a man. The fulfilment of duty is merely the fulfilment of one's true nature, the fulfilment of the divine "idea" of a man. When Anodos has been released by the girl, he puts off his accoutrements of pride and discovers the "delight of being lowly":

> "I am what I am, nothing more. I have failed," I said; "I have lost myself—would it had been my shadow." I looked around: the shadow was nowhere to be seen. Ere long, I learned that it was not myself, but only my shadow, that I had lost. I learned that it is better, a thousandfold, for a proud man to fall and be humbled, than to hold up his head in pride and fancied innocence. I learned that he that will be a hero, will barely be a man; that he that will be nothing but a doer of his work, is sure of his manhood. (*Phantastes*, pp. 164-165)

Anodos has thus learned both the power of the imagination, the power that the poet has to see the "truth" of a flower, which brings him into joyous communion with his surroundings, and the necessity for man to justify his own place in those surroundings by the performance of duty, humbly and without expectation of reward. His final experience provides him with the opportunity to put this knowledge into successful action.

He meets again Sir Percival, whom, although formerly seen as his rival, he is now able to greet warmly. When they arrive at the strange religious ceremony in the wood, it is Anodos who senses its real nature:

The knight whispered to me, "how solemn it is! Surely

they wait to hear the voice of a prophet. There is something good near!"

> But, I, though somewhat shaken by the feeling expressed by my master, yet had an unaccountable conviction that here was something bad. So I resolved to be keenly on the watch for what should follow. (*Phantastes*, p. 174)

What does follow is a human sacrifice, masked by the solemnity of the ceremony. Anodos recognises the fear on the face of the victims, destroys the pedestal into which they are being pushed, and is met by the wolf to whom the victims have been given. He fights with the animal and both are killed. He has seen the truth of the situation and, unthinkingly, sacrificed himself for love of his fellow man; he has not consciously thought of his duty but almost instinctively performed it.

In the time directly after his death, Anodos experiences the union with nature for which he has been searching; the work ends with his reluctant removal from the fantasy world and his return to the real world, in which he may live out his life with the comforting conviction that "What we call evil, is the only and best shape which, for the person and his condition at the time, could be assumed by the best good" (*Phantastes*, p. 182). Without some awareness of MacDonald's presuppositions about man's relationship with God, the process by which Anodos reaches this conclusion seems arbitrary in the extreme.[13] With "The Truth" as a key, *Phantastes* becomes the most carefully embodied and consistently developed allegory.

All of MacDonald's fantasy works respond to this kind of precise reading because the urgency of the message that MacDonald felt moved to preach was always present in his works. They are neither the *jeux d'esprit* of a creatively whimsical mind (like the Alice books) nor impalpable subjective visions born of psychological vagaries. They are, as allegory always is, however dream-like its medium, consciously controlled imaginative works with a clearly directed moral function; *Phantastes*, given MacDonald's statements in the non-fiction prose, is as decipherable as *The Pilgrim's Progress*. Not surprisingly, his poetry shows a similar relentlessness of purpose and perhaps the poem "To an Autograph Hunter" shows most clearly the direction of the quest on which MacDonald sets both Anodos and the reader of his *Unspoken Sermons*:

> Seek not my name—it doth no virtue bear;
> Seek, seek thine own primeval name to find—
> The name God called when thy ideal fair
> Arose in deeps of the eternal mind.[14]

Endnotes

1. Ronald MacDonald, "George MacDonald: A Personal Note," in *From a Northern Window* (London: James Nesbit, 1911), p. 68.

2. J.M. Bulloch, "A Bibliography of George MacDonald," *Aberdeen University Library Bulletin*, V, 30 (February 1925), 682.

3. Greville MacDonald, *George MacDonald and His Wife* (London: Allen and Unwin, 1924)

4. Greville MacDonald, p. 497.

5. Obituary notice in the *Daily News*, September 23, 1905, p. 6.

6. Obituary notice in *Outlook*, LXXXI (September 30, 1905), 247.

7. At the time or writing, Wheaton College, Illinois, announces the appearance or a new annual review, entitled *Seven*, to be devoted to studies of the work of seven British authors: G.K. Chesterton, C.S. Lewis. J.R.R. Tolkien, Charles Williams, Dorothy Sayers, Owen Barfield—and George MacDonald, the one pre-twentieth century writer to be included.

8. Ronald MacDonald, "George MacDonald: A Personal Note," *From a Northern Window* (London: James Nisbet, 1911), pp. 66-67.

9. Gary K. Wolfe, "David Lindsay and George MacDonald," *Studies in Scottish Literature*, 12 1974), 138.

10. George MacDonald, "The Truth," *Unspoken Sermons: Third Series* (London: Longmans Green, 1889), p. 69. The whole discussion of an object's truth has very strong echoes, however different the doctrinal framework, or Gerard Manley Hopkins's sermons: see especially *The Sermons and Devotional Writings of Gerard Manley Hopkins*, ed. Christopher Devlin (London : Oxford University Press, 1967), p. 239.

11. George MacDonald, *Robert Falconer* (London: Hurst and Blackett, 1868), p. 403.

12. George MacDonald, *Phantastes* and *Lilith*, with an

introduction by C.S. Lewis (London: or Gollancz, 1962), p. 49.
13. See, for example, the discussion of *Phantastes* in Richard H. Reis, George MacDonald (New York: Twayne Publishers Inc., 1972), pp. 86-94.
14. George MacDonald, "To an Autograph Hunter," *Poetical Works* (London: Chatto and Windus, 1893), v. II, p. 290.

Wells and Cisterns: *Phantastes*
Rolland Hein
From *The Harmony Within*

"I knew now, that it is by loving, and not by being loved, that one can come nearest the soul of another."
—Anodos in *Phantastes*

C. S. Lewis tells of his first discovery of *Phantastes* and of the change it made in his life:

> *It must be more than thirty years ago that I bought—almost unwillingly, for I had looked at the volume on the book-stall and rejected it on a dozen previous occasions—the Everyman edition of* Phantastes. *A few hours later I knew that I had crossed a great frontier. . . . What it actually did to me was to convert, even to baptise . . . my imagination. . . . The quality which had enchanted me in his imaginative works turned out to be the quality of the real universe, the divine, magical, terrifying and ecstatic reality in which we all live.*[1]

Lewis had crossed into the land of Faerie, the land of all MacDonald's fantasies. It is a higher land, existing in the imagination, and entered by a willingness to leave our actual world behind and to follow the author on an adventure in which anything can happen.

In Lewis's case, apparently, MacDonald's theory about how this imagined land should function in the spiritual experience of his readers was valid. The authority for this theory, which we have discussed in the previous chapter in connection with MacDonald's view of the sacramental nature of all things—including the symbols of a truly Christian writer—lies ultimately with Novalis. The epigraph to *Phantastes* contains the essence of his view. Briefly, this prescription for the construction of fairy tales calls for a narrative surface bustling and incoherent, supported by an underlying musical harmony. The subsurface harmony derives from an orchestration of themes, as I hope to show.

For a fantasy to function at its best sacramentally, MacDonald felt that a person should read it simply for his own pleasure, not consciously for his edification, as he would read, say, a parable. It is, of course, intuitive perceptions that MacDonald has in mind. Mere intellectual analysis alone tends to leave the spirit emaciated, not strengthened. He is confident that to the proper reader some incidents will seem to convey moral and spiritual truths; others will remain incorrigibly enigmatic. The type and quantity of truths perceived will depend upon the reader's spiritual state and special needs at the time.

Whether or not we approach the fantasy as MacDonald intended depends, of course, on the extent to which we are willing to accept his basic literary and theological assumptions. In any case, to trace the themes, as we are attempting to do, is to note the underlying harmony. In *Phantastes*, the main theme appears to address the problem of man's search for satisfactions for his personal desires and longings. The Christian concern arises because the natural process of seeking satisfactions for human desires is self-centered, and self-centeredness is spiritually destructive.

What is man to do? MacDonald does not advocate the classic answer of Christian asceticism—that human passions are to be repressed, and many natural satisfactions denied. He shows, rather, that it is better to serve others than ourselves, and that our desires can be satisfied indirectly through this service. Real love endeavors to give, not get, and in so doing, finds inner satisfactions that self-centered love cannot begin to know, together with a joy not otherwise attained. This theme is summarized in a poem found in Chapter Nineteen:

> Better to sit at the waters' birth,
> Than a sea of waves to win;
> To live in the love that floweth forth,
> Than the love that cometh in.
>
> Be thy heart a well of love, my child,
> Flowing, and free, and sure;
> For a cistern of love, though undefiled,
> Keeps not the spirit pure.

Spiritual maturity consists in being like a well that gives and is always fresh, rather than like a cistern that is full to stagnation. How one becomes the former and avoids being the latter is carefully illustrated in the hero's adventures.

THE HERO

The hero of the tale, Anodos, has various, rapidly occurring adventures in Fairy Land, each of which helps him to grow morally and spiritually. His name itself is instructive, being a transliteration from a Greek word which has two meanings: "having no way" and "rising."[2] Anodos wanders through Faerie in a seemingly aimless manner, but all that happens to him has the power to make him rise, or grow, so that he is in the process of becoming a better person. He enters Faerie when he turns twenty-one, and he remains in that land twenty-one days; in other words, having reached physical and legal maturity, he is brought by his adventures to moral and spiritual maturity as well.

For growth to take place, Anodos must first accept the reality of the supernatural world. This requires both a certain inherent sensibility and a desire to cultivate it. At the beginning of the adventures, Anodos is concerned whether he has "fairy blood," and whether he can see the fairies in the woods. He learns from the lips of the country maiden whom he meets in Chapter Three that he could not have come so far in the woods if he did not have "fairy blood" within him. She takes him into the Cottage of the Four Oaks to her mother, who tells him that his ability to appreciate Fairy Land and to see the fairies there is determined by the strength of his fairy nature. He is much concerned about himself until he discovers that he can in fact see the fairies clearly. His fascination with their antics and affairs in the remainder of the chapter shows us that Anodos is indeed the right type of person to profit from these adventures. His having fairy blood does not, in itself, indicate that he has attained moral maturity; it simply assures us that he is such a person who may acquire it.

In Chapter One his attitudes and concerns reveal his need for spiritual growth. He is a young man who desires material and physical things. The story opens with his awakening in bed, and his morning thoughts concern his "legal rights," because he is in the process of inheriting wealth from his deceased father. He recalls that the day before, as he was searching through his father's things, he was interrupted by a visit from a tiny "womanform," who excited within him certain desires, both admirable and unadmirable.

In his conversation with her, he makes three mistakes: he hesitates to believe in her because he has seen her only once; he belittles her because of her smallness; and, when she accommodates his prejudices and becomes "normal" size, he is physically attracted to her and tries to embrace her. These mistakes rest upon assumptions common to ordinary people in the world at large. The first is that the authority of any supernatural event is strengthened by the number of times it is repeated, an assumption to which the scientific mind is inclined. The second is that the larger something is, the more important it must be, an assumption made by dull minds in general. The third is that what is physically attractive must be immediately possessed, an assumption made by sensual people.

Crossing a Great Frontier

For these mistakes, he receives her rebukes. The rebuke to his sensuality is strengthened by her suggesting that she may be the spirit of one of his deceased grandmothers. The suggestion increases the mystery that surrounds her, and Anodos, looking into her eyes, is filled with an "unknown longing" for Fairy Land, which she assures him he will find tomorrow.

What is happening here must be carefully noted, for it suggests a pattern for much that follows. Two types of desire—the one for sexual gratification, and the other for joyous experiences in the supernatural world—follow rapidly one upon another, and both are associated with the same woman. MacDonald suggests that, for man in a low state of spiritual development, these two desires are not all that different from each other. Anodos must learn to distinguish carefully between them and handle each one correctly. This theme is worked out in detail in the episodes of Anodos's experiences with his marble lady, and is orchestrated in both the story of Cosmo in Chapter Thirteen and "The Ballad of Sir Aglovaile" in Chapter Nineteen.

One should note as well, in this important opening chapter, the use of male and female figures as symbols. The fairy woman tells Anodos: "'I dare say you know something of your greatgrandfathers a good deal further back . . . ; but you know very little about your great-grandmothers on either side.'" Apparently, male ancestors symbolize the concerns of the everyday and commercial world; female ones symbolize the less known, mysterious side of experience. It is through the woman that one reaches to the highest truths—so elusive and difficult to express, yet so nourishing to the spirit of man—that give meaning to existence. One recalls the presentation of the female figure in the Curdie books and in *At the Back of the North Wind*: in the former, the aged queen Irene is both the essential human and the divine; in the latter, the North Wind acts as Diamond's entrance into the higher realm of life beyond death. Frequently in the fantasies, women have finer natures and keener sensibilities than men, guarding truth and guiding men to it. Therefore, physical desires which men feel toward women, kept chaste and tastefully expressed, are ready symbols of man's deep longing to possess a knowledge of ultimate truth.[3]

MacDonald, then, presents two attitudes toward sexual desire. In its baser form as lewd and promiscuous desire, he condemns it as being a certain evidence of need for moral and spiritual development. But in its higher expressions—regulated according to Christian principles—it is an aid to moral and spiritual development. Elsewhere in his writings (see, for instance, the essay "Individual Development" in *Orts*, or the novel *Paul Faber, Surgeon*), he makes clear that a proper sensuality may become a means of renewing one's conviction of the reality of the spiritual world. Many today may see this distinction of two types of sensuality as curious, but MacDonald sees a large difference between them and would argue that his interpretation is biblically sound.

FIRST ADVENTURES

We believe with delight in Anodos's entrance into Faerie, feeling wonder with him as the items in his bedroom gradually change into the natural surroundings of the new land. As soon as he is within this land of the imagination, he meets a country maiden who warns him concerning the trees: "'Trust the Oak, and the Elm, and the great Beech. Take care of the Birch, for though she is honest, she is too young not to be changeable. But shun the Ash and the Alder; for the Ash is an ogre—you will know him by his thick fingers; and the Alder will smother you with her web of hair, if you let her near you at night.'" The warning is dramatic, preparing us for fierce conflicts between good and evil beings, both interested in Anodos's allegiances. In Anodos's later meeting with the beech tree, we learn of "an old prophecy" that trees will one day become men and women. Clearly the life that animates all of nature is full of significance for man, both for the present and the future.

Four oak trees form the corners of the first cottage he sees, indicating the trustworthiness of the country maiden's mother who dwells there. She, too, warns him about the ash tree, but avoids being specific about the danger; all she will say is that the ash's favorite tactic is to kill his victims with fright. The reader is deep within the story before he discovers the precise nature of the evil that the ash represents: the spiritual disaster which comes from being consumed with a selfish sensuality.

Another important person in Anodos's spiritual education is now introduced—the knight, Sir Percival. In the cottage Anodos discovers a large old book containing "many wondrous tales of Fairy Land," and in it he reads a fragment of the legend of Sir Percival. It pictures Sir Galahad, in wondrously shining armor, meeting Sir Percival, whose armor is red with rust and whose horse is "smirched with mud and mire." Percival's condition is a result of his seduction by the "damosel of the alder-tree." The account reinforces the warning given Anodos concerning the evil trees and suggests the danger he too will face.

Crossing a Great Frontier

Fleeing in horror from the spirit of the pursuing ash tree, Anodos stumbles and falls, stunned, at the root of a large beech. Suddenly he is enveloped by "two large soft arms" and hears the reassuring voice of a woman murmuring, "'I may love him, I may love him; for he is a man, and I am only a beech tree'" (an incident described in the previous chapter). After giving him a tress of her hair to protect him from the dangers of the ash, she sings:

> *I saw thee ne'er before;*
> *I see thee never more;*
> *But love, and help, and pain, beautiful one,*
> *Have made thee mine, till all my years are done.*

Love that gives of itself—that helps another though that help means personal pain—unlocks the secret of life and bliss. This, Anodos comments, is the "secret of the woods, and the flowers, and the birds." It is a far cry from the love that desires to possess another for the satisfaction of selfish passions.

Spiritually exhilarated by this experience, Anodos next discovers his marble lady. While walking through a seemingly friendly portion of the wood, he enters a mossy cave for rest. He begins to daydream, thinking about "lovely forms, and colors, and sounds," until he realizes he is lying on a moss-covered block of alabaster. When he removes the moss from his couch, he is startled to find that it encases the marble form of a sleeping woman; she is perfectly lovely. Seized with a deep desire to awaken the woman, he finds himself "rejoicing in a song" and begins to sing. The power of his songs is effective; she arises and flees, with Anodos following. (We will consider in our final chapter why MacDonald refers so often in his writings to the power of song.)

The incident pictures Anodos possessed by desire or love in its highest and purest form. The marble lady appears to symbolize the spirit of the Ideal, or the Perfect, and, as such, is in MacDonald's thought a surrogate for the divine Presence. She is the spirit that weds perfect beauty—and ultimate truth. Something deep within Anodos's soul answers to her: he comments that her perfect loveliness was "more near the face that had been born with me in my soul, than anything I had seen before in nature or art." These deep longings toward the Ideal which men feel have often been prime motivations for artists, and much of what MacDonald is saying in *Phantastes* intrigues those who are interested in a Romantic theory of art. At the time he wrote *Phantastes*, MacDonald was the fledgling artist, with growing convictions about the power of literary art to perceive and express spiritual truths. Anodos mirrors him: he is a singer whose songs have on this occasion freed the marble lady, and will evoke her later. But readers who are not artists need not feel as though the symbolism applies to them only in a secondary sense. Anyone who entertains an ideal and expends his energies pursuing it will find that Anodos's experiences serve as a mirror, showing him much about himself.

FACING INITIAL DANGERS

The ideal is fleeting and elusive. One is compelled to follow by the love he feels for it, but the way is beset with spiritual pitfalls. Each pitfall Anodos faces is a variation on the theme of the nature of love. When love's energies flow exclusively toward the self, they are spiritually disastrous; only when its energies flow outward, so that all self-centered considerations are obliterated, can one commune satisfyingly with his ideal. The end of such selfless devotion to the ideal is union with it. Anodos summarizes at the end of Chapter Twenty-two what he learns: ". . . my ideal soon became my life; whereas, formerly, my life had consisted in a vain attempt to behold, if not my ideal in myself, at least myself in my ideal."

The first of Anodos's vain attempts to selfishly possess the ideal results in his falling into the hands of the Maid of the Alder. After he again meets Sir Percival, who warns him to beware of her, he resolves to profit from the knight's example, but nevertheless goes straight to his undoing. He composes another song, and a white lady immediately appears. The substance of the song, however, is quite different from the theme of the former ones: it addresses the "Queen of the Night" and asks to be secluded with her in a night of love. On the story level, Anodos is showing the same animal sensuality that he showed in the opening chapter toward his "grandmother" from Faerie. MacDonald has already warned against such passion, and will continue to do so in many episodes yet to come.

In this episode, the reader is subtly but definitely made concerned for Anodos's safety. First, in his song he dismisses the moon, hoping it will not rise this particular night. A frequent and complex symbol in MacDonald's writings, the moon here seems to suggest the beneficent providence of God that pervades the universe. For Anodos, it functions throughout his adventures as his guardian spirit. For him to dismiss it indicates he is laying himself open to danger. As he does so he feels a certain uneasiness, but he ignores it, yielding to the sensuous pull of the moment.

Crossing a Great Frontier

As Anodos's beautiful companion takes him to her grotto, he is enchanted with her "intense loveliness" and "extreme beauty." His sensual longings show him to be in a spiritual state of complete self-centeredness. Lying entranced with her loveliness, he is engrossed in the tale she tells him, in which he and she are the principal characters. He becomes ecstatic as he surrenders himself to self-centered imaginings.

But Anodos awakes from his swoon in the gray dawn to be confronted with horror. (In the dream world of Faerie, beauty and ugliness, the ethereal and the grotesque, can be swiftly juxtaposed without offending the reader's credulity.) His enchantress appears now at the mouth of the cave "like an open coffin set up on one end . . . a rough representation of the human frame, only hollow," tearing at hair held in her hands. She commits the terrified Anodos to her monstrously ghoulish companion, whom he now recognizes as the Ash tree. The Ash, he now realizes, is the symbol of spiritual death, and his beauty is the famed Maid of the Alder, who has undone the knight and is now about to destroy him. About to be seized by the Ash, Anodos is narrowly saved when "the dull, heavy blow of an axe" echoes through the woods, and his would-be abductor shudders, groans, and then flees. His seductress, with a disdainful look, flees as well. Exhausted and dejected, Anodos, too, leaves the cave, a perplexed and humbled man. How, he asks himself, can "beauty and ugliness dwell so near"?

Thus the warning given Anodos upon entering Faerie is largely fulfilled: "'. . . the Alder will smother you with her web of hair, if you let her near you at night.'" So, too, the warning of the beech-tree maiden is fulfilled, who had admonished him there were beings in the wood resembling herself whom he should beware of, and he should try to avoid the "very beautiful." His unpracticed eye was deceived into mistaking the Maid of the Alder for his marble lady. He unwisely pursued what was beautiful for selfish rather than selfless ends. His mistake has almost meant his death, for all selfishness is spiritually destructive.

THE CHALLENGE OF RATIONALISM AND DOUBT

A related pitfall for one pursuing his ideal is that of succumbing to a sterile, analytical rationality. It may offer a challenge to the existence of the entire supernatural world, as the episode in the farmer's cottage does, or it may be destructively analytical of one's experiences, robbing him of the joy he should otherwise know, as the many incidents of the shadow plaguing Anodos suggest. In any case, this cynicism is a result of self-centeredness. In the next adventure, Anodos accepts the hospitality of a farm family of four. The mother is a devotee of Faerie lore, and the daughter is fascinated with fairy stories; the husband, however, believes all fairy matter to be a hoax, and, the son agrees, adding contempt to his father's denials. Through these two characters MacDonald shows the antagonism of empiricism and rationalism to all imaginative activities. The temptation is to disbelieve in Fairy Land altogether, viewing it as only a delusion. The farmer is the congenial "outsider" who simply lacks the capacity to perceive anything intuitively. It is ironic, of course, that he himself dwells in the very land the existence of which he would deny.

Leaving the farmer's family in a despondent mood, Anodos goes deeper into the forest and comes upon a hut, built against a tall cypress (symbol of dejection), and enters. It is the house of the ogre, against whom the farmer has warned him. That the warning came from the male symbol of rationality suggests that no fine discrimination is required to avoid this danger. Anodos finds within a woman reading aloud from an ancient volume, a philosophy of negation and despair, the very opposite of all MacDonald himself teaches.

This dark philosophy, together with Anodos's mood, causes his cynical self to emerge. Probing in the cottage, Anodos comes upon a closet door which opens to "a narrow, dark passage." As he peers into the darkness, a "dark figure" runs toward him and, to Anodos's alarm, fastens itself to him as his shadow. The woman tells him that anyone who has come from a meeting such as his recent one in the forest is almost certain to be visited by his shadow. That is, Anodos there encountered his ideal—his marble lady—and he is now beset by its opposite, his lower self. Until Anodos masters the shadow with a spirit of humility at the end of Chapter Twenty-two ("'I have lost myself—would it had been my shadow.' I looked round: the shadow was nowhere to be seen"), it intervenes and interferes in various incidents, defeating the good that could otherwise issue, and often working definite harm.

The theme of the possibility of many selves is a basic one in MacDonald's thought, and we will note its fuller development in *Lilith*. The "self" in this sense is not man's true person, but rather its negative underside, and control by the self is an open possibility for an individual, not a necessity. This idea is directly related to MacDonald's doctrine of becoming: each of the successive possibilities of inferior selfhood must be met and successfully denied as one journeys spiritually toward oneness with God. That Anodos's shadow emerges when it does is itself a mark of Anodos's spiritual growth, an indicator that he has so far advanced in inner development that his true self is beginning to be aware of a lower self that, when indulged, negates good and works harm. That the shadow most often expresses a cynical "common sense" or worldly-wise attitude underscores MacDonald's insistence that a healthy Christian spirit is a childlike, imaginative one.⁴

As he continues his journey Anodos finds that now his relation to all things is affected by his shadow. When he rests on the grass, the flowers upon which he lies revive; those the shadow lies upon do not. His attendant appears "blacker in the full blaze of sunlight," and, as Anodos's fascination for his shadow increases, it becomes as bold as to smite "the great sun in the face." The sun seems to be a symbol for God, the source of all spiritual light; the shadow is doubt, rooted in rational analysis. Succeeding incidents in Chapter Nine reveal the shadow's disastrous effects: he transforms the mysterious into the commonplace, and creates distrust between friends. Soon Anodos begins to think the shadow is indispensable to his well-being. He says to himself:

> In a land like this, with so many illusions everywhere, I need his aid to disenchant the things around me. He does away with all appearances, and shows me things in their true color and form. And I am not one to be fooled with the vanities of the common crowd. I will not see beauty where there is none. I will dare to behold things as they are. And if I live in a waste instead of a paradise, I will live knowing where I live.

This is the creed of the cynic, a result of a "common sense" approach to life. It is an avowed enemy of the visions of the imagination.

This conclusion leads Anodos to injure another by being crassly inconsiderate. In the forest he meets a little maiden, happy and dancing, who carries a small crystal globe. Touching the globe makes it pour forth a torrent of harmonious music. (It probably symbolizes the imagined story-world of a child's delight.) The girl is most gentle with the globe, but Anodos, emboldened by his shadow, seizes it, and it bursts. The child is heartbroken, and Anodos is thereafter haunted by the incident, until he meets her again later in his adventures.

Another result—but Anodos says he is not certain this one is owing to the shadow—is that people become grotesque to him when he gets very close to them: "I soon found that . . . to feel I was in pleasant company, it was absolutely necessary for me to discover and observe the right focal distance between myself and each one with whom I had to do." The suggestion is that human relationships are marred by a too-close analysis of what people are; to love one's fellowmen requires seeing them imaginatively, not only as they are but as they are capable of becoming.

THE FAIRY PALACE

Just as a stream flowing through Anodos's bedroom took him into Fairy Land, so now he discovers a streamlet which, as he follows it, leads him to the Marble Palace at the center of Faerie. Before he arrives, he is filled with joy, fed by his harmonious interaction with nature. The marble of the palace is like that of the lady he is pursuing, and we rightfully expect he is about to have experiences nearer the ideal than his former ones. These events further develop the themes we are tracing through the work.

Within the palace, he is pleasantly surprised to discover a room with this description on the door: "The Chamber of Sir Anodos." He enters to find a chamber the very copy of his own, with all his peculiarly individual needs met by "invisible hands." The incident neatly points up MacDonald's emphasis upon individuality in his writings. It stands in interesting relation to the emphasis upon community of the Christian Socialist movement—and the thought of F. D. Maurice—which, as we noted earlier, somewhat influenced MacDonald. God has made each man unique, MacDonald insists, and God intends that each maintain his uniqueness, that he might serve and worship the Lord in a way no one else can. The result is that each man both learns and teaches something of God in his relations with his neighbors.

On the third day after his arrival at the palace, he finds the library, and is delighted to discover that, in Fairy Land, to read a book is to become alive in the imagined world of history or fiction, or to become himself the philosopher in a book of metaphysics. In one volume he reads about a world in which children are produced not by sexual generation, but by a type of natural generation from the earth itself. As he explains the sexuality of earth to the inhabitants there, their reactions are mixed, but some long to die in order to be born into this world where they may know physical love. Though living in the Victorian Age, famous for its prudery, MacDonald does not hesitate to champion the role of sex, not as an end in itself, but as a means to a higher form of love, and hence, spiritual well-being.

But though sexual love, as distinguished from mere lust, may augment spirituality, it still falls short of what the imagination may envision as ideal love. This theme, together with that of the necessity to abandon all self-centeredness, is central to the tale of Cosmo, which Anodos reads next in the Fairy Library. MacDonald also uses the tale to probe further his concept of the nature of art. Thus he presents the story at this juncture to counterpoint the themes we have been exploring, and to indicate more firmly how each theme eventually will be resolved.

Cosmo, a university student in old Prague, has a mirror upon his wall which periodically shows him the image of a lovely woman. Falling in love with her, he uses magic conjuration to compel her to enter his own world. She rebukes him for his use of magic, and tells him she cannot be sure of his love for her or of hers for him until they both are free from all enchantments. He must break the mirror, setting her free, though he thereby risks losing her. This he does, after a difficult inner struggle, but, in the convention of Victorian melodrama, he is wounded in the end of the tale, and dies in his princess's arms.

At the point in the story when Cosmo's fascination for the princess turns to passion, MacDonald quotes, without comment, this line: "Who lives, he dies; who dies, he is alive."[5] The climax of the tale neatly works out this paradox. Cosmo must be willing to destroy the mirror and risk never seeing the princess again in order truly to have her. He must completely relinquish his power over her before they can experience love on any other but a physical level; only this renunciation, a type of spiritual death, can open to him a higher experience of life and love. In this manner, the two types of sensuality are vividly illustrated in the story: the baser lust must be renounced, in order that higher love (which, like good dreams, is another means of grace in Fairy Land) may be experienced.

MacDonald's doctrine of the self comes vividly to mind, with the emphasis that he places upon the death of the self in his sermons on self-denial. In every phase of experience, denying indulgence in any pleasure that simply gratifies the self gives one a higher realization of the potential for true enjoyment inherent in that very pleasure. When Cosmo's love "withers" into passion, it becomes mere craving for self-satisfaction, and makes the princess a possession. To break the mirror is to give her her full selfhood; the love she will then freely choose to give him will be a much higher love. MacDonald will rework this theme very often in his fiction and make it one of the central themes of *Lilith*, as we shall see. To give one illustration from the novels, this theme occurs in the sequels *Sir Gibbie* and *Donal Grant*: in the first novel the shepherd-poet Donal relinquishes the girl whom he loves to Gibbie, only to enjoy a yet higher experience of love in the second novel.

The second theme of the Cosmo story concerns the imperfect nature of any experience of love between the sexes. The tale is prefaced by a direct announcement of this idea: "Sometimes it seemed only to represent a simple story of ordinary life, perhaps almost of universal life; wherein two souls, loving each other and longing to come nearer, do, after all, but behold each other as in a glass darkly." (MacDonald is echoing Paul in I Corinthians 13:12: "For now we see through a glass darkly; but then face to face. . . .") Taken in conjunction with the previous myth in Chapter Twelve, this one implies that, whereas the love relation in this life is more complete than that of the existentially prior world of the myth, it is still imperfect and will perhaps in a succeeding world be still more complete. In the midst of relating Cosmo's tale, Anodos comments: "Nay, how many who love never come nearer than to behold each other as in a mirror; seem to know and yet never know the inward life; never enter the other soul; and part at last, with but the vaguest notion of the universe on the borders of which they have been hovering for years?" Cosmo's longings for his beloved can never be satisfactorily consummated so long as the mirror exists; nor can the princess be a free agent, sure of the truth of their love, until the mirror is destroyed. So, MacDonald seems to be saying, love relationships in this world fall short of perfection because of the limitations inherent in the human condition. That he sees this as universally true to human experience is probably the reason for the name Cosmo, from *cosmos*, meaning "world," and hence, universal.

The story of Cosmo also complements Anodos's quest for the marble lady. Cosmo's first fascination for the princess in the mirror is like Anodos's enthrallment with his ideal beauty in the marble block, and when his love degenerates into passion, it is like the sensual attraction Anodos felt for the Maid of the Alder. Anodos's continued pursuit of his marble lady, which is about to be resumed, will also culminate in an act of renunciation, an act that is just prior to and necessary for his final spiritual maturation into full understanding of the basic moral truths of life.

DISOBEDIENCE, DESPAIR, AND DEATH

In the Hall of Statues in the Fairy Palace, Anodos again determines to evoke his marble lady through song. As he sings, she gradually materializes upon a pedestal, as if an invisible veil were being lifted upward from her. Overcome by her beauty and determined to "tear her from the grasp of a visible Death," he flings his arms about her. He is immediately rebuked, for he was strongly warned upon entering the hall not to touch anything. Fleeing from his presence, his marble lady disappears through a door he is forbidden to enter. He rushes through it, unheeding, to find himself in a wasteland, where, beside a great hole in the earth, he sits down to weep.

The Anodos who seeks to grasp his beautiful lady is not the Anodos in the grotto of the Maid of the Alder; his character has developed since then. In this instance he is prompted not by base sensuality, but by a determination to keep the lady in his sight.[6] His vision of her is of "the highest Human," which "faints away to the Divine," we are told in his song, and MacDonald in his published sermons develops the idea that humanity when it realizes its highest spiritual potential will differ in nowise from divinity.[7] Anodos wants to retain this revelation of glory he is receiving. But the momentary vision appears only in the context of his song; to try to compel it by an act of will is "in defiance of the law of the place," and he suddenly finds himself outside the palace.

Although despairing as he begins his trek through the wasteland, he makes a series of morally admirable decisions in response to his next experiences. He is now willing to relinquish his right to his marble lady in the presence of a "better man," and he sings a little song that summarizes an important lesson he has learned:

> In thy lady's gracious eyes
> Look not thou too long;
> Else from them the glory flies,
> And thou doest her wrong.

One must allow his visions their fleeting nature, and not attempt to capture any experience in order to prolong its effects.

Although he is no longer vulnerable to the appeal of base sensuality, as the next episode of the meeting with the elderly hag confirms, his self-centeredness is still present in his pride that it is his songs that have called the marble lady to life. This pride is stifling to his spirit. Crawling through a rocky tunnel, Anodos comes upon a gray and barren sea, the epitome of desolation. Overcome with despair, he determines to die. He walks out upon a low promontory, plunges headlong into the sea, and discovers instantaneously he has plunged into unspeakable joy. Death to the self is the final answer to pride.

References to water have been too closely associated with Anodos's crucial experiences for the reader not to suppose that water has symbolic significance. A stream of water flows from Anodos's bedroom into Fairy Land in the beginning of the tale, another takes him into the Fairy Palace, and a pool in a hall of the palace affords him a spiritually rejuvenating swim. Now in a sea he symbolically dies and is reborn. Similarly, water figures prominently in *Lilith*, as well as elsewhere in MacDonald's writings. Each association with water in Anodos's adventures marks his emergence onto a higher plane of spiritual existence, a transformation that generally occurs wherever one meets this imagery in MacDonald's works. [8]

THE BALLAD OF SIR AGLOVAILE

Anodos goes on his way, exhibiting an informed simplicity and confident childlikeness that MacDonald often associates with maturing spirituality. On an island after his sea journey, he enters a little cottage and is there ministered to by a woman whom he sees as both very old and very beautiful. But the beauty that Anodos now responds to is spiritual rather than physical, residing in her eyes and voice, so that he feels a "wondrous sense of refuge and repose." Having fed him, she sings him a ballad which repeats and develops the theme found in the Cosmo story and in Anodos's adventures to this point: that, since love and desire in this life are all but inextricably allied, spiritual death into newness of life is essential to be able to experience a higher love apart from base desire.

"The Ballad of Sir Aglovaile" begins with the knight Aglovaile's discovery, as he rides through the churchyard cemetery at night, of a ghost wailing a lament in the moonlight. Her song is certainly among the most charming that MacDonald ever composed:

> Alas, how easily things go wrong!
> A sigh too much, or a kiss too long,
> And there follows a mist and a weeping rain,
> And life is never the same again.
>
> Alas, how hardly things go right!
> 'Tis hard to watch in a summer night,
> For the sigh will come, and the kiss will stay,
> And the summer night is a winter day.

This is the plight of the natural human condition. As the ballad illustrates, it is all but impossible to keep to the narrow path of truth and right apart from spiritual death.

Crossing a Great Frontier

Aglovaile discovers the ghost to be that of a woman whom he once had betrayed and who had died together with his child. When he exclaims about her transformation, she replies: "'Thou seest that Death for a woman can / Do more than knighthood for a man.'" In response to his admiration for her beauty, she invites him to come closer, but with a condition similar to the one the marble lady gave Anodos: "'Come, if thou darest, and sit by my side; / But do not touch me, or woe will betide.'" They enjoy for a time a blissful love, but the prohibition is one that Aglovaile cannot keep for long. Awakening from a dream in which she has fled him, he is overjoyed to find her still by his side:

> And lo! beside him the ghost-girl shone;
>
> Shone like the light on a harbour's breast,
> Over the sea of his dream's unrest;
>
> Shone like the wondrous, nameless boon,
> That the heart seeks ever, night or noon:
>
> Warnings forgotten, when needed most
> He clasped to his bosom the radiant ghost.

As he takes her to himself, she turns into a corpse and disappears. Aglovaile is left only with the recurring lament which he hears "when winds are wild": "Alas, how easily things go wrong. . . ."

The simile above—the longing for the ghost girl suggesting the spiritual longings of the human heart—should not go unnoticed. The theme of the spiritual significance of love for woman is thus given another imaginative development. Feminine beauty answers to something deep within man that is quite other than animal passion, but sensual man misreads his own spiritual longings, understanding them only in terms of physical desires. Physical love, when it is only an appropriation of the beloved for self-centered pleasure, frustrates this higher purpose; yet man in his lower stages of moral development cannot help himself. Spiritual death and rebirth is the answer; for it results in a capacity to love in an unselfish and outgoing manner. To MacDonald, the passions are essentially pure and holy, but they "go wrong" more readily than most other things. The further experiences of Anodos in the beautiful old woman's cottage continue to illustrate this point.

THE FOUR DOORS

The woman's cottage has four doors leading outward, each of which Anodos enters. Three of them lead him into environs that recall past experiences; the fourth opens into timelessness. (Both these adventures and others in the remainder of the fantasy seem to refer to MacDonald's own past.)[9] The woman tells Anodos he may return to her whenever he sees her mark, a dark red cipher, upon a door. At least two of these doors lead him to experiences directly relevant to the themes we are tracing. Songs, which now appear more frequently, begin to repeat the more basic themes of *Phantastes*—namely, the nature of true love and the power of death.

One of the doors is labeled the "door of Sighs." Going through it, Anodos discovers he must assume second place to Sir Percival in the heart of the marble lady. (The knight is morally superior to Anodos, because he has been accomplishing good deeds while Anodos has been, up to this point, passively learning.) Anodos's noble response is to accept the situation, and to continue to love her with an outgoing love. Returning with sighs of agony to the woman of the cottage, he hears her celebrate further in song the beauty of this nobler type of love. The song concludes that it is better to express love like a well gives water, keeping itself pure and fresh by its endless giving, than to be like a cistern, growing stagnant and impure because it only receives for itself, without outlet. As we noted above, this nicely summarizes the major theme of the entire fantasy. The result of Anodos's resignation of his beloved to the knight is that he now loves her as he "had never loved her before." To serve is better than to appropriate to oneself.

After various adventures through other doors, Anodos is forced by rising waters to leave the ancient woman's cottage. Her parting advice to him is "'Go my son, and do something worth doing.'" When Anodos previously overheard the knight and the marble lady talking about him, the knight had remarked: "'There was something noble in him, but it was a nobleness of thought, and not of deed.'" Clearly essential to MacDonald's prescription for moral growth is action, the willingness to work out in life the duties one's conscience lays upon him by his recognition of truth.[10] Anodos's next adventures shows him nobly acting out the higher love, the nature of which he is beginning to understand. In a land exploited and tyrannized by three giants, he allies himself with the ruling family to break the power of the usurping monsters and successfully expel them.

Not all the effects of the "first worthy deed" of his life, however, are happy ones. No sooner does he contemplate his triumph than his shadow, which forsook him when he first entered the Fairy Palace, reappears, but in altered form. The feelings of pride his feat nourishes within him give rise to another severe spiritual peril.

FINAL BATTLES WITH THE SELF

Absorbed in thoughts of self-congratulation, Anodos rides on through a forest "strangely enchanted." He is pleased to note that his shadow is not now with him, but he is startled to encounter a sinister-appearing knight who is the counterpart of himself, and who he suspects is one with the shadow. He is a "resplendent knight, of mighty size, whose armour seemed to shine of itself, without the sun." This knight is another of Anodos's alter-egos, possessed with a sense of self-sufficiency and independence from God, who threatens to enslave the true Anodos. The strength of his pride has given his shadow additional substance. In spite of all his prior adventures and the moral lessons each has taught, he succumbs to the trap; pride is the easiest sin to indulge. Finding himself helpless to do anything except follow his captor, he is imprisoned in a dark, dreary tower with a single small opening high in the top. When the moon shines in upon him, Anodos feels released; when the sun's rays penetrate the tower, he feels wretched and disconsolate. A dream of his childhood innocence and shamelessness increases his longings to be freed.

As previously suggested, these two planets appear to symbolize aspects of God. The sun suggests God's holiness—His love that is at once burning and life-giving; the moon suggests God's beneficent providence, an expression of His grace and mercy. One can readily see how God as the sun is displeased with Anodos's imprisonment in the cell of his pride, for it cuts him off from effective service. But it is not as easy to see why the moon should conflict with the sun, seemingly fostering an illusion. Perhaps MacDonald means to indicate that even though God in His holiness is displeased with Anodos's present predicament, He does not forsake him. God's mercy and beneficence are constantly extended to him in spite of his present folly, ready to turn this present trial to good when Anodos's humility returns.

Anodos is freed from his tower into the liberty of humility through the power of song—not his own this time, but that of another. Opening the door and emerging into the open air, Anodos is startled to find the singer to be the girl whose globe he had broken, now become a woman able to sing powerfully. When he begs her forgiveness, she tells him she has nothing to forgive, because when the globe upon which she relied for song was broken, she was compelled to sing for herself—a valuable change. We recall the theme of the sacramental character of adversity developed in *At the Back of the North Wind*. This woman discovered her own talent through what seemed at the time a catastrophe. Her songs do people good, and her moral radiance is an inspiration to Anodos.

As she goes, she sings one of MacDonald's favorite songs, which appears here and elsewhere:

> Thou goest thine, and I go mine—
> Many ways we wend;
> Many days, and many ways,
> Ending in one end.
>
> Many a wrong, and its curing song;
> Many a road, and many an inn;
> Room to roam, but only one home
> For all the world to win.

To bring all men "home" is God's chief purpose and goal in His working in the world. In fulfilling it, He may overrule evil, creating good out of it. The main ally of God's working thusly, perhaps the very channel of His creating power, is love of the highest type, the outgoing love that through the woman has affected Anodos. Now he is about to go forth, doing deeds worth doing, motivated by his love. But first MacDonald takes the opportunity to reinforce the moral insights of the tale by presenting Anodos, at the end of Chapter Twenty-two, meditating upon what he has learned.

When he removes his armor, a symbol of pride in its subtler form, and leaves it behind, he discovers that now his shadow has completely disappeared. Its demise is simultaneous with his finally achieving selfless humility, about which he muses:

> I learned that it is better, a thousand fold, for a proud man to fall and be humbled, than to hold up his head in his pride and fancied innocence. I learned that he that will be a hero, will barely be a man; that he that will be nothing but a doer of his work, is sure of his manhood. In nothing was my ideal lowered, or dimmed, or grown less precious; I only saw it too plainly, to set myself for a moment beside it. Indeed, my ideal soon became my life; whereas, formerly, my life had consisted in a vain attempt to behold, if not my ideal in myself, at least myself in my ideal.

Perhaps nowhere in his writings does MacDonald define more precisely the meaning of humility and the attitude of the humble man toward his ideal. Here is the fulfillment of MacDonald's epigraph to this chapter, taken from the writings of Cyril Tourneur, a dramatist contemporary with Shakespeare: "Joy's a subtil elf. / I think men happiest when he forgets himself." Not seeing oneself in his ideal, but rather forgetting the self through absorption in the ideal, marks the narrow distinction between pride and humility.

Even so, this humility does not affect the annihilation of all false selves. Another self arises in Anodos that takes pleasure in self-degradation; this false self, too, must die. MacDonald concludes: "Self will come to life even in the slaying of self; but there is ever something deeper and stronger than it, which will emerge at last from the unknown abysses of the soul. . . ." In *Lilith*, this idea will be compellingly symbolized in the scene of Lilith's "death," in which the spot on her side and the worm destroy all but the very essence of her being.

CONFLICTS WITH ANTAGONISTIC RELIGIOUS SYSTEMS

Anodos is now depicted as undertaking further deeds "worth doing." His spiritual development, which is progressing fairly well, is a means to an end, rather than an exclusive end in itself. MacDonald emphasizes in all his writings that righteousness is nothing unless it is practically expressed in good deeds; one must become a being capable of performing righteous acts by the process of doing them. The adventures of Chapter Twenty-three show Anodos acquitting himself admirably as Sir Percival's squire. Two episodes particularly attract our attention. They illustrate the destructive effects that self-centered religious leaders and people in authority have upon sincerely seeking, childlike individuals. This knight tells Anodos that "notwithstanding the beauty of this country of Faerie . . . there is much that is wrong in it," and proceeds to relate the incident of the wooden men, which is followed by that of the forest chapel.

The first incident concerns a little girl who is in search of wings to enable her to fly back to the country from which she has come. She has but to acquire them from obliging butterflies and moths, but when she asks for them, she is trampled upon by grotesque monsters "like great men, made of wood, without knee or elbow-joints, and without any noses or mouths or eyes in their faces." The knight learns that to cut down these creatures with the sword only results in more pieces that join in the attack. He finally succeeds in thwarting them by tripping them and setting them upon their heads, which renders each helpless.

The wooden men seem to represent leaders of cultic mentality in Christianity. Their religious set of mind is inhuman (wooden), inflexible (without joints), and oblivious to the obvious (without noses and other sensory organs). Instead of helping the sincerely devout, who look to them to nurture the better aspects of their natures, these obtuse creatures do nothing but frustrate and hinder their spiritual aspirations. When attacked, they react by quickly producing others of similar mentality. The knight's solution—that of setting them on their heads, which renders them ineffectual—suggests showing them the intellectual shortcomings of their own system. MacDonald spent his life doing this, imaginatively in the symbolism of his fantasies and the realistic depictions of his fiction, and discursively in his sermons and essays.[11]

In the second episode, Anodos comes upon a portion of the forest in which separate trails of felled trees seem to lead to a "common center," and he and the knight enter a forest chapel with walls of yew trees. Within are rows of white-robed, priestly figures reciting liturgical chants, and a large, attentive crowd. The sun has set, and darkness prevails, pierced only by starlight. Young initiates are being taken by groups of the white-robed figures to the farther end of the long chapel, where a "majesticlooking figure" is seated high upon a throne; they are then coerced into entering a door in the pedestal of the throne, where they disappear.

The ceremony fills the knight with reverence and awe: "Incapable of evil himself, he could scarcely suspect it in another, much less in a multitude such as this." Anodos, however, his sight being "so much more keen than that of most people," suspects evil here, and, donning the robe of an initiate, makes his way to the front as though to present himself to the image on the throne. Arriving before the image, he boldly approaches and attacks it, hurling it from its seat. A "great brute, like a wolf" emerges from the chamber in the pedestal and attacks him, they struggle, and Anodos strangles the wolf. Anodos is, however, attacked by the indignant multitude of worshippers, and killed.

Institutionalized religion, with its strong centers of authority and more formal patterns of worship, may be symbolized here. In a manner remarkably anticipatory of twentieth-century trends, religious people appear to be exercising what MacDonald would identify as an injudicious tolerance—that of assuming all religions have a commonality in truth, inasmuch as all are expressions of the human search for the divine. Such "believers" fool the knight, but not Anodos, who actively tries to expose the emptiness of their forms of humanism, and is killed in the attempt. To expose with purified motives and spirit the error of mistaken religious attitudes is, in MacDonald's thinking, close to the noblest deed the true Christian thinker can perform.

Such exposure is necessary, but not for the sake of creedal purity. It is important to notice in each of the above episodes that it is action based upon attitudes, not creedal errors that is being condemned. MacDonald insists theology is not an end in itself; its end is Christian action. But wrong thinking—which invariably springs from wrong attitudes toward the self and which issues in mistaken conclusions about the nature and end of religious experience—produces conduct that is spiritually outrageous.

THEMES RESOLVED

In the closing chapters of *Phantastes* MacDonald gives final expression to the main themes that he has firmly controlled and developed throughout the story. The first theme concerns the nature of passion. Now "dead," Anodos is lamented and buried by his knight and lady. But, far from being unconscious, he is experiencing the bliss of a more complete life and love. (The theme of the nature of death, with MacDonald's view of its sanctifying powers, is also a strong element in *Lilith* and *At the Back of the North Wind*.) That which was coarse within him is now refined and pure: "If my passions were dead, the souls of the passions, those essential mysteries of the spirit which had embodied themselves in the passions, and had given to them all their glory and wonderment, yet lived, yet glowed, with a pure, undying fire. They rose above their vanishing earthly garments, and disclosed themselves angels of light. But oh, how beautiful beyond the old form!"

One is reminded of Sir Aglovaile, who mistook the soul of his passion for its physical fulfillment, and ravished the ghost-girl to his own undoing. The passions themselves are pure. In this life they can lead one astray swiftly, yet they are not thereby to be despised; there is a "glory and wonderment" in them. In a future life man will not be bereft of them, but rather he will be enabled by his passions—then purified—to know the full blessedness of "the land of Death." Thus MacDonald brings to culmination the theme he has been exploring most persistently in this fantasy.

The next theme, that of the vital role of nature in spiritual growth, also culminates in these closing chapters. *Phantastes* contains many key passages expressing this aspect of MacDonald's thinking, some of which we have already discussed.

The theme of the nature and power of love, however, is the focus of the penultimate chapter. Anodos discovers that he now is able to love others without needing to be loved in return. And he has developed a fuller knowledge of what love is:

> I knew now, that it is by loving, and not by being loved, that one can come nearest the soul of another; yea, that, where two love, it is the loving of each other, and not the being beloved by each other, that originates and perfects and assures their blessedness. I knew that love gives to him that loveth, power over any soul beloved, even if that soul know him not, bringing him inwardly close to that spirit; a power that cannot be but for good; for in proportion as selfishness intrudes, the love ceases, and the power which springs therefrom dies. Yet all love will, one day, meet with its return. All true love will, one day, behold its own image in the eyes of the beloved, and be humbly glad.

All love, including that between the sexes, is here defined. Base sensuality—any form of appropriation of another for personal satisfaction alone—destroys true love, because love is in its essence self-giving. The altruistic act of giving of oneself for the pleasure or uplifting of the beloved brings blessedness to the lover. It effects an intimacy otherwise impossible, a power to do the other good, and, in the future, a still greater return of personal likeness in the beloved.

BACK HOME

But Anodos's "death" is not permanent. With a "pang and a terrible shudder" he finds himself transmitted back to the confines of a "more limited, even a bodily and earthly life," and he returns to his castle to assume his duties as overlord of his lands. That he is now spiritually mature is indicated by the fact that his experiences in Faerie have taken twenty-one days, and that he has lost his shadow. His chief concern is whether he can "translate the experiences of my travels there, into common life." He muses: "I have a strange feeling sometimes, that I am a ghost, sent into the world to minister to my fellow-men, or, rather, to repair the wrongs I have already done." Because he has learned selflessness and humility, Anodos can now perform these deeds effectively.

Endnotes

1. *Anthology*, pp. 20, 21.

2. Liddell and Scott, *A Greek-English Lexicon*, rev. ed. (Oxford: Oxford University Press, 1940), p. 145. An instance of ἄνοδος being used to mean the "ascent of the soul to its original source" is given from Hierocles Platonicus's *Carmen Aureum*. Woolf defines the meaning of Anodos's name as "pathless" (GK, p. 47), and Reis suggests "a way back" (p. 87). Manlove notes the meaning of "an upwards direction" (p. 275).

3. Joseph Sigman, "Death's Ecstasies: Transformations and Rebirth in George MacDonald's *Phantastes*," *English Studies in Canada*, 2 (Summer 1976), 203-36, offers an alternate interpretation. He explores similarities between *Phantastes* and Jungian psychology, and suggests that the male and female images symbolize the conscious and subconscious aspects of Anodos's psyche.

4. After a presentation of the *doppelgänger* tradition upon which MacDonald seems to be drawing, Woolf laments that MacDonald shifts the symbolic significance of the shadow from "intellectual skepticism" to "consciousness of self" to personal "pride" (*GK*, p. 103). Reis agrees, concluding that the shadow's "symbolic meanings are multifold," but acknowledges a "subtle unity among the significances" (p. 93). He also sees similarities to Jung's "Shadow" archetype (pp. 116, 117). The point is, it seems to me, that these various manifestations of the shadow's nature are all consistent aspects of the cynical underside of Anodos's character with which he will contend throughout much of the tale, and which he outgrows spiritually through humility and altruism. Consult the sermons "Self-Denial" (*US* II) and "The Heirs of Heaven and Earth" (*HG*).

5. This line does not appear in the early editions; apparently MacDonald added it in a later revision (he frequently reworked his material). It appears in the 1905 edition (along with several new and fascinating illustrations by Arthur Hughes), published in London by Arthur Field. It also appears in the current paperback edition (Grand

Rapids, Mich.: Wm. B. Eerdmans, 1964).

6. Woolf gleefully celebrates the eroticism he sees in this passage (*GK*, pp. 80-87). Here and elsewhere he seems to overlook the way in which Anodos's spiritual and moral development is shaping his behavior.

7. "God is man, and infinitely more. Our Lord became flesh, but did not *become* man. He took on him the form of man: he was man already. And he was, is, and ever shall be divinely childlike" ("The Child in the Midst," *US* I; italics his). Cf. the ancient grandmother Irene in the Curdie stories, whose symbolic import is similar.

8. In harmony with his Freudian concerns, Woolf sees Anodos achieving a return to the womb in his immersion, with water signifying "the maternal element par excellence" (GK, pp. 69, 70). In a footnote he dismisses Jerome Hamilton Buckley's discussion of water images in *The Victorian Temper* (Cambridge; Harvard University Press, 1951), pp. 97-105, as irrelevant to his interests (*GK*, p. 394, n. 17). But Buckley's discussion about the Victorians' inventive use of water symbols to suggest the spiritual new-birth is apropos. MacDonald's imagination is biblically oriented, and Scripture, not Freud, is the safer guide to his meaning. See especially the use of the water-life metaphor in such apocalyptic passages as Ezekiel 47 and Revelation 22.

9. Both Woolf (GK, p. 104) and Reis (pp. 90-91) venture some speculations about these autobiographical details. But, as Reis observes, to push such reading is unwise, and does not add to the appreciation of the literary merit of *Phantastes*.

10. Reis speculates that MacDonald "surely adopted" his emphasis on active obedience from Carlyle's precept, "Do the Duty which lies nearest thee, which thou knowest to be a Duty! Thy second Duty will already have become clearer" (p. 41). But this seems improbable to me, given the difference between MacDonald's tone and Carlyle's bombastic tone, the pervasiveness of this type of insistence in MacDonald's writings, and the extent to which it is present generally in Scripture.

11. See the sermons "Jesus and His Fellow Townsmen" and "The Yoke of Jesus" (*HG*) for delineation of this religious set of mind.

Circularity in Fantasy: George MacDonald
Colin Manlove
From *The Impulse of Fantasy Literature*

Unlike the traditional fairy tale, in which the hero often betters himself in the world and may move place, most modern fantasy involves the notion of a return to a starting point so that one ends where one began. This motif of circularity is an image of the preservation of things as they are, and thus one expression of fantasy's delight in 'being'. It may take the form simply of coming home at the end of one's adventures. Thus Gluck in Ruskin's *The King of the Golden River* returns to the wasted valley from which he and his cruel brothers were forced to leave, to find it blooming once more as at the beginning of the story; George MacDonald's Anodos in *Phantastes* and Vane in *Lilith* find themselves back in their castles after their journeys; William Morris's Ralph in *The Well at the World's End* returns to Upmeads, and Birdalone in *The Water of the Wondrous Isles* to Utterhay; E. Nesbit's children come back to London after their visits to the remote past in *The Story of the Amulet*; C. S. Lewis's Ransom returns to Earth from Mars and Venus; Tolkien's Bilbo and Frodo come back to the Shire from their distant adventures at the end of *The Hobbit; or, There and Back Again* and *The Lord of the Rings* respectively: Peake's Titus returns to Gormenghast (though Peake would have it believed that thereafter he left it finally); and Ursula Le Guin's *The Farthest Shore* begins and ends on the island of Roke in Earthsea. Sometimes there is the sense of circling about a fixed point, as when in David Lindsay's *A Voyage to Arcturus* the hero Maskull finds himself, at the culmination of his journey on the star Arcturus, in that same Scottish tower from which he set out originally from Earth (Lindsay owes something to MacDonald for this method).

Even when a character does not return to his actual place of origin, the impression is given that he has gone 'home'; that is, that he has returned to his rightful place, rather than that things have been changed. Kingsley's Tom, though he does not return to the Yorkshire town with which *The Water-Babies* began, is by the end linked with Ellie, with whom he goes 'home'—presumably to heaven. E. Nesbit's Dickie in *Harding's Luck* finds his true home in Elizabethan times. C. S. Lewis's 'Narnia' children, who find at the end of *The Last Battle* that they are no longer able to return to this world because in it they were killed in a train smash, travel home to heaven; and his Ransom, who felt on Perelandra that he was bound to that planet by primordial ties of longing, perhaps returns there at the end of *That Hideous Strength*. In some fantasies the plot itself can be circular. In E. R. Eddison's *The Worm Ouroboros*, the adventures of the characters are by divine gift at the end made recurrent; T.H. White's *The Once and Future King*, closing with the departure of Arthur, states beneath the text, 'THE BEGINNING'.

A further mode in which fantasy often returns to its starting point is in the departure of the supernatural. The magic realms, creatures, objects, actions or persons appear, disrupt 'normal' life and then depart once more at the end of the story. Thus Thackeray's Fairy Blackstick in *The Rose and the Ring* helps Giglio become a good king and then disappears; or in the works of F. Anstey, E. Nesbit and Charles Williams, a genie, a phoenix or a magic stone throw life into chaos until they are removed. Such removal need not always be final: the Psammead in Nesbit's *Five Children and It* is found again by the children at the start of their adventures in *The Story of the Amulet*. Nor does it suppose a return to happy ignorance or indifference. Thanks to the supernatural the world is by the end seen differently, and characters may have been altered spiritually through their experience of it, as in the work of Kingsley, MacDonald, Lindsay, Williams, Lewis, Tolkien, Peake, White or Le Guin. Here there is not only a circular mode of 'There and Back Again', but a spiral one, whereby the return is at a higher level of insight.

One of the most remarkable examples of the circular in fantasy may be observed by a comparison of George MacDonald's *Phantastes* (1858) with his *Lilith* (1895).[1] *Phantastes* and *Lilith* stand out both among MacDonald's writings and Victorian literature generally as attempts to express and imitate the wholly unconscious mind.[2] MacDonald's deepest links are with extreme Romantic writers such as Novalis, Blake or the E. T. A. Hoffmann of *The Golden Pot* (1814).[3] Like them, if not always for the same reasons, he was absolute and uncompromising in his rejection of rationalist or empiricist approaches to the world and in his advocacy of the unconscious imagination as the source of truth. Unlike them, however, he valued the imagination because he believed it to be the dwelling-place of God in men, and hence the fount of absolute rather than possibly subjective truth. God, and not man, was for him the author of all thoughts in the mind, which 'from the vast unknown, where time and space are not . . . suddenly appear in luminous writing upon the wall of . . . consciousness'. For

> God sits in that chamber of our being in which the candle of our consciousness goes out in darkness, and sends forth from thence wonderful gifts into the light of that understanding which is His candle. Our hope lies in no most perfect mechanism even of the spirit, but in the wisdom wherein we live and move and have our being. Thence we hope for endless forms of beauty informed of truth. If the dark portion of our own being were the origin of our imaginations, we might well fear the apparition of such monsters as would be generated in the sickness of a decay which could never feel—only declare—a slow return towards primeval chaos. But the Maker is our Light.[4]

The human artist must therefore try to avoid imposing patterns or meanings on the gifts of his imagination, for he is expressing God's patterns, which can be understood only in the imagination and by the childlike mind, and not in the intellect: 'The greatest forces', MacDonald declared, 'lie in the region of the uncomprehended.'[5] *Phantastes* is prefixed by a quotation from Novalis on fairy tales (*Märchen*) as dream-like successions of images. *Lilith*, MacDonald told his son Greville, seemed to him to have been 'a mandate direct from God, for which he himself was to find form and clothing'.[6] At the close of *Lilith*, the central character Mr. Vane is given a revelation of the true source of his dreams: 'When a man dreams his own dream, he is the sport of his dream; when Another gives it him, that Other is able to fulfil it.' MacDonald especially valued *Phantastes* and *Lilith*, almost the first and last of his works, and his dearest literary aims[7] find expression in them.

MacDonald lived a life of almost total isolation from his intellectual and social milieu. He was a Highland Scot living in England, a minister deprived of a pulpit for heterodoxy, a man of uncompromising refusal to bend to the world's standards to make money, a soul longing for death as the door to meeting God; one who lived from the resources of his family and his own spirit rather than from any wider community.[8] This partly explains how he could write works so obscure and severed in character from those of his contemporaries. It may also explain why his work does not do the Victorian 'thing' and evolve, change in character or treat new ideas. Indeed the very fact that he ends his career with a work not dissimilar in basic form from one of his earliest[9] underlies this; it also closes the circle of his literary life just as he himself lived in a sense in a circle of his own.

Crossing a Great Frontier

The similarities of *Phantastes* and *Lilith* are clear enough. With the exception of the very different tale of Celtic second sight, *The Portent* (1864), they are the only romances for adults that MacDonald wrote. Both are dream-structured: that is to say, they each consist of a sequence of often inexplicable but suggestive images, described with a curious mixture of precision and vagueness;[10] and the landscape is that of both the unconscious mind and the world imaginatively seen. In both there are recurrent primordial images (most of them to be paralleled in the works of C. G. Jung, where they are given psychoanalytic explanation[11])—mothers, the 'anima' figure, shadows, water, trees, caves, mirrors, and sun and moon. Both works describe death, whether out of the conscious self or life. In each there is one central and isolated human figure who has just come of age and into the management of his estate, and who goes from his house into a fairyland. In these fairylands each hero brings to life a woman enchanted or near death, is repulsed by her, and subsequently pursues her. At the end of each work the hero is returned to 'this' world to await a great good which he believes is coming to him (in both books evil is felt to be finally unreal [pp. 182, 262]). There are several smaller likenesses. Mirrors are used as magic apparatus in both works: Cosmo's mirror in the inset story in *Phantastes* has enslaved a princess to appear in the reflection of any room in which it is set; and the mirror apparatus in Mr. Vane's garret in *Lilith* is the means of his entry into the region of the seven dimensions. Anodos in *Phantastes* finds his evil shadow; Vane is opposed by a Great Shadow. There are feminine doubles in *Phantastes* such as the evil Maid of the Alder-tree and the pure white lady, and in *Lilith* there are a spotted leopardess that is Lilith and a white one that is Mara, child of Eve. The evil Ash and Alder of *Phantastes* have, like Lilith, a spiritual 'hole in the heart' which makes them devourers (pp. 39, 56-7, 325).[12] In both books songs have magical power, whether in binding Lilith (p. 319) or in loosing the white lady from imprisonment as a statue (pp. 45-8, 114-19). Both have halls of dancers (pp. 110-14, 262-6, 309-10), palaces, and cottages. In each the same poem on the home of life occurs in roughly the same position from the end:

> Many a wrong, and its curing song;
> Many a road, and many an inn;
> Room to roam, but only one home
> For all the world to win. (pp. 164, 398)

After that in *Lilith* Vane reflects, 'I thought I had heard the song before.'

Yet while there is not 'evolution' or difference in basic form between the two works, they are radically to be distinguished in subject-matter. Just as they circle MacDonald's literary life, so the one completes the circle begun by the other. That circle has nothing to do with development, but rather with completing a pattern. For *Phantastes* deals with some of the First Things; and *Lilith* with the Last. *Phantastes* has as its subject a man embarking on life, and describes a fall (Anodos's enslavement to his evil shadow after an act of disobedience) and a Christ-like act of sacrifice for others by Anodos in the evil forest-church at the end; after which, back in his own world, he finds that his wicked shadow has gone. Anodos concludes: 'Thus I, who set out to find my Ideal, came back rejoicing that I had lost my Shadow' (p. 182). The narrative in *Lilith*, however, moves towards the Last Days, and describes the morning of eternity when resurrected souls make their way into heaven; the story focuses on the gradual acceptance by the recalcitrant hero Mr. Vane of his need to lie down and sleep with the dead in Adam's house so that he may waken to eternity. In a sense *Phantastes* and *Lilith* together make up a single fantasy.

Throughout *Phantastes* Anodos is occupied in waking people up. In a cave he finds a block of alabaster in which he can see the indistinct outline of a woman: on an impulse he sits by this '"antenatal tomb"' (p. 45) and sets about waking the woman by singing a song against sleep, darkness and death, until the lady actually breaks free from the stone and glides away into the surrounding woods (p. 47). Again by song Anodos later renders visible the figure of the lady in a hall of statues in a fairy palace; and when he seizes her from the black pedestal on which she is set she comes to life and escapes from him (pp. 115-20). Anodos's last act in Fairy Land is designed to waken his master the knight to the evil of the religious ceremony in the forest church (p. 175). The story of Cosmo and his mirror is also one of an awakening: first the princess, who has hitherto been a passive victim of the mirror, not knowing that she is seen in it, becomes aware of Cosmo; and then, when by an act of sacrifice which prefigures that of Anodos Cosmo dies to smash the mirror, she is released from its power and from the deadly trances it produces. In *Lilith*, however, the object of Mr. Raven, or Adam, is to persuade people to lie down and sleep in his house of death. Where Anodos invokes movement and consciousness—'"Rest is now filled full of beauty, / and can give thee up, I ween; / Come thou forth, for other duty/ Motion pineth for her queen"' (p. 46)—all motion in *Lilith* save the one act of climbing on to one of the slabs in the dormitory of the cold sleepers and losing consciousness is seen as evanescent.

Phantastes could be said to portray the gradual wakening of the hero, who is at first unconscious. Though the first words of the book are 'I awoke one morning' the mode of Anodos's entry into Fairy Land is like a gradual lapse out of consciousness, into a dream:

> [I] became aware of the sound of running water near me; and looking out of bed, I saw that a large green marble basin, in which I was wont to wash, and which stood on a low pedestal of the same material in a corner of my room, was overflowing like a spring; and that a stream of clear water was running over the carpet, all the length of the room, finding its outlet I knew not where. And, stranger still, where this carpet, which I had myself designed to imitate a field of grass and daisies, bordered the course of the little stream, the grass-blades and daisies seemed to wave in a tiny breeze that followed the water's flow; while under the rivulet they bent and swayed with every motion of the changeful current, as if they were about to dissolve with it, and, forsaking their fixed form, become fluent as the waters.
>
> My dressing-table was an old-fashioned piece of furniture of black oak, with drawers all down the front. These were elaborately carved in foliage, of which ivy formed the chief part. The nearer end of this table remained just as it had been, but on the further end a singular change had commenced. I happened to fix my eye on a little cluster of ivy-leaves. The first of these was evidently the work of the carver; the next looked curious; the third was unmistakably ivy; and just beyond it a tendril of clematis had twined itself about the gilt handle of one of the drawers. Hearing next a slight motion above me, I looked up, and saw that the branches and leaves designed upon the curtains of my bed were slightly in motion. Not knowing what change might follow next, I thought it time to get up; and, springing from the bed, my bare feet alighted upon a cool green sward; and although I dressed in all haste, I found myself completing my toilet under the boughs of a great tree, whose top waved in the golden stream of the sunrise with many interchanging lights, and with shadows of leaf and branch gliding over leaf and branch, as the cool morning wind swung it to and fro, like a sinking sea-wave. (pp. 19-20)

Throughout the passage (which is very reminiscent of Hoffmann's *The Golden Pot*[13]) there is a steady increase of change from one mode of being to another, mirroring the collapse of the empirical mode of presentation and entry into the unconscious mind and the world it perceives. (It is of a piece with the character of *Phantastes* as a whole that what is described is not only a change of being, but a shift from stillness into motion.) First it could appear that the basin was overflowing for quite ordinary reasons, and that the stream of water was equally natural—though rather more of a spreading flood might be expected; and despite Anodos's 'stranger still' it would still be possible to believe that his impression of the movement of the grass and daisies of the carpet both beside and beneath the stream was an optical illusion. But the possibility of illusion is removed in the same way that the solidity of the carvings of leaves on the oak dressing-table turns through increasing uncertainty into twisting vegetation. With the movement of the branches and leaves on the bed-curtains being heard as well as seen, the reader is still further in; and when Anodos leaps out of bed onto a lawn instead of a carpet, the reader feels sure that little remains of the bedroom itself. The ironic fact is that when Anodos finally rises from his bed he is most fully asleep.[14]

During the first half of the story Anodos (whose name is Greek for 'pathless', or 'having no way') experiences events in a chance manner, without any specific object in view: he wanders into the cave containing the lady in alabaster, he meets the Ash and Alder by apparent accident, a stream leads him to the fairy palace, he sojourns in the palace for some time. Though he wanders in a generally eastwards direction,[15] he does not know why, and can speak of 'my custom since I entered Fairy Land, of taking for a guide whatever I first found moving in any direction' (p. 75). Random impulse governs many of his actions, such as his clearing the moss from the alabaster in which the white lady is imprisoned, and then singing to release her (pp. 44, 45); entering the cottage of an ogress and, despite her warning, opening the door of her cupboard and thus being found by his evil shadow (pp. 62, 63); or singing in the fairy palace (p. 109). He declares, 'it is no use trying to account for things in Fairy Land; and one who travels there soon learns to forget the very idea of doing so, and takes everything as it comes; like a child, who, being in a chronic condition of wonder, is surprised at nothing' (p. 33). This is partly true, but Anodos has to learn how to unite child-likeness with true consciousness. He finds false consciousness in the form of his shadow-self, which is a symbol of intellectual and materialist modes of perception, and removes enchantment from all about him: it turns a beautiful fairy child with magic toys into 'a commonplace boy, with a . . . multiplying glass and a kaleidoscope' (p. 66), and leads Anodos to covet, seize and so break the wonderful music-emitting globe of a little girl (pp. 68-9).

In the fairy palace he begins to be more purposive, and to plan ahead. Around the central hall of the palace are twelve radiating halls, each filled with human statues and curtained off. Anodos becomes convinced that the statues are often dancing and tries to surprise them at it, but in vain, for they are always motionless on their pedestals when he enters. He discovers that 'a premeditated attempt at surprise, though executed with the utmost care and rapidity, was of no avail' (p. 113): if he has any preformed intention of catching the statues before he lifts one of the curtains he is bound to fail, for what is needed is 'a sudden thought suddenly executed' (ibid.). By trial and error, giving his mind to other thoughts and images than the dancers, he arrives at a moment when the impulse to catch them comes just as he is next to one of the curtains, and can dart through on the instant. Clearly there has to be a fusion of conscious and unconscious intention: the wish to surprise the statues must be 'put to sleep' until the right moment arrives. Elsewhere in the second half of *Phantastes* there is emphasis on the notion of being at once prepared and unprepared. Faced by the evil Ash-tree, the knight of the rusty armour knows that '"earthly arms availed not against such as he; and that my soul must meet him in its naked strength"' (p. 139); and later he tells Anodos that a man will do none the worse in Faerie for not being '"burdened with provision and precaution"' (p.169). In the battle with the giants the brothers and Anodos have no time to don their carefully prepared armour (p.155), though their resolution, training and some of their weapons remain to them. In the church in the forest, when Anodos wishes to expose the evil he feels there, he hands his battle-axe to one of the congregation, 'for I wished to test the matter unarmed, and, if it was a man that sat upon the throne, to attack him with hands bare' (p.176).[16]

Thus the reader finds that, in the second part of *Phantastes*, Anodos's actions emerge from rather more sustained desires and sequences of motive and act than hitherto, though these are combined with the previous unconscious mode.[17] When, early on, he brought to life the white lady in the alabaster, his search for her lasted little further than his unhappy confusion of her with the Maid of the Alder. But when he makes her both visible and mobile in the fairy palace he sets off in a pursuit of her which becomes an intermittent motif during the remainder of his experience in Fairy Land. Gradually, however, he learns to yield her to the knight of the (formerly) rusty armour, whom she loves; and eventually he serves the knight as his squire; in his death the two lay him in his grave. Interpolated with this is another causal sequence, beginning with the old lady of the strange island cottage in the ocean, who sends Anodos forth to help two princes slay a group of giants that are despoiling their country; Anodos, the sole survivor of the contest, is feted by the people, and then, becoming vain of his prowess, meets a double of himself in the forest, and is shut up in a tower until he learns humility. This motif, and that of the white lady, are, however, relatively disconnected from one another, and there are still numbers of episodes with no clear relation to either of them— the island—cottage itself with its four mystic doors, the dead dragon with which Anodos finds the knight of the rusty armour encumbered (pp. 166-9), and the little girl who is searching for butterflies to make wings for herself but who is continually being knocked over by invisible wooden creatures (pp.169-72).

In the end, Anodos finally loses his evil shadow in what is an act at once conscious and unconscious: he senses in his soul that there is evil in the forest church, and he perceives with his keen eyesight that something suspicious is being done to the people led to the central throne (p. 174). Together these sensations bring him to a decision and an act which is more his own than anything previously in the book (if there is still an evil tincture of revenge in his motivation (p. 176)). It is the culmination of a development of true consciousness, and with it the false consciousness of the shadow goes for ever. The product of that consciousness is also death, but it is a death in which Anodos's perceptions are more fully awake than ever before.

> The hot fever of life had gone by, and I breathed the clear mountain-air of the land of Death. I had never dreamed of such blessedness. It was not that I had in any way ceased to be what I had been . . . If my passions were dead, the souls of the passions, those essential mysteries of the spirit which had imbodied themselves in the passions, and had given to them all their glory and wonderment, yet lived, yet glowed, with a pure, undying fire. They rose above their vanishing earthly garments, and disclosed themselves angels of light. But oh, how beautiful beyond the old form! (p.178)

This was anticipated by the framing stanza of the song Anodos sang to the princes before the battle with the giants: "'Oh, well for him who breaks his dream / With the blow that ends the strife; / And, waking, knows the peace that flows/ Around the noise of life!'" (p.154). In that peace, waking and dreaming, conscious and unconscious, are one.[18] Anodos has one further stage to go, however, for he has to 'die' back out of Fairy Land into this world and mortality once more; so that in a sense, just as he is divided from Faerie, so he is divided from the true unconscious life once more.

The idea that to be truly dead or asleep is to be truly alive and awake is also central in *Lilith*, but is demonstrated from the opposite direction (illustrating the words of the song in both works—'Many a road.../ ...but only one home / For all the world to win' (pp.164, 398)). In *Lilith*, the hero moves from a condition of stubborn consciousness into unconsciousness. The means by which Mr. Vane finds himself in the region of the seven dimensions[19] is an apparatus whose magical workings are described in quasi-scientific terms concerning the polarisation of light: it is a mirror, which in this context is a symbol of the intellect, the conscious self,[20] and is thus quite opposite in character to the gateway to Fairy Land in *Phantastes*. Unlike Anodos, Vane enters the strange realm of his story in a wakeful, questioning state, and in pursuit of something specific, the strange librarian, Mr. Raven. He is constantly surprised at what he sees, and unlike Anodos spends much time inquiring into the nature of the new world he has entered: 'Could it be that I was dead, I thought, and did not know it? Was I in what we used to call the world beyond the grave? and must I wander about seeking my place in it? How was I to find myself at home?' (pp.196-7). Mr. Raven, whom he meets in this other world, baffles his questions with riddles and paradoxes which themselves continue the intellectual, conscious element—for example, "'you have not yet left your house, neither has your house left you. At the same time it cannot contain you, or you inhabit it!'" (p. 202). Later he tells Vane by intellectual means that he must do without intellect (pp. 326-7). The 'wakeful' condition of Vane throughout *Lilith* is part of the reason for that work's being more consistently connected in structure and motivation than *Phantastes*.

The topography of the region of the seven dimensions is clear, with the Bad Burrow, the Evil Wood, the dried watercourse, the two cottages, the home of the Little Ones and the giants, and the town of Bulika all fairly clearly placed in relation to one another. Vane follows a steady sequence of motive and act in a way that Anodos does not till near the end of his history. He refuses Mr. Raven's invitation to lie down in the house of the dead; he meets the Little Ones and eventually leaves them in the hope of eventually helping them in their development and in their difficulties with the giants; he finds the almost-dead Lilith and revives her; he pursues her to Bulika where she feigns love for him in order to gain access to 'this' world, whence she is beaten off by Mr. Raven. Once more offered death by Mr. Raven, Vane refuses and sets off on the horse of his futile passions (pp. 329-33) to help the Little Ones, but finds them already prepared, under the guidance of Lilith's daughter Lona, to do battle against the giants and set off to assault Bulika and Lilith. The latter aim results in the capture of Lilith, who eventually agrees to lie down with the dead, whereupon Vane does also. Vane remains at a consistent level of truant wakefulness for much of *Lilith*, unlike Anodos, who as we have seen, gradually loses his state of simple, passive unconsciousness.

In keeping with the injunction to more consciousness in *Phantastes* and less in *Lilith*—and also with the fact that Anodos in the former is portrayed as a spiritual child at first—the reader finds that where Anodos is often asked to resist something, Vane and Lilith are required to give way. Anodos is forbidden to touch his fairy-grandmother (p.17), told to guard against the evil Ash and Alder trees, and warned by the ogress of the peril of opening the cupboard door in her cottage. Despite the inscription "'TOUCH NOT!'"(p.111), he lays hands on the female statue he renders visible by his singing in the fairy palace, and then pursues her through a door over which is the command, "'No one enters here without the leave of the Queen'"(pp.119-20). Later he is told in vain by the old lady of the cottage in the sea not to go through the fourth door of the cottage, the door of the Timeless: as a result he has to leave and the sea rises to cover the cottage for a year (pp.143-5). Lilith and Vane, on the other hand, are told to do rather than not to do something. They wrongfully resist for long the injunction to lie down and sleep. Where Anodos is asked to refuse, they are asked to accept. Lilith is told that to do so is to do what her deepest and truest will wants, and that "'There is no slave but the creature that wills against its

Creator'" (pp. 371-2).[21] The imperative here is to go with the grain of the universe, in which one finds oneself borne forward by a will deeper than one's own; while for Anodos the need is often to stand back, to remove himself from absorption in himself and phenomena. In a sense Anodos finds his true self by a process of separation, Vane by one of immersion: the one has to do with what is needed for living, the other with dying.

Much of this difference stems from the theme of maternity in *Phantastes*, and the fact that the history of Anodos is one of gradual removal from over-dependence on mother-figures and a condition of unthinking passivity.[22] These mother-figures include the fairy he meets before his adventures (p.18), the Beech tree in the fairy forest who protects him from the ravening Ash (pp. 37-40), the 'old nursing earth' itself (p.50), the matron of the second forest cottage (p. 56), 'mother Nature' as he floats down a river (p.72) and the old lady of the mid-ocean cottage, who soothes his distress (pp.131, 144). It is when the last finally sends him forth saying, '"Go, my son, and do something worth doing"', that he feels 'as if I were leaving my mother for the first time' (p.145). Thereafter Anodos meets no more mother-figures during his time in Fairy Land: when at one point he feels 'unmanned' by a weak desire for maternal comfort, he 'dashe[s] away the tears, ashamed of a weakness which I thought I had abandoned' (p. 162). In his death, however, which is the product of a fully 'adult' decision and sacrifice, he enters that higher childhood of union with earth, of solid self with solid self, which the earlier mothers have in part prefigured, 'I seemed to feel the great heart of the mother beating into mine, and feeding me with her own life, her own essential being and nature' (p.178).[23]

After Anodos leaves the island cottage, his journey is no longer connected with water or baths, symbols both of the womb and of the melting of one's identity in an infant state of dependency on the mother: there are no more streams, deep rivers, or seas, but only dry land, the upland of the conflict with the giants, the royal city and the forest. In *Lilith*, however, Vane is to be seen as an adult who, with an adult's consciousness, is active rather than passive, until he learns a self-surrender which has nothing to do with flight to a refuge, but is rather the opening of the self to the living stream of the universe. For much of *Lilith* the landscape is waterless and arid, reflecting this insistence on the conscious and personal self: when Lilith gives herself up, the river wells up from the subterranean depths in which it was lost (p. 394).[24]

One of the central themes of *Phantastes* is possession. To seek to 'get' is to be possessed or helpless.[25] Even the voracious Ash-tree, with its need to devour all that it meets, is in a sense a passive victim: the Beech-tree tells Anodos that '"he has a hole in his heart that nobody knows of but one or two; and he is always trying to fill it up, but he cannot"' (p. 39). It is because Anodos lacks a truly 'born' self that he himself feels the need to possess things, to lay hands on the lady of the fairy palace, or, through the effect on him of his evil shadow, to seize the little girl's beautiful crystalline ball of harmony (pp. 68-9). Because most of his acts of seizing are impulsive and childlike rather than actively malignant, he is frequently being mothered. But when he learns to be a separate individual, he learns also to let things be separate from him. He sees the course of his story as a gradual doing without greed and pride, for these are functions of infancy: 'I learned that he that will be a hero, will barely be a man; that he that will be nothing but a doer of his work, is sure of his manhood' (p.165). Thus at the end of the story he finds his true self by giving rather than getting, in his sacrifice in the forest church.

In the first part of *Phantastes* there is a sense of enclosure: Anodos is wandering through forests, or entering cottages or palaces. After he leaves the sea-cottage there is more sense of openness in the upland site of the battle with the giants. Later he returns to woodland: but the tower of his pride in which Anodos is shut is one out of which he can walk simply by opening the door (p. 163).[26] The forest church in which he later finds himself is full of the sense of being confined, 'enclosed by four walls of yew . . . These trees grew to a very great height, and did not divide from each other till close to the top' (p.173). (The yew tree is a death-symbol.[27]) The eyes of the circular congregation are directed inwards, the avenue of white-robed men narrows in the distance, and it is growing dark in 'the enclosure' (p.174). The sacrificial victims are constantly 'surrounded' and 'crowded' towards the central throne (pp. 174-5). It is out of this constriction that Anodos breaks, by smashing the idol and suffering death. In the account of his brief 'life after death' in Fairy Land (pp. 177-80), confinement and freedom, like all other opposites, are reconciled. Anodos lies down in his grave 'like a tired child . . . in his white bed . . . with a more luxurious satisfaction of repose than I knew'; but he also then rises above the ground, first in the form of a primrose, and then floating on a cloud in the free air. But then he is returned into this mortal world, becoming 'once again conscious of a more limited, even a bodily and earthly life', sinking from his 'state of ideal bliss, into the world of shadows which again closed around and infolded me' (p.180). He now has to await the final deliverance of death out of this world. But at least he has broken free of the womb, and can truly begin his life (at the opening of the story it was emphasised that he was just twenty-one); thus the description of his return to this world is somewhat like that of a birth, 'a pang and a terrible shudder went through me; a writhing as of death convulsed me; and I became once again conscious of a more limited, even a bodily and earthly life'.

In *Lilith* the procedure is the reverse: a man who wanders for much of the narrative in the open country ends by entering the house of Adam. But the houses in each story are on the whole different: in *Phantastes* it is the house of life, from which one must break free to realise one's own being; in *Lilith* it is the house of death, in which one is once more joined with the earth (but difference ceases in the death-states of the protagonists, when life and death, womb and grave are reconciled). Life is circular, but for MacDonald as for Blake, in spiral form: one must move from innocence to experience as in *Phantastes*, but thence to a higher innocence which is a return at a different level to the childlike state.

Anodos in *Phantastes* follows a roughly linear path, if the direction is not always constant. He is told by the woman of the second cottage he comes to, "'I have heard, that, for those who enter Fairy Land, there is no way of going back. They must go on, and go through it. How, I do not in the least know'" (p. 61). Thus Anodos never covers the same ground twice, but is always happening on new experiences. First he journeys through the fairy forest, encountering the Ash, the Alder and the Beech, the lady in the alabaster and his own shadow; then he moves downriver to his sojourn in the fairy palace with its statue-halls; and thereafter through the sequence of subterranean journey, wintry sea, island cottage, battle with giants, tower in forest, forest church, death, resurrection and return to this world. Narrative is matched by spiritual progression, as we have seen: *Phantastes* is a *Bildungsroman*, Anodos's experience gradually bringing him nearer true selfhood and humility.

The book is also in a sense centrifugal. Anodos leaves his castle to enter Fairy Land; he starts two female statues into motion and flight; his story is interspersed with other narratives, such as those of the strange 'loveless' planet and of Cosmo that he reads in the library of the fairy palace (pp. 82-108), or the ballad sung to him by the woman of the island cottage about Sir Aglovaile and his ghost-wife (pp.131-5); in the fairy library he often lapses out of his own consciousness into those of the authors or characters of the books he reads:

> if the book was one of travels, I found myself the traveller. New lands, fresh experiences, novel customs, rose around me. I walked, I discovered, I fought, I suffered, I rejoiced in my success. Was it a history? I was the chief actor therein. I suffered my own blame; I was glad in my own praise. With a fiction it was the same. Mine was the whole story. For I took the place of the character who was most like myself, and his story was mine. (pp. 81-2; see also pp. 53, 87, 89)

In *Lilith*, however, Vane in a sense never moves from his house: Mr. Raven tells him: "'You have not yet left your house, neither has your house left you'" (p. 202). In *Lilith* MacDonald portrays a condition in which objects from different dimensions can co-exist in the same place; this is the burden of the epigraph to the book from Thoreau's 'Walking'. In the realm beyond the mirror Mr. Raven shows Vane a tree which '"stands on the hearth of your kitchen, and grows nearly straight up its chimney"', and says that some heads of Faerian wild hyacinth are among the strings of the piano that Vane's housekeeper's niece is playing in the breakfast-room of the house, '"and give that peculiar sweetness to her playing"' (pp. 203-4). Another tree grows '"in the ruins of the church on your home-farm"' (p. 205). Later Vane is smitten with terror, 'I was lost in a space larger than imagination; for if here two things, or any parts of them, could occupy the same space, why not twenty or ten thousand?' (p. 215). Distance is telescoped: Vane is told by Mr. Raven that the closet in the library of his house, into which he emerged immediately on leaving the vaults of the dead (as he does on leaving heaven at the end of the story (p. 419)) '"is no nearer our cottage, and no farther from it, than any or every other place"' (p. 326). Thus it is that during the narrative Vane several times returns to his house as Anodos did not (pp. 197, 217, 315, 405).

Unlike Anodos's wanderings, those of Vane are centripetal, about the cottage of the dead he for much of the narrative resists, and he traverses the same landscape continually, visiting the Little Ones twice, Bulika twice and the Bad Burrow of hideous monsters four times. Where Anodos follows a linear path that of Vane is a circular or spiral one. There is mention of an ancestor Sir Upward (pp. 190, 219-21), and at the end Vane is told of his awakening, '"here all is upwardness and love and gladness"' (p. 408). To reach the mirror-apparatus in his house Vane must ascend a spiral staircase (p. 197). MacDonald found deep and sacramental meaning in spirals, stairs, heights and churchspires. He found 'co-substance between the stairs of a cathedralspire and man's own "secret stair" up to the wider vision';[28] and declared: 'the movements of man's life are in spirals: we go back whence we came, ever returning on our former traces, only upon a higher level, on the next upward coil of the spiral, so that it is a going back and a going forward ever and both at once'.[29]

This linear/spiral, centrifugal/centripetal contrast between *Phantastes* and *Lilith* partly reflects the fact that while Anodos develops spiritually throughout, Vane does not. For most of *Lilith* Vane is simply truant, trying to cling to the ledge of what he considers to be his identity, despite being twice invited to lie down with the dead (pp. 209-17, 327-32). He is constantly in the spiritual condition described by MacDonald in one of his *Unspoken Sermons*:

> The liberty of the God that would have his creature free, is in contest with the slavery of the creature who would cut his own stem from his root that he might call it his own and love it; who rejoices in his own consciousness, instead of the life of that consciousness; who poises himself on the tottering wall of his own being, instead of the rock on which that being is built. Such a one regards his own dominion over himself—the rule of the greater by the less, inasmuch as the conscious self is less than the self—as a freedom infinitely greater than the range of the universe of God's being.[30]

Hence, in part, the name 'Vane'. All he has to do is to give way, to stop, whereas Anodos has to move and change. With *Phantastes* the question is: 'What is it properly to be?' With *Lilith* it is, 'What is being?' The one is concerned with ethics, the other with ontology. Vane and Lilith do not *become*: they simply find out what they are. Thus Lilith is brought to Mara's house solely to relinquish her fancied picture of herself, and to see herself as she really is (pp. 371-8). Such a seeing will involve transformation into what God meant her to be. During the process, Mara tells Vane: "'The central fire of the universe is radiating into her the knowledge of good and evil, the knowledge of what she is. She sees at last the good she is not, the evil she is'" (p. 373).

> Mr. Raven's first question of Vane is, "'Who are you, pray?'", at which: I became at once aware that I could give him no notion of who I was. Indeed, who was I? It would be no answer to say I was who! Then I understood that I did not know myself, did not know what I was, had no grounds on which to determine that I was one thing and not another. As for the name I went by in my own world, I had forgotten it, and did not care to recall it, for it meant nothing, and what it might be was plainly of no consequence here. I had indeed almost forgotten that there it was a custom for everybody to have a name! So I held my peace, and it was my wisdom; for what should I say to a creature such as this raven, who saw through accident into entity? (pp. 195-6; see also p. 198)

Mr. Raven then declares, "'No one can say he is himself, until first he knows that he *is*, and then what *himself* is. In fact, nobody is himself, and himself is nobody'" (p.196). Later again, the issue of Vane's true self is raised, when he finds that he cannot even remember his own name, and Mara tells him, "'Your real name, indeed, is written on your forehead, but at present it whirls about so irregularly that nobody can read it'" (p. 253).³¹ (It may occur to the reader here that 'Vane' is a partial anagram of 'Raven'.) There is a motif of metamorphosis, or uncertainty of identity, in *Lilith*, which is not to be found so much in *Phantastes*. Lilith and Mara can change to leopardesses and back again. Mr. Raven keeps shifting between appearing as a raven and as a librarian (pp. 196, 210, 271, 273, 315, 329). In the Evil Wood the trees and leaves keep turning, to Vane's sight, into the shapes of beasts or men or dancing cadavers and back again (pp. 232-4, 262-6).

Because of the emphasis on finding what one truly is, rather than what one may become, time and place are of less moment in *Lilith* than in *Phantastes*. Regarding place, it has been seen that the story circles about one centre, Adam's cottage, and that there is stress on the notion of 'bi-locality'. Mr. Raven tells Vane:

> 'Home is ever so far away in the palm of your hand, and how to get there it is of no use to tell you. But you will get there; you must get there; you have to get there. Everybody who is not at home, has to go home. You thought you were at home where I found you: if that had been your home, you could not have left it. Nobody can leave home. And nobody ever was or ever will be at home without having gone there.' (pp. 225-6)

And Vane later reflects: 'But what mattered where while everywhere was the same as nowhere! I had not yet, by doing something in it, made anywhere into a place!' (p. 261). As for time, when Vane apologises for his lateness in lying down with the dead, he is told: '"There is no early or late here"' (p. 399); and while he is asleep he remarks: 'For centuries I dreamed—or was it chiliads? or only one long night?—But why ask? for time had nothing to do with me; I was in the land of thought— farther in, higher up than the seven dimensions, the ten senses: I think I was where I am—in the heart of God' (pp. 400-1). There is not even a clear finality to the duration of the universe: the sleepers in the house of the dead rise and go to heaven at different times; the last chapter is entitled 'The "Endless Ending"'.

What idea of development there is in *Lilith* refers primarily to the state of death, not what one does when one is 'alive'; and it is a circular rather than a linear concept of growth, whereby one goes forward by going backwards. Vane learns that his mother lying in the house of the dead '"will go on steadily growing younger until she reaches the perfection of her womanhood—a splendour beyond foresight"' (p. 399); and the Little One, Odu, after his wakening from the dead, is told of the still cold princess Lilith, '"Her wake is not ripe yet . . . she is busy forgetting. When she has forgotten enough to remember enough, then she will soon be ripe, and wake'" (p. 411). It is Lilith in her corrupt state who thinks of ripening and development in purely linear terms of forward movement: "'the older we grow, the nearer we are to our perfection . . . ours is a ceaseless ripening. I am not yet ripe, and have lived thousands of your years'" (p. 305). But true change in Lilith involves a return, through experience, to childhood. Lilith is told, "'A slave thou art that shall one day be a child!'"(p. 378). The rhetorical correlative of this process of going forward by going back is the use of paradox throughout the book. Thus Mr. Raven informs Vane that "'the more doors you go out of, the farther you get in'" (p. 194), "'No one who will not sleep can ever wake" (p. 225), "'Nothing but truth can appear; and whatever is must seem'" (p. 272), "'you will be dead, so long as you refuse to die'"(p. 331); and Vane himself says—when he has found his true being in death—"'no one can die who does not long to live'" (p. 395).

Lilith involves a losing of the self, a merging with others. The title of the book speaks of a figure who shares the central position in the novel with Vane, a figure who like Vane refuses to yield her will and go to sleep in Adam's house. In the end Vane lies down together with Lilith and the Little Ones in the company of the vast hosts of the dead, in a universal dormitory; the grave in Lilith is no fine and private place. Beings appear constantly in groups—Adam and Eve, the Little Ones, the giants, the dancing dead, the quarrelsome skeletons (pp. 266-71), the Bad Burrow full of monsters, the 'society' of Bulika. *Phantastes*, on the other hand, which is much more concerned with progressive growth and separation of the self, usually involves single figures—the women of each of the three cottages, the Ash, the Alder, the Beech, the knight of the rusty armour, the lady in the alabaster, the fairy child, the girl with the globe, the statue in the fairy palace. Even the story of Cosmo and his mirror involves his not meeting his beloved princess until he has his death-wound;[32] and the reader learns that on the strange planet of which Anodos reads in another story, when two people fall in love, 'instead of drawing nearer to each other, they wander away each alone, into solitary places, and die of their desire' (p. 87). Though towards the end of the story Anodos becomes somewhat more social, in helping the brothers against the giants, or acting as squire to the knight, his isolation from the white lady is constantly felt, and at the end of his life in Fairy Land his act of sacrifice in the forest church is uniquely his own, no others seeing the evil till he reveals it.

Anodos's dream clearly springs from his own unconscious, but

Vane is often not sure whether he is dreaming or being dreamt by others. In the black hall of Lilith's palace, he realises that 'in the black ellipsoid I had been in the brain of the princess!' (p. 313; cf. p. 303); and when at the end he seems to have been returned once more to his house and severed from his fellowdead, he says: 'I had fled from my dream! The dream was not of my making, any more than was my life: I ought to have seen it to the end!' (p. 406). In *Phantastes* the concern is with the individual, in Lilith with the corporate subconscious.[33] Even the individual in *Lilith* is multiple: Mr. Raven, the bird-man, tells Vane:

> 'Every one, as you ought to know, has a beast-self—and a bird-self, and a stupid fish-self, ay, and a creeping serpent-self too—which it takes a deal of crushing to kill! In truth he has also a tree-self and a crystal-self, and I don't know how many selves more—all to get into harmony.' (p. 211)

The motif of metamorphosis, by which apparent identity is not sacrosanct but rather shared with other modes of being, is here again significant: all the figures in *Lilith* are, as it were, parts of one huge imagination. Even unconsciousness itself is not certain: increasingly towards the end Vane does not know whether he is waking or dreaming: 'Can it be that that last waking also was in the dream? that I am still in the chamber of death, asleep and dreaming, not yet ripe enough to wake?' (p. 419). The root of this multiple identity, this corporate mind, is God: thinking does not come from the one, but from the Many who is also the One. MacDonald said, writing of the human imagination, 'a man is rather *being thought* than *thinking*, when a new thought arises in his mind';[34] and young Harry Arnold in his *David Elginbrod* (1863) says: "'I never dream dreams; the dreams dream me'".[35]

The landscape of *Lilith* is shared by all minds, and is ultimately God's dream; that of *Phantastes*, however, is usually felt to be an extension of the mind of the solitary hero Anodos.[36] In *Phantastes* Anodos finds his evil shadow; in *Lilith* Vane encounters the Great Shadow. In *Phantastes* Anodos tells the reader that he set out to find his Ideal (p. 82). The lady in the alabaster seems to him 'perfectly lovely; more near the face that had been born with me in my soul, than anything I had seen before in nature or art' (pp. 44-5). It is this personal image of the desirable that he seeks in this lady, in the Maid of the Alder and in the statue-lady in the fairy palace. In his search he at length learns to go beyond the merely personal and the possessive, but his journey remains one into the interior, to discover some hint of the root of his true being. Unlike Vane, however, he never directly encounters God, who is the ultimate source of his desire or *Sehnsucht*, immanent in, but not to be identified with, the white lady he for long tries to possess. *Lilith*, on the other hand, is directly concerned with matters of heaven and hell (for example, pp. 322-3, 408). Vane, standing 'in the burial ground of the universe' (p. 208), moves outward to an understanding of the nature of all being: the figures in his story constitute the whole human race, and in particular the great personages of Christian history—Adam, Eve, Lilith, the Great Shadow, Mara (probably Mary), Christ; and finally God Himself, met, if not quite face to face, in the journey to heaven of the risen sleepers at the end.[37]

Phantastes is geared to mortal, *Lilith* to immortal, existence. Perhaps expressing this difference, *Phantastes* is rather more dialectical in character. Anodos has to learn to live the dialectic of desiring without seeking to possess. In Fairy Land he finds good and evil forms of his white lady; his experiences with his evil shadow partly embody the ancient struggle of darkness with light which the ogress describes before he opens the forbidden cupboard door (pp. 62-3). The book is shot through with such opposites as art and nature (the ladies Anodos brings to life are both originally statues), active and passive, conscious and unconscious, dream and reality, opacity and translucency,[38] age and youth. Many of these are, as has been seen, married in Anodos's death. Yet at the very end Fairy Land and this world remain divided: Anodos accepts that he is no longer in the Faerian realm and wonders: 'Could I translate the experience of my travels there, into common life? This was the question. Or must I live it all over again, and learn it all over again, in the other forms that belong to the world of men, whose experience yet runs parallel to that of Fairy Land?' He goes on: 'These questions I cannot yet answer. But I fear' (p. 181).

Vane, however, does not know whether he is awake in this world or still sleeping and dreaming in Adam's house (p. 419). This uncertainty in part expresses the greater emphasis on the reconciliation of opposites that is found prefigured throughout *Lilith*. The book could be called apocalyptic in that it continually looks to a future, to death and resurrection. Lilith is eschatology, and eschatology is not finally dialectical. '"When you are quite dead, you will dream no false dream"' (p. 403). Evil will cease: Lilith lies down among the dead in peace, and the Great Shadow will do so also (p. 388). Where Anodos seeks to remove his evil shadow, the Shadow in Lilith is to be redeemed.[39] This bringing of things together is expressed in the motif of atonement. Eve tells Lilith of the latter's daughter Lona, '"Death shall be the atonemaker; you shall sleep together'" (p. 386). When Vane wakes on his resurrection-morning,

> Nothing cast a shadow; all things interchanged a little light. Every growing thing showed me, by its shape and colour, its indwelling idea—the informing thought, that is, which was its being, and sent it out. My bare feet seemed to love every plant they trod upon. The world and my being, its life and mine, were one. The microcosm and the macrocosm were at length atoned, at length in harmony! I lived in everything; everything entered and lived in me. (p. 412)

The language of paradox in *Lilith*, in which opposites are yoked together, is also functional here.

A sentence from MacDonald's *Unspoken Sermons* serves to describe the circle that is begun in *Phantastes* and completed in *Lilith*: 'The final end of the separation is not individuality; that is but a means to it: the final end is oneness—an impossibility without it.'[40] Seen in this light *Phantastes* and *Lilith* themselves together form a larger dialectic: the one concerning itself with the First Things, and with true birth, self-realisation and movement into the world; the other treating the Last Things, and true death and the merging of the self with the greater consciousness which is its root. Yet there is, as has been seen, something of an 'atonement' between the two works also, in the marriage of opposites in the death-state which the one briefly describes and the other continually praises and prefigures. Having lived in his imagination, and hence, for him, in God, through the total pattern of Christian history, MacDonald felt himself to have moved out of time towards eternity. Shortly after the publication of *Lilith* he entered a long silent vigil that preluded the death (in 1905) to which he had looked forward all his life.

Endnotes

1. For the present writer's previous accounts of these works, see Manlove, *Modern Fantasy*, pp. 71-2, 75-9. There they are treated more as expressions of MacDonald's ideas and beliefs than in their own right, and are identified rather more than contrasted.
2. C. L. Dodgson's Alice books, though dream-like, are informed with dreamlogic as MacDonald's fantasies are not. Dodgson was, it should be said, on terms of close friendship with the MacDonald family.
3. *Phantastes* has many similarities with Novalis's *Heinrich von Ofterdingen* (1802) and with Hoffmann's tale, the latter of which MacDonald had been re-reading in 1856 with great admiration (Greville MacDonald, *George MacDonald and His Wife* (Allen and Unwin, 1924) pp. 259, 297-8).
4. George MacDonald, *Orts* (Sampson Low, 1882) pp. 24, 25. For a critical account of MacDonald's thought on the imagination, see *Modern Fantasy*, pp. 60-71.
5. MacDonald, 'The Fantastic Imagination' (1893), repr. in MacDonald, *A Dish of Orts: Chiefly Papers on the Imagination, and on Shakspere* (Sampson Low, 1893) p. 319.
6. *George MacDonald and His Wife*, p. 548.
7. For these, see particularly MacDonald, 'The Imagination: its Function and Development', *Orts*, pp. 1-42, and 'The Fantastic Imagination', op. cit., pp. 319-22. For some appraisal, see *Modern Fantasy*, pp. 64-71.
8. For a full account, see *George MacDonald and His Wife*; a more critical view is offered in *Modern Fantasy*, pp. 55-60.
9. On the lack of change in MacDonald's vision and thought, see *George MacDonald and his Wife*, p. 403; and, more critically, in relation to the ideas in the novels, Robert L. Wolff, *The Golden Key: A Study of the Major Fiction of George MacDonald* (New Haven: Yale University Press, 1961) p. 305.
10. For some account of this in relation to *Phantastes*, see *Modern Fantasy*, pp. 75-9.
11. See particularly Carl G. Jung, *Symbols of Transformation* (2nd ed., 1970), *The Archetypes and the Collective Unconscious* (2nd ed., 1969), *Aion: Researches into the Phenomenology of the Self*

(1959), *Psychology and Alchemy* (2nd ed., 1968) and *Mysterium Coniunctionis: An Inquiry into the Separation and Synthesis of Psychic Opposites* (1963)—respectively vols 5, 9 Parts I and II, 12 and 14 of *The Collected Works of C. G. Jung*, trans. R. F. C. Hull, 20 vols (Routledge & Kegan Paul, 1957-79), and cited here as *ST, ACU, AI, PA* and *MC*. On mothers, see *ST*, pp. 207-393 and *ACU*, pp. 75-110; on water, trees and caves, *ST*, pp. 218-22, 274, and *ACU*, p. 135; on mirrors, *PA*, pp. 108, 110, 111; on sun and moon, see esp. *MC*, pp. 92-110, 129-46, 173-83; on the Shadow, *ACU*, pp. 20-2 and *AI*, pp. 8-10; on the anima, *ACU*, pp. 27-30, 54-72 and *AI*, pp. 11-22.

12. On devouring mother see Jung, 'The Dual Mother', *ST*, pp. 306-93. Lilith is portrayed as a child-devourer in the Cabbala—see *The Jewish Encyclopaedia*, ed. Isidore Singer, 12 vols (New York: Funk and Wagnalls, 1901-6), s.v. 'Lilith'; and *The Zohar*, ed. Harry Sperling and Maurice Simon, 5 vols (Soncino Press, 1949) 1, 60, 82-3.

13. See E. T. A. Hoffmann, *The Golden Flower Pot*, trans. Thomas Carlyle (1827), repr. in *The Best Tales of Hoffmann*, ed. E. F. Bleiler, pp. 4-5, 31-2.

14. Compare Vane's feeling at the end of *Lilith*, 'It may be . . . that, when most awake, I am only dreaming the more!' (p. 420).

15. See pp. 27, 35, 37, 55, 59, and 164.

16. Some preparations may be made for one, such as 'The Chamber of Sir Anodos' that the hero finds in the fairy palace (p. 76), or Anodos's part in the battle with the giants (pp. 149-50).

17. This to some extent reverses the present writer's earlier view, in *Modern Fantasy*, pp. 75-8, that the two elements are opposed and express a division in MacDonald's creative purpose.

18. See also the epigraph (from Jean Paul Richter) to ch. 28 (p. 125): "'From dreams of bliss shall men awake / One day, but not to weep: / The dreams remain; they only

break / The mirror of the sleep.'"

19. In September 1895, shortly before the publication of his *The Wonderful Visit* (1895), H. G. Wells wrote to MacDonald remarking the coincidence of their independent use of the notion of travel into or from dimensions beyond the three that we know. Both, however, may have been recalling the speculations of A. Square (pseud. of Edwin A. Abbott), *Flatland: A Romance of Many Dimensions* (1884). Wells went on to say: 'Your polarization and mirror business struck me as neat in the extreme': it may be that this was a partial source for his *The Invisible Man* (1897). (Letter quoted in Greville MacDonald, *Reminiscences of a Specialist* (Allen and Unwin, 1932) pp. 323-4.)

20. On this see also Jung, *PA*, loc. cit., citing Schopenhauer.

21. This expresses MacDonald's benign determinism—on which see *Modern Fantasy*, pp. 60-2.

22. On this see also Jung, *ST*, Part II, chs 4-6, respectively entitled 'Symbols of the Mother and of Rebirth', 'The Battle for Deliverance from the Mother' and 'The Dual Mother'. Significantly the next chapter and stage is called 'The Sacrifice' (pp. 394-440) and can clearly be paralleled in Anodos's final sacrificial death—see esp. pp. 414-15 on the 'unconscious compulsion' of the child-state.

23. Cf. Jung, *ACU*, pp. 177-9, 'The Child as Beginning and End'. Jung declares that the 'child' symbolizes the pre-conscious and the post-conscious essence of man. His pre-conscious essence is the unconscious state of earliest childhood; his post-conscious essence is an anticipation by analogy of life after death. In this idea the all-embracing nature of psychic wholeness is expressed. Wholeness is never comprised within the compass of the conscious mind—it includes the indefinite and indefinable extent of the unconscious as well (p. 178).

24. This is done by Vane's burying Lilith's now severed evil hand at a certain point in the desert sand of the dried-up watercourse.

25. See MacDonald, "Σπεα" Απτεα, *Unspoken Sermons, Second Series* (Longmans, Green, 1885) pp. 21-2.

26. The walls also vanish by moonlight (pp. 160-1).

27. See also p. 158, where on approaching the last forest Anodos finds an unarmed youth 'who had just cut a branch from a yew growing on the skirts of the wood'.

28. *George MacDonald and His Wife*, p. 482; see also pp. 348, 349-51. MacDonald also uses the stair-symbol in his 'The Golden Key' (1867), *The Princess and the Goblin* (1872) and *The Princess and Curdie* (1883).

29. MacDonald, *England's Antiphon* (Macmillan, 1874) p. 56. See also MacDonald, "Σπεα" Απτεα, *Unspoken Sermons* (Strahan, 1867) p. 196, 'The whole system of the universe works upon this law—the driving of things upward towards the centre.'

30. MacDonald, "Σπεα" Απτεα, *Unspoken Sermons*, Third Series (Longmans Green, 1889) pp. 91-2.

31. For further account of man's God-given true name or signature, see *Unspoken Sermons* (1867) pp. 105-7.

32. Cosmo reflects, "'how many who love never come nearer than to behold each other as in a mirror; seem to know and yet never know the inward life; never enter the other soul; and part at last, with but the vaguest notion of the universe on the borders of which they have been hovering for years?'"(p. 99).

33. This may explain why *Phantastes* lends itself more to a Freudian, and *Lilith* to a Jungian reading: see Wolff, op. cit., and Roderick F. McGillis, 'The Fantastic Imagination: The Prose Romances of George MacDonald', University of Reading Ph.D. Thesis (1973), respectively.

34. *Orts*, p. 4. See also MacDonald, *A Book of Strife in the Form of The Diary of an Old Soul* (Allen and Unwin, 1882), July 18, 'not that thou thinkest of, but thinkest me'.

35. Op. cit. (Hurst and Blackett, 1863) vol. iii, p. 194. 36. See e.g. pp. 44-5, 71, 72, 78, 127, 129-30, and 166.

36. See e.g. pp. 44-5, 71, 72, 78, 127, 129-30, 166.

37. It is difficult to understand R. F. McGillis's claim in his 'George MacDonald—the *Lilith* Manuscripts', *Scottish Literary Journal*, vol. 4, no. 2 (Dec. 1977) 56, that 'MacDonald clearly intended to avoid . . . direct references to God' in order to encourage us 'not to read *Lilith* as a Christian document, as many readers do'.

38. On relative translucency, see pp. 36, 44, 53, and 137.

39. Incorporation in rather than rejection of the Shadow by the self is seen as the key to psychic wholeness by Jung: see e.g. *ACU*, pp. 20-2.

40. *Unspoken Sermons, Second Series*, p. 169.

The Psychology of the Self in MacDonald's *Phantastes*

Max Keith Sutton

From *VII: Journal of the Marion E. Wade Center*

George MacDonald's first adult fairy tale, *Phantastes* (1858), both invites and frustrates interpretation. Its most influential modern admirers, C. S. Lewis and W.H. Auden, praised MacDonald as a mythmaker, and Lewis told how reading *Phantastes* "baptized" his imagination, but he never tried to interpret it.[1] Neither did MacDonald himself, who insisted that "there is always more in a work of art" than the artist realised.[2] To offer a schematic interpretation would risk drawing limits around the imagination, even around the divine spirit working in the unconscious, as MacDonald believed, to inspire true fantasies. A scornful Victorian reviewer made him most uneasy by calling the book an allegory—"as if nothing but an allegory could have two meanings!"[3] But while maintaining that a "fairy tale is not an allegory,"[4] he expected a good one to have multiple implications, like the name of his youthful narrator in *Phantastes*: the Greek word ⊠nodos can be read as at least a triple pun meaning (1) "a way back" (2) "pathless, having no way," and (3) "a way up."[5] The name teases, like the story itself. Critics since 1961 have interpreted *Phantastes* from both Freudian and Jungian viewpoints; more recently they have read it also in the light of MacDonald's own views of psychology and religion. The best efforts have used multiple perspectives in looking for his multiple meanings. Yet even with the theories of Freud, Jung, and the author himself at their service, critics still leave certain crucial matters unexplained. Perhaps, as C. N. Manlove has suggested, the story was not written for the "querulous academic": MacDonald, after all, implied that "the best way" to read a fairy tale was "not to bring the forces of our intellect to bear upon it, but to be still and let it work on that part of us for whose sake it exists."[6] That part is the imagination, more cultivated among critics than the silence which MacDonald recommended.

Anyone who breaks the rule of silence and tries to speak about the deeper levels of meaning in *Phantastes* should address at least three puzzling aspects of the story:

(1) the narrator's underlying problem, which provides the context of his quest into Fairy Land (an Oedipus Complex? Narcissism?)

(2) the unifying action of the story ("a way back" as the name *Anodos* suggests, or "a way up" toward spiritual wholeness, or a "pathless" journey leading nowhere?)

(3) the relevance of the central tale within the tale (does it deserve its place in the middle chapter of *Phantastes*, or should it have been omitted?)

Because these three points have invited conflicting interpretations, they may serve as touchstones to reveal the strengths and weaknesses of a particular critical approach. Believing that any single approach is too narrow to deal with all three of these issues, I shall try to supplement the Freudian and Jungian analyses with concepts from the new "psychology of the self" being developed by Heinz Kohut. His perspective provides help in understanding the narrator's problems and gaining a view of the action. In addition, work begun by Richard Reiss, followed by C. N. Manlove, Stephen Prickett, and Keith Wilson, has shown the relevance of MacDonald's views of psychology and religion to his literary fantasies. His perspective can serve as a needed corrective to our impulse to twist an older work to fit a modern theory. Still, as he realized, the tale may mean more than the artist intended and invite interpretation from other perspectives than his own. Light from any quarter should be welcome, for in trying to understand the narrator, the unifying action, and the function of the interpolated tale in *Phantastes*, we need all the help we can get.

I

The most sustained effort to analyse the narrator and read *Phantastes* in the light of modern psychology is still Robert L. Wolff's Freudian interpretation in *The Golden Key* (1961). His motto is William Empson's claim that "To make the dream-story from which *Wonderland* was elaborated seem Freudian one has only to retell it."[7] Wolff's chapter is essentially a careful retelling of *Phantastes*, supplemented with valuable information concerning MacDonald's indebtedness to such German romantics as Novalis and E. T. A. Hoffmann. Following Empson, Wolff assumes that the story is a "dream adventure," like the one written soon afterwards by MacDonald's friend Lewis Carroll.[8] This assumption is itself highly suspect, even though MacDonald's epigraph from Novalis draws an analogy between a *Märchen* and a dream. If *Phantastes* not merely resembles but "is a dream," as Wolff assumes,[9] then the dream has strange powers, for it takes Anodos out of his castle two days after his twenty-first birthday and keeps him absent in Fairy Land until twenty-one days later, when he finds himself on a hilltop overlooking his estate. Furthermore, after his room transforms itself into a forest glade with a steam flowing through it on the morning of his "disappearance," his sisters come and find the floor "flooded."[10] (This awkward detail prompts Manlove's assertion in 1975 that Anodos goes to Fairy Land not in a dream but "in cold fact"—though in 1983 he reverses his position to agree with Wolff, without explaining why he changed his mind.[11]) Because details in the text objectify the journey, it makes better sense to consider the world that Anodos enters as in some way invading his own: Fairy Land is more substantial than a dream and perhaps less susceptible to Freudian interpretation.[12]

Proceeding upon the questionable assumption that *Phantastes* is a "dreamnarrative," Wolff finds it reflecting the Oedipal conflict which he sees in the life of George MacDonald. Biographical evidence for this conflict is sketchy. MacDonald's mother died when he was eight, and he kept in his desk a letter describing her reluctance to wean him. Largely from these two facts, Wolff assumes that keeping the letter indicates an infantile fixation and that her death "dealt him a blow which never healed." So far as the boy's father is concerned, outward signs indicate a positive relationship, but Wolff further assumes that the son repressed his rebellious "filial resentments" and struggled "all his life to conceal the guilt he felt so deeply."[13] Presumably *Phantastes*, as a dream narrative, will reveal more openly what the author in his personal life tried to conceal: Fairy Land, after all, is a realm where a person will do just as he wishes.[14]

But the young man who goes there is in many ways quite different from his creator. He is, first of all, about fifteen years younger than MacDonald, who by 1858 had a devoted wife and five small children. MacDonald knew ill-health and poverty; his youthful narrator lives in a castle and has no pressing family responsibilities; he has never struggled to make a living, or lost a position because of his religious beliefs, or coughed bright blood. It is true that the fictional Anodos lost his mother in childhood, but she died much earlier than MacDonald's mother did, and the youth's father has been dead for some years, while the elder George MacDonald lived until August 1858, several months after the manuscript had gone to the publisher. Although definite reflections of MacDonald's life appear in at least two episodes—as when Anodos hears his father's voice warning him and his brother not to trample the meadow grass, and later in the deaths of two brothers[15]—the protagonist in the fantasy seems almost free-floating in his comparative lack of family attachments. Unlike the novelist, the narrator knows nothing of his father's "personal history" (16); the haziness of his family background makes him more like the archetype of romantic youth in Shelley's *Alastor* (the source of the epigraph for Chapter I) than like the proud clansman of the MacDonalds.

These differences between author and narrator could be interpreted as signs of wish-fulfillment, for a man who secretly resented his father might well create a protagonist without one, just as he might escape in fantasy from sickness, poverty, and the burden of supporting a wife and children by making the character healthy, rich, and unmarried. But to read *Phantastes* as evidence for MacDonald's alleged Oedipus complex involves circular reasoning: the very thing in question—the alleged complex—becomes the means for detecting in the fiction the signs of its existence. Wolff would raise fewer logical difficulties by simply interpreting the text without trying to analyse the author. In the behavior of Anodos, Wolff finds plausible evidence of Oedipal conflict. The youth longs for his unknown mother just before his journey; he seeks comfort from a series of mother figures, and he acts impulsively like a child. On the basis of such evidence, Wolff concludes that Anodos seeks his mother in the women of Fairy Land and never finds sexual fulfillment because his deepest desire conflicts with the incest taboo.[16]

Yet this reading neglects certain differences between the youth's behavior toward the maternal figures and his behavior toward the women he pursues. With the motherly beech tree who protects him in the forest and again with the old woman in the four-doored cottage, Anodos behaves like a child, remembering his childhood as he falls asleep in the beech-tree's arms (40) and letting himself be fed "like a baby" by the old woman with the young eyes (131). But toward the object of his desire, the Lady of Marble, he takes an active masculine role, first releasing her from stone by means of his knife, his "penetrative" look of love, and his song (47); later he sings her to life once more with what Wolff terms a "thoroughly erotic" love song celebrating her naked beauty.[17] Nowhere in his pursuit of this woman does he show a need to be mothered. The central quest in the story thus fails to support Wolff's claim that Anodos (to say nothing of MacDonald) suffers from an unresolved Oedipus complex. The fact that he will give up the quest and resign the lady to a "better man," Sir Percivale, only fits the Freudian theory if the knight is interpreted as a father. But Percivale enters the story simply as a more experienced peer of the youth, warning him against the wiles of the Alder-Maiden, who has just seduced Percivale and will soon seduce Anodos. The narrator never sees Percivale as a father, although at one point when the hero tends a wounded child he compares the knight's gentleness to a mother's (169). By then Anodos sees Percivale as the hero whom he will serve as a squire, but he does not make a parent of him. Wolff neglects the question of how Anodos perceives the man in order to maintain the view that Percivale wins the white lady because he "is the father" and she "was all along forbidden to Anodos-Oedipus."[18]

As Wolff virtually admits, his Freudian reading leaves several "loose ends" and "unexplained details."[19] While these may be due to the disorderly nature of the alleged dream which forms the story, they might as easily be the result of forcing the wrong theory upon the narrator's experience. Instead of seeing Anodos as a repressed Oedipus, the critic might be better advised to consider him as a potential Narcissus and make use of the new "psychology of the self" that has been developed by Heinz Kohut. For much in the narrator's personality suggests the "secondary narcissism" discussed in Kohut's *Analysis of the Self* (1971) and *The Restoration of the Self* (1977) and, less clinically, in Christopher Lasch's *Culture of Narcissism* (1979). While these works identify the disorders of a narcissistic personality as hallmarks of our own era, similar problems appear in the mid-Victorian protagonist of *Phantastes*. The little that he tells of his past reveals not the intense attachments and rivalries of the Oedipal situation but the isolation and parental neglect that hinder the development of a "cohesive self." He lacks the two basic experiences that Kohut finds essential to normal development. He grows up with no mother to serve as a "mirror" and help him gain a strong self-concept by loving attention and encouragement. His father fails to fill this role and to provide the other basic experience that might have compensated for the lack of "mirroring."[20] By keeping himself so remote that the boy learns nothing of his "personal history," he deprives his son of the chance to idealize him as a "parental imago" and thus take the first step toward developing a firm sense of ideals and purpose.[21] In view of the youth's neglected childhood, his name quite rightly includes the meaning of "pathless."

As a result of these deprivations, Anodos grows up with an "enfeebled self"[22] and reveals the symptoms of narcissistic disorder. When the story begins, the young man lacks close ties with anyone: he mentions no friends, no teachers, and no living relatives except his uncharacterised sisters; later he alludes to an unhappy love affair with a girl whom he apparently seduced and left in misery. He will identify her in a vision as "a form well-known to me (*well-known*—alas, how weak the word!)"; he cannot bear to meet her face to face (141). When he becomes the one seduced in the reversed mirror-world of Fairy Land, erotic delight turns to horror: abrupt shifts in mood mark his journey, just as they mark the life of a narcissistic personality, whose flashes of excitement and momentary grandeur barely hide "low self-esteem and depression."[23] Anodos moves from enchanted forests to rocky wastelands, from a fairy palace to a hellish cavern, from a sense of omnipotence as a knight in shining armor—the equal, as he thinks, of Sir Galahad (159)—to feelings of helpless submissiveness and imprisonment in a "dreary square tower" (160). His "grandiose fantasies" as knight and lover have no power to ward off "loneliness and depression."[24]

Fairy Land turns out to be no realm of wish-fulfillment but an intensified reflection of mortal experience, combining "great splendours" with "corresponding horrors" (169). Continually it exposes the weaknesses of his "chaotic and impulse-ridden character"[25] as he violates taboo after taboo, opening forbidden doors and trying to grasp what he is forbidden to touch. While it is true that in Fairy Land he may act upon his wishes, the woman who told him this failed to add that acting has no guarantee of satisfaction. His impulsiveness is accepted in Fairy Land, just as "delinquent" and sometimes "destructive" acting out is accepted by Kohut as a natural response in a narcissistic patient during long-term psychoanalysis.[26] Only by acting out his impulses can Anodos discover what he can and cannot achieve; by learning his limits, he may gain a clearer sense of who he is. With help from a kindly "mirror," a guide on his pathless journey, he may strengthen the "enfeebled self" that is the legacy of his childhood.

II

A Kohutian analysis of the narrator's problems points directly toward a way of understanding the action of the story. The Journey through Fairy Land can be read as a symbolic "working through" of the disorders of a narcissistic personality. "Acting out" is part of the healing process, and Fairy Land affords on open field for any impulse that Anodos wants to follow. Of course, he lacks an R. D. Laing or a Heinz Kohut to make the trip with him, but he does meet spiritual guides along the way. The most important of these is the old woman with young eyes, who serves as the mother he had never known, providing the experience of "mirroring" with her compassionate attention. When he comes to her cottage after trying to seize, and thus losing, his ideal lady, the old woman welcomes him with perfect empathy, letting him weep upon her bosom and accepting his temporary return to infancy: "Poor child; poor child!" she says, embracing him (131). But she directs his mind toward his adult crisis by singing the ballad of Sir Aglovaile, whose double loss of a beloved woman through impulsive action mirrors the experience of Anodos. This indirect approach to his problems avoids alarming him, while it prepares him for a series of visions which deal directly with the wounds to his psyche. Throughout this episode, her songs, speech, and gestures convince the rejected young man that he is both understood and loved.

Although her means are supernatural, she acts like a therapist in allowing him to face once more the key figures from his past. He sees the brother who drowned in childhood the morning after they had quarreled, the beloved Lady of Marble whom he lost to Sir Percivale, and the girl whom he seduced or at least left miserable shortly before entering Fairy Land. He even makes contact with dead ancestors, as the past, which he had previously suppressed in his narrative, comes flooding in under the old woman's influence. She provides both the opportunity for, and the shelter from, these confrontations. Three of the four doors of her square, windowless cottage open to worlds of painful but bearable vision—the doors of weeping, of sighing, and of dismay. Each time he can return to her safe presence whenever the vision threatens to overpower him. But the forbidden "door of the Timeless" which he recklessly opens would have left him in oblivion, apparently, had the old woman not brought him back, unconscious, to her cottage (144). Whatever the timeless is, it could destroy his fragile self; the past is as much as he can deal with.

By helping him deal with his past, this wise woman is performing a central task of psychoanalysis. In Kohut's view, any progress toward healing depends less upon interpreting the old experiences than upon "repeatedly" reliving them.[27] They need to be relived in the new context of a maturing psyche, ideally with such support as the wise woman provides. Not only in this episode, but perhaps all along, Anodos ("a way back") symbolically relives his past, since his twenty-one day journey seems to him as long as the twenty-one years of his life.[28] Whether it does him permanent good is left unanswered at the end, but after his intense, visionary therapy in the old woman's cottage he goes out and performs his first deed "worth doing," as he joins two brothers to rid the land of giants (145). That triumph is followed by another fall ("ego inflation" when he compares himself to Sir Galahad) resulting in his self-imprisonment; but the worthy deed shows that in facing past losses and finally accepting the pain of them he grows in power to act responsibly. As the wise old woman says, "Past tears are present strength," and "Tears are the only cure for weeping" (149, 150).

If the action of *Phantastes* is a Kohutian "restoration of the self," then the climax should demonstrate the achievement of "self-cohesion" through productive work and creativity.[29] But the book ends without showing how the narrator comes to terms with the mortal world. The only tangible creative act that he performs on his return is the impressive one of telling his story, but he sounds far less confident as a learner and a teacher than Coleridge's Ancient Mariner does in telling his fantastic ordeal. Whatever Anodos may have gained from Fairy Land he suspects he will have to "live" and "learn" all over "in the other forms that belong to the world of men" (181). His doubts suggest that his name still deserves to be read as "pathless"—as Wolff read it in his Freudian interpretation, which leaves "Anodos-Oedipus" with nothing more to do than wait for union with his mother earth in death.[30]

But the narrator's readiness for death is not based upon a wish for self-destruction and oblivion: it comes from his spiritual transformation after his climactic deed in Fairy Land. There he strangled a wolf-monster that devoured the victims in disguised ritual of human sacrifice, and he was slain in the process; in death he found himself at last able to love without having to be loved in return. While the supernatural aspects of this event resist psychoanalytic interpretation, from a Kohutian viewpoint the final act is positive. The courage to seek out and attack the monster shows that Anodos has "internalized" the ideal image of Sir Percivale, who kills a dragon shortly before the climactic episode. That the deed costs Anodos his life does not subtract from his achievement, for Kohut sees in "Tragic Man" something other than the Freudian death-wish. There can be a "*triumphant* death . . . which (for the persecuted reformer of real life, for the crucified saint of religion, and for the dying hero on the stage) puts the seal of permanence on the ultimate achievement of Tragic Man: the realisation, through his actions, of the blueprint for his life that had been laid down in his nuclear self."[31]

Kohut's language indicates a leaning away from Freud toward a Jungian view of the psyche. The "nuclear self" that provides a "blueprint" for life sounds a good deal like the Jungian "Self," the "organizing center" of the psyche, which serves as guide and goal in the long inward journey toward wholeness in the process called individuation.[32] Any critical approach to *Phantastes* can hardly ignore Jungian concepts because the work is so full of archetypes—the *Athenæum* called it a "second-hand symbol shop" in 1858,[33] and today one has to fight the anachronistic suspicion that MacDonald cribbed from Jung. Since neither Freud nor Kohut accounts for the mythic aura of archetypal figures, Jung's more mystical view of the psyche holds better promise of doing them justice. Moreover, his sense that individuation never teaches completion is especially appropriate to an open-ended work like *Phantastes*.

While no sustained Jungian reading of the story has yet been offered, the basis for one lies in the parallels between the Narrator's journey and the process of individuation. From the moment Anodos opens the locked cabinet and finds a fairy godmother inside, he encounters one archetypal figure after another: the shadow, first seen as an ogrish ash-tree; the positive anima in the Lady of Marble, and the negative anima in the Alder-Maiden, who masquerades as his ideal and, like Duessa in *The Faerie Queene*, promptly seduces him. Early in his wanderings he meets a potential image of the Jungian Self, of psychic wholeness, in the hero Percivale, but the knight's glory is in eclipse from his own seduction by the Alder-Maiden: Anodos fails both to recognize his heroism and to heed his warning. Without Percivale's unseen intervention, the youth would have been destroyed by the shadow and the negative anima, the representatives of his incompleteness. The ash-tree "has a hole in his heart . . . and is always trying to fill it up, but he cannot" (39), while the Alder-Maiden is literally hollow. Like Lilith in MacDonald's last major fantasy, she tries to compensate by winning a man's love—"not for the sake of his love, but that she may be conscious anew of her own beauty, through the admiration he manifests" (57). Unseen, in this episode the inner guide, the Jungian "Great Man" imaged in Sir Percivale as a symbol of the Self,[34] works to deliver Anodos from his own psychic flaws—the destructive greed embodied in the ash-tree and the narcissistic impulses of the Alder-Maiden. Meanwhile, the Narrator himself may not recognise his reflections, but he soon gets an inkling of their meaning in responding to a matter-of-fact farmer, who finds nothing remarkable in the enchanted forest: "'I dare say you saw nothing worse than yourself there?' 'I hope I did,' was my inward reply. . ." (58). From a Jungian viewpoint, Anodos needs to see Fairy Land as a mirror if he is to reach deeper self-awareness. The key figure to recognise as a reflection is the one called by MacDonald, as by Jung, the "Shadow," which returns in starker form after Sir Percivale lays his ax to the demonic ash-tree. It rushes out when Anodos opens the first of his forbidden doors, and the female ogre in the cottage of darkness says, "Everybody's shadow is ranging up and down looking for him . . . yours has found you, as every person's is almost certain to do who looks into that closet . . ." (64). From this point on, the Shadow haunts his journey, vanishing at times but returning at crucial moments, like Gollum in *The Lord of the Rings*. It can turn his world into a desert, even darkening the sun (66); it can give him a prideful sense of power to see through illusions of beauty and nobleness; it can make him mistrust his friend, Sir Percivale. Even after he slays the giant, the Shadow lies before him, "black in the sunshine" (156).

In his pride over this triumph, Anodos suffers what Jung would call "psychic inflation," brought about by the attempt of his ego to identify with an archetype of the Self, the hero.[35] Since the Self is vastly more than the ego, the identification distorts his whole psyche, setting him up for another downfall. With fantasies of being a match for Sir Galahad, he rides out in shining armor only to fall before his Shadow, seen now as his splendid, larger-than-life double, mounted as another knight on horseback. Admiring this unmistakable reflection, yet feeling that he should fight it, he yields meekly to its commands and lets it lead him off to prison. When the double vanishes, the Shadow lies in its place: at last Anodos gains "the terrible conviction that [the Shadow] and the knight were one" (160). He has finally learned that the Shadow reflects something in himself.

His deliverance from the tower of his wounded pride comes through the songs of a sisterly anima, who reawakens his love of nature and bids him come forth into the sunlight. He opens the door, begs her forgiveness for an earlier wrong he had done to her, and renounces the splendid armor of knighthood: "I learned that he that will be a hero, will barely be a man; that he that will be nothing but a doer of his work, is sure of his manhood" (165). Accepting the role of a squire, he has escaped from the disastrous effort of his ego to identify with the Self. He has escaped also from the Shadow, until it returns in its most dangerous form as the wolf-monster in the ceremony of human sacrifice. This time he seems aware that it represents a part of himself, for upon approaching the unseen killer, he finds "something of an evil satisfaction, in the revenge I was thus taking upon the self which had fooled me so long" (176). While the revenge might be interpreted as the death that he expects to meet in this venture, he more likely refers to the death he plans to inflict upon the murderer whom he identifies with the deceptive self that has repeatedly "fooled" him as his Shadow. In killing that self he foresees that he will die. Following his death and his discovery of unselfish love in the afterlife, he returns to this world freed of his dark companion. In these often-quoted words he sums up his experience: "I, who set out to find my Ideal, came back rejoicing that I had lost my Shadow" (182).

But from a Jungian viewpoint, what has he accomplished? Jung believed that rejecting the Shadow is a negative act, detrimental to the goal of psychic wholeness;[36] the fate of Dr Jekyll and Mr Hyde illustrates the danger. Yet Jung's disciple Marie-Louise von Franz concedes that knowing whether to repress or accept "our dark partner" is "one of the most difficult problems that we encounter on the way to individuation."[37] If the monstrous wolf that Anodos kills only embodies his animal energies, as Mr Hyde embodies that part of Dr Jekyll, then the act leaves him less whole than ever. But throughout the story his Shadow has behaved like something other than a spontaneous vital force. It has "fooled" Anodos into doubting when he should have trusted; it has taken on a disguise and sent him off to prison in the tower, and in the climactic scene it has crouched beneath a wooden idol in a ceremony that deceives even Sir Percivale with its religious solemnity. Like its prefigurings in the greedy ash tree and the AlderMaiden, the Shadow has sought victims, and those it devours in the disguised ritual in the forest represent its ultimate goals. When Anodos confronts and kills it, he rids himself of a destructive aspect of his character; he dies but, unlike Dr Jekyll, he does not deprive himself of true life.

His progress toward individuation can be further tested by the presence or absence of symbols of the Self in the story. These should emerge if he deals effectively with the Shadow and the anima. Given his sacrificial death and MacDonald's Christianity, an expected symbol of the Self for him would be the figure of Christ, but Anodos shows no awareness of this figure. The symbols that he does meet include the hero Percivale—seen both singly and with his new wife, the Marble Lady—and the wise old woman with the young eyes. The embracing knight and lady form a union of opposites and thus represent the wholeness of the Self.[38] When Anodos sees them together in a vision given him by the wise woman, one symbolic detail holds promise that he will find his true being in the Self, for in Sir Percivale's shining armor he sees his own dim reflection (139). Another symbol of wholeness is the wise old woman in her four-square cottage with its four doors of vision. Four is the Jungian "number of totality,"[39] the number of the functions of the psyche. The contrast between the woman's wrinkled face and her young eyes indicates that aspect of the Self which the Jungians believe "is not entirely contained in time."[40] While von Franz implies that feminine personifications of the Self appear mainly in women's fantasies, the old yet beautiful woman of wisdom returns in MacDonald's stories (notably in the two tales of the Princess and Curdie); her male counterparts who express the timeless aspect of the Self include the ancient yet youthful Adam in *Lilith* (1895) and the "oldest man," the "Old Man of the Fire," who turns out to be a naked child in a mossy cave in "The Golden Key" (1867). With the paradox of her age and youth, the woman in *Phantastes* embodies much more than the ultimate mother-figure which Wolff identifies through Freudian lenses. Rather than keeping the narrator in a state of infantile regression, she helps him face the pain of his life that he must accept if he is to function as an adult. Yet she is even more than the ideal Kohutian analyst pictured earlier. From the Jungian viewpoint, she embodies the wholeness which she tries to help Anodos achieve; as a symbol of the Self, she represents the goal of individuation.

Since she is a figure of such power, meeting her and opening her doors of vision brings a certain peril, just as in Jungian analysis the emergence of the archetype of the Self threatens the conscious ego. In opening the forbidden door of the Timeless, Anodos risks annihilation; and though the wise woman retrieves him, waters rise that will submerge her cottage, as if to symbolize the danger of "drowning in the unconscious."[41] Yet she will survive by keeping her hearth-fire burning, and she guides the young man to solid ground. His task is not only to perform his first deed "worth doing"; it is also to trust her in sorrow and disappointment as one who "knows something, though she must not always tell it, that would quite satisfy [him] about it, even in the worst moments of [his] distress" (144). Anodos is to carry with him this image of the Self as the wise "inner friend," ready to help, though she sits by the fire in her square cottage under a "great firmament" of risen waters (144). "Go," she says, but she assures him that he will not lose her: "You will come back to me some day. . . ."

Because Anodos encounters figures of wholeness and finally acts in accordance with their examples, his journey eventually ceases to look "pathless" or regressive ("a way back"). From either a Jungian or Kohutian viewpoint, it can be seen as progressive ("a way up"). A positive view of the journey also gains support from MacDonald's own ideas about the self and the process of spiritual growth. Although his ideas are expressed in religious contexts, they prefigure those of modern psychologists. Like Freud and Jung, he assumes that the unconscious forms the greatest region of the mind: "our consciousness is to the extent of our being but as the flame of the volcano to the world-gulf whence it issues."[42] But unlike Freud, as Richard Reiss points out, he finds divinity here: "in the gulf of our unknown being God works behind our consciousness."[43] His early poem, *Within and Without* (1855), expresses this view of divine process within the psyche in terms that suggest both Jung's concept of individuation and Kohut's belief that the "nuclear self" lays down a "blueprint" for personal development. In MacDonald's theistic context, individuation involves loving consent to the divine will, and the protagonist prays,

> let thy design in me work on,
> Unfolding the ideal man in me;
> Which being greater far than I have grown,
> I cannot comprehend.[44]

The unfolding of the "ideal man," like the inward journey toward realising the Jungian Self, is a long process, taking many births and perhaps more than a lifetime (MacDonald, like his disciple C. S. Lewis, makes a strong case for purgatory.) His "Sketch of Individual Development" (1880) outlines three stages in the process: (1) the birth of "self-consciousness," when the infant begins to "learn that the world is around, and not within him—that he is apart, and that is apart"; (2) the birth of conscience, when he learns that his impulses may conflict with his mother's will, and (3) the birth of the will—"the real Will, not the pseudo-will, which is mere desire, swayed of impulse, selfishness, or one of many a miserable motive."[45] This development may take years: understandably, it takes most of the time that Anodos spends in Fairy Land, and even then it may be incomplete. For in spite of his right-willed achievement in killing the monster, he still stops short of the awareness that marks this "birth from above."[46] Anodos never reaches an awareness of the God whose will he is to delight in doing; he does not see Christ as the "live Ideal," the vitalizing "design" or "soul" that "informs, gives shape to our souls," working to bring the "ideal man" into active being.[47]

If divine awareness eludes Anodos, he does go through many of the experiences that MacDonald finds typical in maturation. The youth in the essay longs to explore new places, to perform "heroic deeds"; he fails and suffers shame; he loses delight in the natural world under the shadow of his new cynicism.[48] He regains temporary freedom from this attitude when he falls in love and glimpses truth through windows no longer blocked "by the shadow of himself"; but he loses the vision and falls prey to his shadow self once more, just as Anodos does after his frustrating encounters with the beautiful Marble Lady. The Shadow in *Phantastes* corresponds with what MacDonald in his *Unspoken Sermons* terms the "usurping Self," the egocentric consciousness which lives by the "principle of hell" and cries, "I am my own. I am my own king and my own subject. . . . My right is-what I desire. . . . I will be free with the freedom that consists in doing whatever I am inclined to do, from whatever quarter may come the inclination."[49]

In grasping after forbidden things, Anodos at first lives by this principle. Only as he learns "the hardness of the way" does he experience the conflict between the egoistic "self of his consciousness" ("the mere ugly shadow of the self that God made") and his soul, which waits for the hidden "deeper soul," the "infinite Life" of Christ, to rise up into "the Self we call *I* and *me*."[50] When Anodos finally renounces the usurping self by taking off his knightly armor and resolving to be a squire, a new self seems "to arise like a white spirit from a dead man," prompting him to wonder if spiritual death and rebirth will be continual, until "something deeper and stronger" than each slain self "will emerge at last from the unknown abysses of the soul" (165). In Jung's terms, this emergence would complete the process of individuation; in MacDonald's, it would mark the perfection of "the undeveloped Christ" within him.[51] Although the story ends long before Anodos approaches so climactic a development, he has traveled far enough from his initial impulsiveness to earn the best meaning of *nodos*—"a way up"—the "true name" which after all his pathless wanderings "expresses the character . . . the meaning of the person who bears it."[52]

III

As a final test for the positive interpretations of *Phantastes*, we may consider the significance of the central tale within the tale, the story of Cosmo and his magic mirror. Whether this piece deserves its central place in the thirteen of the twenty-five chapters, or should have been omitted altogether (as Wolff argues),[53] is an important question; yet Reiss and Prickett ignore the tale; Wilson makes a brief reference to it; while Manlove, after mentioning it only once in his earlier book, finally notes its relevance to the theme of awakening in *Phantastes* in his latest study.[54] The artistic justification for the story of Cosmo and the mirror lies not only in its thematic relevance but also in the way it involves the reader with the question of how (and if) a work of fantasy can affect life through its interplay with the imagination. Read by Anodos in the Fairy "Palace of Art,"[55] the tale mirrors his still incomplete story of romantic longing, of trial and error and eventual growth; his response to it and his subsequent actions invite but do not answer the question of whether a fantasy can foster the growth it dramatizes.

The magic mirror becomes a symbol of the imagination and of art itself through the development of the motif of reflections in *Phantastes*. Anodos has already noted the power of mirrors to transform ordinary reality into art: "The commonest room is a room in a poem when I turn to the glass" (73). Now, in the fantastic story, he sees his own life reflected: "While I read it, I was Cosmo" (89). Like himself, Cosmo is young and dreamy; the mirror, like Fairy Land, awakens the imagination and starts Cosmo upon an inward journey which reveals his anima, a woman in white like the Marble Lady, whom he loves, pursues, and loses. The mirror has a "wondrous affinity" with the imagination (94) because it, too, reveals the essences of things,[56] including an archetype within the psyche. But its power has a sinister side and must eventually be broken, like the mirror in Tennyson's "Lady of Shalott." Cosmo learns that he must give it up after weeks of watching the white lady glide into his reflected room and lie wearily upon his reflected couch, as if by magic compulsion. When he finally uses magic in an effort to make her meet his admiring eyes, she leaves the glass to enter his actual room, but only to confront him with a plea for freedom: "Cosmo, if thou lovest me, set me free, even from thyself: break the mirror" (103). Understandably, the young man hesitates, thinking that to break the mirror would be to "banish out of his universe the only glory it possessed." In his urge to own his beloved, he reflects Anodos, who has tried to possess the Marble Lady and will try again before learning his mistake.[57] By hesitating as one "not yet pure in love," Cosmo loses both the woman and the mirror; soon he suffers the torments of knowing that it has fallen into the hands of a brutal man of "reckless habits and fierce passions" (106). This new archetype, the Shadow, threatens the lady, who lies at the brink of death until Cosmo at last smashes the mirror and sets her free. The act costs him his life, but he dies assured of her love: the sacrifice anticipates the last confrontation of Anodos with his shadow in Fairy Land.

Cosmo's sacrifice becomes all the more significant in the light of the German tales that apparently inspired this one. As Wolff points out, a mirror is the "essential prop" in E.T.A. Hoffmann's "Story of the

Lost Reflection," framed by a scene in which an absent woman's face appears uncannily in a mirror.[58] In this tale, a *femme fatale* persuades a young married man to give her his reflection. She then lures it out of the glass and keeps this shadowy lover as a means of blackmail: only if the man destroys his wife and son can he regain his reflection and her favors. If MacDonald remembered this tale of Hoffmann, he must have deliberately reversed the situation by casting the man, Cosmo, as the character who tried to control the beloved by means of a mirror, and the woman as the one who pleads to be set free. Despite this reversal, however, both authors treat the same theme: the violation of a lover's freedom. But unlike Hoffmann's *femme fatale*, Cosmo in breaking the mirror renounces the power that threatens to corrupt his love. Long before Anodos, he learns to let others be, even if their freedom means separation from himself.[59]

The parallels with the main story demonstrate the artistic function of the interpolated tale. Wolff's argument that it should have been omitted reflects the limitations of his Freudian perspective: the little story has no function because it shows no signs of the Oedipus complex that he was looking for. It shows instead the theme of "awakening," as Manlove demonstrates; as an encounter with archetypes, it suggests the steps toward individuation which Anodos is taking. Cosmo becomes one of Kohut's tragic men who fulfill their being in actions that demand their lives. He thus becomes a prototype for the still-erring narrator. Both men attain enough wholeness to offer themselves for the sake of others; both in acting leave behind the realms of reflections, the mirror and the psychic mirror of Fairy Land which foster their inward journeys. Accepting death, they accept also the independent value of other persons' lives and step beyond the "charmed circle" of the psyche into a still greater realm of the unknown.

But does reading Cosmo's story have anything to do with the narrator's personal growth? Does he, like the young farmer in MacDonald's poem, "The Hidden Life" (1857) find "a larger Self" by reading of "other selves"?[60] Naturally, as a didactic writer, MacDonald hoped that such things would happen. In *Adela Cathcart* (1864), the telling of interpolated tales (including "The Light Princess") serves as a mode of therapy to restore a depressed young lady to health. Fantastic stories are like our dreams, which the curate in that novel recommends taking "seriously," for dreams mark "wells of feeling and delight which have not yet broken out of their hiding-places in our souls."[61] Cosmo's strange story may end with his death, but it forms a living source of "comfort" within Anodos, returning in "after hours of deserved or needful sorrow" (108). The comfort suggests what Tolkien terms "consolation" in his essay on fairy tales; its benefits are not to be measured by any didactic standard, for Anodos apparently learns nothing in a cautionary sense from Cosmo's mistake and eventual triumph. Soon after reading the story he acts as impulsively as ever, clutching at the Marble Lady in the magic gallery where gold letters say "TOUCH NOT!" Only later does he learn to stop saying "my white lady" (121) and to renounce his claim upon her as Cosmo gave up his claim upon the lady in white. If Cosmo's awakening helps to awaken Anodos, it does so on the unconscious level, where MacDonald believed the "deepest self," the "indwelling God," works to make man whole.

Perhaps the question of how the tale affects Anodos should be subordinate to the question of how *Phantastes* affects ourselves. If it really is a story of spiritual growth, can reading it help us grow, too? For at least one reader, the answer is a strong yes: C. S. Lewis claimed that *Phantastes* "baptised" his imagination ("the rest of me," he reported, "took longer").[62] The book did not work upon his intellect, nor did it make him conscious of what his deeper self was learning: "I should have been shocked in my 'teens if anyone had told me that what I learned to love in *Phantastes* was goodness."[63] Lewis is an extreme case, but thirty years before him G. K. Chesterton spoke in similar terms of the "revolution" brought about in his life from reading MacDonald's *Princess and the Goblin*.[64] Other fantasies—for some "The Golden Key," for shallower readers like me "The Light Princess"—may tap hidden "wells of feeling and delight" that bathe the archetypes (those "second-hand" symbols) with fresh life. For some, the experience may be religious, although here the critic, as Manlove says, "can do no more than shyly point to the possibilities."[65] Perhaps these may be cut off, as MacDonald feared, by the critical search for symbolic meanings. But if we can maintain empathy with a character while using psychological concepts to understand his problems and his movement toward wholeness, we may find something to strengthen us, some guiding image, in Joseph Campbell's words, to "carry the human spirit forward."[66] We *may*, but of course there is no guarantee. Like Anodos, we may be left wondering how to "translate" the experience of fantasy into common life and dreading that we shall have to "live it all over, and learn it all over again." For that task, something tells us that even with Freud or Jung or MacDonald himself at our elbows, we still would need a stronger guide.[67]

Endnotes

1. *Surprised by Joy: the Shape of My Early Life* (New York: Harcourt Brace Jovanovich, 1955), p. 181.

2. Stephen Prickett, *Victorian Fantasy* (Bloomington: Indiana Univ. Press, 1979), p. 174. See MacDonald's essay on "The Fantastic Imagination," in *A Dish of Orts* (London: Sampson Low, 1893), p. 320.

3. Quoted in Greville MacDonald, *George MacDonald and His Wife*, intro. by G. K. Chesterton (New York: Dial Press, 1924), p. 297. The offending review appeared in the *Athenaeum*, No. 1619 (6 Nov. 1858), p. 580.

4. "The Fantastic Imagination," p. 317, quoted in C. N. Manlove, *Modern Fantasy: Five Studies* (Cambridge: Cambridge Univ. Press, 1975), p. 87.

5. Liddell and Scott's *Greek-English Lexicon* lists a fourth meaning of *ánodos*—a journey into central Asia. This suggests the easterly direction that Anodos normally follows through Fairy Land.

6. See Manlove, *Modern Fantasy*, p. 66, quoting from "The Fantastic Imagination," p. 321.

7. Empson's sentence serves as an epigraph to the chapter on *Phantastes* in *The Golden Key: A Study of the Fiction of George MacDonald* (New Haven: Yale Univ. Press, 1961).

8. Wolff, p. 108.

9. Wolff, p. 98.

10. *Phantastes*, originally subtitled "A Faerie Romance for Men and Women," reprinted in *Phantastes* and *Lilith*, intro. by C. S. Lewis (Grand Rapids, Mich.: Wm. B. Eerdmans, 1964), p. 11. Subsequent page numbers will be given in the text.

11. See *Modern Fantasy*, pp. 71-72, and *The Impulse of Fantasy Literature* (Kent, Ohio: Kent State Univ. Press, 1983), p. 77.

12. See Prickett, *Victorian Fantasy*: "MacDonald's two adult fantasies depend upon the interrelation and tension between two separate worlds," p. 178.

13. Wolff, p. 13. In contrast, Manlove argues that Anodos "finds his true self by a process of separation," his "history" being one of "gradual removal from overdependence on mother-figures and a condition of unthinking passivity": *The Impulse of Fantasy Literature*, p. 82.
14. "You shall do just as you wish," says the woman in the first cottage, p. 24.
15. See Greville MacDonald, p. 186, for the novelist's memory of his father warning the boys to keep off the grass; for the parallel between the two brothers in the story and his own brothers, see Richard Reis, *George MacDonald* (New York: Twayne, 1972), p. 90.
16. Wolff, pp. 90-91.
17. Ibid., p. 85.
18. Ibid., p. 98.
19. Ibid.
20. See Kohut, *The Restoration of the Self* (New York: International Universities Press, 1977), p. 190.
21. See Kohut, *The Analysis of the Self: A Systematic Approach to the Psychoanalytic Treatment of Narcissistic Personality Disorders* (New York: International Universities Press, 1971), p. 28.
22. *The Restoration of the Self*, p. 286.
23. Ibid., p. 5.
24. Ibid.
25. Christopher Lash, *The Culture of Narcissism: American Life in an Age of Diminishing Expectations* (New York: Warner Books, 1979), p. 81; see also Kohut on narcissistic "impulsivity" in *The Analysis of the Self*, p. 156.
26. *The Analysis of the Self*, p. 156.
27. *The Restoration of the Self*, p. 30.
28. See Reis, p. 90.
29. *The Restoration of the Self*, p. 158.

30. See Wolff, p. 108.

31. *The Restoration of the Self*, p. 133.

32. See Marie-Louise von Franz, "The Process of Individuation," in *Man and His Symbols*, ed. Carl Jung (New York: Dell, 1964), p. 161.

33. Quoted in Greville MacDonald, p. 296.

34. See von Franz, pp. 161-162, and Jung, Symbols of Transformation, *The Collected Works of C. G. Jung*, ed. Herbert Read et al., trans. R. F. C. Hull (New York: Pantheon, 1956), V, 392: the hero is "an archetype of the self."

35. *Symbols of Transformation*, p. 392.

36. See Manlove, *The Impulse of Fantasy Literature*, p. 166.

37. "The Process of Individuation," p. 184.

38. See Ibid., p. 216.

39. Barbara Hannah, *Striving towards Wholeness* (New York: G. P. Putnam's Sons, 1971), p. 2.

40. See von Franz, "The Process of Individuation," p. 208.

41. See von Franz, pp. 234-236, who tells an Iranian fairy tale in which "rising waters" are interpreted in this way.

42. "Man's Difficulty Concerning Prayer," *Unspoken Sermons, Second Series* (London: Longmans, Green, 1886), p. 94. These sermons have been abridged for modern readers in *George MacDonald: Creation in Christ*, ed. Rolland Hein (Wheaton, Illinois: Harold Shaw, 1976.)

43. Ibid., see Reis, p. 42; and Manlove, *The Impulse of Fantasy Literature*, p. 72.

44. *The Poetical Works of George MacDonald* (London: Chatto and Windus, 1893), 1, 17-18.

45. "A Sketch of Individual Development" in *Orts* (London: Sampson Low, Marston, Searle, and Rivington, 1882), p. 48.

46. Ibid., p. 48.

47. "The Mirrors of the Lord," *Unspoken Sermons, Third Series* (London: Longmans, Green, 1889), p. 53.

48. "A Sketch of Individual Development," pp. 53-54.

49. "The Voice of Job," *Unspoken Sermons, Second Series*, p. 195; and "Kingship," *Unspoken Sermons, Third Series*, p. 102.

50. "The Hardness of the Way," *Unspoken Sermons, Second Series*, p. 33; and "The Mirrors of the Lord," *Unspoken Sermons, Third Series*, p. 53.

51. "The Truth," *Unspoken Sermons, Third Series*, p. 79.

52. "The New Name," *Unspoken Sermons, First Series* (London: Longmans, Green, 1887), p. 106.

53. Wolff, p. 78.

54. See *The Impulse of Fantasy Literature*, p. 75. The theme of the awakening of the imagination as a necessary step toward recognising essential reality is carefully treated by Keith Wilson, who uses MacDonald's sermon, "The Truth," as a key to the story: see "The Quest for 'Truth': A Reading of George MacDonald's *Phantastes*," *Etudes Anglaises*, 34 (1981), pp. 140-152.

55. See Wilson, p. 148.

56. See Ibid.

57. Lust, says MacDonald in "The Way," is "the desire or pleasure of having": *Unspoken Sermons, Second Series*, p. 14.

58. See Wolff, p. 78; Wolff does not mention the preliminary scene with its reflection of the absent woman: see *Die Abenteuer der Silvesternacht* in Hoffmann's *Poetische Werke* (Berlin: Walter Gruyter, 1957), I, 318. Parallels appear in Hoffmann's "Golden Pot," as well as in Book III of *The Faerie Queene*, when Britomart sees a young knight in her father's magic mirror, and, more immediately, in MacDonald's *Within and Without*, when Lord Seaford sings of a youth who falls in love with a woman's image in a magic mirror. It shatters when he rushes forward to grasp the forbidden form. (See *Poetical Works*, 1, 77-78.) In "The Mirrors of the Lord," MacDonald deals at length with this symbol, arguing that for St. Paul in II Corinthians 3: 18, mirroring

Christ means internalising his image, absorbing his nature—an interpretation which corresponds to the folk-belief that mirrors have the power to absorb a person's soul. But he warns against interpreting the symbol "*after the flesh*" in some fashion "that partakes of the mere physical, psychical, or spirituo-mechanical." (See *Unspoken Sermons, Third Series*, p. 52.) Hoffmann's handling of reflections stays within the "psychical" realm: see Robert Muhlher's exploration of the motif of magic mirrors in Hoffmann as a revelation of the dream world between actuality and ideal truth, and of thought itself: *Dichtung der Krise: Mythos und Psychologie in der Dichtung des 19. und 20. Yahrhunderte* (Vienna: Herold, 1951), pp. 78, 83.

59. See Manlove, *The Impulse of Fantasy Literature*, p. 83: when Anodos "learns to be a separate individual, he learns also to let things be separate from him." MacDonald previously worked on this theme in *Within and Without*: Lord Seaford chides himself for "grasping" at God's work (the beautiful woman):

That woman-splendour was not mine, but thine.
Like a foolish child, I reached out for the star,
Nor kneeled, nor worshipped. (*Poetical Works*, I, III.)

60. *Poetical Works*, I, 141.

61. *Adela Cathcart* (Philadelphia: David McKay, n. d.), pp. 209-2rn.

62. *Surprised by Joy*, p. 181.

63. Introduction to *Phantastes* and *Lilith*, p. 12.

64. Introduction to *George MacDonald and His Wife*, p. 9. Chesterton read the book in childhood.

65. *Modern Fantasy*, p. 97.

66. *The Hero with a Thousand Faces* (1947; New York: World Publishing Company, 1967), p. II.

67. I regret that this article was completed before I had an opportunity to read the dissertation by Roderick F. McGillis, "The Fantastic Imagination of George MacDonald" (Reading, 1973). McGillis offers an astute

analysis of the two tales within the tale of *Phantastes* as part of his thorough reading of the whole story.

Phantastes and *Lilith*
David S. Robb
From *George MacDonald*

If any single work of MacDonald's has a claim on the attention of posterity, that work is surely *Phantastes* his first major piece of prose fiction. Written rapidly, in two months at the end of 1857, it was published in October 1858 with the subtitle, 'A Faerie Romance for Men and Women'. This is itself enough to hint distantly at Spenser's influence, and a glance at the many mottoes and quotations which MacDonald bestows on his chapters reveals that the work grew not only from a fertile interest in German and English romantic writing (Novalis, Goethe, Fouqué, Schiller, Heine, Jean Paul, Schleiermacher, Shelley, Wordsworth, Coleridge, Beddoes), but also from a considerable knowledge of the English Renaissance (Spenser, Fletcher, Tourneur, Shakespeare, Suckling, Lyly, Cowley, Sidney, Decker) as well as Chaucer, ballads, and the Bible.

The strange title is helpful. 'Phantastes' is a character in a poem by one of Spenser's imitators, 'The Purple Island' by Phineas Fletcher, and is the embodiment of 'the fancie'—the mind's fecund capacity to invent ideas and to clothe them in attractive imagery. MacDonald misquotes two lines of this poem on the title-page. The entire stanza from which they come is as follows:

> *Phantastes* from the first all shapes deriving,
> In new abiliments can quickly delight;
> Of all materiall and grosse parts depriving,
> Fits them unto the noble Princes sight;
> Which soon as he hath view'd with searching eye,
> He straight commits them to his Treasurie,
> Which old Eumnestes keeps, Father of memorie.
> (Canto 6, st. 48) [1]

(MacDonald's substitution of 'their fount' for 'the first' was conceivably intended to bring out more clearly what he took to be the essential meaning Fletcher intended, namely that man's thoughts all derive from the divine fountainhead.) The poem's elaborate allegory is an anatomy of 'the isle of man', and 'the noble Prince' is the Intellect or Understanding. *Phantastes* is the second of the three chief counsellors of this 'highest Soveraigne' and so a faculty of immense importance and responsibility. MacDonald's implication, therefore, is that this book, a product of the fancy, is not merely, or primarily, written for an outside reader, but is a manifestation of a process going on within its creator himself. *Phantastes* is part of the means whereby the individual accumulates knowledge and experience. His presence is a sign that an inner growth is taking place, irrespective of outside observers, and his function is to provide the material which the memory stores once the understanding has vetted it. Memory, as we shall see, is a central thematic and structural element: the chapter mottoes alone indicate that MacDonald's mind was full of memories of other literature as he composed the work. Furthermore, it is hard not to believe that in this tale of how Anodos (whose name has several facets of meaning, but whose root meaning seems to be 'the pathless one') wanders through a bewildering Fairyland until he finds a purpose to give him direction, MacDonald is not also remembering the false starts and changes of direction in his own first thirty-three years.

Despite its being rich in literary roots, *Phantastes* strikes readers with its originality, even when they are ignorant of the work's importance as landmark in the tradition of modern fantasy. Its formal innovations are less important in its appeal, however, than the enduring quality of imaginative freshness which pervades it. The heart of MacDonald's success lies in the quality of imagination which created the landscape of Fairyland and devised the adventures which Anodos encounters within it. The over-riding impression is of a startling fecundity of invention from which pours a tale pleasing to the mind's eye, bewilderingly at odds with our sense of reality, yet harmonious with a lurking coherence and weighted with a convincing moral seriousness. MacDonald's formal starting-point is the German *märchen* as practised by Novalis, Fouqué and Hoffmann, but the quality of many of his episodes derives much from his English sources (one of which, although not represented by a chapter-motto, is assuredly *A Pilgrim's Progress*), while the basic imaginative texture is provided by the dream. This dream-vision, at first reading, seems fully to attain the Novalis-inspired goal of bewildering incoherence. Nevertheless, its landscape is, throughout, a projection of Anodos's mood and his degree of insight: at first the impression is of abundant colour and vitality in a living forest, but as he accumulates experiences of terror and disappointment, the glowing forest gives way to bleaker landscapes of cave, desolate shore and grim, level moor. This Fairyland is peopled by goblins, witches, malevolent creatures of various kinds, and by Anodos's mysterious Shadow, as well as by more normal mortals who all, nevertheless, derive as much from the traditions of the fairytale as they do from everyday life. Time and again, MacDonald invents a character or situation which strikes us with the power of an archetype. Overt references to Christianity are shunned (even though readers with a wide knowledge of MacDonald's beliefs and other writings will find echoes of them on many of its pages). MacDonald is completely successful in devising a book which lives up to his ideal of the fairytale: it has its own clear harmony of imaginative and moral integrity, while remaining open to every reader to develop his own interpretation. Of all his full-length works of fiction, this is the one with the greatest ability to please both with its imaginative quality, and with the conviction with which the achieved form lives up to the apparent intention.

It can seem fruitless to speculate on what prompted this radical innovation in British fiction. Nevertheless, *Phantastes* may perhaps be, in part at least, a response to a recently encountered stimulus. Conjecture rules here, but in the description of the nadir of Anodos's fortunes, when he finds himself on the desolate seashore, we may have a recollection of Arnold's 'Dover Beach':

> I stood on the shore of a wintry sea, with a wintry sun just a few feet above its horizon-edge. It was bare, and waste, and gray. Hundreds of hopeless waves rushed constantly shorewards, falling exhausted upon a beach of great loose stones, that seemed to stretch miles and miles in both directions. There was nothing for the eye but mingling shades of gray; nothing for the ear but the rush of the coming, the roar of the breaking, and the moan of the retreating wave. No rock lifted up a sheltering severity above the dreariness around . . . I wandered over the stones, up and down the beach, a human imbodiment of the nature around me. The wind increased; its keen waves flowed through my soul; the foam rushed higher up the stones; a few dead stars began to gleam in the east; the sound of the waves grew louder and yet more despairing. (p.127)[2]

At this point, MacDonald's novel shares a bleakness comparable with Arnold's, and uses similar imagery and language to express it. A further similarity is between the openings of the two works. Just as Arnold's speaker is at a window looking out over an attractive nocturnal seascape, which puts him in mind of the Sea of Faith, so Anodos comes round from the swoon induced by his 'grandmother's' gaze and finds himself beholding a scene like Arnold's at Dover: 'I forgot all the rest, till I found myself at the window, whose gloomy curtains were withdrawn, and where I stood gazing on a whole heaven of stars, small and sparkling in the moonlight. Below lay a sea, still as death arid hoary in the moon, sweeping into bays and around capes and islands, away, away, I knew not whither. Alas! it was no sea, but a low fog burnished by the moon. 'Surely there is such a sea somewhere!' said I to myself. A low sweet voice beside me replied—'In Fairy Land, Anodos' (p. 18).

'Dover Beach' was not published until 1867, ten years after *Phantastes* was written. Arnold had written it, however, in the early 1850s (probably late June 1851); were MacDonald to have seen it, therefore, he would have to have been shown it in manuscript.[3] We do not know that this happened but it is certainly possible, for Greville records that by 1859 Arnold knew the MacDonalds—indeed, he 'ranked among their intimates' (*GMDW*, p. 300)—and the association seems to have lasted at least into the early 1870s (*GMDW*, p. 412). The outlook expressed in the poem is very different from MacDonald's characteristic optimism, of course, though from his student days MacDonald had associated dreary sea-shores with moods of depression (*GMDW*, p. 80). Arnold's poem moves from the view of the sea from the window, to a consciousness of 'the eternal note of sadness' in the nature of things, a sadness exacerbated for his generation by the loss of faith. He admits that the world 'seems / To lie before us like a land of dreams' but

> Hath really neither joy, nor love, nor light,
> nor certitude, nor peace, nor help for pain.

And he concludes with his famous metaphor of the darkling plain and the ignorant armies. It is a poem without metaphysical hope. Even if this conjecture is wrong, and MacDonald had not yet glimpsed the famous poem, Arnold nevertheless gives us later readers a profound distillation of the mood against which *Phantastes* is directed.

MacDonald also starts with a seascape seen from a window, but proceeds to test the world's dream-like promise with a thoroughness which never occurs to Arnold. As his exploration of the world as dream progresses, Anodos becomes aware, to the full, of sadness: indeed, his journey is an accumulation of disappointments and thwarted longing, but whereas Arnold's poem lets despair prevail, MacDonald's novel places sadness in a larger context in which it is less than final. For MacDonald, despair on the sea-shore is not the cul-de-sac it seems; Anodos positively accepts unhappiness when he plunges into the sea, an act which is immediately rewarded by his finding a little rainbow-coloured boat, which can only signify Hope and which carries him to the cottage on the isthmus. There he finds an old woman who not only provides him with the joy, the love, the light, the certitude, the peace and the help for pain which he immediately needs and which Arnold denies, but, in his subsequent forays into other areas of his life reached by passing through the doors of the cottage, he finds that this haven is always merely a doorway away in the midst of all life's pain. Where Arnold's final consciousness in 'Dover Beach' is of groping across that terrifying plain, Anodos's last thoughts are of the comforting recollection of the wise woman: 'When I am oppressed by any sorrow or real perplexity, I often feel as if I had only left her cottage for a time, and would soon return out of the vision, into it again' (p. 182).

MacDonald's aim is clearly not to deny 'the eternal note of sadness'—indeed, his book is full of it. His attitude is quite different from Arnold's, however, and he appears to welcome it in birdsong: 'As in all sweetest music, a tinge of sadness was in every note. Nor do we know how much of the pleasures even of life we owe to the intermingled sorrows. Joy cannot unfold the deepest truths, although deepest truth must be deepest joy. Cometh white-robed Sorrow, stooping and wan, and flingeth wide the doors she may not enter' (pp.73-74). This insight immediately precedes his arrival at the palace of white marble, which turns out to be a kind of Palace of Art, and where his second crucial discovery of his White Lady as a work of art—a statue—will take place. It is as if his new poised insight into the real meaning of sadness had now equipped him for a deeper experience of art.

It seems significant, also, that his capacity to hear the sadness in the birdsong occurs very soon after he has acquired his Shadow. As most commentators agree, the Shadow is a symbol of many facets, but the variety of detailed interpretations which have been offered is worrying: we are told that it means such things as guilt, worldly-wise cynicism and disillusionment, selfcentredness, intellectuality and materialism, loss of innocence and optimism, and many more. This is in stark contrast to the implication of the ogre (in whose house Anodos acquires his shadow) that there is a single label for it: 'I believe you call it by a different name in your world' (p. 64). What name does MacDonald have in mind? Chapter Nine is devoted to the blighting effects of the shadow on Anodos's behaviour, attitudes and surroundings. That chapter has, as a motto, a few lines from Coleridge's 'Dejection: An Ode' (11.47-9; 53-8), in which the source of the world's life and beauty—but also of its deadness and emptiness—is seen as lying within us: 'Ours is her wedding garment, ours her shroud!' Anodos's shadow seems to be MacDonald's version of Coleridge's 'Dejection,' and it is notable that in all the shadow's later comings and goings, Anodos's mood seems to be the triggering factor. Thus, the strange reappearance of the shadow immediately after the fight with the giants, where we might have expected Anodos to exult after surviving a worthy battle, is the embodiment of that depression which can so easily afflict us when we relax after a mighty effort. When Anodos says finally that he has come back 'rejoicing that I had lost my Shadow', what he has lost is that capacity for despair which is death to our ability to see the world as lying before us like a land of dreams.

His first loss of the shadow occurs in the fairy palace, where his denunciation of it causes the landscape to be flooded with sunlight 'as with a silent shout of joy' (p. 78). Similarly, 'joy' is the keyword which echoes three times through the six lines succeeding his final realisation that his shadow has left him (p. 181). Coleridge's great antidote to Dejection is clearly MacDonald's counterpoise to the shadow, and his novel can be seen as an exploration of the eternal struggle between Joy and Dejection, to see which is the more fundamental. But whereas joy is the first of the elements which Arnold denies at the climax of his poem, it is the prevailing mood which finally ushers Anodos home. Joy does indeed exist, despite Arnold, to clear away Dejection, and leave untramelled 'the eternal note of sadness' which flings open the doors to the deepest truth: as a result of his experiences, Anodos is always reminded by sorrow of the wise woman in the cottage, with her words of comforting assurance, 'A great good is coming to thee'.

To emphasise the theme of sadness and joy as a key to the book is not to deny the importance of other interpretations which have been placed upon it. Thus, Colin Manlove has eloquently described it as 'concerning itself with the First Things, and with true birth, self-realisation and movement into the world', while Rolland Hein stresses the loss of self, and David Holbrook the urge to reunite with the lost Mother (a reflection of MacDonald's own early loss of his mother).[4] The reader can find all these and other ways of understanding *Phantastes*, for it is particularly rich in interpretative possibilities and would seem to embody MacDonald's own belief that a fairytale ought to be open to whatever meaning each reader can find in it. MacDonald certainly believed that no meaning should be imposed on a fairytale by its author, and that the artist's unconscious should be free from the dictates of the rational, materialist part of his mind. In such circumstances, the creative impulse would be most open to the promptings of God, and the resulting work as near as could be to an embodiment of God's truth. Hence his substantial quotation from Novalis, which acts as a kind of preface. Part of this can be translated: 'A fairy story is like a disjointed dream-vision, an ensemble of wonderful things and occurrences, for example, a musical fantasy, the harmonic sequences of an Aeolian harp, nature itself...'

In a sense, the book lives up to this prescription, but not completely. It is impossible to believe that MacDonald's unconscious enjoyed untrammelled sway, for many episodes seem to contain a firmness of intention which their lack of surface explicitness cannot conceal. Thus, Anodos's concluding adventure in Fairyland, his self-sacrificing exposure of the destruction at the heart of the great ceremonial in the twenty-third chapter, is usually taken as reflecting the author's own antagonism to the prevailing religious orthodoxy. Occasionally, too, MacDonald's allegorical instinct peeps through, as when, during the desolate underground journey following the second loss of the White Lady (a journey in which Anodos encounters, and shrugs off, the torments of goblins), Anodos's state of mind is explored in terms of allegorical abstractions. 'Besides being delighted and proud that my songs had called the beautiful creature to life, the same fact caused me to feel a tenderness unspeakable for her, accompanied with a kind of feeling of property in her; for so the goblin Selfishness would reward the angel Love' (p. 126).

C. S. Lewis's formulation, that MacDonald's fantasy 'hovers between the allegorical and the mythopoeic' seems an excellent statement of the mixture of conscious control and mysterious imaginative spontaneity which *Phantastes* presents.[5] It is both a mental wonderland with an appeal which, in part, brings out the childlike in each sympathetic reader while, at the same time, it is an elaborate organisation of symbols which perpetually tease us to interpretation. Yet the impulse to allegories, to decode meanings which then, as it were, supercede their narrative source, seems particularly insensitive in the case of such a work as this, in which the imagined narrative is of such prominence and attractiveness.

In fact, the 'world' which is *Phantastes* is no mere means to an end. The book itself contains suggestions that the sheer experience of entering the domain which MacDonald's imagination has created is the heart of what the book has to offer. For example, Hein is right to stress the loss of self as a theme, but his account veers towards presenting this as a moral which is to be taken, as it were, from a reading. This is in the tradition of C. S. Lewis's view that MacDonald's genius is such that 'its connection with words at all turns out to be merely external and, in a sense, accidental'.[6] In fact, this is never true of MacDonald at his best, and least of all is it true of *Phantastes*, which rewards in corresponding measure however much attention we pay to the details of verbal expression and formal structuring. Thus, while we may, if we like, describe the work as an illustration 'that it is better to serve others than ourselves, and that our desires can be satisfied indirectly through this service'; it seems truer to our experience of reading it to stress how both Anodos and the reader grow, unsuspectingly, into that loss of self which can be described as entering another world.[7]

The process of Anodos learning to lose himself, however, is not completed until late in the narrative—if, indeed, it is really completed within the narrative of his Fairyland journey at all. Even his final ejection from Fairyland seems due to a sudden resurgence of self, or of pride. Having apparently attained to the acme of selflessness in giving his 'life' to destroy the evil ceremony, and thereafter enjoying death as an afterlife of service to others, he finds himself floating on a cloud, like a god, over a great city. Looking down; it toiling humanity, he exclaims, 'O pale-faced women, and gloomy-browed men, and forgotten children how I will wait on you, and minister to you, and, putting my arms about you in the dark, think hope unto your hearts, when you fancy no one is near! Soon as my senses have all come back, and have grown accustomed to this new blessed life, I will be among you with the love that healeth' (pp. 179-80). In this moment of supreme giving, he seems to even himself with Christ: with supreme insight, MacDonald creates the limits of human perfection by an ultimate ambiguity. Is the ejection from Fairyland, which seems a consequence of this exclamation, a sign that the final moral benefit of Anodos's fairy journey has been reaped, or is it a punishment for allowing self to enter in the moment of ultimate selflessness? 'With this, a pang and a terrible shudder went through me; a writhing as of death convulsed me; and I became once again conscious of a more limited, even a bodily and earthly life' (p.180). Are these birth-pangs a reward or a penalty?

And just as the struggle between self and selflessness is still being played out at the end, so, at the outset (when, in many interpretations, Anodos has not even started on his moral journey) he is already showing the first signs of that capacity for selflessness which eventually become a conscious ideal in him. For what else is his initial curiosity about his father's story, and his regarding of the contents of the secretary as 'this long-hidden world', but an instinct to explore the world of the non-self? Curiosity, or the desire to appropriate the outlook of another, is merely an inferior degree of that union of self-giving and self-glory, which causes his final return to each. Similarly, such moments as his encounter with the beech tree (whom he quits with some sense of guilt as well as with the knowledge that their encounter has given her something valuable) and his two releases of the White Lady (which are a giving of life to her, but also spring from a selfish desire to possess her) continue the meditation on man's entrapment in the net woven by the nearly related threads of his selfishness and selflessness. Accounts of the book which reduce it to a tale of simple moral education reduce its subtlety.

Nevertheless, there is a progress in the book in terms of the deepening of Anodos's understanding of the issues, and of his desire for moral improvement. And in this deepening, his willingness to enter world after world is a key factor. Thus his entry into the world of the secretary is followed by his impulse to encounter the sea glimpsed from the window, then by his willingness to accept, without the surprise which is the result of judging by one's familiar expectations, all the strange events Fairyland has to offer. It continues with, in particular, his willingness to share the task of the two princes and his acceptance of brotherhood with them. Furthermore, he develops an insatiable appetite for the worlds proffered by the many works of literature he encounters in his travels. Such moments reveal what is positive in him, but they are always succeeded, sooner or later, by phases of self-centredness. The alternation is the heartbeat of life itself.

What MacDonald understands so well about such a theme as self and selfishness has not so much told us, however, as enshrined in the book's structure, or even in its very nature. If MacDonald's habitual note of didacticism is not entirely banished, it is reduced almost to nothingness, partly because the narrative is in the first person. Consequently, the moral explicitness, when it occurs, is Anodos's, rather than MacDonald's. This point is no mere critical sleight-of-hand: the choice of narrative person is a function of that avoidance of the personality of the historical author which so crucially sets *Phantastes* and *Lilith* apart from the rest of MacDonald's fiction. Fantasy, especially as MacDonald creates it here, is a less than explicit medium. In writing the work, MacDonald is giving the Phantastes within him its head: a part, at least, of the benefit of the creation of the book lies in the enrichment of his own 'noble Prince' (his understanding) as a result of the insights gained during its creation and stored in his memory. Indeed, if *Phantastes* is, as I suspect, in part a debate with the outlook Arnold expresses in 'Dover Beach', then the fact that the poem was not public property would mean that MacDonald's work has, more than ever, a private dimension which has not hitherto been suspected.

If this is so, then *Phantastes* is a work of art with an important role to play in the life of its author as well as (MacDonald must have hoped) the lives of its readers. It is one of the surprises which define Anodos's Fairyland that art and life exist on equal and interchangeable terms. The note is sounded at the outset, as Anodos muses on how his father 'had woven his web of story' and as the fairy grandmother promises that Anodos will enter the fairyland for which he had yearned when he read a fairytale to his little sister. His White Lady, whom he releases from encasement in the alabaster block by means of his singing, is, in one sense, the living work of art which he has created—an interpretation strengthened by her later preference for remaining as a statue in an art gallery. One of the most important characters, the knight Sir Percival, is first encountered in a book read by Anodos in the cottage which provides him with his first refuge in Fairyland, and the manifold tales and poems embedded in the narrative all interact with, and reflect, the main story in a number of ways. The world of art—and especially its literary subdivision—is a constant and equal presence alongside the more obviously living constituents of the fairy country. What Anodos learns and experiences in literature is of comparable moment with any of his other encounters. Indeed, Anodos is quite explicit in this matter: in summarising his voluminous reading in the library of the fairy palace, he describes how he entered fully into whatever book he read, identifying with it completely. 'Mine was the whole story' (p. 81).

The implication is clear both that a human life is a tale and that what one finds within the covers of a book can be as vital a part of one's understanding of reality as anything encountered in 'real life'. And equally clear is the implication, for MacDonald's reader, that this general truth is especially true of the particular book he holds in his hand. Not only do numerous incidents illustrate the interfusion of life and literature, but at many points literature is shown having an effect in the world around it: the tale of Sir Percival is a warning against the Maid of the Alder; Anodos's songs twice reveal and release the White Lady; the Wise Woman's songs soothe Anodos's distress; Anodos sings to the brother princes songs which make them weep but which consequently strengthen them; the maid of the globe releases Anodos from the dreary tower by her singing (as she says, 'wherever I go, my songs do good, and deliver people' (p. 163); even the sight of a child reading helps Anodos to believe in Fairyland once again.

It is clear, too, that memories of other literature have been crucial in helping form *Phantastes*: an awareness of sources does not merely help us explain the work's genesis, but can conceivably take us to the heart of it. This applies even to the chapter-mottoes, which are much more intimately related to the rest of the work than is normally the case. Whereas Scott, for example, adds chapter-mottoes less as an integral element or guide to meaning, than as a kind of decoration, and as a game between himself and his reader, MacDonald's mottoes can be extraordinarily helpful: because this rhetorically indirect work lacks his own commentating voice, they are the sole direct aid that he, as author, provides. Furthermore, they often seem to pinpoint the actual source in MacDonald's reading which gives rise to the contents of a chapter.

What books contain is the result of the activity, within authors, of Phantastes, and one's memories of books can be as precious as the memories of what Phantastes has prompted in one's own mind. Memory, indeed, is seen by MacDonald as the faculty which transforms the power of one's formative experiences into a permanent resource. Nor is it a neutral medium, but it adds beauty and power to what is remembered: 'Even the memories of past pain are beautiful; and past delights, though beheld only through clefts in the grey clouds of sorrow, are lovely as Fairy Land' (p.73). The memory is, like a mirror or a still sea, one of the agents of reflection (there is an element of punning in MacDonald's use of the word) which he extols at several points: 'Why are all reflections lovelier than what we call the reality?—not so grand or so strong, it may be, but always lovelier? Fair as is the gliding sloop on the shining sea, the wavering, trembling, unresting sail below is fairer still . . . All mirrors are magic mirrors. The commonest room is a room in a poem when I turn to the glass . . .' There must be a truth involved in it, though we may but in part lay hold of the meaning. Even the memories of past pain are beautiful . . .' (pp.72-3). A memory is thus an enhancement of the reality it looks back on. Not only can Anodos salve his conscience on leaving the Beech Tree by thinking how comforting the memory of their encounter will be to her, but he himself, echoing the Wordsworth of 'Tintern Abbey', relishes the idea that his reading in the fairy palace has had long-term effect. His reading there has been one of the many deaths and resurrections in his life:

> From many a sultry noon till twilight, did I sit in that grand hall, buried and risen again in these old books. And I trust I have carried away in my soul some of the exhalations of their undying leaves. In after hours of deserved or needful sorrow,

portions of what I read there have often come to me again, with an unexpected comforting; which was not fruitless, even though the comfort might seem in itself groundless and vain. (p.108)

It is in this context that Anodos tries so assiduously to remember and record his experiences in Fairyland, at times apologising for the limitations of his memory, as when he attempts to reproduce the two stories he read in the palace library, or when he recalls the Wise Woman's singing of the Ballad of Sir Aglovaile, or when, having acquired his shadow, he 'can attempt no consecutive account of my wanderings and adventures' (p. 65), until he reaches the palace. Such comments serve two purposes. They are ways of communicating the inevitable gap, when an artistic vision is given a concrete embodiment, between the two: the attempt to catch the living inspiration is like the attempts of Anodos, in the palace, to burst in on the dancing figures behind the curtain by quelling his conscious intention and relying entirely on irrational impulse. Secondly, these comments are reminders that the whole work is a piece of recollection. *Phantastes* is the enactment of a mind trying to reach the bliss of which it has knowledge, and memory is the tool which that mind must use. Not only does Anodos have the recollection of his reading in the fairy palace, or his knowledge of how comforting the memory of the Wise Woman's promise can be, but he also has the example of how memory got him into Fairyland in the first place. The opening chapter is itself made up of the recollection of the strange events of the night before, and it seems to be the act of recollection which causes him to be translated to Fairyland: 'While these strange events were passing through my mind, I suddenly, as one awakes to the consciousness that the sea has been moaning by him for hours, or that the storm has been howling about his window all night, became aware of the sound of running water near me . . .' (p.19). Thus, the whole book is a double attempt to achieve a wondrous translation into Fairyland—double in that it is both Anodos's and George MacDonald's. MacDonald's art, here and elsewhere, is an art of memory. At the outset of his career as a writer of fiction, he here creates an illustration of how he views art as a matter of reaching the goal of comfort and understanding through the creation of works based on the contents of his mind—based, that is, on his recollections of his life and his reading. Assiduous as they would remain throughout his career, Phantastes and old Eumnestes never served him, their noble Prince, better.

In a passage from a much later work, *The Diary of an Old Soul*,

MacDonald, looking towards a time when writing will come hard to him, confirms how memory interacts with present utterance to the benefit, in the first instance, of himself:

> Not what I think, but what thou art, makes sure
> This utterance of spirit through still thought,
> This forming of heart-stuff in moulds of brain
> Is helpful to the soul by which 'tis wrought,
> The shape reacting on the heart again;
> But when I am quite old, and words are slow,
> Like dying things that keep their holes for woe,
> And memory's withering tendrils clasp with effort vain,
> Thou, then as now, no less wilt be my life . . .
> (*Old Soul*, p. 137; 'October', 18, 7 -20, 1)

How much of his writing, one wonders, was the creation of shapes which reacted again upon his heart?

In his last years, words ceased altogether, but in nearly his final effort of literary utterance he created in *Lilith* a work which gives no hint that the words had become any slower. Indeed, *Lilith* is conspicuous for the stylistic poise and tight verbal control for which it has no superior in his output. What has changed, to some extent, is the reliance on memory: the absence of chapter mottoes may be an outward sign of a different genesis from that of *Phantastes*, although, at first glance, it would appear that it is to the method of that youthful work that he had returned. In place of the comforting contemplation of the past, we find in the later fantasy an urgent message for a comfortless present. Greville MacDonald tells us that his father 'was possessed by a feeling' that *Lilith* 'was a mandate direct from God, for which he himself was to find form and clothing' (*GMDW*, p. 548). If God seems to be intervening directly, there is perhaps less need to draw on a purely human resource such as memory; certainly, MacDonald embarked on a composition of remarkable speed and freedom, swiftly creating the book's essential symbols, 'over which he did not ponder' (*GMDW*, p. 548). It was as if the symbols were the mandate, and the search for 'form and clothing' committed him to a process somewhat unusual in his writing of fiction: the work went through a long series of revisions so that although it was embarked upon in 1890, it was not published until 1895.[8] Hence the impression it gives of combining arresting, living imagery with an unusual control in style and structure.

It is obviously a much more highly wrought work than *Phantastes*. While the basic narrative is MacDonald's familiar one of the journey, it is far from the predictably linear, picaresque sequence of the earlier fantasy. Indeed, the convolutions of Vane's interweavings between the worlds of three and seven dimensions, and the complexity induced by apparent retreats which turn out to be further stages of progress, suggest what many critics have denied: MacDonald does have a profound and sure sense of structure. The aura of control, so marked in the total shape, is repeated in detail. For example, the riddles and paradoxes which so frustrate Vane when Mr. Raven utters them in the early stages of their relationship reappear in Vane's mouth at the end, when, having buried Lilith's hand, he is confronted by the greyheaded man who longs to die (p. 395): the structural echo, revealing just how far Vane has come, is deft and telling.

One notes, too, that the wealth of interpolated poems and narratives, so deliberately characteristic of *Phantastes*, has been banished almost completely. When such things do appear, as in 'My Father's Manuscript', and in the extracts from the poem with which Adam masters Lilith in Chapter Twenty-Nine, their purpose is clear and intimately entwined with the progress of the work. The complexity, and challenge to interpretation, of the book's symbols and incidents is acute enough for MacDonald to have no need to impose a narrative maze as he had delighted in doing in the earlier work. Echoes and parallelisms are the order of the day, rather, as when he works towards a unity by the repeated use of the motif of reflected sunlight. Regularly, through the book, crucial developments are initiated by the sudden reflection of beams of sunlight from a shiny surface on to an object to be highlighted—a picture, or a book in the library, or the mirror in the attic, or Lilith herself in the elliptical chamber of her brain.

Similarly, the verbal expression is clear, poised and controlled. McGillis has demonstrated how MacDonald worked towards greater simplicity and concentration in successive versions. Even without such scholarly information, however, the reader can appreciate the strange but effectively calculated combination of natural, simple clarity with elevated, enriching, faintly archaic structures and language, as in (at random) 'When I came to the precipice, I took my way betwixt the branches, for I would pass again by the cottage of Mara, lest she should have returned: I longed to see her once more ere I went to sleep; and now I knew where to cross the channels, even if the river should have overtaken me and filled them' (p. 394). This enriched style proves an entirely satisfactory medium for this tale, and appears to come to MacDonald with a natural inevitability echoing the naturalness of his lifelong heightened sense of reality.

Lilith, in fact, is designed less as an experience into which the reader must plunge, as *Phantastes* with its over-arching offer of imaginative delight pre-eminently is, than as a riddle which must be solved—like the universe described to Vane as he sets off on his journey through the strange land: 'The universe is a riddle trying to get out' (p. 226). The urgency of the message makes MacDonald strive to communicate where, in *Phantastes*, the reader's bewilderment was a conscious intention. MacDonald frequently indicates to his reader that if something is not understood, maturity will eventually bring understanding. Comprehension, both by Vane and the reader, seems much more immanent than it did in *Phantastes*. Meaning is obscured merely by the thin surface of appearances rather than by the deeper inconsequentiality of the earlier work, and so the indirections *Lilith* adopts are the transparent ones not only of allegory and symbol, but even those of satire, with an open freedom quite alien to *Phantastes*. In *Phantastes* the applicability to the reader of what is encountered in Fairyland is left delightfully compromised by its dream-status and by the stress (as we have seen) on Anodos's wondering exploration of his own memory, but in *Lilith* the reader is encouraged to believe in the reality of what is displayed. Vane presents his recollections firmly: though he again claims that his words are inadequate to embody his memories, the prevailing sureness of utterance leaves us little scope for doubting what he describes. Nor does Vane seem to be using memory to bring about wondrous benefits to himself, as Anodos does. The reader, rather, is Vane's concern. While it is true that, in reading of Anodos's experiences, we believe in the fairyland he traverses and remembers or imagines, the world into which Vane stumbles has an additional quality of being there. It has a firm, objective geography capable of being traversed many times: it has a physical independence which can be calculated upon, and entering or quitting it can be chosen and organised, to some extent. Indeed, at times Vane's attitude to it is that of the Victorian explorer with a duty to bring back the secrets of dark continents. MacDonald is insisting on the inescapable tangibility of a region where eternal choices are made and conflicts fought out. He is insisting, too, on its proximity to, and inter-relatedness with, the familiar world. Therefore, its machinery of Wellsian sciencefiction replaces the age-old dream-convention which served well enough in *Phantastes*: the pseudo-science of reflected polarised light provides a link between the two worlds which seems more difficult to gainsay.

The world of *Lilith*, furthermore, is a much more terrifying place than that of its predecessor, where horrors such as the Alder-maiden and the Ash are fairly rare. Vane's first encounters with the very fact of another world induce in him fears which have no counterpart in Anodos and, once properly into it, he finds it full of utterly horrific experiences. Where the opening of *Phantastes* is in a fairytale mode, the manner of *Lilith*'s opening is that of the ghost-story. Poe is sometimes mentioned, rightly, as a comparison and as a possible influence, but the intensity of such scenes as that in which Vane is attacked by Mara's cats (pp. 333-34), or the arrival of Vane in Bulika (pp. 298-300)—let alone the power of *Lilith*'s final scenes with Mara and Adam—negate any suspicions that MacDonald's solemn gothic power is essentially second-hand. Much of the book's imagery derives from a charnel vein which MacDonald always loved but which in this book about death receives its full justification. It was this quality of imagery which so upset MacDonald's wife (*GMDW*, p. 548). If MacDonald risks overdoing the imagery of nightmare, so that the novel seems to shriek at times, it is a sign of his urge to create a clear and forceful message about the reality of evil and the nature of death.

In line with this urge to vehement clarity is the explicit religiousness of some of the imagery and references. In his discussion of 'The *Lilith* Manuscripts', Roderick McGillis is pleased to report that, in successive versions, MacDonald deletes more and more direct references to God with a view to broadening the interest of the work beyond the theological and dealing, instead, with states of being.[9] While it is true that *Lilith* is far less explicit about its religious allegiances than the novels are, it is still far more openly Christian in its colouring than *Phantastes*, and unequivocal enough by any standards in its references to 'the perfect meal' of bread and wine (p. 211), to Adam and Eve, to resurrection and to heaven and hell. It keeps its distance from God, who is mentioned only rarely, but this is because the point of view is that of the groping Vane who at best is allowed only fleeting proximity to the throne of the Ancient of Days. MacDonald is reserved about referring to God, not because he wants to be understood in a sense wider than the religious (I doubt if he could imagine a wider sense than that) but because he had that sturdy Calvinist belief in the distance between God and man—and between God and man's imagination. The novels can refer frequently and intimately to God because their clear confinement to our own fallen world retains the sense of the great gulf. In fantasy works, however, the barrier is down and the creation of worlds where higher and deeper truths are visible might give the appearance of a claim to insight which the author would never wish to make. Restraint, indirection, and the drawing of parallels are the necessary methods of a Calvin-formed fantasist like MacDonald; indeed, what is remarkable about *Lilith* in this respect is how explicit it is.

Both the early and late fantasies succeed in suggesting that man is embedded in a much vaster and more mysterious system of truth than he normally realises, but the universe in *Lilith* has the firmer, more schematic structure: Vane has to fit in to it and discover its secrets, where Anodos wandered through a landscape which was more completely orientated towards him. In *Lilith*, more is at stake than Vane's inner growth: his behaviour brings responsibilities beyond his own improvement and his actions can be decisive in aiding or retarding the spread of evil as a whole. Hence, in part, the greater urgency and seriousness which marks the later work. That moral urgency, too, seems instrumental in greatly reducing the importance of art in the book's scale of values, when compared with *Phantastes*. The theme has lost most of its earlier prominence, though it can still be discerned at moments such as Vane's first stumbling through the mirror—he first views the scene in the frame as a painting and leans forward, connoisseur-like, 'to examine the texture of a stone in the immediate foreground' (p.193). This minimal moment of selfforgetful awareness tips him into the other world. More generally, his bookishness seems to be a rudimentary factor in rendering him a candidate for other-worldly adventures, as the centrality of the library in the early action indicates. Other hints of a lingering concern with art may be found in the scene with the skull-headed dancers, whose dance 'vaguely embodied the story of life, its meetings, its passions, its partings' (p. 263). This seems a rather earth-bound set of implications, however, far from the other-worldly communications that art sometimes achieved in *Phantastes*.

What is *Lilith* about? Greville tells us that his father wrote it as a warning against 'the increasingly easy tendencies of universalists, who, because they had now discarded everlasting retribution as a popular superstition, were dismissing hell-fire altogether, and with it the need for repentance as the way back into the Kingdom. With hell incarnate in ugliness and falsehood all about and within, we are prone to find comfort in declaring that Evil is but shadow cast by the Light, the devil but an imagined symbol of the distress caused by darkness; and to find Hell a tolerably comfortable caravanserai' (*GMDW*, pp. 551-52). As we have seen, evil, in this book, is no longer naturally overcome by the mere onward flow of events: the narrative twists back on itself and lays the onus for a happy outcome much more firmly on the moral choices of the hero. In comparison, too, with the evil creatures of *Phantastes*, Lilith herself is much more of an independent and tangible character—she is no mere shadow of the hero's psyche. Furthermore, the Shadow of this book is more than absence of light but, rather, a tangible blackness, as little Odu describes after the Shadow passes through him (p. 360). More fundamentally still, the state that finally induces Lilith to acquiesce in Mara's demands for submission is worse than the absence of God. MacDonald strives to suggest that that ultimate absence is, more menacingly, a fearful presence so awful as to terrify Lilith into submission as well as to be tangible to an onlooker like Vane: 'A horrible Nothingness, a Negation positive infolded her; the border of its being that was yet no being, touched me, and for one ghastly instant I seemed alone with Death Absolute! It was not the absence of everything I felt, but the presence of Nothing' (p. 375). In such a passage, MacDonald risks even the impression of Manicheism in his urgent attempt to insist on the reality and danger of evil.

Not that MacDonald has reverted to a simple belief in the Calvinist scheme of things: he has the harder task (harder than merely accepting or rejecting the notion of the fiery pit) of redefining hell as a state which, while terrible, is part of a benign scheme—a state which actually induces the self-knowledge and revulsion which propels erring creatures into accepting the will of God. A clear-cut example is the skeleton lord and lady who, comically, continue their earthly bickering and folly until they begin, out of sheer necessity, to build a better relationship with each other. Beholding them, Mr. Raven is quite explicit that hell is a state, not a place: 'You are not in hell. Neither am I in hell. But those skeletons are in hell!' (p. 271). So, undoubtedly, is Lilith as she is subjected, by Mara, to the torture of self-knowledge: As this phase begins, Vane is aware that 'a soundless presence as of roaring flame possessed the house' and Lilith burns 'in the hell of her self-consciousness' (pp. 372; 373).

If a large part of *Lilith* is the redefinition and vivification of the notion of hell, an even larger part of the book's purpose is to do the same for death. As ever, MacDonald intimately links the idea with that of a break-through into selflessness, thus preaching two hard lessons at once: overcoming one's selfishness is as hard and as fundamental as dying while, conversely, dying is simply the stage at which one becomes a better person. The moral climax of *Phantastes* is reached when Anodos sacrifices himself for the sake of others by destroying the evil ceremony, thereby liberating himself to a state of blissful love and service to others. He has become a resurrected primrose, to be gathered to the bosom of his lady. Vane's corresponding death lacks all the attractive trappings of chivalrous action: he must coldly, consciously lie down in the grave, and the imagery of plant-life is transmuted from Anodos's primrose-resurrection to the bulb itself dormant in the frozen earth. This serves to underline the physical burial ('I lay at peace, full of the quietest expectation, breathing the damp odours of Earth's bountiful bosom') and forces on the reader the paradox that the traditional horrors of the grave ('How cold I was, words cannot tell . . .') are themselves the transition—point between woe and bliss ('. . . yet I grew colder and colder—and welcomed the cold yet more and more'.) For 'I grew continuously less conscious of myself, continuously more conscious of bliss, unimaginable yet felt' (p. 400).

In the geography of the other world, Adam's cottage, with its vast graveyard containing Vane's allotted resting-place, lies nearest, of all the other-worldly locations, to Vane's house: the challenge of, and opportunity for, death (especially in its sense of dying to oneself) is the first of the higher realities to be encountered. At first, of course, Vane cannot do so and flees in horror from the graveyard. When he returns soon after, however, having changed his mind, he is judged to be not ready for death, after all, and instead must undergo the various adventures which make up the main body of the narrative. Right knowledge of death is the book's ultimate goal. When Vane first flees from the nocturnal hospitality of Mr. and Mrs. Raven, he does not fully know what it is that he is rejecting, so that his contrary impulse, after having read his father's manuscript, to take up their offer is equally ill-founded. Full, accepting knowledge is needed, in MacDonald's view, before one can fully die, for only thus can the self be destroyed. It is to gain this knowledge that Mr. Raven sends him off on his journey, having denied him a place among the dead for the moment. Vane gains that knowledge primarily by encountering two embodiments of inadequate knowledge of death, Lilith and the Little Ones, and by watching their correction.

Lilith is not merely an embodiment of evil: more crucially, she is the incarnation of the belief that death is a horror—hence her rebellion against God and Adam. The poem with which Adam penetrates through to her undisguised self in Chapter Twenty-Nine is a versification of her (and our) revulsion against the physical corruption of the grave: her belief that that is all that physical death amounts to is also allowed to stand as a symbol for her concept of the loss of self.

Crossing a Great Frontier

Lilith's evil is seen as rooted in an obsession with the corruption of the flesh which utterly perverts what is divine in her nature.

An overriding result of that perversion is the utter negation of maternal feeling in her, and her consequent hatred of the Little Ones, especially her own daughter, Lona. The colony of the Little Ones clearly represents innocent goodness, but they, too, are in a state of unhealthy ignorance of the truth of death, because they are as ignorant of the end of earthly life as they are of its beginnings. They do not fear death, therefore, as Lilith does, but they are aware of, and fear, one who is closely related to Adam and his world of death, namely Mara, whose name signifies bitterness (see Ruth, 1, 20). Their fear of the cat-woman Mara is an allegory of the human instinct to shun pain and sorrow, and it is a fear they must overcome if they, too, are to die—as they, like all things created, must. MacDonald's final urgent message to the world is to teach us to die.

As he sets off on the journey which will involve him with Lilith and the Little Ones, Vane is provided by Mr. Raven with a rainbow-coloured 'bird-butterfly'—one of those symbols, like the air-fish in 'The Golden Key' and the rainbow imagery of *Alec Forbes*, by which MacDonald suggests the transitory goals which draw us into and through experience. After stumbling after it for a little way, however, Vane grasps at the gorgeous light, only to find that 'a dead book with boards outspread lay cold and heavy in my hand' (p. 228). Critics such as Wolff and Hein have been hard on Vane at this point, believing that the episode embodies the dire effects of supplanting unthinking delight with the grasping rationalism of the human intellect.[10] Yet in this of all books, images of death, cold and 'boards outspread' are not elsewhere deplored— nor are books otherwise objects of scorn. The creature, gorgeous as it appeared, was hardly a suitable guide for Vane (any more than Mr. Raven's riddles convey information to him): attempting to follow it, he keeps stumbling and once knocks himself out. Furthermore, it is happy to give itself to Vane, for it sinks towards him. It may be that Vane's fault is in rejecting 'the treasure of the universe' in the bookish form which he is capable of grasping and benefiting from. The despised rationality of its contents might have saved him from the terrors which he now endures as he crosses the Bad Burrow, where the monsters, we learn near the end of the book, symbolise the unhealthy thoughts of which the human mind is capable (see p. 413). At any rate, the creature, evanescent and temporary like all MacDonald's rainbow-guides, has served its purpose in pointing out an initial direction.

There is clearly scope for some disagreement and confusion in the interpretation of this little episode. (Not even those who accuse Vane of culpable, rationalistic grasping eschew a rational, allegorical reading of the incident.) It is a confusion, moreover, symptomatic of the heart of a work which, despite all its excellence, seems unclear as to how Vane and his actions are to be assessed. During the argument later in the book, when Vane succumbs to the temptation to ride to the aid of the Little Ones without first sleeping in the House of the Dead, Adam proclaims that 'nearly the only foolish thing you ever did, was to run from our dead' (p. 331), an assessment at variance with his earlier view that 'your night was not come then, or you would not have left us' (p. 224). In the same argument, Adam is dogmatic, with all the weight of the book's apparent authority behind him, that Vane can achieve nothing without first sleeping the sleep of death. Vane disobeys, however, and certainly runs into a catalogue of perils, disappointments and disasters, culminating in the death of Lona. Nevertheless, the prophecy concerning the downfall of *Lilith* is achieved, the Little Ones are rescued from their unknowing innocence, and Vane is at last endowed with enough knowledge of the rights and wrongs of the universe for him to accept death. Despite Adam's alternative advice, Vane appears to have done the right thing.

When Vane and Adam next meet, *Lilith* having been released into the sleep of death, the hero's disobedience and its consequences are slurred over in two brief sentences ('Is he forgiven, husband?' 'From my heart'. —p. 391). It was open to MacDonald to make a point about good being brought about from evil had he wanted to. That he does not would suggest that his heart is with the broad implication of the narrative, that Vane, with all his imperfection, is the necessary agent for the eventual triumph of good. The conflict goes deeper than this one book, for it is really a reflection of how MacDonald's creed of the virtue of action essentially conflicts with his belief that God is all in all and human effort, considered as a thing itself, vain. The key moment is Vane's disobedience. Adam urges him, above all things, to wait and sleep, causing Vane to exclaim 'But surely sleep is not the first thing! Surely, surely, action takes precedence of repose!' (p. 328). These are not questions, as we might have expected, but (with the reiterated 'surely') cries from the heart, and they seem to come ultimately from the heart of the creator of such athletically active heroes as Malcolm, Gibbie and the young Alec Forbes. All MacDonald's instincts were towards the active assault upon evil, but he also realised that in even the most righteous fights there is some self-glorification. The lesson of

Lilith seems to be that righteous action should not be undertaken until the self is utterly dead, but such an impossible condition was of no use to an author who was, in his son's words, 'always a fighter'.[11]

If MacDonald cannot wait to finally obliterate self in order to render righteous action pure and possible, nor can he finally imagine death, though the closing chapters of his book seem to commit him to doing so. It is not simply that, not having physically died, he does not know what it is like. More fundamentally still, death cannot even be imagined in its ultimate fullness because to do so would require the complete abandonment of any last sense of the self. As MacDonald understands it, death is the utter abandonment of self—the complete negation of identity. (Such, too, is William Golding's conception in *Pincher Martin*, where the imagined survival after physical death is the result of Pincher's ferocious selfishness.) The final obliteration of self is not in the scope of the creature—any more than the completion of the final needful act, the opening of her hand, is within *Lilith*'s power, so God's representative, Adam, cuts it off instead. For Vane, the equivalent of that blow from Adam's sword would be to have been admitted into the 'deep folds' of God's cloudy skirts, disappearing irrevocably into a region beyond the scope of human imagination.

The ending is designed to enact the supreme state of possible human detachment from the everyday world, and to convey the limitations of that state, for the final chapter is shot through with tension, doubt and sadness. The denial of self means total reliance on God, even for the contents of one's thoughts and dreams. Even when doubt is challenged, it is not by Vane himself, but by Hope personified. Yet, having foresworn all the activity which defines and creates our world in our perception, Vane finds that world itself becoming insubstantial and dreamlike, an awareness which maintains the steady pressure of doubt on the fringes of his consciousness. Vane is caught between Self and God, between ignorance and knowledge, between frustration and contentment. Hence the tension in the bald final statement of what he knows: 'I wait; asleep or awake, I wait'. He stresses the little he is sure of His waiting and the repetition enacts his commitment to the self-thwarting which is killing his self, but he cannot restrain the self, with its doubt, ignorance, and weariness, from momentarily swelling out with the alternatives which plague him. The sentence suggests a man grimly and wearily adhering to the abandonment of earthly life. We sense his momentary relief as he escapes into the hopeful words of another—Novalis—in the final sentence.

ENDNOTES

1. Giles and Phineas Fletcher, *Poetical Works* (2 vols.), ed. F. S. Boas, Cambridge, 1909, II, 79.

2. All references are to the edition of *Phantastes* and *Lilith* first published by Gollancz in 1962 and reprinted several times.

3. *The Poems of Matthew Arnold*, ed. Kenneth Allott, 2nd edition, ed. M. Allott, London and New York, 1979, p. 253.

4. C. N. Manlove, *The Impulse of Fantasy Literature*, London, 1983, p. 92; Rolland Hein, *The Harmony Within: The Spiritual Vision of George MacDonald*, Grand Rapids, 1982, pp. 54-84; David Holbrook, 'Introduction' to Phantastes, London, Melbourne & Toronto, 1983, pp. vii-xxv.

5. C. S. Lewis, *George MacDonald: An Anthology*, London, 1946, p. 14.

6. Lewis, p. 16.

7. Hein, p. 55.

8. Roderick F. McGillis, 'George MacDonald—The *Lilith Manuscripts*' in *Scottish Literary Journal*, 4, 2, December 1977, pp. 40-57.

9. McGillis, p. 56.

10. R. L. Wolff, *The Golden Key: A Study of the Fiction of George MacDonald*, New Haven, 1961, pp. 340-41; Hein, p. 91.

11. Greville MacDonald, *Reminiscences of a Specialist*, London, 1932, p. 322.

From *Bildungsroman* to Death-Romance: *Phantastes, Lilith,* and German Romanticism
Stephen Prickett
From *Victorian Fantasy*

Ever since its publication, George MacDonald's *Phantastes* has baffled many readers, critics, and even many admirers. Nor is that bafflement easily assuaged by its subtitle, *A Faerie Romance for Men and Women*, and a string of prefatory quotations from the German Romantic poet, Novalis, which seem to imply that the story is modeled on German Märchen-folk, or fairy stories. They can be translated as follows:

> One can imagine stories which have no coherence, but only association of events, like dreams; poems, which simply sound lovely, and which are full of beautiful words, but which lack sense or coherence, or at most have single verses which can be understood, like fragments of the most varied objects. This true poetry can at most have a general allegorical meaning and an indirect effect like music. For that reason, nature is as purely poetic as a magician's room, or a physicist's, a children's nursery, a padded cell and a larder. [. . .]
>
> A fairy story is like a disjointed dream-vision, an ensemble of wonderful things and occurrences, for example, a musical fantasy, the harmonic sequences of an Aeolian harp, nature itself. [. . .]
>
> In a real fairy tale everything must be wonderful, secret and coherent; everything must be alive, each in a different way. The whole of nature must be marvellously mixed with the whole of the world of spirits; here the time of the anarchy, lawlessness, freedom of nature in its natural state, the time before the world, comes in. [. . .] The world of fairy-tale is a world which is the very opposite of the world of reality, and for that very reason is as thoroughly like it as chaos is to completed creation.[1]

Thus whether or not MacDonald was "tainted" by German theology—as the Elders of the Arundel Congregational Church had charged—German literary influence is thus clearly, if ambiguously, acknowledged at the outset of MacDonald's first novel. But what was it about Germany that was to prove so influential not merely on MacDonald, but on the whole development of English fantasy?

Crossing a Great Frontier

In the early nineteenth-century Germany was immensely fashionable in Britain. The British royal family maintained strong links with its Hanoverian roots. Britain and Prussia enjoyed not merely close military, but ever closer cultural ties since their victory at Waterloo in 1815, culminating in Queen Victoria's marriage to her beloved Prince Albert of SaxeCoburg-Gotha in 1840. The wedding had even been followed by a proposal for a joint Anglican-Lutheran bishopric of Jerusalem in 1841 (anticipating eventual union between the English and Prussian state churches). Nevertheless much of the popular picture of Germany was based on sheer ignorance. Though things had improved slightly since 1821 when Edward Bouverie Pusey, the future Regius Professor of Divinity at Oxford, on setting out to learn about new developments in German theology had discovered that only two people in the entire university knew any German at all, German was still not taught in British schools or universities. Those who, like Carlyle, Coleridge, De Quincey, or George Eliot, had attempted to create a wider awareness of German culture through translation and articles appealed only to a narrow section of the reading public.[2]

The revolutionary philosophy of Kant and Hegel, like the no less iconoclastic theology of Strauss and Feuerbach, was largely untranslated until midcentury, and much of the work of the German Romantics, including Novalis, the Schlegels, and Schleiermacher was not translated until the twentieth century.[3] For most people, Germany was not so much the land of advanced thought as one of dark forests, romantic castles, and musical boxes.[4]

That this image from German folklore, based not merely on the pioneering researches of the brothers Grimm but on the writings of Novalis and his fellow Romantics, not to mention Mme de Stael's propagandist French portrait of the country in her book *De l'Allemagne*,[5] was part of a cohesive national effort to reinvent a truly German culture that might effectively unify a country humiliated by the Napoleonic Wars and still divided politically into over three-hundred independent states was, of course, little understood by the British. Nor did they understand the degree to which this elevation of fairy stories was not only because they represented something truly German enough to satisfy an increasingly nationalistic readership, but because there was, in truth, very little else to work on.

For a variety of historical reasons, the novel as a form had never enjoyed the kind of prestige in eighteenth-century Germany that it had come to hold in England.[6] A reference book published in Leipzig in the 1770s, for instance, has no entry at all under novel, the noun, and under the adjective, novelistic, merely comments tartly: "Thus one describes whatever in content, tone, or expression bears the characteristics which prevailed in earlier novels—such as fondness for adventures, stiltedness in actions, events, feelings. The natural is more or less the exact opposite of the novelistic."[7] In Martin Swales's memorable phrase, the novel in Germany was born with "a bad conscience." It is hardly surprising, therefore, that the first German novels of note had the loose episodic structure and fantastic events more commonly associated with fairy stories than with the kind of closely plotted, realistic structures pioneered by Jane Austen in English and which had rapidly become the norm of the nineteenth-century novel. As we shall see, this is as true of Goethe's *Wilhelm Meister* by the self-styled leader of German "classicism" as it was of Novalis's ultra-Romantic (and romantically incomplete) novel, *Heinrich van Ofterdingen*—both of which were to prove hugely influential in the development of MacDonald's own work.

This problem of the relationship of the parts to the whole—central to all fantasy—has always been at its most acute in *Phantastes*. Despite its superficially fragmented construction, some readers have found an innate underlying unity in the whole work. Robert Lee Wolff, in his pioneering study of MacDonald,[8] was one of the first to discuss this tension between the apparently episodic and even picaresque arrangement of incidents and raise the possibility of an overall allegorical or symbolic structure. Like all his fellow German Romantics, Novalis had not been afraid of contradicting himself, but, as Wolff points out, the problem of intention here is com, pounded by the fact that in the passages by MacDonald quoted at the beginning of this chapter, Novalis had originally written not that "everything must be wonderful, mysterious and coherent" (thereby contradicting the first paragraph) but that it should be "incoherent" (*unzusammenhängend*). It was his friends and posthumous editors, Ludwig Tieck and August Schlegel, who made the alteration for purposes of their own. For Wolff s largely Freudian interpretation any sense of unity overriding the apparently fragmented construction can be attributed more to the degree to which its author reveals his own unconscious needs and fantasies than to any deliberate constructional subtlety,[9] but for others the novel's total coherence (however achieved) has been its essential feature. C. S. Lewis, for instance, records that a key step in his conversion to Christianity was triggered by the chance finding of a copy of *Phantastes* on a railway station bookstall in 1916.

The more one studies Lewis's account of this particular accident of fortune, indeed, the more bizarre does it become. Admittedly any "conversion" narrative is likely to be a more than usually edited and subjective version of the facts, but, if Lewis's telling of the story is to be even half believed, it makes the conversions of Augustine, Wesley, or Newman seem events of the severest necessitarian logic by comparison. Here is part of his account of that first reading of *Phantastes*:

> Turning to the bookstall, I picked out an Everyman in a dirty jacket, *Phantastes*, a faerie Romance, George MacDonald. [. . .] That evening I began to read my new book.
>
> The woodland journeyings in that story, the ghostly enemies, the ladies both good and evil, were close enough to my habitual imagery to lure me on without the perception of change. It is as if I were carried sleeping across the frontier, or as if I had died in the old country and could never remember how I came alive in the new. For in one sense the new country was exactly like the old. I met there all that had already charmed me in Malory, Spenser, Morris and Yeats. But in another sense all was changed. I did not yet know (and I was long in learning) the name of the new quality, the bright shadow, that rested on the travels of Anodos. I do now. It was Holiness. For the first time the song of the sirens sounded like the voice of my mother or my nurse. Here were old wives' tales; there was nothing to be proud of in enjoying them. It was as though the voice which had called to me from the world's end were now speaking at my side.[10]

Here certainly is that sense of wonderful and secret coherence that MacDonald had discovered (however illegitimately) in the Novalis quotations, but in recollecting that coherence Lewis immediately and naturally enters into the allegorical imagery of the story he is describing. It was as if, almost like Anodos, the hero of *Phantastes*, he had been "carried sleeping across a frontier" to somewhere where the allurements of the most exotic literary forms—which clearly included for him the Arthurian cycle and *The Faerie Queene*—were one and the same with the stories of his mother or nurse. Here Lewis slips easily into the imagery of the "grandmother" and "wise-woman" that pervades not just *Phantastes*, but so many of MacDonald's other stories. Yet the inversion of the sinister "dark shadow" of the novel into the "bright shadow" of holiness seems in context almost willful.

Take, for instance, the path of Anodos (whose name means "pathless") towards self-knowledge through disobedience in *Phantastes*.

Essays on George MacDonald's *Phantastes*

He enters a lonely cottage in the forest and finds a woman reading. Beyond her is a door, and he is seized at once by an irresistible desire to know what is beyond it. She warns him, but he persists and looks in through it. It is an ordinary broom cupboard but as his eyes get used to the darkness he realizes that it has no back:[11]

> All at once, with such a shiver as when one is suddenly conscious of the presence of another in a room where he has, for hours, considered him, self alone, I saw that the seemingly luminous extremity was the sky, as of night, beheld through the long perspective of a narrow, dark passage, through what, or built of what, I could not tell. As I gazed, I clearly discerned two or three stars glimmering faintly in the distant blue. But, suddenly, as if it had been running fast from a far distance for this very point, and had turned the corner without abating its swiftness, a dark figure sped into and along the passage from the blue opening at the remote end. I started back and shuddered, but kept looking, for I could not help it. On and on it came, with a speedy approach but delayed arrival; till, at last [. . .] it [. . .] rushed up to me, and passed me into the cottage. [. . .]
>
> "Where is he?" I said, in some alarm, to the woman, who sat reading.
>
> "There, on the floor, behind you," she said, pointing with her arm half outstretched, but not lifting her eyes. I turned and looked, but saw nothing. Then with a feeling that there was yet something behind me, I looked round over my shoulder; and there, on the ground, lay a black shadow the size of a man.[12]

Anodos's subsequent struggle to rid himself of his shadow illustrates MacDonald's theory of the fairytale perfectly. As we discover, the shadow cannot merely be read as "original sin," or the "unconscious," the Jungian "shadow," or even some prototype of the Freudian "id," for it operates at two levels in the story. At one level it may indeed stand for some, or indeed all, of these. Anodos is both frightened and disgusted by the dark menacing presence of the shadow always with him: it insidiously destroys all sense of beauty and wonder in the world around him as he travels, imprisoning him into something like Blake's "cavern'd man" lit only by the fragmented evidence of the five senses as Locke imagined them to be. Simultaneously, however, the discovery of this dark shadow through the forbidden door illustrates the process by which this comes about. It is part of the psychodrama: forming a symbol of his own mental processes. The image itself enlarges our own self-understanding by illustrating its own function. There is, to put it simply, more than we intend in any allegorical image simply because behind it is the forbidden door and the shadow.

> Between the conception and the act
> Falls the shadow.[13]

Nevertheless, though it is one thing to read the novel as both a moral allegory and a psychodrama—as Lewis was well aware, the novel's name is lifted from Phineas Fletcher's *The Purple Island* (1633) where "Phantastes," or "Fancie," is the second of the three allegorical councillors who control the castle of the mind—it is surely quite another to find in it a gateway to the whole doctrinal panoply of institutional Christianity. Fairy stories, whether German or English, have played a significant underground role in European cultural history, but they have not been especially noted in either country for causing religious conversions. Indeed, they have more often been the object of gravest suspicion by guardians of culture and orthodoxy![14]

It may be that part of the clue to Lewis's reaction to *Phantastes* is to be found in the meaning he attached to that word *holiness*. Though at that stage he does not seem to have been particularly well read in German literature, by the early 1930s, when he came to reflect on what had happened to him, he was certainly enough of a classically trained philologist to know that *hagios*, the New Testament word most often translated into English as "holy," like its Hebrew Old Testament counterpart, *quadosh*, came from a root meaning "separate" or "set aside" for a deity or deities[15]—with suggestions of an even earlier meaning of "polluted" or "unclean."[16] Indeed, his final comments on the unexpected effects of his casual purchase seem to be an implicit reference to such connotations of the word:

> Up till now each visitation of Joy had left the common world momentarily a desert—"the first touch of the earth went nigh to kill." Even when real clouds or trees had been the material of the vision, they had been so only by reminding me of another world; and I did not like the return to ours. But now I saw the bright shadow coming out of the book into the real world and resting there, transforming all common things and yet itself unchanged. [. . .] That night my imagination was, in a certain sense, baptised; the rest of me, not unnaturally, took longer. I had not the faintest notion what I let myself in for by buying *Phantastes*.[17]

The language of the Wordsworthian visionary reaches back

through a whole literary tradition to the classical world, both pagan and Christian. Thus for Lewis holiness is not so much an attribute of particular characters in the narrative, nor even of plot structure, but rather the transformation of the mundane world into something new, set aside by divinity, and transcendent. Indeed, the transformation of the shadow from what was originally "polluted" and destructive into a source of inspiration and joy is precisely the kind of metaphor of redemption that would have appealed to his philological imagination. But, of course, as we have seen from the earlier quotation, Lewis's previous sense of the mundane world (even at the stage where he then was of what he was later to call "popular realism") was already essentially a literary one of a particular kind. As Lewis himself was to note afterwards, his road to conversion via Philosophical Idealism, Pantheism, and finally Theism, though it seemed a natural enough one to him at the time, was in fact a highly unusual one for the early twentieth century.[18] What he does not add, but seems clear in retrospect, is the degree to which his route was influenced by his literary taste. The world of his imagination was, we note, that of Malory, Spenser, Morris, and Yeats. None of them, it is true, were notably Christian writers (indeed, two of the four were distinctly hostile to the Christianity they knew) but all four were not merely writers of fantasy but also the creators and users of potent literary myths. All four were creators not just of fictions, but of complex metafictions—creating from the material of myth and legend highly self, conscious mythopoeic works of art. The "baptism" of Lewis's imagination was thus, it seems, a baptism and a sanctification not so much of literature per se as a means of approaching the transcendent (a view Lewis was both drawn by and, for that reason, highly sceptical of) but more specifically of the particular kind of literary synthesis such works implied.

What *Phantastes* seems to have given to Lewis above all was a glimpse of the possibility of a developing synthesis in which language, literature, and thus the entire record of human imaginative experience could be brought into a unified whole. It had showed him a way (or, at least, perhaps the possibility of a way) in which the literary or poetic transformation of sense-experience could be given some kind of objective meaning and validity. Thus Anodos awakes on the morning of his twenty-first birthday to find himself already, literally, in transition from one world to the other:

> While these strange events were passing through my mind, I suddenly [. . .] became aware of the sound of running water

near me; and looking out of bed, I saw that a large green marble basin, in which I was wont to wash, and which stood on a low pedestal of the same material in a corner of my room, was overflowing like a spring; and that a stream of clear water was running over the carpet, all the length of the room, finding its outlet I knew not where. And, stranger still, where this carpet, which I had myself designed to imitate a field of grass and daises, bordered the course of the little stream, the grass blades and daises seemed to wave in a tiny breeze that followed the water's flow; while under the rivulet they bent and swayed with every motion of the changeful current, as if they were about to dissolve with it, and, forsaking their fixed form, became as fluent as the waters.

My dressing table was an old fashioned piece of furniture of black oak, with drawers all down the front. These were elaborately carved in foliage, of which ivy formed the chief part. The nearer end of this table remained just as it had been, but on the further end a singular change had commenced. I happened to fix my eye on a little cluster of ivy leaves. The first of these was evidently the work of the carver; the next looked curious; the third was unmistakably ivy; and just beyond it a tendril of clematis had twined itself about the gilt handle of one of the drawers. Hearing a slight motion above me, I looked up, and saw that the branches and leaves designed upon the curtains of my bed were slightly in motion. Not knowing what change might follow next, I thought it high time to get up; and, springing from the bed, my bare feet alighted upon a cool green sward; and although I dressed in all haste, I found myself completing my toilet under the boughs of a great tree.[19]

This is MacDonald at his best. What in the hands of many writers would remain merely a set piece becomes in MacDonald's hands also a symbolic event. The flowering of the manmade decorations in the carpet and the carvings immediately suggests that this other world, Fairyland, is to be in some sense more real than the one Anodos is leaving. What with us is artificial, there is natural. The stream of water overflowing from the basin is literally the River of Life: as it flows across his carpet it brings to life everything it touches.[20] Imitation becomes what it imitates. Presumably, by inference, we are also meant to assume the same of Anodos himself—and the final chapter of the book suggests that this is so. It is the morning of his twenty-first birthday, and, appropriately, his first action in this new world is to stoop and wash himself in the stream. But this explicit archetypal symbolism has an unexpected side effect. We are suddenly enabled to see the old room as it vanishes with a new intensity of detail. The unexpected metamorphosis of the room from "art" to "life" shows us the clichéd luxuriance of flower and vegetation patterns dear to mid-Victorian bedroom taste with the shock of seeing the familiar for the first time. The juxtaposition with the "other" world shows us our own in a new way. And that, of course, is the purpose of MacDonald's whole technique. The deliberate aesthetic inversion provides an ironic second layer of meaning: in the story we are suddenly brought from art to life; in reality, since the story we are reading is itself a work of art, we are moving from life to art. The "new reality" is being created by MacDonald as author in order to reveal what is latent, but not explicit in the old.

In *Lilith*, MacDonald's last novel, in a parallel scene the hero, Mr. Vane, enters the other world by a device already made familiar to us by Lewis Carroll—a mirror:

> The small chamber was full of light. [. . .] A few rather dim sunrays, marking their track through the cloud of motes that had just been stirred up, fell upon a tall mirror with a dusty face, old fashioned and rather narrow-in appearance an ordinary glass. It had an ebony frame, on the top of which stood a black eagle with outstretched wings, in his beak a golden chain, from whose end hung a black ball.
>
> I had been looking at rather than into the mirror, when suddenly I became aware that it reflected neither the chamber nor my own person. I have an impression of having seen the wall melt away, but what followed is enough to account for any uncertainty:— could I have mistaken for a mirror the glass that protected a wonderful picture?
>
> I saw before me a wild country, broken and heathy. Desolate hills of no great height, but somehow of strange appearance, occupied the middle distance; along the horizon stretched the tops of a far off mountain range; nearest me lay a tract of moorland, flat and melancholy.
>
> Being short sighted, I stepped closer to examine the texture of a stone in the immediate foreground, and in the act espied, hopping toward me with solemnity, a large and ancient raven, whose purply black was here and there softened with gray. [. . .] Nowise astonished at the appearance of a live creature in a picture, I took another step forward to see him better, stumbled over something—doubtless the frame of the

mirror—and stood nose to beak with the bird: I was in the open air, on a houseless heath![21]

These are just two of a series of images of the relation of art to life in the course of the stories—as we shall see, another example in *Lilith* is a book in the library which is half in the other world, half in this. Here, however, the other world literally holds up a mirror to our own. The symbolic significance is obvious: the work of art, in this case *Lilith* itself, reveals to us our own world in a new light. Many of Mr. Raven's speeches are designed to ram this point home. This is as much the proper function of fantasy as it is of any realistic novel, but whereas the events of the realistic novel must perforce work at one remove from spiritual realities, fantasy can show them in a much more direct (though still symbolic) manner simply by the kinds of event it can portray. Abstractions can thus be shown as concrete entities.

Though this may seem at first sight a very far cry from Novalis's idea of a fairy story, it may nevertheless serve to illuminate certain elements in what MacDonald was attempting with his new and highly potent fictional form. In any case there were other elements from German Romanticism besides Novalis at work on MacDonald's imagination.

Among the epigraphs in *Phantastes* are quotations not merely from Lewis's favorites, the Arthurian legends and Spenser, but also Shakespeare, the Metaphysical poets, Coleridge, Wordsworth, and Shelley; and from the Germans: Heinrich Heine, Jean Paul (Richter), Fredrich Schiller, Schleiermacher, and Goethe. Though such a heterogeneous selection of writers could hardly be accused of any kind of religious orthodoxy, what they do have in common is that they are all creators of "Romances" of one kind or another. Whatever MacDonald was attempting to do in creating his adult fairy story, Lewis was clearly right in detecting in him an eclectic literary taste in many ways akin to his own: in its mode of operation at once metafictional and intertextual.

Notably absent from this list, interestingly enough, is E. T. A. Hoffmann, whose novella, *The Golden Pot*, has, following Greville MacDonald's suggestion in his biography of his father, regularly been cited as being the probable model for *Phantastes*.[22] Yet, despite MacDonald's clear appreciation of Hoffmann, such a statement is, in fact, highly misleading. Though certain incidents in *Phantastes*, such as the whispering voices in the tree that begin Hoffmann's story and end MacDonald's, are clear examples of the latter's borrowing (be it said, to good advantage), any structural resemblance between *The*

Golden Pot and *Phantastes* is in fact very slight. Hoffmann's story, with its tightly constructed sequential narrative and plethora of irrelevant magical wonders offers no suggestion of hidden allegory nor even development of character. In no way does it offer the kind of model for a sustained full-length allegorical Romance that MacDonald by his network of epigraphs and quotations seems to be so self consciously striving to recreate in his new form.

For this the influence of Goethe was much more important. Goethe was still little more than a name to the British public—known chiefly through a bad translation of Werther—even after the appearance of Carlyle's classic translation of *Wilhelm Meister* in 1824, the year of MacDonald's birth. Though Carlyle had previously contributed translations for serialization in the *London Magazine* (including a *Life of Schiller*) and was later to translate *The Golden Pot* in 1827, *Wilhelm Meister* was his first independently published literary work and, as such, it was undoubtedly chosen with the aim of furthering the reputation of its twenty-nine-year-old translator as well as its original author. In this he was at least partially successful: if the initial public response was not over-whelming, demand was strong enough for a second edition in 1839. As Carlyle was well aware, nothing quite like it had appeared in English before.

From its first publication in 1796, *Wilhelm Meisters Lehrjahre* had attracted controversy. Goethe had begun his loose and episodic novel as early as 1777, when he was both a Minister of State in Weimar and director of the Court Theatre, and he worked on it spasmodically until 1785, by which time he had completed the fifth book. He did not resume writing until 1794, in very different circumstances, when he rapidly completed the remaining three books.[23] By that stage what had seemingly begun as an autobiographical novel of theatrical life had turned into the first (and arguably the greatest) example of the genre later to be known as a *Bildungsroman*.

The degree to which the novel reflects this checkered writing-history is a matter of controversy. The earlier books tell the story of how young Wilhelm rejects the middle-class commercial world in which he was brought up, and, under the guise of a business trip financed by his father, joins and eventually runs a troupe of itinerant actors. While on this extended period of absence from home he has a series of more or less disastrous and unsuitable love affairs with women ranging from two actresses to a countess, in the process acquiring a number of dependents including a small child which, as he afterwards learns, is his own—borne by Marianne, his first love who has subsequently died. In the midst of these adventures he learns that his father has also died. The loosely strung episodes of this narrative are given further shape by a second, metafictional plot based on Shakespeare's *Hamlet*. On first being introduced to the play by the mysterious Jarno, Wilhelm takes the play to himself, undertaking not merely to rewrite it in accordance with the needs of the time, but also to direct it, and even to act the part of the prince himself. The parallels with his own life are carefully highlighted. He is haunted by guilt over the neglect of his father (significantly, less so over Marianne—a not-so-innocent but equally misused Ophelia). His closest friend and confidant is even known as "Horatio" (though we are told that is not his real name). In the later sections of the book direct references to the players in *Hamlet* and his own troupe are stressed: culminating in a scene where Jarno points out, in a passage reminiscent of Act. II, Sc. 2, the symbolic parallels between the playhouse and the world.[24]

In the final books of the *Apprenticeship* and in its sequel, the *Travels*, all semblance of conventional naturalism is set aside. Jarno, along with several other equally enigmatic figures, turns out to belong to a secret society, the Society of the Tower, which takes its name from the tower of the mysterious rambling castle of a nobleman called Lothario. This organization, it transpires, has been keeping a beneficent watch over Wilhelm almost from the start, limiting the potentially disastrous consequences of his mistakes, and eventually, in a scene echoing the initiation of Tamino in *The Magic Flute*, admitting him to the mysteries of their Order. At the end of the novel, he is finally rewarded with the hand of the beautiful lady, the Amazon, with whose image he has been in love (when he remembers) for most of the novel, and who conveniently turns out to be the sister of the Countess for whom he has long also nourished a hopeless passion.

He is not to be allowed to enjoy his lady at this stage, however. Once safely betrothed, he is immediately sent off again on his travels-the subject of the next volume. For its metafictional structure this sequel, the *Travels*, relies less on Shakespeare than on the work of another, no less metafictional English writer: Sterne's *Sentimental Journey*—at one point Wilhelm is even casually referred to as "Yorrick," Sterne's mouthpiece and protagonist as well as the one-time owner of the skull in Hamlet's graveyard scene. Throughout the narrative level there are a good many "shandian" interludes; at a philosophical level the emphasis is less on the gaining of worldly experience than on the stages of religious awareness.[25]

Any reader of MacDonald is immediately struck by the startlingly familiar imagery from which these complex allegories are created. We have already mentioned the rambling castle, with the secret in the tower (and even, at one point, hobgoblins!)—so central to *The Princess and the Goblin*—but these borrowed elements of the *Apprenticeship* pale into insignificance with the flood of ingredients MacDonald has culled from the *Travels*. Miners "allured by the metallic veins," boring through the rock, are held up by Jarno as types or exempla of the "enquiring thinker" "in a thousand ways endeavouring to solve the hardest problems"; [26] there is a golden casket with a (missing) golden key—in connection with which a character even has, in the words of Carlyle's translation, to toil "through moss and tangle";[27] the protagonists are at another point led on a preordained route by mysterious arrows; there are even, for those who like to mix MacDonald with Tolkien, dwarves (who, like MacDonald's goblins, have chosen to go underground and shun the light), and dragons.

Such elements, however, are less significant for our understanding of MacDonald than the way in which the episodic plots of both novels are constructed around a sense of the larger whole in which it is suggested that there is a hidden order permeating all existence, and that the growth of the youthful but symbolically named "Meister" is achieved both through its guidance and, eventually, by discovery of it. That this discovery is at the same time a self-discovery is made clear in the ceremony of Wilhelm's admission to the Society of the Tower when he is presented with an already printed book of his own life. The constant cross-reference to other works of literature, moreover, serves to create the impression that there is, similarly, a hidden meaning and order to be discovered through literature, and that there, too, understanding and self-discovery are but twin aspects of the same process. As a spiritual advisor to the "fair saint," a noblewoman who comes under the influence of Count Zinzendorf's Moravian sect, says:

> Life lies before us, as a huge quarry lies before the architect: he deserves not the name of architect, except when, out of this fortuitous mass, he can combine, with the greatest economy, and fitness, and durability, some form, the pattern of which originated in his spirit. All things without us, nay, I may add, all things on us, are mere elements: but deep within us lies the creative force, which out of these can produce what they were meant to be; and which leaves us neither sleep nor rest, till in one way or another, without us or on us, that same has been produced.[28]

In effect, what Lewis was to find with such astonishment in MacDonald was a redeployment not just of individual motifs and elements culled from Goethe, but a whole way of structuring experience, part-fantasy, part-realism, which go to make up the origins of the German *Bildungsroman*.

The German word *Bildung* is almost untranslatable in English. The most literal meaning would be that of "formation" or "growth" with the implication of internal organic self-development rather than merely the acquiring of a skill or training (as in the parallel word, *Ausbildung*). Thus Goethe's contemporary, the philologist Wilhelm von Humboldt, wishing, as he put it, to study "the faculty of speech in its inward aspect, as a human faculty" insisted that it must be understood in the context of a "philosophical survey of humanity's capacity for formation (*Bildung*) and with history."[29] Such connotations of "inwardness," "culture," and even introspectiveness have sometimes led to the word *Bildungsroman* being rendered in English as "the novel of self-cultivation"—a genre which no less a literary figure than Thomas Mann saw as being Germany's most distinctive cultural form.[30]

Though the term seems to have been coined in the early 1820s by Karl Morgenstern[31] it did not achieve wide currency until the end of the nineteenth century when it was taken up by Wilhelm Dilthey, who at first simply defined it in terms of what he saw as the first example: "I propose to call those novels which make up the school of *Wilhelm Meister* [. . .] *Bildungsromane*."[32] This he later summarized as: "A regulated development within the life of the individual [. . .] each of its stages has its own intrinsic value and is at the same time the basis for a higher stage. The dissonances and conflicts of life appear as the necessary growth points through which the individual must pass on his way to maturity and harmony."[33] Morgenstern's original definition, however, had been more subtly reflexive. For him the term should apply not merely to the *Bildung* of the hero, but also to that of the reader, whose own personal formation and self-development is fostered through involvement with the text.[34] Without plunging into the interesting question of his anticipation of later reader-response theories, it is worth noticing how closely such an idea of the *Bildungsroman* foreshadows the effect of *Phantastes* at least on a reader such as Lewis—not to mention his friend Arthur Greeves with whom he corresponded at length about his discovery.[35]

But Dilthey's concentration on the character of the hero should not allow us to lose sight of the degree to which such novels were always self-conscious literary artefacts. In an echo of Morgenstern's idea of the self-conscious reflexiveness inherent in the genre, one modern critic, Michael Beddow claims:

> We are invited to view the entire narrative as a piece of fiction which requires of us a response that includes an awareness of reading an imaginative construction, rather than an empirically accurate representation. At this level of reading, the mimetic claim to be "about" the hero's development is relativised by the wider claim that the narrative of the hero's experiences, precisely insofar as we perceive it to be a piece of fiction, offers insights into human nature which could not be adequately conveyed either in the form of discursive arguments or through a rigorously mimetic, non-self-conscious fictional work.[36]

Such an inherently metafictional description applies not merely to Goethe's *Wilhelm Meister*—still for Beddow, as for Dilthey, the supreme example of the genre—but also with extraordinary accuracy to *Phantastes*, and to the new form of "Faerie Romance" in English that we would now see as probably MacDonald's most significant stylistic achievement. It also suggests the degree of MacDonald's debt to Goethe.

But so what? What difference does it make to our reading of *Phantastes* if we see it in terms of the organic unity of a *Bildungsroman* rather than the a-logical fragmentation of a fairy story? Do we really need to refer to German literary theory to discover that Anodos's spiritual growth and development is a central theme of the story? Are there in fact any elements that we might be led to look for in the story by such a reclassification that we might otherwise be inclined to miss?

The most obvious answer is irony—especially irony in that peculiar new sense that we find with Goethe and the German Romantics.[37] Though we are familiar enough with it in Augustine, Dante, the metaphysical poets, and even in Bunyan, irony is not a quality that we are necessarily quick to associate with Victorian religious writing. Yet the moment we formulate the question it is clear that *Phantastes* is in fact a pervasively ironic work—at many levels. Most obvious is the constant disconfirmation of Anodos's expectations—from his first meeting with his variable-sized grandmother in the bureau to his mistakes over the various "white" and "marble" ladies he pursues with such energy throughout the narrative. It is clear throughout that this "fairy land" in fact corresponds neither to his wishes nor his expectations—derived mostly from other literature on the subject. This brings us at the metafictional level to the truly Goethean irony in the use of other parallel literary texts—not least, of which, as we have seen, is the one from Novalis stressing the fragmentary and elliptical nature of fairy stories. Not merely are we to bear Novalis in mind when reading *Phantastes*, we need also to read the Novalis in the light of *Phantastes*.

This pervasive sense of irony is also the clue to so much of the relationship between MacDonald's novel and the other literature on which it draws.[38] As we have seen, there was a very real sense in which the folktale or fairy story occupied in Germany the same cultural niche as the novel had come to do in Britain, but as a result it was normal for prose narrative to be judged not in its own terms, or in terms of prose realism, but rather for its poetic content. Thus Friedrich Schlegel, reviewing the first part of *Wilhelm Meister* in 1798, eulogizes it as "all poetry—high pure poetry. Everything has been thought and uttered as though by one who is both a divine poet and a perfect artist; and even the most delicate secondary features seem to exist in their own right and to rejoice in their own independent life, even against the laws of petty, inauthentic probability."[39] Sadly, Schlegel's own novel, *Lucinde*, whose vagueness and abstraction might well pass for poetic, proved so lacking in either plot or narrative as to be largely incomprehensible to the reader, then—or subsequently. Similarly, Tieck, comparing Cervantes with Shakespeare, takes it for granted that both are poets, working in a common medium.[40] In this connection it is revealing, for instance, that, in MacDonald's quotation from Novalis with which we began, the fairy story is discussed not as narrative (which it is taken for granted will have "no coherence") but as poetry—and the word used in the German is not *dichterish*, which would be employed in connection with actual verse and imaginative writing, but *poetisch*, which has a much more theoretical, abstract, and spiritualized flavor to it.[41]

Thus *Wilhelm Meister's* enormous popularity and prestige in early nineteenth-century Germany stemmed not least from the fact that it seemed to rehabilitate what had hitherto seemed to many critics as a dubious and even illegitimate fictional form. In his introduction to the first edition of his English translation Carlyle quotes Schlegel on the contrast between it and its predecessors.

> To judge of this book,—new and peculiar as it is, and only to be understood and learned from itself, by our common notion of the novel, a notion pieced together and produced out of custom and belief, out of accidental and arbitrary requisitions,—is as if a child should grasp at the moon and stars, and insist on packing them into its toy-box.[42]

What was felt to be the inwardness and dignity of the way in which Goethe handled the new medium gave the lie to the eighteenth-century English stereotype of German literature summed up by Wordsworth in 1798 in his attack on "frantic novels, sickly and stupid German Tragedies."[43] This perception helped to pave the way for the great reappraisal that, helped by Carlyle's influence, was to fire the next generation of young Scots (in particular)[44] such as MacDonald with an enthusiasm for German literature, culture, and theology.

Yet the general improvement in status of the German novel with Goethe's great *Bildungsroman* served only to highlight a paradox that had always been latent in any literary expression of "self-development" as an aesthetic form. In his comments on the novel in his *Aesthetics*, Hegel puts in general terms what is, in effect, the central problem of *Wilhelm Meister*. The heroes of such novels, he writes,

> stand as individuals with their subjective goals of love, honour, ambition, or with their ideals of improving the world, over against the existing order and prose of reality which from all sides places obstacles in their path. [. . .] These struggles are, however, in the modern world nothing but the apprenticeship, the education of the individual at the hands of the given reality. [. . .] For the conclusion of such an apprenticeship usually amounts to the hero getting the corners knocked off him. [. . .] In the last analysis he usually gets his girl and some kind of job, marries and becomes a philistine just like the others.[45]

In other words, the very process of self-formation and the gaining of worldly wisdom, essential as it is to growth and maturity, is actually toward a goal that is fundamentally less interesting and less morally worthy than the raw immature idealism that preceded it![46] Certainly the ending of *Wilhelm Meister*, where our hero is paired with a beautiful aristocrat and given the job of managing a large estate purchased as an investment by a business syndicate, is highly ambiguous.

It is part of the ironic literary structure of MacDonald's *Bildungsroman* that the ending of *Phantastes* can be read not merely in relation to the narrative that precedes it, but also in relation to this problem in its progenitor: *Wilhelm Meister*. Thus Anodos, at the end of his experiences, so far from being better fitted for accommodation with the real world (in a question, that, as we have seen, was to be echoed by Arthur Machen fifty years later[47]) is left wondering how far he is now actually unfitted for it.

> I began the duties of my new position, somewhat instructed, I hoped, by the adventures that had befallen me in Fairy Land.

> Could I translate the experience of my travels there, into common life? This was the question. Or must I live it all over again, and learn it all over again, in other forms that belong to the world of men, whose experience yet runs parallel to that of Fairy Land? I cannot yet answer. But I fear. [. . .]
>
> I have a strange feeling sometimes, that I am a ghost, sent into the world to minister to my fellow-men, or, rather to repair the wrongs I have already done. [. . .]
>
> Thus I, who set out to find my Ideal, came back rejoicing that I had lost my Shadow. [. . .]
>
> What we call evil, is the only and best shape, which, for the person and his condition at the time, could be assumed by the best good. And so, Farewell.[48]

Whereas *Wilhelm Meister*, at the end of the *Apprenticeship*, is compared with Saul, the son of Kish, "who went out to seek his father's asses, and found a kingdom,"[49] Anodos, can be certain not of present happiness, like Goethe's hero, but only of future good. Though he is in some ways a sadder and a wiser man, there is no suggestion that his final condition involves any kind of moral compromise with the values of the world. His "formation" has, on the contrary, given him a stronger sense of his own ideals—even if he is also correspondingly more humble both about their value and of his capacity to attain them. Notably, he does not get any of the women he has been pursuing so earnestly. This strangely hesitant agnosticism of MacDonald, the religious believer, similarly loses something of its quiet irony if we fail to set it alongside the formulaic certainties of the agnostic religious instruction of Goethe's ideal community at the end of the *Travels*:

> Two duties we have most rigorously undertaken: first, to honour every species of religious worship, for all of them are comprehended more or less directly in the Creed: secondly, in like manner to respect all forms of government; and since every one of them induces and promotes a calculated activity, to labour according to the wish and will of constituted authority, in whatever place it may be our lot to sojourn, and for whatever time. Finally, we reckon it our duty, without pedantry or rigour, to practise and forward decorum of manners and morals, as required by that Reverence for Ourselves. [. . .] All this, in the solemn hour of parting, we have thought good once more to recount, to unfold, to hear and acknowledge, as also to seal with a trustful Farewell.[50]

Though one might wish for a little more of Novalis's incoherence at points like this, nevertheless, if the striking parallels between *Phantastes* and *Wilhelm Meister* suggest that MacDonald in creating his "fairy romance for men and women" was in fact transplanting Goethe's *Bildungsroman* into the alien but highly fertile context of English literature, we need to recognize first of all the inevitable and ironic transformation wrought by that subtle change of air. Whereas the prose romance in German was scarcely recognized, in England it had a lineage reaching back to Malory; while the indigenous German theater was of little account, England had Shakespeare. In this sense the context of metafictional reference available to MacDonald was far richer and more evocative than was possible for Goethe in his own literature. It is highly significant that when Goethe, comparing the demands on the hero of the drama (Hamlet, naturally!) with the hero of the novel, needed to evoke a string of protagonists from novels, his entire selection was from England: "Grandison, Clarissa, Pamela, the Vicar of Wakefield, Tom Jones. [. . .]"[51] Contrarywise, in returning the compliment, MacDonald by his references to Novalis, Hoffmann, Jean Paul, Schleiermacher, Heine, Schiller, and Goethe, is in fact doing something very different: whereas Shakespeare and the English eighteenth-century novelists were comparatively familiar in Germany, German writers of the late eighteenth-century literary renaissance, were, in contrast, little known, and even exotic figures to the more insular British readership of the 1850s. Goethe's literary references had the effect of placing his novel in relation to what he saw as the mainstream development of prose realism; MacDonald contrives to suggest that behind the veil of normality in that tradition was something marvelous and magical that could not be wholly eradicated from everyday life. In the very literature where Goethe had assiduously sought bourgeois reality, MacDonald discovers romance—awaiting only the mysticism of Novalis and his fellow Germans to be awakened into new life.

But the ironies of the change in referential context are minor compared with the consequences of the shift in medium from realism to fantasy. Though *Wilhelm Meister* is hardly realistic by the later standards of the nineteenth century, it is certainly no fairy story either. MacDonald was one of the few nineteenth-century writers to recognize that realism and fantasy are two sides of the same coin: that realism is as much an arbitrary and literary convention as fantasy, and that fantasy is as dependent on mundane experience as realism.[52] By invoking Novalis as his mentor, and moving his own *Bildungsroman* overtly into the realm of the fantastic, MacDonald was able to bring out latent resources of irony in the genre that were unavailable even to Goethe himself in his more overtly naturalistic mode. Anodos's adventures in Fairy Land, after all, conclude with his account of his own death—the acceptance of which, as we know from *Lilith*, MacDonald saw as being an essential factor in any kind of spiritual maturity. The irony of Christ's maxim "He that would save his life, must lose it" is always present in MacDonald's imagination. Moreover, the structural technique of placing the process of self-formation not in this world but in a fantastic other world immediately circumvents what we have seen is the major thematic problem of Goethe's *Bildungsroman*. If there is, as I believe, a sense in which *Phantastes* is the most satisfactory English adaptation of the *Bildungsroman*—much more so than, say, Dickens's *Great Expectations* or George Meredith's *Ordeal of Richard Feverel*, which have been commonly advanced as examples of the genre[53]—it is not so much because it is the most faithful replica of its outward characteristics, but because (to use a very German argument) it is the truest expression of its spirit. In adapting and radically changing the original form to suit his particular needs, MacDonald in fact solved the problem that had dogged Goethe and his successors working, however loosely, within the tradition of realism. The contradiction between moral idealism and worldly accommodation that worried Hegel is ultimately, of course, a theological one, and can in the end only be solved in theological terms. But theological solutions do not necessarily make good novels. To find through Goethe's irony an appropriate literary and aesthetic form for such an abstraction is an extraordinary achievement—perhaps in its own way one of the greatest achievements of Victorian fiction.

But important as this metaphysical transformation of the *Bildungsroman* undoubtedly is in terms of literary history, it would still hardly explain the impact that *Phantastes* had on the eighteen-year-old Lewis, who, at that stage of his life and in the middle of the First World War, was most unlikely to have known or cared about the problems of the German novel. What seems to have excited Lewis is the manner in which MacDonald had managed to give a new relevance and meaning to the fantastic romances of Malory, Spenser, Morris, and his other heroes. By showing the limitations of conventional realism to portray vital aspects of human growth and development, MacDonald had not merely helped to legitimize Lewis's own literary taste, he had also obliquely and ironically suggested a profound critique of genre and, incidentally, of contemporary assumptions about realism. To suggest that, for Lewis, *Phantastes* served as an introduction to what we would now, with rather a parochial sense of history, call "postmodernism" seems at first sight an unlikely perspective, yet, as we have seen, there is a good argument for such a case. It should also make us look more carefully at our own conventional assumptions about postmodernism.

. . .

Endnotes

1. MacDonald, *Phantastes*, and *Lilith*. The passage has had a chequered history since two further mistakes were made in the transliteration at the initial printing of the novel. [See Wolff, *Golden Key*, 42-44.] The corrected German text reads as follows:

   Es lassen sich Erzahlungen ohne Zusammenhang, jedoch mit Association, wie Träume, denken; Gedichte, die bloss wohlklingend und woll schöner Worte sind, aber auch ohne allen Sinn und Zusammenhang, höchstens einzelne Strophen verständlich, wie Bruchsrucke aus den verschiedenartigsten Dingen. Diese wahre Poesie kann höchstens einen allegorischen Sinn im Grossen, und eine indirecte Wirkung, wie Musik haben. Darum ist die Natur so rein poetisch, wie die Stube eines Zauberers, eines Physikers, eine Kinderstube, eine Polterund Vorrathskammer. [. . .]

   Ein Mährchen ist wie ein Traumbild ohne Zusammenhang. Ein Ensemble wunderbarer Dinge und Begebenheiten, z. B. eine Musikalische Phantasie, die harmonischen Folgen einer Aeolsharfe, die Natur selbst.

   In einem echten Mährchen muss alles wunderbar, geheimnissvoll und zusammenhängend sein; alles belebt, jeders auf eine andere Art. Die ganze natur muss wunderlich mit der ganzen Geisterwelt gemischt sein; hier tritt die Zeit der Anarchie, der Gesetzlosigkeit, Freiheit, der Naturstand der Natur, die Zeit vor der Welt ein. [. . .] Die Welt des Mährchens ist die, der Welt der Wahrheit durchaus entgegengesetzte, und eben darum ihr so durchaus ähnlich, wie das Chaos der vollendeten Schopfung ähnlich ist.

2. See Rosemary Ashton, *The German Idea: Four English Writers and the Reception of German Thought, 1800-1860* (Cambridge: Cambridge University Press, 1980).

3. See ibid; also Andrew Bowie, *Aesthetics and Subjectivity from Kant to Nietzsche* (Manchester: Manchester University Press, 1990), and *From Romanticism to Critical Theory* (London: Routledge, 1997).

4. See, for instance, the opening paragraphs of Mme. De Stael's influential book, *On Germany: On the Appearance of Germany*, in *Selected Writings of Germaine de Stael*, translated and introduction by Vivian Folkenflik (New York: Columbia University Press, 1987):

> Many vast forests are the sign of a new civilization: the ancient land of the South has almost no more trees, and the sun falls straight down on earth ravaged by men. Germany still offers some traces of uninhabited nature. From the Alps to the sea, between the Rhine and the Danube, you see a countryside covered with chestnut and fir trees, crisscrossed by impressively beautiful rivers, and cut across by picturesque mountains. [...]
>
> The ruined castles one glimpses on mountaintops, the houses built of earth, the narrow window, the snow that buries the plains in winter all give a harsh impression. (292)

5. See John Claiborne Isbell, *The Birth of European Romanticism* (Cambridge: Cambridge University Press, 1994).

6. For a discussion of one aspect of this imbalance, see Hans Frei, *The Eclipse of Biblical Narrative: A Study in Eighteenth-and Nineteenth-Century Hermeneutics* (New Haven, Yale University Press, 1974), 142; also Stephen Prickett, *Origins of Narrative: The Romantic Appropriation of the Bible* (Cambridge: Cambridge University Press, 1996), ch. 5.

7. Johann Georg Sulzer, *General Theory of the Fine Arts* (Leipzig, 1773-1775), cited by Martin Swales, *Thomas Mann: A Study* (London: Rowman & Littlefield, 1980), 19.

8. See Wolff, *Golden Key*, 43-45.

9. Ibid., ch. 2.

10. Lewis, *Surprised by Joy*, 169.

11. This cupboard is almost certainly the origin of C. S. Lewis's backless wardrobe in *The Lion, the Witch, and the Wardrobe* (London: Macmillian 1950).

12. MacDonald, *Phantastes and Lilith*, 63-64.
13. T. S. Eliot, "The Hollow Men," *Complete Poems and Plays* (New York: Harcourt Brace, 1952).
14. See above, 7-8.
15. Gabriel Josopivici, *The Book of God* (New Haven: Yale University Press, 1988), 6-7.
16. Alan Richardson, ed., *A Theological Word Book of the Bible* (London: SCM Press, 1950), 215.
17. Lewis, *Surprised by Joy*, 70-71.
18. C. S. Lewis, *The Pilgrim's Regress* (London: Collins, 1980), 9.
19. MacDonald, *Phantastes and Lilith*, 19-20.
20. An image which could well have come straight out of his friend John Ruskin's *King of the Golden River*.
21. MacDonald, *Phantastes and Lilith*, 192-93.
22. See *GMD and Wife*, 73, 259; Wolff, *Golden Key*, 45; Manlove, *Modern Fantasy*, 274; Rolland Hein, *The Harmony Within: The Spiritual Vision of George MacDonald* (Grand Rapids: Eerdmans, 1982), 7.
23. W. H. Bruford, *The German Tradition of Self-Cultivation: "Bildung" from Humboldt to Thomas Mann* (Cambridge: Cambridge University Press, 1975), 31-32.
24. Johann Wolfgang von Goethe, *Wilhelm Meister's Apprenticeship and Travels*, trans. Thomas Carlyle, 2 vols. (New York: J. D. Williams, 1882), 2: 14.
25. For a partial but interesting discussion of some of the religious symbolism of the *Travels*, see Ruth ap Roberts, *The Ancient Dialect: Thomas Carlyle and Comparative Religion* (Berkeley: University of California Press, 1988), ch. 2.
26. Goethe, *Wilhelm Meister*, 2:225.
27. Ibid., 2:230. The link with Mossy and Tangle in MacDonald's *Golden Key* is obvious.
28. Ibid., 1:444.

29. Wilhelm von Humboldt, *On Language*, trans. Peter Heath, introduction by Hans Aarsleff (Cambridge: Cambridge University Press, 1988), xiv.

30. Bruford, *German Tradition*, vii.

31. Martin Swales, *The German Bildungsroman from Wieland to Hesse* (Princeton University Press, 1978), 12.

32. Wilhelm Dilthey, *Leben Schleiermachers*, 2 vols. (Berlin: G. Reimer, 1870), 1:282. Cited by Michael Beddow, *The Fiction of Humanity: Studies in the Bildungsroman from Weiland to Thomas Mann* (Cambridge: Cambridge University Press, 1982), 1.

33. Wilhelm Dilthey, *Das Erlebnis und die Dichtung: Lessing, Goethe, Novalis, Hoklerlin* (Leipzig & Berne, 1913), 394. See Swales, German Bildungsroman, 3.

34. Swales, *German Bildungsroman*, 12.

35. Walter Hooper, ed., *See They Stand Together: The Letters of C. S. Lewis to Arthur Greeves* (1914-1963) (London: Collins, 1979), 92-93, 94, 96, 106, etc.

36. Beddow, *Fiction of Humanity*, 5.

37. For a fuller discussion of this sense see Kathleen Wheeler, ed., *German Aesthetic and Literary Criticism: The Romantic Ironists and Goethe* (Cambridge: Cambridge University Press, 1984), viii.

38. Ibid. This applies to nearly all the works called by Wheeler in this volume.

39. "On Goethe's Meister" (1798), cited by Wheeler, *German Aesthetic*, 64.

40. "The Old English Theatre" (1811), cited by Wheeler, German *Aesthetic*, 120.

41. For a further discussion of the implication of these two terms and their historical significance, see Stephen Prickett, *Words and the Word: Language, Poetics, and Biblical Interpretation* (Cambridge: Cambridge University Press, 1986), 83.

42. Goethe, *Wilhelm Meister*, 1:7.

43. William Wordsworth, *Preface to the Lyrical Ballads*, ed. R. L. Brett and A. R. Jones (London: Methuen, 1965), 249.

44. For an account of the impact of German literature in Edinburgh in the 1820s, see Ann-Marie Jordens, *The Stenhouse Circle* (Carlton: Melbourne University Press, 1979), ch. 1.

45. G. W. F. Hegel, *Vorlesungen über die Ästhetik*, ed. F. Bassenge (Berlin: Aufbau-Verlag 1955), 557-58. Cited by Swales, *The German Bildungsroman*, 20-21.

46. Swales, *The German Bildungsroman*, 21. As James Heffernan has pointed out, this is, of course, also the ending of Mel Brooks's *Young Frankenstein* ("Looking at the Monster," 142).

47. See Introduction, 2-3.

48. MacDonald, *Phantastes*, 166.

49. Ibid., 2:189.

50. Ibid., 2:415-16.

51. Ibid., 1:345.

52. For an extended discussion of this point without mentioning MacDonald, see Paul Coates, *The Realist Fantasy: Fiction and Reality Since Clarissa* (London; Macmillan, 1983).

53. See, for instance, Jerome Buckley, *Season of Youth: The Bildungsroman from Dickens to Golding* (Cambridge, Mass.: Harvard University Press, 1974). . . .

The Sources of *Phantastes*
John Docherty
From *North Wind: A Journal of George MacDonald Studies*

MacDonald's *Phantastes*, with its numerous literary allusions and its considerable autobiographical content, is a typical novel. In most other respects, of course, it is highly atypical, not least in its relationship to its sources. David Robb[1] suggests that "an awareness of sources does not merely help us to explain the work's genesis, but can conceivably take us to the heart of it." MacDonald quotes from many authors for his chapter headings. However, most of these quotations—with the notable exceptions of those from Novalis—seem to do no more than underscore what is already self-evident in MacDonald's text. Several could have prefaced almost any chapter. Robb[2] draws attention to the passage from Coleridge's "Dejection" ode which heads Chapter IX, noting that the alternation of Joy and Dejection is a major theme throughout *Phantastes*. This is true, but these contrasting moods are part of a deeper pattern of systole and diastole which MacDonald seems to borrow from the mainstream tradition of Scottish story telling.

Robb suggests that "Anodos's shadow seems to be MacDonald's version of Coleridge's Dejection." But it may be truer to say that MacDonald is responding to the criticism of the "Dejection" ode in Shelley's short collection of poems *Alastor* (1815). The first chapter of *Phantastes* is prefaced by a quotation from the final part of Shelley's title poem, where the poet seems to lose his avenging demon (his *Alastor*) as he approaches death. In this poem the demon is only alluded to obliquely. However, in "Oh! There are spirits of the air," a critical poem addressed to Coleridge in the same volume, Shelley describes an apparently similar demon as "This fiend whose ghastly presence ever / Beside thee like thy shadow hangs."

MacDonald seems to draw much of the character of Anodos from Shelley, as he appears as the protagonist of *Alastor*, reflecting his negative as well as his positive traits. He makes extensive use of inversion, so that, for example, the Shelley quotation heading the first chapter of *Phantastes* appears to allude primarily to the end of the story, just as the Novalis quotation heading the last chapter appears to allude primarily to the beginning. In *Phantastes*, MacDonald uses Shelley's *Alastor* as his starting point in an imaginative effort to penetrate the heart of the Romantic dilemma.

Crossing a Great Frontier

While some of MacDonald's chapter-head quotations have not been understood, the quotation he appends to his title has proved actually misleading. "Phantastes from 'their fount' all shapes deriving, / In new habiliments can quickly dight," is modified from Phineas Fletcher's *The Purple Island*. Phantastes, in Fletcher's allegory of the human body, is the creative imagination, one of the counsellors of the brain. However, Phantastes is not the only hero of MacDonald's story. The same stanza of Fletcher's also mentions old "Eumnestes," the memory, and Robb[3] explains the importance, in *Phantastes*, of the interaction of Phantastes and Eumnestes. MacDonald himself emphasises this in his exquisite myth of the dung beetles in Chapter IV. The behaviour of these beetles is a clever development of their traditional role as symbols of rebirth. The Egyptian Kephri daily brings the fructifying dunghall / sun to the world; MacDonald describes an opposite ritual. His beetles, in the evening, bring light to the dung, causing each fragment to shoot into the air as a glorious sky-rocket. (Of course, as true myth, the episode is not exhausted by extracting this one meaning. It is noteworthy, for example, that both sexes of beetle appear to be necessary to perform the operation.)

What is sometimes forgotten about MacDonald's allusion to Fletcher is that Fletcher borrows all his essential imagery from Spenser's allegory of the human body, the House of Alma, in Cantos IX to XI of Book II of *The Faerie Queene*. MacDonald presumably alludes to Fletcher's Phantastes because this character approximates more closely to his own conceptions than does Spenser's Phantastes. Otherwise, however, all MacDonald's very many borrowings from *The Faerie Queene* seem to be directly derived from Spenser, not via Fletcher. We should, it seems, take MacDonald's misquotation seriously and ourselves look to "the fount."

Spenserian symbolism is evident throughout *Phantastes*. The story proper begins in the second chapter with the much-quoted transformation scene, where Anodos's bedroom metamorphoses into a meadow. This is a literal fulfilment of Novalis's dictum that "*Unser Leben ist kein Traum, aber es soll und vielleicht einer werden*," but its immediate source appears to lie in the transformation scenes which were very popular in stage productions at that time. Ostentatious naturalism on the stage is less esteemed today. Nevertheless, we can accept such representations of the Ideal as the Ideal, because the naturalism is primarily intended to assist the imagination, not to deceive it. In Anodos's bedroom, however, art and nature seem to be interchangeable, and when this occurs we become deeply uneasy.

One of the best-known examples of utilisation of such unease for didactic purposes is Spenser's Bower of Bliss (F.Q. II, XII). Immediately upon encountering the artificial ivy the ordinary reader has an instinctive urge to see the bower torn down. And the naked young women whom we meet immediately afterwards are traditional inhabitants of "Enchanted Ground." MacDonald clearly wants us to believe that his Fairy Land is in a sense more real than the world Anodos leaves, yet ivy forms "the chief part" of the metamorphosing ornamentation on his furniture, and upon entering Fairy Land he is soon pursuing, if not a naked, at least a diaphanously-clad maiden.

MacDonald loved *The Faerie Queene* and could scarcely have forgotten Spenser's negative use of these symbols. It seems likely, therefore, that he is consciously opposing Spenser in order to disorient us and shake us into awareness. By temperament he was more prone to associate diaphanously-clad maidens with the Golden Age than with Acrasia's bower. The "ideal woman" pursued by Anodos seems to be one element in MacDonald's recreation of the theme of the fifth of Novalis's *Hymns to the Night*, which describes the Golden Age, its undermining by Fear, and Man's subsequent redemption through the sacrifice of Christ. This pattern recurs frequently in *Phantastes*. "Inversions" of episodes from *The Faerie Queene* are underpinned at a deep level by concepts derived from works of Novalis which MacDonald had himself translated.[4]

Robert Lee Wolff[5] recognises one such crucially important but inconspicuous allusion to Novalis. The marble lady whom Anodos sings into visibility in the fairy palace has some affinities with the maiden Shamefastnes whom Sir Guyon accosts in Alma's hall (*F.Q.* II, IX). However, Anodos addresses the lady as Isis, and Wolff points out that this is an allusion to where Hyacinth unveils Isis (Wisdom) and discovers Rosebud (Erotic love) in Novalis's parable *Hyacinth and Rosebud*. Wolff does not mention that the song Anodos sings draws upon Novalis's *Hymn*, the seventh of his *Sacred Songs*. Of this, Owen Barfield comments:[6]

> Is there not in this poem a certainty, a grounded *knowledge*? It is not content to stop in imagination and hint and suggestion. One feels that its meaning, its *openly expressed* meaning, reaches right down into the solid earth and right up into the empyrean. It is the resurrection of the body—in terms of the body.

MacDonald himself is attempting a similar stupendous Dantean resolution, but at the crucial moment Anodos fails him.

Crossing a Great Frontier

Only a few of MacDonald's allusions to *The Faerie Queene* can be mentioned here. Most are pieces of subtle self-parody based upon inversions. A good example occurs in Chapters XVIII and XIX where MacDonald inverts the image of Phaedria and her self-propelled boat (*F.Q.* II, VI) to describe Anodos's visit to the wise woman. Both accounts mark a major turning point in their respective narratives, and both Phaedria and the wise woman are at one with nature, although in very different ways. The depraved Cymochles finds "wondrous great contentment" in Phaedria's presence and in her boat, as does Anodos with the wise woman and in her boat; but the sober Sir Guyon does not!

Spenser's preference reproduces a letter to Raleigh indicating that he originally planned to describe the adventures of twelve knights exemplifying the twelve Aristotelian virtues. He never completed this plan, but it is reflected in reverse in the existing text where Maleger leads twelve battalions of vices against the House of Alma (*F.Q.* II, XI). Anodos is oblivious of any evil menacing *his* House of Alma, the "fairy palace." However, this palace contains twelve halls of dancers/statues representing shades of feeling. (These twelve satellite halls reappear as the mood chambers of the wise woman in *The Lost Princess*.) Presumably it is because MacDonald is describing only the areas of life which are the concern of *Phantastes* that his fairy palace is solely a palace of the feelings. Anodos, however, does experience "wilful" aspects of feeling when he pursues the marble lady out of the palace, and "intellectual" aspects of feeling in the library of the palace. And his paraphrasing of two books he reads in the library—as Chapters XII and XIII—recalls Spenser's paraphrasing of the two books which Prince Arthur and Sir Guyon read in the library of the House of Alma (*F.Q.*, II, X).

Spenser's proposed twelve knights were to depart upon their quests over the twelve days of Christmas. MacDonald, by a pun on this, seems to draw another element of his story from *Twelfth Night*. Both *Phantastes* and *Twelfth Night* portray the experience of a young man of high birth who pursues a lady who has "abjured the company and sight of men" but who ultimately weds a better man. Anodos, in switching from a feckless eroticism to what amounts to childish "purity,"[7] ignores the moral of Shakespeare's sub-plot—that both extremes of sexual pretension (exemplified in Sir Andrew and Malvolio) are equally ridiculous.

Anodos adopts his attitude of purity upon leaving the tower of self at the end of Chapter XXII, and subsequently in the story an understanding of the allusions to Spenser becomes particularly crucial. Anodos's first encounter after this is with his old acquaintance the knight, who is in the process of rescuing a babe. The life of the babe is seriously threatened because the knight is wasting precious time taking the body of the dragon which attacked it to display to the child's parents. When he does eventually get round to tend the babe's wounds, MacDonald's text draws directly upon the scene in *The Faerie Queene* where Calepine succors the babe he has rescued (*F.Q.* VI, IV). The crucial point is that Calepine is only able to rescue his babe because: "Well then his chaunst his heavy armes to want, / Whose burden mote empeach his needful speed." MacDonald's knight can make "but slow progress" because the great dragon is a great drag on his horse. The pun is intentional. And we realise we are expected also to laugh at the absurd Romantic trappings: idyllic setting; knight in shining armour; distraught parents in lowly cottage. The knight, valiant and loveable yet obtainless, ludicrous yet noble, must surely be based upon Cervantes's *Don Quixote*. It is noteworthy that we have only his own accounts of his exploits—all described in terms of wood chopping! Anodos nearly always accepts the knight's interpretation of events without question and ultimately becomes his Sancho Panza.

Robb[8] emphasises that "the sheer experience of entering the domain which MacDonald's imagination has created is the heart of what the book has to offer." As the story approaches its end MacDonald must begin to extricate his readers from this domain, encouraging us not simply to adopt Anodos's moral improvements as our own, but to recognise their limitations and, like Sir Guyon, strive for an outlook of Temperance.

For Anodos's final adventure in Fairy Land, MacDonald combines two opposite images from Spenser,[9] the Bower of Bliss and the Garden of Adonis (*F.Q.* II, XIII & III, VI). These are, respectively, negative and positive developments of the mediaeval image of Garden of Love, where the "rites of spring" were formalised into the conventions of courtly love. MacDonald builds up an image of utter decadence, where young people are thoughtlessly sacrificing themselves to an evil religion. Anodos gives to these young people an example of intelligent (far-seeing) self-sacrifice, and, as such, his overthrow of the idol is the culmination of his deeds in Fairy Land. However, his actions are also a terrible self-mutilation,[10] and his perception of events is decidedly biased.

In Spenser's Garden of Adonis, Venus has ensured that the boar is "firmly emprisoned for ay" beneath the central mount; in the outdoor temple Anodos visits, the werewolf beneath the central mount is appeased only by regular human sacrifices. Adonis exists "eterne in mutabilite"; the "king" whom Adonis overthrows is an idol, apparently "eterne" because wooden, but in fact rotten within. After overthrowing the Bower of Bliss, Sir Guyon embarks upon an orgy of destruction in the surrounding groves; after Anodos has overthrown the idol, the knight hews down "like brushwood" the great multitude of priests who rush up to the mount.

Anodos does not undertake the overthrow of the idol out of any sympathy for the youths and maidens, but because he feels the knight may be embarrassed on discovering that he has misunderstood the nature of the religious ceremony! Anodos is under some degree of mental strain, so we can excuse the alliteration in his description of the priest's reaction as one of "rath and revenge and rescue." However, we cannot help smiling when, immediately following this, he tells how there was "a universal hiss of steel, as every sword was swept from its scabbard." And, clearly, MacDonald *intends* us to smile. Subsequently, Anodos's descriptions of his burial is as fine as anything MacDonald ever wrote on "good death." Thus it is extremely disconcerting for the reader when this passage passes into a comic parody of an adolescent fantasy[11] with Anodos's description of the knight and lady weeping over his coffin. This bears no relation to the standard technique of introducing humour directly *after* scenes of high drama, nor to the technique of having an ever-present irony behind the seriousness. It may be an example of Novalis's "*zusammenhangen*," but, if so, is very different from Novalis's use of the concept. More probably it is another deliberate attempt by MacDonald to disorient his readers.

This bathos prepares the reader for Anodos's ultimate insufferable presumption when, floating upon his cloud, he declaims about all the good he intends for suffering humanity. To have him disappear in (literally) a cloud of glory would be contrary to MacDonald's desire to make *Phantastes* a never-ending story. Moreover, Anodos, like the Ancient Mariner, has to be returned alive to be able to tell his story. The comic self-depreciation MacDonald employs here recalls similar techniques used by traditional tellers of fairy tales to close a story and bring the listeners down to earth. However, Anodos's description of his physical symptoms as he leaves Fairy Land is clearly based upon accounts by people who have undergone near-death experiences. In a similar way, his description of the flower-fairies at the beginning of his adventures is, as he claims, in accord with other first-hand reports. These two framing episodes are intended to give an ironic verisimilitude to the story.

It is not particularly remarkable that MacDonald should parody the very ideals he wishes to affirm. Charles Kingsley, for example, does this in *The Water-Babies* (1864). MacDonald was probably inspired by the blend of passionate advocacy and satire in Carlyle's *Sartor Resartus* and, even more, by the style of E.T.A. Hoffmann's fictional writings. Ruskin told MacDonald apropos *The Light Princess*: "you see too deeply into things to be able to laugh nicely,"[12] but depth of perception and boisterous humour are not incompatible; Kingsley's principal source is Rabelais's *Gargantua*, with its comparable combination of both qualities. The humour of Hoffmann, however, is much more subtle, and is closely associated with the other emotions, as well as with the intellect. Either deliberately or unconsciously, MacDonald appears to be attempting to model elements of his style upon Hoffmann's, but in *Phantastes* his shock tactics work against an integration of his humour with his mythopoeia. C. S. Lewis, profoundly affected by the mythopoeia, argues that one can throw the rest away.[13] Many readers probably fare far worse than Lewis, like him rejecting the bathos and other elements of the self-satire as incompetence, but because of this discarding the book without penetrating to the mythopoeia. MacDonald in his later stories does not give up shock tactics, but they are better orchestrated.

In the course of developing his own style out of that of Hoffmann, MacDonald borrows many of Hoffmann's images, but most of his borrowings are not true allusion since a study of the originals does not appreciably enhance one's understanding of MacDonald's text. (In *The Golden Key*, MacDonald seems to forget he has borrowed from Hoffmann, believing Novalis to be the source for an image which actually comes from the first chapter of Hoffmann's *The Devil's Elixirs*.)

The differences between the ways MacDonald borrows from Spenser, Novalis and Hoffmann are considerable, and this applies also to his borrowings from other authors. For example, with *The Divine Comedy*, another of MacDonald's great loves, he copies Dante's Trinitarian framework,[14] but apparently without borrowing any details of incidents from the work.

In that *Phantastes* is a tale of spiritual search and knightly deeds, MacDonald could scarcely ignore Malory, but, in his allusions to the *Morte d'Arthur*, Malory's characters are recognised as characters from a tale. This is very like Spenser's distanced attitude to Mallory.[15] In Chapter III Anodos reads a story written in the style of the *Morte d'Arthur* which alludes to an episode in Chapter X of Book XIV of

Malory's work. The knight refers to this later in the story when he asks Anodos: "'hast thou . . . ever read the story of Sir Percival . . . as it befell him, so has it befallen to me.'" This is unequivocal, yet, strangely, nearly all critics except Wolff refer to the knight as "Sir Percival"! Later again, in Chapter XIX, the wise woman sings the beautiful "Ballad of Sir Aglovaile." And, since Malory's Sir Aglevaile is the brother of Percival, MacDonald's allusions here may be no less deep than those to *The Faerie Queene*.

To consider the Bible as one of the extrinsic sources drawn upon by MacDonald makes little sense, since its teachings are as much a part of him as, for example, is his knowledge of basic syntax. However, one can recognise in *Phantastes* echoes of passages in the Bible where a general teaching is brought into particularly sharp focus. The most notable is Anodos's desire "to be a child again" when imprisoned in the tower of self, which is a total misrepresentation of Christ's teaching that we should become as little children. Also, *Phantastes* has a direct inversion of a biblical text where the ogre woman reads an inversion of John I in Chapter VIII.

Robb[16] makes the interesting suggestion that *Phantastes* may embody a deliberate inversion of Matthew Arnold's view in "Dover Beach" that:

> the world, which seems
> To lie before us like a world of dreams
> So various, so beautiful, so new
> Hath really neither joy, nor love, nor light,
> Nor certitude, nor peace, nor help for pain.

Robb conjectures that a passage in the opening chapter of *Phantastes* is a deliberate reflection of the tranquil opening of "Dover Beach." The story opens with Anodos recalling coming into his material inheritance. On the threshold of the great desk which symbolises this inheritance a "woman-form" appears who, in a sense, symbolises his "spiritual inheritance." At first the creature—Anodos's fairy grandmother—appears to him as tiny, but her eyes soon engulf him:

> They filled me with an unknown longing. I remembered somehow that my mother died when I was a baby. I looked deeper and deeper, till they spread around me like seas, and I sank in their waters. I forget all the rest, till I found myself at the window, whose gloomy curtains were withdrawn, and where I stood gazing on a whole heaven of stars, small and sparkling in the moonlight. Below lay a sea, still as death

and hoary as the moon, sweeping away into bays and around capes and islands, away, away.

"Dover Beach" begins:

> The sea is calm tonight.
> The tide is full, the moon lies fair
> Upon the straits;—on the French coast the light
> Gleams and is gone; the cliffs of England stand,
> Glimmering and vast, out in the tranquil bay.
> Come to the window, sweet is the night air!

Robb's suggestion seems highly likely, since the reflection of the moonlight is not the only double reflection in MacDonald's text at that point. Anodos is looking out of the window of a room strange to him, he has just been comforted in an unusual fashion by a previously unknown relative, and he recalls his dead mother. This must surely reflect David Copperfield's experience at Miss Trotwood's villa in Chapter XIII of Dickens's story. At the end of that chapter David recalls looking out of the window of the room he was given: "I remember how I still sat looking at the moonlight on the water, as if I could hope to read my fortune in it, as in a bright book, or see my mother with her child, coming from heaven along that shining path . . . I seemed to float, then, down the melancholy glory of that track upon the sea, away into the world of dreams." And Miss Trotwood's villa overlooks . . . Dover beach!

There must be many other literary allusions in *Phantastes* which, if recognised, would contribute greatly to our appreciation of the story. William Raeper, for example, shows that MacDonald introduces a note of humorous irony at the very beginning. Anodos's fairy grandmother—herself a humorous substitution for the more usual fairy godmother—alludes to a popular farce of the time—*You Can't Marry Your Grandmother*.[17]

Most critics recognise that, in *Phantastes*, autobiographical sources are in some respects as important as the literary sources. For example, the source of the battle with the three rather stupid giants in Chapter XXI is probably MacDonald's battle with the Arundel deacons—as representatives of a particularly religious outlook—transposed into traditional fairy-tale imagery. The valiant little tailor of fairy tales primarily represents the intellect. Since the garment Anodos fashions during his apprenticeship with the king's sons is "a shirt of steel plates and rings," we may take it that his intellect is something out of the ordinary! His subsequent social successes at the court may, at this autobiographical level, recall the many female admirers MacDonald attracted by his lecturing.

Chapter XXIII seems to begin with biography rather than autobiography. The description of the knight's rescue of the babe looks very like the portrait of a social worker whose tendency to romanticise his work sometimes has near-fatal consequences for his clients! MacDonald had been involved with social workers in Manchester in 1854, and also had contact with such people through F. D. Maurice. Subsequently in Chapter XXIII, in a wonderful and unique allegory, the knight describes to Anodos how he assisted a striving young person against stupid didacticism, standing faceless wooden men on their heads when they threatened the imaginative integrity of the child. His description of the beggar-child is highly reminiscent of Lewis Carroll's famous 1858 photograph of Alice Liddell as a beggar-girl (a photograph which Tennyson described as the most beautiful he had ever seen). The knight's behaviour towards this child is likewise reminiscent of Carroll's attitude towards Alice. For example, the knight is confused by the child's incipient wings, which, at one level, certainly symbolise an emerging sexuality. The knight's thoughtful behaviour in this episode is totally out of character with his personality as depicted in the rest of the book, and the whole episode gives every indication of being a late insertion. Robb,[18] on the basis of other photographic evidence, suggests that MacDonald and Carroll had become friends before *Phantastes* finally went to the printers. Carroll did not get to know the MacDonald children, with the possible exception of the eldest, Lilia, until 1860, when he met Greville and Mary at Alexander Munro's London studio. However, this is easily explained by the strict discipline which prevailed at the MacDonald's home in Hastings.[19]

What makes *Phantastes* so remarkable a work is the extent of MacDonald's reliance upon his own Phantastes to create his images and, equally, the depth of his understanding of other writers—particularly of Dante, Novalis and Spenser—and the way this enables him to create a complex dynamic structure for the material generated by his unconscious. As a writer in the Romantic tradition, he seeks to relate his own experience, including the experiences he has gained from literature, to his world picture; thus gaining a better understanding of the latter and assisting his readers to do the same for themselves. Clearly *Phantastes* does not represent a total assimilation of all the important experiences in MacDonald's life and reading up to the time it was written, still less does it comprehend an exhaustive statement of his future aims. MacDonald attempts no less, but he is still too close to much of his experience to achieve that synthesis of attachment and detachment for which he strives. Yet, without the catharsis he achieved completely through the creation of Phantastes, he would never have been able to write such superbly balanced and positive stories as *The Light Princess* and *Cross Purposes* a few years later.

Endnotes

1. David Robb, *George MacDonald* (Edinburgh, Scottish Academic Press, 1987, p. 91).
2. Robb (op.cit., pp. 83-4).
3. Robb (op.cit., pp. 91-94).
4. MacDonald's Novalis translations were published in *Exotics* (1876) and reprinted with revisions in *Rampolli* (1897).
5. Robert Lee Wolff, *The Golden Key* (New Haven, Yale U.P., 1961 p.86).
6. Owen Barfield, *Of the Intellectual Soul, in Romanticism Comes of Age* (London, Anthroposophical Publishing Co., 1944).
7. John Docherty, "A Note on the Structure and Conclusion of *Phantastes*," *North Wind*, VII, (1988, pp.25-30).
8. Robb (op.cit., p.86).
9. MacDonald here also borrows from (but does not seem to allude to) the temple with its monster in *F.Q.* V, XI.
10. Docherty (op.cit.).
11. Wolff (op.cit.) recognises the adolescent fantasy, although not as a parody.
12. Letter of 22/7/63 quoted by William Raeper in *George MacDonald* (Tring, Lion, 1987, p. 222).

13. C. S. Lewis, *George MacDonald, An Anthology* (London, Geoffrey Bles, 1946, pp.14-16). Illogically, Lewis goes on to maintain (p. 21) that "There was no question of getting through to the kernel and throwing away the shell; no question of a gilded pill. The pill was gold all through"!

14. Docherty (op.cit.).

15. Vide C S. Lewis, *English Literature in the Sixteenth Century, Excluding Drama*, (Oxford, O.U.P., 1954, pp. 381-2).

16. Robb (op. cit. pp. 80-3).

17. Raeper (op.cit., p.4 01).

18. David S. Robb, "The Fiction of George MacDonald," *VII*, VI, (1985).

19. The effects of this discipline are charmingly described by a lady visitor who is quoted by Greville in his biography of his parents and by Raphael Shaberman in "George MacDonald and Lewis Carroll," *North Wind*, I (1982, p.10).

The Community of the Centre: Structure and Theme in *Phantastes*
Roderick McGillis
From *For the Childlike*

My title derives from chapter 12 of George MacDonald's *Phantastes* (1858). Here MacDonald writes: "The community of the centre of all creation suggests an interradiating connection and dependence of the parts." The sentence is helpful in many ways: we understand MacDonald's notion of multiplicity of dimensions interpenetrating and inter-influencing; we understand that all creation is within a centre and hence all created things are special; at the same time, we understand that individuals are part of a larger entity, a community of the centre. The familiar Romantic paradox of unity in multeity takes yet another expression. A "centre" also suggests inwardness. Something in the centre, something beyond the capability of scientific thought to tabulate or to formulate into an "external law" is at work in the universe bringing creation together. This community of the centre, best articulated in literary fantasy, is a way of knowing that brings humanity together in harmonious variety. This way of knowing is not antirational, but it is imaginative rather than ratiocinative.

Let me explain this point. The passage I began with is from a story that Anodos reads in the library of the Fairy Palace. The story is about "a world that is not like ours," and Anodos cannot recall whether or not the story "was all a poem." The story, as he relates it, is partly in prose and partly in verse. Clearly, this other world is meant to "befull of mysterious revelations of other connexions with the worlds around us." Quite simply, the story warns us that unfulfilled desires breed pestilence. The lives of the people of this planet are long, lonely, and tedious. But this is not the only interesting aspect of the story. How can a revelation be mysterious? What is revealed is uncovered, shown for what it is. Sex is a joy! Yet, as Anodos's overactive libido points up, sex can be joyless, an expression of thoughtless self-gratification. The story teaches Anodos that desire need not be ugly, but that it may be ugly, and certainly it will be so perceived by angelic women, white ladies, and the like.

The story also teaches him about literature. While reading the story, Anodos discovers that he participates in it. In fact, he becomes a character in the action. This happens when he becomes a visitor to the strange land, and it happens again more clearly in the story of Cosmo von Wehrstahl. Reading this second story, Anodos "was Cosmo, and his history was mine." Reader participation, MacDonald says, breeds a "double consciousness" that perceives a "double meaning" in the story, perhaps a personal meaning and a universal meaning. In other words, the story of the strange planet has application to Anodos's particular problem in understanding his desires, and it also applies to the human condition. But the story also draws the reader into a centre, the story. As a detached, analytical reader, Anodos would be outside the centre, at the circumference of the book, but by moving into the story he enters a centre that welcomes all readers who are willing to go beyond the book as formal object and know it from inside. This kind of knowing means having sympathy with the story and understanding how it works. The moral truths apparent in the themes of selfishness and love (evident in both stories read by Anodos in the library) are of less importance than the knowledge that the stories themselves offer. They teach us to know our imaginations. Such knowledge humanizes: to know not only how our minds function, but also to know that literature brings us out of ourselves and into a community of shared images, themes, characters, etc. is to participate in a humane imaginative enterprise. Knowledge gained through story is not irrational or anti-intellectual; it is the result of imaginative sympathy and imaginative understanding. The subjective response and the objective one have validity in relationship.

 This is why the revelations are, paradoxically, mysterious. What stories attempt to reveal is beyond the capability of language to articulate. This explains why the story of the strange planet is partly in verse and partly in prose. MacDonald directs our attention to language in its metaphoric role. Literature communicates through image and metaphor, not through concept or abstraction. Yet the quest for the image is endless. MacDonald reminds us throughout his work that what we gain from literature is comforting, but not final. Literature does not realize apocalypse, but it can tell us how to understand apocalypse, not as historic fact but as human possibility. Shelley's *Epipsychidion* comes to mind as a work close to *Phantastes*, not only in incident, but also in mood. It is hopeful, yet sceptical. Shelley's poem presses language to the limits; it attempts to articulate that deep truth which is imageless. But this entails reducing the imageless to the image, and consequently poetry always fails to present deep truth; it must mediate vision. If it didn't, there would be no need for more poems. Anodos must return from his death in Fairy Land in order for this point to be made clear. Once back at his own home, Anodos tells us that in Fairy Land he both found and lost his Shadow. One does not, however, lose one's shadow; one incorporates it. Literature reminds us of dualisms such as shadow and self, and it also reconciles them. But can we reconcile them? *Phantastes* closes with the question: "Could I translate the experience of my travels there (in Fairy Land), into common life?"

Fairy Land, or what we might simply call poetry, provides a community of the centre, a place where the imagination is freed from the pressures of desire and convention. This is why Anodos spends so much time reading the "wondrous volumes" in the Fairy Palace Library. In this way, he gains knowledge of himself and of himself in relation to others. The two stories he relates to us illustrate the difference between self-centeredness and the community of the centre. The angel-woman in the first story dies because she will not accept the desire that brings us out of ourselves; and Cosmo in the second story learns that the mirror that encloses the lady must be shattered before true union is possible. The circle he draws when conjuring the lady from the mirror signifies separation, not community. Only by breaking circles of selfhood can we enter centres of community.

The sentence we began with has provided us with a clue to a thematic aspect of the book. It helps us understand the references to mirrors, lakes, reflections, Shadow, globes, circles, and other images of enclosure that abound in the book. All such centres must be shattered in order that a larger community of the centre be revealed. The community of the centre works, then, on at least two levels: the human and the poetic. Anodos is a self-centered young man whose experiences teach him that he is not alone in the universe. His Shadow attempts to keep Anodos from a knowledge of the individuality of others by presenting others as objects, dark fragments of a universe detached from the self. Anodos is at the centre of his world and everything else is outside and useful only as it can gratify his desires. In other words, the Shadow narrows and darkens Anodos's perceptions. Fairy Land (call it poetry or imaginative experience) finally cleanses Anodos's perceptions. He dies. His death gains him entry into the true centre of the universe which is the community of the centre, at once centre and circumference. This ties in with poetry because Anodos's experience is clearly "poetic": he sings many songs; he is a poet. And the true poet, as MacDonald's poem "Of the Son of Man" (1852) makes clear, is "a living lyre" (*Poetical Works*, vol. 2, 269-275); he poeticizes the universe by realizing in life what is searched for in art. Syllables become deeds. However, Anodos returns to this life, and the struggle begins again. The poem, Fairy Land, gives hope—a hope, as Shelley presents it in

Epipsychidion—that poetry and love build a world divine, if not here, then beyond the grave.

What we are seeing in all this is not merely a theme, but also a structure. *Phantastes* has always been deemed a structureless book, sometimes even a confusing one. The *Athenæum* review is well known; it calls *Phantastes* a "Wilderness of wilderment" (580).The *Spectator* reviewer finds himself "in the wildest regions of fairy and fancy" (286), while the *British Quarterly Review* cautions some readers that "a verdict of 'determination of nonsense to the brain'" (296-297) may be the result of reading *Phantastes*. Even a favorable review in *The Globe* indicates a quality of "dreaminess" and "seeming incoherence," although it does not find these defects. An appreciation by E. S. Robertson in 1906 (308-309) accepts the notion of incoherence that MacDonald offers in his epigraph from Novalis finding such mistiness a beauty; after all, shouldn't art aspire to the condition of music?

Even more recent commentators, although differing in their attitude toward incoherence, perceive in *Phantastes* an aimless structure. W. H. Auden implies that *Phantastes*' "allegorical structure" is loose: "there seems no particular reason, one feels, why Anodos should have just the number of adventures he does have." Richard Reis calls the structure "loose" and suggests we are to allegorize the incidents as events in Anodos's childhood, but as Reis admits, "this is not easy to do" (90). He concludes that the "looseness and unevenness of *Phantastes* must be counted as defects" (94). Colin Manlove, in a closely argued chapter on MacDonald in *Modern Fantasy*, says *Phantastes* is "perhaps" MacDonald's "most disconnected" fairy tale (75). More recently, in discussing the circularity of *Phantastes* and *Lilith*, Manlove has described *Phantastes* as "centrifugal" (85). In my reading, it is centripetal and centrifugal. Max Keith Sutton, in a reading that considers Freudian, Jungian, and Kohutian paradigms, refers to "the disorderly nature of the alleged dream which forms the story" (12). And Joseph Sigman, in what is the most complete reading yet of *Phantastes*, finds structure through applying a Jungian paradigm to the book. Consequently, he reads through the episodes from beginning to end to correlate the images with Jung's individuation process. This can appear neat, but why apply apriori structures to a book that provides us with its own structural pattern, a structural pattern that turns out to be poetic rather than psychological? What I mean by this is simply that the structure of the book teaches us to understand what the book means. Structure reflects image and like images it is a way of communicating meaning.

For example, just prior to Anodos's journey to the Fairy Palace he finds his Shadow in a cottage situated in a forest clearing. This cottage, with its cypress tree at one end, is the structural counterpart of the oak tree-cornered cottage Anodos comes upon when he first enters Fairy Land. In the second half of the book, however, there are two more cottages which, structurally, balance the two in the first half: the island cottage with four doors, and the tower that imprisons Anodos. The first of these recalls the oak tree cottage, and the second should remind us that the cypress tree rose at one end of its cottage "like a spire to the building." Two cottages represent hospitality, protection, and nurture; the cypress cottage and the tower represent selfhood, vulnerability, and despair. In every case, the building is a centre, but a polarity exists between a dark, enclosed centre and a bright, expansive centre. The cottage as enclosure in self-centeredness is apparent when Anodos enters the cypress tree cottage. The place has no windows. The woman inside reads, head down, by a reddish light. The place is dim. Negation abides here. Anodos finds his own dark self lurking within.

Opposite to this is the cottage of the old lady who spins in chapter 19. MacDonald's creation of this still centre is as fine an example of what he means by the community of the centre as any in the book. Whereas the notion of permanence in the earlier cottage centred on the book and its doctrine of darkness, here permanence is given a human centre. On a flat island in the sea, Anodos finds a homely cottage, windowless like the earlier one, but differing in essential import. This cottage is an eternal centre in a sea of mutability. Mutability is also apparent in the "few plants of the gumcistus, which drops every night all the blossoms that the day brings forth," that grow near the cottage. Inside sits an old woman who spins by a fire, instead of reading by a lamp. She is old, but beautiful; her eyes are the eyes of a twenty-five-year old. She welcomes Anodos and feeds him like a baby. Later, she sings him an old ballad and then spins; her spinning is musical. (The image is an inversion of the folk tale motif of the spinning witch or wise woman; she becomes for MacDonald a *god*-mother. Compare his *The Princess and the Goblin*, 1872.) Whereas the hag in the earlier cottage reads sophistic philosophy, this lady warms Anodos with poetry. And instead of one door that leads to the narrow closet of the self, this cottage has four doors of tears, of sighs, of dismay, and of the timeless[1] that take Anodos in stages toward an experience of complete integration. Together they reflect wholeness, symbolized by the cottage itself with its maternal and poetic centre. Anodos's experience here does not darken him to others; it reconciles his inner and outer selves. The cottage is a centre from which Anodos explores his past, present, and future; it is a centre of serenity he must learn to internalize if he wishes to get beyond enslavement to his desires and fears. That familiar Romantic paradigm of self-consciousness leading to anti-self-consciousness finds expression in this cottage. Even the sign ∾ that marks the entrance to the cottage through its four doors reflects the idea of an open circle. The circularity of this mark is countered by its open ends that stretch outward. The sign suggests embrace, but not enclosure. Here is the community of the centre: the willingness—indeed, the desire—to embrace others, yet the refusal to bind them to us. This is what the old wise woman does; she willingly succours Anodos, she sacrifices her island for him, and she does this in order not to keep him with her. It is with wisdom that MacDonald chooses a mother for his metaphor of a centre that does not restrict. Mothers remain centres of emotion and understanding for children even while they teach them independence.

Thematically, this incident in the cottage with four doors articulates the community of the centre. Structurally, it balances earlier episodes dealing with the same theme and carries those episodes a stage further. It reminds us that each episode is a centre whose meaning radiates to that larger centre of meaning, the book. Finally, the images—fire, spinning *wheel*, cottage, mother, door— communicate themes and structures: the cottage is a centre of poetry, warmth, selflessness, and natural harmony. What happens in this episode—Anodos learns about himself and experiences love and death—is what happens in the romance as a whole. What should be evident in all this is that the community of the centre as a thematic element provides a way of structuring the book; we need not look elsewhere for help in reading *Phantastes*. The community of the centre is a clue to that structure, both in a thematic sense and in a more strictly "structural" sense. We have already seen the thematic manifestation of this structure in the stories of the strange planet and Cosmo, in the role of the Shadow, and in the incident in the cottage of four doors. But perhaps another example will help prepare us for a move from theme to structure, a move that will illustrate the fact that structure is theme. This is the episode of the country maiden.

The country maiden appears twice in the book, once shortly after Anodos has found his Shadow, and again after he and his dreaded Shadow are locked together in a tower. Incidentally, the first of these appearances occurs one chapter before Anodos lands at the Fairy

Palace and three chapters before the middle of the book, while the second appearance occurs one chapter before Anodos's death and three chapters before the end of the book. This sequence ought to suggest that some structural principle is at work, and as we will see later, such a suggestion is absolutely correct.

Before recounting his first meeting with the country maiden, Anodos tells us that the incident "quite cured" him of his fascination for the Shadow. What he does not grasp at the time is the significance of the event beyond its obvious sexual moral. The ultimate significance he could not know at least until he had read the stories in the Fairy Palace Library. Until he reads these, he, and we, can have only partial knowledge of what has happened. But what does happen? The little maiden joins Anodos "One bright noon" as he proceeds on his path through a forest. She is both childlike and womanly, suggesting, as in so many fairy tales, that she is ready to learn the sad truth of what it means to be a woman. She carries a "small globe" which is as bright "as purest crystal." To this she is devoted. In fact, the crystal globe, like Blake's crystal cabinet, keeps the maiden in her child world; Anodos says the maiden "produced on me more the impression of a child, though my understanding told me differently." Anodos and the maiden travel together by day, but separate discreetly at night. But by day the maiden proves a coy mistress, "smiling almost invitingly" at Anodos when he desires to touch the globe. First she tells him he must not touch it, then she changes her mind. When touched the globe emits "a tiny torrent of harmony." The globe is the self-enclosed, artificial and selfish world of childhood. Anodos, influenced by his Shadow, sees the globe as a desirable object, something to gratify his senses; he lusts after it. Clearly his reaction is judged wanting, but so is the girl's.

The maiden and the man satirize each other, as do Blake's states of innocence and experience. Close reading of the passage reveals the complexity of the reactions on the part of the two characters, but without either a reading of the two stories in the Fairy Palace Library or a reading of the maiden's return later in chapter 22, the full implication of the incident is not apparent. We are left, again as in Blake's "Crystal Cabinet," with the notion that the libido casts us out of childhood; it breaks the illusion of a safe, harmonious world. The maiden's wail, "You have broken my globe, my globe is broken," is a complaint against an unregenerate Anodos. What is not yet manifest is that the breaking of the globe constitutes the necessary prelude to the removal of the self as centre to a larger community of the centre.

Crossing a Great Frontier

The two stories that Anodos recounts prepare us for the return of the maiden. The first, as we have seen, illustrates the inchoate existence of life without fulfilled desires, and the second tells us that Cosmo can love completely only by accepting sacrifice, separation, and death. He learns, however, that "good" death is not separation, but completion. For the Lady, the breaking of the mirror is liberation, but also sorrow. We will see what this sorrow can mean when the country maiden returns.

Much later in the book, after his triumphant battle with a Giant, Anodos lapses into pride and finds himself locked in a tower with his shadow. The country maiden now returns. She proves the regeneration of Anodos. As he lies in his self-prison, Anodos experiences by day the agony of self-hate under the cold glare of sun, and by night the release of moonlight dreams. During one of his nightly dreams, he wishes he were a child again, "innocent, fearless, without shame or desire." The next day, "about noon," he hears "the voice of a woman singing." The song refreshes and cleanses him; its effect is reminiscent of the bath Irene takes in her great-great-grandmother's bedroom in *The Princess and the Goblin*. It "unmans" (MacDonald's word) him; that is, it returns him to childhood innocence in order to regenerate him. He is reborn! The song that accomplishes all this ends with two lines that recapitulate our theme:

> From the narrow desert, O man of pride,
> Come into the house, so high and wide.

The tower is a "narrow desert," a centre of self-waste; what lies outside the tower (Fairy Land) is a house that contains many mansions, each a centre of a larger centre.

The song's invitation works mysteriously, and Anodos opens the door. Outside he sees a "beautiful woman" who turns out to be the maiden whose globe he had broken. She tells him her story which sounds remarkably similar to his. Her globe broken, she took the pieces to the Fairy Queen, who merely took them and put them aside, presumably as childish things. Then the Fairy Queen made the maiden "go to sleep in a great hall of white, with black pillars, and many red curtains." Upon waking in the morning, the maiden leaves the house without her globe, no longer feeling the need for it. She has, she says, "something so much better." Sorrow has proved beneficial, providing a necessary fall from innocence. After all, Mr. Vane is right when he says the Little Ones in *Lilith* are incomplete. They know nothing of sorrow and therefore they cannot be fully human. The fairy maiden is now a poet whose songs are deeds that deliver people. She now lives by her songs which manifest her relationship with others; with "room to roam" she has found that there is "only one home / For all the world to win."

The community of the centre waits for Anodos. By merely opening the door to his tower, he leaves it behind, and soon—by offering himself in a gesture of self-sacrifice—he attains the community. Lying dead in the bosom of the earth, Anodos enjoys participating in "the whole earth, and each of her many births." He has gone one better than the maiden. She sings of relationship; he experiences relationship. Anodos enters flowers, floats above the earth, and feels a limitless power of understanding and sympathy. This is possible, however, "in the realms of lofty Death." He returns to earth; he dies into moral life to continue his "more limited" bodily life. Here he can only hope to translate his experiences in Fairy Land into action, to further a day when a true community will exist.

What the book deals with, then, is what Keats calls "Identity." *Phantastes*, as its many references to Novalis, Wordsworth, Shelley, Coleridge, Schiller, Heine, and other of their contemporaries suggests, is a "Romantic" statement. It deals with the struggle to attain consciousness and to overcome self-consciousness. It reconciles opposites. It tries to intellectualize the imagination, to reassociate sensibility. A famous passage in Shelley's *Defence of Poetry* provides a gloss on MacDonald's book:

> The great secret of morals is love; or a going out of our nature, and an identification of ourselves with the beautiful which exists in thought, action, or person, not our own. A man, to be greatly good, must imagine intensely and comprehensively; he must put himself in the place of another and of many others; the pains and pleasures of his species must become his own. The great instrument of moral good is the imagination; and poetry administers to the effect by acting upon the cause. Poetry enlarges the circumference of the imagination by replenishing it with thoughts of ever new delight, which have the power of attracting and assimilating to their own nature all other thoughts, and which form new intervals and interstices whose voice forever craves fresh food. (Shelley 487-488)

The mention of "circumference" reminds us of our theme. This widening of our vision is not mere emotionalism. Rather it is a way of knowing. As MacDonald writes in his essay, "The Imagination," we can know a flower in two ways: the way of the botanist who tears it to shreds, and the way of the poet who understands what the flower is by understanding imagery.² And we can only know this by understanding the different imagery possible in flowers and weeds, and knowing further that these images are products of our imaginations. The garden of flower fairies offers Anodos a lesson in selfishness, possession, and class that is merely an expression of what he already knows but only now has the strength to imagine.

Since the book is so clearly structured around this theme of a centre, it is reasonable to look more closely at the structure itself to see whether it communicates to us in this imaginative way. As we have seen, most readers look for an order and a progression of incidents unfolding logically from beginning to end, and most readers are disappointed when they discover a looseness about MacDonald's plotting.³ This looseness, however, will only appear if we read the book in a conventional manner, something we inevitably do on a first reading. Once we have the whole book in our minds a different structure begins to take shape, a structure based on the notion of a centre. M. H. Abrams has taught us to read Romantic works as spiral journeys beginning where they end, but ending on a higher level of consciousness. This is brilliant and instructive. I should, however, like to adjust this pattern by shifting attention not to beginning and ending, but to the centre. The structure I suggest is apparent in such Romantic texts as *The Rime of the Ancient Mariner*, *The Prelude*, *La Belle Dame Sans Merci*, and *Heinrich von Ofterdingen*. MacDonald undoubtedly got his structure from Novalis's unfinished romance where it is both clearer and more complex than in *Phantastes*. The idea of the community of the centre is, of course, pervasive in Romantic works.

Phantastes has twenty-five chapters. Chapter 13, the central chapter in the book, contains the story of Cosmo von Wehrstahl. Cosmo's name is a clue to the theme of centre and circumference. In this central chapter Anodos, who claims he is Cosmo, learns the true nature of love as a going out of ourselves. Cosmo dies with a smile on his face; he has attained his desire: relationship and community. This central chapter looks backwards and forwards. The book both moves towards this centre and away from it, expressing the idea that the revelation presented here is not final. Romanticism constantly reminds us that we move towards revelation and back from it. Revelations constitute good moments, eternal centres amid the flux of events in time and space. This central chapter in *Phantastes* tells us we move toward death, but before we die, we ought to strive for constant rebirth within the mutable world. At the end of *Phantastes*, Anodos returns a new man, but he faces the task of maintaining his newness until he achieves the "great good" which is evident in the smile on Cosmo's dead lips.

However, the importance of the centre is clearer still. Chapters 10 through 16, the middle seven chapters, leaving nine on either side, take place in the Fairy Palace. The first three chapters of this group (10 to 12) recount Anodos's arrival at the Palace and his exploration of it. The centre chapter takes place in the Palace Library. The final three chapters (14 to 16) tell of the dancing statues and the veiled maiden. The Palace is an ideal. In it Anodos is fed and refreshed. He is instructed through literature and art, but he departs because he has not yet achieved the permanence of the image. He shares Cosmo's experiences, but he wants the marble lady to share his experiences. His selfish desire cannot end happily. He brings the lady to life through the power of song, but he drops poetry for sexuality and loses her. But the Fairy Palace has served its purpose; in it the dance continues. In art we find relaxation, relationship, and freedom from false desires. By reducing art to sensual life, we profane it.

The art/life complex also divides on either side of this centre. Chapters 1 to 9 deal with, among other things, Anodos's attitude toward women. He idealizes them. For example, the lady which he perceives in a block of alabaster is "more near the face that had been born with me in my soul, than anything I had seen before in nature or art." His interest is in females that represent art (marble lady), fairyland (the tiny fairy in chapter 1), or childhood (the country maiden). When he falls willing victim to the Alder-Maiden, he mistakes his ideal for a natural woman, a femme fatale who incorporates throughout Romantic poetry the notion of nature as object as separate from us and as desirable. Anodos succumbs to the actual, to the fiction that the natural world has an existence separate from him. His stay in the Fairy Palace ought to tell him that all things exist together as products of the human imagination. Ideals remain ideals and only wither when we touch them. This is the problem raised by all Romantic literature. If ideals are to benefit us they must be actualized. And any actualization can only reduce them much as criticism inevitably reduces art.

The second part of the book, after Anodos leaves the Fairy Palace, not only confronts Anodos with his past (in the episode in the Old Woman's cottage with the four doors), but also with his desire for an ideal woman. He learns that the marble lady is, in fact, a lady of flesh and blood complete with a lover. He learns to accept this and love the lady anyway. He meets the country maiden, now a full-grown woman dedicated to her art. He is welcomed back home by his sisters. He must accept the female for what she is, another human being with worries and responsibilities just like him. Both male and female must strive to achieve an ideal, not to reduce an ideal to their level. And perhaps they can work together strengthening each other. Sir Percivale and the lady would seem to substantiate this.

What this examination hopes to illustrate is that the structure of *Phantastes* is not accidental. In directing our attention both toward the central chapter and chapters and out toward the beginning and ending, the structure reflects a prominent theme: the community of the centre. Each episode in this episodic book not only repeats ideas but also clarifies them. Anodos's adventures lead him towards a centre where he is alone and not alone. He must learn to tell the difference between being alone and sharing his existence with others. The book, by directing us inward and outward at the same time, reminds us that at the centre we can find the cosmos. At the centre we might well be at the circumference. At the very least, by moving toward this centre, Anodos "enlarges the circumference of his imagination."

Endnotes

1. What lies beyond each door roughly corresponds to Blake's four levels of existence: Ulro, Generation, Beulah, Eden. The first door, of tears, takes Anodos to his childhood, a time of lost innocence, separation, guilt, and fear. For him it is agony. The second door, of sighs, picks up the theme of separation, but when Anodos plucks up courage to enter the door leading to the bedroom of the white lady and her lover, Sir Percivale, he accepts a world of generative sexuality. The door of dismay, which comes next, leads to reconciliation: Anodos becomes reconciled with his past, his ancestors, and with death. We have also moved from the country (vale) of tears to the city, a premonition of Jerusalem. Logically, the fourth door will take us that extra level to Eden (in Blake's sense), but MacDonald is, of course, not Blake, and what he gives us is a fleeting and tantalizing glimpse of the timeless. Max Keith Sutton, in his article "The Psychology of the Self in MacDonald's *Phantastes*," examines the lady in this cottage as a "therapist" who allows Anodos "to face once more the key figures from his past" (14).

2. In this same essay, MacDonald writes: "science may pull the snowdrop to shreds, but cannot find out the idea of suffering hope and pale confident submission, for the sake of which that darling of the spring looks out of heaven" (*A Dish of Orts* 10). Keith Wilson cites a similar passage in MacDonald's sermon "The Truth" from *Unspoken Sermons: Third Series* (1889) in his analysis of the imaginative act that perceives "a natural object's 'truth'" (142).

3. An exception is John Docherty, who notices a "threefold organisation" in *Phantastes* (26). Docherty's discussion of the structure of *Phantastes* is remarkably close to mine; I might point out that my paper was written long before Docherty's fine article appeared.

Works Cited

Abrams, M. H. *Natural Supernaturalism*. Oxford: Oxford UP, 1971.

Athenæum. Review of *Phantastes*. November 6, 1858, 580.

Auden, W. H. "Introduction." in *The Visionary Novels of George MacDonald*. Ed. Anne Freemantle. New York: The Noonday Press, 1954. Reprinted in W. H. Auden. *Forewords and Afterwords*. New York: Vintage Books, 1973, 268-273.

British Quarterly Review. Review of *Phantastes*. Vol. 29, 1859, 296- 297.

Docherty, John. "A Note on the Structure and Conclusion of *Phantastes*." *North Wind: A Journal of George MacDonald Studies* 7 (1988): 25-30.

The Globe. Review of *Phantastes*. December 30, 1858.

MacDonald, George. *A Dish of Orts*. London: Sampson, Low, Marston, 1895.

—. *Phantastes*. London: Smith, Elder, 1858.

—. *Poetical Works*. Vol. 1. London: Chatto and Windus, 1893.

Manlove, C. N. *Modern Fantasy*. Cambridge: Cambridge UP, 1975.

—. *The Impulse of Fantasy Literature*. Kent, OH: Kent State UP, 1983.

Reis, Richard. *George MacDonald*. New York: Twayne, 1972.

Robertson, E. S. "A Literary Causerie: *Phantastes*." *Academy* 70 (1906): 308-309.

Shelley's Poetry and Prose. Ed. Donald H. Reiman and Sharon Powers. New York: Norton, 1977.

Sigman, Joseph. "Death's Ecstasies: Transformation and Rebirth in George MacDonald's *Phantastes*." *English Studies in Canada* 2 (1976): 203-226.

Spectator. Review of *Phantastes*. December 4, 1858, 1286.

Sutton, Max Keith. "The Psychology of the Self in MacDonald's *Phantastes*." *Seven* 5 (1984): 9-25.

Wilson, Keith. "The Quest for 'The Truth': A Reading of George MacDonald's *Phantastes*." *Etudes Anglaises* 34 (1981): 140-152.

Meta-*Phantastes*:
A Self-Referential Faerie Romance for Men and Women
Graeme A. Muirhead
From *Scottish Literary Journal*

> There is always more in a work of art . . . than the producer himself perceived while he produced it . . . .[1]

Metafiction has been described as 'fictional writing which self-consciously and systematically draws attention to its status as artefact in order to pose questions about the relationship between fiction and reality'.[2] The succinctness and clarity of this definition conceal the confusion of often competing theories and terminologies that have proliferated around metafiction. Reviewing some of the literature of metafictional theory and criticism, Zadworna Fjellestad draws attention to a particularly helpful distinction between overtly and instantly recognisable self-referential novels such as Laurence Sterne's *Tristram Shandy*, John Barth's *Lost in the Funhouse*, and John Fowles's *The French Lieutenant's Woman*, which she terms 'auto-thematic', and a class of fiction in which 'the artifice is not flatly self-evident' and 'the employed narrative strategies, conventions, themes, and the language itself function on two levels: telling a seemingly traditional story, they demonstrate at the same time their own functioning as strategies, conventions, themes, and medium'.[3] This category is named 'duplex fiction' because of its capacity to transmit two messages simultaneously. Alongside texts such as Thomas Pynchon's *Gravity's Rainbow* and Umberto Eco's *The Name of the Rose*, we find Lewis Carroll's *Alice's Adventures in Wonderland* cited as representative of this class. *Alice* was first published in 1865, only seven years after George MacDonald's *Phantastes*, at a time when the friendship between the two writers was at its closest. The writings of both men show signs that some cross-fertilisation took place, and while these two works are clearly very different in many respects, they are alike in that both are works of fantasy that have been subjected to a multiplicity of interpretative approaches, and present in each is an undercurrent of self-consciousness. For this reason it may not be inappropriate to use Zadworna-Fjellestad's discussion of *Alice* as a framework for an analysis of *Phantastes* as a covert metatext. Indeed, by doing so it is possible to gain new insights into this complex and challenging work.

Crossing a Great Frontier

Central to duplex fiction is the kind of reading it demands. ZadwornaFjellestad proposes three categories of reader. First, the 'naive reader' who 'would read the text for its obvious story and respond to the meaning of the tale emotionally; he would not attempt a conscious intellection about the text as a separate unity' (26). The 'self-reflexive reader' on the other hand is 'able to deal interpretatively with the text in the same ways as the author deals generatively with it. This reader is able to fully actualize the text's network of messages; although he responds emotionally and psychologically to the text . . . he is capable of conscious intellection about the text' (26). Third, there is the 'critical reader', whose awareness of the incompatibility of the naive and selfreflexive readings leads him to consider the act of interpretation itself: 'The critical reader's aim is not to zero in on one meaning and thus to master the text, but rather to notice how meaning can never be fixed, to see how the emerging sense is provisional' (111). Because, in *Phantastes*, there is a direct relationship between the reader and Anodos, without the intervention of a narrator, the handling of this character is crucial in determining the reader's response, and will therefore provide a useful point of departure to illustrate the relevance of these three types of reader to MacDonald's work.

The name 'Anodos' has been interpreted as meaning either 'pathless', 'having no way'[4] or alternatively 'a way back'.[5] Either way it is an apt choice as this ambivalence is fundamental to the portrayal of Anodos. During the first part of his adventures he is characterised above all by his passivity. From the very outset he conveys no clear purpose as he drifts eastwards, guided by nothing more than a vague longing and a superficial and intermittent curiosity to find out as much as possible about Fairy Land. He receives impressions and is acted upon, but seldom initiates actions for himself. His first positive behaviour occurs when he casts himself on the ground between the moon and the shadowy hand of the Ash. Yet this is a reckless impulse rather than a predetermined plan, and it places him utterly at the mercy of his hunter. Shortly afterwards, his discovery of the White Lady is quite accidental, and he is able to free her from her tomb only by the gift of song, which comes to him unpredictably and without his own volition. On both occasions his actions lead him into situations from which he has to be rescued by other characters, first the beech tree, then the Knight of the Soiled Armour. When he finds his Shadow, the impression is not so much that he has made a discovery as that the Shadow has been lying in wait, ready to pounce on him.

This initial lack of intent on the part of Anodos contributes to the absence of structure in the book as a whole. Plot was never one of MacDonald's strong points. His novels are often formulaic, slack in their overall construction, and at times highly contrived. Probably this is because MacDonald, unlike many of his contemporaries, was interested in the novel less as literary artifice than as a vehicle for his preaching. It must also be borne in mind that *Phantastes* was written extremely rapidly, in the space of just two months. But what we find in the shape of this book is more than just carelessness or haste. It is as if MacDonald is deliberately practising the theory outlined in the Novalis quotation which prefaces his work. There is little sense of an authorial hand guiding and manipulating the events that occur. Rather, the story progresses in an almost chaotic manner that seems to mimic the workings of the unconscious mind. Short chapters are punctuated by quotations and frequently interrupted by poems, songs or digressions. There are repeated changes of scene as Anodos encounters a sprawling series of apparently unrelated adventures, strung together sequentially with no strong impression of causality or of mounting tension as events move to a climax.

Apart from his short-lived pursuit of the White Lady, Anodos continues in an essentially passive role until well into his stay in the fairy palace. He is transported there involuntarily in a little boat, and once there he is waited on by unseen servants while he spends his time reading and dreaming. It is during this section of the narrative, however, that a transformation begins to take place. While his two most decisive actions are essentially negative in that they are acts of disobedience to the commands 'touch not!' and 'No one enters here without the leave of the Queen', they do represent a more sustained attempt to follow the White Lady. Thereafter Anodos shows determination and fortitude in adversity, a sense of duty towards others, a positive and beneficial use of his gifts, and a gradual self-renunciation which culminates in the ambivalence of his ritual self-sacrifice, a single act which fuses together the two aspects of his character.

Concurrently with this change of behaviour, a development takes place in his style as a narrator. This first appears in his use of abstractions to generalise from his own experience: '. . . the same fact caused me to feel a tenderness unspeakable for her, accompanied with a kind of feeling of property in her; for so the goblin Selfishness would reward the angel Love';[6] 'Wrong and Sorrow had gone together, hand-in-hand as it is well they do' (141). It is seen most clearly later in two lengthier passages, one following his release from the tower in the forest, and the other in the closing chapters, in which he analyses his experiences and reflects on the lessons they have taught him (166, 181-5).

We can say then that Anodos, from being a model of the naive, imaginative response implicit in the Novalis quotation at the start of the book, which stresses a passive surrender to the irrationality of Fairy Land and the primacy of the unconscious, has undergone a transformation into someone whose behaviour and thinking are notable for the positive qualities listed above.

This change, I would suggest, reflects and to some extent nurtures a similar change which has already begun to occur in the reader. The conscious mind, confronted with what seems incomprehensible, will almost certainly try to perceive underlying meaningful structures. This is especially true, for example, with regard to language. As Geoffrey Leech has written, 'it seems to be an incontrovertible principle of semantics that the human mind abhors a vacuum of sense; so a speaker of English faced with the absurd sentences will strain his interpretative faculty to the utmost to read them meaningfully'.[7] MacDonald was not unaware that his audience, unable to latch on to the familiar conventions of a representationally realistic novel, would try to impose meaning. So it is that in *Phantastes* we find, alongside the ostensible disorder, textual features which suggest the operation of an organising intellect. These elements actively encourage us to distance ourselves from the imaginative flow of the story and apply our reason in an effort to decode the hidden substructure of meaning—they encourage us, that is, to make the progression from naive to sophisticated readers.

If, for example, the quotations at the head of each chapter contribute to the fragmented quality of the narrative by interrupting its continuity, they do so with an unvarying regularity, and, more important, tempt the reader to seek in them some clue to the meaning of the story. Again, there are several sections of the narrative which leave a firm impression of order and pattern beneath the chaos: the square construction of the island cottage, with its pyramidal roof and four doors, each leading to another world where new connections and parallels are set up between past, present, and future; the ceremony and ritual of the final sacrificial scene in the forest; and above all, in the fairy palace, where the symmetry and design of the architectural features, and the precision with which they are described, suggest the presence of a creative intelligence which although invisible like the half-glimpsed inhabitants of the palace, is nonetheless revealed through its handiwork. Finally, there is MacDonald's suggestive use of recurrent characters and symbols. While it is true that *Phantastes* is in essence what W.H. Auden has called a 'chain adventure story',[8] several episodes are linked by more than just the presence of a common protagonist. Sir Percival, the White Lady, the Shadow, and the little girl with the crystal globe all reappear once or more, and there is a group of female characters who, though not identical, can be categorised together as manifestations of the Wise Woman archetype. These characters give some continuity to the narrative and introduce an element of causality and purpose to Anodos's adventures, as, for example, he pursues the White Lady and, later, tries to lose his Shadow. Similarly, water, music, statues, mirrors, cottages, and the Shadow are some of the symbols that hint at broader structural and thematic patterns. But it remains difficult to articulate these themes without resorting to either vague generalisations on the one hand, or unacceptably narrow and reductive allegorical readings on the other.

'Duplex fictions', writes Zadworna-Fjellestad,

> start off with strong signals of well-established and easily recognizable conventions—of fairy tale, detective novel, or sports commentary. The reader is thus activated in his inferences about the text; he is led to expect a certain kind of narrative and a final closure, or disclosure, of the text's 'meaning'. . . . However, whereas in traditional or modernist fiction such signals do indeed lead the reader to an uncovering of patterns that unify the meaning of the text, in duplex fiction the same signals lead instead to various cul-de-sacs or, at best, to a very fragmentary and overly simplistic final 'message'. . . .Thus the reader's elicited expectations and forecasts are constantly frustrated; instead of progressing, he is jammed in the narrative. No matter which of the signals of coherence he chooses, he will be left with residues of meaning that cannot be recuperated by his interpretation. (108)

In much the same way, MacDonald begins with an unmistakable statement that his story belongs to a literary tradition which can be traced back to the German *Märchen* of Novalis, Fouqué, and Hoffmann. By making this association, he is attributing to the fairy story a seriousness of purpose which in English literature it had lost. As Tolkien has pointed out in his famous essay 'On Fairy-stories', the relegation of fairy tales to the domain of the nursery is 'an accident of our domestic history'.[9] It is also clear that if the fairy tale is a bearer of meaning, the correct response is not to try to comprehend it cerebrally, but to respond imaginatively and intuitively. After preparing the ground thus, MacDonald proceeds to send conflicting signals which, as we have seen, prompt the reader to think more critically, to rationalise, and to search for a consistent message—a message which, however, eludes any attempt to state it in precise terms. As C.S. Lewis has well expressed it, what MacDonald does best is 'fantasy that hovers between the allegorical and the mythopoeic'.[10] Out of this situation in which opposing ways of reading fairy tales are brought into close proximity, and in which expectations of coherence are aroused but not wholly satisfied, emerges a reader whose response resembles that of the critical reader of duplex fiction, able to 'savour the friction' between these conflicting readings, and, induced by their incompatibility, to go on the consider the very nature of fairy tales. Ostensibly a work of fantasy, *Phantastes* is, at a deeper level, a work about fantasy, a kind of 'metafantasy'.

Throughout the story signs of this covert self-consciousness filter through to the surface of the text in ways that find close correspondence with ZadwornaFjellestad's description of duplex fiction. Just as '*Alice* draws the selfreflexive reader's attention to the text's self-awareness of its genre' (31), so MacDonald's original subtitle, 'a faery romance for men and women', alerts us at the very outset to his unusual choice of genre, and indicates something of the complexity of the responses it will generate: on the one hand, an imaginative response appropriate to a fairy tale; on the other, an inquisitive, searching, adult reading. The quotation from Novalis which follows suggests that the former should predominate, and seems therefore to exclude an intellectual approach. At the same time, though, it is itself making us think about how fairy tales work. As the story progresses, generic self-consciousness is present in the many remarks about the strangeness of Fairy Land. We are told that Anodos's little sister had been reading him a fairy story, and as he recounts his adventures he is always aware that he is in a 'fairy-country' like, the one in his sister's book, 'full of oddities and all sorts of incredibly ridiculous things, which a man is compelled to meet and treat as real—existences, although all the time he feels foolish for doing so' (173). Examples of this are scattered throughout the book, but two stand out for the way they refer to other fairy stories. Sitting down to his first meal in the fairy palace, Anodos comments: 'And now I found, as in many instances before, how true the fairy tales are; for I was waited on, all the time of my meal, by invisible hands' (70). Next morning, 'agreeably to all authentic accounts of the treatment of travellers in Fairy Land, I found by my bedside a complete suit of fresh clothing, just as I was in the habit of wearing' (71). The effect of these remarks is to remind us that we are reading a fairy tale and that the phenomena we encounter will seem queer in comparison with the everyday world of our own experience.

Generic self-consciousness is not restricted to *Phantastes*. The fairy tales for children furnish many other examples similar to those given above. Like Anodos, Colin in 'The Carasoyn' likens his own situation to that of characters he had read about: '"People in fairy stories", he said, "always find what they want. Why should not I find this Carasoyn?"' Similarly, the prince in 'Little Daylight' parallels his forced exile with the journeys of princes in fairy tales: 'He had read of princes setting out upon adventure; and here he was out in similar case, only without having had a choice in the matter' (173). In 'The Golden Key' we are informed that 'it is well known that the little creatures commonly called fairies, though there are many different kinds of fairies in Fairyland, have an exceeding dislike to untidiness' (213). Shortly afterwards, Tangle's Grandmother tells her that 'in Fairyland . . . the ambition of the animals is to be eaten by the people' (218-19). The norms and practices of Fairy Land are not those we are accustomed to in this world, and by explaining them MacDonald is reminding us that we are reading a fairy tale.

However alien this world may seem, it is nonetheless predictable, governed by fixed laws and conventions. This point is the basis of the comedy in the cursing scene in 'Little Daylight'. The wicked fairy can claim a second chance to bewitch the princess because the good fairies, by interrupting her, have contravened an inviolable law (170). The same rules that allow Colin to say that 'people in fairy stories . . . always find what they want' are invoked in 'The Light Princess': 'It must have been about this time that the son of a king . . . set out to look for the daughter of a queen' (35). The prince sets out to look for a princess because that is the sort of thing princes do. When, on his travels, he loses sight of his retinue in a forest, MacDonald comments, 'these forests are very useful in delivering princes to their courtiers, like a sieve that keeps back the bran' (35-6). Forests are a useful narrative device, that is, for the writer of fairy tales. MacDonald's humour in this story verges at times on the heavyhanded, but his tone of detached amusement skilfully invites the reader to collude with him in his game as he pokes fun at the conventions and trappings associated with the classic fairy tale.

A final example can be found in the hybrid nature of *At the Back of the North Wind*, which flits back and forth between the grave hardships of nineteenth-century London and the land at the back of the North Wind, and thus focuses attention on the problem of classifying a work which unites characteristics from more than one literary category.

Another feature of duplex fiction is its concern with intertextuality. 'Duplex narratives force the self-reflexive reader into an awareness of his acts of decoding in the light of other texts.'[12] In *Phantastes* there are constant references to other texts in the quotations which open each chapter. More interesting, the act of reading is given special prominence: several characters are shown or said to have been reading—Anodos's sister, the child at the farm house where Anodos spends the night after his escape from the Maid of the Alder Tree, the ogress in the cottage where he discovers his Shadow, and of course Anodos himself. In itself, this is scarcely worth commenting on. What is remarkable is that whenever Anodos reads, complications set in which direct the reader's attention from the story to the act of reading itself and the relationship between the fictional world and reality. Thus there is an interaction between Anodos's activity as a reader and his actual experience in Fairy Land when the characters he reads about in the legend of Sir Galahad and Sir Percivale subsequently play a part in his own adventures. When he discovers the White Lady entombed in a block of alabaster, he interprets this in terms of other myths and stories he has read—Pygmalion, Ariel, Niobe, the Sleeping Beauty, Orpheus (35-7). And there is a merging of fictional worlds so that their characters become indistinguishable, first when Anodos listens to the 'strange tale' with which the Alder-maid seduces him (46), and later in the library of the fairy palace.

In his triple role as narrator, protagonist, and reader, Anodos stands astride the fictional world to which he belongs and the world of the reader. A similar bridging function is fulfilled by MacDonald's own presence as narrator in his realistic novels, addressing his readers directly, and at the same time professing a personal acquaintance with his characters, often in the form of a feigned ignorance of their inner feelings and motivations. MacDonald is fond of the analogy between God's creative activity and that of the writer:

> We discover at once, for instance, that where a man would make a machine, or a picture, or a book, God makes the man that makes the book, or the picture, or the machine.... All the processes of the ages are God's science; all the flow of history is his poetry.... As the thoughts move in the mind of a man, so move the worlds of men and women in the mind of God, and make no confusion there, for there they had their" birth, the offspring of his imagination. Man is but a thought of God.[13]

Essays on George MacDonald's *Phantastes*

It follows that if the world is a book of which God is the author, the demarcation line between fictional characters and us as readers is less distinct than might be supposed. Fiction and reality are not then clear-cut categories but can be seen as gradations on a continuous scale which may be extended in either direction or interpenetrated by lines in other elevations.

The story of Cosmo von Wehrstahl illustrates this point well. MacDonald has already prepared us for the idea of an enchanted mirror during Anodos's journey along the river to the fairy palace (66), and we are reminded of Cosmo's story later, when Anodos finds that his own image is not reflected in the mirror through the door of Sighs (137). The image of the magic mirror echoes backwards and forwards in the text, establishing links between two separate fictional worlds. It is significant that Cosmo's story is set in a real city, Prague, and that its characters are all human beings identified by names and surnames. This is so out of place in Fairy Land that one immediately becomes aware of the multiple layers of fiction that are being superimposed on each other: Anodos, a fictional character, having left his own world for the fantastic world of Fairy Land, is absorbed into the world of a book he is reading, which turns out to be a geographically identifiable place in the real world of the reader. In Fairy Land the 'real' world has become a fairy tale.

Such complexities are less common in the fairy tales for children, which are self-reflexive in a much weaker sense. One notable instance occurs near the beginning of 'The Golden Key', at the point where the fairies are trying to frighten Tangle into running away. Although her home is only 'on the borders of Fairyland', Tangle, abandoned by her father, imprisoned and illtreated by his servants, is a stereotyped fairy tale character. She is also a reader of fairy tales, as we learn when she imagines that the three bears from the story of Silverhair are approaching the door of her room. This intrusion of characters from a traditional fairy tale creates a momentary overlap between two imaginary worlds. A further twist is that it is only an imagined intrusion—the actual events are stranger still: fairies impersonating fictional characters!

The final aspect of this undercurrent of textual self-consciousness in *Phantastes* is MacDonald's use of and discussion of language. 'Duplex texts foreground language to varying degrees.... Linguistic puns, riddles and jokes; conscious exposure of the dialogic nature of the text; deliberate stylizations that multiply this dialogism; diversity of languages employed in one text—these are some of the ways in which duplex fiction draws the reader's attention to its medium.'[14] The techniques used by MacDonald are less conspicuous and less playful than those listed by Zadworna-Fjellestad. There are frequent shifts from prose to verse, and at one point Anodos comments on this: 'Whether or not it was all a poem, I cannot tell; but, from the impulse I felt, when I first contemplated writing it, to break into rime, to which impulse I shall give way if it comes upon me again, I think it must have been, partly at least, in verse' (76). Although these fragments of verse or song are often expressive of elevated feelings or are attributed with powers which mere prose does not possess, they are almost invariably preceded by an apology for their failure to convey what Anodos really heard or said. This may be merely implied. Several times we are told that the song that follows 'went *something like* this . . .'. This is a phrase which recurs frequently in MacDonald's other works. But there are also a number of quite explicit statements about the constraints of language:

> I sang something like this: but the words are only a dull representation of a state whose very elevation precluded the possibility of remembrance. (37)

> The wondrous account, in such a feeble, fragmentary way as is possible to me, I would willingly impart. (76)

> One story I will try to reproduce. But, alas! it is like trying to reconstruct a forest out of broken branches and withered leaves. In the fairy book, everything was just as it should be, though whether in words or something else, I cannot tell. It glowed and flashed the thoughts upon the soul, with such a power that the medium disappeared from the consciousness, and it was occupied only with the things themselves. (84)

This is more than just a failure of memory or of expression on the part of Anodos. It is a limitation inherent in the very nature of linguistic expression. MacDonald's belief in the importance of the unconscious is well known: 'The greatest forces lie in the region of the uncomprehended.'[15] The tension in much of his work between opposites such as age and youth, life and death, imagination and reason, order and chaos, art and nature, dream and reality, good and evil, requires the reader to embrace seemingly contradictory propositions and thus, in a sense, to go beyond the bounds of rationality and recognise the limitations of our habitual categories of thought. It is only in the unconscious mind that contact with what is real is achievable. This 'chamber of our being in which the candle of our consciousness goes out in darkness' is nothing less than the dwelling place of God in each one of us. It is, however, impossible truly to express our most perceptive insights and highest visions in the 'broken branches and withered leaves' of language, as words are part of the apparatus by which the conscious mind processes and packages these experiences. As Geoffrey Leech puts it, language is 'the means by which we, interpret our environment, by which we classify or "conceptualize" our experiences, by which we are able to impose structure on reality'.[16] Hence it is not the denotative or descriptive content of words that MacDonald stresses in his essay 'The Fantastic Imagination', but rather their appeal to the ear and their power to 'impress' by connotation.[17] And in 'The Imagination: its Functions and its Culture' he contrasts the freshness and vitality of the poetic 'symbol' with the staleness of the mere 'sign', which, 'by commonness of use', has 'lost its poetic aspect' and mummified into prose.[18] It is this contrast above all that provides MacDonald with a way out of the paradoxical situation in which communication is only possible using the signs and structures of a linguistic system, yet in thus exposing ideas and feelings to such a system, they are robbed of the essential qualities that make them worth transmitting. Stephen Prickett has shown the extent to which MacDonald is indebted to Coleridge for his conception of the symbol.[19] To use language symbolically meant, for MacDonald, imaginatively seeking out and exploiting the limitless network of analogies and correspondences between man's inner life and the external world of nature. The potency of the symbol derives from the fact that these correspondences are not merely arbitrary or subjective, but are indicative of the immanent presence of the divine in both man and nature:

> We have already said that the forms of Nature . . . are so many approximate representations of the mental conditions of humanity. The outward, commonly called the material, is *informed* by, or has form in virtue of, the inward or immaterial—in a word, the thought. The forms of Nature are the representations of human thought in virtue of their being the embodiment of God's thought. As such, therefore, they can be read and used to any depth, shallow or profound.[20]

Used thus, words become 'live things'. While their divine origin gives them a universality and objectivity, they remain dynamic, indefinite, expansive, multifarious, pointing beyond their immediate referent to an infinite storehouse of meaning, actively involving each reader in interpreting them at a level appropriate to his or her spiritual development:

> One difference between God's work and man's is, that, while God's work cannot mean more than he meant, man's must mean more than he meant. For in everything that God has made, there is layer upon layer of ascending significance; also he expresses the same thought in higher and higher kinds of that thought: it is God's things, his embodied thoughts, which alone a man has to use, modified and adapted to his own purposes, for the expression of his thoughts; therefore he cannot help his words and figures falling into such combinations in the mind of another as he had himself not foreseen, so many are the thoughts allied to every other thought, so many are the relations involved in every figure, so many the facts hinted in every symbol.[21]

MacDonald's reputation as a fantasist rests largely on his successful use of symbols in this way. For C.S. Lewis this ability to 'move by suggestion, to cause to imagine' is not primarily literary, 'since it can coexist with great inferiority in the art of words—nay, since its connection with words at all turns out to be merely external and, in a sense, accidental'.[22] This view probably tells us as much about Lewis as it does about MacDonald. According to David Robb, it is 'never true of MacDonald at his best, and least of all is it true of *Phantastes*, which rewards in corresponding measure however much attention we pay to the details of verbal expression and formal structuring'.[23] Robb goes on to demonstrate this with reference to the theme of Anodos's loss of self, which is developed not as a simple moral progression, but as a succession of advances and regressions, acts of selfishness alternating with acts of selfgiving, within the overall framework of a gradual movement towards selfrenunciation. The intrusive narrative voice and moral explicitness of many of MacDonald's other works is notably absent from *Phantastes* so that the lessons to be learned from Anodos's education are not detachable, but embodied in this very movement of events around which the book is structured. Whatever its mythopoeic qualities, therefore, which made it so appealing to C.S. Lewis, *Phantastes* is a literary work in which the linguistic structures and narrative techniques contribute significantly to its impact.

This argument can, I believe, be extended to include the metalinguistic and metatextual features discussed earlier. The mere fact of their presence surely contradicts Lewis's opinion that once the work has 'done the trick', 'you can throw the means of communication away'. What is more, these techniques are supportive of the book's main themes. MacDonald's uncharacteristic use of the first person narrative voice has the effect of drawing the reader into a more immediate relationship with Anodos. Absorption in his adventures is, however, counteracted by the underlayer of self-consciousness which periodically distances us from these events. The overall effect is one of identification with Anodos, of loss of self, interrupted by periods of reflection, during which the illusion of being in Fairy Land is broken, such that the reader re-enacts and participates in Anodos's fitful progress. Whether one interprets this progress as 'loss of self' or in some other way, the metafantastic elements, the surface structure drawing attention to itself, function at a moral level too, communicating experientially the book's meaning.

It is clear then that MacDonald's readers have an experience which is quite the opposite of that described by Anodos in the library of the fairy palace. Words do not become transparent, the medium does not disappear. On the contrary. By frequent changes from prose to verse, by commenting on these changes, and by explicitly discussing language, MacDonald distracts us from the story to the medium through which it is expressed, and so makes language itself one of the themes of his narrative.

When *Phantastes* was published in 1858, MacDonald, with as yet only two volumes of verse to his name, was at the very outset of his literary career. Moreover, he had recently been deprived of the pulpit as a vehicle for communicating his message of God's truth. These circumstances must surely have forced him to reflect on where his talents as a writer lay and on how literature could most effectively be used to express his beliefs. It is hardly surprising, therefore, that in one of his earliest serious literary efforts these preoccupations should be particularly conspicuous.

This self-conscious strain was to continue throughout his long career, persisting even into his last major publication, albeit in a somewhat attenuated form. *Lilith's* concern with its own textuality is manifest not so much in the extensive use of the technical devices that are so pervasive in *Phantastes*, though there is still some residual self-consciousness in the inserted manuscript, the fragments of poetry and song, the footnotes, and the literary, classical, and biblical allusions. It is present, rather, in Vane's discourse, particularly in the interruptions and asides in which he underlines the incommunicability of his experiences, and in the equivocal and problematic status which names, words, and meanings assume in his debates with Mr Raven. And as in *Phantastes*, books and reading feature prominently. The action begins and ends in Vane's library. Mr Raven is a librarian, though in his later manifestation as the sexton he professes to have gone through the entire library and emerged 'none the wiser'. Vane too is a lover of books and learning, but becomes progressively disenchanted with the pursuit of knowledge to the point where, on returning to his library, he can say that 'there the books were hateful to me—for I once loved them'.[24] MacDonald seems to suggest, however, that it is Vane's attitude that is wrong. It is only when he puts out his hand and grasps the bird-butterfly that its fiery wings become dead boards (46-7). And the power of poetry is revealed in its influence on Lilith (144-7) and on Vane himself (228).

Thus, the themes that were so evident in *Phantastes* are still present in *Lilith*. But in this, the work of MacDonald's old age, they are overshadowed by the urgency of his message in what is altogether a darker and more sombre work.

Duplex fiction is not a watertight compartment. Neither is it 'a term that defines a historically delimited mode of writing. It is, I believe, a mode of writing (and reading) that crosses various periods and genres'.[25] By applying Zadworna-Fjellestad's argument to *Phantastes* it is not suggested that this is a final or definitive reading, but simply one which permits us to reread our literary past in the light of recent critical theory.

In his discussion of *Phantastes*, Colin Manlove concludes that the incompatibility of the two ways of reading the story is an indication of uncertainty on the part of MacDonald and a fundamental flaw in the work:

> In sum, one would go so far as to say that the chaotic element of the story has so frightened MacDonald that he has been driven to impose meaning on it. . . . It is almost as if he first imagined *Phantastes* and then applied his intellect to it—two acts by different areas of his mind. It is not surprising that the products of the two—image or motif, and significance—co-exist rather uneasily. The themes he has put into the story in fact start only half way through the book, making the split even more marked.[26]

By drawing on the concept of duplex fiction with its three types of reader, we can see an underlying unity in *Phantastes*, read not as a closed statement or the embodiment of a single, coherent point of view, but as an open-ended text, in which the inconsistencies and conflicts of MacDonald's theory of fantasy as expounded in the expository essays in *A Dish of Orts* are carried over into a fairy story and are themselves explored as the subject of a work of the imagination. The effectiveness of this exploration is that the critical reader, to whom contradictory critical stances are exposed as such, is invited to share in its preoccupations in a direct and personal way. Seen in this light, *Phantastes* becomes an 'open work' in which the reader interacts with the text in a participatory manner.

For MacDonald, any concern with the hermeneutic activity itself could never be merely sterile theorising. Our response to literature and our response to the created world around us are inseparable, for both literature and nature are embodiments of the divine imagination. Our duty as readers and as individuals is to seek out the meaning latent in all things, and *Phantastes* empowers us to do so by transforming us into virtuoso readers, alert, receptive, and free of 'intellectual greed'. MacDonald's purpose was 'not so much to convey a meaning as to wake a meaning':[27] 'For repose is not the end of education; its end is a noble unrest, an ever renewed waking from the dead . . . an urging on of the motions of life, which had better far be accelerated into fever, than retarded into lethargy.'[28] At the end of *Phantastes* Anodos is left asking questions, uncertain as to the meaning of his adventures. Like Alice, *Phantastes* 'asks the critical reader to embrace ambivalences, to live with questions left unanswered, to face uncertainties';[29] it also asks us to be open to boundless possibilities: 'We are dwellers in a divine universe where no desires are in vain, if only they be large enough.'[30] *Phantastes* is indeed 'a story without a beginning, and it will never have any end'.

Endnotes

1. George MacDonald, *A Dish of Orts: Chiefly Papers on the Imagination, and on Shakespeare*, enlarged edition (London, 1893), p. 25.
2. Patricia Waugh, *Metafiction: The Theory and Practice of Self-Conscious Fiction*. (London, 1984), p. 2.
3. Danuta Zadworna-Fjellestad, *'Alice's Adventures in Wonderland'* and *'Gravity's Rainbow'*: A Study in Duplex Fiction, *Stockholm Studies in English*, 68 (Stockholm, 1986), p. 6.
4. C.N. Manlove, *The Impulse of Fantasy Literature* (London, 1983), p. 77.
5. Richard H. Reis, George *MacDonald*, Twayne's English Authors Series, 119 (New York, 1972), p. 87.
6. *Phantastes: A Faery Romance for Men and Women* (London, 1858), reprinted by Lion, 1982, p. 124. Further references in the text are to this Lion reprint.
7. Geoffrey Leech, *Semantics* (Harmondsworth, 1974), p. 8.
8. Introduction to *The Visionary Novels of George MacDonald*, ed. Anne Fremantle (New York, 1954), reprinted in W.R. Auden, *Forewords and Afterwords*, selected by Edward Mendelson (London, 1973), pp. 268-73 (269).
9. J.R.R. Tolkien, *Tree and Leaf* (London, 1964), p. 34.
10. *George MacDonald: An Anthology*, ed. C.S. Lewis (London, 1946), reprinted in Fount Paperbacks, 1983, p. xxvi. Further references are to the Fount reprint.
11. *'The Light Princess' and Other Tales* (London, 1961), reprinted by Canongate, 1987, pp. 130-1. Page numbers in the text refer to this collection.
12. Zadworna-Fjellestad, p. 8.
13. *A Dish of Orts*, pp. 3-4.
14. Zadworna-Fjellestad, p. 108.
15. *A Dish of Orts*, p. 319.
16. *Semantics*, p. 28.
17. *A Dish of Orts*, pp. 318-19.

18. Ibid., p. 9.
19. Stephen Prickett, *Romanticism and Religion: The Tradition of Coleridge and Wordsworth in the Victorian Church* (Cambridge, 1976), pp. 223-48.
20. *A Dish of Orts*, p. 18.
21. Ibid., pp. 320-1.
22. *George MacDonald: An Anthology*, p. xxviii.
23. David S. Robb, *George MacDonald*, Scottish Writers Series (Edinburgh, 1987), pp. 86-7.
24. *Lilith: A Romance* (London, 1895), reprinted by Lion, 1982, p. 237.
25. Zadworna-Fjellestad, pp. 104-5.
26. C.N. Manlove, *Modern Fantasy: Five Studies* (Cambridge, 1975), pp. 77-8.
27. *A Dish of Orts*, p. 317.
28. Ibid., p. 1.
29. Zadworna-Fjellestad, p. 38.
30. *A Dish of Orts*, p. 28.

The Multiple Realms of George MacDonald's *Phantastes*
Adrian Gunther
From *Studies in Scottish Literature*

Critics have often referred to George MacDonald's dualism. Recently a book has been published centered around this concept and opening with an essay entitled "The Two Worlds of George MacDonald."[1] These two worlds are variously seen as those of "reality" and "fantasy", of "intellect" and "imagination", of the traditional and the personal, of the pagan and the Christian and so on. I would suggest that a more useful approach to the understanding of *Phantastes*, is to see it as the embodiment of *multiple* worlds, as a text whose subsuming vision may be seen to embrace, not two realms, but the possibility of an infinity thereof.

Phantastes is structured around a system of interconnecting and co-existing worlds, of multiple realms on different spiritual levels interpenetrating at significant moments in which time and space are transcended. Such a system utilizes an approach to time which is essentially very modern and more typical of twentieth,[2] than of mid-nineteenth century, fantasy. The basic premise of MacDonald's system is, however, profoundly religious, and hinges on his conception of God and His relation to His creation, a relationship which must surely have seemed extremely unorthodox to MacDonald's Christian colleagues. From the sacred center is generated a great flux of energy. This energy is embodied in an infinity of forms falling into patterns of time and space which combine to create realms, "the mighty hosts of life bearing worlds" as he calls them in his sermons.[3] One of his most specific assertions of this process lies at the heart of *Phantastes*, in the first of the book's two central and key chapters. Here he postulates multiple worlds radiating out from the sacred "center" and all, of necessity, interconnected, whether individuals within individual realms can recognize these connections or not. Each individual, it is assumed, has both future and past lives:

> Worlds cannot be without an intermundane relationship. The community of the centre of all creation suggests an interradiating connection and dependence of the parts. Else a grander idea is conceivable than that which is already embodied. The blank, which is only a forgotten life, lying behind the consciousness, and the misty splendour, which is

> an undeveloped life, lying before it, may be full of mysterious revelations of other connexions with the worlds around us, than those of science and poetry. No shining belt or gleaming moon, no red and green glory in a selfencircling twin-star, but has a relation with the hidden things of a man's soul, and, it may be, with the secret history of his body as well. They are portions of the living house wherein he abides.[4] (XII, 97)

Each world of form in its miraculous dance is struggling towards its next embodiment, a process which ultimately leads to the still center which generates and controls this great dance of forms. Some realms parallel each other; others fall into a sequence whose controlling principle is distance from this center. As MacDonald elsewhere expresses it, "The whole system of the universe works upon this law—the driving of things upward towards the center."[5] However, at any particular time, the forms of any one realm (and of any one person within that realm) can be developing towards higher spiritual embodiments or deteriorating towards grosser forms. MacDonald refers to this system of metempsychosis or reincarnation in *The Princess and Curdie*, where he calls it, "the whole science of natural history—the heavenly sort." The princess tells Curdie:

> All men, if they do not take care, go down the hill to the animal's country . . . many men are actually, all their lives, going to be beasts. People knew it once, but it is long since they forgot it . . . it is always what they do, whether in their minds or their bodies, that makes men go down to be less than men, that is, beasts . . . They do not know it of course; for a beast does not know that he is a beast, and the nearer a man gets to being a beast the less he knows it.[6]

When describing the evolution of the goblins' animals in *The Princess and the Goblin* he uses similar terms and in this case, his description is clearly influenced by current theories of evolution:

> In the course of time, all had undergone even greater changes than had passed upon their owners. They had altered . . . their countenances had grown in grotesque resemblance to the human. No one understands animals who does not see that every one of them, even amongst the fishes . . . yet shadows the human: in the case of these the human resemblance had greatly increased: while their owners had sunk towards them, they had arisen towards their owners. But the conditions of subterranean life being equally unnatural for both, while the goblins were worse, the creatures had not improved by the approximation . . . (p. 72).

When Curdie begins to lose his path and become commonplace MacDonald comments: "There is this difference between the growth of some human beings and that of others: in the one case it is a continuous dying, in the other a continuous resurrection" (p. 180). And this concept remains central to all his writings. In his *Unspoken Sermons*, this "resurrection" is seen as "gradations of an *infinite* progress" (my emphasis).[7] All creatures are, of necessity, either going forward towards the sacred center, returning to that center one might say, or drawing further away. How ever, MacDonald's philosophy is essentially optimistic in that he sees all beings as ultimately returning to the source and being reunited with the divine. As he says, all it requires is time and there is an infinitude of that. The princess tells Curdie that she may take "a few thousand years" to answer his questions. "But that's nothing. Of all things time is the cheapest."[8] So too, in his sermons, MacDonald repeatedly refers to the huge periods of time needed to achieve this union: "God . . . takes millions of years to form a soul that shall understand him . . ."; "God's day is a thousand years": "not by a stroke of grandeur, but by years of love, yea, by centuries of seeming bafflement . . . must he grow into the heart of (his) sons and daughters."[9]

Thus the basic challenge offered individuals on their life journeys is to glimpse the sacred process underlying the forms of the adventures that befall them. In this way, they are able to use these experiences, perhaps even transform and thence transcend them. They cannot see the complete pattern, but they can get a glimpse into the true meaning of things, or at least a hint that there is a meaning, a pattern of cause and effect in action.[10] This brief insight is, by definition, elusive, and as so often occurs to Anodos, protagonists spend much of their time struggling to recollect the details of these moments and to express them in words.

The concept of multiple realms controls the text on all its levels. From the moment Fairy Land invades Anodos's bedroom, dissolving its fixed forms into energy, his experiences are characterized by a sense of mystery, of everything being more than it appears to be, of individual forms directing attention beyond themselves to further states towards which they are striving. He feels this sense of expectation all about him:

> here I was struck with utter stillness. No bird sang. No insect hummed. Not a living creature crossed my way. Yet somehow the whole environment seemed only asleep, and to wear even in sleep an air of expectation. The trees seemed all to have an

expression of conscious mystery, as if they said to themselves, "We could, an' if we would." They had all a meaning look about them (IV, 10).

He immediately links this mysterious ambiguity to the processes of the subconscious as embodied in the world of dream and of the night, because it is to these realms that Fairy Land belongs:

> I, being a man and a child of the day, felt some anxiety as to how I should fare among the elves and other children of the night who wake when mortals dream, and find their common life in those wondrous hours that flow noiselessly over the moveless death-like forms of men and women and children, lying strewn and parted beneath the weight of the heavy waves of night, which flow on and beat them down, and hold them drowned and senseless, until the ebb-tide comes, and the waves sink away, back into the ocean of the dark (IV, 10).

Later, as he leaves the first cottage, he notices that the woods are full of a strange "feeling of presences." All about him are creatures whom he cannot quite see, levels of existence which he cannot quite penetrate. As Anodos puts it:

> All this time, as I went through the wood, I was haunted with the feeling that other shapes, more like my own size and mien, were moving about at a little distance on all sides of me. But *as yet* I could discern none of them . . . I constantly imagined, however, that forms were visible in all directions except that to which my gaze was turned; and that they only became invisible, or resolved themselves into other woodland shapes, the moment my looks were directed towards them (IV, 28, my emphasis).

We notice therefore that in Fairy Land a mysterious ambiguity characterizes Anodos's adventures. The different forms taken by these adventures are in flux, in the process of shifting and changing. All is in the process of *becoming* and much of what Anodos experiences has a dreamlike unreality, at times bordering on nightmare. MacDonald captures this nightmare quality brilliantly. What could be more horrific than Anodos's pursuit by the Ash? In this event the horror lies in what is *not* stated, in the suggestion of other dimensions on the verge of breaking through into the "normality" of this one. When Anodos is found by his shadow, the horror lies in exactly this shifting of dimensions. From the depths of some distant realm, from the "luminous extremity" of a "night sky" in the "remote" distance, his shadow rushes at him (VIII, 69-70). Even the first cottage which Anodos enters resonates a sense of sinister anticipation quite at variance with the kind "homeliness" of his treatment there. The woman pushes him back from the window "with an expression of impatience and terror" (III, 13). She predicts "foul weather" and the impression created is one of hostile realms threatening to invade and barely being held at bay. The naive world of garden fairies squabbling and teasing the cat exists side by side with, and in total opposition to, the nightmare world of the Ash which later reduces Anodos to a state where he is "simply imbruted with terror" (IV, 32).

At key stages in Anodos's adventures, worlds merge, space shifts, linear time ceases and words fail to convey what is happening. These experiences take the form of trances or visions. The fairy "form" who enters Anodos's castle "reality" instigates the first of these visionary revelations. On looking into her eyes he "sank in their waters . . . forgot all the rest" and sees the world of form as a great sea of energy, a vision which fills him with an intense longing which she then directs towards the realm of Fairy Land. He experiences a second trance-like vision in the arms of the Beech tree. As always he has trouble describing the experiences her "strange, sweet song" provokes. He is "wrapt in a trance of still delight" and learns the "secret of the woods, and the flowers, and the birds" (IV, 36) and seems to relive "childhood" experiences of nature and its seasons. This reinforcement of childlike insight into the world of nature is an important experience in MacDonald's scheme of things, and it leaves Anodos strengthened and feeling "as if new born" (V, 38). This encounter is also characterized by suggestions of a potential for different future embodiments. The Beech tree longs "for the world of men" as Anodos "had . . . longed for Fairy Land" and she looks forward to being a woman, predicting also that the ash trees will make "horrid men" one day (IV, 35). Anodos's reluctance to leave her is minimized by his comforting himself with the notion that he might meet her again in some different realm: "if ever she is a woman, who knows but we may meet somewhere? There is plenty of room for meeting in the universe" (V, 38).

These trance-like insights into other times and other places are always conveyed in terms of a direct experience defying expression in language. Because they represent revelations into realms transcending that of the protagonist at the time, this fundamental failure of language is inevitable and our attention is repeatedly drawn to it throughout the text. In this experience with the Beech tree, Anodos says of her song that he could not understand it but that it left him with a feeling which he then tries to convey in poetry, at the same time apologizing for the inadequacy of this attempt: "I cannot put more of it into words" (IV, 36). When, transformed by drinking the magic water in the Marble Lady's cave he falls into "a delicious reverie," he describes the "assembly of forms and spiritual sensations" this trance-like state produces as "far too vague to admit of being translated into any shape common to my own and another mind" (V, 41). Then, as he is inspired by this vision to sing the imprisoned form into life, he comments: "I sang something like this: but the words are only a dull representation of a state whose very elevation precluded the possibility of remembrance and in which I presume the words really employed were as far above these, as that state transcended this wherein I recall it" (V, 45). This failure of memory characterizes his next experience also, that with the Alder Maid. She tells him a tale which he cannot recollect but which "at every turn and every pause" focuses him on her "extreme beauty." Once again he lies "entranced" as her tale draws him into its magic realm "till she and I were blended with the tale, till she and I were the whole history." However, where the experience with the Beech tree left him "new born," this trance-like exposure to the realm of the Alder Maid leaves him with such horror that his very memory of it is "almost obliterated" (VI, 55) and he is left feeling emasculated.

The central section in the Fairy Palace provides keys to the understanding of the text as a whole. It also contains key passages where these concepts are embodied in powerful symbolic form. In such passages MacDonald is at his most brilliant. Every detail of description resonates mysteriously with subtle suggestions of other forms just beyond the experience of the protagonist. Other dimensions, other realms, impinge on, lead out of or into, parallel or contradict this one, and this complex of relationships in process is brilliantly captured, for example, in Anodos's baptismal bathing or his experience of the dance at the palace's heart. Water, music and dance are powerful symbols for sacred energy, for the paradoxical concept of unity in multeity or motion in stasis and MacDonald uses them in this way consistently throughout his works. I will look at these two sections in detail.

At the center of the palace courtyard is a "great fountain . . . throwing up a lofty column of water," the top of which "caught the moonbeams, and like a great pale lamp, hung high in the night air, threw a dim memory of light . . . over the court below" (X, 86). Anodos as usual follows this water energy which leads into the heart of the palace building, where he finds next day a "huge basin . . . filled with the purest most liquid and radiant water" in which he has a series of baptismal immersions. These baths are conveyed in terms of a shift in dimension, a movement into another realm where all is enigmatic and elusive yet at the same time profoundly transforming so that with each immersion he feels as if he has gained expanded insight into the true nature of this realm wherein he finds himself. The pool itself is, as already stated, deeply symbolic, embodying as it does this sacred energy underlying all the forms of the palace. It is a "harmonious confusion," thus combining order and chaos. It looks as if "there was no design" but Anodos realizes that "not one little pebble could be displaced without injuring the effect of the whole." Realm upon realm is contained within, and yet at the same time "unfolded" by this pool, which ultimately links to the great ocean itself: "Beneath [the] . . . floor of the water, lay the reflection of the blue inverted roof, fretted with its silver stars, like a second deeper sea, clasping and unfolding the first" (XI, 91). When Anodos plunges in, the waters "seemed to enter and revive [his] . . . heart." He swims "as in a rainbow,"[11] and when he dives, finds himself enchanted, in an underwater realm, in "the heart of a great sea." He is in the great ocean itself, with "wondrous caves," glowing corals and "the glimmer of what seemed to be creatures of . . . human form at home in the waters." When he emerges "deeply refreshed," he feels as if "clothed with a new sense" and finds that his consciousness is subtly altered. He begins "to discern faint, gracious forms" hitherto invisible to him (XI, 92), although they are still unclear: "Nor were they plainly visible to my eyes. Sometimes a group or . . . individual, would fade entirely out of the realm of my vision as I gazed." His insights increase steadily with each bath but he is always aware that he is still only seeing a shadow of what is there. He never sees the Queen for example and is aware that to do so is not his destiny (XI, 93). His needs are different, presumably being on a much lower level than that would imply.

So too his experience of the dancers in the great pillared hall is characterized by this sense of mystery and elusiveness. Just beyond Anodos' consciousness, realms are lying in "misty splendor . . . full of mysterious revelations of other connexions with the worlds around him." He is aware of a great dance of forms and longs to see it in order to glimpse the "music" which controls it:

> I seemed to hear something like the distant sound of multitudes of dancers, and felt as if it was the unheard music, moving their rhythmic motion, that within me blossomed in verse and song. I felt, too, that could I but see the dance, I should, from the harmony of complicated movements, not of the dancers in

relation to each other merely, but of each dancer individually in the manifested plastic power that moved the consenting harmonious form, understand the whole of the music on the billows of which they floated and swung (XIV, 135).

He feels that if he could only see it *completely*, he would understand the music controlling its forms. He struggles vainly to see the solid shapes and patterns of movement and sound with which he *knows* he is surrounded. He *knows* there is a great Truth behind and informing these strange occurrences, but he can never get more than the faintest hint as to its real nature. As he says of the Fairy Palace:

> I was convinced there must be music in it, but that *my sense was as yet too gross* to receive the influence of those mysterious motions that beget sound. Sometimes I felt sure, from the way the few figures of which I got such transitory glimpses passed me, or glided into vacancy before me, that they were moving to the law of music; and, in fact, several times I fancied for a moment that I heard a few wondrous tones coming I knew not whence. But they did not last long enough to convince me that I had heard them with the bodily sense. Such as they were, however, they took strange liberties with me, causing me to burst suddenly into tears, of which there was no presence to make me ashamed, or casting me into a kind of trance of speechless delight, which, passing as suddenly, left me faint and longing for more (XIV, 133, my emphasis).

It becomes evident that the revelations that a quester has are dependent on his spiritual level, a level also controlling the forms created by his imagination. Thus from the multitude of realms with which each quester is potentially surrounded, the path he experiences as his is directly related to this spiritual level. As a consequence of these ideas, time and space as they are normally viewed are revealed as an expression of our own limitations. Moments of insight break through these normal experiences of time and space. The protagonists move onto a different level of consciousness in which moments can seem like years and vice versa; space can be experienced as totally illusory or as shifting according to the state of mind of the protagonist. There is some sense in which any world of forms is objectively real, but how the protagonists experience these forms is very much a product of their spiritual states. In fact the suggestion is that the questers produce the forms out of their own needs. One could express this variously: that they *free* the forms which are specifically needed for spiritual development, or that they attract or even generate these forms from the depths of their imaginations. The imagination, being grounded in the subconscious, is the link which connects human beings to God's divine energy and it is therefore the key factor in a quester's progress.

As MacDonald quite specifically expresses it, the form a man finds to "embody his thought" arises "within him without will or effort" because "Such embodiments are not the result of the man's intention, or of the operation of his conscious nature. His feeling is that they are given to him; that from the vast unknown, where time and space are not, they suddenly appear in luminous writing upon the wall of his consciousness . . . [and he continues] can we not say that they are the creation of *the unconscious portion of his nature?*" (my emphasis). He answers his own question in the affirmative with the proviso that "that unknown region whence such embodiments come" be recognized as finding its ultimate source in God's energy which is, by definition, Truth:

> God sits in that chamber of our being in which the candle of our consciousness goes out in darkness, and sends forth from thence wonderful gifts into the light of that understanding which is His candle. Our hope lies in no most perfect mechanism even of the spirit, but in the wisdom wherein we live and move and have our being. Thence we hope for endless forms of beauty informed of truth. If the dark portion of our own being were the origin of our imaginations, we might well fear the apparition of such monsters as would be generated in the sickness of a decay which could never feel—only declare—a slow return towards primeval chaos. But the Master is our Light.[12]

MacDonald repeatedly asserts this distinction between conscious and subconscious levels of personality. The fact that God works through the latter gives it a quite remarkable importance in his scheme of things. As he elsewhere expresses this:

> To give us the spiritual gift we desire, God may have to begin far back in our spirit, in regions unknown to us, and do much work that we can be aware of only in the results; for our consciousness is to the extent of our being but as the flame of the volcano to the world-gulf whence it issues; in the gulf of our unknown being God works behind our consciousness. He may be approaching our consciousness from behind, coming forward through regions of our darkness into our light, long before we begin to be aware that He is answering our request-has answered it, and is visiting His child.[13]

Thus the freeing of the subconscious is to give play to God's sacred energy, allowing it to find its own forms which will of necessity be the right ones for any person's spiritual development at that time in that place. The freeing of the subconscious in dreams or in trance-like states is therefore of crucial importance.[14] As already stated, it allows individuals key revelations into the true nature of the phenomenal world. In these moments "chinks in time" are created, through which "heaven peepeth out."[15] Time and space are both transformed. The limits of any one realm are briefly transcended and future stages of development embodied in other realms can reveal themselves, thus giving meaning to present yearnings. Realms can thus invade each other and these invasions take many forms. Sometimes more enlightened realms penetrate lesser worlds, in the process thereof revealing the true direction of the latter. However, individuals can experience insights into past experiences and into events from other time periods and other worlds. The insights therefore can be on the level of the macrocosm or of the microcosm. They can be so profound as to take the form of mystic visions or simple enough to consist merely of a shift in the experience of the protagonist from, for example, dark wood to lonely tower. Thus these experiences can be within one realm or between different realms. However, the purpose is always the same: to gain understanding of present experiences, an understanding which then gives direction to the transcendence of those experiences.

As suggested above, Anodos experiences trance-like insights under the influence of each of the four female anima figures in the first half of his journey, the fairy grandmother, the Lady of the Beech, the Marble Lady and the Alder Maid, and his sojourn in the Fairy Palace is characterized throughout by a sense of imminent revelation. He is aware that these mystical experiences of other realms or other levels of being are potentially all around him if he could only break through into them, and he does succeed in doing so many times over this period. These insights are provoked variously by baptismal bathing or by exposure to the magical literature, music and dance of the palace and because this is the nearest Anodos gets to the "harmony of the centre," they are of profound significance in his quest.

The second half of the book, those adventures which occur to Anodos *after* his expulsion from the Fairy Palace take on a more profound multidimensional quality. They are characterized by a more complex and shifting pattern of interweaving dimensions. His experiences through the doors of the wise old lady's cottage are confusing and dreamlike, as are the mysterious transitions between day and night in the square tower. There is no question of dual worlds, of one realm being real and the other not. All is shifting and all is equally *un*real and enigmatic until this irrationality takes on the power of claustrophobic nightmare with life and death implications. MacDonald employs a variety of threshold and transition imagery in this section and makes powerful use of the symbolism of reflection whether through images of water or of mirrors.

I have already noted the way in which the pool in the Fairy Palace reflects the sky/roof "fretted with . . . silver stars." When thrust out of the palace into the subterranean world which brings him to the point of despair, Anodos moves down into a bottomless chasm leading into a shaft "smooth as glass" which yet reflects the world of stars and heaven above. He turns determinedly away from this heavenly upward realm and creeps inwards to a world in which the sky is of rock and "whenever a choice was necessary [he] always chose the path which seemed to lead downwards" (XVII, 151). This symbolic plunge into the abyss (XVII, 150) occurs in some strange timeless realm where Anodos finds "such a discrepancy between the decisions of [his] . . . imagination and . . . judgement, as to the length of time that had passed . . . that [he] . . . gave up all attempts to arrive at any conclusion on the point" (XVII, 158). He is caught in a gray mist which in some mysterious way embodies his past so that when he "looked back towards the past, this mist was the medium through which [his] . . . eyes had to strain for a vision of what had gone by." The shedding of this gray mist of his past life is brilliantly conveyed. With Anodos's despairing yet courageous assertion of will,[16] the gray entombing ocean with its "hopeless" waves "flung . . . in raving heaps upon the desolate shore" is transformed into a benign nurturing force in which the waters themselves lift him "with loving arms" (XVIII, 160). The little "rainbow" boat which then rescues him carries him through another multidimensional water realm where reflections are once more from above and therefore benign ("The stars . . . bent down lovingly towards the waters; and the reflected stars within seemed to float up, as if longing to meet their embraces") and the waves reveal such a vision of his past ("vaguely revealed beneath the wave, I floated above my whole Past" [XVIII, 161]) that he is symbolically freed from its burdens. He awakes "with the feeling that [he has] . . . been kissed and loved to his heart's content," (XVIII, 162) which then frees him to enter the magic sphere of the wise old/young lady's square cottage.

This cottage appears to be another stable center in this flux of shifting interpenetrating realms, although one presumes it is of lesser symbolic importance than the Fairy Palace. Characteristically too it is portrayed as mysterious and enigmatic, resonant with hidden significance which Anodos is as yet unable to grasp. The worlds of form which radiate out from this still center provide Anodos with the final experiences he needs to come to terms with and shed his past, but that this is only a tiny part of its potential is clear. MacDonald brilliantly creates this sense of everything being in process and containing significances beyond the protagonist's (and the reader's) wildest imaginings. It is the essence of his skill as a writer.

The four doors through which Anodos ventures lead him into realms associated with his past and yet different from it and there is some sense in which these realms seem independently real and not merely projections of his own longings. The complex nature of all this is epitomized by the mysterious world he meets through the "door of Sighs." He is in the castle of his white lady and her knight. Significantly, she is quite different from his previous experience of her. She is no longer "marble" but "altogether of the daughters of men," so much so that he feels doubt as to whether it is really she. The implication of this invisible invasion of Anodos into their world is that theirs is the "reality" and he is being granted a glimpse into it His form has no place in their mirror although strangely, he sees "a dim shadow of [himself] . . . in the shining steel" (XIX, 175) of the knight's armor. In this scene Anodos is fully conscious that he is the "unreal" one. He says: "I could not enter the sphere of these living beings . . . I moved in a vision while they moved in life" (XIX, 178). Yet later he is able to rejoin the knight as his squire, even asking him about the conversation he overheard when invisible. This puzzles the knight but provokes his long and apparently irrelevant explanation about the beggar girl. The point here is that yet again multiple realms are interconnecting. The girl is one from the "strange planet" read about by Anodos in the library of the Fairy Palace and sent to Fairyland to gather wings with which to fly back to "the country she came from." Once again, characteristic of this experience is the knight's difficulty in remembering what she said and in expressing it verbally: "it seemed to me, all the time, as if I were hearing a child talk in its sleep. I could not arrange her story in my mind at all, although it seemed to leave hers in a certain order of its own" (XXIII, 222).

As usual, when realms interconnect, memory and language fail. Reason and intellect cannot grasp the insights gained because they speak of necessity to the subconscious and the imagination.

The interlude when Anodos is imprisoned in the square tower has similar irrational and nightmare qualities. Night time, with its connotations of a freeing of the subconscious, rescues him from the nightmare of the day's deathly barrenness. The rays of the moon touch him and he is free, insisting "I should have died but for this" (XXII, 207). All binary distinctions between reality and illusion, dreaming and waking, conscious and subconscious, are however characteristically confused to the point of irrelevance. His night dream experiences are life-giving and "real." In them he returns to his "real" home—the castle he initially left—and is welcomed by his sisters. This is the illusion because he wakes back in the tower—or is it? MacDonald plays quite self-consciously with these confusions, moving the text in and out of different levels of experience in what, one realizes by now, is a totally characteristic fashion. Anodos's night, moon-inspired experiences seem utterly "real"; the deadly tower "vanish[es] away like a mist" and he rejoices: "Oh joy it was only a dream," only to have "the glorious night . . . swallowed up of the hateful day" (XXII, 207). The symbolic connotations of intellect battling with imagination are there but the power of the episode carries it well beyond such a simple opposition. Anodos initially rejoices in the day tower being a dream, but then comes to see his night experiences as "only" dreams, thus reducing them to illusory status, and being unable to get real comfort from them. He is "somewhat consoled" by his dreams, "but all the time I dreamed I knew that I was only dreaming" (XXII, 207). When his "real" world breaks through into this dismal one, provoking the great yearning for primal childlike innocence and thence for freedom, which then permits of his liberation, it is in the form of the original "real" world of his castle, sisters, friends, and the vintage—presaging the events which will actually occur at the end of the book, thus transgressing yet again boundaries of time as well as space. At this point it is the dreams that become reality for Anodos. They are no longer "only" dreams. He is "waiting only for the dreams of the night" to liberate him from the nightmare of the day. Night and day are placed in confrontation but interwoven and confused until Anodos transcends the opposition altogether by discovering that his whole imprisonment was an illusion, his own creation. The door was open all the time. The maiden's songs "suddenly invaded [him] . . . as if something foreign to all [his] . . . senses and all . . . experience" and he strains "to catch every syllable of the revelation from the unseen outer world" (XXII, 208) which then inspires him to open the door and leave. Once again energy from one dimension "invades" another, giving it direction, enabling it to transcend the constraints of conflicting oppositions and thus move onwards towards the next trial.

Crossing a Great Frontier

Experiences of this nature characterize each stage in Anodos's quest but, as already suggested, those insights he is granted in the Fairy Palace are key. They place all the others in their true perspective by establishing the scheme of which they are part. The possibility of a "music" governing and subsuming the dance of forms is established. So too is the "harmony of the centre" to which all "worlds" relate in "an interradiating connection." As one might expect, the stories Anodos reads in the palace are clear illustrations of what MacDonald is saying here. The first opens with the statement establishing the existence of multiple worlds (XII, 97) and then proceeds to give an example of these worlds, in the "strange planet." The second story opens with MacDonald's most specific statement of the failure of language in attempting to convey these experiences, then establishes the nature of the great yearning which drives beings upwards towards the center, through realm after realm in an endless process. The story of the "strange planet" propounds exactly this system of different realms of existence interpenetrating and influencing each other. The world described in the story is profoundly limited; its inhabitants are undeveloped in key ways, in particular in terms of sexuality and loving relationships. However, the very fact that they *are* undeveloped creates in them, as they approach death, "an indescribable longing" for the next phase in this development and this controls the form (and presumably the world) of their next incarnation. Anodos, coming as he does from a realm *beyond* that of this planet, acts as a kind of spiritual guide to these people. He sees that their wings, "glorious as they are, are but undeveloped arms" (XII, I 03) and that their male/female relationships are essentially deficient, and he tells these people about birth and sexuality on earth, "in the vaguest manner I could invent" (XII, 102). However, this vagueness is nevertheless sufficient to meet with an instant response, giving form as it does to what these people already feel as "an indescribable longing for something, they know not what, which seizes them, and drives them into solitude, consuming them from within, till the body fails" (XII, 102), so much so that two of them immediately go off and die in order to hasten this next stage which they now understand to be their direction. There is no suggestion that these deaths have any negative connotations whatsoever. "A great light shone in the eyes of one maiden" (XII, 102) who instantly walks away to her death.

Anodos, during this experience, is shifting in and out of different realms changing function as he does so. He moves from his role as narrator of a fiction into a role as one of its characters; he shifts from outside to inside the text and does it so that we barely notice, yet to such an extent that he directly alters the events he is describing. His penetration into his own story extends his function further, because as already suggested he becomes a spiritual guide to these people, able from the wider knowledge of his own realm to help them direct their energies towards their true future embodiments, instead of merely experiencing a vague longing for they know not what and therefore, presumably, quite possibly, from ignorance, dissipating this energy. In his own quest, the various guides he meets function in a parallel way, giving him insights into how to direct the vague yearning which drives him towards the future forms his spiritual development requires.

The self-reflexive quality of the text, as Anodos relates these central stories, is therefore quite remarkable. As he puts it: "But see the power of this book, that, while recounting what I can recall of its contents, I write it as if myself had visited the far-off planet, learned its ways and appearances, and conversed with its men and women. And so, *while writing*, it seems to me that I had" (XII, 103, my emphasis). Anodos has slipped from reader of, to narrator of, to writer of, to protagonist in the fiction, these shifts in function reflecting the shifting nature of the worlds of form in which he finds himself Sometimes one realm is "real," sometimes another, and sometimes contradictory realms seem to coexist and interact as if they shared the same reality and the same time period. Underwater worlds coexist and interact with magical boat trips, chivalric knights and dragons with winged maidens from distant planets and with invisible wooden figures of enigmatic origins. Only the Fairy Palace and the island cottage remain stable centers in this flux of forms. All else is like Anodos's bedroom, in the process of dissolving and becoming "fluent as the waters" (II, 7).

The text, in its confusing interweavings of different realms, of different historical periods, of different levels of fiction and literary genre, even of the different roles filled by Anodos himself (as writer, reader, singer, protagonist, narrator) becomes itself an embodiment of this concept.

We are thus presented with a continuum of parallel and complementary worlds of form, which together participate in a process, a great movement of energy striving to regain the harmony of the center from which it came. Through "chinks of Time" (XII, 97) in the veils between worlds, at each level glimpses are given of further stages in this process. "Forgotten" past lives lie "behind the consciousness" like a "blank," while future lives, with all their "misty splendour," lie before this consciousness and "may be full of mysterious revelations of other connections with the worlds around us" (XII, 97). Inevitably these glimpses are difficult to communicate. In particular the language of any one planet or realm or stage in this process, will be unable to do more than hint at the full import of these mystical insights, because naturally this language is restricted to the experiences of this world and has no vocabulary for those resonated back by realms on more advanced spiritual levels. As already suggested Anodos, on the strange planet, can only hint at the extraordinary complexities of human sexuality. So too the wise old lady on the island can only suggest to him what he needs for his spiritual development. She is restricted to his language and the "forms" with which he is familiar. She uses his past earthly life, his failures and his fears, in order to push him beyond them. It is therefore the *feelings* associated with these revelations which leave the most powerful impression, and words fail totally to convey these feelings because there is always something deeply mysterious about them, which Anodos cannot quite remember. At moments like this, all forms become symbols hinting at mysterious meanings resonating out from them and transcending obvious significances.

The first story in the Fairy Palace establishes the process of progressive and interrelating worlds. The second develops this concept by indicating what drives this process. The motivating force behind the quests of both Cosmo and Anodos is *need*, a need which translates into a great longing. Initially this yearning is vague and directionless. Anodos's vague yearning for Fairy Land is what sets him on his journey. Cosmo lies, overwhelmed with a great longing, dreaming day and night, but having no specific object to give form to his needs (XIII, 108) until he finds the lady in the magic mirror. For both Anodos and Cosmo, this yearning is for the ideal feminine. Both must then learn to transcend this kind of egocentric longing or love and move onto the next stage in the process, which is an unselfish love where the welfare of the beloved is more important than one's own. Love is another term for the great longing which MacDonald sees as driving both individual protagonists and individual worlds ever upward towards the center. This is the driving energy. Each new insight or stage in this process opens up the next. As MacDonald expresses it in his sermons: "Nothing is inexorable but love . . . there is nothing eternal but that which loves and can be loved, and love is ever climbing towards the consummation . . ." and what he stresses here is once again the process that this involves: "It may be centuries of ages before a man comes to see a truth—ages of strife, of effort, of aspiration . . . [but] to see a truth, to know what it is, to understand it, and to love it, are all one. There is many a dim longing for it as an unknown need before at length the eyes come awake" (*Unspoken Sermons*. Series One, p. 37); and elsewhere he expresses this principle thus: "The true revelation rouses the desire to know more by the truth of its incompleteness" (Ibid, p. 36).

These are the two key principles behind *Phantastes*, and Anodos' adventures are an embodiment of this process. As already indicated, death is only a stage in an infinite number of embodiments. Any one realm is merely a stage in a process of realms. Nothing could be more compassionate, open-ended, tolerant and undogmatic than MacDonald's philosophy here. He is far from being a conventional or narrow-minded Christian. It is *because* MacDonald sees individual experience as relative to a person's spiritual level that this system is so appropriate. The world of forms shifts and changes according to this ever shifting level. As the quester's needs and consequent yearnings develop, so do the forms which characterize his journey. His imagination finds the forms needed by him at any one time because this realm of form in which he finds himself is merely one of an infinite number. The particular "reality" he inhabits at any one time is in constant flux in the process of development which will carry it towards its next stage, driven always by that great yearning "upwards" towards the center of all creation.

George MacDonald's *Phantastes* is then on all levels an embodiment of these ideas. In terms of its story, in terms of its use of language, metaphor and symbol, and in terms of its employment of the quest archetype, it depends on this concept of multiple realms. All these interweavings of different realms and times culminate in the final two chapters. Anodos's "death" experience is, on all levels, a revelation. As usual the prologue establishes the key ideas, in this case those already established in the stories he read in the Fairy Palace: life as one in a series, worlds as interradiating from a sacred center, and language as inadequate to convey real truth ("the meagre and half-articulate speech of a savage tribe" [XIII, 106]). We imagine this life to be "our Dwelling Place" when it is in fact only "one step" in the "Race," a mere "wretched Inn" along the way. Death is one stage in a long process of passages through lifetimes and through worlds on the long struggle back to the center. The "enlightened" recognize that this death is actually a birth. They also recognize the limited nature of our language and "scorn" its "nonsense." Death and the shedding of "these vanishing earthly garments," as both Cosmo (smiling as he dies) and the winged creatures of the strange planet learned to recognize, is a blessing. Anodos is emphatic: "I was dead and right content" is how this section opens. "I had never dreamed of such blessedness" (XXIV, 231). For a moment the process of death and rebirth and interradiating realms pauses; Anodos briefly lives "an unradiating existence . . . [his] soul a motionless lake, that received all things and gave nothing back."[17] He experiences the power of being able to embody his spirit at will. ("I felt that I could manifest myself in the primrose" [XXIV, 232].) The world of form is revealed for what it is, a transitory manifestation of "the essential being and nature" of the great mother earth. As has been implied throughout the book, the great play of form with its multiple realms is all illusion. The truly "real" is the sacred energy underlying these forms, giving them their fragile and transitory beauty, and established once again is the key importance of love in this process. As the Epigraph (from Sir John Suckling's "Song") to Cosmo's story states, "Love is such a Mystery" (XIII, 106) and its transforming power is what drives these shifting forms through their "infinite progress" towards the center. In this final section Anodos affirms this power as the key lesson he has so far learned in this quest. This is the culmination of all his experiences and it is no accident that MacDonald stresses it as an essential aspect of these death revelations. Love is "a power that cannot be but for good" and "all love will, one day, meet with its return . . . All true love will, one day, behold its own image in the eyes of the beloved" (XXIV, 233).

Anodos's return to bodily form is a return to "the world of shadows" through "the door of Dismay," a return in which he feels like a "ghost" (XXV, 236). Death is "bliss." The return to the world of "normal reality" is conveyed in terms of death and limitation: "a writhing as of death convulsed me; and I became once again conscious of a more limited even a bodily and earthly life" (XXIV, 233). Back in his castle Anodos longs to return to the cottage of the wise lady which he recognizes as a stable factor beside which his present life is a brief vision ("I often feel as if I had only left her cottage for a time, and would soon return *out of the vision* into it again" [XXV, 236, my emphasis]) from which he can only escape "through [his] . . . tomb." Life is a dream from which one needs to awaken, as Anodos is reminded in this concluding section of the book. He dreams under the ancient beech tree with which the revelations on his quest began. The sacred energy subsuming form is all around him, threatening to break though the illusory surface of things, taking the shape of the wise ancient woman's voice and leaving him and us with the final revelation on which all others hinge. Amidst all these paradoxical oppositions, interacting worlds of form, multiple interradiating realms and mysterious interconnecting dimensions of experience, there is this single great and optimistic truth. Ultimately all things are driven by love upwards to the harmony of the center. "Good is always coming; . . . What we call evil, is the only and best shape, which, for the person and his condition at the time, could be assumed by the best good. And so, *Farewell*."

ENDNOTES

1. *For the Childlike: George MacDonald's Fantasies for Children*, ed. Roderick McGillis (Metuchen, NJ & London, 1992).

2. See for example, Clive Barker, *Weaveworld* (London, 1988), in which many of MacDonald's favorite ideas are utilized.

3. *Unspoken Sermons.* Series One, (Eureka, CA, 1989), p. 132. All references are to this edition.

4. George MacDonald, *Phantastes: A Faerie Romance.* Introd. Greville MacDonald (London, 1940), Ch. XII, p. 97. Chapter and page numbers will be included in the text.

5. Ibid., p. 195.

6. George MacDonald, *The Princess and the Goblin. The Princess and Curdie*, ed. Roderick McGillis (Oxford, 1990), pp. 219-20. All references are to this edition.

7. *Unspoken Sermons.* Series One, p. 36.

8. *The Princess and Curdie*, p. 208.

9. *Unspoken Sermons.* Series One, pp. 23, 153, 197.

10. Cf. *Phantastes*, XIII, 107.

11. This is another favorite MacDonald symbol for this elusive and magical energy.

12. George MacDonald. *A Dish of Orts* (London, 1893), pp. 24-5.

13. *Unspoken Sermons.* Series Two (Eureka, CA, 1989), p. 94.

14. Cf. MacDonald's statement: "The mind, in the quiescence of its consciousness in sleep, comes into a less disturbed contact with its origin, the heart of creation" (*Wilfred Cumbermede* [London, 1872], Ch.48).

15. See *Phantastes*, Epigraph, Ch. XII, 97.

16. "I will not be tortured to death . . . I will meet it halfway" (XVIII, 160).

17. Cf. The Fairy Palace where there was "no reflection . . . only . . . a ghostly shimmer" (X, 85).

George MacDonald, Julia Kristeva and the Black Sun
William Gray
From *Death and Fantasy*

Most of the main critical readings of George MacDonald's *Phantastes* have recognized that the text is highly susceptible of a Freudian or (more frequently) a Jungian interpretation. Robert Lee Wolff's ground-breaking book *The Golden Key: A Study of the Fiction of George MacDonald* is, if perhaps not actually a "vulgar" Freudian reading, then certainly an example of what Norman Holland has called "first phase" psychoanalytic criticism, intent on disinterring the latent content (the game of "hunt the phallic symbol" popular in first year seminars in university "theory" courses).[1] But however unsatisfactory Wolff's psychoanalytic reading of *Phantastes* may have been, it does not seem necessary on that account to turn instead (as Edmund Cusick has argued) to Jungian psychology.[2] Unlike some other commentators (for example Richard Reis, Colin Manlove and William Raeper) who seem to take it for granted that Carl Jung's approach and terminology have some kind of natural resonance with MacDonald's writing,[3] Cusick does actually argue that we need to choose between the Freudian and Jungian approaches, and that the latter is more helpful. Cusick concedes that his opposition between Sigmund Freud and Jung is very crude, but somehow he seems to want to blame this on Wolff.[4] However, the fact that in 1961 Wolff was interested in the latent content of MacDonald's work hardly seems to justify Cusick in suggesting thirty years later that Freudian approaches *as such* are "biological, deterministic and negative"[5] and seemingly only interested in latent content, thus leaving the Jungian approach as the only viable option.

On the contrary, there have of course been major developments in Freudian approaches since the first phase id-psychology and its rather narrow concern with latent content. The term "Freudian approaches" should surely include the work not only of Anna Freud, Melanie Klein, Donald Winnicott, and Erik Erikson, but also of Jacques Lacan and Julia Kristeva (not to mention the later writings of Freud himself). Indeed *pace* Cusick and the Jungians, it seems to me that the best reading of MacDonald in terms of depth psychology is still that sketched out by David Holbrook in his 1983 introduction to *Phantastes*, a reading which is certainly Freudian, though it is heavily influenced by the British "object relations" school, and especially by Winnicott.[6] Holbrook's interpretation focuses on the themes of death, melancholy, and the longing for a lost maternal love, and in particular reads *Phantastes* as a quest for what was lost in a premature and traumatic weaning. Even apart from the remarkable biographical evidence we happen to have to support such a reading,[7] it is difficult to resist Holbrook's interpretation of the novel as a quest for the beginnings of being or identity in what Erik Erikson called "the primary maternal matrix"—or we might call, following Kristeva, the "semiotic *chora*", a term for the original "womb" or "receptacle" that Kristeva derives from Plato's *Timaeus*.[8] Rather than rehearse Holbrook's argument here, I propose to take further his psychoanalytical reading of *Phantastes* by using some themes from the writings of Kristeva. Although Kristeva is influenced by Lacan, she also departs from him in certain respects, and links back in some interesting ways precisely to those "object relations" theorists (Klein, W.R.D. Fairbairn and Winnicott) who influenced Holbrook. The texts by Kristeva which seem to link most interestingly with *Phantastes* are: *Powers of Horror: An Essay on Abjection*; *Tales of Love*; and, above all, *Black Sun: Depression and Melancholia*.

The opening of *Phantastes* could be described in several respects as liminal, that is, having to do with the borderline. The hero, whose name Anodos means "pathless" or also perhaps "the way up" or "the way back", has just reached the age of twenty-one, and has been invested with various legal rights, including access to his late father's papers contained in an old desk or "secretary". However, this so-to-speak transition into the "symbolic order" is far from straightforward; there is something uncanny in these opening pages, a sense of anxiety. Anodos is driven by a curiosity about his father's personal history to break into a secret compartment in the secretary where he finds some withered rose leaves, a small packet of papers, and a "tiny woman-form" who proceeds to berate men, who are, she says, only convinced by "mere repetition". "But I am not going to argue with you" she says "but to grant you a wish".[9] The wish, however, is never put into words, but is rather conveyed by a sigh—the sigh with which Anodos had on the previous evening answered his sister's question about Fairyland, after she had read him a fairy-tale. Fairyland, in MacDonald's writing, has to do with the pre-linguistic, or with Kristeva's "semiotic"[10] and is very much the realm of "the mothers". As Anodos's fairy grandmother points out, while he may know something about his male ancestors, he knows very little about his great-grandmothers on either side. When Anodos again tries to argue with her, she replies: "Never mind what I seem to think. You shall find the way into Fairy Land tomorrow. Now look into my eyes." (*PH* 5) Eagerly Anodos does so: "They filled me with an unknown longing. I remembered somehow that my mother died when I was a baby. I looked deeper and deeper, till they spread around me like seas, and I sank in their waters. I forgot all the rest." (*PH* 5) Anodos has a vision of a sea "sweeping into bays and round capes and islands, away, away, I know not whither." (*PH* 5) But this suggestion of *jouissance*, of an ecstatic loss of self in the unlimited, in the "oceanic feeling," is a mirage: "Alas! it was no sea, but a low bog burnished by the moon." (*PH* 6)[11] The "imaginary" is a kind of fiction, and the "real" not so easily encountered.

Anodos's journey begins when his room quite literally dissolves into Fairyland. The figures in his carpet, which he had himself designed in imitation of grass and daisies, "bent and swayed with every motion of the changeful current, as if they were about to dissolve with it, and forsaking their fixed form, become fluent as the waters." (*PH* 7) The realm of representation, of which Anodos had thought himself in control, what we might call with Kristeva (following Lacan) the realm of the "symbolic", begins to slip and slide into what Kristeva says in *Tales of Love* is "the very space of metaphorical shifting".[12] Here we move into a realm that is, as we shall see, not able to be represented, but only evoked in sound, rhythm, colour, music, above all poetry; the realm of the semiotic, "the maternal vessel," where "metaphor . . . as if to blur all reference . . . ends up as synesthesia".[13]

Anodos's first encounter in Fairyland is with a rather strange country maiden who informs him of what to expect from the various trees that turn out to be some of the major characters in *Phantastes*. The main villains are the Ash who is an ogre and the Alder who "will smother you with her web of hair, if you let her near you at night." (*PH* 10) In this and the following chapter, the threatening presence of the Ash gradually intensifies, culminating in a genuinely chilling account of a chase through the woods when the Ash almost catches up with Anodos. Characteristic of the Ash are his admittedly rather phallic fingers—described as "bulbous," with "knotty joints and protuberances"—which contribute to Holbrook's interpretation of the Ash in oedipal terms.[14] However such a reading does not altogether fit what is most striking and uncanny in the appearance of the Ash; he has no centre: "I saw the strangest figure; vague, shadowy, almost transparent, in the central parts, and gradually deepening in substance towards the outside, until it ended in extremities capable of casting such a shadow as fell from the hand, through the awful fingers of which I now saw the moon." (*PH* 30-1) MacDonald was fond of playing around with the categories of outside/inside; here he seems to be saying that the Ash has no inside or, as it is put later, "has a hole in his heart that nobody knows of but one or two; and he is always trying to fill it up, but he cannot. That must be what he wanted you for." (*PH* 35) Rather than identifying the Ash as an avenging oedipal father-figure, one might take literally the indication that he is not yet a man, or in psychoanalytical terms, not yet an "object". The Ash seems more like Kristeva's "abject", that which is not yet clearly one thing or another, that which has not yet separated out into an object or a subject, and whose threat resides precisely in this borderline, undecided status in which the inside is not clearly demarcated from the outside. The abject can also pose in a primitive way threats that only crystallize more sharply at the oedipal stage. Thus the threatening Ash may *anticipate* the avenging oedipal father-figure, but the anxiety and terror here is perhaps more to do with the mother, or more precisely with the mother-infant dyad (since the mother at this stage has not yet become a separate object). Since the inside is still all mixed up with the outside (or the processes of projection and introjection are in continual flux), the terrifying greed and aggression are as much *in the infant* at the breast as in the mother. As MacDonald writes: "[the eyes] seemed lighted up with an infinite greed. A gnawing voracity which devoured the devourer, seemed to be the indwelling and propelling power of the whole ghostly apparition. I lay for a few moments simply imbruted with terror." (*PH* 31-2) This is surely in psychoanalytical terms a classic case of the "biter bit".

Anodos is saved from the Ash by the entrance of the Beech. Again this has been read as the appearance of the oedipal mother; even the fact that the beech-woman is "rather above the human size" is interpreted as indicating the perspective of a child towards his mother (*PH* 33).[15] But again we might take literally the statement that the Beech is not yet a woman (*PH* 34). The Beech seems to embody the holding, the giving, the lulling, the sweetly sensual aspects of the "maternal vessel", the *chora*. What pervades this section is her "low, musical, murmuring voice," which is "like a solution of all musical sounds," and blends in with the sound of the wind in the leaves (*PH* 34). Then the Beech sings "a strange, sweet song" which, Anodos says, "I could not understand, but which left in me a feeling like this—": a short poem follows, after which Anodos says he cannot put any more of it into words (*PH* 36). This is a move typical of MacDonald in which (partly perhaps out of an insecurity about his own poetic talent) he claims to offer an inferior version of an original which in its quality, and indeed in its sometimes unknown language, is very different from what the reader is actually given. His own poetry is presented as a pale imitation of some transcendent "song without words". This idea is related to another favorite MacDonald device of running natural sounds and rhythms in and out of language. The music of the beech-tree reappears in the final page of the novel: "I began to listen to the sounds of the leaves overhead. At first, they made sweet inarticulate music above; but, by-and-by, the sound seemed to begin to take shape, and to be gradually moulding itself into words, till at last, I seemed able to distinguish these, half-dissolved in a little ocean of circumfluent tones." (*PH* 237) Here again we seem on the borders of the semiotic. MacDonald's actual poetry may be unremarkable; what is remarkable is the extent to which he privileges the poetic, in a gesture that certainly harks back to Novalis, and also seems to hint forward to Kristeva.

After some further wandering through the woods in which, in the best German Romantic tradition, Anodos "began to feel in some degree what the birds meant in their songs, though [he] could not express it in words, anymore than you can some landscapes" (*PH* 39), he stumbles into a small cave, in a manner reminiscent of the opening dream sequence of *Heinrich von Ofterdingen*. As in the latter, the cave contains a well or basin with obviously magical properties; and like Heinrich's cave, Anodos's "antenatal tomb" (*PH* 44) contains an image of his ideal woman "more near the face that had been born with me in my soul, than anything I had seen before in nature or art." (*PH* 43) But Anodos's image of the ideal woman takes the form not of nature (as in Heinrich's "blue flower") but of art; it is a reclining marble statue, locked in a block of alabaster. After failing to penetrate his ideal woman with his knife, Anodos resorts to the magical power of song to release her. Again this sequence has been read in fairly vulgar Freudian terms, and sometimes it is obviously true that a knife is not just a knife. But it is again interesting to take a step back from the oedipal scenario where the marble woman is the inaccessible, frigid love object, to the pre-oedipal dyad where the frozen woman represents not only the withheld maternal body (or breast) but also the frozen "false self" of the baby. It is only the power of the semiotic that can break open the castrating hold of the oedipal/symbolic, as well as counteracting the more primitive denial of the maternal body/breast that is also the denial of the emerging infantile self. It is not a case of playing off the pre-oedipal against the oedipal; the former is the condition of the possibility of the latter. And the revolution of poetic language needs to be perpetual, for as soon as the frozen maternal body has been released by the semiotic pulse of song, it is immediately lost again, leaving Anodos in despair by the forsaken cave.

Anodos sets off in quest of his "white lady," and almost immediately comes across the Knight, Sir Percival, about whom he had previously read in the fairy cottage, and who in his rusty armour is literally a picture of dejection or perhaps of abjection. In his defiled armor, Percival is an outsider, "jettisoned from the symbolic system" as Kristeva puts it in *Powers of Horror*,[16] and also uncannily like the disinherited Knight of Gerard de Nerval's "El Desdichado" ("The Disinherited") which gives Kristeva her title *Black Sun*.[17] Percival's problem is that he has been tainted by his encounter with the evil Alder-maiden. Anodos has been warned. As he continues his quest for his lost lady of the marble, he experiences an ecstatic sense of union with Mother Earth: "Earth drew me towards her bosom: I felt as if I could fall down and kiss her." (*PH* 50) "In the midst of this ecstasy" the idea that somewhere his lady was "waiting (might it not be?) to meet and thank her deliverer in a twilight which would veil her confusion" turns the whole night into "one dream-realm of joy." (*PH* 51) The very thought of such a night of love leads to an involuntary semiotic outburst of song, which draws the response near to him of "a low delicious laugh . . . not the laugh of one who would not be heard, but the laugh of one who has just received something long and patiently desired-a laugh that ends in a low musical moan." (*PH* 52) Announcing herself as indeed his "white lady", and thus "sending a thrill of speechless delight through a heart which all the love-dreams of the preceding day and evening had been tempering for this culminating hour" (*PH* 52), the mysterious female figure invites Anodos to her grotto. There she entrances him with a tale of love: "I listened till she and I were blended with the tale; till she and I were the whole history . . . What followed I cannot clearly remember. The succeeding horror almost obliterated it." (*PH* 55)

This horror is the replacement of the damsel by "a strange horrible object" that looks like "an open coffin set on one end." (*PH* 55) This hollow, rough representation of the human frame seems made of decaying bark, which is seamed "as if [it] had healed again from the cut of a knife." (*PH* 55) This "thing" literally displays the backside of the enchantress. The obvious Freudian reading of this is that it expresses a horror and disgust of the vagina both as a displaced anus and as the site of castration. However, it is also possible to read this passage in the light of Kristeva's work on depression and melancholia, especially as this scene with the Alder-maiden marks the outset of Anodos's depression. Kristeva writes in *Black Sun*: "The depressed narcissist mourns not an Object but the Thing. Let me posit the 'Thing' as the real that does not lend itself to signification, the centre of attraction and repulsion, seat of the sexuality from which the object of desire will become separated." (*BS* 13) Kristeva continues in a way that uncannily echoes the movement of MacDonald's narrative: "Of this Nerval provides a dazzling metaphor that suggests an insistence without presence, a light without representation: the Thing is an imagined sun, bright and black at the same time." (*BS* 13) Indeed, what she writes next could almost be summary of the plot of *Phantastes*:

> Ever since that archaic attachment the depressed person has the impression of having been deprived of an unnameable, supreme good, of something unrepresentable, that perhaps only devouring might represent, or an *invocation* might point out, but no word could signify . . . Knowingly disinherited of the Thing, the depressed person wanders in pursuit of continuously disappointing adventures and loves; or else retreats, disconsolate and aphasic, alone with the unnamed Thing. The "primary identification" with the "father in individual prehistory" would be the means, the link that might enable one to become reconciled with the loss of the Thing. Primary identification initiates a compensation for the Thing and at the same time secures the subject to another dimension, that of imaginary adherence, reminding one of the bond of faith, which is just what disintegrates in the depressed person. (*BS* 13-4)

We will have cause to refer back to this passage in our reading of MacDonald's text. But already here it is significant that the figure who saves Anodos from the "unfathomable horror" of the Alder-maiden, and the Ash "with his Gorgon-head" who now appears, turns out to be the Knight, figuring as "the father in individual prehistory" who precedes and makes possible the subsequent oedipal father of the symbolic order (*BS* 56).

However, although saved from "unfathomable horror" by the as yet unnamed Knight, Anodos enters the depression that will haunt the remainder of the book. The daylight has become hateful to him, "and the thought of the great, innocent, bold sunrise unendurable." (*PH* 57) The birds are singing, but not for him. After an interlude in a farm-house which contains one of the many nurturing mothers in the book, Anodos comes to a different kind of house containing a different kind of mother: this is the house of the ogre, or as it will later be called, "the Church of Darkness." The epigraph to this chapter is from the "Mother Night" speech of Mephistopheles in Goethe's *Faust*: "I am a part of the part, which at first was the whole".[18] The epigraph is directly relevant to this chapter, for Anodos finds in this house a woman reading aloud from "an ancient little volume" what amounts to a kind of hymn to darkness. This could certainly be seen as an inversion of Christian Orthodoxy, and seems in part to be derived from the passage from Faust that provides this chapter's epigraph. But there is another, perhaps less obvious, intertext at this point. For what the woman reads in the ancient volume bears a strong resemblance to Novalis's *Hymns to the Night*, which MacDonald must have known in the 1850s and would later translate (in 1852 he had already published a translation of Novalis's *Spiritual Songs*). We may go with the Goethe intertext, in which Mephistopheles, the "spirit of negation" ("*der Geist der stets verneint*"), is the unwilling servant of the greater good, and darkness ultimately assists in the triumph of light; or we may go with the Novalis intertext in which night is positively hymned as the great Mother. In neither case is darkness seen as unambiguous and absolute evil. Like the German Romantics who influenced him, and indeed like some postmodern thinkers with whom he has been compared, MacDonald resisted absolute dualisms, or binary oppositions.[19] The Shadow acquired by Anodos in the Church of Darkness, after his intrusion into the forbidden cupboard, is a *necessary* Shadow; his fall here is a *felix culpa*. Kristeva, too, in her *Powers of Horror* refers to the *felix culpa* idea in the chapter entitled "Qui tollis peccata mundi." She refers to Duns Scotus's spiritual revolution, which allowed the remission of sin by bringing sin into speech in confession and absolution: "It is owing to speech, at any rate, that the lapse has a chance of becoming fortunate: *felix culpa* is merely a phenomenon of enunciation."[20] Underlying Kristeva's theological point is a psychoanalytical one: to acquire a subject position in language, or in the symbolic order, requires a breaking loose from, and a rejection of, the abject, ultimately the mother. Therefore the fault that is necessary and ultimately blessed is matricide, for matricide is the condition of the possibility of subjectivity and speech. Kristeva writes provocatively in *Black Sun*: "Matricide is our vital necessity, the sine-qua-non of our individuation." (*BS* 27-8)

But this fall, fault, rejection, and loss have to be *felt* as fall, fault, rejection, and loss, and consequently there occurs mourning, melancholia, and abjection. As Kristeva puts in *Black Sun*: "The child king becomes irredeemably sad before uttering his first words; this is because he has been irrevocably, desperately separated from the mother, a loss that causes him to try to find her again, along with other objects of love, first in the imagination, then in words." (*BS* 6) So if *Phantastes* ends in hope, as Anodos hears the following words in, and permeated by, the semiotic music of the rustling beech leaves: "A great good is coming—is coming—is coming to thee, Anodos" (*PH* 237), such hope is only bought at the price of *really going through* the guilt and mourning of the so-called "depressive position" of Klein, Winnicott, and Kristeva. Night may ultimately be transfigured, as in Novalis; evil may in the end turn out be, as in Goethe, merely a rather serious joke; but in the meantime the Shadow, with all its distorting and blighting effects, has to be lived with. In a passage that strikingly echoes Nerval, and anticipates Kristeva, Anodos says of his Shadow: "it began to coruscate, and shoot out on all sides a radiation of dim shadow. These rays of gloom issued from the central shadow as from a black sun, lengthening and shortening with continual change. But wherever a ray struck, that part of earth, or sea, or sky, became void and desert, and sad to my heart . . . one ray shot out beyond the rest, seeming to lengthen infinitely, until it smote the great sun on the face, which withered and darkened beneath the blow." (*PH* 73)

One of the baleful influences of Anodos's "evil demon" is that it disrupts his ability to offer a connected account of his experiences (*PH* 73). He says: "From this time until I arrived at the palace of Fairy Land, I can attempt no consecutive account of my wanderings and adventures. Everything, henceforward, existed for me in its relation to my attendant." (*PH* 72) This lack of a consecutive account not only follows Novalis's description of the *Märchen*, given in the epigraph to the whole novel[21]; it is also, according to Kristeva, related to melancholia. Whether it results from "an inversion of aggressiveness" or from some other cause, "the phenomenon that might be described as a breakdown of *biological and logical sequentiality* finds its radical manifestation in melancholia." (*BS* 20) What Kristeva calls "shattered concatenation" or simply "nonconcatenation" is for her a result of the failure to mourn successfully the archaic maternal pre-object, "the Thing." She writes later in *Black Sun*: "From the analyst's point of view, the possibility of concatenating signifiers (words or actions) appears to depend upon going through mourning for an archaic and indispensable object . . . Mourning for the Thing—such a possibility comes out of transposing, beyond loss and on an imaginary or symbolic level, the imprints of an interchange with the other articulated according to a certain order." (*BS* 40)

More simply put: "If I did not agree to lose mother, I could neither imagine nor name her." (*BS* 41) It is significant that Anodos says that his inability to give a consecutive account of his wanderings lasts until he arrives at the palace of Fairy Land (*PH* 72). Anodos's stay in the palace is at the centre of *Phantastes*, and central to his time there are the hours spent reading in the marvellous palace library. Reading in this library is a magical experience. Anodos finds that his identity is taken over by the text; he *becomes* the text, or conversely, the text gives him an identity. One of the stories he reads forms the central chapter of *Phantastes*. This story is a Hoffmannesque tale within a tale about Cosmo von Wehrstahl, a student in Prague, though of course as Anodos says: "while I read it, I was Cosmo, and his history was mine. Yet, all the time, I seemed to have a kind of double-consciousness, and the story a double meaning." (*PH* 106) Cosmo/Anodos/the reader— for as Stephen Prickett says, this *Bildungsroman* is above all about the formation of the *reader*[22]—acquires a magic mirror in which he discovers in his *reflected* room a beautiful woman with whom he falls obsessively in love. The tale is about Cosmo's quest to be united with the object of his longing desire, which he only achieves in the end at the cost of his own death, after having smashed the mirror. That the centre of this *Bildungsroman* should be occupied by a tale about a magic mirror, which is explicitly compared with the imagination (*PH* 112-3), invites reference to Lacan's "mirror stage" and "the imaginary." Yet more interesting from Kristeva's point of view is the way that here the concept of identity, union with the loved object, and a death bordering on suicide come together in a kind of *jouissance*. This mutual interplay of the themes of identity, love, the maternal, and death by suicide, dominates the remainder of *Phantastes*.

After the mirror episode, in a scene that reverses the ending of Novalis's *Märchen* "Hyacinth and Roseblossom", Anodos finally unveils his Isis only to have her writhe from his arms and disappear, leaving him desolate. He continues his journey "with a dull endurance, varied by moments of uncontrollable sadness" and comes to a bleak shoreline, "bare and waste, and gray." (*PH* 157; 159) The following powerful evocation of desolation and despair, which one critic thinks may be in part a response to Arnold's "Dover Beach," seen in manuscript form,[23] culminates in the simple statement: "I could bear it no longer." (*PH* 159) Anodos throws himself into the sea:

> I stood one moment and gazed into the heaving abyss beneath me; then plunged headlong . . . A blessing, like the kiss of

a mother, seemed to alight on my soul; a calm, deeper than that which accompanies a hope deferred, bathed my spirit. I sank far into the waters, and sought not to return. I felt as if once more the great arms of the beechtree were around me, soothing me after the miseries I had passed through, and telling me, like a little sick child, that I should be better tomorrow. (*PH* 160)

Saved by a little boat that miraculously appears, Anodos lies in a trance: "In dreams of unspeakable joy . . . I passed through [a] wondrous twilight. I awoke with the feeling that I had been kissed and loved to my heart's content." (*PH* 161-2) Kristeva's comment in *Black Sun* seems remarkably apt at this point: "One can imagine the delights of reunion that a regressive daydream promises itself through the nuptials of suicide." (*BS* 14) It is as if Anodos is plunging from the unbearable symbolic order back into the sweet annihilation of self in the primal chaos that Kristeva associates with suicide: "The depressive denial that destroys the meaning of the symbolic also destroys the act's meaning, and leads the subject to commit suicide without anguish of disintegration, as a reuniting with archaic non-integration, as lethal as it is jubilatory, 'oceanic.'" (*BS* 19)

Suicide is the way back to "the non integrated self's lost paradise, one without others or limits, a fantasy of untouchable fullness." (*BS* 20) And it is quite fitting that Anodos's way should now take him back to the most explicitly maternal figure in the book, the wise old woman with young eyes who lives in a magic cottage. It is fitting because, according to Kristeva, the act of suicide is a way of avoiding matricide, which is, as we have seen, "our vital necessity, the sine-qua-non condition of our individuation." (*BS* 27-8) She writes in the same passage in *Black Sun*: "The lesser or greater violence of matricidal drive . . . entails, when it is hindered, its inversion on the self: the maternal object having been introjected, the depressive or melancholic putting to death of the self is what follows, instead of matricide. In order to protect mother I kill myself." (*BS* 28) Having killed himself, Anodos has saved his allproviding mother: "While she sung, I was in Elysium . . . I felt as if she could give me everything I wanted; as if I should never wish to leave her, but would be content to be sung to and fed by her, day after day, as years rolled by." (*PH* 171) Anodos does nevertheless attempt to leave her by going through each of the four doors in the cottage, but returns each time after having encountered, respectively: the death of his brother; the disappearance of the Knight and his lady behind an obviously parental bedroom door; a dead lover and/or mother; and whatever lay behind the fourth door, which he cannot bring to consciousness. In other words, behind each door lies obviously oedipal material which Anodos cannot face; he must return to "the floor of the cottage, with my head in the lap of the woman, who was weeping over me, and stroking my hair with both hands, talking to me as a mother might talk to a sick and sleeping, or a dead child." (*PH* 182) However, the old woman finally persuades Anodos to leave, gently pushing him away with the words "Go, my son, and do something worth doing." The last sentence of this chapter reads: "I felt very desolate as I went." (*PH* 184)

Nevertheless, in the next section Anodos does do something worth doing. He teams up with two brothers in order to kill three giants who have been terrorizing the countryside, and is feted as the conquering hero in the court of the grateful king, whose two sons died in defeating the giants. Superficially, then, Anodos seems to have successfully entered the symbolic order; but he is still haunted by the Shadow. As he enters an enchanted wood, the Shadow suddenly disappears. Anodos becomes euphoric and begins to develop an inflated sense of self, until he encounters a more powerful *Doppelgänger* who totally deflates his sense of self-worth, and leads him, cowed, to a "dreary square tower" in which he is imprisoned with his Shadow, which has meanwhile reappeared (*PH* 205). Again, Kristeva's version of psychoanalysis seems to fit MacDonald's text uncannily well. In her discussion of borderline cases in *Powers of Horror* she calls this kind of patient a "fortified castle," and writes:

> Constructed on the one hand by the incestuous desire of (for) his mother and on the other by an overly brutal separation from her, the borderline patient, even though he may be a fortified castle, is nevertheless an empty castle. The absence, or the failure, of paternal function to establish a unitary bent between subject and object, produces this strange configuration: an encompassment that is stifling . . . and, at the same time, draining. The ego then plunges into a pursuit of identifications that could repair narcissism—identifications that the subject will experience as insignificant, "empty", "null", "devitalized" and "puppet-like". An empty castle, haunted by unappealing ghosts—"powerless" outside, "impossible" inside.[24]

But not for the first time, Anodos is liberated by the semiotic: a song enters his prison-house: "it bathed me like a sea; inwrapt me like an odorous vapour; entered my soul like a long draught of clear spring-water; shone upon me like essential sunlight; soothed me like a mother's voice and hand." (*PH* 208) Anodos is able now simply to walk out the door of the castle, where he finds the singer, a beautiful woman whose magic globe he had shattered long before, just after he had acquired his Shadow. The woman has, through the power of the Fairy Queen, become a wandering agent of liberation, delivering people by the power of her song. Anodos can now give up his "vain attempt to behold, if not my ideal in myself, at least myself in my ideal" (*PH* 212); that is, perhaps, the vain pursuit of "insignificant" identifications that would repair narcissism (to use Kristeva's terms). He experiences what Kristeva says we are all ultimately looking for, and especially in psychoanalysis—a new birth: "Another self seemed to arise like a white spirit from a dead man, from the dumb and trampled self of the past. Doubtless, this self must again die and be buried and again from its tomb spring a winged child . . . Self will come to life even in the slaying of self." (*PH* 212)[25]

Underway again, Anodos once more hears a voice singing, but this time a manly voice. It is the Knight, dragging behind his horse the hideous corpse of a dragon, described in lurid detail, surely an instance of the abject. However the conquering Knight is hardly the stern oedipal father figure one might perhaps anticipate; rather his feminine qualities are stressed. He has "all the gentleness of a womanly heart" (*PH* 216); he tends to a wounded child "if possible even more gently than the mother." (*PH* 217) Anodos begs to become the Knight's squire, and although this could be read in straightforwardly oedipal terms, the Knight has enough of the maternal and the semiotic about him to suggest that he is perhaps rather the *Black Sun*'s pre-oedipal "father in individual prehistory"(*BS* 13), "primary identification" with whom allows reconciliation with loss of "the Thing." Such reconciliation, which allows the transition from the presymbolic (or pre-object-choice) stage into the symbolic order, is very much the province of religion. As Kristeva says in *Powers of Horror*: "it is within that undecidable space, logically coming before the choice of the sexual object, that the religious answer to abjection breaks in: *defilement, taboo*, or *sin*."[26] Or *sacrifice*, Kristeva might have added at this point.[27] And indeed it is to a strange religious ceremony that the Knight leads Anodos, where they witness a ritual human sacrifice, in which the victims are devoured by being pushed into a door in a great pedestal supporting an enthroned image. The Knight seems to acquiesce in all this, but Anodos does not. In a violent gesture which resists the institutionalized violence of the sacrifice which founds the symbolic order, he strides up to the image, overthrows it and grapples with the beast which emerges from the gaping hole under the displaced image. Though he dies in its embrace (and there is a strong suggestion of suicide), Anodos manages to kill the devouring monster. One suspects that although he seems finally to have managed to kill his mother, by dying himself he has achieved ultimate union or identification with her in a state which seems as much pre-natal as postmortem: "Now that I lay in her bosom, the whole earth, and each of her births, was as a body to me, at my will. I seemed to feel the great heart of the mother beating into mine, and feeding me with her own life, her own essential being and nature." (*PH* 232)

Anodos enjoys not being. The following (and penultimate) chapter begins: "I was dead, and right content." (*PH* 230) There follows an at times sentimental, at times didactic, and at times bizarre evocation of "a state of ideal bliss" with echoes of Plato, Novalis, Goethe, and William Blake, and the suggestion of an identification of Anodos with Christ himself (*PH* 234). From this "state of ideal bliss" Anodos is wrenched: "a pang and a terrible shudder went through me; a writhing as of death convulsed me; and I became once again conscious of a more limited, even a bodily and earthly life." (*PH* 233) Paradoxically, it is a death agony that brings Anodos back to *this* life, a life that "seemed to correspond to what we think death is, before we die." (*PH* 234) There is also a strong suggestion of *jouissance*, a violent "coming" into contact with "the real." And in a literal sense, Anodos has come home, back to quotidian reality.

Yet what constitutes "the real" is precisely the issue which remains undecided at the end of *Phantastes*. On one level there is the theme, typical of German Romanticism, of a banal common life that needs somehow to be synthesized with the free play of fantasy. But MacDonald at the end of his novel backs off from the radically Utopian vision whose traces haunt the margins of the Novalis quotations which preface *Phantastes*. The promised "great good coming" to Anodos (*PH* 237) is not the radical poeticization of reality projected by Novalis's "magic idealism". Despite its semiotic trappings, the promise seems to amount to little more than the platitudinous: "what we call evil, is the only and best shape, which, for the person and his condition at the time, could be assumed by the best good." (*PH* 237) And if MacDonald fails to follow through the dialectic of Novalis, it might equally be said that he fails to follow through Kristeva's dialectic of the semiotic and the symbolic. The consequent precariousness of the subject-position achieved at the end of *Phantastes* is confirmed by MacDonald's later fantasy work *Lilith*, where things start to fall apart in a spectacular and disturbing way.²⁸ The question remains of course as to whether the projects of personal and social transformation in the writings of Novalis and Kristeva are in reality more than desperate attempts by what Kelly Oliver calls "melancholy theoreticians" to come to terms with profound feelings of personal loss through the practice of writing.²⁹ Perhaps the modest, ambiguous ending of *Phantastes* is not without a certain courage, the "corage" to which George MacDonald aspired when he took as his motto the anagram of his name "Corage: God mend al." That courage is in the first place "the courage to be" or to use Kristeva's terms in *Black Sun*, the resistance to the *"I AM THAT WHICH IS NOT"*. (*BS* 146)

Endnotes

1. Robert Lee Wolff, *The Golden Key: A Study of the Fiction of George MacDonald* (New Haven: Yale University Press 1961); Norman N. Holland, "Literary Interpretation and Three *Phases* of Psychoanalysis," *Critl* 3, 2 (Winter 1976) and reprinted in Alan Roland (ed.), *Psychoanalysis, Creativity and Literature*, (New York: Columbia University Press, 1978), pp. 233-47.

2. Edmund Cusick, "George MacDonald and Jung" in William Raeper (ed.), *The Gold Thread: Essays on George MacDonald*, (Edinburgh: Edinburgh University Press, 1990), pp. 56-86, 57-9.

3. Richard Reis, *George MacDonald* (New York: Twayne Books, 1972); C. N. Manlove, *Modern Fantasy: Five Studies* (Cambridge: Cambridge University Press, 1975); William Raeper, *George MacDonald* (Tring: Lion, 1987). A decade after the first appearance of this piece, I'd be less inclined to disagree with them. Doubtless a Jungian would have told me so.

4. Cusick, "George MacDonald and Jung", p. 58.

5. Ibid.

6. David Holbrook, Introduction to *Phantastes*, by George MacDonald (London: Everyman Paperback, 1983) pp. vi-xxv. Holbrook subsequently published *A Study of George Macdonald and the Image of Woman* (New York: Edwin Mellen, 2000).

7. In a secret drawer in MacDonald's desk were found, after his death, a lock of his mother's hair and a letter by her containing the following reference to his premature weaning: "I cannot help in my heart being very much grieved for him yet, for he has not forgot it ... he cryed desperate for a while in the first night, but he has cryed very little since and I hope the worst is over now." See Greville MacDonald, *George MacDonald and His* Wife (London: George Allen and Unwin, 1924), p. 32.

8. On the "semiotic" and the "*chora*" see Julia Kristeva, *Revolution in Poetic Language* (trans. Margaret Waller) (New York: Columbia University Press, 1984);

extracts in *The Kristeva Reader* (ed Toril Moi) (Oxford: Blackwell, 1986).

9. George MacDonald, *Phantastes: A Faerie Romance for Men and Women* [1858] (London: Dent Everyman, 1915), p. 4. Subsequent references are to this edition and will be cited as *PH* parenthetically in the text

10. See footnote 8 above.

11. Some editions of *Phantastes* read "a low fog burnished by the moon".

12. Julia Kristeva, *Tales of Love*, (trans. Leon S. Roudiez) (New York: Columbia University Press, 1987), p. 38.

13. Julia Kristeva, *Tales of Love*, pp. 277-8.

14. David Holbrook, Introduction to *Phantastes*, p. xix.

15. David Holbrook, Introduction to *Phantastes*, p. xvii.

16. Julia Kristeva, *Powers of Horror: An Essay on Abjection*, (trans. Leon S. Roudiez) (New York: Columbia University Press, 1982), p. 65.

17. Julia Kristeva, *Black Sun: Depression and Melancholia*, (trans. Leon S. Roudiez) (New York: Columbia University Press, 1989). Subsequent references to this edition will be cited parenthetically as *BS*. The first quatrain of "El Desdichado" runs as follows:

    Je suis le ténébreux, le veuf, l'inconsolé
    Le prince d'Aquitaine á la tour abolie;
    Ma seule étoile est morte, et mon luth constellé
    Porte le soleil noir de la mélancolie

    I am saturnine, bereft, disconsolate,
    The Prince of Aquitaine whose tower has crumbled;
    My lone star is dead, and my bespangled lute
    Bears the black sun of melancholia.
    (translation as in the English version of *Black Sun* by Leon S. Roudiez, p. 140).

18. Johann Wolfgang von Goethe, *Faust, Part One*, trans. David Luke (Oxford and New York: Oxford University Press, 1981), lines 1349-50. Quoted in *Phantastes*, p. 67.

19. See Stephen Prickett, "Fictions and Metafictions: 'Phantastes,' 'Wilhelm Meister,' and the idea of the 'Bildungsroman,'" in William Raeper (ed.), *The Gold*

Thread, pp. 109-25; Roderick McGillis, Introduction to MacDonald's *The Princess and the Goblin*, and *The Princess and Curdie* (Oxford: Oxford University Press, 1990), pp. vii-xxviii, xvi. On MacDonald's resistance to binary thinking see also Roderick McGillis "*Phantastes* and *Lilith*: Femininity and Freedom" in *The Gold Thread*, pp. 31-55.

20. Kristeva, *Powers of Horror*, p. 131.

21. "A *Märchen* is like a dream image without coherence . . . In a genuine *Märchen* everything must be miraculous, mysterious and incoherent . . . here begins the time of anarchy, of lawlessness, freedom . . . the world of the *Märchen* is a total opposition to the world of truth and for that very reason has the total likeness to it that chaos has to the completed creation." In MacDonald's text the epigraph is untranslated; the translation here is mine. On the history of omissions and misprints relating to these Novalis extracts see Wolff, *The Golden Key*, pp. 42-5.

22. Prickett, op. cit., in Raeper (ed.), *The Gold Thread*, p. 117.

23. David S. Robb, *George MacDonald* (Edinburgh: Scottish Academic Press, 1987) pp. 80-3.

24. Kristeva, *Powers of Horror*, pp. 48-9.

25. Cf. Novalis's concept of *Selbsttödtung* (which Thomas Carlyle translates as "annihilation of self"), and which MacDonald would have known from Carlyle's essay on Novalis if not from Novalis himself. See Thomas Carlyle, "Novalis" in *Critical and Miscellaneous Essays*, vol. 2 (London: Chapman and Hall, 1899), pp. 1-55.

26. Kristeva, *Powers of Horror*, p. 48.

27. For Kristeva on sacrifice, see John Lechte, *Julia Kristeva* (London: Routledge, 1990), pp. 73-5, 148-9; also Kelly Oliver, *Reading Kristeva: Unraveling the Double-bind* Bloomington: Indiana University Press, 1993), pp. 40-1.

28. George MacDonald, *Lilith* [1895] (Grand Rapids: Eerdmans, 1981).

29. Oliver, op. cit., p. 143.

From Fact to Fantasy in Victorian Fiction: Dickens's *Hard Times* and MacDonald's *Phantastes*

John Pennington

From *Extrapolation*

> In an utilitarian age, of all other times, it is a matter of grave importance that Fairy tales should be respected.... To preserve them in their usefulness, they must be as much preserved in their simplicity, and purity, and innocent extravagance, as if they were actual fact.
> —Dickens, "Frauds on the Fairies"

Dickens's comments on the fairy tale in the partly satiric essay "Frauds on the Fairies" (1853) is an important midcentury manifesto on the importance of the imagination to the Victorians. Dickens's agenda in the essay was at least twofold: he wanted to chastise his colleague George Cruikshank, who began bowdlerizing classic fairy tales and retelling them as moral tracts for the young; and he felt the need to defend the fantastic imagination because he saw it as a liberating force in a factdriven utilitarian age. As he claims in his essay: "It [fairy literature] has greatly helped to keep us, in some sense, ever young, by preserving through our worldly ways one slender track not overgrown with weeds, where we may walk with children sharing their delights" (435).

It is significant that Dickens's next novel after "Frauds on the Fairies" is *Hard Times* (1854), often dubbed an industrial novel or anti-utilitarian tract, and certainly the atypical work in his canon. Thematically, *Hard Times* explores the tension between fact and fantasy: Gradgrind's philosophy stresses that "facts alone are wanted in life" (7); the Coketown ethic spurns that which is contrary to fact and productive behavior. Sleary's circus and the Pegasus's Arms, on the other hand, represent the imaginative side of life, the fantasy realm where horses are more than quadrupeds with forty teeth. *Hard Times* can be viewed as Dickens's attempt to integrate his beliefs expressed in "Frauds on the Fairies" into his novel: he balances fact with fantasy, commenting on the entire realistic tradition that privileges fact—realism—over fancy—fairy tale and fantasy. The novel, then, demonstrates Dickens's personal trust in the imagination, shrouded in the guise of a serialized realistic novel. As Harry Stone claims in *Dickens and the Invisible World*, after "Frauds on the Fairies" the "fairy tale now stood at the center of his imaginative and social beliefs; it was a shorthand way of referring to and dramatizing those beliefs" (15).

Dickens certainly inspired others. Another contemporary of Dickens would take his lead and carry his ideas even further. George MacDonald, Scottish preacher, essayist, novelist, and fantasist, wrote *Phantastes* (1858) in response to this growing schism between fact and fantasy. In fact, pardon the pun, MacDonald appears to be directly answering *Hard Times*, for in *Phantastes* MacDonald literally transforms fact—the mundane world—into fantasy. He creates a whole fairyland where "truth" resides in the faith in imagination, not in the faith in reason. Whereas the government official tells the fledgling Bitzers that "you don't walk upon flowers in fact; you cannot be allowed to walk upon flowers in carpets" (11), MacDonald seduces the reader to imagine that flowers on carpets are real—that is, they are real in fairyland, in the imagination. As Dickens explored the importance of fantasy through realism, MacDonald explored the nature of reality through fantasy. As Dickens explored the importance of fantasy in the imagination thematically in *Hard Times*, MacDonald explored these concerns thematically *and* structurally in *Phantastes*.

"Now, what I want is, Facts . . . . Plant nothing else, and root out everything else" (7) begins *Hard Times*. *Fact* with a capital *F*. "Louisa, never wonder," orders Mr. Gradgrind to his daughter. "Never wonder. By means of addition, subtraction, multiplication, and division, settle everything somehow, and never wonder" (41), spouts the narrator, mimicking what Mr. M'Choakumchild drills into the young children he teaches. The irony residing behind *Hard Times* is that it is a deadly serious—a factual—work. There is less imaginative play in the novel, less of Dickens's broad stokes of humor and whimsy. It is direct, didactic, and sentimental in places, often mechanical and telegraphic in its construction. Yet this deadly serious realistic novel uses fairy-tale motifs to contrast and complement the thematic focus on the imagination (or lack of imagination). David Lodge equates Dickens's technique in *Hard Times* to Brecht's "alienation effect": "By invoking the world of fairy-tale *ironically*, making the inhabitants of this drab, gritty, Victorian mill town re-enact the motifs of folk-tale and legend, he drew attention to that repression or elimination of the human faculty of imagination . . . which he believed was the culturally disastrous effect of governing society according to purely materialistic, empirical criteria of 'utility'" (45). Thus the realistic novel becomes an ironic commentary on the lack of imagination during the nineteenth century, *and* it becomes a commentary on the more complex problem of belief—or lack of belief—that was part of the growing industrialized world, which privileged fact over fiction, fact over faith.

In "*Hard Times* and Dickens' Concept of the Imagination," Robert Higbie persuasively argues that Dickens "is trying to redeem imagination by finding a new way of using it, by giving it a serious purpose so that it will no longer be separate from faith . . . but rather allied with it" (100). To Higbie, "the novel both asks and demonstrates how imagination can survive realism" (107). Of course, *Hard Times*'s pessimistic ending complements such claims, for Dickens the realist and Dickens the social commentator do not want the reader to find the imagination a mere escape from the workaday world; he wants the reader to see what the curtailment of the imagination can lead to. Mr. Gradgrind, Mr. Bounderby, Tom, and Louisa are all tainted by utilitarian fact-bound reasoning. Stephen Blackpool is destroyed because humane actions conflict with factual and practical action; Mr. James Harthouse is a mere shadow of a potentially productive creature. Only Sissy, fruitfully married with children, "grown learned in childish lore," who beautifies "lives of machinery and reality with those of imaginative graces and delights, without which the heart of infancy will wither up" (219), has a satisfactory and productive life. As Higbie suggests, "One must learn that imagination's childlike belief in wish-fulfillment is not enough; one must face the unidealness of reality in order to learn the need for serious belief, chastening oneself into looking for something higher than one's own fancy, giving up the illusion that one can create an ideal oneself as the endings to the earlier novels do" (101). Thus in *Hard Times* Dickens appropriates the imagination to comment on the need for realistic uses of such enchantment: the pathos of the ending is redeemed by Sissy's imaginative and childlike ways. The fairy tale works itself through tragedy to hope, what Tolkien would call "eucatastrophe" (68).

In chapter 2 of *Hard Times* Dickens satirizes utilitarian moral calculus: the government official presiding over the children's class attempts to teach the youngsters that "you must discard the word Fancy altogether" (11). He proves his case with simple logic: since you do not see horses walking up and down your wall, then you do not put horses on wallpaper. Since "you don't walk upon flowers in fact; you cannot be allowed to walk upon flowers in carpets"; thus, you must use "mathematical figures which are susceptible of proof and demonstration. This is the new discovery. This is fact. This is taste" (11). Apparently George MacDonald disliked such a taste, for in chapter 2 of *Phantastes* he appears to answer the government official. In chapter

Crossing a Great Frontier

1, Anodos, the narrator, has been warned by a tiny woman he has discovered in his family bureau that he will eventually find fairyland; in chapter 2 Anodos is careful to describe the metamorphosis into this new realm:

> I suddenly, as one awakes to the consciousness that the sea has been moaning by him for hours . . . became aware of the sound of running water near me; and looking out of bed, I saw that a large green marble basin, in which I was wont to wash . . . was overflowing like a spring . . . And, stranger still, where this carpet, which I myself designed to imitate a field of grass and daises, bordered the course of the little stream, the grass-blades and daises seemed to wave in a tiny breeze that followed the water's flow; while under the rivulet they bent and swayed with every motion of the changeful current, as if they were about to dissolve with it, and, forsaking their fixed form, become fluent as the waters. (9)

His dressing table, carved with foliage, also comes to life, as do his curtains, which depict branches and leaves. It seems fairly certain that MacDonald has *Hard Times* in mind as he writes such a scene.[1] The bedroom is an apt metaphor for this transformation: imagination is the act of dreaming, the dream or fantasy world becoming as real and significant as the mundane world of 1858. Flowers can indeed be alive on wallpaper *if* one is allowed to use imagination. In *Unspoken Sermons* MacDonald writes:

> Ask a man of mere science, what is the truth of a flower: he will pull it to pieces, show you its parts, explain how they minister each to the life of the flower . . . and doubtless many more facts about it. Ask the poet what is the truth of a flower, and he will answer: "Why, the flower itself, the perfect flower, and what it cannot help saying to him who has ears to hear it." The truth of the flower is, not the facts about it . . . but the shining, glowing, gladdening, patient thing throned on its stalk-the compeller of smile and tear from child and prophet. (145-46)

Stephen Prickett, in *Romanticism and Religion*, calls the transformation passage in *Phantastes* "a *symbolic* event" that "suggests that this Fairyland is in some sense to be apprehended as more 'real' than the world in which Anodos had hitherto been brought up" (232). Art or imagination is brought to life, "the imitation is liberated into reality" and the result becomes "the shock of seeing the familiar for the first time" (232). In *Victorian Fantasy* Prickett adds, "What with us is artificial, there [Faerie] is 'natural.' The stream of water overflowing from the basin is literally the River of Life: as it flows across his carpet it brings to life everything it touches" (179-80). MacDonald delivers what Dickens requests: a world where the magical informs the mundane. Or as Anodos explains, "So doth Faerie invade the world of men, and sometimes startle the common eye with an association as of cause and effect, when between the two no connecting links can be traced" (85). The imagination, then, requires faith and belief and becomes the hope and salvation of humanity. MacDonald performs no fraud on fairies in *Phantastes*.

MacDonald's choice of writing fantasy is important, for he seems to be challenging the very notion of realistic literature that defined the age. C. S. Lewis, the greatest admirer and populizer of MacDonald, writes that MacDonald was "seduced into writing novels," most of which are utterly forgettable, because "a dominant form tends to attract to itself writers whose talents would have fitted them much better for works of some other kind" (232). As editor of *Good Words for the Young*, MacDonald published serially *At the Back of the North Wind* and *The Princess and the Goblin*; the latter work he considered one of his finest. As readership plummeted, MacDonald wrote to his wife: "Strahan [his publisher] thinks it [lagging readership] is because there is too much of what he calls the fairy element. Perhaps I could find a market for that kind of talent in America—I should wonder" (Greville MacDonald 411-12).Years earlier, George Murray Smith, who had published and liked *Phantastes*, and who had just rejected a drama by MacDonald, wrote to him suggesting, "If you would but write novels, you would find all the publishers saving up to buy them of you! Nothing but fiction pays" (Greville MacDonald 317-18). Dickens's popularity defined literary taste, and his brand of realism satiated the reading public; MacDonald, more radical than Dickens in his attempt to remythologize the Victorians, stumbled. His fantasies were too far in fairyland, too far from fact.

When *Phantastes* was published in 1858, the *Athenæum*, the purveyor of critical taste, contended that MacDonald "seems to have lost all hold of reality." The reviewer called the fantasy "a confusedly furnished second-hand symbol shop" that is "not anchored fast to the earth on which we stand" (580). Equating successful allegory to the "firm grasp of reality," the reviewer argued that *Phantastes* gives "us the shadow without the life. Thus . . . [the book] is a riddle that will not be read" (580). MacDonald, in this reviewer's eyes, paled in comparison to the more stately and conservative Spenser and Bunyan. What MacDonald attempts in the fantasy, however, is much more than allegory; as he wrote in a letter to Mrs. A. J. Scott, "I don't see what right the *Athenaeum* has to call it an allegory and judge or misjudge it accordingly—as if nothing but an allegory could have two meanings!" (Greville MacDonald 297). In a sense, MacDonald intends for his fantasy to wake up the fancy or imagination in the reader, not necessarily to provide a one-to-one correspondence to reality. A woman Anodos meets in fairyland explains, "I should be ill if I did not live on the borders of fairies' country, and now and then eat of their food" (13). Fantasy becomes the food of faith, the tonic from fact. Later in his career, MacDonald wrote "The Fantastic Imagination" in order to explain his theory of the fairy tale. MacDonald believes that "we spoil countless precious things by intellectual greed" (322) and that "the greatest forces lie in the region of the uncomprehended" (319). Thus, MacDonald could meld fantasy with belief in a higher power—God—with the purpose of a fairy tale being to "wake things up that are in him [the reader]" and to "make him think things for himself" (319). This anti-rational—or anti-intellectual—discussion by MacDonald aligns him with Dickens: we must preserve our childlike freedom and imagination. McDonald's most concrete definition of a fairy tale is highly emotional and geared toward the reader's personal—and innocent—response: "A fairytale, a sonata, a gathering storm, a limitless night, seizes you and sweeps you away: do you begin at once to wrestle with it and ask whence its power over you, whither it is carrying you?" (319).

If Dickens and MacDonald agreed on the importance of fantasy and fairy tale, it is MacDonald who ultimately—and radically—integrated theory into practice. As we have seen, Dickens used fairy-tale motifs as an ironic commentary on the fact-based structure of Coketown. MacDonald, on the other hand, left realism behind after two paragraphs in *Phantastes*, breaking from realistic conventions. The epigraphs at the beginning of the fantasy define its strategies. MacDonald's work begins with various quotations from his master, Novalis: "In fairy-story is that world which is opposed throughout to the world of rational truth, and precisely for that reason it is so thoroughly an analogue to it, as Chaos is an analogue to the finished Creation." To Novalis, "One can imagine stories without rational cohesion and yet filled with associations, like dreams; and poems that are mere lovely sounding . . . but also without rational sense and connections . . ." (3). *Phantastes* follows this pattern: Anodos, in his first person *Bildungsroman*, wanders through fairyland encountering a world "full of oddities and all sorts of incredibly ridiculous things, which a man is compelled to meet and treat as real existence, although all the time he feels foolish for doing so" (173). Yet the chaotic nature of the text mirrors the overall thesis of the fantasy, that the world is comprehensible only through the imagination and faith.

Anodos is returned to the real world at the end of the fantasy, awaiting passage once again to fairyland, now a metaphor for death and a new beginning. Melancholy is balanced by the understanding that a higher reality awaits Anodos, MacDonald, and the reader. Fantasy becomes an alternative religion for MacDonald; in fantasy one finds the belief in God. Higbie argues that Dickens used imagination in *Hard Times* to underscore that "imagination and faith are both necessary, acting together to defeat unbelief. Thus imagination can help lead to something like spiritual salvation" (103). Anodos writes at the end of his narrative: "Yet I know that good is coming to me—that good is always coming; though few have at all times the simplicity and the courage to believe it. What we call evil, is the only and best shape, which, for the person and his condition at the time, could be assumed by the best good. And so, *Farewell*" (185). Dickens ends *Hard Times* with: "Dear reader! It rests with you and me, whether, in our two fields of action, similar things shall be or not. Let them be! We shall sit with lighter bosoms on the hearth, to see the ashes of our fires turn grey and cold" (219). To Dickens and MacDonald faith conquers all—and faith in the imagination leads to this ultimate belief.

Dickens wrote "Frauds on the Fairies" to condemn the rationalizing of imaginative literature, and though Dickens would venture into the world of fantasy—especially in his ghost stories—he always had a solid footing in reality, for his breadand-butter was the realistic novel. He would only leave this world for a short time, always returning to the *Hard Times* of the nineteenth century. MacDonald, however, was able to suspend his disbelief more radically than Dickens; in *Phantastes* he could achieve thematically and structurally what Dickens would only hint at in his major novels. "Fairyland lay before me, and drew me towards it with an irresistible attraction" (54), says Anodos, symbolizing MacDonald's belief in the power of the imagination. Tempted by the fairies, MacDonald relinquished his hold on fact in order to find a much higher truth in the apparent chaos of fantasy. Anodos tells us how we are to read such fantasy: "But it is no use trying to account for things in Fairyland; and one who travels there soon learns to forget the very idea of doing so, and takes everything as it comes; like a child, who, being in a chronic condition of wonder, is surprised at nothing" (24). Dickens would have liked Anodos.

Endnote

1. In *The Golden Key* Robert Lee Wolff includes a picture entitled "MacDonald with a Group of Contemporary Writers," which is originally printed in Greville MacDonald's *George MacDonald and His Wife*. Thackeray, Macaulay, Bulwer Lytton, Carlyle, Dickens, Froude, Collins, Trollope, and MacDonald are pictured. Though the photograph is obviously a composite, it does indicate that MacDonald was part of the literary circle of the day. Wolff posits that "Dickens is said to have praised *Phantastes*" (5), but in a note he admits that he cannot find a reference to the book in Dickens's letters. Michael Kotzin suggests that Dickens may have read *Phantastes*, but he too is unable to substantiate such a claim. H. Crago contends that Dickens did indeed influence MacDonald, concluding that "MacDonald certainly found Dickens' use of the fantastic one of his great resources, and in adapting and extending certain symbolic elements sometimes produced conceptions that are in many ways worthy of the greatness of their inspirer" (90). Crago sees *Little Dorrit* as an influence on *Phantastes*. It seems safe to say, consequently, that MacDonald did read Dickens, particularly "Frauds on the Fairies" and *Hard Times*.

Works Cited

Crago, H. "Charles Dickens and George MacDonald." *Dickens Studies* 5 (1969): 86-90.

Dickens, Charles. "Frauds on the Fairies." *Miscellaneous Papers*. Vol. 1. London: Chapman and Hall, 1911. 435-42.

—. *Hard Times*. 2d. ed. Ed. George Ford and Sylvere Monod. New York: Norton, 1990.

Higbie, Robert. "*Hard Times* and Dickens' Concept of the Imagination." *Dickens Studies Annual* 17 (1988): 91-110.

Kotzin, Michael. *Dickens and the Fairy Tale*. Bowling Green: Bowling Green U Popular P, 1972.

Lewis, C. S. *The Allegory of Love*. Oxford: Oxford UP, 1936.

Lodge, David. *Working with Structuralism*. Boston: Routledge, 1981.

MacDonald, George. "The Fantastic Imagination." *A Dish of Orts*. London: Edwin Dalton, 1908. 313-22.

—. *Phantastes*. Grand Rapids: Eerdmans, 1981.

—.*Unspoken Sermons*. Ed. Rolland Hein. Wheaton, IL: Harold Shaw, 1976.

MacDonald, Greville. *George MacDonald and His Wife*. London: George Allen, 1924.

Review of *Phantastes*, by George MacDonald. *Athenæum*, Nov. 6, 1858, 580.

Prickett, Stephen. *Romanticism and Religion*. Cambridge: Cambridge UP, 1976.

—.*Victorian Fantasy*. Bloomington: Indiana UP, 1979.

Stone, Harry. *Dickens and the Invisible World*. Bloomington: Indiana UP, 1979.

Tolkien, J. R.R. "On Fairy-Stories." *The Tolkien Reader*. New York: Ballantine, 1966. 26-84.

Wolff, Robert Lee. *The Golden Key*. New Haven: Yale UP, 1961.

George MacDonald's *Phantastes*: The Spiral Journey to the Goddess
Bonnie Gaarden
From *The Victorian Newsletter*

George MacDonald, though chronologically a Victorian writer, owes an immense intellectual debt to the English and German Romantics. Key elements of the world view he preached are clearly and explicitly derived from Romantic writers. His model of spiritual development as an ascending circle (which he called "Ethical Evolution") closely corresponds to what M. H. Abrams describes as the spiral journey of the Romantics, which "fuses the idea of the circular return with the idea of linear progress" (184). As young children, this model runs, we enjoy a primitive unity with our surroundings in the oceanic bliss of infancy; however, as we develop self-consciousness we fall from this primal unity and begin to see ourselves as divided from and even opposed to nature and our fellows as ego and non-ego, subject and object, etc. Our spiritual education consists of a gradual re-appropriation of unity through the process that is perhaps best known as set forth in Hegel's *Phenomenology of Spirit*: consciousness divides into two opposing elements which then synthesize into a third higher state which incorporates, while transcending, the original distinction. As this process continues, we keep returning to the same developmental point, but on progressively higher levels: thus the figure of the spiral, which frequently appears in MacDonald's fantasy and fiction in the form of the winding stair. Abrams notes that the Romantic spiral differs from the Neo-Platonic circle in that the Romantic process occurs entirely in this life, while the journey described by Plotinus culminates only after death, in God. MacDonald's affinities here are with Plotinus rather than the Romantics. Not so, however, in the other distinction Abrams notes: The recovered unity of Plotinus is identical with the primitive unity that was the starting point of the process. For the Romantics, though, the recovered unity is an improvement over our originally blissful consciousness because it incorporates the individuality that has been developed during the process. The final unity is complex, not simple, preserving distinctions, yet without division: Coleridge's "multeity in unity" (186). MacDonald's description of the individual's final relationship to God in his sermon "The New Name" (*Sermons* I: 100-17) unquestionably favors the romantic development here.

Crossing a Great Frontier

At MacDonald's eschaton, when God is finally All in All, one might describe the universal condition as Abrams describes the Absolute, the end-point of the Hegelian dialectic: "that undivided unity which, having overcome yet preserved all preceding individuation, incorporates in itself not less that everything" (187).

Another Romantic tenet in MacDonald's canon is one which he himself labeled "Christian pantheism" and attributed to Wordsworth. In his essay "Wordsworth's Poetry," he explains the term thus: "This world is not merely a thing which God hath made, subjecting it to laws; but it is an expression of the thought, the feeling, the heart of God himself.... God is in everything, and showing himself in everything. ... [H]e has embodied his own grand thoughts thus that we might see them and be glad" (*Orts* 246-47). This notion that God is expressed but not contained in nature is more familiar to modern theologians under the term "pantheism" (Fox 50; Russell, *Lucifer* 34). It was, at any rate, a key belief of MacDonald's, reiterated over and over in sermons, fiction, and fantasy. Because nature is God's direct self-expression, she is an appropriate tutor for the person who wishes to learn of the Divine nature, and it is nature's face, not her secret workings discovered by the analysis of natural science, that best conveys God's heart (*Sermons* 3: 61). God's heart expressed in nature communicates to man's heart more significant truth about the Deity than any doctrinal system could possibly convey to the intellect. As related points, MacDonald's valuing the feelings and intuition over the intellect as a means of perceiving the truth and his correspondingly high regard for innocents close to nature such as children, animals, and the mentally disabled, also echo the preferences of the Romantics. The "rational horizon," MacDonald said, is too narrow to accommodate the truth (Greville MacDonald 336-39). I think it probable that MacDonald's giving priority to Western culture's *Mother* Nature as Divine self-revelation and his reliance on the heart over the head (traditionally a "feminine" preference) as the guide to truth find expression in his tendency, in his fantasy writing, to portray Deity or Divine forces as feminine. The grandmothers in the *Princess* books and "The Golden Key," North Wind in *At the Back of the North Wind*, the Wise Woman in "The Lost Princess," are only some of the goddess-figures in his fairy tales.

Phantastes was MacDonald's second published literary work, and first published fantasy. Since the author needed to make money, the critical and popular failure of this "fairy romance" determined MacDonald's decision, much lamented by later critics, to devote himself to writing novels, a genre for which his imaginative abilities were much less suited.

Phantastes is widely recognized as having been influenced by Novalis's *Heinrich von Ofterdingen* and Hoffman's "The Golden Pot." Like them, it is a *Bildungsroman* of a poet, or the tale of a young man following the Way of Imagination. For MacDonald as for other Romantics, the proper exercise of the imagination was vital to humanity's maturation/sanctification, but for MacDonald most plainly the imaginative function was a means and not an end. The journey Anodos makes is, essentially, the journey from infantile narcissism to the blessedness of self-giving, and the theme of the book is summed up in this song of its principal divinity:

> Better to live at the water's birth
> Than a sea of waves to win;
> To live in the love that floweth forth,
> Than the love that cometh in.
>
> Be thy heart a well of love, my child,
> Flowing, and free, and sure;
> For a cistern of love, though undefiled,
> Keeps not the spirit pure.

A simple concept and a simple theme, but the concept intellectualizes a spiritual state notoriously difficult to attain. Both the wandering journey of Anodos (who often seems, according to one meaning of his name, truly path*less*) and the density of MacDonald's symbolism reflect this difficulty. Several writers have applied the concepts of Jungian psychology to illuminate parts of the story, though some fail to note the ways in which MacDonald's psychological/theological concepts, though surprisingly similar to and compatible with Jung's, do in some respects differ from that of the psychoanalyst.[1] Critics such as Max Sutton and Roderick McGillis have also discerned structure in the apparently aimless series of Anodos's adventures. Here, I wish to suggest that the book is built around the spiral pattern MacDonald and other Romantics found so suggestive of human spiritual development. I see the plot of *Phantastes* as tracing a spiral with four turns, each turn a repetition of the basic pattern set by the first, but each describing a more advanced developmental state. The turns correspond, respectively, with the chronological periods of youth, young adulthood, maturity, and late maturity. Each turn is introduced by birth or rebirth imagery. The rebirth process introduces a period of nurture and spiritual growth. From this psychic expansion, Anodos advances to achieve some important accomplishment, vision or victory. But his victory quickly leads to a situation he is unprepared to deal with, and he makes a serious mistake. The error, reflecting some flaw in his character, leads to a descent or depression— a dark night of the soul—before yielding, again, to rebirth. As Anodos matures, the turns of the spiral become tighter. The first two, those of youth and young adulthood, each constitutes fifty-plus pages of text, while the third requires only thirty-six and the last, twelve.

Each of these turns is introduced by water imagery: a torrential rain, a stream that grows into a river, the ocean. In the first phase (of nurture and growth) of each turn we find goddesses, the female representations of Divinity that so pervade MacDonald's fantasies. The Woman of the Beech Tree, I will argue, represents God in Nature. The Fairy Queen and her palace are God in Art. The old woman with the young eyes in her island cottage is a figure of God in Christ. In the fourth turn, Anodos is not reborn again through water, but the singing of a maiden who represents his own true soul, his Christself or God Within, and whose maturity liberates him to enter the service of his ideal. In this final cycle, his triumph over the wolf (which Sutton, I think correctly, reads as the destruction of his false self) signals his attainment of spiritual manhood and leads to his graduation into the bliss of what C. S. Lewis has called "good Death": the experience of his unity with all creation in an outpouring of "the love that floweth forth."

So read, the text offers a Christianized version both of modern developmental psychology and of the Hindu notion of reincarnation, that is, constant rebirth and return to the cycle of being until one is worthy of Nirvana.

Prolegomena

Anodos, we are told as the story opens, is a young aristocrat who has just turned twenty-one and received the initiatory symbol of the keys to his dead father's desk. As he opens a hidden pigeonhole, out steps a tiny woman, who implies that she is his great-grandmother and tells him that she will grant him his wish to get into Fairy Land. When she assumes normal human size and he, struck with her attractiveness, stretches his arms toward her, she warns him, "A man must not fall in love with his grandmother, you know" (17-18).

This encounter, though hardly obviously, introduces Anodos's psychological predicament He is parentless; his mother died when he was a baby (15, 18). As Sutton observes, parental loss, particularly of the mother, often contributes to the development of neurotic or pathological narcissism, for the young child is thus deprived of the person most likely to reflect back to him his own existence as a person of worth. This "mirroring" function is critical to the child's developing sense of self; if he does not get it, he remains selfcentered and grasping for the rest of his life, forever consuming things and people in a desperate search for worthiness, lovability, completion. Anodos's inclination to "fall in love with his grandmother" signifies two inappropriate tendencies. Falling in love implies both emotional fascination and a desire for sexual possession; one's grandmother is both a part of oneself (an ancestress) and an authority-figure. (The grandmothers of MacDonald's fantasies tend to be spiritual authorities of no mean import.) And while indulging in emotional fascination with oneself (or a projection of oneself) is narcissistic, to wish to sexually possess an authority-figure indicates psychic inflation.[2] It is suggested here, then, not necessarily that Anodos has a character disorder such as full-blown narcissism, but that he is radically immature, perhaps having been deprived of the parenting that would have enabled him to grow up emotionally.

Back to Fairy Land

Anodos enters the Fairy Land the next morning, when his bedroom, which he designed himself, comes alive around him: the carved ivy of his bed becoming real ivy; his washbowl overflowing into a small stream bordered by living daisies which used to be a pattern in his carpet. Clearly this indicates that the regions of Anodos's own mind are enveloping him as a second world. He follows the stream back into infancy. The huge unbroken forest, the hut built around live oak trees, from whose chairs and tables "even the bark had not been removed" (22) which is occupied only by the fairyblooded woman and her daughter: all this suggests infancy, dominated by the raw nature of the unconscious and the feminine presence of the mother. The male principle is present at a distance and in two opposing forms, suggesting a male demon/hero generated by a child from his divided experience of his more distant father: the spectral, threatening Ash, and the knight whom the book in the cottage associates with Percivale. (Interestingly, Anodos's hostess sets the book in the window to screen out the Ash, as though trying to shield her guest from the male demon by means of the masculine ideal.) The flower-fairies Anodos watches in the hut's garden fit a small child's idea of Fairy Land.

Crossing a Great Frontier

The First Turn: Youth and God in Nature

When Anodos leaves the safe area of the woman's cottage, he is terrorized by the Ash in the forest until, having been drenched by a sudden rainstorm (the rebirth symbol in this turn) he is embraced by the Woman of the Beech Tree. Safe in her arms, he learns about the Ash (who devours to fill "a hole in his heart"), dreams all night "in a trance of still delight" about communing with nature in all seasons, and receives a protective girdle of the Woman's hair (beech leaves by daylight). Anodos goes on his way at daybreak "with a vague compunction, as if I ought not to have left her" (41).

In psychological terms, to be devoured by the Ash is to become the Ash. The interlude with the Beech represents the mothering Anodos has received from God in nature, which evidently provided him with enough sense of his own person and worth to keep the child Anodos from becoming a narcissistic devourer. His vague guilty feelings as he continues his journey suggest both the maturing child's uneasiness at his growing separation from his mother, and the feelings of toss and guilt that might accompany a child's fall into consciousness from his previous unconscious unity with the rest of the natural world.[3]

Fortified and protected by this encounter with the goddess, Anodos goes on to the major accomplishment of this turn, realizing the power of his imagination.

MacDonald in his essay "The Imagination: Its Function and Culture" denied that humans could properly be called "creative." That particular word he would reserve for acts of God. The human activity that most resembled the Divine creativity was, he said, the finding of natural forms to properly express the ideas that God, from his seat in the subconscious, releases into our conscious minds. In this essay he uses two major images to express imaginative activity: freeing a prisoner and lighting a lamp.[4] As we will see, in describing Anodos's freeing of the White Lady of the Marble and his seduction by a lamp-illuminated Alder Maid, MacDonald uses both of these images.

After leaving the Beech, Anodos comes upon a little rocky cell filled with a harmony of ferns and moss, with a well in one corner and a mossy mound at one end. He drinks from the well, lies on the mound, and is entertained by a reverie in which "all lovely forms, and contours, and sounds seemed to use my brain as a common hall" (43). Afterwards he notices a representation of Pygmalion on the wall, and, beginning to remove the moss from the stone upon which he has been lying, soon sees the form of a lovely marble woman in the alabaster of the stone, who has a face "more near the face that had been born with me in my soul, than anything I had seen before in nature or art" (45). He speculates that the cave is the "home of essential Marble—that spirit of marble which, present throughout, makes it capable of being molded into any form" (45). The imagery here suggests that Anodos's reverie has impregnated the receptive "spirit of the marble" with this particular form: his own feminine ideal. Many recent critics agree (as I do) in seeing her as a figure of his anima, the Jungian "inner woman" who, among other things, enables the imaginative flow. In older terms, we might say she is the personification of his Muse. When he proceeds, literally, to sing her out of her alabaster prison, she evasively flits off into the woods.

To identify the White Lady as Anima explains both Anodos's fascination with her and his final necessity of relinquishing her as a sexual love object. In contrast to MacDonald's Fairy Land, where Anodos may have a direct, personified experience of the anima, males in the real world free their animas into physical existence by projecting them onto living women. (Jung noted that certain women seemed especially liable to attract such projections and so were particularly adept at attracting men.)[5] But a relationship with one's own projection is only a relationship with oneself, thus, an exercise in narcissism. (In his sermon "Love Thy Neighbor," MacDonald observes that only otherness makes real love possible (*Sermons* 1: 201- 2121.) As part of himself (in imagery of the book, almost his own child) the White Lady, like Anodos's grandmother, is not an appropriate object for a mature, sexual love.

In thinking of her as *my* white lady, and himself as her deliverer, Anodos is correct in the same sense that a parent is correct in speaking of *my* child or an artist of *my* picture. Yet according to MacDonald, just as a child is born through his parents but is, in the ultimate sense, born from God, the creative flow of the imagination does not originate with the artist. Both the thought that is expressed and the form that the artist chooses to express it comes from God; the former from God in the subconscious, the latter from God in nature. Anodos, therefore, is not only mistaken in expecting to be rewarded for his act of deliverance with sexual favors, but is mistaken about his agency in the act itself. In the last analysis, he neither made nor freed the White Lady: God did.

Compare the figures of Serpentina in "The Golden Pot" and Matilda in *Heinrich von Ofterdingen*. Anselmus's union with Serpentina at the conclusion of the former symbolizes his triumphant entry into the imaginative life despite the bourgeois claims upon him, and Henrich's marriage to Matilda, the poet's daughter, is coeval with his undertaking the poetic vocation. These women, too, appear to be anima figures, and the symbol of marriage used to represent integration. Novalis's unfinished tale takes the poet's story farther than Hoffman's, for it encompasses Heinrich's toss of his wife—possibly to represent the psychological necessity for getting on with the other tasks of one's spiritual development. In MacDonald's thinking, the imagination as revealer of the truth is primarily of value in forming godly ideals which we may then serve (*Orts* 35). This revelation of truth is to the will, not the intellect, and the goal of such revelation is deification—that is, voluntary subscription to God's will and consequent divine union. Because for MacDonald imaginative vision is not an end in itself, Anodos must renounce the White Lady *as a mate* in order to properly integrate her as an internal capacity. (Similarly, in the New Testament, the disciples have to give up Jesus' bodily presence in order to receive the internal presence of the Holy Ghost.)

The inflation of pride and possessiveness that follow Anodos's imaginative activity in birthing his feminine ideal set him up for his fall: his seduction by the Maid of the Alder. If the White Lady represents Anodos's pure imagination, the Alder Maid symbolizes its corruption: an imagination that has stopped seeking after the ideal and has instead "remained at home to be sensual" (*Orts* 30). The story she tells Anodos centers in and always returns to "her own loveliness" (53); she desires the love of men only to shore up her conviction of her own beauty. As the White Lady is the female counterpart of the heroic knight, the Alder Maid is the female counterpart of the devouring Ash, for whom she prepares Anodos by destroying his beech-leaf girdle. While the mothering love of the nature goddess could protect Anodos from the narcissism born of a "hole in the heart," it is ineffective against the self-centeredness of a powerful imagination that endlessly returns to "building airy castles of vain ambition, of boundless riches, of unearned admiration," thus working "for evil . . . for falsehood . . . for death" (*Orts* 30, 29).

What saves Anodos this time is a double confrontation. Consciously, he sees the Alder Maid as a "living sepulchre" (55), while his masculine Ideal comes face-to-face with the hideousness of the Ash (139-40).[6] Anodos still thinks the Alder Maid is beautiful, but knows her as dangerous, and in horror he rejects the greedy self-involvement and sterile fantasizing the two represent. In fact he is deeply ashamed of his indulgence, which shows his developing moral sense. His next encounter with Fairy Land's inhabitants shows, as well, the developing intellectual complexity of adolescence. The next cottage in which he takes refuge has both male and female inhabitants. Mother and daughter believe in the unseen phenomena or Fairy Land; father and son do not. This family represents Anodos's divided mind; he himself changes belief depending on which individual he listens to (57-61). The kind, genial father and his sneering son suggest that materialism itself is not evil, but generates evil. Though the rest of the family agree that Anodos had better avoid the ogress of nihilism, the son leads him directly to her Church of Darkness where he finds his shadow.

MacDonald's shadow does indeed resemble Jung's concept of that name, but there are significant differences as well. For Jung, the shadow consists of those parts of the personality rejected by the conscious ego, repressed and thereby distorted. Yet they remain real parts of the personality. MacDonald's shadow in *Phantastes*, though, seems clearly to represent, not simply the "bastard self" of our consciousness (as opposed to the "Christ-self," or the real personality made by God, which corresponds closely to the Jungian concept of the self) but, more subtly, Anodos's *consciousness* of that "bastard self." It is the bastard self which, according to MacDonald, clutches and clings, because it does not realize its true relationship to God and to the world. The bastard self is the result of our being "born in sin": that is, in MacDonald's terminology, into ignorance and error. The essential difference between MacDonald's bastard self and Jung's shadow is that the latter is "real," in some essential sense, and in most cases ought to be brought to consciousness and at least some of its material integrated, while the former is not. The bastard self must also be brought to consciousness, but not to be integrated or accommodated. According to MacDonald it must simply be denied—that is, killed. It is the self of which Jesus was speaking when he told his disciples to deny themselves, take up their crosses and follow him. It is the self that must be crucified (*Sermons* 2: "Self-Denial" 210-32). It is, in agreement with MacDonald's Platonism and mainstream Christian theology, actually "no thing," and to lose it is no loss, but sanctification. In the earlier parts of the book, Anodos's bastard self was represented by the Ash and the Alder, his own potential for self-centeredness and greedy devouring (Cf. Sutton 15-16). The ogress tells him that his seduction by the Alder Maid has made his shadow more likely to find him: in other words, Anodos's experience of his own bastard self, combined with the shakiness of his faith in the unseen (which would include his unseen true self), generates a negative self-consciousness—that is, a consciousness merely of his negative self—

and that consciousness is his shadow.

In *Robert Falconer*, MacDonald writes:

> Men call the shadow, thrown upon the universe where their own dusky souls come between it and the eternal sun, life, and then mourn that it should be less bright than the hopes of their childhood. Keep thou thy soul translucent, that thou mayest never see its shadow; at least never abuse thyself with the philosophy which calls that show life.

The "dusky soul" referred to here is the bastard self, and the shadow of Anodos, his negative self-consciousness, blackens the world. This following part of his adventures constitutes the descent of this turn. The shadow scorches flowers, darkens the sun, makes the wonderful seem commonplace. Anodos sees an alternative to his own situation in his ideal, the knight who "had met the Alder-Maiden as I, but . . . had plunged into the torrent of mighty deeds, and the stain was nearly washed away. No shadow followed him . . . ; he had not had time to open the closet door." But his shadow leads him to distrust ideals (67). Anodos begins to think his darkened perspective is the true one, and to be proud of it as shrewd or worldly-wise, until the episode of the child and her globe.

The incident is particularly interesting in that it recapitulates all that has happened to Anodos till this point in his adventures. The child/woman takes his own role, while he plays the part of the Alder-Maid in his own story. The girl cherishes a harmonic globe in the same way Anodos cherished the White Lady; both are symbols of the imagination. Under the influence of the shadow, Anodos grasps the globe, causing it to vibrate and "sing" until it breaks into blackened fragments, and the child runs off lamenting. In the same way, Anodos's youthful imaginative activity has been broken and blighted; he has lost his White Lady as the child her globe. Both scenes are highly charged with the imagery of sexual seduction. This episode makes him hate the shadow again. The maid, who as a child on the brink of womanhood, is at about the same developmental stage as is symbolized by this part of the turn, would seem to represent Anodos's own innocence, his true or Christ-self,[7] which Anodos has been seduced into abusing. Under the influence of the Ash/Alder/shadow, Anodos has become his own corrupter.

Now the descent reaches its lowest point, the "dark night" of this turn. Anodos travels through a sand desert populated by mocking goblins, possibly his own self-hating thoughts. But the low point precedes rebirth. He finds and drinks from a spring which generates a small stream, and, like Coleridge's Ancient Mariner looking at the happy watersnakes, a "kind of love to the cheerful little stream" rises in his heart. He follows it till it becomes a river and has made the desert beautiful countryside, whereupon he cries with joy, falls in love again with Nature and Imagination ("Could I but see the Spirit of the Earth, as I saw once the indwelling woman of the beech tree, and my beauty of the pale marble . . . how gladly would I die of the light of her eyes!"), sleeps deeply, and rises "as from the death that wipes out the sadness of life" (71-72). Shortly thereafter he finds the boat that carries him over the river and to the fairy palace.

The Second Turn: Young Adulthood and God in Art

The fairy palace is Anodos's second divine refuge of nurture and education, and seems clearly to be MacDonald's version of the palace of art. Like the White Lady, it is made of white marble, and everything in and around it represents culture at its most beautiful and gracious: lovely architecture, halls and chambers, jeweled baths, fine food served by invisible attendants, and wonderful grounds offering "the most varied and artistic arrangement" of landscape, water, birds and animals. The fairies of the palace, though largely invisible to Anodos, receive him like a prince: he finds his name on a chamber that replicates his own room in his own castle. Here he is home, indeed. But the center of the palace, for him, is the enormous library, where he spends most of his afternoons engrossed in books which absorb him into their own virtual reality.

This library, like all the many impressive libraries in MacDonald's writing, is thought to have been modeled on the nobleman's library in northern Scotland that MacDonald spent a few months cataloguing when he was eighteen. According to William Raeper: "This library introduced MacDonald to all that was to mark him and his writing for the rest of his life: romance, the sixteenth-century divines, romantic poetry and German literature" (49). In MacDonald's fiction, his protagonists' experience with literature and other arts mark important steps in their moral and spiritual education. Here, for Anodos, is a place of rest and spiritual expansion.

The two interpolated stories that Anodos retells from his reading in the palace library bear on his own internal state and foreshadow his own end in Fairy Land. The first describes a world in which each season lasts for years, the men and women live essentially separate lives (infants are found by, not born to, young women) and the women have wings, which, "glorious as they are, are but underdeveloped arms" (87).

Crossing a Great Frontier

The general atmosphere of the tale is gentle, yearning melancholy, as it describes a girl who wanders off and dies of longing after hearing about the relations between the sexes in our own world, and another young woman, born in winter, who dies crossing her globe searching for spring. But the tale is also hopeful, for it implies that the people of this planet are reborn into our own world, where at least some of their dreams have a better chance of fulfillment. This tale can be read as a picture of Anodos's current state of psychic incompletion. In him, the masculine and feminine principles have not matured and come together into a generative union; he has neither learned to master and direct his own impulses, not to submit to an authority higher than his conscious ego. Consequently, he has borne no fruit of useful deeds. The second tale and its relevance to Anodos has been well analyzed by Sutton (20-21). Like the tale's hero, Cosmo, Anodos must learn to free the one he loves; like Cosmo, he will graduate into death when he releases his egoistic grasp on his lady (anima) and himself. The fact that Cosmo's princess appears to Cosmo in a mirror points to the White Lady's relation to Anodos as an anima projection.

The vision or accomplishment of this turn is actually a re-vision; as a young man Anodos rediscovers in art the divine inspiration that nature held for his youth. Sitting on a throne in a marble hall of the fairy palace, he is revisited with "a succession of images of bewildering beauty" of the kind he experienced in the marble cave (109-110). But this time such experiences are more under his own control. He returns regularly to this hall, where he dreams, acts, invents epics, sings. In the privacy of his own imagination, he has become a poet.

As a climax, the White Lady reappears, freed from invisibility by Anodos's singing, as before she was freed from her alabaster block. In his renewed imaginative activity he reconnects with his anima and rediscovers his feminine ideal. But he still misunderstands the nature of his relationship with her and makes the serious mistake of this turn by trying to grasp her in defiance of the imperative "TOUCH NOT!" inscribed on the pedestal where she appears. The anima, the imaginative flow, is essentially outside the artist's control, and to stay in contact with her one must respect her autonomy.

The White Lady flees—again—and Anodes pursues, through a rough-hewn door marked "*No one enters here without the leave of the Queen*" (120). The descent of this turn is quite literal, as Anodos follows the White Lady down a hole in the earth, where he finds a desert of rocks and again encounters jibing goblins. This suggests that his revivifying encounter with the Divine through art, both contemplated and created, has devolved into an introspective struggle as Anodos, deserted by his muse, tries vainly to find and possess the source of his inspiration. Finally, defeated, he gives up. He relinquishes his claim on the White Lady in favor of that of a "better man." This is the bottom of the pit, and ironically, as soon as he makes this mental gesture, he is (albeit sadly) inspired into song once more—song of renunciation.[8] Immediately afterward he rejects the temptation to the demonic imitation of imaginative power presented by the ugly old woman who turns herself into a lovely girl, and the rocky desert into a pristine landscape. She might represent, like the Alder Maid, sensuous and self-centered fantasy, or even artificial stimulation of the visionary power of drugs.

After more desolate travel, he squeezes through the last of the rock cavern (birth imagery) to find himself on the bleak shore of a wintry ocean. Determined to renounce his very life before it is forced from him, he flings himself into the waves, to be greeted with "a blessing, like the kiss of a mother," reminding him of the Beech Tree's arms. Rising to the surface he is met by a little boat, which nudges him till he climbs in. After resting, he opens his eyes to a summer sea, with stars above like children's eyes, and in the waters below he beholds the re-creation of his whole past, ending with what seem to be dreams of reunions with dead loved ones. He wakes "feeling I had been kissed and loved to my heart's content" (128-29). This womblike bath of nurturing love, embracing his past, present and future, prefigures the experiences he will have in the next turn, with the goddess of the island cottage.

The Third Turn: Maturity and God in Christ

Anodos is born again onto an island that is full of center imagery;[9] he seems at the center of his soul, the center of Fairy Land. It is humble, full of "delicate lowly things" such as "the flowers of my childhood," but no trees. It is calm, subject to neither tide nor storm. The cottage is square (typical of Jungian symbols of the self) with a fire in the center of the floor whose smoke issues from a hole in the center of the roof, and over the fire stands a tall, straight woman with a wrinkled face and young eyes, cooking something in a pot. Anodos loves her at once, crying with happiness, and she calls him "poor child," feeds him like a baby, and sings to him:

> While she sung. I was in Elysium, with the sense of a rich soul upholding, embracing, and overhanging mine, full of all plenty and bounty. I felt as if she could give me everything I

wanted: as if I should never wish to leave her, but would be content to be sung to and fed by her, day after day, as years rolled by. At last I fell asleep while she sang. (135-36)

This could serve as a speculative excursion into the mind of a nursing infant. Such similes are not unusual in describing a mystical experience of Divine presence. According to Julian of Norwich, "Jesus our mother" gave us birth in his passion, feeds us with his own body and shelters us in his wounds (*Revelations* 169-70). At conversion[10] and immediately after, the mystic feels embraced and nourished by God as by a mother. The Blessed Henry Suso describes his own early states of spiritual illumination thus:

> Whilst he was thinking . . . of the most lovable Wisdom, he questioned himself . . . saying, "O my heart, whence comes this love and grace, whence come this gentleness and beauty, this joy and sweetness of the heart? . . . Come! let my heart, my sense and my soul immerse themselves in the deep Abyss whence come these adorable things." . . . He was like a baby which a mother holds upright on her knees . . . by the movements of its little head, and all its little body, tries to get closer and closer to its dear mother. . . . Thus did the heart of the Servitor ever seek the sweet neighbourhood of the Divine Wisdom . . . altogether filled with delight. (qtd. in Underhill 254)

But like the mystics Underhill describes, Anodos does not linger long in this blissful infant condition. He wakes to see his hostess turn to each of the hut's four doors and evince, in turn, weeping, sighs, dismay, and shuddering; she then feeds the fire and begins to spin. Her facing of the doors indicates her participation in human suffering, while the spinning wheel is the ancient symbol of the goddess as fate, spinning the web of human destiny. This paradoxical combination of images, suggesting that the woman is both a determiner and a partaker of the human condition, is appropriate to the divine/human nature of Christ.[11] As Anodos earlier left the Beech's nurturing embrace, he now feels an urge to explore the island, and discovers that in fact his hostess is leading him in an exploration of his own life's experience. The four doors are four ways to God, all of them painful, but most passable. The door of Weeping takes Anodos back to his childhood and the loss of his brother. He returns to the goddess through the door of a barn. The way "back," to childhood and the animals, is a way to God, for it is from God that we and all of Nature originate. The door of Sighs leads Anodos into the private chambers of the (now enfleshed) marble lady and her husband, the knight. This represents the way to God through psychological maturity, the union of opposites in the soul. In renouncing the White Lady as a sexual love-object, Anodos has freed her to take her proper place as the feminine counterpart of his masculine ideal, giving him a complete ideal that he can passionately love as well as intellectually approve. The door of Dismay leads Anodos to witness the symbolic death of a girl he once loved and left, and to pass from her tomb to his own, where he experiences the dead as loving presences. Death, of course, is also a way to God, and to a reunion with lost loved ones in which all the wrongs we have experienced or inflicted can be set right. The fourth door, the door of the Timeless, would appear to lead to a direct experience of God as Transcendent, which Anodos only survives through the mediation of the divine/human goddess who goes through the door herself to drag him back. As a result, she and her cottage will be covered by the ocean for a year, and Anodos must leave her (though he feels as if he is leaving his mother) to do, as she instructs, "something worth doing." He will, she assures him, come back to her one day (144-45).

This encounter markedly alters Anodos. Not only has he received in full measure the nurturing love he had largely missed in his childhood, but he knows from experience that all of life's weeping, sighs and dismay are given by Love for one's own strengthening and growth in love (as the goddess says, "Past tears are present strength" [149]) and thus are only doors back into Love. He has learned that Love does not cling to its object, but gives and serves without thought of itself. In pursuing the White Lady he was not loving her, but himself; in setting her free he has allowed her to ascend to his ideal. Now, his love for that ideal can go forth into useful action: "something worth doing."

The accomplishment of this turn marks Anodos's entry into maturity. For the first time, he dedicates himself to a cause outside himself (a cause that the old woman with young eyes has arranged for him) in joining with the two brothers to slay the giants. In this cause he finds real human fellowship for the first time. He has also learned that art is God's gift to be given to others, and is not a possession of the artist. He tells the brothers, when they ask him to sing, that he must wait for the power of song to come upon him, and when it does, he sings so that they, too, weep the tears that strengthen their souls for the coming combat. To prepare for death at the hands of the giants, one brother must give up his father, the other, his lady-love; Anodos through his songs helps them to do so.

Crossing a Great Frontier

The three young men kill the giants. The two brothers, as they had foreseen, graduate into death. As Anodos will do later, they have "left their lives to [their] people" (157). Anodos himself is not ready for death yet; he survives. Yet immediately after killing his giant, he again beholds his shadow;[12] that is, his attention turns inward again in an uprush of both vanity and self-deprecation (156)—equally inappropriate, by MacDonald's lights, because equally self-centered. This victory in battle leads to his being received into the court of the king, acclaimed a hero, dubbed a knight, and created by the young nobles and ladies as one of themselves. And all the time, he is plagued by the shadow's presence. When he leaves the court on a journey, he is met by a larger, stronger version of himself which he knows he should fight, but (in the serious mistake of this turn) cannot. The *doppelgänger* leads him, unresisting, to a ruined tower and shuts him up inside. And Anodos knows that his shadow is both his imprisoner and his fellow-prisoner (158-60).

Though Anodos has matured greatly in this turn, he is not a spiritual grown-up yet. In joining with his fellows and accomplishing a genuine good, in assuming the role of a knight and winning a place in a society, he has reached the level that Jung described as typical of adulthood: the development of a persona, a social face that identifies one with an accepted cultural role and conforms to cultural mores.[13] The spiritual downside of this developmental stage is that the persona allows realization to only a very limited part of one's self. Therefore, as has been widely popularized lately in the concept of the mid-life crisis, sooner or later most people begin to feel imprisoned by the very role that earlier in life provided them with an empowering self-definition. Anodos's shadow takes the form of his role, a knight like himself, only bigger and better (a pointed comment on self-images) and shuts him up with only his self-consciousness for company.

The period of imprisonment is the descent of this turn. Anodos is immobilized by his idea of and his pride in his role; he could walk out of the tower at any time, but the idea does not occur to him. Only at night, in dreams and visions, is his spirit free to roam. Then, from the tower, he hears a woman singing a song "like an incarnation of Nature" which soothes him "like a mother's voice and hand" (162) urging him to come from the "narrow desert" to the house of mother Earth, "so high and wide." After listening for a while, he is reborn as a free man: "Hardly knowing what I did, I opened the door. Why had I not done so before? I do not know" (163).

The Fourth Turn: Late Maturity and God Within

Anodos issues from the tower to discover that the singing woman is the now-matured child whose globe he broke. Her story, again, mirrors his own.[14] She took the pieces of her globe to the Fairy Queen, who sent her to sleep in the white marble Hall of Phantasy and dismissed her; whereupon she discovered that she did not need her globe any longer, for she had internalized it. Now she goes singing everywhere and her songs "do good and deliver people" (163). Similarly, Anodos hoped to regain the White Lady but was instead led to internalize her. Again, it seems that the now-mature maiden represents Anodos's own true self, which has gained enough voice through his stay in the cottage of the old woman with young eyes that its liberating promptings could be heard even within the Tower of Pride. Her story gives him the vision of a new spiritual possibility: "I could hardly speak to her. . . . She was uplifted, by sorrow and well-doing, into a region I could hardly hope ever to enter. I watched her departure, as one watches a sunset. She went like a radiance through the dark wood, which was henceforth bright to me, from simply knowing that such a creature was in it" (164).

This encounter is supremely healing for Anodos. Having encountered God Within, his self-consciousness is no longer negative: the dark wood of his psyche now becomes bright to him, and he can emotionally afford to discard all that is not truly himself. Like a person on the far side of the midlife crisis whose motto, according to Gail Sheehy, is often "No more bullshit," Anodos renounces his pretentious claims to knighthood, piles his rusty armor at the foot of a tree, and goes off seeking service as a squire, armed only with a short ax and "the delight of being lowly; of saying to myself, 'I am what I am, nothing more.'" He discovers he has lost his shadow, for now he no longer thinks of himself: "whereas, formerly, my life had consisted in a vain attempt to behold, if not my ideal in myself, at least myself in my ideal." However, in his new work serving his ideal, the knight, "my ideal . . . became my life" (165).

His period of apprenticeship to the knight constitutes the achievement of this turn. Interestingly, the two adventures of the knight which Anodos describes consist of delivering children from peril or persecution. Since children are often MacDonald's symbol for the Christ-self in people (the little girl making wings to fly to her home country seems clearly a child of this son), the knight, and now, in a humbler capacity, Anodos, are embarked on the same work

MacDonald himself felt called to do.[15]

In this turn, when Anodos is confronted with a circumstantial test of sorts, we see that he has finally developed passing instincts. Focused on preserving the blight rather than himself, determined to give rather than grasp, he is able to slay the monstrous, wolflike idol of the yew-tree enclosure, which Sutton identifies as a figure of his false self (17). Avoiding the serious mistake that, in the other turns, has led him to a negative descent, he here attains a positive descent: he dies and, "right content," is buried. The rebirth is immediate: in yet more womb imagery he feels the "great heart of the mother [Earth] beating into mine, and feeding me with her own life, her own essential being and nature" (178). Then he rises, first into a primrose and then onto a cloud, knowing that now he can "love without needing to be loved again" (179) and anticipating a future of ministering to all humankind with "the love that healeth" (180). It is at this point of transfiguration that he, with a terrible shudder, dies back into "a bodily and earthly life" and finds himself on a hill above his own castle.

The Fairy Land spiral has gone right up into glory, into the bliss of felt love toward all that lives, and the felt power of benediction with which to express that love. In MacDonald's terms, such a state constitutes unity with the God who is, ultimately and fundamentally, Love Itself, and unity with the Divine will, which is, ultimately and fundamentally, to save, to bless, and to gather home all s/he has in love created (*Sermons* 1: 24-25). The turns of the spiral have taken Anodos through the perilous developmental tasks of kindling the imagination, using the imagination to discover true ideals, striving to realize those ideals in human society, finally forgetting (and thus slaying) one's false self in that service, and so freeing one's true self, which shares in and conducts the divine essence, the "love that healeth."

The question presenting itself to Anodos on his return to his own world is "Could I translate the experience of my travels [in Fairy Land) into common life? . . . Or must I live it all over again, and learn it all over again, in the other forms that belong to the world of men . . . ?" (181). The text suggests ambiguous answers. If Anodos at times feels like a ghost sent to minister (thus identifying with his last blissful state in Fairy Land), he at other times finds that blessedness "too high for me to lay hold upon it and hope in it" (182). Sutton would apply this question to the problem of how far people can learn from literature: can we really grow spiritually through vicarious experience (22)? I think Anodos's experience in Fairy Land is more analogous to the experiences described in medieval dream-visions than to those garnered from reading, and would suggest that the question also applies to the seemingly inevitable distance between the human spiritual reach and grasp. We can always *see* more than we can *be*. But even a passing taste of the bliss at the water's birth might give anyone what his Fairy Land journey seems most certainly to have given Anodos: an end for which to hope. He hopes to return to the old woman with the young eyes. "I have come through the door of Dismay; and the way back from the world into which that had led me, is through my tomb. Upon that the Red sign lies, and I shall find it one day, and be glad" (182). This, I suggest, is MacDonald's literary version of the New Testament's promise of an eternity "with the Lord."

The book ends with a conflation and evocation of two of its goddesses—God in Nature, and God in Christ—and an assertion of faith in Fairy Land. Anodos, resting beneath a "great, ancient beech-tree," begins to hear, in the wind murmuring though the branches, the voice of "the ancient woman, in the cottage that was foursquare," saying "'A great good is coming . . . to thee, Anodos.' . . . I opened my eyes and, for a moment, almost believed that I saw her face . . . looking at me from between two hoary branches of the beech overhead." Once again, the vision fades into common day, but even in the common day one can see the transcendent gazing through immanent nature: "But when I looked more keenly, I saw only twigs and leaves, and the infinite sky, in tiny spots, gazing through between. Yet I know that good is coming to me—that good is always coming . . ." (182).

Yet I know. It is the affirmation everywhere of romantics and mystics and all others who deduce the Real, not from proofs of sense or logic, but from the yearnings of the heart and the reaches of the imagination. Thus it was that George MacDonald *knew* that the end of the spiral journey, and the fundamental Reality of the universe, was the Goddess of Outgoing Love.

ENDNOTES

1. For a review of recent critics who have used Jungian concepts to elucidate MacDonald's work in general and *Phantastes* in particular, see Cusick.

2. Robert Lee Wolff has noted and explored the Oedipal overtones in many of the incidents of the book. They are strong. However, though certain events seem almost to demand a Freudian interpretation, a Freudian reading of the text leaves many parts irrelevant or incomprehensible (cf. Sutton 12). Cusick argues that Jungian concepts make *more* sense of more of MacDonald's work than does strict adherence to Freud (58).

3. Baring and Cashford discuss the Eden myth as representing this development of the psyche of humanity as a whole.

4. MacDonald says that in refining existing literary material to reveal splendidly what it has said only crudely before, poets like Shakespeare "rescued the soul of meaning from its prison of uninformed crudity, where it sat like the Prince in the 'Arabian Nights,' half man and half marble; they have set it free in its own form, in a shape, namely, which it could 'through every part impress'"(*Orts* 22). On using the forms provided by nature to express thought, he writes: "God has made the world that it should thus serve his creature, developing in the service that the imagination whose necessity it meets. The man has but to light the lamp within the form; his imagination is the light, it is not the form. Straightway the shining thought makes the form visible, and becomes itself visible though [sic] the form" (*Orts* 5).

5. See "Marriage as a Psychological Relationship," in *The Development of Personality* (*Collected Works* Vol. 11).

6. I am more hesitant than Sutton to identify the knight with the Jungian self. It seems to me more likely that the knight represents Anodos's conscious ideal of manliness, which, according to MacDonald, he ought to try to live out (See *Sermons* 1:203-05 on the importance of doing the best one *knows* as the path to further spiritual enlightenment.)

7. Another MacDonald fantasy-character whose Christ-self represented in the opposite gender is Tangle in "The Golden Key," who meets her Christ-self as a male child.

8. This reminds me of Madeline L'Engle's response to a particularly discouraging period in her writing. Having decided she would simply give it up, she immediately began plotting a new story—about failure.

9. Cf. McGillis. "The Community of the Centre" 56. See this article for the use of center imagery as a key to the structure of *Phantastes* as a whole.

10. Not usually in the modem sense of a conversion from unbelief to belief, but conversion from formal religious belief to immediate personal experience of The Divine.

11. In Sutton's reading, Anodos does not encounter God or Christ, though he notes that MacDonald, in his essay "Sketch of Individual Development," declared that such an encounter was vital for full spiritual growth (*Orts* 48).

12. "Am I going to do a good deed?" writes MacDonald in "The Hands of the Father." "Then of all times,—Father, into thy hands; lest the enemy should have me now" (*Sermons* 1:184).

13. See "The Persona as Segment of the Collective Psyche" in "The Relations between the Ego and the Unconscious," *Two Essays on Analytical Psychology* (*Collected Works* Vol. 7).

14. Roderick McGillis has noted the similarity of this part of the girl's story to that of Anodos.

15. Compare the tale of the little girl begging wings from butterflies and the mindless wooden figures who walk over her with MacDonald's sermon "The Higher Faith" (*Sermons* 1: 50-65) in which he complains that the aspiring child who sees, through imagination, God in nature and humanity, "is often checked by the dull disciple" who objects to any vision not expressly endorsed by his own dead interpretation of Scripture. MacDonald may well have seen himself as the literary knight whose job it was to succor children.

WORKS CITED

Abrams, M. H. *Natural Supernaturalism: Tradition and Revolution in Romantic Literature.* New York: Norton. 1971.

Baring, Anne, and Jules Cashford. *The Myth of the Goddess: Evolution of an Image.* New York: Viking, 1991.

Cusick. Edmund. "George MacDonald and Jung." Raeper. *The Gold Thread.* 56-86.

Fox, Matthew. *The Coming of the Cosmic Christ: The Heading of Mother Earth and the Birth of a Global Renaissance.* San Francisco: Harper, 1988.

Hegel, George Wilhelm Friedrick. *Phenomenology of Spirit.* New York: Oxford UP, 1977.

Hoffman, E. T. *Tales of E. T. Hoffman.* Ed. and trans. Leonard J. Kent and Elizabeth C. Knight. Chicago: U of Chicago P, 1972.

Julian of Norwich. *Revelations of Divine Love.* Trans. Clifton Wolters. New York: Penguin, 1966.

Jung, Carl G. *The Collected Works of Carl G. Jung.* 2nd ed. Trans. R. F. C. Hull. Bollingen Series XX. Princeton: Princeton UP, 1970.

MacDonald, George. *A Dish of Orts: Chiefly Papers on the Imagination and Shakespeare.* London: Dalton, 1908.

—. *The Golden Key and Other Stories.* Elgin. IL: Chariot, 1978.

—. *Phantastes and Lilith.* Grand Rapids, MI: Eerdman's, 1980.

—. *Robert Falconer.* Sunrise Centenary Editions of the Works of George MacDonald. Novels. Vol. 3. Eureka, CA: Sunrise, 1990.

—. *Unspoken Sermons.* 3 vols. Eureka, CA: Sunrise, 1989.

MacDonald, Greville. *George MacDonald and His Wife.* New York: Johnson Reprint, 1971.

McGillis. Roderick. "The Community of the Centre: Structure and Theme in *Phantastes.*" McGillis, *For the Childlike* 51-66.

—, ed. *For the Childlike: George MacDonald's Fantasies for Children*. Metuchen, NJ: The Children's Literature Association and the Scarecrow P, 1992.

Novalis. *Heinrich von Ofterdingen*. Trans. Palmer Hilty. New York: Ungar, 1964.

Raeper, William. *George MacDonald*. Tring, England: Lion, 1988.

—, ed. *The Gold Thread: Essays on George MacDonald*. Edinburgh: Edinburgh UP, 1990.

Russell, Jeffrey Burton. "Lucifer." *The Devil in the Middle Ages*. Ithaca: Cornell UP, 1984.

Sutton. Max. "The Psychology of the Self in MacDonald's *Phantastes*." *Seven* 5 (1984): 9-25.

Wolff. Robert Lee. *The Golden Key: A Study of the Fiction of George MacDonald*. New Haven: Yale UP, 1961.

The Angel in the Cosmos:
Phantastes's Recasting of the New Gentleman

Kelly Searsmith

From *The Journal of Pre-Raphaelite Studies*

"O man of pride, / Come into the house, so high and wide."
(The Woman Artist, *Phantastes*, 164)

By the early nineteenth century, England's upper and middle classes had reinvented the gentlemanly ideal in their own images. His upper-class transformation into a modern-day knight was most influentially encouraged by Kenelm Henry Digby. Digby's *The Broad Stone of Honour* (1822), a contemporary courtesy book that became a bible for Young Englanders, described an England that was divided by politics and sectarianism and corrupted by mercantilism and the contagion of secularism. Digby wrote *Broad Stone* as a "counteracting force," to unify and ennoble England through reforming its idea of manhood (lv-lvi). Mark Girouard has distinguished Digby's contribution from Walter Scott's: "He brought chivalry up to date, as a code of behaviour for all men, not just for soldiers; he enabled modem gentlemen who had never been near a battlefield to think of themselves as knights. . . . Scott saw the knight ultimately developing into the gentleman. Digby used 'knight' and 'gentleman' as virtually interchangeable terms" (60). Men who patterned themselves upon his chivalric ideal would find their superior character gave them a new common ground, regardless of the allegiances that divided them. At the same time idealists of the upper class like Digby were forming the gentleman along chivalric lines, serious Christians of the middle class were remaking him in Christ's image. The old style of gentleman was displaced by this Christ-like model of a man who was physically and morally strong yet as gentle and sentimental as a woman. Like Digby's chivalric new gentleman, this middleclass version was defined not by his occupation, wealth, or social class but by his Christian character.

George MacDonald's *Phantastes* seems to have a mission similar to Digby's *Broad Stone*, for the romance posits that read or dreamed experiences affect readers as strongly as lived ones and presents these potentially transformative, vicarious experiences as the struggle of a privileged male to find a reformed identity that is stable yet benign. In depicting this developmental struggle, the fantasy directly articulates some of the key conflicts and compromises that were occurring at midcentury between present and emergent masculine identifications.[1] Specifically, this compressed, masculine *Bildungsroman* (Prickett) portrays its protagonist, Anodos, as a conventional, young squire who comes to emulate both middle- and upper-class styles of the new gentleman.

The romance makes explicit the relation between the new gentleman and conceptions of the feminine and childlike. The sentimental inspiration of the feminine and humbling identification with the childlike are the catalysts for the gentleman's transformation from old to new. The romance also reveals the uneasy imbrication between the middle-class form of the Christ-like new gentleman and the Romantic artist. Such an artist, although likewise gentled by fine sensibilities, remained too sexually charged for selflessness; at the same time, he threatened effeminacy through his associations with a leisured life of the mind. In my discussion of these (re)genderings below, I adopt Herbert Sussman's guidelines for masculine studies terminology, in which male denotes biological sex; masculinity and manliness, "those multifarious social constructions of the male current within the society"; and manhood, a masculine ideal (13).

Although *Phantastes* represents the new gentleman as a morally superior and desirable form of manhood, the romance exposes the role's questionable capacity to ameliorate "the central problematic in the Victorian practice of masculinity, the proper regulation of innate male energy" (Sussman, 3). The anxiety this fantasy expresses about sentimental virtue's domesticating or ennobling potential is especially significant, since the new gentleman was conceived of as an *essentially* disinterested man, defined by the pleasure he gained in serving others rather than indulging himself. Digby portrays the new gentlemen's disinterestedness as unassailable. He imagines such men standing upon a broad stone of honour from whence they might "look down upon their enemies, who are vainly plotting in the plain below; where they may enjoy a purity of feeling, which, like 'the liberal air,' that surrounds that lofty summit, is free from the infection of a base world" (xiii xiv). *Phantastes* marks the new gentleman's lack of such an invulnerable foundation, and offers an even more idealistic form of compensatory manhood in its place: the angel in the cosmos.

The new gentleman was an idealistic formation that rejected conventional upper- and middle-class masculinities. Although still physically vigorous and emotionally controlled, he adopted a domestic sensibility or chivalric *gentilesse* in lieu of the values of "the masculine public sphere," which were "the values of fact—technical proficiency, acquisitiveness, practical utility" (Nelson, 147-48). An *essentially* private and disinterested individual, he worked in the public sphere with the most benign, paternal motivations. He related to others with a sense of charitable fellowship—a Christian conception of the extended human family taken up by both Young Englanders and evangelicals—rather than by what Carlyle derided as "hollow commercial league."

The new gentleman was an egalitarian reformation of the elitist gentleman. Certainly Victorians still recognized a gentleman in the same ways that previous generations had: by his attire grooming, deportment, speech, delicacy, and occupation or lack thereof—all important indicators of class. The social category "gentleman" continued to serve as a standard of inclusion or exclusion from social privilege. Yet, the new gentleman's promoters and adherents no longer tended to conceive of these external attributes as his shibboleth. The outward signs of gentlemanliness became instead indications of an inwardly gentle character, and the inclusiveness, rather than the exclusiveness, of the ideal was celebrated. Like Arnold's "*aliens*"—men of culture who were motivated by a humane rather than a class spirit (73) —the gentleman became a prestigious identification "open to all men, to those who are not of gentle blood, if so be that they can attain to the virtues of chivalry, which are the prescribed qualifications" (Digby, 640). As this statement implies, however, it was not enough for a man to be naturally noble or even noble born; to "attain" a virtuous, gentlemanly character, further cultivation was necessary. Digby thus especially addressed his courtesy book to young men of twenty, just about to attain legal majority—around the same age as MacDonald's protagonist. Young men must choose, Digby tells them, between "approbation" or "censure," "refinement, or "dissoluteness of principle" (2-3)—MacDonald's Anodos faces these same choices. Only once such a youth had fully become a reformed gentleman would he be free from danger, safe atop his fortress of virtue from outward assault or inward taint.

Late in the century, natural nobility became imbued with nationalist significance, a chauvinism whereby English blood was thought to run bluer than continental or colonial (even Digby, who finds gentlemen come from every Christian nation, touts England's special distinction). From its earliest conceptualization, however, the egalitarian redefinition of gentlemanliness held the promise for social determinations to be made on a more meritocratic basis. The new gentleman's upper-class proponents advocated gentlemanliness as a means of maintaining social order in the face of democratization, both because it would provide a single standard of manhood for all Englishmen and because that standard was modeled upon the traditional ruling class. They did not usually imagine middle-class men might qualify. Just as Arnold had condemned the middle-class's philistinism, they rebuked its commercialism. Digby believed the getting of money and gentlemanliness were irreconcilable: "The spirit of a gentleman is opposed to these narrow schemes of selfish enjoyment . . . so frequently adopted by rich mechanics and persons in the middle ranks of life" (209-10). For Digby, gentlemen might only serve in the clergy, parliament, law, or military (492-93).

Not surprisingly, the middle class resisted this aristocratic identification, seeking an independent basis of social value. The serious Christian middle class insisted on "the primacy of the inner spirit" as the measure of an individual (Davidoff and Hall, 450-51). They tended, in contrast to Digby, to reason that a man could get a living commercially and still be a gentleman so long as he used his worldly gain to the support of his family and good works (Davidoff and Hall, 21- 22). Evangelicalism gave the middle class the rhetorical ground from which to argue their equality with the landed upper class. Thus, the egalitarian ground for the middle-class's style of new gentleman was not chivalry, but evangelical Christianity.

For middle-class evangelicals, the new gentleman was also a means of dissociating ideal manhood from a conventional masculinity that already transcended class. Although physical virility became less important to a conventional definition of masculinity than occupation in the early nineteenth century (Davidoff and Hall, 229), men continued to be thought of as having undesirable aggressive and sexual drives. Men were, the Victorians believed, "better able to feel and less able to control their lower natures than women" (Nelson, 527). MacDonald's mentor, F.D. Maurice, acknowledged that men felt two equally natural but competing impulses: the urge to satisfy their own desires set against the pull of mutual affection:

> We cannot be acquainted with a family, or be members of a family, without knowing in others, without feeling in ourselves, certain inclinations which tend to the dissolution of its bonds, and to the setting up of that separate independent life . . . . *These inclinations are kept down by discipline, and the affections which attract us to the members of our family.* (my emphasis; Maurice, 76)

Victorian narratives of masculine development were especially concerned with depicting how young men negotiated this struggle. More conventional narratives, such as *The Mill on the Floss*'s Tom Tulliver's, stressed how young men tamed habitual male inclinations like lustiness, aggression, drunkenness, and profligacy through practising discipline. As conventional men successfully matured, they changed their behaviour to conform to society's standard of respectability. The new gentleman, in contrast, internalized the sentiments that civilized in order to attain manhood. New gentleman's narratives, such as Allington's Johnny Eames's, emphasized young men's gradual domestication, demonstrating how idealized romantic and family affection helped them to resist the world's temptations and inspired them to become better men. When successfully matured, the new gentleman was the kind of man who could not conceive of violating his own inward standard of respectability. Both types of masculine narrative regularly culminated in marriage, but the marriage functions differently. In conventional narratives of masculine development, nearly *pro forma* marriage both rewarded men for the self-control they had achieved and somewhat imperfectly assured their continued compliance. For the new gentleman, marriage was not a surety, and, when it did happen, functioned purely as reward; he was not in any danger of slipping.

Middle-class stories of new gentlemanly formation were especially concerned with the feminization, or gentling, of maleness. Early in the nineteenth century, serious Christians thought the feminine qualities of selflessness and sympathy were so morally and spiritually desirable that the masculine ideal should incorporate them. "Feminine elements" were often conceived of as "a corrective to the faults . . . in the purely masculine character" (Christ, 157). In *Boys Will Be Girls*, Claudia Nelson argues that up through mid-century, the ideal for boys was "essentially androgynous" (525). The best boys were emotional and passive, their narratives more likely to climax with a pious sickbed or deathbed scene than a physically rousing victory over pirates or bullies. Evangelicalism's adult masculine ideal incorporated some feminine attributes, but it also presupposed that men were constituted along otherwise normative lines.

Stories of new gentlemanly formation regularly included elements that established and maintained those lines. Although Tennyson often depicted ideal men as knights, he typified this evangelical formation when he "attributed to Christ a union of male and female qualities, of sweetness and strength, which he called the man-woman in him" (Christ, 156). Carol Christ points out that Tennyson was careful to distinguish between the man-woman and the womanly, or effeminate, man, which he firmly and specifically rejected in "On One Who Affected an Effeminate Manner" (157). The Prince of *The Princess* likewise expresses the view that the Christ-like man is feminized but not effeminate. Men and women, says he, are "distinct in individualities." Growing "liker" through close association, they each increase in the other gender's essential virtues; from woman, man "gain[s] in sweetness and in moral height" (II 250-79).

The evangelical construct of the "man-woman" shared an affinity with the Romantic model of manhood, which emphasized "emotive openness and imaginative inwardness, passivity, and even the drive toward dissolution and death" (Sussman, 82). The Romantic masculine represented, however, a more wholesale rejection of bourgeois masculinity, for it did not presume the value of a public role, aside from a vatic one. Yet, because of their ideological similarities, the evangelical man-woman was often blurred with the Romantic model of manhood in Victorian texts written by liberal, religious writers such as MacDonald.

Roderick McGillis has argued that Anodos's development is one of feminization ("The Community of the Centre"), but it is more accurately described as a special form of infantilization. MacDonald believed adults who evolved spiritually became increasingly childlike. The Wordsworthian child who served as the standard for this formation was obedient; unselfconscious, generous, loving, and trusting. He or she was Christ-like, for "God" himself, MacDonald asserted, "is childlike" (*Unspoken Sermons*, 18). That adults should strive to remain or seek to grow more childlike was a view shared by other Victorians influenced by a Romantic sense of what children were. They believed children's naturally imaginative, plastic natures gave them a ready faith adults could only struggle toward. Whether they identified with the upper or middle classes, these idealists' affinity for the childlike and conception of what childlikeness represented was the same. Digby expresses such a sentiment in *Broad Stone*, saying that gentlemen "must be content to . . . become as little children" (xxix-xxx). Despite his loathing for Young England, Dickens echoes this feeling in many of his fictions. In *The Chimes* (1844), for instance, Mrs. Chickenstalker praises the poor ticket-porter Trotty Veck as "the simplest, hardest-working, *childest-hearted* man, that ever drew the breath of life" (my emphasis; 229). MacDonald's infantilization of normative, bourgeois manhood does not significantly differ from Tennyson's feminization of it—perhaps because the infantile and the feminine shared so many defining characteristics in common. Victorians infantilized the style of femininity that was characterized by physical delicacy, innocence of the world's vices or complexities, passivity, and sentimentality. Tennyson, for example, hoped that as women gained "mental breadth" from their association with men, they would not "lose the childlike in the larger mind" (1. 268). MacDonald was, however, less concerned with preserving the distinction between masculine and feminine than he was in creating one between the "childish" and the "childlike." It was the nonnative, bourgeois man, with his selfish desires and ego demands, that he viewed as undesirably childish and far from childlike.

Once fully domesticated, and rendered to some degree Christ-like—or, to use MacDonald's term, childlike—the new gentleman had mastered his baser impulses. A direct analogue of the angel in the house, he embodied manhood attained, rather than manhood at struggle with itself. Yet, he was only analogous to a feminine angel; he was not himself angelic. His model character was still housed in a man's body and relegated to a man's social role. Because his maleness was at odds with his disinterestedness, within him were always the traitorous seeds of sexual desire and without him were external forces impelling him to emerge into the world to do its work. Although formed in reaction to conventional masculine traits, the new gentleman could not escape the cognitive dissonance aroused by their lingering associations. The formation entailed an inherent ideological contradiction, one for which *Phantastes* provides a tenuous, symbolic resolution. I turn now to discuss how MacDonald's romance fantastically explores the redemptive possibilities of new gentlemanly identifications, only to find them wanting.

Phantastes is not typically read as a story of specifically masculine development, but this coming of age tale is concerned with how a conventional, privileged youth might adopt a more idealistic, even heroic, masculine identity. At the beginning of the romance, Anodos, just come of legal age, explores his deceased father's effects. Instead of finding "the records of lands and moneys, how gotten and how secured" (6), he releases his ancestral fairy grandmother who informs him that his father travelled to Fairy Land in his youth and invites him to do the same. The Victorian trope of a secret birthright inevitably leads the inheriting son to question his identity, and forces him to reconstitute it anew through retracing his father's experiences. Anodos wonders if he "was to learn how my father, whose personal history was unknown to me, had woven his web of story" (6). In Fairy Land, however, Anodos's journey is one of self-discovery rather than paternal revelation—his father's having gone before only authorizes him to do the same, and suggests that the inheritance he should be seeking is not a material, but an imaginative and spiritual one.

Anodos's experience of Fairy Land is meant to resocialize him, to give him a different way of thinking about the natural and social worlds and his relation to them. His journey in Fairy Land spans twenty-one days, one for each year of his life. Although Anodos has no clear goal, and thus cannot properly be described as being on a quest, the romance has a quest-like structure. He receives hints that his sojourn in Fairy Land has a greater meaning than he can yet discern and that his impulsive wending along the way is purposeful.[2] "No one comes here," one of Fairy Land's wise women tells him, "but for some reason, either known to himself or to those who have charge of him" (15). This implicit providential ordering of events provides the logic for the narrative of Anodos's development. In one of the books Anodos reads in the fairy palace's library, a narrator states this theme explicitly: "They who believe in the influences of the stars over the fates of men, are, in feeling at least, nearer the truth than they who regard the heavenly bodies as related to them merely by a common obedience to an external law" (77). Neither can Anodos, once set upon this transformative journey, turn back. That he can only move forward in Fairy Land (53-54) implies the journey will end when he crosses the threshold to maturity. Yet. Anodos's maleness and privilege make his spiritual development significantly more difficult and its outcome more certain than it might otherwise have been.

In presenting Anodos as an individual ripe for reform, *Phantastes* does not so much condemn his character as it does the worldly values that underwrite his traditional gentlemanliness, mores grounded in a privileged masculinity he has had little cause to question before his journey. Fairy Land's egalitarian and cooperative values are diametrically opposed to Anodos's, for he has the unexamined sense that social relations outside of one's family are inherently hierarchical and commercial. During his first encounter with fairies, Anodos learns they operate on an idealized system of social exchange that includes no acknowledgement of rank or payment. The goodwife in whose kitchen garden Anodos meets the fairies tells him it is just as well he finds his purse empty, for money is "not of the slightest use" in Fairy Land. In fact, "nothing offended them [fairies] so much [as trying to pay them]. 'They would think,' she added, 'that you were making game of them'" (18-19). Later, at a low point in Anodos's journey, kobolds (German mine spirits) do lampoon his superior sense of his own station, one of them saying "with mock humility—'Honoured sir, vouchsafe to withdraw from thy slaves the lustre of thy august presence, for thy slaves cannot support its brightness.... You are so big, you keep the sun from us'" (119). Through their satiric interpolation of Anodos's imagined thought processes, the kobolds suggest that his arrogance stems from an undue admiration of his own social status and physical dominance. Their sarcasm might read as merely loosely flung barbs, but for the fact that they prove that they know more of Anodos's quest than he does himself, foretelling that his white lady shall choose a "better man" (120).

The unpleasant consequences of Anodos's thoughtless actions reinforce the reader's impression that Anodos takes undue liberties because of his assumption of privilege. Anodos has the sense that he has the unquestioned right to go where he likes, such as rashly entering the forest where the Ash lurks at night or the house of the ogress; to take and touch what he wishes, such as the crystal globe of the girl with whom he briefly travels or the statue of the white lady in the fairy palace; and, by extension, to possess the women he desires. Anodos's objectification of others is made to seem most harmful when it leads him to eroticize women. What readers might take as Anodos's singular obsession with a particularly ideal woman is revealed to be a pattern of behaviour for him as well as other men. A dream vision Anodos experiences in the cottage of the "old woman with the young eyes" discloses that not long before coming to Fairy Land, he seduced a woman and then abandoned her. We know little of Anodos's relationship with her, only that "Wrong and Sorrow had gone together" (141). Readers may suppose the rest, for they are encouraged to find Anodos's and Sir Aglovaile's stories alike. This revelation about Anodos's past comes soon after the wise woman sings a ballad about Sir Aglovaile. The ballad tells of how Sir Aglovaile impregnated and then cast off a poor village maid, who later died with their child. When he encounters her ghost, he finds that death has elevated her above him, because she is measured now by her spiritual rather than her social station; "Death for a woman can / Do more than knighthood for a man" (132). Aglovaile renews his courtship of this now worthy lady, only to violate the prohibition against touching her. In doing so he loses her, just as Anodos has lost the white lady by touching her statue in the fairy palace.

Anodos's pursuit of the white lady, whom he has sung to life from the block of marble in which she lay trapped, is a condemnation not only of his own desires, but of the eroticizing masculine imagination. Anodos's white lady is drawn with such broad symbolism that she represents the conventional female wish-fulfilment of heterosexual men. She is Helen, Iseult, the Sleeping Beauty in the Wood. She is even "essential Marble," the artist's material shaped to fulfill his fantasy (37). Such a description is an almost metafictive acknowledgement of the Victorian male's narcissistic imagination, in which he both manufactures his desire and then seeks to master it (Danahay). Anodos's struggle with his ghostly white lady parallels that of Cosmo, a character with whom Anodos strongly identifies after reading about his conflict over whether to free a woman trapped every evening in his magic mirror. As Anodos develops spiritually, he begins to understand Cosmo's choice to free her, for he comes to realize that other beings have their own equally valued integrity. An older Anodos (the romance's nostalgic first-person narrator) admits to having had a "feeling of property in her," and labels such a feeling monstrous by identifying his younger self with "the goblin Selfishness" (124). The thrust of Anodos's love-plot therefore seems plain: His self-imposed quest for the white lady has been superimposed upon some greater transformative schema. Like so many heroes of the West, the inspiration for his spiritual betterment is a woman who serves as his holy grail, embodying all that is worth fighting and dying for. Yet, she is not the grail itself, nor can his love of her quench a pilgrim's yearning.

As this line of ethical development suggests, the significant twist MacDonald adds to the normative narrative of masculine development, in which a young man must learn to regulate his own desires, is that Anodos's degree of self-mastery is proportional to his investment in a Romantic hermeneutic (Hein, McGillis). Anodos finds Fairy Land's Romantic values stated in a story he encounters in the palace's library: "the community of the centre of all creation suggests an interradiating connection and dependence of the parts" (77). To become a "true man" (174), much after the style of the middle-class new gentleman, Anodos must team to relate to others as if his connection to them were not defined hierarchically, commercially, or desirously; he must learn to see and respond to their essential, spiritual value. Anodos is impeded, however, by not only his innate male energies, but also his ego-bound skepticism.

For MacDonald, the old gentleman's ethical failings are not rooted in poor self-control so much as they are in his inadequate epistemology. As if taking up Digby's call for men "to lay aside all that harsh and acrimonious and proud wisdom that constitutes the worldly wise" (xxix-xxx), *Phantastes* depicts men, with their commitment to reason and fact over feeling, as less likely to believe in the invisible world of fairies and spirits, and, by extension, the divine. This ignorance of the spiritual connections between all things permits men to think and behave selfishly. What is at stake in Anodos's moral development is whether he will foster this mystical, Romantic sensibility within himself—only a minor, uncultivated strain of his character when he enters Fairy Land—or whether he will suppress it even further, to render himself more conventional.

Phantastes clearly marks a positivist perspective as masculine. Anodos's fairy grandmother links his reluctance to believe in the unseen with his gender: "Ah! that is always the way with you men, you believe nothing the first time" (7). Indeed, Anodos's early discourse is often that of the hero of rational inquiry, an amateur scientist who will not give up his old mode of interpretation even though the fantastic evidence before him calls it directly into question. He is a "geologist . . . about to turn up to the light some of the buried strata of the human world, with its fossil remains charred by passion and petrified by tears" (6). Rather than literally turning up the bones and fossils of alien fauna and flora, Anodos imagines he will uncover an emotional past that has been long buried, a figurative turn that underscores his all-but-latent affinity for the sentimental. Yet, Anodos thinks of the Platonic ideal naively, as if it were composed of material he could root out and put beneath the glass for closer inspection. Moreover, Anodos's specific comparison of himself to a geologist must have seemed especially significant to mid-Victorian readers at a time when geological science had offered significant challenges to the Christian fundamentalist conception of creation. The year before *Phantastes* was published, Philip Henry Gosse's *Omphalos: An Attempt to Untie the Geological Knot* (1857) argued that God might have placed fossils within layers of sedimentary rock, creating a false record of evolution to test humanity's faith. Anodos's faith is undermined by the tacit positivism against which Gosse was reacting. "Whether all the flowers have fairies, I cannot determine," Anodos says, "any more than I can be sure whether all men and women have souls" (18). His reluctance to believe what he cannot observe is the tie that binds together feminine Fairy Land and utopian Heaven and sets them up in mutual opposition to a masculine real that dominates Anodos's thinking even when he finds himself physically outside of it.

That the romance explicitly thematizes Anodos's progress as a shift from a conventionally masculine and positivist to a subversively feminine and Romantic hermeneutic is best demonstrated by his understanding of and relationship to Fairy Land as Mother Earth. Just before Anodos accidentally attracts the false Aldermaiden with a desirous song, he imagines "Earth drew me towards her bosom; I felt as if I could fall down and kiss her. I forgot I was in Fairy Land.... It seemed an old, old forest, perfect in forest ways and pleasure" (42). Anodos portrays the Earth as having seduced him, creating in *him* the desire to kiss *her*. He projects his own eroticism onto the feminine, just as he does with the Alder-maiden after. The Alder-maiden, though, is wily in the ways of men. She uses Anodos's false impression of her to lure him to her lair; but, her only desire has been to destroy him, to procure him for the terrible Ash. Just as in Coleridge's *Rime of the Ancient Mariner*, Anodos's reductive view of and exploitative relationship with the natural world is described as sepulchral, a form of death in life (the Alder-maiden has a coffin shape; she and the Ash are each a "walking Death"). Consider how differently Anodos describes his relationship with the Earth after the death of his own desire: "Now that I lay in her bosom, the whole earth, and each of her many births, was as a body to me, at my will. I seemed to feel the great heart of the mother beating into mine, and feeding me with her own life, her own essential being and nature" (180-81). Anodos's initial sexualization of the Earth is revealed to have been a fanciful projection of his desire. When Anodos is in sympathy with "her own essential being and nature," he perceives the Earth as maternal and himself as a suckling child. Anodos's unstable hermeneutic leads to a Platonic confusion about women's bodies: about whether they should be defined by their material form, and so rendered as desirable, sexual objects, or by their ideal form, and so considered as vessels for a sacred, maternal spirit. His shifting perception leads him to wish for a new understanding of himself and his relationship to others, for he begins to want to do no harm.

 In the second half of the romance, Anodos therefore self-consciously adopts the roles of artist and knight, metonymies of the middle- and upper-class formations of the new gentleman. Anodos's artistry helps to feminize and even to infantilize him, creating a growing division between the new gentleman he is becoming and the conventional male whom he perceived himself to be at journey's beginning. Prior to coming to Fairy Land, he was unable to match his voice to the music for which he had a fine ear (37). Now, he surprises himself with an innate gift for song. At first, his singing is only an impromptu expression of the imaginative sensibilities that come naturally to him. Later in the romance, Anodos sings more often by design, even singing for his foster brothers as a means of repaying them (152-53). The gift of music with which Anodos comes to identify himself is a feminizing force because of its special associations with the affective, intuitive, and spiritual. Anodos's "inward music" is uplifting, transcendent, instinctive, with the power to make statues dance or come alive. His song wells up clear and true from his soul; it cannot ring false (44). Others' songs as well as his own enable them to connect to others on a deeper emotive level than the social normally allows, bringing comfort and release, as when the beech enwraps Anodos in her dreamy music. Songs in Fairy Land also enable the expression of one's essence, as when the knight sings himself true as he rides through the wood. Thus, Anodos's individual art becomes a better means of connecting to the divinity within and without than does any doctrine or religious ceremony. Since *Phantastes* conceives of the Romantic artist in these terms, Anodos the bard is implicitly rendered an ecumenical analogue for the man of sentimental faith: a middle-class new gentleman.

The romance expresses anxiety, however, about the manliness of such artistic work, even when it is put to the service of others. Anodos's artistry can be highly sexualized, as when he lingeringly sings of the white lady's loveliness from toe to tip, and thus unequivocally male, but it elsewhere also suggests a "convergence of domestic and intellectual labor" (Sussman, 1). Anodos's gift of song is not necessarily coded as masculine, for the woman who sings him free of the prisonhouse of his own pride has songs of greater power and the old-woman-with-the-young-eyes's are more beautiful. Concern about his effeminacy comes to the fore when Anodos finds that he is not as manly as the foster brothers with whom he fights the giants. "I am ashamed of my white hands beside yours so nobly soiled and hard, "he tells them, vowing to alter this condition with physical labour (150). Despite his efforts, he remains the "least worthy," finding he is physically weaker and less skilled in making armour or waging war. He shores up the value of his songs, all that he really can effectively offer, by emphasizing their utility (152).

To become a new gentleman, then, Anodos must not cultivate the feminine traits associated with his artistry alone, for that might lead to a life of private leisure, as during his stay at the fairy palace final wise woman's cottage, or in the king's palace after Anodos's carries news to him of his sons' deaths. He must adopt a more masculine role in order to understand his work as a public function, rather than merely as a private expression. At the same time, he must not roughly put aside his tender sensibilities, for the compensating masculine ideal he is to emulate, the rusty knight, is a soldier "with all the gentleness of a womanly heart" (169).

The Knight's appeal is not androgynous, or even feminine, but a powerful masculinity feminized. Anodos admires the Knight's ability to melt strength into tenderness. Having slain a dragon and brought its infant victim home to her mother, the Knight's "powerful hands turned it [the child's seemingly dead body] and shifted it, and bound it, if possible even more gently than the mother's" (170). Anodos finds the Knight's transition from mildness to fierceness equally noble. In fact, the two are positioned one directly after the other, encouraging readers to appreciate the affective, chiasmic spectacle of the man-woman:

> Loving-kindness beamed from every line of his face. It seemed as if he would repay himself for the late arduous combat by indulging in all the gentleness of a womanly heart. But when the talk ceased for a moment, he seemed to fall into a reverie. . . . The whole face grew stern and determined, all but fierce, only the eyes burned like a holy sacrifice, uplift on a granite rock. (170)

The Knight holds his strength and fierceness in abeyance among those who merit his tenderness and sentiment, but is capable of swift and terrible action when presented with those who would harm innocence or disrupt domestic order. The effect is not a blending of masculine and feminine traits, neither is it an equal balance between the two. It is, rather, an aesthetic appreciation of masculine power that gives way to feminine gentleness when it need not do so, and an admiration for the sentimental and chivalric virtue that so inclines it.

Not only appropriate feminization, but muscular masculinity and the channeling of desire into work are the Knight's themes. The masculine dialectic the Knight himself sets up is "noble men and weaklings" (174), with a noble man defined as one who attempts to "better what he can," going "to his work with a cool brain and a strong will" (174). Even in the feminized new gentleman, muscularity, logic, and mastery are exclusionary characteristics that prevent womanly weakness of body, mind, and spirit from overcoming him—the kind of effeminacy Tennyson railed against. Anodos admires the self-mastery the rusty knight has achieved through his labours, an inner state of undivided virtue that Anodos himself despairs of ever realizing. The Knight has conquered his male energies so thoroughly that each new combat strikes some of the tarnish from his armour—a reminder of the folly of his youth, his own tryst with the corrupt Alder-maiden from whom he could not warn Anodos away.

Anodos's adopted roles of artist, with its feminizing influence, and the knight, with its compensating manliness, are each presented as fairly efficacious modes of masculine heroic agency. As an artist, Anodos does free the white lady and inspire his foster brothers to slay rapacious giants. As a knight in training, Anodos slays a giant and saves innocent sacrificial victims by killing the Fenris-like wolf that has been devouring them—only to earn his escape from Fairy Land by being killed in return. Becoming a knight, however, seems to be Anodos's ultimate destiny, the fulfilment of his masculine reformation in Fairy Land. Readers are likely to feel this not only because Anodos dies out of Fairy Land attempting to act as a knight, but also because he once found a door in the fairy palace inscribed *"The Chamber of Sir Anodos"* (70). Anodos's fairy palace, where the id is manifested, is reminiscent of Tennyson's "Palace of Art." that "lordly pleasure-house" created by the poet for his soul "wherein at ease for aye to dwell" and sing its songs alone (1-2). Furthermore, the rusty knight's teachings, expressed as generalizations based upon his personal experiences, imply that men universally mature into wisdom in the same way he has.

The martyred Anodos has never achieved, however, the stable new gentlemanliness of the legendary rusty knight. Almost right up to his death in Fairy Land, he has continued to fan. Anodos expresses despair over his lack of self-mastery, despite all his efforts to be of service: "I felt quite indifferent as to my own fate; not feeling, after the late events of my history, that I was at all worth taking care of" (178). This pattern of error brings to the surface the tension inherent in the patterns upon which he has modeled himself: a heroic masculinity that remains inevitably linked to treacherous, male impulses.

When the artist and knight have failed to provide unwavering manhood, Anodos turns toward the child, a formation that partly achieves selflessness through genderlessness (a radical form of unselfconsciousness). He longs to become as "innocent, fearless, without shame or *desire*" as a child (my emphasis; 162). Throughout the romance, in those moments when Anodos gives up his narcissistic, privileged persona and rational world view, he assumes a more childlike persona. Colin Manlove has argued that Anodos's development is away from the infantile toward the manly (81-82). I agree that Anodos grows less childish as he matures; however, paradoxically, he becomes more childlike. As a childish man, Anodos tries to make sexual contact with his fairy grandmother, and she rebukes him as a "foolish boy" (8). Similarly, when he meets the second goodwife after having fallen prey to the Alder-maiden, she tells him, "It is no wonder they could delude a child like you" (49). As a childish man, he views the world as he *fancies* it, reading only its surfaces, wherein he finds reflected his own desires. When Anodos focuses on feeling for others, he "learns to forget the very idea of doing so [accounting for things], and takes everything as it comes; like a child, who, being in a chronic condition of wonder, is surprised at nothing" (24). In this infantilized state, Anodos has a more powerfully perceptive vision; he is able to imaginatively penetrate the surfaces about him, to see into the "true" nature of things. Since that mystery is feminine-identified in this romance's Fairy Land, Anodos's development is a process of "immersion" rather than "separation" from the maternal, the opposite of what Colin Manlove has argued (82).

To recuperate Anodos, MacDonald does not regress him back to the condition of a child, as he might have in a fantasy medium; neither does he safely extinguish Anodos's impulses in marriage—a near-ubiquitous trope in the realistic Victorian novel and a resolution manifested in the coupling of the rusty knight with his lady. Instead, the narrative fantastically strips Anodos of his complicating maleness and transforms him into a masculine angel. Anodos's desire for individuated, sexual, and amorous union is likewise transformed into a longing for collective healing and agapic communion. The death of his body has meant the death of his passions, but "the souls of the passions, those essential mysteries of the spirit which had embodied themselves in the passions . . . yet lived" (180). In that moment of ecstasy, at once dead and yet so marvellously alive, Anodos invokes the inhabitants of the great city over which his soul hovers: "How I will wait on you, and minister to you, and, putting my arms around you in the dark, think hope unto your hearts. . . . I will be among you with the love that healeth" (182). As Anodos spiritually embraces the troubled city and promises its suffering inhabitants his disinterested love, he resonates more fully than the new gentleman as a masculine cultural icon that might serve as a twin to the feminine "angel in the house"—selfless, nurturing, morally empowered, and as literally disembodied as she was figuratively etherealized.

The construction of an angel in the cosmos is firmly rooted in the middle-class identity formation of the serious Christian. Within this sub-culture, many men and women earnestly attempted to model their lives on Christ's, refraining from sensuousness and making personal sacrifices for the public good. They understood their society to be a series of ever-expanding domestic spheres, from the individual family home, to county or parish, to nation, to empire, to the cosmos itself, in which God was a benign and loving father and heaven all humankind's true home. In dying out of Fairy Land, then, Anodos has become an even more potent figure of the masculine heroic than he was as artist or knight: a purely domestic hero whose essentially male energies are quenched by a state of utter and ecstatic self-abnegation. No longer the "man of pride," he has finally answered the call to "Come into the house" that is "so high and wide" it constitutes the very cosmos (164).

This utopian state, however, proves unstable, for Anodos remains fundamentally tied to the mortal world. At the very end of the romance, Anodos returns to his body and to the real from whence he came, what Anodos now names "the world of shadows" (182). His sudden and disappointing return to a male body and masculine identity leaves him uncertain of his power to morally master himself. He asks, "Could I translate the experience of my travels there, into common life? Or must I live it all over again, and learn it all over again, in the other forms that belong to the world of men, whose experience yet runs parallel to that of Fairy Land?" (184). Denied the surety he would find in a continued communion with the divine, a freedom from the struggle to regulate his desires that he described as "ideal bliss" (182), Anodos longs for death. His only consolation are the whispers he hears in dreamy visions th.at now assure him that this "great good" is coming (184). The disappointing return from Fairy Land is a narrative move common in the long Victorian fairy tale, one that in *Phantastes* presses readers to wish for "natural" utopian ideals even as it calls into question the possibility of their being enacted in a social world so fallen.

Anodos's return from an angelic state to his physical body and former social role may have much the same effect as the return to "dingy Hammersmith" of Morris's utopian sojourner, the aptly named Guest, of *News from Nowhere*. Readers are encouraged to want Guest's journey to the "epoch of rest" to have been more than a dream, even as they are aware that it can be nothing other than a beautiful dream because it is, in reality, a fiction. The distinct distance between the beauty of that dream and the unpleasant reality that ends it is emphasized by his expressions of disappointed longing. At the same time, his continued belief in the "vision" he has had keeps him from despair. Like Guest, Anodos has brought back with him a vision of a better world, one that is as haunting as it is personally transformative. Significantly, however, MacDonald's Anodos has never seen the best of all possible worlds for which he finally yearns; he has only had a foretaste of the country from whence the shadows fall, has only journeyed to a land that lies somewhere between the earthly plain and heaven. He has not been to heaven itself. Hence, Anodos is left with the sense that he must strive to maintain his faith in a world where matter discloses little of its innate spirit and where even a gentleman may only hope to imperfectly regulate his own desires through serving others rather than satisfying himself. MacDonald does not depict Anodos as having achieved some kind of manhood that is beyond mortal ken. Instead, he finally represents Anodos as a squire who has been infused with a renewed sense of faith, to believe in what he cannot see, and spiritual purpose, to be a better man than he had been before.

Although Anodos's transformation into an angel in the cosmos may seem to have limited consequences—MacDonald is, after all, depicting the reformation of just one man—it is ideologically profound. Within Victorian culture, the angel in the house was widely reproduced as a standard of conduct and ideation with far-reaching cultural consequences. The construct of the new gentleman was based, in part, on men's attempt to emulate such gentle virtues, but such emulation did not extend to men the same kind of cultural capital as was accorded to women, who were the natural source of them. Women's virtues were functions of their very bodies, which were without sexual desire but replete with maternal feeling. Men's bodies, on the contrary, were a source of betrayal; they had to use their intellect and will to overcome its basic drives. What makes *Phantastes* an important contribution to the ideation of Victorian manhood is that it constructs yet another new version of the gentleman that provided an idealistic ground for men's virtue. Since the source of men's virtue could not be in their bodies, it would be in their spirits, the vital divine essence that underwrote all physical forms. MacDonald trades biological essentialism for spiritual essentialism with some degree of metaawareness. As he lies in his grave in Fairy Land, his body falling away, Anodos tells us that he feels Mother Earth infusing him, as if she were "feeding me with her own life" (181). Through this exchange of symbolic economies, *Phantastes* authorizes men to assume a role of ethical importance on a scale even grander than that accorded to women. If women naturally constituted the domestic sphere, and by extension the nation and empire, the angel in the cosmos revealed men's potential to constitute a universal sphere of benign patriarchy. Anodos has a strong desire, in the end, to manifest this new sense of divine agency in his public role: "I have a strange feeling sometimes," Anodos tells us, "that I am a ghost, sent into the world to minister to my fellow men, or, rather, to repair the wrongs I have already done" (184).

ENDNOTES

1. For arguments that contribute to understanding masculinity in *Phantastes*, see Gray, Hein, Manlove, and McGillis.

2. Rolland Hein suggests that Anodos's name is transliterated from a Greek word with two meanings: "having no way" and "rising," which accounts for Robb and Wolff's reading it as "pathless," and C.N. Manlove's definition of the name's origin as "an upward direction" (Hein, 56). We can see how both are true of Anodos in the tale, who must literally and figuratively lose himself before he may rise in wisdom and in spirit toward heaven.

WORKS CITED

Adams, James Eli. *Dandies and Desert Saints: Styles of Victorian Masculinity*. Ithaca: Cornell UP, 1995.

Arnold, Matthew. *Culture and Anarchy*. 1869. Ed. Samuel Lipman. New Haven: Yale UP, 1994. Christ, Carol. "Victorian Masculinity and the Angel in the House." *A Widening Sphere: Changing Roles of Victorian Women*. Ed. Martha Vicinus. Bloomington: Indiana UP, 1977, 146-62.

Dale, Peter Allan. *In Pursuit of a Scientific Culture: Science, Art, and Society in the Victorian Age*. Madison: U of Wisconsin P, 1989.

Danahay, Martin. "Class. Gender, and the Victorian Masculine Subject." *A-B: Auto-Biography Studies*, 5 (Fall 1990), 99-113.

Davidoff, Leonore, and Catherine Hall. *Family Fortune: Men and Women of the English Middle Class*, 1780-1850. Chicago: U of Chicago P, 1987.

Dickens, Charles. "The Chimes." *The Christmas Books: Vol. 1. A Christmas Carol/The. Chimes*. Ed. Michael Slater. New York: Penguin, 1985, 149-246.

Digby, Kenelm Henry. *The Broad Stone of Honour: or, Rules for the Gentlemen of England*. 1822. Rev. ed. London: C. & J. Rivington, 1823.

Eliot. George. *The Mill on the Floss*. Ed. James Kincaid. Oxford: Oxford UP, 1980.

Gosse, Philip Henry. *Omphalos: An Attempt to Untie the Geological Knot*. London, 1857.

Girouard, Mark. *The Return to Camelot: Chivalry and the English Gentleman*. New Haven: Yale UP, 1981.

Gray, William N. "George MacDonald, Julia Kristeva, and the Black Sun." *Studies in English Literature, 1500-1900*, 36 (Autumn 1996), 877-93.

Hastings, A. Waller. "Social Conscience and Class Relations in MacDonald's 'Cross Purposes.'" *For the Childlike: George MacDonald's Fantasy Stories for Children*. Ed. Roderick McGillis. Metuchen. NJ: Children's Literature Association and Scarecrow Press, 1992, 75-86.

Hein, Rolland. *The Harmony Within: The Spiritual Vision of George MacDonald*. Washington D.C.: Christian UP. 1982.

Knowles, Murray, and Kirsten Malmkjaer. *Language and Control in Children's Literature*. New York: Routledge, 1996.

MacDonald, George. *Phantastes: A Faerie Romance*. 1858. Grand Rapids, Mich: Erdmans.1981.

—. *Unspoken Sermons*. London; George Routledge & Sons, 1871.

Manlove, C.N. "Circularity in Fantasy: George MacDonald." *The Impulse of Fantasy Literature*. Kent Ohio: Kent State UP, 1983. 70-92.

Maurice, F.D. *An Abridgement of Maurice's Kingdom of Christ: The Original Two Volumes Abridged into One based on the 1842 Edition Emended with an Introduction*. Ed. William J. Wolf. Lanham, Maryland: UP of America, 1983.

McGillis, Roderick. "The Community of the Centre: Structure and Theme in *Phantastes*." *For the Childlike: George MacDonald's Fantasies for Children*. Ed. Roderick McGillis. Metuchen. NJ: Children's Literature Association and Scarecrow Press, 1992, 51-65.

—. "*Phantastes* and *Lilith*: Femininity and Freedom." *The Gold Thread: Essays on George MacDonald*. Ed. William Raeper. Edinburgh: Edinburgh UP, 1990, 31-55.

Nelson, Claudia. *Boys Will Be Girls: The Feminine Ethic and British Children's Fiction 1857 1917.* New Brunswick, NJ: Rutgers UP, 1991.

Poovey. Mary. *Uneven Developments: The Ideological Work of Gender in Mid-Victorian England.* Chicago: U of Chicago P, 1988.

Prickett, Stephen. "Fictions and Metafictions: 'Phantastes,' 'Wilhelm Meister,' and the Idea of the 'Bildungsroman.'" *The Gold Thread: Essays on Gorge MacDonald.* Ed. William Raeper. Edinburgh: Edinburgh UP, 1990. 109-25.

Sussman, Herbert. *Victorian Masculinities: Manhood and Masculine Poetics in Early Victorian Literature and Art.* Cambridge: Cambridge UP, 1995.

Tennyson, Alfred Lord. *Tennyson: A Selected Edition.* Ed. Christopher Ricks. Berkeley: U of California P, 1989, 222-330.

Trollope, Anthony. *The Small House at Allington.* Oxford: Oxford UP, 1989.

Mirrors in MacDonald's *Phantastes*: A Reflexive Structure

Fernando Soto

From *North Wind: A Journal of George MacDonald Studies*

1. Introduction: *Phantastes* and Present Scholarship

"The Soul of Man," says my father in the unpublished Seekers and Finders, "is the world turned outside in"; and in *Paul Faber* he speaks more poetically of a little child being a "mirrored universe." (Greville MacDonald 404)

How much Gibbie even then understood of the lovely, eerie old ballad, it is impossible for me to say. . . . Certainly it was the beginning of much. But the waking up of a human soul to know itself in the mirror of its thoughts and feelings, its loves and delights, oppresses me with so heavy a sense of marvel and inexplicable mystery, that when I imagine myself such as Gibbie then was, I cannot imagine myself coming awake. . . . When by slow filmy unveilings, life grew clearer to Gibbie, and he not only knew, but knew that he knew, his thoughts always went back to that day . . . Then first he saw nature reflected, Narcissus-like, in the mirror of her humanity, her highest self. (*Sir Gibbie* 97)

MacDonald's *Phantastes* had remained a type of literary "black box" for nearly one hundred and forty years. Ever since its introduction to the public, little had surfaced regarding two interrelated aspects of importance for an understanding of this puzzling book: its meaning and structure. Because few instances of solid internal meaning or direct references to outside sources were easily extracted from MacDonald's complex book, many reviewers and later scholars, it seems, concluded that *Phantastes* had neither plot nor structure, and/or that it was loosely written.[1]

The critical tide began to turn a little more than a decade ago, after John Docherty and Roderick McGillis convincingly argued for the existence of a structure in *Phantastes*. Their general conclusions, however, tended to divide scholarly opinion. There still appears to be little accord among some of the most influential and active MacDonald scholars regarding the type(s) of structure(s) in *Phantastes*.[2]

Without a general, coherent, and persuasive structure for readers to follow, few relevant examples and references are likely to surface from the enigmatic and complex world of *Phantastes*. Too general, too disconnected, or overly conjectural examples and references appear to breed discordant and unconvincing possible structures, and this formidable dialectical circle, externally perceived, continues to prevent a confident entrance to the inner sanctum of MacDonald's complex masterpiece.

In this article I will attempt to present a coherent central structure underlying *Phantastes*, and some inter-textual examples as well as extra-textual references reflecting and supporting this structure. Outlining some internal examples of the book's reflective or looking-glass nature, ultimately focused on Cosmo von Wehrstahl's Magic Mirror, permits analysis, delineation, and explanation of the "reflective" structure in the book. Using this structure as a guide, I examine further external reflexive references used by MacDonald. Ultimately, this provides a coherent, descriptive structure of *Phantastes* that should withstand critiques likely to emerge from the various "camps" in the somewhat discordant present scholarship devoted to MacDonald.

Before proceeding to some of the complex examples of mirroring and the mirror structure these reflect, some background and a short history of MacDonald's interests and education should be presented. Greville MacDonald, in the biography of his parents, mentions that his father received his MA in Chemistry and Natural Philosophy (i.e., Physics), and that he was very interested in working with the famous German biochemist, Justus von Liebig (68).[3] The only impediment that kept MacDonald from joining Liebig in Germany was lack of money (Broome 89). However, this did not keep him from studying Liebig's works. Nor, perhaps, did pecuniary reasons keep him from hearing Liebig speak in Glasgow in 1840.[4]

It seems MacDonald's study of Liebig's theories proved fruitful for the budding novelist, at least in his gaining of contemporary knowledge in regards to scientific discoveries, theoretical models, and their possible meanings: "Liebig . . .was prone to making 'chemical analogies'—as was MacDonald, who made Swedenborgian transformations of chemical equations for his classes at Bedford College—and provided the process which led to the silvering of mirrors, an important image in MacDonald's works" (Broome 90). MacDonald's interest in Liebig and chemistry may thus have led him directly toward the subject of mirrors and reflections.

2. Reflections on Mirrors, Images and Inversions

> Why are all reflections lovelier than what we call the reality?—not so grand or so strong, it may be, but always lovelier? Fair as is the gliding sloop on the shining sea, the wavering, trembling, unresting sail below is fairer still. Yea, the reflecting ocean itself reflected in the mirror, has wondrousness about its waters that somewhat vanishes when I turn toward itself. All mirrors are magic mirrors. The commonest room is a room in a poem when I turn to the glass. (*Phantastes* 123)

Because mirrors give the appearance of the existence of two related worlds, or because reflecting surfaces seem to divide the world in two (the "real" and the "reflected"), they are of great interest to MacDonald (Broome 90; Prickett, "Worlds" 17-29).[5] Reflections or images in a looking glass, however, portray to the observer the object(s) reflected and something quite different—the perceived reversal of the object(s) in the image. In *Phantastes*, MacDonald's awareness of these optical phenomena (the perceived repetition and "inversion" of objects) is evident. This awareness is partially understood by considering the relationship between mirrors and the imagination, two crucial components of this and many of MacDonald's other books. MacDonald provides many detailed and imaginative passages about mirrors and the imagination in *Phantastes*. For example: "What a strange thing a mirror is! and what a wondrous affinity exists between it and a man's imagination! For this room of mine, as I behold it in the glass, is the same, and yet not the same. It is not the mere representation of the room I live in, but it looks just as if I were reading about it in a story I like. All its commonness has disappeared. The mirror has lifted it out of the region of fact into the realm of art" (161-62).

In *Phantastes*, MacDonald is also cognizant of the optics involved with more complex types of mirrors and reflecting surfaces. For instance, Anodos narrates a "strange thing" regarding the focal distance between himself and the inhabitants of a village he visited in Fairy Land:

> I observed, that whenever I came within a certain distance of any one of them, which distance, however, varied with different individuals, the whole appearance of the person began to change; and this change increased in degree as I approached. When I receded to the former distance, the former appearance was restored. The nature of the change was grotesque, following no fixed rule. The nearest resemblance to it that I know, is the distortion produced in your countenance

when you look at it reflected in a concave or convex surface—say, either side of a bright spoon. (115-16)[6]

Thus, it may be gathered that MacDonald's interest in all types of mirrors and reflections is an important component of this and other of his books.

The centrality of the mirror is an intellectual and a material structural component of *Phantastes*. MacDonald presents the reader with the above explicit, theoretical descriptions of the three types of mirrors (plane, concave, and convex), and with many actual instances of mirrors, reflecting surfaces, and literary "reflections." In addition, a very important component of the story is the special "place" given to Cosmo's Magic Mirror. This mirror is found in the middle chapter of *Phantastes*, very near the actual centre of the book. Consequently, the Magic Mirror intellectually and physically bisects the story, and structurally reflects both sides of *Phantastes* in almost equal proportions.

Some of MacDonald's individual examples of reflectivity are superficial, while others are found deep below the more exterior aspects of *Phantastes*.[7] Easily identifiable instances of reflection occur in chapters 1 and 10. The first examples of two related "images" are found when Anodos refers to the scent of rose-leaves and the colour of a ribbon curiously having departed together: "in one corner lay a little heap of withered rose-leaves, whose long-lived scent had long since departed; and in another, a small packet of papers, tied with a bit of ribbon, whose colour had gone with the rose scent" (15-16).

This type of direct association among colour, scent, and roses is recalled in chapter 10:

"Roses, wild roses, everywhere! So plentiful were they, they not only perfumed the air, they seemed to dye it a faint rose-hue. The colour floated abroad with the scent, and clomb, and spread, until the whole west blushed and glowed with the gathered incense of roses" (121). MacDonald, therefore, presents the reader with two events that reflect each other, yet mirror-like, the two "images" are inverted in terms of the existence and non-existence of the main entities involved.

Among the "hidden" similarities within the above examples is Anodos' awareness of the reflecting "images" surrounding the two rose-colour-scent episodes. In chapter 1, it is immediately after Anodos opens the last door into Fairy Land that he perceives the scentless rose-leaves and the colourless ribbon. It is the opening of this last chamber that allows the tiny woman to emerge and "invite" him to enter Fairy Land—something Anodos later does by following the stream/rivulet whose source is in his overflowing wash basin (20-23).

By continuing to follow Anodos' stream of consciousness presented in chapter 10, the reader finds "deeper" correspondences between the above two related sections of *Phantastes*. In chapter 10, Anodos follows a river to a castle, which he enters through "a wide gateway, but without gates." In the castle he finds "a large fountain . . . throwing up a lofty column of water . . . into a basin beneath; overflowing which, it ran in a single channel towards the interior of the building" (127). He follows the "stream from the basin of the fountain" to a "great open door, beneath the ascending steps of which it ran through a low arch, and disappeared" (128). He ceases to follow the stream by going through this doorway, and once inside, encounters "a great hall, surrounded with white pillars" (129). He then finds himself in a darkening hall and later in a dark corridor—with "seemingly innumerable pillars." Then, while searching for a "hospitable chamber," he locates exactly what he requires, a chamber that perfectly mirrors his own bedchamber. While he reflects on this "strange" coincidence, he correctly intuits a part of the reflective nature of what is occurring: "But what surprised me more than all, was, that the room was in every respect a copy of my own room, the room whence the little stream from my basin had led me into Fairy Land" (130).

These above events and insights give the strong impression that Anodos is retracing his steps—following a river across the landscape of Fairy Land to his own castle, walking beside the stream which is now flowing back to his basin, through his secretary, and back to his own chamber (20-23; 120- 131).[8] As shown above, the finer points of this "mirror-image" are not lost on Anodos: before he encounters the roses and their colour/smell, he is aware of the similarities when he exclaims: "I felt as if I were entering Fairy Land for the first time" (121). Given the many close correspondences between both episodes, this "insight" (and the one related to him finding a "copy" of his own bedroom) should not be surprising for the reader or Anodos. Indeed, there are many reasons for the second event to feel like a mirror-reflection of Anodos' first entrance to Fairy Land. MacDonald likely intends some readers to make this connection when he includes the verse which heads chapter 10: "From Eden's bowers the flail-fed rivers flow, / To guide the outcasts to the land of woe: / Our Earth one little toiling streamlet yields, / To guide the wanderers to the happy fields" (119). However, as may be expected, the above order inherent in the quotation is reversed: Anodos had first followed a streamlet out of his chamber, whereas in chapter 10 he follows a river back to his point of origin.

There are many other "reversals" in some of the above reflecting sections of the book. The most obvious individual inversion is where a lack of rose scent and colour of the roses in the chamber of the secretary in chapter 1 are reflected by the overabundance of the roses' colour and scent in chapter 10. The same is generally true regarding the light available for both events: the first occurs in the morning and the second at night The "opposite" times of day also allow for Anodos to be first awakened to "consciousness" by the sound of the running water emerging from his basin, while it is once more the sound of water, from the mirror-image of this basin, that lulls him to sleep in the second episode. One "image" shows the negative and the other the positive in relation to roses and colour and scent, the time of day, and the changes of consciousness (in this case, brought on by listening to the sound of water) that usually occurs in the morning and at night (20; 231). And mirror-like, the first episode relates to Anodos' entrance to Fairy Land, and the second to his exit.

Another revealing example of mirroring becomes apparent by considering the two following episodes of *Phantastes*. Soon after Anodos enters Fairy Land in chapter 3, he reflects upon the difference between the creatures of the day and those of the night: "Then I remembered that night is the fairies' day, and the moon their sun; and I thought—Everything sleeps and dreams now: when the night comes, it will be different. At the same time I, being a man and child of the day, felt some anxiety as to how I should fare among the elves and other children of the night who wake when mortals dream" (26).

While Anodos is imprisoned in the tower in chapter 22, he completely reverses most of his previous conclusions:

> But as soon as the first faint light of the dawn appeared, instead of shining upon me from the eye of the morning, it stole like a fainting ghost through the little square hole above my head; and the walls came out as the light grew, and the glorious night was swallowed up by the hateful day. The long dreary day passed. My shadow lay black on the floor. . . . Thus night after night passed away. I should have died but for this. Every night the conviction returned, that I was free. (280)

This reversal within Anodos is partially explained by considering that dreaming and wakefulness had also been inverted for him by this point in the story. The mirror-reversal of these two states of consciousness is further inferred from the *Phantastes* passage prior to the above:

> I sat down on the floor, in listless wretchedness. I think I must have fallen asleep, and have slept for hours; for I suddenly became aware of existence, in observing that the moon was shining through the hole in the roof. As she rose higher and higher, her light crept down the wall over me, till at last it shone right upon my head: Instantaneously the walls of the tower seemed to vanish away like a mist. I sat beneath a beech . . . I thought with myself, "Oh, joy! it was only a dream; the horrible narrow waste is gone, and I wake beneath a beech-tree." (279)

The above example presents the reader with a type of mirror-image—where Anodos' conceptions regarding the "reality" of wakefulness and the "fictitious" nature of dreams are reversed. Also, the "positivity" regarding day and the "negativity" of night are again inverted from one image to the other, as dreaming and wakefulness had similarly been reversed. The reversal or confusion of the dream and waking states is an important theme and perhaps a major psychological aim of *Phantastes*. This is reflected in one of MacDonald's favourite aphorisms of Novalis (used in key sections of *Phantastes* and other of his books, notably at the very end of *Lilith*): "*Our* life is no dream; but it ought to become one, and perhaps will" (315).

Another such mirroring and reversal of similar events occurs with the deaths of two primroses. These floral deaths are respectively found in chapters 3 and 24. In the first instance, a flower fairy, the Pocket, bites the stalk of a Primrose and hastens its demise. The events surrounding the death of the first primrose are partly described as: "During the latter part of the song-talk, they had formed themselves into a funeral procession, two of them bearing poor Primrose, whose death Pocket had hastened by biting her stalk, upon one of her own great leaves. They bore her solemnly along some distance, and then buried her under a tree. Although I say *her* I saw nothing but the withered primrose-flower on its long stalk" (40). The mirror image of this incident is found after Anodos is killed by the warrior-priests, and, like the first primrose, is buried beneath some trees. In this episode, a disembodied Anodos momentarily "inhabits" a primrose:

> They buried me in no graveyard. They loved me too much for that . . . but they laid me in the grounds of their own castle, amid many trees; where, as it was spring-time, were growing primroses, and blue bells, and all the families of the woods. . . . I rose into a single large primrose that grew by the edge of the grave, and from the window of its humble, trusting face, looked full in the countenance of the lady. I felt that I could

> manifest myself in the primrose; that it said a part of what I wanted to say . . . . The flower caught her eye. She stooped and plucked it, saying, "Oh, you beautiful creature!" and, lightly kissing it, put it in her bosom. It was the first kiss she had ever given me. But the flower soon began to wither, and I forsook it. (312-13)

This is the opposite of the relationship of flower fairies to their flowers. During Anodos' description of his early encounter with flower fairies he comments that "the conclusion I arrived at from the observations I was afterwards able to make, was, that the flowers die because the fairies go away, not that the fairies disappear because the flowers die" (36). We learn nothing more about these later observations.

These two curious botanical incidents share many similarities: both events take place in the late evening, both primroses are occupied by living entities, both flowers "wither" and are forsaken by their inhabitants, both entities are buried under trees soon after their "funerals," and so on. Identification and analysis of one of the main reversals, however, begins by considering that the gender of the inhabiting entity is changed from female in the first instance to male in the latter. The first primrose is a female—described by the pronoun "her"—whereas Anodos remains a male throughout the story (even as he becomes a disembodied entity). Another reversal may be considered in relation to the actions performed by the mouths of the Pocket and the Marble Lady. It is an envious bite that hastens the death of the first primrose, whereas a loving kiss may quicken the death of the flower Anodos temporarily inhabits. Hate and jealousy, in the first instance, are replaced by love and faithfulness in the second.

The examples of mirroring presented thus far give some idea of the reflective complexity of *Phantastes*; however, there are many other highly abstract examples to consider regarding this important structural component of the book. For example, the Alder-maiden has her wooden, mirror-counterparts in the latter sections of the book. Here is how Anodos describes the Maid of the Alder in chapter 6:

> I woke as a grey dawn stole into the cave. The damsel had disappeared; but in the shrubbery, at the mouth of the cave, stood a strange horrible object. It looked like an open coffin set up on one end; only that the part for the head and neck was defined from the shoulder-part. In fact, it was a rough representation of the human frame, only hollow, as if made of decaying bark torn from a tree. It had arms, which were only slightly seamed, down from the shoulder-blade by the elbow, as if the bark had healed again from the cut of a knife. (84)

The counterparts of the Maid of the Alder are the wooden men who keep the little beggar girl from gathering her butterfly wings in chapter 23. These wooden men are described by the little maiden whom they tread underfoot as being "like great men, made of wood, without knee or elbow-joints, and without any noses or mouths or eyes in their faces" (297).[9] Later, the knight describes the first wooden man he sees: "This being, if being it could be called, was like a block of wood roughly hewn into the mere outlines of a man; and hardly so, for it had but head, body, legs, and arms—the head without a face, and the limbs utterly formless" (300).

All three of the above descriptions of the evil wooden creatures are very similar. Complementing these shared characteristics are some implicit similarities within MacDonald's accounts of both types of wooden images. The curious way in which MacDonald describes the "set up" of both wooden creatures is one of these more hidden correspondences. In the first of the above accounts, MacDonald conveys to the reader that the Maid of the Alder "looked like an open coffin set up on one end." This "set up" reflects the clever method by which the knight first subdues a wooden man: "I tripped one of them up, and, taking him by the legs, set him up on his head" (300). In case the reader did not mark the importance of this method of "setting up" the wooden men, MacDonald has the knight repeat it: "Whenever one appeared, I followed the same plan—tripped him up and set him on his head." The similar descriptions and "set up" of both wooden creatures tend to make both events and wooden characters closely mirror each other. The main reversals are: the actual physical inversion of the latter wooden creatures (the Alder maid is "set up" pointing up and the wooden men are "set up" pointing down); the shift from concentrating on the facial beauty of the Maid of the Alder compared to the lack of any aesthetic features where the face ought to be on the wooden men; and finally the reversal of the gender of the creatures under question (58).

The Ash, like the Maid of the Alder, has his wooden counterpart in a later section of *Phantastes*. Before proceeding, one important identifying attribute or description of the Ash ought to be mentioned: this tree-spirit's voracious nature. The Beech-tree woman describes the Ash as wanting to bury Anodos at the foot of his tree because: "this one has a hole in his heart that nobody knows of but one or two; and he is always trying to fill it up, but he cannot. That must be what he wanted you for" (58).

The reader encounters the mirror-image of the Ash in chapter

23. As Anodos and the knight enter the yew-tree enclosure, where the human sacrifices are taking place, they encounter something strikingly reminiscent of the Ash. The relationship between both the evil things becomes simple to detect by considering Anodos' actions in the presence of this "wooden image":

> I walked right up the stairs to the throne, laid hold of a great wooden image that seemed to sit upon it, and tried to hurl it from its seat . . . I strained with all my might; and, with a noise as of the cracking, and breaking, and tearing of rotten wood, something gave way, and I hurled the image down the steps. Its displacement revealed a great hole in the throne, like the hollow of a decayed tree, going down apparently a great way. (307-8)

Supplementing the above description, Anodos claims to have previously witnessed the pushing of a boy into the hollow beneath the throne: "The company ascended to the foot of the throne, where they all knelt for some minutes; then they rose and passed round to the side of the pedestal upon which the throne stood. Here they crowded close behind the youth . . . and one of them opened a door in the pedestal, for the youth to enter. I was sure I saw him shrink back, and those crowding behind pushed him in" (305).

After witnessing the same type of sacrifice performed with a girl, Anodos appears to conclude that the priests are attempting to fill the deep hole at the foot of their wooden image. This fact, and the descriptions of both wooden entities, certainly reflect what the reader already knows of the insatiable nature of the Ash, and his custom of burying young people in an attempt to "fill up" the hole in his heart. Moreover, most of the people witnessing the sacrifice, including the knight, seem unaware of the nature of the sacrificial part of the ceremony. Hence, it seems that while more than one or two priests know what is occurring to the young man and woman, the secret of the hole in the heart of the Ash is still not known widely by this point of the story.

Again, there are many reversals in this latter reflection of the first meetings of Anodos and the Ash ogre. It is a cunning Anodos who now attacks the immobile image of the Ash ogre, and kills its wolf-spirit by a method learned from the grasping, knobbly handed, Ash-ogre itself. Anodos strangles the wolf-spirit with one, and, only one, hand. By directly attacking the Ash effigy and exposing the brutal nature of the ceremony, Anodos "saves" the knight. This action reflects the way the knight had previously saved Anodos by his timely assailment of the tree inhabited by the Ash spirit. The situations are further reversed when we consider that the Ash had attempted to attack Anodos with his bare hand (in the grotto of the Maid of the Alder), and that the knight had saved Anodos by attacking the Ash tree with an axe (241-2). In the latter episode it is Anodos, leaving his axe behind, who attacks the Ash-idol, and the idol's wolf-spectre with his bare hand(s). He has learned from overhearing the conversation between the Knight and the White Lady that "earthly arms availed not against such as" the Ash's spectre and perhaps suspects a similar foe here. His unarmed state allows him to approach the idol, but then it allows the priests easily to kill him with their swords.

3. Mirrors, Chemistry and Life-force

To appreciate better the depth and meaning of the next mirroring example, it must be recalled that MacDonald was interested in the more theoretical aspects of his era's Science.[10] Hal Broome argues convincingly that Justus von Liebig particularly influenced MacDonald with some of his own and adopted bio-chemical and bio-electrical theories. Liebig's conclusions which interested MacDonald include: i) "life force was analogous with electricity"; ii) "[l]iving things were endowed with 'vital force'"; iii) "vital force" was of two types—the "vegetative" and the "animal"; iv) females had more "vegetative" force; v) "the life-force within the individual changed with the amount of light available to him/ her" (Broome 89-92). In addition, Broome claims that Müller, to a lesser degree than Liebig, also influenced MacDonald with his related biochemical theories. Broome argues that it was Müller who first presented the theory—of interest and use to MacDonald—that "men were more likely positive and women negatively electrical" (Broome 94). But is any of this biographical and "scientific" material reflected in *Phantastes*?[11]

In chapter 3 of *Phantastes*, the reader is provided with a comical scene that at first appears to hold little meaning or justification. One daytime prank of the flower fairies involves adhering to a cat, holding it in place, and proceeding to remove sparks from the feline. MacDonald, through Anodos, describes this electrical process:

> By this time the party which had gone towards the house, rushed out again, shouting and screaming with laughter. Half of them were on the cat's back, and half held on by her fur and tail, or ran beside her, till, more coming to their help, the furious cat was held fast; and they proceeded to pick the sparks out of her with thorns and pins, which they handled

like harpoons. Indeed, there were more instruments at work about her than there could have been sparks in her. One little fellow who held on hard by the tip of the tail with his feet planted on the ground at an angle of forty-five degrees, helping to keep her fast, administered a continuous flow of admonitions to Pussy. (41)

In addition, the fairy that held the tip of the cat's tail provides a type of "altruistic" and "scientific/psychological" reason for the fairies' actions:

"Now, Pussy, be patient. You know quite well it is all for your good. You cannot be comfortable with all those sparks in you; and, indeed, I am charitably disposed to believe" (here he became very pompous) "that they are the cause of all your bad temper; so we must have them all out, every one; else we shall be reduced to the painful necessity of cutting your claws, and pulling out your eye-teeth. Quiet! Pussy, quiet!" (41-2)

Near the end of this charged episode, the female cat manages to escape from her "helpers": "But with a perfect hurricane of feline curses, the poor animal broke loose, and dashed across the garden and through the hedge, faster than even the fairies could follow" (42).

The above, by itself, holds some possible similarities with Liebig's and Müller's theories. However, by including the literary mirror-image of the above event—found in chapter 17—many of the possible similarities become actualities.

Chapter 17 has many explicit and implicit references to things electrical. One possible reference to Liebig's theories is given when Anodos, while pursuing the Marble Lady, descends into a dark chasm and has to "quit the sunlight" (209). As Anodos leaves the daylight behind, or above him, and unsuccessfully pursues the Marble Lady, he enters an "underground country" lit by "sad sepulchral illumination" (217). In this underground cavern "instead of trees and flowers, there were only fantastic rocks and stones" (210). Like the above-ground fairies who inhabited the flowers, the underground creature whom Anodos first encounters emerges out of, or from behind, one of the rocks that had "replaced" the flowers: "At length I began to find that these regions were inhabited. From behind a rock a peal of harsh grating laughter, full of evil humour, rang through my ears, and looking round, I saw a queer, goblin creature, with a great head and ridiculous features, just like those described, in German histories and travels, as Kobolds" (211).

In the semidarkness of this underground country, it is this Kobold who first refers to Anodos' bio-electrically charged state: "Honoured sir, vouchsafe to withdraw from thy slaves the lustre of thy august presence, for thy slaves cannot support its brightness" (211).

It is directly following this bio-electrical reference that a "whole pandemonium of fairy devils" joins the first Kobold in mocking Anodos. They attempt to insult Anodos through verbal and gesticulatory acts very reminiscent of the above-ground fairies' theatrics, although there it is the cat they torment that is described as a "demon" (30). The woman there tells Anodos that the fairies are "very amusing, with their mimicries of grown people and mock solemnities. Sometimes they will act a whole play through before my eyes" (34). These "amusing mimicries," "mock solemnities" and "whole plays" are all present in Anodos' meeting with the underground "goblins." Though the woman looks upon such antics positively, Anodos understandably reacts negatively to the goblin's pranks. So they resort to more direct methods in their attempts to injure him: "Inexpressible laughter followed, which broke up in a shower of tiny stones from innumerable hands" (212).

The tiny stones are too small to cause Anodos much damage. As he attempts to run away, however, the fairies grab hold of him in almost the exact fashion as the cat had been seized: "I attempted to run away, but they all rushed upon me, and laying hold of every part that afforded, a grasp, held me tight. Crowding about me like bees, they shouted an insect-swarm of exasperating speeches up into my face, among which the most frequently recurring were—'You shan't have her; you shan't have her; he! he! he! She's for a better man; she's for a better man; how he'll kiss her! how he'll kiss her!'" (212-13). As the above-ground fairies that Anodos sees are connected with flowers, it is interesting that he compares the goblins to bees and interprets their shouts as an "insect swarm." But, given the electrical nature of the whole episode, he may be hearing the buzzing of a growing electrical build-up.

It is directly following this outpouring of verbal and physical abuse that the more explicit references to Anodos' electrical state emerge: "The galvanic torrent of this battery of malevolence stung to life within me a spark of nobleness, and I said aloud, 'Well, if he is a better man, let him have her'" (213). Thus, by being held down and "rubbed the wrong way," Anodos reacts (just as the cat had) by releasing a "spark." It is directly after this conduction of "electrical" energy (i.e. the biochemical, bio-electrical "spark"), that the underground goblins, mirroring the above-ground fairies, allow Anodos to escape:

"They instantly let go their hold of me, and fell back a step or two, with a whole broadside of grunts and humphs, as of unexpected and disappointed approbation" (213-14).[12]

To reiterate and analyse these two important "electrical connections" (between the treatment of the cat and Anodos), let us review these two parallel events and sets of characters side by side: Both the cat and Anodos are held tight by many fairy beings grasping at "every part that afforded a grasp," both are forced to release "sparks," and both are admonished for their supposed rectification. On the other hand, while this "electrical reading" of the episode clearly joins the cat and Anodos, MacDonald appears to want also to convey some information regarding the cat's and Anodos' distinct "polarities."

Before breaching the topic of polarity, however, let us pay closer attention to the outcome of Anodos' "treatment" when he states: "The galvanic torrent of this battery of malevolence stung to life within me a spark." This interesting outburst strongly implies that Anodos and the cat are, or become, types of galvanic batteries, which when "rubbed" or "stimulated" tend build up a galvanic torrent (stream/current?). This build-up, it is implied, naturally produces sparks. Also, when the cat and Anodos discharge the sparks, they can escape. The release of the sparks directly leads to their own release from the fairies. The consequences of these electrical releases are, however, different for those who receive the sparks. As the "demon-like" cat is being relieved of her "negative" sparks, the "good" fairy at the receiving end of the tail becomes "pompous." With Anodos' "positive" electrical release the "fairy devils" become much more civil.

Of further interest is MacDonald's brilliant electrical expansion of the name "Anodos." By recalling an electrical word, coined by Faraday, MacDonald gives the readers of *Phantastes* an important dimension of the protagonist's name and a "positive" identification of the hero:

"*Anode*. . . .1841. (ad. Gr. Anodos, way up.) Elect, strictly: the path by which an electric current leaves the positive pole, and enters the electrolyte, on its way to the negative pole (Faraday), loosely: the positive pole in both senses, opp. Cathode" (Onions 70). As there is little chance that MacDonald is not aware of the word "Anode" and its meanings, due to his scientific education and training in Chemistry and Physics, it is safe to say that he includes this electrical aspect of the word *Anodos* in his brilliant narrative. Furthermore, this reading (of Anodos as an Anode) is supported and in turn supports/reflects the identity of the negatively charged, sparking female cat. Here is the definition of an important word and mirror-image of Anode: "*Cathode* ... Also Kath-. 1834. (ad. Gr.; see prec.) Electr. The path by which an electric current leaves the electrolyte and passes into the negative pole; the point or surface in contact with the negative pole. opp. to anode." (O.E.D.).[13]

Brilliantly, the cat becomes the Cat(hode) in this electrical reading of the above highly charged and meaningful episode.[14] Thus MacDonald directly, yet covertly, uses the then modern scientific meanings attached to the derivative *Anode* from the Greek *Anodos*, and *cat* from the Greek word *Cathodos*.[15] These electrical words and meanings directly reflect each other, and similarly represent the exact polar reversals in MacDonald's imaginative mirror/book. Thus MacDonald introduces "outer" scientific words and meanings which reflect and support numerous dimensions of his mirror structure in *Phantastes*.

Given the above information, we can proceed to examine the polarity of the Cathode and Anode as represented by the female cat and the male protagonist, Anodos. Of course, anyone with a basic knowledge of Chemistry knows that the Cathode is the negative pole and the Anode is the positive pole by which electricity enters an electrical device. This must be the motive for MacDonald, the biochemist writer of fantasy and student of Liebig's and Müller's works, to make the cat into a female negative pole, while keeping the male positive pole for Anodos. Furthermore, MacDonald is very specific regarding the amount of light available for both short-circuiting events. The female cat is assailed in the evening, as the outer light and her energy became weaker, while Anodos is treated to a similar fate, for similar reasons, in the semi-darkness of the underground caverns. In addition, the cat, by being a female, possesses more vital or "vegetative" force, and can therefore release many sparks. Anodos, the male protagonist, on the other hand, is only capable of generating one spark or outburst of this curious bio-electrical energy.[16]

MacDonald is creatively following and expanding upon Liebig's and Müller's biochemical or bio-electrical theories.[17] The cat's sparks are caused by the static electrical build up within the feline, while in Anodos' case, it is a biochemical, "ego-centred" spark that must be released. The forced release of his "too positive" egocentric spark allows Anodos to begin to love without needing to possess—a "positive" outcome.[18] It is stated in the narrative that the release of the cat's negative sparks will be beneficial in curbing her aggressive and "negative" impulses. The procedure of removing the cat's sparks is done to reduce her "bad tempers"—otherwise she would need to have her claws and eye-teeth removed.

By considering the above examples and the mirror structure these complex examples reflect, we may begin to use this structure to detect the deep connections between Anodos and Cosmo von Wehrstahl—Anodos' mirror-image in the world of "fiction" within the "reality" of *Phantastes*. Cosmo (i.e., the Greek word Kosmos or "world") is literally a mirror image of Anodos in this other "world" reflected in the Magic Mirror. And, as stated earlier, Cosmo's Magic Mirror is situated in the middle of *Phantastes*, thus marking the centrality of the mirror motif and mirror structure for MacDonald's book.

Another story Anodos read, of which he tells fragments in chapter 12, is the shadow precursor and complement of the Cosmo chapter.[19] The planet there described does not appear to have any reflecting surfaces other than the men's and women's eyes and a distant, distorting sky. It is only on the rare occasions when the inhabitants reflect (by looking into each other's eyes or by questioning Anodos) that they begin to long for a more meaningful life and they mature enough to be able to leave their "unreflective" existence behind.

4. Phantastic Mirroring and St. Paul

Anodos sees himself reflected in three figures in *Phantastes*: in the polished armour of the knight in the knight's own castle where Anodos, invisible, perceives this in chapter 19; in the polished armour of the evil knight whom Anodos recognises as his own shadow in chapter 22; and in the story of Cosmo von Wehrstahl. "Von Wehrstahl" means "of the steel arms" and he "was considered an authority in every matter pertaining to arms, ancient or modern."

It is in the centre of *Phantastes*, in the middle chapter of the book, that Anodos perceives himself reflected directly in Cosmo. Anodos and Cosmo, unlike the other characters (and episodes) so far considered, stand directly across from each other in the opposite sides of the Magic Mirror.[20] The connections that MacDonald makes between mirrors and books here play a crucial part: Anodos reads about Cosmo in a book that acts as a mirror, joining and reflecting both protagonist's lives. Thus, it is no surprise that Cosmo's and Anodos' lives and loves parallel each other so very closely.[21] In general terms, both men love "ideal" women; "attract" these ideal women; lose them due to their "masculine" selfishness; gain the women's love by overcoming their own possessiveness; receive one and only one kiss from their lovers; and, lastly, die violent deaths by the sword. It is perhaps for these and many additional reasons that MacDonald has Anodos begin chapter 13 by comparing some things, persons, and concepts of crucial depth and importance for *Phantastes* (his fairy book) and for its readers:

> In the fairy book, everything was just as it should be, though whether in words or something else, I cannot tell. It glowed and flashed the thoughts upon the soul, with such a power that the medium disappeared from the consciousness, and it was occupied only with the things themselves. My representation of it must resemble a translation from a rich and powerful language, capable of embodying the thoughts of a splendidly developed people, into the meagre and half- articulate speech of a savage tribe. Of course, while I read it, I was Cosmo, and his story was mine. Yet, all the time, I seemed to have a kind of double consciousness, and the story a double meaning. Sometimes it seemed only to represent a simple story of ordinary life, perhaps almost of universal life; wherein two souls, loving each other and longing to come nearer, do, after all, but behold each other as in a glass darkly. (153-4)

MacDonald borrows much of the above imagery, concepts, and language from an important external literary source, Saint Paul's First Letter to the Corinthians, and their deep relationships are easier to identify and analyse if we refer to Paul's statement:

> When I was a child, I spake as a child, I understood as a child, I thought as a child; but when I became a man, I put away childish things. For now we see through a glass darkly; but then face to face: now I know in part; but then shall I know even as also I am known.

> And now abideth faith, hope, charity, these three; but the greatest of these is charity. (1Cor.13.11-13)

The original Greek upon which this "translation of a rich and powerful language" is based (i.e., either the Greek or the "language" of the Holy Spirit) also translates as:

> When I was a child, I used to talk like a child, and see things as a child does, and think like a child; but now that I have become an adult, I have finished with all childish ways. Now we see only reflections in a mirror, mere riddles, but then we shall be seeing face to face. Now I can know only imperfectly; but then I shall know just as fully as I am myself known. As it is, these remain: faith, hope and love, the three of them; and the greatest of them is love.

Crossing a Great Frontier

By identifying and analysing the full Biblical passage, and the surrounding texts and different translations, the reader of *Phantastes* may begin to appreciate the meaning of these paramount words for Anodos, and the importance of maturity and true love found at the core of the story.[22] Anodos must put away childish things and become a man, just as the "little maiden," on the verge of physical maturity, is also forced to put away her globe after Anodos breaks it and the Fairy Queen refuses to repair the broken toy. (Without her globe, the maiden is forced to come of age and later to conclude that the loss was necessary for her growth and for her understanding of her life's mission.)

By coming upon the Fairy Book/Magic Mirror, Anodos has to learn, by seeing himself reflected in Cosmo, that he must, like Cosmo, become a man. Cosmo, like the little maiden, must discard his childish toys—the skeleton, dried bat, porcupine skin, and stuffed sea-mouse (along with his dark magic, jealousy and possessiveness)—before he can begin to love Princess Hohenweiss with a mature, honourable love. He twice wishes to see the Princess, "face to face," instead of only as a reflection in a mirror, and ultimately realizes this wish—in the middle of this central and crucial story—in the personal interview that allows him to begin to love in an unselfish way.

Anodos too must become aware of deceiving appearances, images, and words, and even as he loses faith and hope, he must trust in love. Then he can begin to truly understand, and see "face to face." Thus, by getting to "know (Cosmo) just as fully as I am myself known," and by understanding his mirror image's sacrifice, Anodos can begin to incorporate the idea of unselfish, non-possessive love. This proves paramount for his moral and spiritual development in the Fairy Land of *Phantastes*. Anodos, exactly as Cosmo had done with the Princess, attempts to control what he thinks of as *his* Lady of the Marble. When he ignores the warnings "TOUCH NOT!" and attempts to embrace the lady she rejects his crude advances and chastises him with "You should not have touched me!" (207), reflecting the Princess' rebukes of Cosmo. Like Cosmo, his loved one deserts him and he must learn the nature of loving without needing to possess. And soon he can claim that "I no longer called her to myself my white lady" (211).

The voyage to Fairyland, as many have intuited, is a "rite of passage" from childhood to adulthood both for Anodos and perhaps for readers of *Phantastes*.[23] Anodos is very aware of his coming of age, metamorphosis, and the putting away of childish things. After he sacrifices himself, by courageously destroying the idol and its evil wolf-spectre, a "dead" yet mature Anodos, inspired by Saint Paul, exclaims: "Ere long, they bore me to my grave. Never tired child lay down in his white bed, and heard the sound of his playthings being laid aside for the night, with a more luxurious satisfaction of repose than I knew" (310-12).

The scientifically and theologically trained MacDonald, by means of the above Pauline passage, can focus most of his book on the central Magic Mirror and add several dimensions to *Phantastes*. The reference to St. Paul's mirror adds a great amount of external, traditional meaning and context to the story. This reference to Corinthians I also allows the reader directly and indirectly to compare himself with many things: with Cosmo; with the women both men love; with "reality"; with "appearance"; everyday life with the universal (Kosmos'/Cosmo's) life; as well as comparing word and thought, the types of consciousness reflected in the fairy book and its counterpart the looking-glass, childhood and adulthood, ego-centred love and other-centred love, and so on. As Cosmo reflects Anodos in the fairy book, MacDonald mirrors St. Paul in *Phantastes*.[24]

It is clear from a reading of MacDonald's other books that he was particularly attracted to St. Paul's words.[25] It is also apparent from his published letters that he was drawn to St. Paul, and particularly to the above passage from Corinthians I. MacDonald directly refers to and uses the relevant quotations from St. Paul at least three times in his published letters (69, 292, and 308). Two of these letters are written to Mrs. Cowper-Temple. In one he writes: "Some day God will, I trust, reveal himself to me as he has never done yet, and I shall be as sure as St. Paul" (292). A few months later he exclaims: "But God comes nearer and nearer I think. How can I be sure till he actually comes, and I know as I am known!" (308).

Thus, MacDonald was inspired by St. Paul and his famous passage from Corinthians I both in his "real life" and correspondence and in its reflection: his imaginative fiction, *Phantastes*.

5. Further Complex Imagery in *Phantastes*

It is in chapter 13 where most of *Phantastes* is reflected and where the most important parts of the book come into focus. However, perhaps the best method to visualize this reduction and inversion of *Phantastes* into chapter 13 is to use MacDonald's idea, related to the optics involved with mirrors and reflections, of "the ever-changing field of a camera obscura."

Crossing a Great Frontier

This "scientific" model by which to understand the relationship between chapter 13 and the rest of *Phantastes* is supplied by MacDonald in the central chapter of the book (174). To give a few examples of MacDonald's *camera obscura* effect, it should be noticed that it is Anodos—in a conversation with his sister (narrated by his "Fairy grandmother")—who originally wishes to enter Fairy Land: "'Is there a Fairy-country, brother?' You replied with a sigh, 'I suppose there is, if one could find the way into it'" (18).

It must be recalled that between Anodos' conversation with his sister and the emergence of the Fairy Grandmother, a whole night elapses (18-20). On the other hand, Cosmo's identical wishes to "enter" the world of the Magic Mirror are "answered" by a similarly described female almost instantaneously:

> "I should like to live in that room if I could only get into it."
>
> Scarcely had the half-moulded words floated from him, as he stood gazing into the mirror, when, striking him as with a flash of amazement that fixed him in his posture, noiseless and unannounced, glided suddenly through the door into the reflected room, with stately motion, yet reluctant and faltering step, the graceful form of a woman, clothed all in white. (163-4)

Thus the time, place, and characters in this latter episode are reflected, reduced in "size" and inverted: the time that elapses is much shorter, the great expanses of Fairy Land are replaced by a room in Prague, and a mortal woman is substituted for the Fairy Grandmother. Nevertheless, it is from Cosmo's "projections" in the Magic Book that Anodos must draw MacDonald's and St. Paul's lessons regarding self-knowledge, maturity and love. It is by means of Anodos immersing himself into the story of Cosmo that in the second part of the book he learns to think like a man, love unselfishly, and finally die the "good death." This is exactly the self-reflective method MacDonald uses (through Anodos) to describe the process of reading fairy books (like *Phantastes*):

> If, for instance, it was a book of metaphysics I opened, I had scarcely read two pages before I seemed to myself to be pondering over discovered truth, and constructing the intellectual machine whereby to communicate the discovery to my fellow men. With some books, however, of this nature, it seemed rather as if the process was removed yet a great way further back; and I was trying to find the root of a manifestation, the spiritual truth whence a material vision

sprang; or to combine two propositions, both apparently true, either at once or in different remembered moods, and to find the point in which their invisibly converging lines would unite in one, revealing a truth higher than either and differing from both; though so far from being opposed to either, that it was that whence each derived its life and power. Or if the book was one of travels, I found myself the traveller. . . . With a fiction it was the same. Mine was the whole story. For I took the place of the character who was most like myself, and his story was mine; until, grown weary with the life of years condensed in an hour, or arrived at my deathbed, or the end of the volume, I would awake, with a sudden bewilderment, to the consciousness of my present life. (140-41)

It is by means of this type of self-conscious passage that MacDonald continually underscores the complex reflective nature of his book, and invites the reader to reflect on and utilise its many brilliant devices, not least its mirror structure.

6. Conclusions

> It is God who gives thee thy mirror of imagination, and if thou keep it clean, it will give thee back no shadow but of the truth. (*Paul Faber* 29)

Docherty, McGillis, and Gunther were correct regarding the existence of structures in *Phantastes*. In this paper I identify and explain one such structure, while attempting to provide enough solid examples to convince even the more sceptical of readers of the relevance and coherence of the mirror structure embedded in MacDonald's early masterpiece. On the other hand, I hope this mirror structure paves the way for discoveries of further complex examples of mirror images, and/or other similarly complex structures. It must be remembered that their pioneering work provided us with examples that appear to mirror each other (the two pairs of cottages, the women inhabiting the cottages, the immature Globe Maid and the adult Singing woman into whom she grows, and so on). At the same time, the discovery of a mirror structure may help account for other "singular" examples found by theorists who cannot as easily account for them or locate them within their own conceptions of a unified structure or literary matrix.

I hope that some of the examples above, and the mirror structure they reflect and support, are enough to convince most rational scholars that *Phantastes* is an extremely abstract, sophisticated, and self-reflective book. But, although the book is perplexing, it is by no means beyond a critical understanding. Thus, while there are many further instances of mirroring, and more than one plot and structure in MacDonald's enigmatic book, we are well on our way to understanding some of its hidden secrets and mysteries. Certainly researchers must perform much more work if we are to further lift the veil of Isis from MacDonald's first masterpiece. But the feet, if not the legs, of the work appear exposed! Let us henceforth be cautious and carefully chose our logical and poetic song to awaken the spirit of the book, instead of rushing at it with further conjectural conclusions that deny meanings and structures. Too many commentators may have been attempting to embrace possible meanings and structures, which in the light of reflection turn out to be somewhat wooden and disappointing. The significance of MacDonald's book, like that of his Marble Lady, is not easily grasped.

Endnotes

1. There is a general discussion of original reviews of *Phantastes* in McGillis (54).

2. Adrian Gunther followed Docherty's and McGillis' articles with two of her own papers on *Phantastes*. Graeme Muirhead, while presenting many insights, does not recognise the importance of some of these. And neither of these critics provide a possible structure for the book. Earlier, McGillis had mentioned a type of general structure centred on chapters 12 and 13 but not specifically on the mirror in chapter 13 ("Femininity" 34). He makes no references to any of MacDonald's many other more covert mirrorings. Gunther theorises that there may be more than one coherent plot in *Phantastes*. Colin Manlove continues to deny the existence of any coherent structure (*Modern* 55-98; *Impulse* 70-92; *England AT*, 65, 93,122). For an account of another plot, co-existing with that described in the present paper, see Soto's "Chthonic Aspects of MacDonald's *Phantastes*."

3. For an autobiographical reference to Liebig and Chemistry, see *Warlock O' Glenwarlock* (326-27).

4. If MacDonald did not attend Liebig's lectures or "Report on the Present State of Organic Chemistry" in 1840, surely he heard about this report, and much more, from William Gregory. Gregory had studied with Liebig and later became editor of his main works in English. According to Broome, Gregory (while Professor of Medicine and Chemistry at King's College, Aberdeen for four of the five years spanning MacDonald's studies at Aberdeen) "was undoubtedly the man who encouraged MacDonald's attempts" to study with Liebig. For Liebig's and Gregory's influence on MacDonald, see Broome. For the state of Organic Chemistry in 1840, see Liebig's *Animal Chemistry*.

5. MacDonald's *Paul Faber, Surgeon* has vivid passages relating the human imagination and understanding to a mirror. See particularly pages 8, 29, 60, 106 and 138.

6. This example also presents the reader with an ironic device

MacDonald uses in many sections of *Phantastes*. After providing several fixed rules that describe the above phenomena, Anodos goes on to claim that no such rules exist to explain these same phenomena.

7. McGillis is often close to identifying some of the mirror images in *Phantastes*. But he is mainly concerned with "the community of the centre" and "poetry" and does not explore the significance of the Magic Mirror at the centre of the story. While making the connection between the "community of the centre" and the imagination (51), he stops short of linking the imagination directly with mirrors. Gunther and Muirhead also identify the mirror as a theme in *Phantastes*, but fail to classify this important component as anything more than one theme among many.

8. A river appears again in *Lilith*. Its waters are rejuvenating; it flows down a "stair" and issues from a rock into a cave, then finds its outlet through the "door" of the cave.

9. The "descendants" of these wooden men seem to make their appearance in *Lilith*—in many ways a literary "mirror" image of *Phantastes*—in the form of the "bad giants" (94-95)! The "little ones" fear being stepped upon by these creatures, and Vane easily, trips them up. In *Lilith* "E" the connection between the wooden men and the bad giants is made even clearer. The giants are described as "a tribe of well-carved wooden dolls into which something that resembled a mind had entered" (244); and Vane is told that a small child had in fact been killed by "a crush of one of [a giant's] horrid, clumsy feet" (245).

10. Much of the following material dealing with the mirroring of two electrical episodes in *Phantastes* was published as "The Phantastic Spark that Binds all Life" in *Inklings* 20 (2002): 186-98.

11. For more information on the above biochemical theories, see Liebig's *Animal Chemistry* 1, 11, 31, 219, 230, 233, 260 and so on.

12. McGillis is not only aware of some structural counterparts and the importance of "images," but is also familiar

with some types of polarity in *Phantastes*. Some of these insights are also explored and slightly pursued in Gunther ("Structure" 43-47). Docherty also is aware of connections between some above-and-below-ground fairies (*Literary* 17-76).

13. The words "Cathodic" and "Anodic"—first recorded in 1852 and 1853 respectively—are described in the O.E.D. as used in medicine and physiology. Cathodic means: "Of nerve force: Efferent" and Anodic means: "Of nerve force: proceeding upwards." These terms provide additional direct links to the biochemical and bio-electrical mirroring that MacDonald, with the help of Liebig and Müller, utilizes in *Phantastes*.

14. In *Lilith*, MacDonald uses, expands and reverses aspects of the cat-cathode/ Anodos-anode incidents. Vane tells us that "the cats were all over me in a live cataract, biting wherever they could bite, furiously scratching me anywhere and everywhere. A multitude clung to my body; I could not flee" (252). When he does struggle free he describes how: "They accompanied me in a surrounding torrent, now rubbing, now leaping up against me, but tormenting me no more." Hence, in this complex electrical mirroring episode it is Vane (whose original name of Fane, in *Lilith* "A" means "Fairy") who is rushed upon, and it is the cats that hold "every part that afforded a grasp." However, he is not "held tight" Instead of holding Vane down and forcing him to release a spark, the cats force him to release kinetic energy: to "run" all night. The outcome of this "lesson" administered to him by the cataract of cats is that Vane learns not to be so reckless in disregarding Mr Raven's good advice.

15. For MacDonald's extensive use of the Greek religious meanings of the words "Anodos" and "Kathodos," see Soto ("Chthonic" 20-47).

16. This was pointed out to me by Clarice A. Kuhling.

17. MacDonald may have been expanding Liebig's and Müller's theories in the Swedenborgian direction of "correspondences." Here is how Greville describes his father's interests in this direction: "He knew enough of Swedenborg's teachings to feel the truth of *correspondences*, and would find innumerable instances of physical law tallying with metaphysical, of chemical affinities with spiritual affections" (my emphasis, 216).

18. In *There and Back*, MacDonald describes the hero Richard

watching a wholly positive type of bio-electric transfer from one young woman to another: "it was a revelation to him as he watched the electric play of love that passed from the strong, tender child-like girl to the delicate, weary, starved creature to whom she was ministering" (165).

19. McGillis and Gunther periodically appear to view chapter 12 as the centre of *Phantastes*. However this neither ties up in a numerical fashion nor is there much support within the book for this reading other than a mention of a "community of the centre," which McGillis interprets as "poetry." Docherty sees a structural parallel with MacDonald's chapters 12 and 13 in the play and the preceding mime at the centre of *Hamlet*; and also in the two books that Arthur and Sir Guyon read in the library of the house of Alma in Edmund Spenser's *Faerie Queene* 2.10 (*Literary* 48- 49). Docherty, however, fails to perceive clearly that in each of these cases the more "shadowy" account (or performance) is a necessary compliment to the more material one.

20. In *Lilith*, Vane's first encounter with the Raven is "nose-to-beak" across the mirror that is no longer a barrier between them (8).

21. The connection between Cosmo and Anodos is found by once again analysing carefully the different *Lilith* manuscripts. In *Lilith* "C" it is Sir Cosmo's portrait that hangs in the library (235-36). In most other versions it is Sir Upward (i.e. Anodos) who is depicted in the important portrait. Moreover, it was Sir Upward who used two mirrors in his polarised light contraption to transport himself to Fairyland (*Lilith* 13; 61-65).

22. In *Lilith*, MacDonald uses the same biblical reference at a more advanced stage of his hero's development, where Vane begins to feel he is near to seeing God "face to face" (370-71).

23. C. S. Lewis, who claimed MacDonald as his "Master," appears to intuit some of this "Christian Message" when he claims that after a few hours of reading *Phantastes*, "I knew I had crossed a great frontier." Unfortunately,

he disdains the style and language used by MacDonald to such a degree that most of the profound and brilliant messages and lessons (primarily Classical/pagan and only secondarily Christian) in *Phantastes* were, it appears, completely lost on him. For Lewis' bizarre understanding of *Phantastes*, MacDonald, and some types of literature and mythology, see the preface to his *George MacDonald: An Anthology* or his equally strange accounts in *Surprised by Joy* (Soto, "Chthonic" 45-46). When Lewis was not in preaching mode, however, but writing to his boyhood friend Arthur Greeves, he could write very perceptively upon MacDonald, as Stephen Prickett notes ("Death" 159-62).

24. Rolland Hein, in *The Harmony Within* (70), mentions—in parentheses—that "MacDonald is echoing St Paul in I Corinthians 13.12." But, though his whole analysis is ultimately from a Christian perspective, he fails to pursue the crucial implications of this biblical reference. This oversight may be partially explained by the fact that Hein claims that in *Phantastes*, "It is, of course, intuitive perceptions that MacDonald has in mind. Mere intellectual analysis alone tends to leave the spirit emaciated, not strengthened."

25. St. Paul is referred to in many of MacDonald's books, particularly those novels where a clergyman is an important character. MacDonald alludes to this particular passage from I Cor. in *The Marquis of Lossie* (297).

Works Cited

Breul, Karl (reviser). *A German and English Dictionary*. London, 1929.

Broome, Hal. "The Scientific Basis of MacDonald's Dream Frame." *The Gold Thread*, 87-108.

Docherty, John. *The Literary Products of the Lewis Carroll-George MacDonald Friendship*. 2nd ed. Lewiston NJ: Mellen, 1997.

—. "A Note on the Structure and Conclusion of *Phantastes*." *North Wind* 7 (1988): 25-30.

Grant, William and David Murison, eds. *The Scottish National Dictionary*. Edinburgh, 1929-74.

Gunther, Adrian. "The Structure of MacDonald's *Phantastes*." *North Wind* 12 (1993): 43-59.

—. "*Phantastes*: The First Two Chapters." *Scottish Literary Journal* 21 (1) (1994): 32-43.

Hein, Roland, ed. *Lilith: A Variorum Edition*. 2 vols. Whitethorn: Johannesen, 1997.

—. *The Harmony Within*. Grand Rapids: Christian UP, 1982.

Liebig, Justus von. *Animal Chemistry or Chemistry in its Applications to Physiology and Pathology*. Trs. and Ed. William Gregory. London, 1843.

MacDonald, George. "The Cruel Painter." *Adela Cathcart*. (1864). Whitethorn: Johannesen, 2nd. ed. 2000.

—. *Lilith: First and Final*, c. 1891 and 1895. Whitethorn: Johannesen, 2nd ed. 1998.

—. *Lilith a Variorum Edition*. Ed. Rolland Hein. Whitethorn: Johannesen, 1997.

—. *The Marquis of Lossie*. 1877. Whitethorn: Johannesen, 1995.

—. *Paul Faber Surgeon*. 1879. Whitethorn: Johannesen, 2nd ed. 1998.

—. *Phantastes*. 1858. Whitethorn: Johannesen, 2nd ed. 2000.

—. *Salted with Fire*. 1897. Whitethorn: Johannesen, 1996.

—. *Sir Gibbie*. 1879. Whitethorn: Johannesen, 3rd ed. 2000.

—. *There and Back*. 1891. Whitethorn: Johannesen, 1991.

—. *Thomas Wingfold, Curate*. 1876. Whitethorn: Johannesen, 2nd ed. 2002.

—. *Warlock O' Glenwarlock*. London, 1887.

MacDonald, Greville. *George MacDonald and his Wife*, 1924. Whitethorn: Johannesen, 1998.

Manlove, Colin. *The Fantasy Literature of England*. London: Macmillan, 1999.

—. *The Impulse of Fantasy Literature*. London: Macmillan, 1983.

—. *Modern Fantasy: Five Studies*. Cambridge: Cambridge UP, 1975.

McGillis, Roderick, ed. *For the Childlike: George MacDonald's Fantasies for Children*. Metuchen NJ: Scarecrow, 1992.

—. "The Community of the Centre: Structure and Theme in *Phantastes*." *For the Childlike*, 51-65.

—. "*Phantastes* and *Lilith*: Femininity and Freedom." *The Gold Thread*, 31-55.

Muirhead, Graeme. "Meta-*Phantastes*: A Self-Referential Faerie Romance for Men and Women." *Scottish Literary Journal* 19 (2) (1992): 36-49.

Onions, C. T. ed, *The Oxford Universal Dictionary*. Oxford: Clarendon Press, 1956.

Prickett, Stephen. "Death in *Lilith*." *Inklings* 13 (1995): 159-68.

—. "The Two Worlds of George MacDonald." *For the Childlike*, 17-29. [44]

Raeper, William, ed. *The Gold Thread: Essays on George MacDonald*. Edinburgh: Edinburgh UP, 1990.

—. *George MacDonald*. Batavia IL: Lion, 1987.

Sadler, G. E. ed, *An Expression of Character: The Letters of George MacDonald*. Grand Rapids: Eerdmans, 1994.

Soto, Fernando J. "Chthonic Aspects of *Phantastes*: From the Rising of the Goddess to the Anodos of Anodos." *North Wind* 19 (2000): 19-49.

—. "Cosmos and Diamonds: Naming and Connoting in MacDonald's Works." *North Wind* 20 (2001): 30-42.

—. "Some Linguistic Moves in the Carroll-MacDonald Literary Game." *North Wind* 18 (1999): 45-53.

—. "The Phantastic Spark that Binds All Life." *Inklings* 20 (2002): 186-98.

Allegory and Aestheticism in the Fantasies of George MacDonald

Yuri Cowan

From *North Wind: A Journal of George MacDonald Studies*

> "The demand for perfection is always a misunderstanding of the ends of art." —Ruskin, "The Nature of Gothic."

George MacDonald's first work of fantasy for adults, *Phantastes*, was published in 1858, the same year as William Morris's *The Defence of Guenevere and Other Poems*. Morris's collection received a great deal of attention, and was the foundation of his reputation as a poet; MacDonald's fairy romance, on the other hand, sank almost without a trace. Walter Pater looked back on *The Defence of Guenevere and Other Poems* as "the first typical specimen of aesthetic poetry" (*Appreciations* 521), but *Phantastes* was neglected until its rehabilitation by the Christian fantasists C. S. Lewis and G. K. Chesterton in the early twentieth century. Chesterton's and Lewis's own particular interpretations of MacDonald have since become orthodoxy.

MacDonald has consequently been seen by recent scholars primarily as a "mythopoeic" writer, to the detriment of our understanding of him as a Victorian novelist, as David Robb has pointed out (279), as well as of our understanding of him as an allegorist in the context of the Aesthetic Movement in nineteenth-century literature. To see MacDonald as a shaper of Christian myths is to ignore both the non-dogmatic nature of his views on moral and social renewal and the emphasis on individual interpretation that colours his views on art, both of which are characteristic of the concerns of the Aesthetic Movement in general.

George MacDonald is certainly not the first writer one would include in a study of the movement. His tone, though genial, is too serious, and his preoccupation with good and evil has few parallels in the more worldly Aesthetic Movement (and certainly not among the near-amoral Decadent coterie). Where Pater and his followers saw life as a series of ecstatic aesthetic moments, MacDonald saw it as a journey like Anodos's in *Phantastes*, and the world as a vale of soul-making (he was above all a Christian, and a product of Romanticism). Where the aesthetic movement claimed art was important in and for itself, MacDonald wanted his fantasies to help his readers better come to terms with their own spirituality.

But MacDonald was associated with many of the major figures of the early Aesthetic Movement, and of fantastic Victorian literature in general. He and John Ruskin, for example, were fairly close, and it was at MacDonald's home in Hammersmith that Ruskin met with Rose LaTouche after her parents had forbidden her to see him (Greville MacDonald 370). That same house, then known as The Retreat, was, after MacDonald's family left, taken over by William Morris and renamed Kelmscott House (MacCarthy 391-2). The Burne-Joneses were also numbered among the MacDonalds' "intimate" friends (Greville MacDonald 503), and the MacDonald children were enthusiastic guinea pigs for the Reverend Charles Dodgson's *Alice's Adventures Under Ground* (Greville MacDonald 342).

The Aesthetic Movement encompassed more than a simple devotion to blue china and sunflowers. It was best characterised by the belief that Art could change people's lives for the better—socially, politically, and even morally. For John Ruskin and William Morris, this meant giving the worker contentment in his work. For Walter Pater, art would "give nothing but the highest quality to your moments as they pass" (*Renaissance* 220). And for Oscar Wilde, the aesthetic life and one's everyday life were inextricably linked. "Life and literature, life and the perfect expression of life" ("Critic as Artist" 1114)—and Wilde's pronouncement here shares an earnest exalted tone, and an intentional infuriating vagueness of terminology, with some of MacDonald's own formulations—were for Wilde the two highest arts, and he prized individual expression and expressiveness above all else. For many writers in the nineteenth century, from the Oxford Movement in the 1840s to the Decadents at the *fin de siècle*, art was seen as a possible medium of social renewal. The industrial revolution had brought with it a century of social upheaval, and the Victorian project was to make sense of its consequences, to come to grips with them, and if possible, to solve them. The Victorian intelligentsia grasped at Utilitarianism, Darwinian capitalism, Communism, Catholicism and a host of other religious, moral, and political systems to make sense of the era's hard times. Aestheticism was simply one of many possible solutions, and it attracted a diverse mix of adherents, from nostalgic advocates of paternal social orders (Ruskin), to radicals like Morris, to decadent Catholics such as Lionel Johnson.

Hilary Fraser finds in the work of the Oxford Tractarians in the 1830s the origins of the Aesthetic Movement's involvement with religion. John Keble and John Henry Newman sought to renew their religion through poetry, and their emphasis on individual development and imagination prefigures the theories of the later movement. For example, Fraser traces the influence of religion on Pater's aesthetic theory:

> For Pater . . . it was important to distinguish between the rigid, dogmatic forms of religion, and the flexible, developing, imaginative aspect. Only the latter could fit in with the preoccupation with relativism which is characteristic of both [Pater's] essay on 'Coleridge's Writings' and his most-quoted work, *The Renaissance*. (214)

If we take the journey through Fairy Land to represent spiritual growth, then MacDonald's view of religion is not that different from Pater's. If, as the woman in the cottage on the outskirts of the forest tells Anodos, "[f]or those who enter Fairy Land, there is no way of going back. They must go on, and go through it. How, I do not in the least know" (*Phantastes* 53-4), then MacDonald has as individualised a notion of religion as Pater does in his writings.

MacDonald was on the fringes of both the nineteenth-century British religious ferment and the growing social justice movement. The story of MacDonald's "entertainments" for the tenants of Octavia Hill's experiments in low-income housing is illustrative of his passion for storytelling, his devout spirituality, and, above all, the non-authoritative character of his narrative style:

> The basement of one house was converted into an entertainment room, and there George MacDonald would gather round him the worst of characters; or rather Octavia Hill did so in the first place.
>
> 'Will you come and hear a friend of mine read something fine on Sunday?' she asked them one day.
>
> 'Parson, Miss?' 'No.'
>
> 'White choker, Miss?'
>
> 'No, he generally wears a red tie.' 'Done! I'll come!'
>
> And hands were shaken on the bargain. So in that room in tweeds and a red tie my father would tell them stories and awaken keen and sympathetic interest; he would touch 'the red spot.' And when his stories were gradually understood to have originated in a man named Jesus Christ, the audience forgot any suspicion they may have had of a white choker; and many became constant attendants and helpers at such entertainments. (Greville MacDonald 383)

He had rejected his strict Calvinist upbringing (although he never ceased to admire and love his father's stern devotion), but he spent time as minister of a Congregational church in Arundel, and his particular brand of non-conformist Christian spirituality must colour all his storytelling. It is important to recognise here MacDonald's emphasis in his storytelling, first upon the universally human and only second upon the specifically Christian. His sermons are thereby made more accessible to all, more palatable to the skeptic, and more effective in general. It is in MacDonald's nature to preach; but the literary forms he chooses to preach in—the romance, the fairy tale, the dream-vision—and the allegorical mode he adopts, prevent his moralising from becoming a burden to the reader.

Allegory (defined here as a non-restrictive, open-ended mode that relies for its interpretation upon the reader, rather than as a system of concordances) is essential to understanding George MacDonald's fantastic works, MacDonald's theology as a whole, and his place in the Aesthetic Movement. Gordon Teskey, in his tightly-argued entry in *The Spenser Encyclopedia*, proposes a model of allegory as

> a game designed by the writer and played by the reader . . . Allegory differs from the related forms, parable and fable, by including in its narrative conspicuous directions for interpretation (such as naming the serpent of F[aerie] Q[ueene] I i 18 'Errour'). Whereas in parable or fable we are offered a complete (and sometimes surprising) interpretation when the story is over, in allegory we find only the iconic rudiments of an interpretation we must build for ourselves, within certain constraints, as we proceed. (16)

Those "constraints" are important, however. They consist partly in the "directions for interpretation," and partly in the overall structure of the allegorical work. It would be no use reading about the kitchen in the Castle of Alma (*Faerie Queene* II.ix.29-32) out of context, for instance, since it only makes sense as part of a coherent whole, just as a book on the workings of the digestive system would be too specific for a devotee of holistic medicine.

Readers of allegory are like the aptly named hero of *Phantastes*, Anodos ("the person without a path"—a conspicuous direction if ever there was one). The reader who joins the allegorical game is faced in the text with a series of landmarks, which there are a number of ways to interpret; some are easier to understand than others, and taken together they make a whole. A complete and inflexible meaning is not necessarily in the text waiting to be discovered, but a recognizable truth can be read in part by each participant in the game. It is significant, moreover, that each participant in the game will probably recognize a different truth, within the constraints laid out by the text.

This theory of allegorical reading is entirely consistent with the emphasis in the writings of the Aesthetic Movement on the role of the appreciator of a work of art. The Oxford Movement's John Keble, for example, was a rare and early advocate of nineteenth-century allegory. To him, allegory was a mode that met "the demands of expression and concealment . . . For Keble, there was an inherent similarity between reserve in poetry and mysticism in religion, and the poet, through his use of ideas, images, similes, and poetic forms, should, he thought, stimulate religious and moral associations in the imagination of the reader" (Fraser 17-18).

Both art and religion, then, seek to give some portion of the "truth" to their participants, whose duty it is in turn to actively involve themselves in the search for meaning, since ultimate truth stands always outside the text or sermon. Such active and ongoing individual participation, it was thought, would lead to the ultimate religious renewal of the Anglican Church; when such widespread aesthetic education was not forthcoming, the Oxford Movement's major proponents secluded themselves or turned to Catholicism. A similar fate met Pater's disciples at the end of the century.

Oscar Wilde in "The Critic as Artist" gave the critic a creative role. Indeed, he claimed, all readers should be critics and artists at once. Social renewal would come from bringing the world of art into the world of everyday life; where Morris was an advocate of daily artisanship or creation with one's hands, Wilde advocated going to the raw materials of art and creating in conversation and on paper new and more beautiful worlds. The act of criticism, he says, "treats the work of art simply as a starting-point for a new creation . . . it does not confine itself . . . to discovering the real intention of the artist and accepting that as final" (1127). MacDonald himself recognises the highly individualised nature of allegorical reading. In his essay on "The Fantastic Imagination," he imagines his reader asking, "'How am I to assure myself that I am not reading my own meaning into it, but yours out of it?'" To which he answers, quite rightly, "Why should you be so assured? It may be better that you should read your meaning into it. That may be a higher operation of your intellect than the mere reading of mine out of it: your meaning may be superior to mine" (*A Dish of Orts* 316). This denial of authorial intention is both characteristic humility on MacDonald's part and a shrewd strategy to incite the reader's own creativity, an interpretative activism that

MacDonald's own characters tend to find themselves pursuing, often to their own surprise.

Anodos, like the aesthetic critic or the reader of an allegory, stumbles through Fairy Land attempting to find the right course of action, and occasionally acting impulsively.[1] Unlike most conventional fairy-tale heroes, he often goes against the advice of his supernatural helpers ("'I told you,' said the woman, 'you had better not look into that closet,'" 57). In the end, the things he carries away from his experience are imperfect, but they are his own:

> I began the duties of my new position, somewhat instructed, I hoped, by the adventures that had befallen me in Fairy Land. Could I translate the experience of my travels there, into common life? This was the question. Or must I live it all over again, and learn it all over again, in the other forms that belong to the world of men, whose experience yet runs parallel to that of Fairy Land? (184)

When MacDonald calls experience in this world "parallel to that of Fairy Land," he is giving a concrete geographical dimension to the spiritual development he wants to invoke. This reification of spirituality is typical of MacDonald's writing, and typical of allegory as a whole.

Theorists from C. S. Lewis onward have recognized the interpenetration of the real and ideal in allegory. Lewis tells us to read allegories "as they are meant to be read: by keeping steadily before you both the literal and the allegorical sense and not treating the one as a mere means to the other but as its imaginative interpretation, by testing for yourself how far the concept really informs the image and how far the image really lends life to the concept" (125).

For Teskey, the place where concept and image meet is a "rift" ("Allegory, Materialism, Violence" 295) and a place of conflict, but I prefer to see it, as Lewis does, as the site of a more creative union. This would probably have been MacDonald's point of view, as well:

> As through the hard rock go the branching silver veins, as into the solid land run the creeks and gulfs from the unresting sea, as the lights and influences of the upper worlds sink silently through the earth's atmosphere, so doth Faerie invade the world of men, and sometimes startle the common eye with an association as of cause and effect, when between the two no connecting links can be traced. (*Phantastes* 85)

And at the end of the novel, when he has returned to the "real" world, Anodos sees for an instant in the leaves of the beech tree the face of the lady of the beech (185). The aesthetic project is to sustain that sense of wonder; to find the Earthly Paradise; to make "modern art . . . so to rearrange the details of modern life, so to reflect it, that it may satisfy the spirit" (Pater, *Renaissance* 215); and to bring the art world into the real world, making them both that much richer.

Mr. Vane, the hero of MacDonald's last fantasy *Lilith* (published in 1895), finds his spiritual vision reified in much the same manner as Anodos does. *Lilith* concludes with an even higher vision than *Phantastes*—with an ascent to the enclouded throne of God itself from which issues "the river of the water of life," and the tactile image inside the cloud of a "hand, warm and strong" (chapter 46, 250)—and ends even more abruptly. The hand only leads Mr. Vane back to the library of his home, where his strange adventures began. Unlike some of his contemporaries in the Aesthetic Movement, MacDonald is no medievalist; but if he were, his reader would be reminded of the narrator of *Pearl*, who, in attempting to cross over and join the pearl-maiden in the heavenly city on the other side of the stream, is rudely awakened from his allegorical vision.

Allegory, then, does not pretend to absolute knowledge; in fact, it denies outright such absolutes. Part of this is due to the limitations of language itself, and in his awareness of those limitations, George MacDonald anticipates modern allegorical theory. His imaginary interlocutor exclaims that "'words at least are meant and fitted to carry a precise meaning!' It is very seldom indeed [answers MacDonald] that they carry the exact meaning of any user of them! And if they can be so used as to convey definite meaning, it does not follow that they ought never to carry anything else" (*A Dish of Orts* 318). The limitations of language become, in MacDonald's works, its strengths. Later he writes in a characteristic passage that "the best thing you can do for your fellow, next to rousing his conscience, is—not to give him things to think about, but to wake things up that are in him; or say, to make him think things for himself" (319).[2] This is the red tie, not the white choker, model of moral storytelling.

In the most simple kind of allegory, only a few, mostly similar, meanings may be found by any number of readers; in more complex ones, various readers may find that the same texts call up vastly different images. Teskey writes that

> because the reader, in seeking to close up the gaps perceived in the text, only opens up more, and because the work is designed precisely to sustain that effect, the goal of a complete interpretation always recedes beyond grasp . . . This may be accounted for in part by the conventions of the form. But

> it is also a consequence of a theory of language of which allegory is the most extreme expression, a theory in which meaning, at some ideal level of visual form, always floats free of any acoustic involvement with words. Words, therefore, are thought of as imperfect pictures of meanings that exist in their purest state, outside the linguistic requirement of sound, in icons and symbols. These may be combined, like pixels, into larger pictures of states of affairs. We may then think of language as an organized whole composing a universe of signs in a total picture that is a "mirror of nature." ("Allegory," *Spenser Encyclopedia* 21)

Teskey might merely have used the verb *evoke* here to describe what allegory does. But his discussion of the relationship of meaning to sign is central to any application of allegory (his location of meaning in its "purest state . . . in icons and symbols" seems wrong here, however, since so much in the uncovering of allegorical meaning relies upon the reader). A number of analogies can be made along the same lines: the relationships of content and form, of body and soul, of real and ideal, of a text and its interpretations. When C. S. Lewis writes of the "fundamental equivalence between the immaterial and the material" (44) in allegory, he might as well be referring to the equivalence between the art world and the real world which was the Aesthetic Movement's primary contribution to nineteenth-century social and artistic thought.

In both *Phantastes* and *Lilith* MacDonald acknowledges the weakness of language in its inability to properly capture expressions of the ideal. In *Phantastes*, for example, Anodos always claims to have forgotten more than he tells: "This was one of the simplest of her songs, which perhaps, is the cause of my being able to remember it better than most of the others" (134). That is a romance convention: the clothes are always more rich, the women always more beautiful, and the knights always braver than words can relate. And in *Lilith*, Mr. Vane claims that his experiences in the other world (he does not call it Fairy Land, as Anodos does) are so indescribably different from what he is used to "that I can present them only by giving, in the forms and language of life in this world, the modes in which they affected me—not the things themselves, but the feelings they woke in me . . . A single thing would sometimes seem to be and mean many things, with an uncertain identity at the heart of them, which kept constantly altering their look" (46). The ideal always floats beyond any attempt to capture it in words or images. Because it is a prime tenet of allegory and of Aestheticism that images can often come closer to the ideal than words can, however, Anodos and Mr. Vane speak in images, the better to evoke insofar as possible the spiritual experiences they have had. What is more, MacDonald's protagonists want to describe "not the things themselves, but the feelings they woke in me," integrating their experiences into their lives just as the aesthetic critic and the interpreter of an allegory are supposed to do.

The signs in an allegory, then, must point beyond themselves to something larger: to a moral system, a macrocosm, and/or a world of interrelated parts, even to a way of reading the allegory itself. The larger concern might be something as basic as the body (Spenser's Castle of Alma or Phineas Fletcher's *The Purple Island*, incidentally a favourite mine of epigraphical ore for *Phantastes*) or as complicated as the emotional and social consequences of courtly love (the *Roman de la Rose*). Allegory is fantasy, in a way, since its outward shows are so alien to the experience of everyday existence, but the things or concepts to which it points are always comprehensible to the reader in one way or another. As J. R. R. Tolkien writes in his essay "On Fairy-Stories," "creative Fantasy is founded upon the hard recognition that things are so in the world as it appears under the sun; on a recognition of fact, but not a slavery to it. So upon logic was founded the nonsense that displays itself in the tales and rhymes of Lewis Carroll" (55). "To the aesthetic temperament, the vague," as Wilde says, "is always repellent" (1137).

MacDonald clarifies his views on fantastic writing in his essay "On Polish": "True polish in marble or in speech reveals in lying realities . . . I would admit of no ornament [in style] whatsoever . . . But let me explain what I mean by ornament. I mean anything stuck in or on, like a spangle, because it is pretty in itself, although it reveals nothing. Not one such ornament can belong to a polished style. It is paint, not polish" (*A Dish of Orts* 184-5). It might seem odd that MacDonald, a writer with such an imaginative pen for fantastic incident, should be so disapproving of writing that is meant to please the reader's eye. Can this have been written by the author of the passage describing the mad rout of fairies in the third chapter of *Phantastes*, certainly a bit of Pigwiggenry such as J. R. R. Tolkien rightly derided in "On Fairy-Stories" (7)? What MacDonald really means, however, is that everything in his stories is (or should be) significant to his overall allegorical direction.[3]

It is also significant that MacDonald connects polish very distinctly with the reader-critic's response: "The most polished style will be that which most immediately and most truly flashes the meaning embodied in the utterance upon the mind of the listener or reader" (184). The language he uses here is more evocative than exact ("most immediately and most truly flashes the meaning. . ."), suggesting that MacDonald has not betrayed the principle he states in "The Fantastic Imagination." The utterance still does not contain a particular meaning to be read out of it, but relies upon the reader's critical faculty to extract one or more of many possible interpretations. Feelings are not objects to be described scientifically in clinical, exact language; their description should rather be felt in the blood, and felt along the heart, than laid upon a table and dissected. Lewis finds in fourteenth-century allegory a particular manner of writing that relies upon reading: "Descriptions of the act (or passion) of falling in love tend to be among the most banal passages of fiction . . . A love story of considerable subtlety and truth is hidden in the *Romance [of the Rose]*. It would be a work not of creation, but of mere ordinary dexterity, to strip off the allegory and retell this story in the form of a novel. Nor would the change be an improvement" (129, 135). Allegory was so immensely popular in the fourteenth century, argues Lewis, because the readers of the time were—far from being confused by the apparent fantastic incongruities of allegory—particularly open to reading allegorically. Such readers were precisely the type that MacDonald describes in "The Fantastic Imagination," and that Pater wanted to create in his famous "Conclusion" to *The Renaissance*. The Aesthetic Movement was diverse and, far from attempting to impose a particular kind of art upon the populace, sought to educate people in the appreciation of all art, no matter how apparently obscure. Just as William Morris called for a society in which everyone was an active artisan and Pater called for a society in which everyone was an active lover of beauty, MacDonald wanted to encourage his readers to have active spiritual imaginations, engaging at once with the world as created by God and with the sub-created worlds of allegory and art.

How, then, are we to actively read MacDonald's allegories? What is the solid subject-matter of, say, *Phantastes*, *Lilith*, or "The Golden Key"? MacDonald's primary concerns are right action and the growth and development of the individual psyche, up to and after death (when, in his optimistic theology, *life* in the sense of aesthetic perception and spiritual knowledge really begins). To illustrate those concerns, he uses a mode— allegory—that takes into account the variety of individual experience and the importance of individual effort in action and interpretation. Reading MacDonald's fantastic allegories one is struck, not by the ethereality of his work, but by its constant grounding in real experience. The dreamlike shifts in, say, *Phantastes* from one fantastic scene to another simply denote the variety of encounters a person experiences over the course of a "real" life. His protagonists may find themselves in extraordinary situations, but they react in the same, often flawed, manner that we act in our mundane lives. No person today has met with a knight in soiled armour, still less with one whose armour was once soiled and now gleams, and who approaches dragging the corpse of a dragon behind his steed. Most of us, however, know the experience of reacting with "surprise and pleasure . . . [and] a sudden pain" (*Phantastes* 168) to some enviable stroke of kindness, genius, or strength on the part of an acquaintance. Apprenticeship to such a one may be the best— albeit most difficult—course we can take, and it is part of Anodos's spiritual development when he does exactly that, offering himself as squire to the unnamed knight.

Apprenticeship is, in the real world and in the context of a lifetime, brief. Since MacDonald's protagonists are involved in no less a project than lifelong spiritual growth, such interludes are also fleeting; it is this that accounts for the often confusing episodic nature of *Phantastes* and "The Golden Key" (*Lilith* is less disjointed). Just as in real life there is no one teacher at whose feet one learns everything one needs to know, Anodos and Mossy and Tangle receive the aid of many natural and supernatural helpers. Most importantly, perhaps, MacDonald's heroes remain rightly imperfect, even unto their lives' conclusions. The knight, for all his strength and chivalry, is unable to sense the real nature of the ritual he and Anodos witness in the clearing among the yew trees:

> I looked up at my master: his noble countenance was full of reverence and awe. Incapable of evil himself, he could scarcely suspect it in another, much less in a multitude such as this, and surrounded with such appearances of solemnity. I was certain it was the really grand accompaniments that overcame him; that the stars overhead, the dark towering tops of the yew-trees, and the wind that, like an unseen spirit, sighed through their branches, bowed his spirit to the belief, that in all these ceremonies lay some great mystical meaning, which, his humility told him, his ignorance prevented him from understanding. (*Phantastes* 177)

It is not an irony that Anodos's fallen state and his capacity for wrong action enable him to see, where the good knight does not, the sinister nature of the proceedings. Human imperfection, for MacDonald, serves to open up possibilities rather than to restrict spiritual growth: if we had never sinned, we would not need forgiveness. If an allegory were capable of only one interpretation, it would be incapable of properly evoking the great variety of individual experience in the real, fallen world, and would not be successful.

Accordingly, the endings to MacDonald's fairy tales—*Lilith*'s above all, but *Phantastes*'s too—do not offer authoritative and final conclusions. Even though he has done his great deed and experienced a fitting end ("I was dead, and right content," 179), Anodos sinks back again from his bliss to the sublunary world. In the coda to *Phantastes* he even wonders whether he will have to relearn the lessons he learned in Fairy Land. The great vision of the throne of God that comes to Mr. Vane after his death in *Lilith* is the cause of equally great confusion after he is returned (or so it seems) to his library: "Can it be that that last waking also was in the dream? that I am still in the chamber of death, asleep and dreaming, not yet ripe enough to wake? . . . If that waking was itself but a dream, surely it was a dream of a better waking yet to come, and I have not been the sport of a false vision! Such a dream must have yet lovelier truth at the heart of its dreaming!" (251).[4] It is an important characteristic of allegory that it at once holds out the possibility of ultimate truth and denies that truth's immediate attainment. The abrupt ending, whether intended or not, to Chaucer's *House of Fame*, with its silent and undescribed "man of grete auctorite . . ." is entirely apt in its denial of an authoritative summation of the allegory.

It is true that MacDonald once rejected the characterisation of *Phantastes* as an allegory: in a letter to Mrs. A. J. Scott, he writes that "I hope Mr. Scott will like my fairy tale. I don't see what right the *Athenæum* has to call it an allegory and judge or misjudge it accordingly—as if nothing but an allegory could have two meanings!" (qtd. Greville MacDonald 297). The *Athenæum* article to which he refers is a rather patronizing review of *Phantastes* that concludes—"One mistake is said to be permitted to every writer of books: Mr. MacDonald has made his. Happy is the author who makes only one!"—a comment that would make any author wince. Patronizing as the review may have been, the reviewer does seem to have grappled with the work, and to have thought deeply about allegory in general:

> Now the great masters of allegory succeed by their firm grasp of reality . . . Mr. MacDonald has given us the shadow without the life which should cause it to him, and account for it to us.

> Thus 'Phantastes' is a riddle that will not be read. He has made his voyage into Dreamland with the Phantom bark, but when he tries to bring it home to us and reveal something of the far wonder-world we cannot get on board. He has not anchored fast to the earth on which we stand. (580)

Whether it was unfair or not to say that MacDonald has no grasp of reality in his fantasies, much the same judgement would be passed on the Aesthetic Movement in general. The pernicious doctrine of *l'art pour l'art* was to damage the movement in the eyes of the sensible Victorian middle classes, accustomed to appraising in terms of utility if not of guineas; and it would prove easy to mistake for ivory-tower escapism the movement's refusal to put a tangible value on art. The failure of the major Aesthetic authors to do more than flirt with respectability would also be grounds for suspicion. Burne-Jones might have received a baronetcy, the moneyed classes might be flocking to Morris's shop in Oxford Street, and there could be little doubt that Ruskin was the preeminent art critic of the age, but by late century there was still something unseemly about Ruskin's quixotic social schemes, Morris's socialism, Wilde's and Pater's barely-disguised homosexuality, and Rossetti's and Swinburne's fleshliness. MacDonald's own non-conformity lost him his parish in Arundel, and the obscurity of his fantasies denied them the popular audience that his novels received. The *Athenæum's* reviewer had off-handedly set the tone for Victorian criticisms of the Aesthetic Movement.

When MacDonald scoffs "as if nothing but an allegory could have two meanings!" he is not rejecting outright the characterisation of *Phantastes* as an allegory, and as Greville reflects, "I do not quite see why my father should object to the definition" (297). At the very least, his statement could be written off as pique. But clearly George MacDonald was hoping at the time of his letter that *Phantastes* would be seen as something greater than the conventional allegory of one-to-one correspondences. It must be remembered that in the staid Victorian age, allegory was an outdated genre appreciated only by antiquarians or a mechanical device for children's tales; it was certainly not one of the acknowledged fashionable modes.

Paul De Man, in his essay "The Rhetoric of Temporality," describes the growth of an allegorical mode in the relation of subject to object and of the individual to nature in the early nineteenth century. De Man makes an important distinction between dogmatic (i.e., eighteenth-century) allegory, with its very straightforward relationship between subject and object (between signifier and signified), and allegory that is "located entirely in the temporal relationships that exist within a system of allegorical signs," a form of allegory that he finds in the very German Romantics, such as Schlegel and Novalis, that were such a formative influence upon MacDonald: "At the very moment when properly symbolic modes, in the full strength of their development, are supplanting allegory, we can witness the growth of metaphorical styles in no way related to the decorative allegorism of the rococo, but that cannot be called 'symbolic' in the Goethian sense" (190). The "decorative allegorism of the rococo" here (a properly Aesthetic association of the decorative and literary arts) is the simple one-for-one allegory used by the neo-classical writers of the eighteenth century: what C. S. Lewis calls "the platitudinous allegory produced in ages to which allegory is a toy—the allegory of Maeterlinck or Addison" (114-5). However, De Man adds, "it does not take long for a symbolic conception of metaphorical language to [re-]establish itself everywhere, despite the ambiguities that persist in aesthetic theory and poetic practice" (208).

Everywhere, that is, save in the pockets of Romanticism that held out in certain aspects of the Aesthetic Movement—and in the poetic theories and allegories of George MacDonald. De Man locates his interpretation of romantic allegory "in the tendency shared by all commentators to define the romantic image as a relationship between mind and nature, between subject and object. The fluent transition in romantic diction, from descriptive to inward, meditative passages, bears out the notion that this relationship is indeed of fundamental importance" (193). It is easy to see here the example of Wordsworth, an important precursor of the aesthetic reader and the subject of one of Pater's "Appreciations." Pater reacts strongly to Wordsworth's capacity for vivid sensation and to his "intense susceptibility" (424) to the influence of natural things around him. MacDonald, in his essay on "Wordsworth's Poetry," frames his study of Wordsworth in much the same manner:

> Let us go further; and, looking at beauty, believe that God is the first of artists; that he has put beauty into nature, knowing how it will affect us . . . Then, let us go further still, and believe that whatever we feel in the highest moments of truth shining through, beauty, whatever comes to our souls as a power of life, is meant to be seen and felt by us . . . Now, Wordsworth is the high priest of nature thus regarded . . . the life of Wordsworth was so ordered as to bring this out of him, in the forms of his art, to the ears of men. (*A Dish of Orts* 247)

Wordsworth, in MacDonald's view, is both reader and writer, leading a life of experience and expressing that experience in his life's work. His book is (God's) nature, and his work the record of his reading therein. The religious aspect of Romanticism survived, as I have hinted and as Stephen Prickett describes more fully in *Romanticism and Religion*, well into the nineteenth century; Hilary Fraser traces its influence upon the Aesthetic Movement in *Beauty and Belief*. It is an error to see the nineteenth century's "religion of art" (Fraser 228) as diametrically opposed to religion proper, for the devout far outnumbered the atheists in the Aesthetic Movement. If George MacDonald is to be excluded from the Aesthetic canon, it cannot be on the grounds of his religion, or on the basis of his Romantic antecedents.

It must be cautioned that the Victorians were the product of the Enlightenment as well as of the Romantic era: orthodoxy and literalism were, if anything, more prevalent than individualism and aestheticism (as the *Athenæum*'s clear-headed critic, longing for solidity, attests). Citing Edwin Honig, Lynette Hunter writes that in the post-Renaissance period, "Allegory became moralising without art, rhetoric without imagination, symbolism without mastery, and . . . fantasy without reality. No tension remained between the fictional and the actual and there was a correlative attempt to control within the extent of its man-made authority" (141). It is quite possible to see examples of Hunter's "moralising without art" in the period; allegory was enlisted heavy-handedly in moral tales for children, a vast industry in the nineteenth century (see, for example, Bratton 69-80). That the suppression of tension between "the fictional and the actual" is designed to control the reader and should be avoided is a primary tenet of the Aesthetic philosophy. "Life," proclaims Vivian in Wilde's "Decay of Lying,"

> imitates art far more than Art imitates life. We have all seen in our own day in England how a certain curious and fascinating type of beauty, invented and emphasised by two imaginative painters, has so influenced Life that whenever one goes to a private view or an artistic salon one sees, here the mystic eyes of Rossetti's dream . . . there the sweet maidenhood of [Burne-Jones's] 'the Golden Stair'. . . And it has always been so. A great artist invents a type, and Life tries to copy it, to reproduce it in a popular form, like an enterprising publisher. (1082-3)

But the process cannot end there: Wilde would hardly be one to call for a merely imitative existence. The Aesthetic project is one of continuing to receive impressions of art and to create new forms from them, and of absorbing them into one's life on a daily basis, thereby making one's character more refined and individual.[5] If there is one agreement among the diverse writings of the Aesthetic Movement, it lies in their desire to maintain the tension (or harmony) between the fictional and the actual, the real and the ideal, life and art. It is not "the Truth" that will make us free, it is Art.

"Allegory, besides being many other things, is the subjectivism of an objective age" (Lewis 30). Allegory is a particular kind of subjectivism—one that simultaneously embodies and denies an objective truth. The "objective age" to which Lewis refers here is the late Middle Ages, with its reliance upon the absolute model of the Christian Church, but his characterisation might well be applied to nineteenth-century England. The Victorians were systematic thinkers: their religion and their science were systematic, as were their social philosophies (utilitarianism and the industrial complex). Just as high medieval Europe, however, could never quite create a uniform religious society (individualist heresies like Lollardy and self-fashioning geniuses such as Chaucer continued to thrive), so Victorian England had to be the (often unwilling) heir to Romanticism's subjectivity and individualism.

Although allegory was not one of the genres or modes that the Aesthetic Movement claimed for its own, the movement's desire to realise dreams and its emphasis on the individualised nature of the reading, interpretation, and appreciation of art are entirely in tune with the allegorical mode. Pater's *Marius the Epicurean*, like MacDonald's, works an extended examination of the spiritual growth of an individual soul, ends in no dogmatic manner. Marius gains a new portion of truth from each of his experiences, and the work finally places the responsibility with the reader to decide whether Marius is an example of Hebraism or of Hellenism or of both, in a process like that of allegorical reading. Wilde's *Picture of Dorian Gray* is probably a moral allegory on the dangers of finding too much significance in the artistic critical existence that Wilde, following Pater, encouraged. Its signs can, over the course of successive reading, be read in a number of ever more intriguing ways. Even Ruskin's chapter in *The Stones of Venice* on "The Nature of Gothic" at first offers its social commentary in the form of an analogy, giving the reader Ruskin's interpretative account of the medieval artisan at work. It is only when Ruskin drops the veil and makes his point by addressing the reader directly—ironically in such phrases as "You must either make a tool of the creature, or a man of him. You cannot make both" (177)—that the red tie comes off and the white choker puts in an appearance. The clerical collar constricts its wearer's voice; but MacDonald found (in his life and in his art) his own ways of avoiding its narrow compass, and the emphasis in his allegorical fantasies on individual growth and choice indicates that he wanted to extend that freedom to his readers as well.

ENDNOTES

1. It might be argued here that one can hardly imagine Wilde's elegant artist-critics "stumbling"—but it should also be noted that in their ongoing search for the *mot juste*, his protagonists do not always succeed. A consistently high level of style is, after all, impossible to maintain, and the form of the dialogue relies upon incomplete comprehension between its participants.

2. In the next sentence, MacDonald shows his debt to Romanticism, and especially to Wordsworth: "The best Nature does for us is to work in us such moods in which thoughts of high import arise. Does any aspect of Nature wake but one thought? Does she ever suggest only one definite thing?"

3. There is no doubt a place for the fairies in an allegorical interpretation of *Phantastes* if the reader is willing to look deeply enough for it. For example, the fairies are Anodos's introduction to geographical Fairy Land: they acclimatize him. They even set up the allegorical distinction between real and ideal, form and matter: "whether all the flowers have fairies, I cannot determine, any more than I can be sure whether all men and women have souls" (18).

4. The passage continues: "In moments of doubt I cry, 'Could God Himself create such lovely things as I dreamed?' 'Whence then came thy dream?' answers Hope. 'Out of my dark self, into the light of my consciousness.' 'But whence first into thy dark self?' rejoins Hope." There is a foreshadowing in this passage of J. R. R. Tolkien's theory of subcreation ("Fantasy remains a human right: we make in our measure and in our derivative mode, because we are made: and not only made, but made in the image and likeness of a Maker," "On Fairy-Stories" 55). Oddly enough, while C. S. Lewis in his autobiography *Surprised by Joy* acknowledges *Phantastes* and *Lilith* as enormous influences on his writing, Tolkien is less than enthusiastic about MacDonald in his letters, although he remembers having enjoyed the Curdie books as a child.

5. As Arthur Symons writes in his defense of the unsavoury scent of Decadent writing, "and if patchouli pleases one, why not patchouli?" It is, of course, ironic that patchouli, like sunflowers and blue china, became itself an orthodoxy of sorts.

WORKS CITED

Ankeny, Rebecca Thomas. *The Story, the Teller, and the Audience in George MacDonald's Fiction*. Lewiston: Edwin Mellen, 2000.

Bratton, J. S. *The Impact of Victorian Children's Fiction*. London: Croom Helm, 1981.

De Man, Paul. "The Rhetoric of Temporality." *Blindness and Insight: Essays in the Rhetoric of Contemporary Criticism*. 2nd rev. ed. Minneapolis: U of Minnesota P, 1983. 187-228.

Filmer, Kath. "La Belle Dame Sans Merci: Cultural Criticism and Mythopoeic Vision in *Lilith*."

The Victorian Fantasists: Essays on Culture, Society and Belief in the Mythopoeic Fiction of the Victorian Age. Ed. Kath Filmer. London: Macmillan, 1991. 90-103.

Fraser, Hilary. *Beauty and Belief: Aesthetics and Religion in Victorian Literature*. Cambridge: Cambridge UP, 1986.

Hunter, Lynette. *Modern Fantasy and Allegory: Rhetorical Stances of Contemporary Writing*. New York: St. Martin's, 1989.

Lewis, C. S. *The Allegory of Love*. 1936. New York: Galaxy, 1958.

MacCarthy, Fiona. *William Morris: A Life for Our Times*. London: Faber and Faber, 1994.

MacDonald, George. *A Dish of Orts: Chiefly Papers on the Imagination and Shakespeare*. London: Edwin Dalton, 1908.

—. "The Golden Key." *The Victorian Fairy Tale Book*. Ed. Michael Patrick Hearn. New York: Pantheon, 1988. 229-51.

—. *Phantastes*. 1858. Grand Rapids, MI: Wm. B. Eerdmans, 1981.

—. *Lilith*. 1895. Grand Rapids, MI: Wm. B. Eerdmans, 1981.

MacDonald, Greville. *George MacDonald and his Wife*. 2nd ed. London: Allen and Unwin, 1924.

Michalson, Karen. *Victorian Fantasy Literature: Literary Battles with Church and Empire*. Lewiston, NY: Edwin Mellen, 1990.

Pater, Walter. *Appreciations*. 1889. Walter Pater: Three Major Texts. Ed. William E. Buckler. New York New York UP, 1986. 391-550.

—. *The Renaissance: Studies in Art and Poetry*. [1873]. Walter Pater: Three Major Texts. Ed. William E. Buckler. New York New York UP, 1986. 69-220.

Pennington, John. "From Fact to Fantasy in Victorian Fiction: Dickens's *Hard Times* and MacDonald's *Phantastes*." *Extrapolation* 38: 3 (1997): 200-206.

Prickett, Stephen. "George MacDonald and the Poetics of Realism." *The Victorian Fantasists: Essays on Culture, Society and Belief in the Mythopoeic Fiction of the Victorian Age*. Ed. Kath Filmer. London: Macmillan, 1991. 82-9.

—. *Victorian Fantasy*. Hassocks, Sussex: Harvester, 1979.

—. *Romanticism and Religion: The Tradition of Coleridge and Wordsworth in the Victorian Church*. Cambridge: Cambridge UP, 1976. Rev. of *Phantastes*. *Athenæum* 1619 (November 6th, 1858): 580.

Robb, David S. "Realism and Fantasy in the Fiction of George MacDonald." *The History of Scottish Literature, Volume 3: Nineteenth Century*. Ed. Douglas Gifford. Aberdeen: Aberdeen U P, 1988. 275-290.

Ruskin, John. *The Genius of John Ruskin: Selections from His Writings*. Ed. John D. Rosenberg. London: Routledge and Kegan Paul, 1963.

Teskey, Gordon. "Allegory." *The Spenser Encyclopedia*. Ed. A. C. Hamilton. Toronto: U of Toronto P, 1990. 16-22.

—. "Allegory, Materialism, Violence." *The Production of English Renaissance Culture*. Ed.

David Lee Miller, Sharon O'Hair, and Harold Weber. Ithaca, NY: Cornell U P, 1994. 293-318.

Tolkien, J. R. R. "On Fairy-Stories." *The Tolkien Reader*. New York: Ballantine, 1966. 1-73.

Wilde, Oscar. "The Critic as Artist." *Complete Works of Oscar Wilde*. Ed. Owen Dudley Edwards, Terence Brown, Declan, Kibard, and Merlin Holland. 2nd. ed. Glasgow: Harper Collins, 1994. 1108-55.

—. "The Decay of Lying." *Complete Works of Oscar Wilde*. Ed. Owen Dudley Edwards, Terence Brown, Declan, Kibard, and Merlin Holland. 2nd. ed. Glasgow: Harper Collins, 1994. 1071-92.

Riddled with Evil: Fantasy as Theodicy in George MacDonald's *Phantastes* and *Lilith*

Courtney Salvey

From *North Wind: A Journal of George MacDonald Studies*

George MacDonald's life was permeated by a hyper-awareness of death, first through the early deaths of close family members and then through the tuberculosis which constantly threatened his life. Yet MacDonald did not live in fear of death, but in longing for it. In a letter to his wife in 1891, MacDonald writes in comfort about the death of their daughter Lilia, "Oh dear, what a mere inn of a place the world is! and thank God! we must widen and widen our thoughts and hearts. A great good is coming to us all—too big for this world to hold" ("G.M.D. to his Wife" 524). While death is to be desired for MacDonald, this longing is balanced with an equally strong sense of the wonder of this world. Objecting to an Evangelical religion which called for the rejection of the material world in order to win eternity, MacDonald wrote to his father:

> One of my greatest difficulties in consenting to think of religion was that I thought I should have to give up my beautiful thoughts and my love for the things God had made. But I find that the happiness springing from all things not in themselves sinful is much increased by religion. God is the God of the beautiful, Religion the love of the Beautiful . . . . ("G.M.D. to his Father" 108)

For MacDonald, both this world and the next are good, but this world is good because it points to God. Stephen Prickett and Frank Riga recognize in this attitude toward God and the physical world a Platonic idealism in which the physical world is the evanescent image which can lead us to the real in God. However, seeing MacDonald as a Platonist is problematic, which both Prickett and Riga acknowledge in using that label, one calling him a "temperamental Platonist" (Prickett, *Victorian* 170) and the other demonstrating the impurity of that Platonism (Riga 112), because it is contradictory for a Platonist to maintain the goodness of the material world while claiming its unreality. As David Robb observes, MacDonald "is opposed to materialism in all its forms, but his position is complicated by his seemingly opposite tendency to revel in the beauty and variety, the very evanescence, of the thing to be despised" ("Fiction" 38). By making this theoretical move, MacDonald abandons locating the source of evil in the material world. But if evil is not in the illusory material world as Platonists hold, what is it and where is it? How can MacDonald maintain the goodness of this world while personally longing for death?

This theoretical problem does not point to a failure in MacDonald's theology, for as Prickett observes, "Behind the magical beings of MacDonald's universes lies the philosophical and theological principles of a scheme that is as carefully worked out as that of Dante" ("Two" 22). MacDonald's failure to reject the material world by identifying it as evil is not merely a blip in his Platonism, but points to a different theology altogether. His fantasies written for adults, *Phantastes* and *Lilith*, the bookends of his writing career, outline the solution to the riddle of valuing both this world and the next. Instead of Platonism, MacDonald illustrates in these novels different facets of an Augustinian conception of the universe in which evil is the privation of good and all things with substance are good. Written at the beginning of his career and while he was a young man, *Phantastes* demonstrates the value and meaningfulness of the material world and subtly identifies the source of evil as the will of the self. His last major work, written during a time of increasing depression and declining health, *Lilith*, explores the workings of evil as it permeates the world. Ultimately, MacDonald exhibits a Platonism refracted through Augustine with an understanding of evil as the non-substantive privation of good, thereby allowing the celebration both of this life and the next one and laying the theoretical foundation for MacDonald's belief in the future redemption of all people and all things.

British study of Augustine was rejuvenated in 1838 when Edward Pusey published a widely available revised translation of Augustine's *The Confessions* (Cobb). MacDonald's academic and religious training ensures his familiarity with this text and the theology behind it. In *The Confessions* and his Christian writings, Augustine, inheriting Platonism through Plotinus, posits an idealistic universe structured as a continuum with God—as the Supreme Good and That Which Is— at the top, and the created world at the bottom. God, for Augustine, is the Real, the Good, and the Ultimate Substance. Everything else in the world has substance (which is not synonymous with material) in a lesser degree. Because God is good and he created all things, nothing he created can be evil. In *The Confessions*, Augustine claims that "therefore whatsoever is, is good. That evil then which I sought, whence it is, is not any substance: for were it a substance, it should be good" (122). Corroboratively, in *The City of God*, Augustine observes that "evil has no positive nature; the loss of good has received the name 'evil'" (354). While the Platonic hierarchy puts the evil material at the bottom and the good ideal at the top, Augustinian cosmology affirms the goodness and reality of all substances along a continuum which ascends from good but less substance to even better, more real substance, finally terminating in That Which Is. For Augustine, no part of this continuum is in itself bad or evil.

Before his conversion to Christianity, Augustine studied for several years with the Manicheans, who maintained a strict, antagonistic dualism between the evil material world and the good spiritual world. Yet Augustine struggled with this explanation for the existence of evil because it implies that God created evil. After leaving the Manichees because of their failure to expound a satisfying explanation for evil, Augustine formulated the idea that evil is merely the privation of good and therefore has no substance, since all substance is good through its creation by a good God. This facilitated a new attitude toward the material world. Encouraged by the Platonists to "search for incorporeal truth," Augustine began to see God's "invisible things, understood by those things which are made" (*Confessions* 126). According to the Platonists, the seeker begins on the lowest rung of the hierarchy, the created world, and then proceeds upward, abandoning the previous rung with the implication that the lowest rung, although necessary, is evil. Instead, Augustine claims the inherent goodness of even the distant points on the continuum because they are created by God. In *The City of God*, he asserts that "all natures, then, inasmuch as they are, and have therefore a rank and species of their own, and a kind of internal harmony, are certainly good" (384). This attempt to understand God through the created world coupled with an assertion of the goodness of all substance is impossible with the Manicheans and sets Augustine apart from Platonic idealism. Because the natural world is good, Augustine, unlike the Platonists, can embrace it fully and classify evil as the privation of good.

For Augustine, the theoretical challenge was how evil is introduced into the world if all things are good. Augustine suggests that when the will abandons what is above itself, and turns to what is lower, it becomes evil—not because that is evil to which it turns, but because the turning itself is wicked. Therefore it is not an inferior thing which has made the will evil, but it is itself which has become so by wickedly and inordinately desiring an inferior thing (*City* 386).

Crossing a Great Frontier

He adds that "defection from that supremely is, to that which has less of being—this is to begin to have an evil will" (387). In *The Confessions*, Augustine explains how evil works within the individual: "when I did will or nill any thing, I was most sure, that no other than myself did will and nill: and I all but saw that there was the cause of my sin" (110). To have an evil will is to have disordered desires. This implies that all things that can be desired have intrinsic value, but that some things have more value than others, and should be desired accordingly.

Instead of locating evil outside of the person by blaming it on some evil force in the universe as the Manichees did, Augustine conceives of the traditional Devil and his fallen angels as individual examples of the entrance of evil into an individual existence. He explains: "If we ask the cause of the misery of the bad [angels], it occurs to us, and not unreasonably, that they are miserable because they have forsaken Him who supremely is, and have turned toward themselves who have no such essence" (*City* 385). He continues about the nature of angels, "whilst by abandoning Him it should become, not indeed no nature at all, but a nature with a less ample existence, and therefore wretched" (385). To do evil is not to choose the material over the physical as the Manichees would suggest, but is to turn away from God and toward the self, something that is good but is less good than God, causing a disordering of the desires.

MacDonald's *Phantastes*, the story of a young man who unknowingly "set out to find [his] Ideal" (184), reveals a Platonic idealism in the conception of physical things as images of transcendent ideals which a person should seek to understand. Mirroring the experience in Plato's "Allegory of the Cave" from *The Republic*, Anodos is completely unaware of the existence of the ideal, the goal of life, when he enters fairyland, an ignorance betrayed in his constant bewilderment and aimless wandering. However, when he sees the lady imprisoned in the marble, the existence of the ideal flashes upon him. Awed by her, he notes: "What I did see appeared to me perfectly lovely; more near the face that had been born with me in my soul, than anything I had seen before in nature or art" (36). Anodos becomes aware of an ideal for which he yearns and which is beyond the luminous surface of the material marble. This idealism also permeates Anodos's reading in the Fairy Palace, where he "was trying to find the root of a manifestation, the spiritual truth whence a material vision sprang" (75-76). Elaborating the process of this reading, Anodos notes that the fairy book "glowed and flashed the thoughts upon the soul, with such a power that the medium disappeared from the consciousness, and it was occupied only with the things themselves" (84). Through his reading, Anodos almost achieves a Platonic ecstasy in which he perceives the things as they are, bypassing the material of the book which he reads. Anodos's journey, like that in Plato's "Allegory of the Cave," is a gradual realization of the ideal which grounds the existence of material objects.

Yet the idealism of Anodos is not wholly Platonic because it does not reject and devalue the physical, particular embodiment of the ideal after it has been used as a tool for contemplating that ideal. When Anodos finally catches up to the White Lady in the evening dance at the Fairy Palace, his singing her into a fully sensuous life is a positive, not negative, achievement. As he sings, "a real woman-soul was revealing itself by successive stages of imbodiment [sic], and consequent manifestation and expression" (112). Hers is the "face that had been born with [him] in [his] soul" (36), the ideal which he pursues. Yet the celebration of her embodiment suggests that knowing the ideal intellectually is somehow dissatisfying and that an embodiment of the ideal in beautiful material is preferable. This breaks with Platonic idealism and the accompanying dualism which suggests that the spiritual is always better than the material. Instead, material objects formed from the ideal are to be celebrated in themselves. Frank Riga understands this process by suggesting that MacDonald demonstrates an impure Platonism which "accommodated the essential goodness of the flesh and its ultimate purification and resurrection" (112). But instead of merely an impure Platonism, MacDonald brilliantly illustrates an Augustinian understanding of the universe in which all things possessing substance are inherently good because created by a good God.

Phantastes celebrates the entire natural world, pointing toward an Augustinian understanding of the goodness of the universe as created by God. Like Augustine's confrontation with the Manichees over their dichotomy between evil material and good spiritual powers in the universe, MacDonald faced religious people, especially in the growing Evangelical sect, who believed that the material world was evil and the spiritual world was good. In Charlotte Brontë's *Jane Eyre*, Mr. Brocklehurst exemplifies this Victorian Manichean phenomenon: he mortifies the flesh to improve the soul. He chastises the headmistress for feeding the girls bread and cheese instead of burnt porridge and he even requires the cutting of the girls' hair when he thinks long hair will cause the lust of the flesh (53-54). While MacDonald is in "unrelenting opposition to the materialism of the modern outlook" (Robb, *MacDonald* 23), MacDonald, in *Phantastes*, holds what Rolland Hein suggests is a sacramental view of nature (65-66), in which he proclaims the religious power of nature, redeeming the beauty of the physical, material world from Evangelicals who brand it as evil. In Anodos's reading in the Fairy Library, he discovers that "All that man sees has to do with man. Worlds cannot be without an intermundane relationship. The community of the centre of all creation suggests an interradiating connection and dependence of the parts" (77). The natural world is not evil, but is interrelated with the spiritual; the poles of binary dualism are brought together in the "community of the centre."

The lavish descriptions of the natural world through which Anodos travels reveal MacDonald's appreciation of the created order. The very beginning of Anodos's adventure celebrates the beauty of the natural world which invades Anodos's bedroom:

> where this carpet, which I had myself designed to imitate a field of grass and daisies, bordered the course of the little stream, the grass-blades and daisies seemed to wave in a tiny breeze that followed the water's flow; while under the rivulet they bent and swayed with every motion of the changeful current, as if they were about to dissolve in it, and, forsaking their fixed form become fluent as the waters. (9)

Not merely a method of discovering ideals, the natural world is inherently valuable. Later Anodos sleeps in the arms of the earth where "glow-worm was alight here and there, burning out into the great universe. The night-hawk heightened all the harmony and stillness with his oft-recurring, discordant jar" (42). MacDonald portrays the earth as loving and lovely, its beauty a gift from God. Cutting between a Romantic idolization of nature and a Platonic disdain for the material, MacDonald manifests an Augustinian understanding of the created world as inherently good because created by God and as usefully good for man because through it he can think God's thoughts after him.

In opposition to Victorian Manichees, *Phantastes* illustrates that evil is not within the natural world but corrupts it, a parasite on anything with substance, including the psyche. While evil characters scurry through the fantastic landscape, MacDonald never presents the Devil as the ultimate source of all evil, an impulse consistent with Augustinian evil. Evil has no single source in the universe from which it emanates (which would be a reverse structure of the good).

Instead, MacDonald presents evil as a shadow over the self, locating evil within the self. Although the shadow which Anodos acquires at the cottage of the Ogress has been defined in many different ways, a diversity of interpretation which bothers David Robb (*MacDonald* 84), the shadow in each definition is something sinister, something evil: it is a negation of good. The source of Anodos's shadow points to its definition as evil. When Anodos enters the cottage of the Ogress, she is reading:

> "So, then, as darkness had no beginning, neither will it ever have an end. So, then, it is eternal. The negation of aught else, is its affirmation. Where the light cannot come, there abideth darkness. The light doth but hollow a mine out of the infinite extension of darkness. And ever upon the steps of light treadeth the darkness; yea, springeth in fountains and wells amidst it, from the secret channels of its mighty sea. Truly, man is but a passing flame, moving unquietly amid the surrounding rest of night; without which he yet could not be, and whereof he is in part compounded." (55-56)

This strange speech discusses the source of darkness, associated with evil in Christian imagery. The Ogress asserts the substance of darkness, of evil, and suggests that man's existence is grounded in the darkness. Yet the fact that she is an Ogress implies that she is somehow evil so her words must be taken not as MacDonald's own view, but as the opposite of it. Inverted, this speech outlines the Augustinian conception of substance and goodness (light). Darkness and light are in opposition, but light is substance and darkness is the absence of substance. Darkness, or evil, has no beginning or end, it is not eternal but rather non-existent. The Ogress inverts the Platonic Cave paradigm (in which a cave, or mine, is dug out of the "infinite extension" of lightness) by suggesting that the light dug a mine out of the substance of darkness.

Yet even in her falsity, she does not set up an evil ideal around which this dark world is centered. Although the inversion and falsity of her speech is confusing, her chant points toward the meaning of evil as the absence of good.

Anodos's acquisition of the shadow illustrates MacDonald's Augustinian conception of evil and the self. Unfortunately for Anodos, his perverse impulse, his disordered desire, motivates him to open the door of the closet, of the inverted Platonic Cave, out of which his shadow, evil, finds him. After he sees a figure travelling towards him, he "looked round over [his] shoulder; and there, on the ground, lay a black shadow, the size of a man. It was so dark, that [he] could see it in the dim light of the lamp, which shone full upon it, apparently without thinning at all the intensity of its hue" (57). The shadow has no independent existence, does not have its own substance, but is the negation of light, of good. It lives as a parasite on the self of Anodos. After gaining the shadow in the "Church of Darkness" (69), Anodos's vision of the world is distorted by it. When he sees a child with a magical toy, "straightway he was a common place boy" (60) when the shadow affects him. Anodos visits a town where if he gets too close to people they appear terrifically ugly when the shadow falls upon them (63). Eventually his self and his shadow are tangled up together, and he cries, when at the Fairy Palace: "'Shadow of me!' I said, 'which art not me, but which representest thyself to me as me; here I may find a shadow of light which will devour thee, the shadow of darkness!'" (72). Yet there is no evidence or implication that the shadow has a self or a substance separate from Anodos—the shadow was "in [his] heart as well as at [his] heels" (64). Anodos's loss of the shadow reveals the relationship of self and evil. He says,

> Then first I knew the delight of being lowly; of saying to myself, "I am what I am, nothing more." "I have failed," I said, "I have lost my self—would it had been my shadow." I looked round: the shadow was nowhere to be seen. Ere long, I learned that it was not myself, but only my shadow, that I had lost. . . . Indeed, my ideal soon became my life; whereas, formerly, my life had consisted in a vain attempt to behold, if not my ideal in myself, at least myself in my ideal. (166)

When Anodos focuses on himself, when he ignores the advice given to him by others, the shadow begins its terrorization of him when it comes from the depth of the darkness. In that shadowed state, Anodos no longer tries to seek the ideal, but only seeks to serve himself. This turning to self instead of looking toward God, the true ideal, is what Augustine pinpoints as the invasion of evil into the self. All the things which the self-centered try to achieve are good in themselves, but have been distorted by the disordered desires of an evil will which turns to the self, the lower good, rather than focusing on That Which Is, on God. Anodos escapes evil when he turns away from himself and toward the true ideal, making his journey a working through of what Max Keith Sutton calls the "disorders of a narcissistic personality" (13).

Yet the novel does not end merely on Anodos's ecstatic loss of self in ever-increasing union with God. Instead Anodos must return, after he learns these lessons about self, evil, and the ideal, to the regular, non-fantasy, earthly world. In fairyland, Anodos dies and achieves union with and knowledge of the ideal. So when he awakens on the top of an earthly hill, he feels that he is "sinking from such a state of ideal bliss, into a world of shadows" (182). Like Plato's philosopher-king, he must descend back into the world of images in order to lead the people. Yet this is not a true Platonism which disparages the natural world, but a cosmology which values the natural world as good, but just not as good, not as real, as the world which Anodos has recently left. Wondering about what he has learned in Fairy Land, Anodos asks whether he is a "ghost, sent into the world to minister to [his] fellowmen, or, rather, to repair the wrongs [he] had already done" (184). Anodos's sorrow in returning to this world is not that this world is evil, but that it does not have the full reality which imbued Fairy Land. This earthly world is not evil, but because it is not as real, it is not as good.

Finally, the book ends with Anodos speaking with a tone of confidence: "Yet I know that good is coming to me—that good is always coming; though few have at all times the simplicity and the courage to believe it. What we call evil, is the only and best shape, which, for the person and his condition at the time, could be assumed by the best good" (185). For Anodos, evil has no independent existence. Instead, good is always coming because the entirely good world is ever in a movement of tighter and tighter spirals toward the perfection of the "community of the centre," of the top of the hierarchy or the center of the bulls' eye: the Supreme Good, the Augustinian God at the center of the universe, out of whom all of the Platonic ideas spring and then are clothed with good substance to form the good natural world.

The conception of good and evil illustrated by *Phantastes* is an implicit version of Augustine's Plato-informed conception of the universe and of evil. By asserting the value and goodness of the material world through articulation of evil as something which cuts across the material and spiritual as the privation of good, MacDonald rescues material life and makes it meaningful while also celebrating the life which is to come. Yet the novel, because it is almost completely centered around Anodos and his psyche, does not contain a full elaboration of how evil functions in the world at large. MacDonald's late novel, *Lilith*, contains MacDonald's clearer theodicy, his explanation of evil in the universe. In this bitter and weird novel, MacDonald exposes the functioning of evil and illustrates its corruption of the self and its social impact, while still maintaining the goodness of a world shadowed by evil.

From the beginning of the novel, *Lilith* presents, through Vane's journey of upward movement, an Augustinian understanding of the universe as a continuum culminating in ultimate good and of humanity's status in that continuum. Vane's ancestor is identified as a Sir Upward who suddenly disappeared and was never heard from again (9), implying that he moved

"Upward" on the continuum. In the second chapter of the novel, Vane begins this upward journey by following Mr. Raven up the stairs into the garret where a new world is revealed to him through a magical mirror. Paralleling the Platonic "Allegory of the Cave," Vane turns away from the attractive world he sees out of his window and climbs the stairs to the attic and into knowledge of another world. Vane's movement from regular earthly reality into the fairy world is conceptualized as an unwilling upward movement as the magnetism of Mr. Raven compels him toward a fuller understanding of the universe. Once in Fairy Land, Vane continues the upward journey through this higher plane. Mr. Raven attempts to communicate this multi-level conception of reality when he tells Vane that they are "'[i]n the region of the seven dimensions'" (21) which interpenetrate, but that the immature Vane can only see the three regular dimensions.[1] As Mr. Raven is "'widening [Vane's] horizon'" (22), Vane begins to grasp that there are more levels to reality than he comprehends. In an Augustinian fashion, Vane's passage will be through those levels as he "journeys spiritually toward oneness with God," as Rolland Hein labels it (91).

Although often a strange and menacing landscape, the natural world in *Lilith* is affirmed instead of debased. Mr. Raven tells Vane, "'All live things were thoughts to begin with, and are fit therefore to be used by those that think. When one says to the great Thinker:—'Here is one of thy thoughts: I am thinking it now!' that is a prayer—a word to the big heart from one of its own little hearts'" (26). Platonically, the natural world is the flimsy embodiment of an ideal to be discarded when its utility ends; but this passage celebrates the natural thing as a way to understand God and his creation. When Vane returns to his library after his second trip to fairyland, he ponders, "Which was the real—what I now saw, or what I had just ceased to see? Could both be real, "interpenetrating yet unmingling?" (37). The different worlds, interpenetrating yet unmingling," are both real and are intimately knitted together. However, as David Robb points out, "the world into which Vane stumbles has an additional quality of being there" (*MacDonald* 97). It exists on a higher rung of the continuum of reality, where substance and goodness increase as a thing approaches the terminal end of that continuum, That Which Is. Although Fairy Land seems to be a on a higher rung of the Augustinian universal hierarchy, the reality of the earthly world is not negated. Both worlds are real, although possibly not equally real, and both worlds are good, although perhaps not equally good.

Instead of identifying evil as something material, MacDonald illustrates the character of evil through the Shadow, an absence of light, a parasite upon substance, which oppresses Bulika and is especially powerful around Lilith. Entering Bulika, Vane sees the Shadow, the symbol of ultimate evil, in the street:

> At a place where he had to cross a patch of moonlight, I saw that he cast no shadow, and was himself but a flat superficial shadow, of two dimensions. He was, nevertheless, an opaque shadow, for he not merely darkened any object on the other side of him, but rendered it, in fact, invisible. In the shadow he was blacker than the shadow; in the moonlight he looked like one who had drawn his shadow up about him, for not a suspicion of it moved beside or under him . . . . When they passed together from the shadow into the moonlight, the Shadow deepened into blackness. (118-119)

As a symbol, the shadow is often employed to express something which has existence but no substance because it is the negation of light. Shadows are the darkness, the privation of light, as Augustinian evil is merely the non-substantial privation of good. MacDonald builds on this conception, but, because the Shadow is a being, he has a small amount of substance. The Shadow, as the "Prince of the Power of the Air" (75), has turned away from good for so long that his existence has almost dwindled to nothingness—a flat, two dimensional shape which has "'no thick to him'" (187). MacDonald's Augustinian sense of evil as that which has no substance but is a negation of good is darkly expressed in the haunting persona of the Shadow.

Yet the responsibility for sin and evil in the novel does not lie with some independent evil force in the world, but is bound up in the choices of the self. Augustine explains specifically that selves generate evil when they "have forsaken Him who supremely is, and have turned to themselves who have no such essence" (*City* 385). Vane's journeys illustrate this disparity between the real self grounded on "him who supremely is" and the evil self which attempts to form its own identity. Entering fairyland, Vane realizes that he does not know who he is:

Crossing a Great Frontier

"Then I understood that I did not know myself, did not know what I was, had no grounds on which to determine that I was one and not another" (*Lilith* 14). Something outside of himself is required for existence; if he turns to himself to define himself, his identity disappears. In Vane's second excursion to fairyland, Mr. Raven tells Vane that Vane is "'but beginning to become an individual'" (21), as he, like Anodos, works toward overcoming narcissism. Wandering through the Evil Wood, Vane also recognizes that self-focus, a turning to the self and away from God, constitutes hell: "What a hell of horror . . . to wander alone, a bare existence never going out of itself, never widening its life in another life, but, bound with the cords of its poor peculiarities, lying an eternal prisoner in the dungeon of its own being! . . . evil was only through good! selfishness but a parasite on the tree of life" (83). As Colin Manlove observes, the self of the ego is the source of evil in *Lilith* (60). Essentially, hell and evil have no positive existence; they are a lack of supreme good caused by self-focus.

Continuing to illustrate the workings of evil in the world, MacDonald dramatizes through Vane's relationship with the Little Ones that evil is not antecedent to substance but is merely caused by a choice of something that is less good than should have been chosen. When Mr. Raven warns Vane to refuse to complete a task which has been requested by a deceiver and Vane asks what will happen if he does, Raven answers, "'then some evil that is good for you will follow'" (95). Evil does not exist in the thing itself, but in the relationship of that thing to the Good. Originally, Vane decides not to risk educating the Little Ones because he is unsure about the benefit for them. This impulse to protect them is not inherently evil, but it is just not as good as educating them, as Mr. Raven points out to Vane much later in the story (142). The evil is in choosing to do the less good thing. Evil does not attack the self from outside, but from within. Vane again makes this mistake through his selfishness, when he proudly believes that he knows better than Adam when Adam invites him to lie down in death before any attempted rescue of the Little Ones. Instead of dying and then going to rescue the Little Ones, Vane sets off before his death to educate and save them. The result is the tragic (to Vane) death of Lona and the near-defeat of the Little Ones. Vane's affectionate yet misguided relationship to the Little Ones reveals how evil is a parasite on goodness picked up through self-focus.

Like Augustine, MacDonald enters deeply into the exploration of the nature of evil through the consideration of a fallen angel, Lilith. According to Augustine, angels are naturally good because they are beings created by God. The fallen angels, however, "have forsaken Him who supremely is, and have turned to themselves who have no such essence" (*City* 385), which constitutes evil and entry into the hell of the self. Through the Kabbalistic fallen angel, MacDonald illustrates the complete process of creation, fall, and redemption, but focuses in the majority of the novel on the corrupted Lilith, on the time between fall and redemption. Using Lilith to represent that element of society which is evil as Kath Filmer suggests, MacDonald seeks to address the "existence" and eventual end of evil in the universe. Of her creation, Adam recounts the story of God's gift of Lilith to him:

> He brought me an angelic splendor to be my wife: there she lies! For her first thought was power; she counted it slavery to be one with me, and bear children for Him who gave her being. ... Finding, however, that I would but love and honour, never obey and worship her, she poured out her blood to escape me, fled to the army of the aliens and soon had so ensnared the heart of the great Shadow that he became her slave, wrought her will, and made her queen of Hell. (147-148)

Because a good God created all things and Lilith is part of created substance, Lilith herself was also created good. But she lost that complete goodness when she turned to herself for her identity, refusing to submit to Adam and the God for which Adam was the earthly representative. Instead she sets up herself as God, as the source of herself, demanding worship from Adam.

The evil and corruption of Lilith are represented on the surface of her body by the presence of the shadowy wound, the abscess, which is slowly destroying her by dissolving her substance as it corrupts her body. On Vane's first encounter with Lilith, he notices the presence of the spot. He describes the figure he sees: "The eyes in the beautiful face were dead, and on her left side was a dark spot, against which she would now and then press her hand" (50). After the white leopardess, the symbol of uncorrupted good, defeats the spotted leopardess, "the spotted one drew herself away, and rose on her hind legs. Erect in the moonlight stood the princess, a confused rush of shadows careering over her whiteness" (135). When Adam discovers that Lilith has followed Vane into the earthly world, she claims that she is beautiful and that the spots have disappeared, but Adam challenges her "'what is that under thy right hand?'" (149). Obedient yet fiercely reluctant, she reveals the spot and Adam says, "'It is not on the leopard; it is in the woman! . . . Nor will it leave thee until it hath eaten to thy heart, and thy beauty hath flowed from thee through the open wound'" (149). Yet he beseeches her to "'repent, and be again an angel of God'" (149). When Vane, seduced by her beauty, is tempted to help her, Adam explains, "'Nothing will ever close that wound . . . . It must eat into her heart! Annihilation itself is no death to evil. Only good where evil was, is evil dead. An evil thing must live with its evil until it chooses to be good. That alone is the slaying of evil'" (153). Adam's explanation of the wound reveals that evil and annihilation are synonymous because they are the decay and negation of substance, while good is the return, the completion of substance. Evil can neither die nor be killed because it has no substance; instead, it must be replaced by good. Therefore, death in annihilation is only more evil. The abscess on Lilith's body represents the nothingness, the evil, eating into Lilith's body and soul. Life, and the healing of the wound, can only come through turning to the Good, whose presence will nullify the absence (the abscess), which is evil.

Yet even in this despicable character, evil is not her essence but attacks that essence. Lilith's night in Mara's cottage demonstrates that Lilith's evilness is not part of her substance, but is caused by turning toward herself, refusing to orient herself toward God. Mara asks Lilith, "'Will you turn away from the wicked things you have been doing so long?'" (199) and Lilith replies, "'I will not . . . . I will be myself and not another!'" (199), eliding the self and evil and revealing that the evil person turns toward the self and refuses the upward journey. Mara replies, "'Alas, you are another now, not yourself! Will you not be your real self?'" (199). The "real self" is not found through focus on the self, but through turning to the Good and locating the self in relationship to it. Lilith proclaims to Mara that freed from Mara's cottage:

> "I will do as my Self pleases—as my Self desires."
>
> "You will do as the Shadow, overshadowing your Self inclines you?" (199)

Although Lilith perceives her nature through herself, Mara knows that Lilith's inherently good nature is distorted by the shadow of turning toward herself instead of the good. Holding tightly to the self, although it is her hell, Lilith rebuffs Mara's comment that that Self is an illusion:

> "What I choose to seem to myself makes me what I am. My own thought makes me me; my own thought of myself is me. Another shall not make me!"

> "But another has made you, and can compel you to see what you have made yourself." (200)

If the created world is the embodiment of God's thoughts, then Lilith attempts to usurp the position of God when she claims that "my own thought makes me me," instead of merely trying to think God's thoughts after him. Lilith sets herself up as her own creator and the center of her universe, revealing her turning away from God and toward herself.

Even this sinister personality is redeemed at the end of the novel, though, further illustrating MacDonald's universalism. As a creation of God, Lilith still retains her inherent goodness, facilitating her final salvation. Only her will is evil, not her substance. Still in Mara's cottage, Mara tells Lilith how she will be redeemed: "'There is a light that goes much deeper than the will, a light that lights up the darkness behind it: that light can change your will, can make it truly yours and not another's—not the Shadow's. Into the created can pour itself the creating will, and so redeem it!'" (200). Despite her evil, Lilith can be redeemed when she is set again in proper relationship to the hierarchy of the universe. The light which is coming to Lilith will destroy the shadow and will change Lilith's narcissistic volition. Only by turning that will and contemplation away from the self will Lilith ever achieve her "real self" (199). When the "creating will," the ideal thought of God, enters Lilith, she will be redeemed and made more real. After this conversation, the "worm-thing . . . white-hot, vivid as incandescent silver, the live heart of essential fire" crawls into Lilith's abscess and reveals herself to her, placing her in the "'hell of her self-consciousness'" (201), while beginning the restoration of her body and her soul.

Yet Lilith's resistance, MacDonald's testament to the stubbornness of the human spirit, to the coming of that light, leads her to the edge of annihilation, the edge of complete evil through dissolution of substance. After she has seen herself through the light of God, she still refuses to turn away from herself, to "'restore that which [she has] wrongfully taken'" (203). Her refusal to turn toward God leads her to the brink of annihilation. Watching her, Vane notices

> an invisible darkness, a something more terrible than aught that had yet made itself felt. A horrible Nothingness, a Negation positive, infolded her; the border of its being that was yet no being, touched me, and for one ghastly instant I seemed alone with Death Absolute! It was not the absence of everything I felt, but the presence of Nothing. . . . It was the

recoil of Being from Annihilation. (204)

The culmination of her turning away from God and towards herself is "horrible Nothingness, Negation positive" resulting in utter "Annihilation." The more evil she is, the less real she becomes. Ultimately, if she chooses to continue to turn toward the self, that self will be completely destroyed in Annihilation, in Death Absolute, which is the end of being altogether, the absence of the good substance which God created. Yet because she has some being, some goodness, left in her, she rejects Annihilation.

After this brush with Annihilation, Lilith waveringly begins the upward process of the right relationship to God only to fall even lower. Knowing "the one that God had intended her to be, the other that she had made herself" (204), she neither wants to be what she has made herself nor does she want to turn her will toward God. Lilith's defiance returns strongly and she undergoes the "most fearful thing of all. . . . *Life in Death*—life dead, yet existent" (205). When she is in this state, Vane realizes that in her self-centeredness and self-absorption she is truly the "queen of Hell" (206). He notes that "the source of life had withdrawn itself; all that was left her of conscious being was the dregs of her dead and corrupted life" (206) and that she was now "what God could not have created" (206). All that remains is the self willed by Lilith—a self without life or goodness because severed from God, the "source of life." Through this agony, Lilith finally turns toward God after he has left her, by trying to open her hand (207). Her turning away from herself is represented in the tears that she sheds, beginning to release the waters that she had pulled into herself in her selfishness.

Yet even in her repentance Lilith believes she is ending her suffering through some kind of catatonic, ignorant existence away from God, the center of the universe. Although she has already experienced this kind of death in her experience of Annihilation, she tells Adam that "'I cried out for Death—to escape Him and thee!'" (214). But this understanding of death as a cessation, that death cannot be good in any way, is false. Instead, as Adam says to *Lilith*, "Cease thou canst not: wilt thou not be restored and *be*?'" (214). To die in the right sense is to *be* more fully than the person has ever been. To turn away from self in dying is to attain a higher level of existence as the person moves closer to God. For MacDonald, death is not an escape from the earthly physical world but a completion of it through an increase of substance.

Vane's eventual death cements the goodness of MacDonald's conception of death as not some kind of evil annihilation but as a fulfillment and expansion of good life. When Vane awakes, he sees

Lona waiting for him. He notes that "she fell asleep a girl; she awoke a woman, ripe with the loveliness of the life essential" (238). Through her death, Lona, instead of deteriorating, increases in reality and, because of that, she increases in loveliness as she progresses in her upward journey toward God. After his waking, he also meets Adam who tells him that "'you have died into life, and will die no more; you have only to keep dead. . . . Now you have only to live, and that you must, with all your blessed might. The more you live, the stronger you become to live'" (238). In his upward journey, Vane will continue to gain reality as he lives strongly with ever-increasing strength. Eve tells him that "'*the* Life keeps generating ours.—Those who will not die, die many times, die constantly, keep dying deeper, never have done dying; here all is upwardness and love and gladness'" (239). This life-after-death, this life-in-death, is characterized by "upwardness," as the person moves closer and closer to "The Life" which gives him existence. The remainder of Vane's life in the fantastic dreamland is his joyful journey to heaven, the "Journey Home" (243), where "it had ceased to be dark" and "nothing cast a shadow, all things interchanged a little light" (243). Here "every growing thing showed [him], by its shape and colour, its indwelling idea—the informing thought, that is, which was its being, and sent it out" (243). Because things are closer to the Thinker, they are more real by emitting more clearly the idea which is behind them. But he recognizes that "something more than the sun, greater than the light, is coming, is coming. . . . He is coming, is coming" (245). Vane wanders through the wonderful heaven with Lona, marveling at its beauty and reality and longing to meet him whose "substance and radiance were human" (248).

The great joy in Vane's death-into-life is not limited only to himself, but will be shared by everything in existence, including the Shadow. Even the Shadow himself, because he has that tiny two-dimensional scrap of substance, will eventually enter the house of death and begin the upward journey toward life. Eve tells Lilith that the only way the Shadow will enter the house of the dead is to "'lie down and sleep also—His hour will come, and he knows it will'" (218). The negation of good, the Shadow who has almost lost his existence because of that evil, will eventually die into life, substance, and move toward the Good. Once everything is caught in the net of the good death, it will move toward God, toward the real. Augustinian theology and cosmology explain why the Shadow, the Devil, can be redeemed through his turning away from himself and towards God. The ultimate redemption of the Shadow reveals the strength of MacDonald's universalism, a universalism built on the Augustinian conception of evil as the privation of good balanced with the belief in the value of the physical world as part of the good substance of God's creation.

In the final pages of the novel, Vane, like Anodos does in *Phantastes*, returns to the real world, to his library, where he takes up the journey again. Yet despite his longing to be with Lona, he willingly remains in this world, saying that "'all the days of my appointed time will I wait till my change come'" (251). He looks at the created things around him and sometimes, when he looks "they seem to waver as if a wind rippled their solid mass, and another world were about to break through" (251). Within the Platonic context, the good of the other world implies the evil of this world. However, within the text's Augustinian conception of the good of the created world and of evil as the privation of good, this idealism allows a celebration both of the world at which Vane looks and the world which almost breaks through the earthly screen. Through the Augustinian conception of evil and the goodness of the universe, *Phantastes* and *Lilith* point to a reconciliation of materialism and idealism, the kind of breakdown of binaries which MacDonald celebrated. Despite MacDonald's increased focus on evil in *Lilith*, he continues to affirm the goodness of this world presented in *Phantastes*, while he longs for the imminent death of an old man. Ultimately, *Lilith* is not a riddle as Robb suggests (*MacDonald* 97), but is itself a solution to the paradox of MacDonald's personal belief in the goodness of the world and his longing for death.

ENDNOTE

1. Deirdre Hayward argues that the "Seven-fold Pattern of Existence" theology is taken directly from the German mystic Jacob Boehme. In Boehme's theology, man goes through seven specific levels, which exist within himself, before he achieves oneness with God.

WORKS CITED

Augustine. *The City of God*. Trans. Marcus Dods. New York: Modern Library, 1950.

—. *The Confessions*. Revised translation by E.B. Pusey. Oxford: John Henry Parker, 1853.

Brontë, Charlotte. *Jane Eyre*. 3rd ed. Ed. Richard J. Dunn. New York: W.W. Norton, 2001.

Cobb, Peter G. "Pusey, Edward Bouverie (1800–1882)." *Oxford Dictionary of National Biography*. Ed. H. C. G. Matthew and Brian Harrison. Oxford: OUP, 2004. Online ed. Ed. Lawrence Goldman.

Filmer, Kath. "La Belle Dame Sans Merci: Cultural Criticism and Mythopoeic Vision in *Lilith*." *The Victorian Fantasists*. Ed. Kath Filmer. New York: St. Martin's Press, 1991. 90-103.

Hayward, Deirdre. "George MacDonald and Jacob Boehme: *Lilith* and the Seven-fold Pattern of Existence." *Seven* 16 (1999); 55-72.

Hein, Rolland. *The Harmony Within*. Revised Ed. Chicago: Cornerstone Press, 1999. MacDonald, George. "G.M.D. to his Father." Greville MacDonald 108.

—. "G.M.D. to his Wife." 13 October 1891. Greville MacDonald 524.

—. *Lilith*. 1895. Grand Rapids: Eerdmans, 2000.

—. *Phantastes*. 1858. Grand Rapids: Eerdmans, 2000.

MacDonald, Greville. *George MacDonald and His Wife*. New York: Johnson Reprint, 1971.

Manlove, C.N. *Modern Fantasy*. Cambridge: Cambridge UP, 1975.

McGillis, Roderick. "*Phantastes* and *Lilith*: Femininity and Freedom." *The Gold Thread*. Ed. William Raeper Edinburgh: Edinburgh U P, 1990. 31-55.

Plato. *The Republic*. Trans. and ed. Allan Bloom. 2nd ed. New York: Basic Books, 1991.

Prickett, Stephen. "The Two Worlds of George MacDonald." *For the Childlike*. Ed. Roderick McGillis. Metuchen, NJ: The Scarecrow Press, 1992. 17-30.

—. *Victorian Fantasy*. 2nd ed. Waco: Baylor UP, 2005.

Riga, Frank. "The Platonic Imagery of George MacDonald and C. S. Lewis." *For the Childlike*. Ed. Roderick McGillis. Metuchen, NJ: The Scarecrow Press, 1992. 111-132.

Robb, David S. "The Fiction of George MacDonald." *Seven* 6 (1985): 35-44.

—. George MacDonald. Scottish Writers Series, No. 11. Edinburgh: Scottish Academic Press, 1987.

Sutton, Max Keith. "The Psychology of Self in MacDonald's *Phantastes*." *Seven: An Anglo-American Literary Review* 5 (1984). 9-25.

The Shadow of Anodos:
Alchemical Symbolism in *Phantastes*

Aren Roukema

From *North Wind: A Journal of George MacDonald Studies*

Because it is heavily reliant on symbol, interpretative approaches to George MacDonald's *Phantastes* have varied widely. Some critics, such as a reviewer in London's *Athenæum* at the time of the novel's release, have seen it as "a riddle that will not be read" (Cowan 51), while others have been anxious to wade into the sea of imagery and symbol that washes through the novel. Freudian or Jungian interpretations have been especially popular and have come to interesting, though somewhat anachronistic, conclusions. Though MacDonald likely did not intend that Anodos's fearsome nemesis, the Ash tree, be interpreted in oedipal terms, he probably would not have objected.[1] In his opinion, "The truer the art, the more things it will mean" ("The Fantastic Imagination" 317). For many critics, however, a subjective symbolic experience is the extent of what can be gained from a reading of *Phantastes*. The novel is accused by many, including Robert L. Wolff, Richard Reis, Colin Manlove, and William Raeper, as having little to no structure (Reis 89; Manlove 75; Gunther 43-59).[2] However, this interpretation must be questioned because of the allegorical structure provided by several symbols that arch through the whole of the narrative. One such central symbol, which has yet to be properly understood, is the shadow that attaches itself to Anodos in the Ogress's church of darkness (48). Many scholars have attempted to decipher the shadow, but most arrive only halfway. Salvey, for example, sees the shadow as merely a "negation of good," thus drawing MacDonald's theodicy into a sharp dualism, even though MacDonald himself stated that even evil is ultimately good (20).

This paper will interpret the shadow in the light of MacDonald's cosmology and theology, as both are vital for an understanding of this powerful symbol. This interpretation will show that Anodos's shadow is drawn from the alchemical symbols of the *nigredo* and the black sun, which MacDonald uses to represent separation from the divine spirit immanent in creation. When the alchemical significance of the shadow is identified, *Phantastes* emerges as an alchemical fable in which Anodos, the subject of transmutation, undergoes a journey toward reunification with an immanent God.

Christian Pantheism: MacDonald's Immanent God

In order to examine the shadow as an active symbol of separation from God in Nature, which I will refer to as disenchantment, it is necessary to first establish MacDonald's ideal of unity with the Divine, or enchantment. Stephen Prickett states that MacDonald is a "temperamental Platonist, only interested in the surface of this world for the news it gives him of another, hidden reality" (193). However, while MacDonald's cosmology is certainly Platonic, he does not devalue the external world. His view is more similar to forms of Neo-Platonic emanation in which all of Nature is divine by virtue of the one indivisible God's immanence in creation. The universe is God, though in a lower form of gradation. For MacDonald, this Neo-Platonic emanation takes place through the divine Imagination. In his essay "The Imagination," MacDonald states: "As the thoughts move in the mind of a man, so move the worlds of men and women in the mind of God . . . for there they had their birth . . . Man is but a thought of God" (8). The universe is created and sustained through divine Imagination, but man also participates in creation through his own imaginative faculty. Just as God envisioned the world and it was so, man also constructs his own world through participation with symbols present in Nature that indicate spiritual facts and entities which are otherwise hidden from the view of the material senses. There is thus a creative correspondence between the Imagination of God and the imagination of humans: "The imagination…is that faculty in man which is likest to the prime operation of the power of God, and has, therefore, been called the *creative* faculty, and its exercise *creation*" ("Imagination" 8).[3]

MacDonald sets up a cosmological triangle in which God imagines both man and woman and nature into being, while humans participate in the eternal act of creation by recalling forms with their own imagination that God has placed in their mind with which to engage nature. Nature is sustained by the same divine Imagination as humans, and, by virtue of the fact that it is created from the Imagination that is God, is itself divine. If this sounds like pantheism preached with the pen of a devout Christian who was raised as a Calvinist and always saw himself as a minister without a pulpit—it very nearly is. MacDonald unabashedly gives the name "Christian Pantheism" to his belief that "God is in everything, and showing himself in everything" ("Wordsworth's Poetry" 182). To be clear, MacDonald did not believe that spirit and body were the same thing. His pantheism sees the two as intertwined in a constant process of creative imagination. Though the world is seen as constructed the divine Imagination that is God, it is not itself synonymous with God. It is therefore more suitable to speak of MacDonald's cosmology as panentheism.

MacDonald's views on the relationship between God and nature are not always clear. At times he uses language that can support dualistic interpretations. An example of such language is found in "The Imagination": "The outward, commonly called the material, is *informed* by, or has form in virtue of, the inward or immaterial—in a word, the thought" (17). Here we see the thought of God enchanting the material, in the same way that "our spirit informs, gives shape to our bodies" ("Mirrors" 221), but for MacDonald the relationship between spirit and matter is not so simple as the inward giving substance to the outward. The imagination of God enchants, or sustains, a body, but it has also created that body and, in an emanative sense, *is* that body: "This world is not merely a thing which God hath made, subjecting it to laws; but it is an expression of the thought, the feeling, the heart of God himself" ("Wordsworth's Poetry" 182). The person who chooses to see the phenomenal as lifeless, rather than as a repository of signifiers enriched by Imagination, is "living in the outer court, not in the *penetralia* of life" ("Individual Development" 52). Nature, properly viewed by humans, is enchanted by its connection to the spirit of the divine through Imagination. Humans exist in a state of unity with nature and God when they recognize this enchantment.

Disenchantment and the Shadow

When the shadow attaches itself to Anodos in the Ogress's dark church, it removes Anodos from this ideal state of enchantment by changing his perception of nature to a limited, materialist view. Shortly after the shadow has attached itself, Anodos lies down to rest in "a most delightful part of the forest, carpeted with wildflowers." When he rises, he sees that his shadow has desecrated the ground: "The very outline of it could be traced in the withered lifeless grass, and the scorched and shriveled flowers which stood there, dead, and hopeless of any resurrection" (51). As if this insidious effect weren't enough, the shadow gains in power:

> One day, having come out on a clear grassy hill, which commanded a glorious prospect, though of what I cannot now tell, my shadow moved round, and came in front of me. And presently, a new manifestation increased my distress. For it began to coruscate, and shoot out on all sides a radiation

of dim shadow. These rays of gloom issued from the central shadow as from a black sun, lengthening and shortening with the continual change. What wherever a ray struck, that part of earth, or sea, or sky, became void, and desert, and sad to my heart. On this, the first development of its new power, one ray shot out beyond the rest, seeming to lengthen infinitely, until it smote the great sun on the face, which withered and darkened beneath the blow. (51)

The symbolic power of the black sun lends itself well to psychological readings. William Gray, for example, connects it to the black sun motif of Freudian psychologist Julia Kristeva (885). It is possibly more instructive, however, to look to the work of Carl Jung, as he takes his black sun from the symbolic vista of alchemical tradition—likely the same sky in which MacDonald saw his own black sun. Compare the passage above with this description of the nineteenth picture of the *Splendor Solis*, the 16th Century alchemical text by Salomon Trismosin:

> It is a most dismal and curiously dark weird-like subject. A bleakish stunted landscape, with black blighted withered trees in foreground. A MONSTER BLACK SUN [sic] is in great part sunk below the ground, yet visible and partly rising above the ground at the center of the landscape—or middle distance. The rising of this pall-like bristly black sun, overspreads and hides totally the body of the true sun, which lies beyond; for; behind—is to be seen golden radiations of the true sun, which illuminates with its golden tinted light a nice landscape in the extreme distance. (60)

It would be hasty, based on this comparison, to state that MacDonald read *Splendor Solis* or saw one of many different sets of images based on it, but there are interesting similarities. In MacDonald's description the shadow itself adopts the "pall-like bristly" character of Trismosin's sun before it blackens the actual sun, but in both descriptions the black sun ultimately renders the landscape "bleakish." Trismosin's description ends with a hopeful vision of a true sun lying beyond, with a "nice landscape in the distance," while MacDonald's description ends in despair, but, as I will discuss further on, MacDonald's black sun/shadow carries its own hope for the future. Whatever the case, the black sun of *Phantastes* can be safely connected to the black sun of alchemy.

The sources and scope of MacDonald's interest in alchemy are unclear, but we know from Greville MacDonald that his father was familiar with alchemy to some degree. He describes a conversation with his father about his other novel of symbolic fantasy, *Lilith*, in which Mr. Vane bathes Lilith's near-dead body in "the river of life," which his father said was made up of the four elements of medieval alchemy: water, air, earth, and fire. In alchemical terms, the "river of life" can be read as corresponding to the quintessence—the original element from which the material elements were created and to which the substance being transmuted must return. It could also refer to the elixir of life, one of the primary goals of alchemists, and a substance often connected to the quintessence in alchemical texts. Reis, trusting Greville MacDonald's word, states that MacDonald simply borrowed the alchemical imagery from Jacob Boehme (108). Indeed, Boehme was a significant influence on MacDonald, both directly and through Romantics such as Novalis, Coleridge, and Schelling,[4] but Boehme never refers to the black sun. Moreover, while MacDonald's romantic roots lead him to focus more on moon symbolism, Boehme gives symbolic precedence to the sun, the "similitude" of Christ (104). While Boehme was likely an influence, MacDonald must have encountered other alchemical texts as well.

In light of its connection to the black sun, the shadow can be identified with what is known to alchemists as the *nigredo*, the black colour, representing death, which a substance takes on during the transmutation of base matter into the philosopher's stone. In the alchemical tradition, the philosopher's stone can be seen as a substance (equivalent to the quintessence) that transcends the material elements and thereby has the power to manipulate them, or as a human being that has completed a process of spiritual regeneration and has become unified in spirit with the divine, as in the Gnostic and Hermetic traditions. This process goes through many different stages that vary according to the alchemist or alchemical tradition in question, but a process consisting of at least the three main stages of putrefaction, coagulation, and sublimation is usually followed. The *nigredo* is part of the process of putrefaction, or dissolution. "This dissolution," says Trismosin, "Is nothing but a killing of the moist with the dry, in fact a PUTREFACTION, and consequently turns the MATTER black" (38). The "moist," in this context, can be the spirit in a substance or in humans. The "dry" can be seen as elemental matter, separated from spirit (Principe 13). The *nigredo*, then, is the result of the separation of spirit from matter, usually seen as mutually present in phenomena. In MacDonald's symbolic conception, a human under the spell of the *nigredo* is a disenchanted human, a material human, reminiscent of the scientific naturalism that reigned in Victorian Britain at the time of the writing of *Phantastes* in 1858.

Indeed, we soon see that the shadow has transformed Anodos into a rational materialist from the enchanted young man able to see the spirit in things when he first entered Fairy Land, symbolized by his ability to see fairies enchanting the flowers. The "most dreadful" part of this development is that soon he begins to welcome the shadow's disenchanting presence. "In a land like this, with so many illusions everywhere, I need his aid to disenchant the things around me. He does away with all appearances, and shows me things in their true colour and form. . . . And if I live in a waste instead of a paradise, I will live knowing where I live" (53).

MacDonald uses the sun to symbolize this disenchanted way of knowing. Though the shadow is not dependent on Anodos's position in relation to a particular light source, it shows up blacker in the sunlight, while it is not visible by moonlight (146). In the full light of day Anodos experiences Fairy Land as the mechanistic workaday world of industrial Britain. Enchantment, or awareness of the spirit essential in nature, is much more difficult. In other forms of light not connected to the shadow, such as dawn, twilight, and sunlight filtered through trees, Fairy Land is revealed as it is beneath the moon—a panentheist world in which both external and internal meanings are seen in the symbolic repository of Nature. Moonlight is a symbol of knowledge reflected between the self and Nature through Imagination, a guiding light beneath which the enchanted nature of matter is more visible. Moonlight is thus directly connected with a fairy, or dream, or as a way of knowing. "Night is the fairies' day, and the moon their sun" (8). This symbolic structure matches with the role played by the sun and moon in medieval alchemy. In alchemical texts the sun is often related to fire and sulphur, while the moon is connected to water and mercury. Mercury, seen as a literal metal, but even more importantly as a primal element representative of water and earth, is the principle of fusibility, while sulphur, seen as representative of air and fire, is the principle of combustibility. Mercury gives permanence to metals, while sulphur corrupts them (Haage 19). The sun of *Phantastes* is symbolically applied to Anodos in order to begin the alchemical process through a combustible process of putrefaction—a function of sulphur—while both water and the moon elevate him through coagulation—a function of mercury.

The connection of the sun to the industrialized Britain of MacDonald's day represents a critique that is clearly in line with the views of Romantics like Coleridge, Shelley, and Wordsworth, for all of whom he professed deep admiration. MacDonald went beyond the Romantics with his panentheist cosmology however, as his thought remained primarily theological. His ideas were ultimately a product of the minister without pulpit, rather than the Romantic writer of fairy tales.[5] To truly understand the shadow as a symbol of the disenchantment resulting from materialism, we should look past the Romantics and focus on MacDonald's ultimate goal for humans. It is important for humans to view phenomena as living symbols so that they will be aware of their essential unity with Nature, and thus begin to glimpse the face of God. The materialist path is therefore the path away from unity, and for MacDonald, "Oneness with God is the sole truth of humanity. Life parted from its causative life would be no life; it would at best be but a barrack of corruption, an outpost of annihilation" ("Individual Development" 57). MacDonald has often been accused of being vague, but he is very clear on this point: a disenchanted state, such as that symbolized by Anodos's shadow, is death.

The Four Vices of the Shadow

In addition to the black sun, Anodos's shadow is connected to three other symbolic characters in *Phantastes*, who represent four vices that keep the self in a permanent state of disenchantment. The vices of fear, greed, lust, and pride are represented by two evil dryad characters—the Ash and the Alder—and by the shadow's assumption of Anodos's vain image of himself as Galahad. MacDonald leaves clues for the shadow's connection to each of these characters, but they have generally been missed by previous scholarship. The Ash, for example, is usually interpreted as a manifestation of Anodos's psyche, and its connections to fear and greed are often observed, but its direct correspondence to the shadow has not been noted. However, the Ogress in the dark church where Anodos finds his shadow tells him that he has already met it in the forest (50). Indeed, when Anodos meets the Ash in the forest, we see that it is also a projection of Anodos's shadow self, or *nigredo* state. He sees the shadow of the Ash on the ground, but nowhere between the moon that casts the shadow, and the ground upon which it is projected, can he see its source (21). The reason, of course, is that Anodos himself is casting the shadow. The Ash is even described in terms of a shadow rather than a material entity. When Anodos first meets the Ash it is as a "shadow as of a large distorted hand" passing over the blinds of the window as he reads the story of Sir Percivale (11). Even when the Ash materializes, it is as "the strangest figure; vague, shadowy, almost transparent in the central parts, and gradually deepening in substance towards the outside" (21).

The presence of the Ash is brought on when Anodos begins to feel a sensation of fear, which he is "unable to associate with any definite object whatever." This fear, he says, "Continued and deepened, until all my pleasure in the shows of various kinds that everywhere betokened the presence of the merry fairies vanished by degrees" (20). This function of fear is exactly parallel to the disenchanting effect of the shadow. The "merry fairies" are those that live in flowers, which die without the presence of their requisite fairy, and are thus directly analogous to the spirit aspect of matter. The Ash is thus parallel to the motif of the "Dweller of the Threshold," developed by Sir Edward Bulwer-Lytton in his novel *Zanoni*, released six years before *Phantastes*. Bulwer-Lytton's Dweller manifests itself as a spectral figure that frightens the individual from pursuing paths to higher knowledge. The Ash performs the same function by removing knowledge and awareness of the immanent God in Nature and in the self.

The "most awful of the features" of the Ash, however, are its voracious eyes. "These were alive, yet not with life. They seemed lighted up with an infinite greed" (22). This greed has two forms—possession and lust. The Ash as a symbol of possession can be seen as another critique of industrial Britain, a society obsessed, in MacDonald's view, with obtaining knowledge of Nature not to perceive higher realities, but to push toward human acquisition and technological progress. The shadow is also directly connected to greed. It appears each time Anodos experiences a desire to gain empirical knowledge of an object that he initially experiences with a sense of childlike wonder and mystery. An example is Anodos's encounter with a young maiden who possesses a crystal globe that Anodos is not allowed to touch—"Or if you do, it must be very gently." When Anodos touches the globe it produces magnificent harmonies. The spherical shape of the object suggests that it is directly symbolic of the earth and indirectly of Nature itself. Anodos, however, is not content to merely enjoy the beauty of the globe and its harmonies. His desire to possess and empirically know the globe leads him to try and steal it from the maiden. In the process of the attempt, the music grows discordant and the globe begins to vibrate and heave until it bursts. A black vapour breaks from it, a substance so black that it envelops the maiden and makes even the shadow indiscernible. Again the *nigredo* of alchemy is called to mind. The maiden flees from Anodos, crying, "My globe is broken!" MacDonald has her repeat the cry many times, no doubt to accentuate the sense of violation brought upon the innocent maiden by Anodos's forced disenchantment (54).

The second form of greed connected to the shadow is lust. When Anodos is reading the story of Percivale, the Ash's shadow falls across the window just at the moment that he reads of the knight's seduction by the "damosel of the Alder tree." At this point, he is unable to continue reading (11). The Alder tree appears shortly after in Anodos's own story as a personification of lust—a twisted mockery of the Beech tree, who symbolizes pure, selfless love. The Alder ensnares Anodos with her false beauty and attempts to give him over to the Ash. Her association as the Ash's helper, in addition to the fact that the Ash appears in Anodos's perception when she appears on the pages of Percivale's tale, deepens the connection between Alder, Ash and shadow as representative of lust.

The shadow himself manifests as the *doppelgänger* knight, a symbol of Anodos's pride. When Anodos successfully slays a giant, he feels a surge of pride and the shadow arrives in its usual form—lying black upon the ground. Later, while riding through an enchanted forest, he thinks back again on the killing of the giant and counts himself "amongst the glorious knights of old . . . side by side with Sir Galahad." The moment the thought appears in his mind, the shadow manifests as a *doppelgänger* of Anodos himself, except larger, fiercer, and malevolent. This shadow knight then locks Anodos in a tower. The interesting part of this experience is that the door of the tower is not actually locked, and even the tower's existence is a matter of perception. Each day the sun peaks through a window near the ceiling and lights the inside of the tower and Anodos is aware of his shadow lying beside him, "black on the floor." At night, the moon comes out and he becomes "suddenly aware of existence." The walls of the tower melt away: "The open country lay, in the moonlight, for miles and miles around me." When the sun comes out, he becomes aware again of the walls of the tower around him. "Every night the conviction returned, that I was free. Every morning I sat wretchedly disconsolate. At length, when the course of the moon no longer permitted her beams to touch me, the night was dreary as the day" (144-6).

The dichotomy between the sunlit view of scientific rationalism and the moonlit dream seeing of the inner eye is clearly illustrated in this scene, as is the shadow's direct connection to that sunlit materialist view. Chris Brawley follows Robert L. Wolff in seeing the shadow of the tower scene as different from earlier versions of the shadow, which, in Wolff's view, previously represented "the intellectual skepticism that withers the imagination," later represented "consciousness of self," and has now come to represent pride, "or a misconception of one's true role in the world" (qtd. in Brawley 109). As the relation of the shadow to fear, greed, and lust shows, however, the shadow's representation of pride is simply another illustration of a cause of the separation of the self from the divinity that is in nature. Thus, the shadow in its Ash form plays the same function as the shadow manifested as the *doppelgänger* knight.

All four vices represent a selfish, possessive perspective that stands in the way of seeing Nature and the self as enchanted. Reis comes close to this view in connecting the shadow to lust, vanity, and fear, but ultimately comes to a moral conclusion: "The Shadow represents the guilt which comes from not doing one's duty" (92-93). This would seem a logical conclusion, given the usual moral associations of such vices, but the shadow's connection to these vices is far more metaphysically important for MacDonald than a mere representation of guilt. For MacDonald the four vices result in disenchantment, an evil far worse than failure to do one's duty. MacDonald speaks of this in "A Sketch of Individual Development": "Take the eternal thought from the heart of things, no longer can any beauty be real, no more can shape, motion, aspect of nature have significance in itself, or sympathy with human soul. At best and most the beauty he thought he saw was but the projected perfection of his own being, and from himself as the crown and summit of things, the soul of the man shrinks with horror" (48).

The shadow knight is not the only vision of himself as the monstrous summit of things that Anodos shrinks from. The Ash and Alder are also monstrous representations of Anodos's own self that come to dominate his view and lead him to focus thought on himself rather than the "eternal thought."

The Great Work

The connection between these four vices and the disenchantment of the shadow faces us with a logical quandary. MacDonald believed that nothing was ultimately evil: "What we call evil, is the only and best shape, which, for the person and his condition at the time, could be assumed by the best good" (167). In MacDonald's theology, all beings eventually move toward oneness with God. Where then does the vice-tainted experience of the shadow fit? The answer may sound odd at first, but for MacDonald the experience of the shadow is ultimately a positive one, just as the *nigredo* of the alchemists, though it represents death and putrefaction, is a positive stage on a journey toward ultimate perfection.

It is important to see Anodos's journey through Fairy Land as symbolic of alchemical transmutation, as the claim for the shadow as a positive symbol rests on its association with spiritual regeneration. In order to illustrate that *Phantastes* is an alchemical fable, I will look back over the basic plot progression of the novel and treat Anodos as though he were a base metal. Recall that alchemists often sought to transmute base metals in order to produce the philosopher's stone, which, in the case of the self-transformation sought by alchemists with more spiritual goals, symbolizes unification with the Divine.

Anodos's transmutation begins with his first experience of *nigredo* during his fear-stricken encounter with the Ash, which represents an experience of putrefaction because of its connection to the shadow. Following the Ash encounter, he experiences his first coagulation, or, in the language of spiritual alchemy, his first experience of illumination. Leaving the dryad of the Beech tree after she has rescued him from the Ash, Anodos discovers a cave in which there is "a little well of the clearest water." He drinks this water and says, "[I] felt as if I knew what the elixir of life must be" (29). The "elixir of life" is an alchemical term used to denote a substance that gives healing or extended life. MacDonald's use of an alchemical term in this context is likely not accidental. Having drunken of the water, Anodos is thrown into a "delicious reverie . . . during which all lovely forms, and colours, and sounds seemed to use my brain as a common hall, where they could come and go, unbidden and unexcused" (29). The water allows Anodos's imagination to function in an unconscious manner, free of the restrictions of disenchantment. While it does not give him eternal life, it gives him consciousness of the divine Imagination, which is both eternal and life generating. Water, as we have seen, is commonly related to the symbols of the moon and mercury in the alchemical tradition, thus reinforcing the association of this cleansing bath with the alchemical stage of coagulation.

Following this initial process of purification, however, Anodos is thrust back into putrefaction, this time more strongly than before, when he succumbs to the temptations offered by the Alder/Lust. When he arrives in the Palace of Fairy Land, however, he gets another chance at coagulation. Anodos's entire experience in the palace can be read as an experience of illumination—he spends most of his time in the library, reading books as though he were himself the main character: "Was it a history? I was the chief actor therein . . . With a fiction it was the same. Mine was the whole story" (66). These reading experiences indicate a greater connectedness with all things through the operation of the imagination. MacDonald also uses alchemical imagery to link the palace itself with coagulation. Anodos states that in the palace "silver seemed everywhere preferred to gold" (63), an image that reflects the common alchemical association of silver with the moon and gold with the sun (Haage19). This is another example of MacDonald privileging the dream knowledge represented by the moon over the materialistic knowledge represented by the sun. The palace also contains a "fairy bath," in which Anodos swims each day. The hall in which the large pool of water is found is "spangled with constellations of silver stars." The pool itself appears quite deep, and is filled with "the purest, most liquid and radiant water." In addition to employing water symbolism to connect the pool to coagulation, MacDonald leaves a hint of alchemical colour symbolism to tie the pool to coagulation, as the sides of the pool are paved with white marble. While black is the colour of putrefaction, and red the colour of sublimation in alchemy, white (and sometimes yellow) is the colour of the tincture that is added to the base metal after putrefaction to result in coagulation.

When Anodos dives into the fountain, he says, "It clothed me as with a new sense and its object both in one." He describes the experience in terms of a liquid entering him, just as a tincture might mix with the purified substance of the base metal following putrefaction: "The waters lay so close to me, they seemed to enter and revive my heart." While looking at the pool from above, it had seemed to Anodos to be paved at the bottom with "all kinds of refulgent stones, of every shape and hue," suggesting a deeper unity that leads him to say, "I came at last to feel as if not one little pebble could be displaced, without injuring the effect of the whole." After diving in, however, Anodos sees that the pool does not have a bottom, indeed he can see for miles beneath the water and feels that were he to come to the surface he would find himself in the middle of a great sea. Rising to the surface, however, he finds himself in the same fairy bath that he had entered (63-4). Not only does Anodos thus experience a temporary illumination in which he is able to see the greater reality visible in the correspondent external appearance of reality, he is also permanently able to experience the "penetralia" of the "outer court" with his senses. This heightened awareness is highlighted by his newfound ability to see the forms of fairies that he had previously only been able to sense intuitively (64).

While in the Fairy Palace, Anodos comes close to reaching sublimation when he wakes the Marble Lady from her pedestal through song. The Marble Lady can be seen as symbolic of absolute beauty, and Anodos's love for her as symbolic of Romantic Love.[6] An alchemical connection is suggested by the colour symbolism of the hall in which he finds the Marble Lady—he must proceed through red curtains from a central chamber with white pillars and a black floor and walls. Before he peeks behind the curtains he sits upon a red throne beside a white table and falls into a reverie of "images of bewildering beauty, which passed before my inward eye," an experience he compares to his first experience of illumination in the cave (93). However, once more Anodos fails the test of selflessness that he must pass to go beyond the stage of coagulation. He attempts to touch and possess the Marble Lady and she flees from him. He attempts to follow her, but in doing so he passes out of the Palace of Fairy Land into a dark chasm, an underworld in which he lives once more the disenchanted experience of the shadow. This time though, Anodos escapes the shadow by choosing the path of coagulation and illumination. He comes to the edge of a grey sea and throws himself into the "heaving abyss" (112). By doing so he accepts the death of his selfish shadow nature, choosing no longer to fear for himself, lust for himself, and claim his accomplishments for his own. The putrefaction of his selfish nature is successful. Anodos chooses to see himself in unity with God and nature, and as he hits the water he is illuminated: "A blessing, like the kiss of a mother, seemed to alight on my soul" (112).

Emerging from the water, Anodos alights on a green island where he meets a Mother Nature figure, representative of the immanent God, living in a pyramidal cottage in the middle of a great sea. The old woman's face is "older than any countenance I had ever looked upon," while her eyes are "very incarnations of soft light" (115), a reference to the moonlit dream or soul knowledge of the hidden nature of phenomena discussed above. Anodos's arrival at the cottage is a sort of homecoming after all his travails in Fairy Land: "A wondrous sense of refuge and repose came upon me." Anodos is aware of the feeling of peace and unity he feels in her embrace, but he is not yet ready to ascend from coagulation to permanent sublimation through knowledge of his oneness with her and with creation. Just as in his encounters with the Beech tree and the Marble Lady, Anodos descends away from sublimation by choosing to leave Mother Nature on her island. Before he departs through one of the four doors in the four walls of her cottage, she instructs him to look for arrows of a certain colour whenever he is out in the world and seeks to find his way back to her. These arrows are a deep red colour, the red of the philosopher's stone, the red of sublimation.

Anodos returns to an existence in which the immanent God is once more hidden, and once more experiences the return of the shadow with the rush of pride he feels after killing a giant. The shadow manifests as the *doppelgänger* knight and locks him in a tower. In the end, Anodos escapes the tower by simply choosing to open the door. The only lock keeping him in the tower had been his failure to see the world and himself as enchanted. By opening the door, he once more moves from putrefaction to coagulation. This time, however, he has become permanently able to resist lapsing into his shadow self. He will not need to return to the *nigredo* state in his journey toward reunification with the divine, but he does encounter it one more time near the close of his experience in Fairy Land. Before Anodos can reach the final stage of sublimation, he must kill the selfish aspect that still lies dormant within him. The great beast that he throttles on the platform, surrounded by a multitude of its worshippers, carries several potential symbolic meanings, but it is most of all a symbol of Anodos's shadow self. MacDonald clearly describes Anodos's killing of the beast as a slaying of his self: Anodos throttles the beast, but as it dies he also loses consciousness, though he can "remember no blow" (161).

Now that he has killed his selfish self, Anodos achieves true sublimation, the state of being equivalent to the philosopher's stone, when the self realizes its unity with all things by virtue of its creation in the divine Imagination. Lying in his coffin, he perceives himself as one with the earth around him: "Now that I lay in her bosom, the whole earth, and each of her many births, was as a body to me, at my will. I seemed to feel the great heart of the mother beating into mine, and feeding me with her own life, her own essential being and nature" (163). This awareness of the correspondence between the body of the earth and his own body, of the essence of the earth and his own essence, is the end goal of imaginative seeing: "The end of imagination is *harmony*. A right imagination, being the reflex of the creation, will fall in with the divine order of things as the highest form of its own operation . . . will be content alone with growth towards the divine idea, which includes all that is beautiful in the imperfect imaginations of men" ("Imagination" 30). Unlike the experiences of putrefaction and coagulation, the alchemical imagery is limited in the description of sublimation. However, after Anodos achieves correspondence between himself and the whole earth, he sees a feathery cloud in the sky, illuminated by the "rosy" beams of the setting sun. After the sun sets, the cloud remains red, for "it carried its rose-hue within" (163). Thus, we do see some colour connections to the red that represents sublimation. More important, however, is the clear thematic connection between alchemical sublimation and Anodos's achievement of oneness with the panentheist God.

Conclusion

The name *Anodos* stems from the Greek for "the way back" or "the way up." The importance of that name in light of the alchemical journey back, or up, to unity with the divine can now be seen. A non-alchemical interpretation of the shadow has resulted in critics missing the significance of this journey, which unites the novel as a cohesive whole rather than the collection of scattered dream scenes it has been accused of being. Like all the symbols in *Phantastes*, the shadow is open to the many possible interpretations of the reader's imagination. Interpretations that miss or purposefully avoid the alchemical symbolism in the novel are therefore certainly valid. However, the long history of interpreting the shadow as merely a symbol of darkness or negativity in a dualistic theodicy results in an interpretation of the novel that lacks the allegorical depth that MacDonald intended. The shadow is symbolic of disenchantment, representative of
a state of being in which the self sees phenomena as devoid of spiritual essence, even though all created matter is inextricably intertwined with spirit by virtue of its creation by the divine Imagination. The shadow functions as the first, ultimately positive stage of the alchemical transmutation of the self. MacDonald's connection of the shadow to the *nigredo* of alchemy places Anodos in a paradoxical state of being in which he is stripped of his knowledge of the panentheistic God in order that he may, through further processes of transmutation, become more truly aware of him.

Endnotes

1. For a review of oedipal readings of the Ash tree, see Gray 880. The article provides a review of much of the Freudian and Jungian analysis that has been applied to *Phantastes*.

2. Gunther, siding with John Docherty, sees *Phantastes* as carefully structured.

3. MacDonald's theory of imagination was influenced by the German and English Romantics, particularly by Samuel Taylor Coleridge's ideas of primary and secondary imagination. See Coleridge 9.5-17.

4. For a cautious approach to the influence of Boehme on MacDonald, see Nelson 24-36.

5. Before beginning his writing career, MacDonald was dismissed from his position as pastor of a congregationalist church at Arundel, England.

6. See Brawley's "The Ideal and the Shadow" for an excellent illustration of the connection of the Marble Lady to Romantic Love.

Works Cited

Boehme, Jacob. *The Confessions of Jacob Boehme*. London: Methuen, 1920.

Brawley, Chris. "The Ideal and the Shadow: George MacDonald's *Phantastes*." *North Wind* 25 (2006): 91-112.

Coleridge, Samuel T. *Biographia Litteraria*. London: Oxford UP, 1907.

Cowan, Yuri. "Allegory and Aestheticism in the Fantasies of George MacDonald." *North Wind* 25 (2006): 39-57.

Docherty, John. "Dryad Fancies and Fairy Imagination in *Phantastes*." *North Wind* 24 (2005): 16-28. Web. 14 Jan. 2012.

—. "The Sources of *Phantastes*." *North Wind* 9 (1990): 38-53. Web. 14 Jan. 2012.

Gray, William N. "George MacDonald, Julia Kristeva, and the Black Sun. *Studies in English Literature*, 1500-1900 36.4 (Autumn 1996): 877-893.

Gunther, Adrian. "The Structure of George MacDonald's *Phantastes*." *North Wind* 12 (1993): 43-59.

Haage, Bernard D. "Alchemy II." *Dictionary of Gnosis and Western Esotericism*. Ed. Wouter Hanegraaff et al. Leiden: Brill, 2005. 17-34.

MacDonald, George. "A Sketch of Individual Development." *A Dish of Orts*. Pennsylvania: Penn

State Electronic Classics Series, 2006. 36-58.

—. *Phantastes*. Suffolk, Great Britain: Boydell Press, 1982.

—. "Self-Denial." *Unspoken Sermons*. Pdfbooks, n.d. 176-86.

—. "The Creation in Christ." *Unspoken Sermons*. 200-209.

—. "The Fantastic Imagination." *A Dish of Orts*. 232-7.

—. "The Imagination: Its Functions and its Culture." *A Dish of Orts*. 6-35.

—. "The Knowing of the Son" *Unspoken Sermons*. 209-16.

—. "The Mirrors of the Lord." *Unspoken Sermons*. 216-21.

—. "Wordsworth's Poetry." *A Dish of Orts*. 182-97.

Manlove, Colin. *Modern Fantasy*. London: Cambridge UP, 1975.

Nelson, Dale J. "MacDonald and Jacob Boehme." *North Wind* 8 (1989): 24-36.

Prickett, Stephen. *Victorian Fantasy*. Sussex: The Harvester Press, 1979.

Principe, Lawrence M. "Alchemy I." *Dictionary of Gnosis and Western Esotericism*. Ed. Wouter Hanegraaff et al. Leiden: Brill, 2005. 12-16.

Reis, Richard H. *George MacDonald*. New York: Twayne Publishers, 1972.

Salvey, Courtney. "Riddled with Evil: Fantasy as Theodicy in George MacDonald's *Phantastes* and *Lilith*." *North Wind* 27 (2008): 16-34.

The Fairy Palace:
Sabbath Restoration and Twilight Vision

Daniel Gabelman

From *George MacDonald: Divine Carelessness and Fairytale Levity*

In an introductory letter to *The Portent*—written in the same year as *Adela Cathcart* (1864)—MacDonald defends the writing and reading of fantastic stories on the basis of their connection with real human experience: "seeing so much of our life must be spent in dreaming, may there not be a still nook, shadowy, but not miasmatic, in some lowly region of literature, where, in the pauses of labour, a man may sit down, and dream such a day-dream as I now offer to your acceptance."[1] Fantasy through dreams is a major element in everyone's life and therefore has just as great a claim to realism as fiction which only deals with the commonplace world. "Escapism" in literature is justified because escape itself is "realistic," for dreams are a natural and healthy part of life.

In the aforementioned quotation, MacDonald emphasizes how important different modes of vision are for a holistic understanding of reality. Fantasy is "shadowy" in that it dims the full force of the sun's light and stimulates creative imaginings, but this does not make it "miasmatic," that is, false or illusory. Instead, this lessening of the "hot noontide unideal" allows for a special mode of perception:[2]

> We have seldom real positive night in this world—so many provisions have been made against it. Every time we say, "What a lovely night!" we speak of a breach, a rift in the old night: there is light more or less, positive light, else were there no beauty. Many a night is but a low starry day, a day with a softened background, against which the far-off suns of millions of other days can show themselves. The near vision vanishes, the far hope awakes. It is not said of heaven there shall be no twilight there.[3]

Rather than ushering in the time of deception, the setting of the sun allows for a different type of optics. Freed from the distractions of the immediate, the eye can reach "millions of other days," and the shy distant stars can shine. The night of our world is really twilight. It is the time for resting from the labours of the day to renew one's strength and the time for dreaming, for seeing beyond the tyrannous clamour of the nearby and awaking the far hope. Similarly, reading or hearing the words "once upon a time" is like looking through "a rift in the old night." It ushers one into the twilit fairyland, where as we have already seen one can rest in a Sabbath realm, but where in addition "the near vision vanishes" so that in the twilight distance "the far hope awakes."

Thus far, I have consciously avoided in-depth discussion of either *Phantastes* or *Lilith* on the grounds that these two longer "adult" fantasies often overshadow the fairytales because they seem to display more characteristics of "seriousness." Critics by and large take the view of Rolland Hein that "because the tales contain more of the absurd and the tone is more light and playful, fresh breakthroughs into the transcendent are more rare" and that the longer fantasies compel the "adult mind," whereas "the fairy tales dilute and simplify these themes so that children can understand them."[4] Yet in interesting ways, *Phantastes* provides metacommentary on the experience of engaging with and being transformed by fairytales. Though they are "light and playful," fairytales are the primary agents of change that teach Anodos "breakthroughs into the transcendent" by enabling him to take himself lightly. By this line of topsy-turvy thinking, *Phantastes* becomes the derivative, secondary work and fairytales the vital, primary creations.

In a strange sense, *Phantastes* is MacDonald's laboratory for testing the effects of fairytales upon readers. Just after his twenty-first birthday, the first-person narrator, Anodos, awakes to find his room transforming into a magical forest, and the book then records his various adventures in fairyland. Here Anodos not only reads fairytales on several occasions and records his reactions but he also enacts them in different episodic encounters (visiting an ogress' cottage, slaying giants, escaping from a tower prison). The epicenter of this engagement with fairytales is the fairy palace and its enchanted library. Stephen Prickett, in a passing comment, draws attention to how "when Anodos is reading in the magic library, his reading seems to be pointing to our experience of reading about him."[5] The fairy palace and its library thus become symbols of the experience of reading fairytales in an ideal state.

Before arriving at the fairy palace, Anodos has several encounters that reveal the vanity of being to him, many of which his newly found shadow initiates. Though there are moments of respite, as when Anodos visits the two human huts and the willow tree, most of his adventures in fairyland up until he reaches the fairy palace are wearisome, so that just before being led to the palace by the river, he is walking "listlessly and almost hopelessly along" with the shadow "in [his] heart as well as at [his] heels."[6] Yet the time that Anodos spends at the fairy palace is a kind of pause in the action—a Sabbath "breach in the old night."

The palace is "the home of wonder itself" in which Anodos finds an exact "copy" of his own room where his attendant shadow "dares not come."[7] He feasts and drinks to his heart's content and then sleeps "dreamless" yet with "a sense of past blessedness."[8] "All the pleasures to be found in the most varied and artistic arrangement" are present in the palace, and Anodos has constant experiences of rest and refreshment. In short, the fairy palace participates fully in festive, Sabbath time—it brings Anodos into momentary contact with eternity. Whereas fairyland outside of the palace tends to be dangerous, dark, and just a little bit sinister—much closer to Tolkien's definition of "Faerie" as "the perilous realm"—inside everything is beautiful, light, and carefree. The fairy palace thus seems to be located within the same festive, Sabbath temporality as MacDonald's fairytales.

Further examination reveals that it is also a place of twilight. Everything is silver rather than gold. Anodos calls it the "palace of marble and silver, and fountains and moonshine," and he records how after bathing in a bath of "the purest, most liquid and radiant water" he begins "to discern faint, gracious forms," which are most visible in moonlight and when he is in the shade.[9] In premodern cosmology, silver is the metal of the moon (just as gold is for the sun). Symbolically, therefore, MacDonald establishes the palace as a twilight place, a "shadowy," "still nook" of literature "where in the pauses of labour a man may sit down, and dream such a day-dream." Both the moon and silver have associations with mirrors as well. Just before arriving at the fairy palace, Anodos calls the moon "the lovelier memory or reflex of the down-gone sun, the joyous day seen in the faint mirror of the brooding night."[10] Mirrors in this case do not trap the vision of the self as with the creatures in the mirrors in "The Shadows"; rather they function like twilight, allowing a person to see beyond the horizon of the immediate. "All mirrors are magic mirrors," says Anodos, because in them "the commonest room is a room in a poem."[11] Twilight likewise has the same power of unveiling the wonder hidden in the commonplace, as can be seen from MacDonald's poem "My Room" (1857):

> [Twilight] stains the air with power estranging
> Known with unknown clouding, changing.
> See in ruddy atmosphere Commonplaceness disappear!
> Look around on either hand—
> Are we not in fairyland?[12]

While the effect of both mirrors and twilight might be described as "magical," this magic is not deceptive but revelatory. It removes the dullness that accrues as a result of habit and familiarity. What disappears is the room's "commonplaceness" not the things themselves. The items lose a certain manner of their appearing, a manner which is itself a distortion or limited way of looking at things. Mirrors lift things "out of the region of fact into the realm of art" such that the "very representing of it" clothes "that which was otherwise hard and bare" "with interest."[13] The problem lies not in *what* we see but in *how* we see. In this way, the twilight mirror of art is not less true than reality, as it is in a strict Platonic sense, but potentially more true:

> Art rescues nature from the weary and sated regards of our senses, and the degrading injustice of our anxious everyday life, and, appealing to the imagination, which dwells apart, reveals Nature in some degree as she really is, and as she represents herself to the eye of the child, whose every-day life, fearless and unambitious, meets the true import of the wonder-teeming world around him, and rejoices therein without questioning.[14]

MacDonald likely borrows this understanding of art from the Romantics, in particular Coleridge's *Biographia Literaria*:

> [Wordsworth was] to give the charm of novelty to things of every day, and to excite a feeling analogous to the supernatural, by awakening the mind's attention from the lethargy of custom, and directing it to the loveliness and the wonders of the world before us; an inexhaustible treasure, but for which in consequence of the film of familiarity and selfish solicitude we have eyes, yet see not.[15]

And, of course, both writers draw upon the biblical tradition in which people often "have eyes, yet see not." Jesus, for example, claims that he teaches in parables "because seeing they do not see, and hearing they do not hear, nor do they understand" (Matt 13:13). Parables awaken "the mind's attention from the lethargy of custom"; they startle and provoke thought, thereby allowing people to see past the "film of familiarity" and into things as they really are. As Oscar Wilde says, "to look at a thing is very different from seeing a thing. One does not see anything until one sees its beauty."[16] When, therefore, MacDonald depicts the fairy palace as the domain of silver, the moon, pools, and reflections, he intends to affiliate it with the power of twilight and mirrors to transform one's vision from looking to seeing.

In addition to resting and restoring his spirits through feasting and playing in the fairy palace, Anodos renews his fairy vision as well. When he finds his shadow, Anodos' vision becomes "disenchanted." Instead of beautiful fairy creatures, he only sees common peasants. But after one deeply refreshing bath in the palace's rainbow pool, he once again begins "to discern faint, gracious forms" moving all about him, and these forms he can see especially well "when they [come] between [him] and the moon; and yet more especially when [he himself is] in the shade."[17] Like the delicate light of stars, there are some things which can only be seen when the harsh light of day wanes and one is still and restful enough to progress beyond looking at a thing and into seeing its beauty. In this restorative environment, Anodos' far-off hope awakens. He begins to wonder if he might find "a magic word of power to banish the demon [shadow]" or "a shadow of light" to "devour" his shadow of darkness.[18] And, of course, his hope reawakens that he might find his "ideal," the marble lady whom he awoke with his song of love. Hope, as we have already seen, was "the one constitutional power of life" in MacDonald; it was the force that lightened the load of his financial difficulties and lifted him up when so many of his family and friends died before him.[19] Hope is thus, we might say, the fuel of transformation. Without hope, even if a person espies the possibility of *ought* becoming *is*, they do not have the energy to strive toward this transformation.

Even more than this, hope helps figure forth the ideal; it creates a playful link or bridge between *is* and *ought* that aids in actualizing metamorphosis. As Shelley says in *Prometheus Unbound*, "to hope till Hope creates / From its own wreck the thing it contemplates" (4, 570). Thus MacDonald calls twilight "a concentrated tumult of undetermined possibilities" because in it "the germs of infinite adventure and result are floating around you like a snow storm."[20] By entering into a fairytale, a reader must let go of himself, all that he rigidly holds on to as "reality," and see the "germs of infinite adventure" that are floating all around him. Like Shelley's description of hope creating "from its own wreck the thing it contemplates," these "germs of infinite adventure" are the intermediaries between *is* and *ought* that make transformation possible.

From Glory to Glory: Mirrors and Metamorphosis

The effects of fairytales upon readers described so far in this chapter are all prior to the culmination of transformation. Vanity breaks an individual out of the enclosed self, Sabbath revitalizes the weary soul, and twilight both reveals the beauty in the commonplace and awakens hope. These are necessary elements of transformation, but they are not its consummation. While transformation for MacDonald never finally finishes until we are perfectly in the image of the Son, he does suggest that fairytales might even have the power to transform readers at an ontological level. Anodos' reading in the fairy library reflects this idea most clearly.

The fairy palace is the structural center of *Phantastes*, and the library is the center of the palace. There is a sort of chiasm (following the pattern A B C B A) in how Anodos arrives at the palace in chapter 10 of the 25-chapter work, departs in chapter 16, and in chapters 12 and 13—the exact middle of the palace episode and the book as a whole—reads fairytales. Fernando Soto observes how Cosmo's "magic mirror intellectually and physically bisects the story" of Anodos and provides the key to understanding the overarching structure of the apparently chaotic narrative.[21] The whole of the romance pivots upon these two little stories—stories that just happen to have eerie echoes of fairytales.

The first story describes a planet that orbits the sun at a greater distance than the earth and where babies are born without erotic love. When the inhabitants hear about love, their longing and hope for something greater leads them—much like Nycteris—to seek a way out of their world and into ours through MacDonald's favorite gateway, death and rebirth. Cosmo's story, meanwhile, parallels almost exactly the episodes and themes of "The Light Princess" and "Little Daylight"—a young man falls in love with a woman enchanted by an evil witch, and the enchantment both brings them together and keeps them apart. Ultimately; Cosmo's self-sacrifice breaks the spell (as with the princes). Both stories from the fairy library, however, take place outside of fairyland—fairies apparently like telling stories of other worlds, too—on a distant planet and in Prague.[22] Yet an even more important contrast with fairytales in terms of genre is that the stories in *Phantastes* elicit strong, weighty emotions, and both end in tragic death. It is as though to holiday from their levity, fairies tell stories of pathos. Like a mirror retaining form and figure but inverting direction, these stories are the uncanny doubles of MacDonald's fairytales.

Within the ludic landscape of the fairy library—a playful mixture of gothic grandeur and baroque excess—Anodos spends from "noon till twilight" reading on "sumptuous eastern carpets" until "weary; if that can be designated as weariness, which was rather the faintness of rapturous delight."[23] His reading magically transports him into the books. If he reads metaphysics, he instantly ponders the truth and begins "constructing the intellectual machine whereby to communicate the discovery," whereas if it is a book of travels he finds himself the traveler.[24] In fictional stories, he becomes "the chief actor therein," experiencing intimately all the fears and joys of the protagonist. Summarizing these reading encounters, Anodos says:

> I did sit in that grand hall, buried and risen again in these old books. And I trust that I have carried away in my soul some of the exhalations of their undying leaves. In after hours of deserved or needful sorrow, portions of what I read there have often come to me again, with an unexpected comforting; which was not fruitless, even though the comfort might seem in itself groundless and vain.[25]

Anodos is like Wordsworth in "Tintern Abbey," who "oft, in lonely rooms, and 'mid the din / of towns and cities" receives "in hours of weariness, sensations sweet" (26-28) from his recollection of beautiful landscapes, though, unlike Wordsworth, for Anodos it is the memory of reading fairytales and not an experience of nature that produces

> That blessed mood,
> In which the burthen of the mystery,
> In which the heavy and weary weight
> Of all this unintelligible world
> Is lighten'd. (38-42)

Oblique allusions to Christ (death and resurrection) and the Holy Spirit ("exhalation," "comfort") meanwhile charge Anodos' assertion with theological force. Reading fairytales in the magic library has soteriological resonances. These salvific undertones may seem excessive, but the structural positioning of these chapters within the narrative suggests even greater import for the reading of fairytales: they effect some fundamental change in the character of Anodos such that instead of spiralling downward as he does in the first half of the book, in the second half he begins to learn from his errors and slowly ascends until his final triumph of self-sacrifice.[26] Furthermore, this final act perfectly mirrors the two interpolated stories: Anodos gives his life for the freedom of others (like Cosmo), and dies only to rise again in a higher world (like the children of the distant planet). In other words, the reading of these stories actualizes some definite change within Anodos. How does MacDonald think this transformation occurs?

A clue can be found in the sermon "The Mirrors of the Lord" (1889), in which MacDonald comments on 2 Corinthians 3:18 ("But we all, with open face beholding as in a glass the glory of the Lord, are changed into the same image from glory to glory, even as by the spirit of the Lord").[27] MacDonald insists on retranslating "beholding as in a glass" with "mirroring" because Paul, like a poet, utilizes the "outer show of things, which outer show is infinitely deeper in its relation to truth, as well as more practically useful, than the analysis of the man of science."[28] Surface is depth, as Oscar Wilde might say (and as "camp" does say). The surface show of a mirror is not "throwing back the rays of light" but "receiving, taking into itself, the things presented to it." The mirror surrounds "the visage with its liquid embrace." MacDonald cites Dante as support (*Inferno*, XXIII, 25-27) before explaining the theological ramifications: "Our mirroring of Christ, then, is one with the presence of his spirit in us. The idea, you see, is not the reflection, the radiating of the light of Christ on others, though that were a figure lawful enough; but the taking into, and having in us, him working to the changing of us."[29] Something ontological occurs when a person reflects upon Jesus—the image of Christ that is held in the mirror of an individual's mind begins to transform that person into the same likeness through the power of the Holy Spirit. Undoubtedly, MacDonald would make a distinction between Jesus shaping a person's soul and a story transforming that person—Jesus is the "sun-glory," the primal source of life and being, whereas all else is "moonlight."[30] Even so, we can easily make the interpretative leap from St. Paul's symbolism of mirrors in 1 Corinthians to MacDonald's symbolism of mirrors in *Phantastes*.

By opening his imagination to the fairytales, Anodos receives more than just a pleasant tale—he mirrors the stories in his mind (according to MacDonald's poetic understanding of mirrors), thereby initiating his own ontological transformation. Anodos narrates the story of the distant planet in the first person as he finds himself mirrored into the fantastic landscape. Then, though it is told in the third person, Anodos recalls Cosmo's story:

> While I read it, I was Cosmo, and his history was mine. Yet, all the time, I seemed to have a kind of double consciousness, and the story a double meaning. Sometimes it seemed only to represent a simple story of ordinary life, perhaps almost of universal life; wherein two souls, loving each other and longing to come nearer, do, after all, but behold each other as in a glass darkly.[31]

The story begins after this passage, but MacDonald significantly omits a discussion of what the story meant "at other times." The universality of Cosmo (not accidentally named) creates the potential for Anodos simultaneously to mirror himself into the story and to mirror the story within himself. There is thus a "double consciousness."[32] By participating in the story and allowing it to participate in him, Anodos undergoes real metamorphosis as he licenses the shaping of his self into the image of Cosmo. Like a "germ of infinite adventure" in the soil of his mind, the fairytale, held in the imagination's "liquid embrace," begins to take on a life of its own, leading finally to the good fruit of freely letting go of the self for the sake of others.

In this way, MacDonald seems to hope that his fairytales will be mirrors within which readers can see themselves so that they too can have a "double consciousness" and simultaneously mirror the fairytale in their mind. As we have already seen, MacDonald's fairytale characters are universal types that aid the functioning of the stories as mirrors, but MacDonald designs the symbolism of the stories to be polyvalent for the same reason. Thus in "The Fantastic Imagination," MacDonald refuses to offer any interpretations of his fairytales to the interlocutor who complains that a person could imagine "what he pleases" rather than what MacDonald meant: "If he be a true man, he will imagine true things; what matter whether I meant them or not."[33] Here MacDonald is not just posturing, attempting to maintain the mystery of his stories; rather he hopes that his fairytales will take on a transformative life of their own within the reader. They cannot do this, however, if an authorial interpretation were to finalize their meaning. Thus, he constantly compares his fairytales to living things such as butterflies, bees, fireflies, and roses, as if to emphasize their ability to grow, morph, and move independent of his will. "My tales may not be roses," he says, "but I will not boil them."[34] Much like Wordsworth's famous line "we murder to dissect," distilling the moral essence kills the ability of the fairytale to evolve independently within each reader. Alive within their readers, fairytales retain the power to transform "from glory to glory." As readers develop, the tales change their meaning and the reader can reapply them to new situations.

Significantly, though, MacDonald depicts the tales as light, defenseless creatures that require the reader's cooperation to live and flourish: "Let fairytale of mine go for a firefly that now flashes, now is dark, but may flash again. Caught in a hand which does not love its kind, it will turn an insignificant, ugly thing, that can neither flash nor fly."[35] But in the right hands, fairytales can foster the metamorphosis of their readers into similarly lighthearted, defenseless creatures, reminiscent of Dante's words:

> Do you not understand that we are worms,

Crossing a Great Frontier

Each born to form the angelic butterfly,
That flies defenseless to the Final Judge?
Why do your souls' pretensions rise so high,
Since you are but defective insects still,
Worms as yet imperfectly evolved? (XI, 124-29)

Endnotes

1. MacDonald, *The Portent* (Whitehorn: Johannesen, 1999), i.

2. MacDonald, *Poetical Works*, vol. 2 (Whitehorn: Johannesen, 1996), 13.

3. George MacDonald, *Castle Warlock* (Whitehorn: Johannesen, 1998), 47-48.

4. Hein, *The Harmony Within* (Chicago: Cornerstone Press, 1999), 178.

5. Prickett, *Romanticism and Religion* (Cambridge: Cambridge University Press, 1976), 239.

6. MacDonald, *Phantastes* (Whitehorn: Johannesen, 2000), 119.

7. MacDonald, *Phantastes*, 130.

8. MacDonald, *Phantastes*, 132.

9. MacDonald, *Phantastes*, 135-37.

10. MacDonald, *Phantastes*, 124.

11. MacDonald, *Phantastes*, 123.

12. acDonald, *Poetical Works*, vol. 2 (Whitehorn: Johannesen, 1996), 14.

13. MacDonald, *Phantastes*, 162.

14. MacDonald, *Phantastes*, 162.

15. Samuel Taylor Coleridge, *The Major Works*, ed. H. J. Jackson (Oxford: Oxford University Press, 2000), 314. See also Shelley's "Mont Blanc" for a similar view of the power of the imagination.

16. Oscar Wilde, *De Profundis and Other Writings* (London: Penguin, 1986), 79.

17. MacDonald, *Phantastes*, 137.

18. MacDonald, *Phantastes*, 134.

19. Sadler, *An Expression of Character* (Grand Rapids, Eerdmans, 1994), 354.

20. MacDonald, *Robert Falconer* (Whitehorn: Johannesen, 1999), 452.

21. Fernando Soto, "Mirrors in MacDonald's *Phantastes*: A Reflective Structure," *North Wind* 23 (2004): 28. See also John Docherty, "A Note on the Structure and Conclusion of *Phantastes*," *North Wind* 7 (1988); Roderick McGillis, "The Community of the Centre: Structure and Theme in *Phantastes*," in *For the Childlike*, ed. Roderick McGillis (Metuchen: Scarecrow, 1992).

22. Wolff says that on account of its earthly setting, the story of Cosmo is "out of place in the library of the fairy palace," but this surely misses MacDonald's point that "Faerie invades the world of men" (*The Golden Key* (New Haven: Yale University Press, 1961), 78; MacDonald, *Phantastes*, 154).

23. MacDonald, *Phantastes*, 139.

24. MacDonald, *Phantastes*, 140.

25. MacDonald, *Phantastes*, 187.

26. There is a Dantesque ascent via descent. While Anodos still fails in the second half—most notably in allowing himself to be imprisoned by his shadow—these failures spur him on to greater acts of humility and letting go of himself

27. MacDonald here quotes from the revised version. After its release in 1881, MacDonald strongly supported the revised version as the most accurate of all English translations.

28. MacDonald, *Unspoken Sermons* (Whitehorn: Johannesen, 2004), 452. MacDonald interestingly defines mysticism in this sermon as "the exercise of a power of seeing, as by spiritual refraction, truths that had not, perhaps have not yet, risen above the human horizon; at another, the result of a wide-eyed habit of noting the analogies and correspondences between the concentric regions of creation."

29. MacDonald, *Unspoken Sermons*, 454.

30. MacDonald, *Unspoken Sermons*, 457.

31. MacDonald, *Phantastes*, 153-54.

32. Wordsworth in *The Prelude* says that when musing on his childhood "often do I seem / Two consciousnesses, conscience of myself / and of some other Being" (2.31-33). MacDonald takes this concept of personal memory and applies it to the reading of stories, suggesting that the stories have a power as emotive and powerful as that of personal memory.

33. MacDonald, *A Dish of Orts* (Whitehorn: Johannesen, 1996), 320.

34. MacDonald, *A Dish of Orts*, 321.

35. MacDonald, *A Dish of Orts*, 321.

Select Bibliography

Letters

Sadler, Glenn Edward. *An Expression of Character: The Letters of George MacDonald*. Grand Rapids, MI: Eerdmans, 1994.

Biography and Critical Biography

Hein, Rolland. *The Harmony Within: The Spiritual Vision of George MacDonald*. Grand Rapids, MI: Eerdmans, 1982.

Johnson, Joseph. *George MacDonald: A Biographical and Critical Appreciation*. London: Sir Isaac Pittman, 1906.

Lewis, C.S. Preface. *George MacDonald: 365 Readings*. New York: Macmillan, 1947. xxi-xxxiv.

MacDonald, Greville. *George MacDonald and His Wife*. London: George Allen and Unwin, 1924.

—. *Reminiscences of a Specialist*. London, 1932.

MacDonald, Ronald. *From a Northern Window*. London, 1911.

Phillips, Michael R. *George MacDonald: Scotland's Beloved Storyteller*. Minneapolis: Bethany House, 1987.

Prickett, Stephen. "Adults in Allegory Land: Kingsley and MacDonald." *Victorian Fantasy*. 2nd ed. Waco, TX: Baylor UP, 2005. 139-71.

Raeper, William. *George MacDonald*. Tring, UK: Lion, 1987.

Reis, Richard. *George MacDonald*. New York: Twayne, 1972.

Robb, David S. *George MacDonald*. Edinburgh: Scottish Academic Press, 1987.

Saintsbury, Elizabeth. *George MacDonald: A Short Life*. Edinburgh: Cannongate, 1987.

Triggs, Kathy. *George MacDonald: The Seeking Heart*. London: Pickering and Inglis, 1984.

—. *The Stars and the Stillness: A Portrait of George MacDonald*. Cambridge: Lutterworth, 1986.

Wolff, Robert Lee. *The Golden Key: A Study of the Fiction of George MacDonald*. New Haven, CT: Yale UP, 1961.

BIBLIOGRAPHY

Bulloch, J.M. "A Centennial Bibliography of George MacDonald." *Aberdeen University Library Bulletin* 5 (1925): 679-747.

Hutton, Muriel. "The George MacDonald Collection: Brander Library, Huntly." *The Book Collector* 17 (1968): 13-25.

—. "Sour Grapeshot." *Aberdeen University Review* 41 (1965): 85-88.

Shaberman, R.B. *George MacDonald's Books for Children: A Bibliography of First Editions*. London: Cityprint Business Centres, 1979.

—. *George MacDonald: A Bibliographical Study*. Winchester: St. Paul's Bibliographies, 1990.

COLLECTIONS OF ESSAYS

Harriman, Lucas, ed. *Lilith in a New Light: Essays on the George MacDonald Fantasy Novel*. Jefferson, NC: McFarland, 2008.

Himes, Jonathan B., ed. *Truths Breathed Through Silver: The Inklings' Moral and Mythopoeic Legacy*. Newcastle, UK: Cambridge Scholars, 2008.

MacLachlan, Christopher, John Patrick Pazdziora, and Ginger Stelle, eds. *Rethinking George MacDonald: Contexts and Contemporaries*. Glasgow: Scottish Literature International, 2013.

McGillis, Roderick, ed. *For the Childlike: George MacDonald's Fantasies for Children*. Metuchen, NJ: Scarecrow, 1992.

—, ed. *George MacDonald: Literary Heritage and Heirs*. Wayne, PA: Zossima Press, 2008.

Pennington, John, and Roderick McGillis, eds. *Behind the Back of the North Wind: Critical Essays on George MacDonald's Classic Children's Book*. Hamden, CT:

Winged Lion Press, 2011.

—, eds. Phantastes: *A Collection of Critical Essays*. Hamden, CT: Winged Lion Press, 2017.

Raeper, William, ed. *The Gold Thread: Essays of George MacDonald*. Edinburgh: Edinburgh UP, 1990.

Webb, Jean, ed. *A Noble Unrest: Contemporary Essays on George MacDonald*. Newcastle, UK: Cambridge Scholars Publishing, 2007.

Literary Studies of *Phantastes*

Adams, Gillian. "Student Responses to *Alice in Wonderland* and *At the Back of the North Wind*." *Children's Literature Association Quarterly* 10.1 (Spring 1985): 6-9.

Bilbro, Jeffrey. "Phantastical Regress: The Return of Desire and Deen in *Phantastes* and *The Pilgrim's Regress*." *Mythlore* 28 (2010): 3-4; 21-37.

Brawley, Chris. "The Ideal and the Shadow: George MacDonald's *Phantastes*." *North Wind: A Journal of George MacDonald Studies* 25 (2006): 91-112.

Bruce, Sylvia. "Entering the Vision: A Novelist's View of *Phantastes*." *Seven* 9 (1988): 19-28.

Burt, Michael. "*Phantastes* and the Development of the Imagination." *North Wind: A Journal of George MacDonald Studies* 35 (2016): 89-103.

Cowan, Yuri. "Allegory and Aestheticism in the Fantasies of George MacDonald." *North Wind: A Journal of George MacDonald Studies* 25 (2006): 39-57.

Creed, Daniel. "Connecting Dimensions: Direction, Location, and Form in the Fantasies of George MacDonald." *North Wind: A Journal of George MacDonald Studies* 33 (2014): 1-20.

Docherty, John. "A Note on the Structure and Conclusion of *Phantastes*." *North Wind: A Journal of George MacDonald Studies* 7 (1988): 25-30.

—. "The Sources of *Phantastes*." *North Wind: A Journal of George MacDonald Studies* 9 (1990): 38-53.

—. "Dryad Fancies and Fairy Imaginations in *Phantastes*." *North Wind: A Journal of George MacDonald Studies* 24 (2005): 16-28.

Elliott, Nathan R. "A More Rational Hope: The Influence of George MacDonald's Novel *Phantastes* on Hopkins' Short Story 'The Dolphin.'" *Hopkins Quarterly* 28.3-4 (Summer-Fall 2001): 103-13.

Gaarden, Bonnie. "George MacDonald's *Phantastes*: The Spiral Journey to the Goddess." *The Victorian Newsletter* 96 (Fall 1999): 53-69.

Gabelman, Daniel. *George MacDonald: Divine Carelessness and Fairytale Levity*. Waco, TX: Baylor UP, 2013.

Gray, Willian. "George MacDonald, Julia Kristeva, and the Black Sun." *Studies in English Literature* 36.4 (Autumn 1996): 877-93.

—. "A Source for the Trampling Scene in *Jekyll and Hyde*." *Notes and Queries* 52.4 (2005): 493-4.

Green, Melody. "George MacDonald and Celtic Christianity." *North Wind: A Journal of George MacDonald Studies* 35 (2015): 103-13

Gunther, Adrian. "*Phantastes*: The First Two Chapters." *Scottish Literary Journal* 21.1 (1994): 32-43.

—. "The Multiple Realms of George MacDonald's *Phantastes*." *Studies in Scottish Literature* 29.1 (1996): 174-90.

—. "The Structure of George MacDonald's *Phantastes*." *North Wind: A Journal of George MacDonald Studies North Wind* 12 (1993): 43-59.

Holbrook, David. "George MacDonald and Dreams of the Other World." *Seven* 4 (1983): 27-37.

Howard, Susan. "In Search of Spiritual Maturity—George MacDonald's *Phantastes*." *Extrapolation* 30.3 (1989): 280-92.

Knoepflmacher, U.C. *Ventures into Childland: Victorians, Fairy Tales, and Femininity*. Chicago: U of Chicago P, 1998. 228-68.

Litten, Jonathan. "*Phantastes*: All Mirrors are Magic

Mirrors." *North Wind: A Journal of George MacDonald Studies* 35 (2016): 104-25.

MacIntyre, J. "*Phantastes* into Alice." *Newsletter of the Victorian Studies Association of Western Canada* 3.2 (Spring 1977): 6-9.

Manlove, Colin. *Modern Fantasy*. Cambridge, Cambridge UP, 1975.

—. "The Circle of the Imagination: George MacDonald's *Phantastes* and *Lilith*." *Studies in Scottish Literature* 17.1 (1982): 55-80.

—. *The Impulse of Fantasy Literature*. Kent, OH: Kent State UP, 1983.

McGillis, Roderick. "A Fairytale is Just a Fairytale": George MacDonald and the Queering of Fairy." *Marvels and Tales* 17.1 (2003): 86-99.

—. "The Community of the Centre: Structure and Theme in *Phantastes*." In *For the Childlike: George MacDonald's Fantasies for Children*, ed. Roderick McGillis. Metuchen, NJ: Scarecrow, 1992. 51-65.

—. "*Phantastes* and *Lilith*: Femininity and Freedom." *The Gold Thread: Essays on George MacDonald*. Ed. William Raeper. Edinburgh: Edinburgh UP, 1990: 31-55.

Moss, Anita. "'Felicitous Space' in the Fantasies of George MacDonald and Mervyn Peake." *Mythlore* 30 (Winter 1982): 16-17; 42.

Muirhead, Graeme A. "Meta-Phantastes: A Self-Referential Faerie Romance for Men and Women." *Scottish Literary Journal* 19.2 (1992): 36-49.

Pennington, John. "From Fact to Fantasy in Victorian Fiction: Dickens's *Hard Times* and MacDonald's *Phantastes*. *Extrapolation* 38.3 (1997): 200-06.

—. "*Phantastes* as Metafiction: George MacDonald's Self-Reflexive Myth." *Mythlore* 53 (Spring 1988): 26-29.

—. "George MacDonald as Rock Star?" *North Wind: A Journal of George MacDonald Studies* 25 (2006): 124-6.

—. "Let the Wild Rumpus Start: Desire in MacDonald's

Phantastes and Sendak's *Where the Wild Things Are*." *North Wind: A Journal of George MacDonald Studies* 35 (2016): 126.34.

Pionke, Albert D. "The Art of Manliness: Ekphrasis and/as Masculinity in George MacDonald's *Phantastes*." *Studies in the Novel* 43.1 (2011): 21-37.

Prickett, Stephen. *Romanticism and Religion: The Tradition of Coleridge and Wordsworth in the Victorian Church*. Cambridge: Cambridge UP, 1976.

—. "Fictions and Metafictions: 'Phantastes,' 'Wilhelm Meister,' and the Idea of the Bildungsroman. *The Gold Thread: Essays on George MacDonald*. Ed. William Raeper. Edinburgh: Edinburgh UP, 1990: 109-25.

—. *Victorian Fantasy*. 2nd ed. Waco, TX: Baylor UP, 2005.

Roukema, Aren. "The Shadow of Anodos: Alchemical Symbolism in *Phantastes*." *North Wind: A Journal of George MacDonald Studies* 31 (2012): 48-63.

Salvey, Courtney. "Riddled with Evil: Fantasy as Theodicy in George MacDonald's *Phantastes* and *Lilith*." *North Wind: A Journal of George MacDonald Studies* 27 (2008): 16-34.

Searsmith, Kelly. "The Angel in the Cosmos: *Phantastes's* Recasting of the New Gentleman." *The Journal of Pre-Raphaelite Studies* 8 (Fall 1999): 53-69.

Sigman, Joseph. "Death's Ecstasies: Transformation and Rebirth in George MacDonald's *Phantastes*." *English Studies in Canada* 2.2 (Summer 1976): 203-226.

Soto, Fernando J. "Mirrors in MacDonald's *Phantastes*: A Reflexive Stucture." *North Wind: A Journal of George MacDonald Studies* 23 (2004): 27-47.

—. "Chthonic Aspects of MacDonald's *Phantastes*: From the Rising of the Goddess to the Anodos of Anodos." *North Wind: A Journal of George MacDonald Studies* 19 (2000): 19-49.

Sung, Eunai. "The Evolution of British Bildungsroman:

George MacDonald's *Phantastes*." *British and American Fiction* 21.1 (2014: 27-50.

Sutton, Max Keith. "The Psychology of the Self in MacDonald's *Phantastes*." *Seven* 5 (1984): 9-25.

Thomson, Patricia. "*Phantastes* and His Horoscope." *Notes and Queries* 13 (1966): 203-26.

Walsh, Susan A. "Darling Mothers, Devilish Queens: The Divided Woman in Victorian Fantasy." *The Victorian Newsletter* 72 (1987): 32-6.

Williamson, James T. "The Fourfold Myth of Death and Rebirth in George MacDonald's *Phantastes*." *North Wind: A Journal of George MacDonald Studies* 33 (2014): 35-69.

Wilson, Keith. "The Quest for 'The Truth': A Reading of George MacDonald's *Phantastes*." *Etudes Anglaises* 34.2 (1981): 141-52.

Websites

North Wind: A Journal of George MacDonald Studies: Full-text articles from *North Wind*: 1982-most current issue. http://digitalcommons.snc.edu/northwind/

Orts: The Newsletter of the George MacDonald Society. Full-text newsletters from *Orts*: 1981-most current issue. http://digitalcommons.snc.edu/orts/

The George MacDonald Collection: Manuscripts of MacDonald's Writings from Brander Library, Huntly Collection. http://www.aberdeenshire.gov.uk/libraries/information/georgemacdonald/index.asp

The George MacDonald Society: Official webpage of the Society. http://www.macdonaldsociety.org

The Golden Key. http://www.george-macdonald.com

The Victorian Web: George MacDonald. http://www.victorianweb.org/authors/gm/index.html

Wingfold: Celebrating the Work of George MacDonald. http://pages.prodigy.net/b_amell/wingfold1.html

Contributors

Richard Reis was Chair of the English Department at the University of Massachusetts, Dartmouth, United States, and is Professor Emeritus of English at Southeastern Massachusetts University. His book *George MacDonald* (Twayne, 1972) was updated as *George MacDonald's Fiction: A Twentieth-Century View* (Sunrise Books, 1989) and remains a key critical work on MacDonald.

Joseph Sigman—from McMaster University, Ontario, Canada—has published widely on authors ranging from George MacDonald, Thomas Carlyle to Kurt Vonnegut. He is also the co-editor, with James D. Brasch, of Ernest Hemingway's library.

Keith Wilson is Professor Emeritus of English at the University of Ottawa, Canada. His primary research interests include 19th and 20th century British Literature, with secondary expertise in Victorian and Edwardian music hall. He is the co-editor, with Michael Millgate, of *The Collected Letters of Thomas Hardy: Volume VIII* (Oxford UP, 2012) and editor of *The Mayor of Casterbridge* by Thomas Hardy (Penguin Classics, 1997), as well as the author of *Thomas Hardy on Stage* (Macmillan and St. Martins, 1995).

Rolland Hein, Emeritus Professor of English at Wheaton College, Illinois, United States, is involved with the Wade Center at Wheaton, which is a research center devoted to the following authors: Owen Barfield, G.K. Chesterton, C.S. Lewis, George MacDonald, Dorothy L. Sayers, J.R.R. Tolkien, and Charles Williams. His most recent publications include *Christian Mythmakers: C. S. Lewis, Madeleine L'Engle, J. R. R. Tolkien, George MacDonald, G. K. Chesterton & Others* (2nd ed. Wipf & Stock, 2014) and *Through the Year with George MacDonald: 366 Daily Readings* (Winged Lion, 2011).

Colin Manlove is the author of numerous works on fantasy in general and MacDonald in particular, including *Christian Fantasy: From 1200 to the Present* (U of Notre Dame P, 1992); *From Alice to Harry Potter: Children's Fantasy in England* (Lisa Loucks Christenson Publishing, 2003); and *C. S. Lewis: His Literary Achievement* (Winged Lion 2010). His latest work is *Scotland's Forgotten Treasure: The Visionary Novels of George MacDonald* (Aberdeen UP, 2017).

Max Keith Sutton, a teacher of English as the University of Kansas, United States, has published on a variety of authors, including MacDonald, Robert Browning, Sabine Baring-Gould, T. E. Brown, W. S. Gilbert, and Gerard Manley Hopkins. He is the author of *W. S. Gilbert* (Twayne, 1975), *R. D. Blackmore* (Twayne, 1979), and *The Drama of Storytelling in T. E. Brown's Manx Yarns* (U of Delaware P, 2004).

David S. Robb is Professor Emeritus of English at the University of Dundee, Scotland. He has published widely on MacDonald, Sydney Goodsir Smith, Hugh Miller, and Muriel Spark. His recent books include *Auld Campaigner: A Life of Alexander Scott* (Dunedin Academic Press, 2007) and *Robert Louis Stevenson* (Northcote, 2016). He has served as Joint Editor of the Scottish Writers series and General Editor of the Scottish Classics series.

Stephen Prickett is the President of the George MacDonald Society. He is the author of numerous works, including *Romanticism and Religion: The Tradition of Coleridge and Wordsworth in the Victorian Church* (Cambridge UP, 1976; 2008), *Victorian Fantasy* (2nd ed., Baylor, 2005), and (as editor with David Jasper), *The Bible and Literature: A Reader* (Blackwell, 2007).

John Docherty was the editor of *North Wind: A Journal of George MacDonald Studies* and *Orts: The Newsletter of the George MacDonald Society* for many years. He is the author of *The Literary Products of the Lewis Carroll-George MacDonald Friendship* (2nd ed., Edwin Mellen, 1997).

Roderick McGillis is Emeritus Professor of English, the University of Calgary, Canada. He has edited, with John Pennington, the Broadview edition of MacDonald's *At the Back of the North Wind* and an accompanying volume, *Behind the North Wind: Critical Essays on George MacDonald's Classic Children's Book* (Winged Lion, 2011). He is the editor of *For the Childlike: George MacDonald's Fantasies for Children* (Scarecrow, 1992) and *George MacDonald: Literary Heritage and Heirs* (Zossima, 2008). Additional books include *He Was Some Kind of a Man: Masculinities in the B Western* (Wilfrid Laurier UP, 2009) and *Voices of the Other: Children's Literature and the Postcolonial Context* (Routledge, 2012).

Essays on George MacDonald's *Phantastes*

Graeme A. Muirhead studied English at the University of Glasgow, Ireland, before pursuing a career in library services and the software industry. He has edited two books and written a number of articles on library automation, including *Planning and Implementing Successful System Migrations* (1997) and *The Systems Librarian: Role of the Library Systems Manager* (1994).

Adrian Gunther is a teacher and researcher at the University of New England, Armidale, New South Wales. She has focused her research on MacDonald, though she has also written on Frances Hodgson Burnett.

William Gray is retired Professor of Literary History and Hermeneutics at the University of Chichester, United Kingdom. His publications include *Fantasy, Art and Life* (Cambridge Scholars Publishing, 2011), *Death and Fantasy: Essays on George MacDonald, C.S. Lewis, Philip Pullman and R.L. Stevenson*, (Cambridge Scholars Publishing, 2008), *Fantasy, Myth, and the Measure of Truth: Tales of Pullman, Lewis, Tolkien, MacDonald and Hoffmann* (Palgrave, 2008), *Robert Louis Stevenson: A Literary Life* (Palgrave, 2004), and *C. S. Lewis* (Northcote, 1998). He also founded the Sussex Centre for Folklore, Fairy Tales and Fantasy. More about his work can be found at williamgray.org.

John Pennington, editor of *North Wind: A Journal of George MacDonald Studies*, is a professor of English at St. Norbert College, Wisconsin, United States. He is the co-editor, with Roderick McGillis, of MacDonald's *At the Back of the North Wind* (Broadview, 2011) and *Phantastes* (Winged Lion, 2017). With McGillis, he is also editor of *Behind the Back of the North Wind: Critical Essays on George MacDonald's Classic Children's Book* (Winged Lion, 2011).

Bonnie Gaarden is professor of English at Edinboro University of Pennsylvania, United States, where she teaches Mythology and Literature of the Bible. She has published extensively on MacDonald in various journals, including *The Victorian Newsletter*, *Mythlore*, *Studies in the Novel*, *Scottish Studies Review*, and *North Wind: A Journal of George MacDonald Studies*. She is the author of *The Christian Goddess: Archetype and Theology in the Fantasies of George MacDonald* (Fairleigh Dickinson UP, 2011).

Crossing a Great Frontier

Kelly Searsmith is an independent scholar who earned her doctorate in British Victorian literature at the University of Illinois at Urbana-Champaign, United States, completing a dissertation on the reformist poetic in the long Victorian fairy tale. She has served as an associate editor for the *Journal of the Fantastic in the Arts* (she continues as a reader) and as tenure-track faculty at Appalachian State University. Her research focuses on the global nineteenth century and the folkloric and fantastic arts' engagement with and transformations of the collective make-believe of culture.

Fernando Soto, a co-editor of *North Wind: A Journal of George MacDonald Studies*, has published widely on MacDonald in such journals as *Inklings*, *Studies in Scottish Literature*, and *North Wind: A Journal of George MacDonald Studies*.

Yuri Cowan is Professor in the Department of Language and Literature at the Norwegian University of Science and Technology (NTNU) in Trondheim, Norway, specializing in book history, nineteenth-century literature, and medievalism. He has published articles on topics including William Morris's book collecting and the Kelmscott Press; the Aesthetic Movement; ballad anthologies; Victorian sporting periodicals; and the reprinting of Victorian fantasy in the 1970s. He is also a founding editor of the online peer-reviewed open-access journal *Authorship*.

Courtney Salvey explores the intersections of literature, technology, and religion in nineteenth-century Britain in her work. She has written on Joseph Conrad, George MacDonald, and Victorian industrial travel writing. Currently, she is converting her doctoral thesis, which she completed at the University of Kent, into a book manuscript. She teaches at Augsburg University, Minnesota, United States.

Aren Roukema is a Social Sciences and Humanities Research Council of Canada doctoral fellow, currently completing his PhD dissertation at Birkbeck, University of London, United Kingdom. His research focuses on the cultural expressions of esoteric movements and traditions, particularly those related to Anglo-American literature. He is editor of *Correspondences: Online Journal for the Academic Study of Western* Esotericism, and Co-Director of the London Science Fiction Research Community.

Daniel Gabelman received his PhD in literature from the University of St. Andrews, Scotland. He has published articles on Lord Byron, MacDonald, G. K. Chesterton, and C. S. Lewis. His most recent work is *George MacDonald: Divine Carelessness and Fairytale Levity* (Baylor UP, 2013).

PERMISSIONS

Richard Reis, "Phantastes: Full-Length Adult Fantasies." From *George MacDonald's Fiction: A Twentieth-Century View*, Sunrise Books, 1989, pp. 86-94. Originally published by Twayne, 1972, as *George MacDonald*. Used by permission of Sunrise Books.

Joseph Sigman, "Death's Ecstasies: Transformation and Rebirth in George MacDonald's *Phantastes*," *ESC: English Studies in Canada*, vol. 2, no. 2, Summer 1976, pp. 203-26. Used by permission of *ESC*.

Keith Wilson, "The Quest for 'The Truth': A Reading of George MacDonald's *Phantastes*." *Études Anglaises*, vol. 34, no. 2, 1981, pp. 141-52. Used by permission of *Études Anglaises*.

Rolland Hein, "Wells and Cisterns: *Phantastes*." From *The Harmony Within: The Spiritual Vision of George MacDonald*, Eerdmans, 1982, pp. 54-84. Used by permission of the author.

C. N. Manlove, "Circularity in Fantasy: George MacDonald." From *The Impulse of Fantasy Literature*, Kent State UP, 1983, pp. 70-92. An earlier version of this essay appeared as "The Circle of the Imagination: George MacDonald's *Phantastes* and *Lilith*," *Studies in Scottish Literature*, vol. 17, 1982, pp. 55-80. Used by permission of the author.

Max Keith Sutton, "The Psychology of the Self in MacDonald's *Phantastes*." *VII: Journal of the Marion E. Wade Center* (formerly *Seven: An Anglo-American Literary Review*), vol. 5, 1984, 9-25. Used by permission from the Marion E. Wade Center, Wheaton College, Wheaton, IL.

David S. Robb, "*Phantastes* and *Lilith*." From *God's Fiction: Symbolism and Allegory in the Works of George MacDonald*, Sunrise Books, 1989. Originally published as *George MacDonald*, Scottish Academic Press, 1987, pp. 77-108. Used by permission of the author.

Stephen Prickett, "From *Bildungsroman* to Death-Romance: *Phantastes*, *Lilith*, and German Romanticism." From *Victorian Fantasy*, 2nd revised and expanded ed., Baylor UP, 2005. An earlier version of this essay appeared as "Fictions and Metafictions: 'Phantastes', 'Wilhelm Meister', and the Idea of the 'Bildungsroman.'" From *The Gold Thread: Essays on George* MacDonald, ed. by William Raeper, Edinburgh UP, 1990, pp. 109-25. Used by permission of Baylor UP.

John Docherty, "The Sources of *Phantastes*." *North Wind: A Journal of George MacDonald Studies*, vol. 9, 1990, pp. 38-53. Used by permission of the George MacDonald Society.

Roderick McGillis, "The Community of the Centre: Structure and theme in *Phantastes*." From *For the Childlike: George MacDonald's Fantasies for Children*, Scarecrow Press and the Children's Literature Association, 1992, 51-65. Used by permission of the author.

Graeme A. Muirhead, "Meta-*Phantastes*: A Self-Referential Faerie Romance for Men and Women." *Scottish Literary Journal*, vol. 19, no. 2, 1992, pp. 36-49. Used by permission of the author.

Adrian Gunther, "The Multiple Realms of George MacDonald's *Phantastes*." *Studies in Scottish Literature*, vol. 29, issue 1, 1996: 173-90. Used by permission of *SSL*.

William Gray, "George MacDonald, Julia Kristeva, and the Black Sun." From *Death and Fantasy: Essays on Philip Pullman, C. S. Lewis, George MacDonald and R. L. Stevenson*, Cambridge Scholars Publishing, 2009. An earlier version of the essay appeared as "George MacDonald, Julia Kristeva, and the Black Sun." *Studies in English Literature*, vol. 36, 1996, 877-93. Used by permission of the author.

John Pennington, "From Fact to Fantasy in Victorian Fiction: Dickens's *Hard Times* and MacDonald's *Phantastes*." *Extrapolation*, vol. 38, no. 3, 1997, pp. 200-06. Used by permission of *Extrapolation*.

Essays on George MacDonald's *Phantastes*

Bonnie Gaarden, "George MacDonald's *Phantastes*: The Spiral Journey to the Goddess." *The Victorian Newsletter*, vol. 96, Fall 1999, pp. 6-14. Used by permission of *The Victorian Newsletter* and the author.

Kelly Searsmith, "The Angel in the Cosmos: *Phantastes's* Recasting of the New Gentleman." *The Journal of Pre-Raphaelite Studies*, vo. 8, Fall 1999, pp. 53-69. Used by permission of the author.

Fernando Soto, "Mirrors in MacDonald's *Phantastes*: A Reflexive Structure." *North Wind: A Journal of George MacDonald Studies*, vol. 23, 2004, pp. 27-47. Used by permission of the George MacDonald Society and the author.

Yuri Cowan, "Allegory and Aestheticism in the Fantasies of George MacDonald." *North Wind: A Journal of George MacDonald Studies*, vol. 25, 2006, pp. 39-57. Used by permission of the George MacDonald Society and the author.

Courtney Salvey, "Riddled with Evil: Fantasy as Theodicy in George MacDonald's *Phantastes* and *Lilith*," *North Wind: A Journal of George MacDonald Studies*, vol. 25, 2008, pp. 16-34. Used by permission of the George MacDonald Society and the author.

Aren Roukema, "The Shadow of Anodos: Alchemical Symbolism in *Phantastes*." *North Wind: A Journal of George MacDonald Studies*, vol. 31, 2012, pp. 48-63. Used by permission of the George MacDonald Society and the author.

Daniel Gabelman, "The Fairy Palace: Sabbath Restoration and Fairytale Levity." From *George MacDonald: Divine Carelessness and Fairytale Levity* (Baylor University Press, 2013), pages 184-94. Used by permission of Baylor UP.

INDEX

A Dish of Orts, 116, 138, 219, 236, 238-239, 260, 369, 371, 373, 378

Abrams, M. H., 39, 46, 50, 52, 216, 289-290

Aesthetic Movement, 365-366, 368-369, 371-372, 374, 377-380

Alastor, 30, 124, 195

Alder Tree, 58, 105, 230, 415

Alder-Maiden, 19-20, 124, 129, 160, 217, 266-267, 298, 324, 327-328, 342

Alice's Adventures in Wonderland, 223, 238

allegory, 4, 19, 65, 121, 145, 159, 164, 174, 179, 196, 204, 283-284, 365, 365, 368-374, 376-380, 390-391, 396

archetype, 28-30, 32-33, 42-43, 48-49, 92, 116, 124, 129-130, 132, 135-138, 140, 147, 227, 257

Arthurian Romances, 19

Ash, 3, 4, 19, 35-36, 41, 58-59, 73-74, 76, 98, 101-102-, 105-106, 108, 112, 129-131, 160, 224, 244-245, 263-264, 267, 293-294, 296-298, 321, 324, 343-345, 407, 413-417

At the Back of the North Wind, 11, 15, 53, 72, 87, 90, 229, 283, 290

Athenæum, 4, 14, 23, 129, 210,, 230, 283, 376-387, 379, 407

Auden, W. H., 17-18, 121, 230, 227, 238

Augustine, 172, 183, 388-390, 394, 397-398

"Ballad of Sir Aglovaile," 72, 83, 127, 156, 202

Beech Tree, 28, 46, 73-74, 105-106, 124, 153, 155, 224, 245-246, 258, 292, 294, 299, 301, 370, 415, 419

Bible, 46, 145, 202, 313

Bildungsroman, 108, 169, 179, 182-183, 185, 187-188, 193-194, 270, 277, 284, 291, 314, 334, 444

Biographia Literaria, 51, 428

Black Sun, 261-262, 266-269, 271-273, 275, 277, 333, 407, 410-413, 433

Blake, William, 46, 50, 96, 108, 173, 213, 219, 274

Bleak House, 1

Boehme, Jacob, 405, 411, 422

Brawley, Chris, 415-416, 422

Bunyan, John, 183, 283

Calvin, John, 160-162, 367, 408

Carlyle, Thomas, 3, 6, 53, 93, 117, 170, 179, 181, 184-185, 192, 201, 278, 287, 315

Carroll, Lewis, 5, 53-54, 122, 177, 204, 206, 273, 373

centrifugal, 108-109, 210

centripetal, 109-210

chain adventure story, 18, 227

Chaucer, Geoffrey, 45, 145, 376, 380

Chesterton, G. K., 6-7, 53, 137-138, 142, 365

Christ, 26, 42-43, 46, 59, 114, 131-134, 142, 152, 188, 197, 202, 274, 292, 297-298, 301-302, 305, 307, 309, 313-314, 317-318, 329, 367, 411, 431-432

Christian, 4, 7, 26, 42, 54, 69-70, 72, 78-79, 89-90, 114-115, 120, 160, 175, 241, 257, 268, 290, 297, 313, 315-317, 323, 328, 360-361, 365, 368, 380, 388, 393, 408, 442

Coleridge, Samuel Taylor, 3, 36, 44, 51, 61, 128, 145, 149, 156, 170, 178, 195, 215, 233, 239, 289, 299, 324, 367, 411-412, 422, 428, 435

Cosmo, 37, 61, 72, 80-81, 83, 98-99, 108, 112, 119, 134-137, 208, 212, 214, 216-219, 231, 265, 258, 270, 300, 322, 336, 338, 350-354, 360, 430-432, 436

country maiden, 58, 71, 73, 212-214, 217, 263

Cowan, Yuri, 11, 365, 407

Dante, 29, 31, 42, 183, 201, 204, 388, 432-433

The Divine Comedy, 201

David Elginbrod, 62, 113

death, 5, 9, 20, 23, 26, 28, 30-36, 38-39, 43-47, 49, 53-54, 63, 72, 76, 80, 82-85, 88, 90-92, 97-99, 103, 105-108, 111-115, 118, 123, 128, 130-131, 134-136, 148, 150, 152, 155, 160, 162-166, 169, 188, 195, 200, 202, 208, 209, 212-216, 219-220, 232, 244, 251, 253, 254, 257-258, 260-262, 270-271, 274, 276, 285, 289, 292, 296, 299-300, 303-304, 317-318, 321, 324-325, 327-329, 341-342, 351, 354-355, 361, 363, 374, 376, 387-388, 398, 400-404, 411, 413, 417, 419, 430-431, 445

Decadents, 366

Dickens, Charles, 11-3, 6, 8, 53, 188, 194, 203, 279-281, 283-286, 289, 318

Bleak House, 1

Docherty, John, 11, 195, 205, 206, 219, 335, 355, 357, 359, 360, 422, 436

Doppelgänger, 20, 21, 92, 272, 304, 415, 416, 420

"Dover Beach," 147-149, 153, 202, 203, 270

Dr Jekyll and Mr Hyde, 131

Duplex Texts, 231

Eagleton, Terry, 1, 2

ego, 24, 25, 26, 33, 37, 39-41, 43, 44, 86, 128, 130, 131, 134, 256, 272, 289, 297, 300, 309, 319, 322, 349, 353, 398

Eliot, George, 2, 170

Empson, William, 122, 138

Epipsychidion, 35, 208, 210

Erikson, Erik, 261-272

evil, 15, 21, 36, 42, 65, 73, 87, 89, 98, 99, 101-106, 110-114, 118, 120, 152, 160-165, 172, 186, 198, 199, 232, 259, 266, 268, 269, 274, 285, 296, 297, 343, 346, 350, 352, 365, 375, 387-404, 407, 413, 416, 430

Fairy Palace, 39, 42, 62, 79, 81, 83, 86, 99, 101, 102, 105, 106, 108, 112, 113, 126, 150, 154, 155, 197, 198, 207, 209, 211, 213, 217, 225, 226, 228, 230, 231, 235, 246, 248, 250, 251, 252, 254-257, 260, 299, 300, 320, 321, 325, 327, 390, 391, 394, 419, 425-430, 436

Fairy Land, 4, 12, 24-27, 29, 35-37, 42, 44, 57-61, 63, 70-73, 77, 79, 80, 83, 99, 100-102, 104, 106-108, 112, 114, 121, 123, 126-129, 133, 135, 136, 138, 148, 155, 183, 185, 186, 188, 197, 199, 200, 208, 209, 211, 214, 215, 224, 226, 228, 229-231, 243-245, 256, 263, 270, 292, 293, 295-297, 299, 301, 306, 307, 319, 320, 322-325, 327-330, 337-340, 352, 354, 367, 370, 372, 376, 382, 395, 396, 412, 417, 419, 420

Fantasy, 1, 3-8, 10, 11, 15, 16, 23, 27, 47, 54, 59, 62, 63, 65, 69, 70, 85, 90, 95, 96, 99, 116-118, 123, 124, 129, 135, 137-142, 146, 151, 153, 157, 158, 160, 167, 169, 171, 175, 178, 182, 187, 192, 194, 200, 205, 207, 210, 223, 228, 236, 238, 239, 241, 261, 271, 274, 276, 279, 280, 282-285, 289, 290, 301, 309, 313, 314, 322, 328, 349, 365, 371, 374, 379, 382, 387, 395, 411, 425

"The Fantastic Imagination," 116, 138, 142, 284, 369, 374, 407, 433

felix culpa, 268

female, 24, 25, 27-29, 35, 37, 38, 40, 41, 59, 72, 92, 105, 198, 130, 204, 217, 218, 227, 250, 254, 266, 292, 296, 297, 317, 322, 342, 345, 346, 348, 349, 354

feminine, 27-29, 33, 34, 38, 47, 84, 98, 132, 256, 273, 290, 293, 295, 296, 300,

303, 314, 317-319, 323-326, 328

femme fatale, 136, 217

fin de siècle, 366

Fletcher, Phineas, 15, 39, 44, 145, 167, 174, 196, 373

"Frauds on the Fairies," 279, 285

Freud, Sigmund, 10, 93, 119, 121, 128, 129, 133, 137, 261, 308

Gaarden, Bonnie, 11, 289

Gabelman, Daniel, 11, 425

George MacDonald and His Wife, 5, 6, 49, 66, 116, 119, 138, 142, 276, 287, 288, 310, 362, 384, 405, 4390

George MacDonald: 365 Readings, 7

German Romanticism, 4, 23, 49, 169, 178, 274

German Romantics, 122, 170, 171, 183, 268, 289, 378

German Theology, 169, 170

God, 9, 54-57, 60-62, 64, 65, 75, 78, 79, 86, 87, 93, 96, 97, 110, 111, 113-115, 119, 120, 133, 134, 137, 142, 150, 157, 160, 162, 163, 165, 166, 192, 230-235, 241, 243, 249, 275, 284, 285, 289, 290, 292, 294, 295, 297, 299, 301-303, 305, 306-309, 318, 323, 329, 353, 355, 360, 371, 374, 376-379, 382, 387-389, 391, 392, 394-396, 398, 399-405, 407-409, 413, 414, 416, 419-421

Goethe, 31, 35, 36, 45, 49, 145, 171, 178, 179, 182, 183, 185-188, 192, 193, 268, 269, 274, 277

Good Words for the Young, 283

goodness, 8, 137, 164, 387-89, 391, 393, 395, 397-399, 401, 402, 404

Gray, William, 11, 261, 332, 410, 422

Gunther, Adrian, 11, 241, 355, 357-360, 407, 422

Hard Times, 2, 279-282, 285, 287

Hawthorne, Nathaniel, 1, 2

Hegel, 170, 185, 188, 194, 289, 290

Hein, Rolland, 11, 69, 140, 150, 151, 164, 167, 192, 288, 322, 332, 361, 392, 396, 426, 435

Heine, Heinrich, 145, 178, 187, 215

Heinrich von Ofterdingen, 30, 34, 50, 116, 216, 265, 291, 295

hero, 7, 15, 17-19, 21, 26-27, 30-31, 35, 38, 41, 43, 45-47, 50, 56-57, 64, 70, 87, 95, 98-100, 104, 107, 113, 117, 125, 128-131, 140, 142, 162, 165, 172, 177, 182-183, 185-187, 196, 262, 272, 293, 296, 300, 304, 323, 329, 348, 359, 360, 368, 381

Hill, Octavia, 53, 367

Hoffmann, E. T. A., 15, 27, 46, 50, 96, 100, 116, 117, 122, 135, 136, 141, 142, 146, 178, 179, 187, 201, 227, 270, 291, 296

Holbrook, David, 150, 167, 261, 262, 263, 276, 277

Hughes, Arthur, 6, 92

imagination, 2, 3, 7, 8, 20, 27, 36, 44, 55, 57, 60-64, 69, 73, 78, 80, 93, 96-97, 109, 113, 115-116, 119, 121, 135, 137-138, 141-142, 146, 151, 160, 166, 174-175, 178, 188, 196-197, 199, 208-209, 215-218, 230, 232-233, 236-238, 241, 248-249, 251-253, 257, 269-270, 279-285, 291, 294-296, 298-300, 306-309, 322, 337, 355, 357-358, 367, 369, 374, 379, 407-409, 412, 416-418, 420-422, 428, 432-433, 435

Jauss, Hans Robert, 10-11

Jung, Carl, 23-25, 27, 29, 33-34, 37, 48-49, 92, 98, 116-118, 120-121, 129-131, 133-134, 137, 140, 210, 261, 276, 291, 295, 297, 304, 410

Kant, 170, 180

Keats, John, 20, 215

Kingsley, Charles, 5, 53, 95-96, 201

Klein, Melanie, 10, 261-262, 269

knight, 18, 21, 31, 40-45, 63-64, 73, 75-76, 83, 85-86, 88-90, 99, 102, 103, 112, 124, 125-126, 129, 130-131, 141, 154, 199-200, 202, 204, 252, 266, 267, 271, 273, 293, 296, 298, 303-305, 308, 309, 313, 324-329, 343-345, 350, 375, 415-416, 420

Kohut, Heinz, 122, 125-129, 133, 136, 139

Kristeva, Julia, 10, 261-273, 275-278, 410

Lacan, Jacques, 10, 261-263, 270

Levine, George, 3

The Realistic Imagination: English Fiction from Frankenstein to Lady Chatterley, 3

Lewis, C. S., 3, 5, 7-11, 15, 48, 54, 66-67, 69, 95-96, 121-122, 133, 137-138, 151, 167, 171-172, 174-175, 178, 181-182, 188, 191-193, 201, 204, 206, 228, 234, 238, 283, 292, 360-361, 365, 370, 372, 374, 378, 380, 382

The Allegory of Love: A Study in Medieval Tradition, 7

George MacDonald: 365 Readings, 7

library, 1, 23, 37, 61, 66, 79-80, 108-109, 154, 156, 158, 161, 178, 198, 207-209, 213, 217, 230, 235, 236, 252, 270, 299, 320, 322, 360, 371, 376, 392, 396, 404, 418, 426, 430-431, 436

Liebig, 336, 345-346, 349, 357-359

"The Light Princess," 15-16, 136, 201, 205, 229, 238, 430

Lilith, 1, 7, 9, 11, 15, 48, 54, 66, 77, 80, 83, 88, 90, 95-99, 104-115, 117-120, 129, 132, 138, 142, 145, 153, 157-167, 169, 177-178, 188, 190, 192, 210, 214, 235-236, 239, 274, 278, 341, 358-360, 371-372, 374-376, 382, 387-388, 395-396, 398-404, 411, 426

MacDonald, George. Works by

A Dish of Orts, 116, 138, 219, 236, 238-239, 260, 369, 371, 373, 378

At the Back of the North Wind, 11, 15, 53, 72, 87, 90, 229, 283, 290

"Ballad of Sir Aglovaile," 2, 83, 127, 156, 202

David Elginbrod, 62, 113

"The Light Princess," 15-16, 136, 201, 205, 229, 238, 430

Lilith, 1, 7, 9, 11, 15, 48, 54, 66, 77, 80, 83, 88, 90, 95-99, 104-115, 117-120, 129, 132, 138, 142, 145, 153, 157-167, 169, 177-178, 188, 190, 192, 210, 214, 235-236, 239, 274, 278, 341, 358-360, 371-372, 374-376, 382, 387-388, 395-396, 398-404, 411, 426

Paul Faber, 73, 335, 355, 357

Robert Falconer, 56, 62, 66, 298, 435

The Diary of an Old Soul, 156

"The Fantastic Imagination," 116, 138, 142, 284, 369, 374, 407, 433

"The Golden Key" (fairy tale), 10, 15, 16, 119, 132, 137, 164, 201, 231, 290, 375

The Portent, 98, 425, 435

The Princess and Curdie, 15, 119, 132, 242, 260, 278

The Princess and the Goblin, 15, 119, 137, 211, 214, 260, 278, 283

Unspoken Sermons, 54-57, 62-64, 66, 110, 115, 119-120, 134, 140-142, 219, 260, 282, 318, 436

Within or Without, 3

MacDonald, Greville, 5-6,

44, 49, 51, 53, 66, 97, 116, 118, 138-140, 148, 157, 161, 167, 178, 204, 206, 260, 276, 283-284, 287, 290, 335-336, 359, 366-367, 376-377, 410-411

Malory, Thomas, 18, 41-42, 172, 175, 187-188, 201-202

Manlove, C. N., 11, 92, 95, 116, 121-123, 134, 136-140, 142, 150, 167, 192, 210, 236, 261, 276, 327-328, 332, 357, 398, 407

Marble Lady, 28-35, 37-38, 41-42, 44-45, 72, 74-77, 81-82, 84-85, 131, 134-135, 137, 197-198, 217, 246, 250, 342, 346, 356, 419, 422, 429

märchen, 46, 97, 122, 146, 169, 227, 269-270, 278

masculinity, 40-41, 314, 316, 318, 320, 326-327, 332

Maurice, F. D., 53, 79, 204, 316

McGillis, Roderick, 11, 119-120, 142, 158, 160, 167, 207, 260, 278, 291, 309, 318, 322, 332, 335, 355, 357, 358, 360, 436

metafiction, 175, 178, 180, 183, 187, 223, 238, 277

mirrors, 37, 75, 98, 117, 127, 135, 140-142, 155, 209, 227, 251, 285, 305, 335-339, 345, 350, 353, 358, 360, 409, 427, 428-429, 431, 432-433, 436

Morris, William, 26, 63, 182, 185, 198, 376, 379, 384, 393, 472

Morte d' Arthur, 16, 53, 95, 172, 175, 188, 329, 365-366, 369, 374, 377

Muirhead, Graeme A., 11, 223, 357, 358

Müller, Max, 345, 346, 349, 359

myth, 8, 10, 33, 36, 37-39, 43, 46-47, 51, 54, 81, 175, 196, 230, 308, 365

narcissism, 121, 125, 139, 272-273, 291, 293, 295-296, 398

Narcissus, 37-38, 43, 50, 125, 235

Nerval, 31, 266-267, 269

Neumann, Erich, 23, 29, 33, 35, 41, 47, 49, 50, 51, 52

new gentleman, 313, 314, 315, 316, 317, 319, 322, 324, 325, 326, 327, 328, 330

nigredo, 407, 411, 413, 414, 417, 420, 421

Novalis, 15, 27, 30-31, 34, 42, 45-46, 49-51, 69, 96-97, 116, 122, 145-146, 150, 166, 169-172, 178, 184, 186-187, 193, 195-197, 200-201, 204-205, 210, 215-216, 225-228, 265, 268-270, 274-278, 284, 291, 296, 341, 378, 411

Oedipal, , 18, 23, 123, 124, 125, 263, 264, 265, 267, 272, 273, 308, 407, 422

Oxford Movement, 369

Pater, Walter, 365, 366, 367, 369, 371, 374, 377, 378, 380

Paul Faber, 73, 335, 355, 357

Pennington, John, 1, 11, 279

Percival, 68-69, 73-74, 83, 85, 95, 164, 212, 237, 276, 473

Percivale, 58, 59, 63, 64, 73, 75, 85, 88, 154, 202, 227, 266

Pilgrim's Progress, The, 65, 146

Platonism, 297, 387, 388, 391, 395

Plotinus, 48, 299, 398, 473

Prickett, Stephen, 11, 122, 134, 138, 169, 191, 193, 233, 239, 270, 277-278, 282, 314, 337, 361, 379, 387-388, 408, 426, 435

psychoanalysis, 9-10, 16, 126-127, 272-273, 276

Purple Island, 15, 44, 145, 174, 196, 373

Pygmalion, 19, 29, 30-32, 37, 230, 294

Raeper, Willian, 203, 205-206, 261, 276-278, 299, 407

Reis, Richard, 11, 15, 44, 48, 49, 51, 54, 67, 92-93, 122, 133-134, 139, 140, 210, 238, 261, 276, 407, 411, 416

Riga, Frank, 387, 391

Robb, David, 11, 145, 195-196, 199, 202-206, 234, 239, 278, 332, 365, 387, 392-393, 396, 404

Robert Falconer, 56, 62, 66, 298, 435

romantic literature, 20, 46, 50, 217

Roukema, Aren, 11, 407

Ruskin, John, 53, 95, 200, 365-366, 377, 380

Salvey, Courtney, 11, 387, 407

Searsmith, Kelly, 11, 313

Scenes of Clerical Life, 2

Schlegel, 170-171, 184, 378

Schiller, Fredrich, 145, 178-179, 187, 215

Schleiermacher, 145, 170, 178, 187

Scott, Sir Walter, 2, 313

Sehnsucht, 114

self, 3, 21, 37-39, 42-44, 58-61, 63-64, 70, 75-78, 80, 82, 84, 86, 88, 90-91, 98, 101, 104, 105-107, 110, 112-113, 115, 121-122, 125-134, 136-137, 150-153, 162-163, 165-166, 171-175, 179, 181-183, 185, 188, 195, 198-202, 207, 209, 211-215, 223-225, 228-231, 234-235, 253, 255, 263, 265, 271-273, 289-293, 296-298, 301, 304-306, 317, 319, 322, 324, 326-327, 329,

335, 354-356, 380, 388, 390, 393-395, 397-402, 412-414, 416-417, 420-421, 427, 429-431, 433

shadow, 4-5, 8, 20-21, 35-37, 60, 63-64, 77-78, 86-87, 91, 98-101, 103, 106-108, 113-115, 129-131, 133-136, 146, 149-150, 156, 161-162, 172-175, 186, 195, 208-209, 211-214, 224, 227, 230, 242, 244, 247, 252, 258, 263, 268-269, 272-273, 281, 283, 297-298, 304-305, 329-330, 340, 350, 355, 376, 393, 394-395, 397, 399-401, 403, 407-417, 420-421, 425-427, 429

Shakespeare, William, 38, 88, 145, 178, 180, 184, 187, 198

Shelley, P. B., 30, 35, 124, 145, 178, 195, 208-209, 215, 412, 429

Sigman, Joseph, 11, 23, 210

Sir Galahad, 126, 128, 130, 230

Soto, Fernando, 11, 335, 430

Spenser, 15, 18, 39, 41-42, 44, 145, 172, 175, 178, 188, 196-199, 201, 204, 283, 368, 372-373

spiral journey, 289, 307

St. Paul, 141, 350, 353-354, 432

Sussman, Herbert, 314, 318, 325

symbolic, 15, 21, 37-38, 83, 126-127, 131, 137, 171, 176, 178, 180-181, 233? 246-247, 251, 253, 262-263, 265-269, 271-274, 282, 287, 303, 310, 330, 378, 407, 410-414, 417, 419, 420-421, 427?, 272, 273, 275-279, 281-284, 292, 297, 313, 329, 340, 388, 417, 420-424, 427-431, 474

Tennyson, Alfred, 37, 53, 135, 204, 317-319, 326, 324

"The Carasoyn," 229

circuitous journey, 39

The Diary of an Old Soul, 156

The Faerie Queene, 18, 41, 43, 44, 129, 141, 172, 196, 197, 198, 202, 368

"The Golden Key" (fairy tale), , 15, 16, 119, 132, 137, 164, 201, 231, 290, 375

The Golden Key (critical study), see Wolff, Robert Lee

The Golden Pot, 27, 46, 96, 100, 141, 178-179, 291, 295

The Great Mother, 29, 34, 47, 49

The Portent, 98, 425, 435

The Princess and Curdie, 15, 119, 132, 242, 260, 278

The Princess and the Goblin, 15, 119, 137, 211, 214, 260, 278, 283

The Waste Land, 60

The Water-Babies, 5, 95, 201

Tolkien, J. R. R., 3, 5, 10, 15,

48, 54, 66, 95-96, 137, 181, 227, 238, 281, 373, 382, 427

Toward an Aesthetic of Reception, 10

truth, 1-3, 17, 19, 53-60, 62, 63-66, 70, 72, 74-75, 81, 83, 85, 89, 96, 97, 112-113, 133, 141-142, 149-150, 154-155, 160-161, 164, 170, 208, 213, 219, 221, 235, 248-249, 257, 259, 278, 280, 282, 284-285, 290, 296, 320, 354-355, 359, 368-369, 374, 376, 378, 380, 389-390, 413, 431-432, 436

Unspoken Sermons, 54-57, 62-64, 66, 110, 115, 119-120, 134, 140-142, 219, 260, 282, 318, 436

utilitarian, 2, 279, 281, 366, 380

von Franz, Marie-Louise, 131-132, 140

via negationis, 54

White Lady, 62, 63, 75, 98, 101, 102, 112, 114, 125, 135, 137, 149, 151, 153, 154, 219, 224, 225, 227, 230, 252, 266, 294-296, 298-301, 303, 305, 321-322, 325, 327, 345, 352, 391

Wilde, Oscar, 366, 369, 373, 377, 379-380, 382, 428, 432, 435

Wilson, Keith, 11, 53, 122, 134, 141, 219

Wilhelm Meister, 171, 179, 182-187, 192-193

Winnicott, Donald, 110, 261-262, 269

Wolff, Robert Lee, 8, 9-11, 15, 16, 18, 20, 23, 26, 48, 50, 116, 119, 122-125, 128, 132, 134-136, 138-141, 164, 167, 171, 190-192, 197, 202, 205, 261, 276, 278, 287, 308, 332, 407, 415-416, 436

Williams, Charles, 10, 48, 54, 66, 96, 192

Wise Woman, 28-29, 39-40, 43, 45-46, 50, 127, 131, 132, 149, 150, 154, 198, 202, 211-212, 227, 290, 321

Within or Without, 3

Wordsworth, William, 61, 145, 155, 174, 178, 185, 215, 290, 318, 378, 379, 408-409, 412, 428, 431, 433

Zadworna, Fjellestad, 223-224, 227-228, 232, 236

OTHER BOOKS OF INTEREST

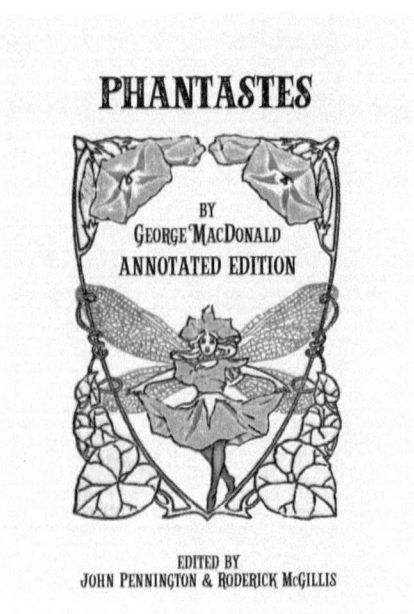

***Phantastes* by George MacDonald: Annotated Edition**
John Pennington and Roderick McGillis, Editors

Phantastes was a groundbreaking book in 1858 and continues to be a seminal example of great fantasy literature. Its elusive meaning is both alluring and perplexing, inviting readers to experience a range of deep feelings and a sense of profound truth. This annotated edition, by two renowned MacDonald scholars, provides a wealth of information to better understand and enjoy this masterpiece. In addition to the text, there are 184 pages containing an authoritative introduction, life chronology, textual notes, book reviews, and comparative source materials. With 354 footnotes to explain obscure words and literary references, this enhanced edition will benefit any reader and provide a solid foundation for future scholarship.

> A good critical edition of George MacDonald's *Phantastes* has long been needed, and now we have it. This fine, comprehensive edition provides an accessible and illuminating introduction to this profound work.
>
> —Colin Manlove, author of *Scotland's Forgotten Treasure: The Visionary Novels of George MacDonald*

C. S. LEWIS

C. S. Lewis: Views From Wake Forest - Essays on C. S. Lewis
Michael Travers, editor

Contains sixteen scholarly presentations from the international C. S. Lewis convention in Wake Forest, NC. Walter Hooper shares his important essay "Editing C. S. Lewis," a chronicle of publishing decisions after Lewis' death in 1963.

"Scholars from a variety of disciplines address a wide range of issues. The happy result is a fresh and expansive view of an author who well deserves this kind of thoughtful attention."
    Diana Pavlac Glyer, author of *The Company They Keep*

The Hidden Story of Narnia:
A Book-By-Book Guide to Lewis' Spiritual Themes
Will Vaus

A book of insightful commentary equally suited for teens or adults – Will Vaus points out connections between the *Narnia* books and spiritual/biblical themes, as well as between ideas in the *Narnia* books and C. S. Lewis' other books. Learn what Lewis himself said about the overarching and unifying thematic structure of the Narnia books. That is what this book explores; what C. S. Lewis called "the hidden story" of Narnia. Each chapter includes questions for individual use or small group discussion.

Why I Believe in Narnia:
33 Reviews and Essays on the Life and Work of C. S. Lewis
James Como

Chapters range from reviews of critical books , documentaries and movies to evaluations of Lewis' books to biographical analysis.
"A valuable , wide-ranging collection of essays by one of the best informed and most acute commentators on Lewis' work and ideas."
    Peter Schakel, author of *Imagination & the Arts in C. S. Lewis*

C. S. Lewis: His Literary Achievement
Colin Manlove

"This is a positively brilliant book, written with splendor, elegance, profundity and evidencing an enormous amount of learning. This is probably not a book to give a first-time reader of Lewis. But for those who are more broadly read in the Lewis corpus this book is an absolute gold mine of information. The author gives us a magnificent overview of Lewis' many writings, tracing for us thoughts and ideas which recur throughout, and at the same time telling us how each book differs from the others. I think it is not extravagant to call C. S. Lewis: His Literary Achievement a tour de force."
    Robert Merchant, *St. Austin Review*, Book Review Editor

In the Footsteps of C. S. Lewis: A Photographic Pilgrimage to the British Isles
Will Vaus

Over the course of thirty years, Will Vaus has journeyed to the British Isles many times to walk in the footsteps of C. S. Lewis. His private photographs of the significant places in Lewis' life have captured the imagination of audiences in the US and UK to whom he has lectured on the Oxford don and his work. This, in turn, prompted the idea of this collection of 78 full-color photographs, interwoven with details about Lewis' life and work. The combination of words and pictures make this a wonderful addition to the library of all Lewis scholars and readers.

Speaking of Jack: A C. S. Lewis Discussion Guide
Will Vaus

C. S. Lewis Societies have been forming around the world since the first one started in New York City in 1969. Will Vaus has started and led three groups himself. *Speaking of Jack* is the result of Vaus' experience in leading those Lewis Societies. Included here are introductions to most of Lewis' books as well as questions designed to stimulate discussion about Lewis' life and work. These materials have been "road-tested" with real groups made up of young and old, some very familiar with Lewis and some newcomers. *Speaking of Jack* may be used in an existing book discussion group, to start a C. S. Lewis Society, or as a guide to your own exploration of Lewis' books.

Light: C.S. Lewis's First and Final Short Story
Charlie W. Starr
Foreword by Walter Hooper

Charlie Starr explores the questions surrounding the "Light" manuscript, a later version of story titled "A Man Born Blind." The insights into this story provide a na ew key to understanding some of Lewis's most profound ideas.

"*As literary journalism, both investigative and critical, it is top shelf*"
  James Como, author of *Remembering C. S. Lewis*

"*Starr shines a new and illuminating light on one of Lewis's most intriguing stories*"
  Michael Ward, author of *Planet Narnia*

C. S. Lewis & Philosophy as a Way of Life: His Philosophical Thoughts
Adam Barkman

C. S. Lewis is rarely thought of as a "philosopher" per se despite having both studied and taught philosophy for several years at Oxford. Lewis's long journey to Christianity was essentially philosophical – passing through seven different stages. This 624 page book is an invaluable reference for C. S. Lewis scholars and fans alike

WWW.WINGEDLIONPRESS.COM

C. S. Lewis' Top Ten: Influential Books and Authors, Volume One
Will Vaus

Based on his books, marginal notes, and personal letters, Will Vaus explores Lewis' reading of the ten books he said shaped his vocational attitude and philosophy of life. Volume One covers the first three authors/books: George MacDonald: *Phantastes*, G.K. Chesterton: *The Everlasting Man*, and Virgil: *The Aneid*. Vaus offers a brief biography of each author with a helpful summary of their books.

"Thorough, comprehensive, and illuminating"
        Rolland Hein, Author of *George MacDonald: Victorian Mythmaker*

C. S. Lewis' Top Ten: Influential Books and Authors, Volume Two
Will Vaus

Volume Two covers the following authors/books: George Herbert: *The Temple*, William Wordsworth: *The Prelude*, Rudopf Otto, *The Idea of the Holy*.

C. S. Lewis' Top Ten: Influential Books and Authors, Volume Three
Will Vaus

Volume Three covers the following authors/books: Boethius: *The Consolation of Philosophy*, James Boswell, *The Life of Samuel Johnson*, Charles Williams: *Descent into Hell*, A.J. Balfour: *Thiesm and Humanism*.

C. S. Lewis Goes to Heaven:
A Reader's Guide to The Great Divorce
David G. Clark

This is the first book devoted solely to this often neglected book and the first to reveal several important secrets Lewis concealed within the story. Lewis felt his imaginary trip to Hell and Heaven was far better than his book *The Screwtape Letters*, which has become a classic. Readers will discover the many literary and biblical influences Lewis utilized in writing his brilliant novel.

C. S. Lewis Goes to Hell
A Companion and Study Guide to The Screwtape Letters
William O'Flaherty

The creator and host of "All About Jack" (a podcast feature of EssentialCSLewis.com) has written a guide to *The Screwtape Letters* suitable for groups or individuals. Features include a topic index of major and minor themes, summaries of each letter, questions for reflection, and over a half-dozen appendices of useful information.

Joy and Poetic Imagination: Understanding C. S. Lewis's "Great War" with Owen Barfield and its Significance for Lewis's Conversion and Writings
Stephen Thorson

Author Stephen Thorson began writing this book over 30 years ago and published parts of it in articles during Barfield's lifetime. Barfield wrote to Thorson in 1983 saying, ""*...you have surveyed the divergence between Lewis and myself very fairly, and truly 'in depth...*'". This book explains the "Great War" between these two friends.

Exploring the Eternal Goodness: Selected Writings of David L. Neuhouser
Joe Ricke and Lisa Ritchie, Editors

In 1997, due to David's perseverance, the Brown Collection of books by and about C. S. Lewis and related authors came to Taylor University and the Lewis and Friends Colloquium began. This book of selected writings reflects his scholarship in math and literature, as well as his musings on beauty and the imagination. The twenty-one tributes are an indication of the many lives he has influenced. This book is meant to acknowledge David L. Neuhouser for his contributions to scholarship and to honor his life of friendship, encouragement, and genuine goodness.

Inklings Forever, Volume X: Proceedings from the 10th Francis White Ewbank Colloquiunm on C. S. Lewis & Friends
Joe Ricke and Rick Hill, Editors

In June 2016, the 10th biennial Frances Ewbank Colloquium on C. S. Lewis and Friends convened at Taylor University with the special theme of "friendship." Many of the essays and creative pieces collected in this book explore the important relationships of Inklings-related authors, as well as the relationships between those authors and other, sometimes rather surprising, "friends." The year 2016 marked the 90th anniversary of the first meeting of C.S. Lewis and J.R.R. Tolkien – a creative friendship of epic proportions

> *What a feast! It is rare that a book of proceedings captures the energy and spirit of the conference itself: this one does. I recommend it.*
>
> Diana Pavlac Glyer, Professor of English at Azusa Pacific University and author of *The Company They Keep* and *Bandersnatch: C. S. Lewis, J. R. R. Tolkien, and the Creative Collaboration of the Inklings*

Mythopoeic Narnia: Memory, Metaphor, and Metamorphoses in C. S. Lewis's The Chronicles of Narnia
Salwa Khoddam

Dr. Khoddam offers a fresh approach to the *Narnia* books based on an inquiry into Lewis' readings and use of classical and Christian symbols. She explores the literary and intellectual contexts of these stories, the traditional myths and motifs, and places them in the company of the greatest Christian mythopoeic works of Western Literature.

CHRISTIAN LIVING

Keys to Growth: Meditations on the Acts of the Apostles
Will Vaus

Every living thing or person requires certain ingredients in order to grow, and if a thing or person is not growing, it is dying. *The Acts of the Apostles* is a book that is all about growth. Will Vaus has been meditating and preaching on *Acts* for the past 30 years. In this volume, he offers the reader forty-one keys from the entire book of Acts to unlock spiritual growth in everyday life.

Open Before Christmas: Devotional Thoughts For The Holiday Season
Will Vaus

Author Will Vaus seeks to deepen the reader's knowledge of Advent and Christmas leading up to Epiphany. Readers are provided with devotional thoughts for each day that help them to experience this part of the Church Year perhaps in a more spiritually enriching way than ever before.

"Seasoned with inspiring, touching, and sometimes humorous illustrations .... I found his writing immediately engaging and, the more I read, the more I liked it. God has touched my heart by reading Open Before Christmas, and I believe he will touch your heart too."
The Rev. David Beckmann, The C.S. Lewis Society of Chattanooga

God's Love Letter: Reflections on I John
Will Vaus

Various words for "love" appear thirty-five times in the five brief chapters of I John. This book invites you on a journey of reading and reflection: reading this book in the New Testament and reflecting on God's love for us, our love for God, and our love for one another.

Jogging with G.K. Chsterton: 65 Earthshaking Expeditions
Robert Moore-Jumonville

Jogging with G.K. Chesterton is a showcase for the merry mind of Chesterton. But Chesterton's lighthearted wit always runs side-by-side with his weighty wisdom. These 65 "earthshaking expeditions" will keep you smiling and thinking from start to finish. You'll be entertained, challenged, and spiritually uplifted as you take time to breath in the fresh morning air and contemplate the wonders of the world.

"This is a delightfully improbable book in which Chesterton puts us through our spiritual and intellectual exercises."
Joseph Pearce, author of *Wisdom and Innocence: A Life of G.K. Chesterton*

George MacDonald

Diary of an Old Soul & The White Page Poems
George MacDonald and Betty Aberlin

The first edition of George MacDonald's book of daily poems included a blank page opposite each page of poems. Readers were invited to write their own reflections on the "white page." MacDonald wrote: "Let your white page be ground, my print be seed, growing to golden ears, that faith and hope may feed." Betty Aberlin responded to MacDonald's invitation with daily poems of her own.

Betty Aberlin's close readings of George MacDonald's verses and her thoughtful responses to them speak clearly of her poetic gifts and spiritual intelligence.
    Luci Shaw, poet

George MacDonald: Literary Heritage and Heirs
Roderick McGillis, editor

This latest collection of 14 essays sets a new standard that will influence MacDonald studies for many more years. George MacDonald experts are increasingly evaluating his entire corpus within the nineteenth century context.

This comprehensive collection represents the best of contemporary scholarship on George MacDonald.
    Rolland Hein, author of *George MacDonald: Victorian Mythmaker*

In the Near Loss of Everything: George MacDonald's Son in America
Dale Wayne Slusser

In the summer of 1887, George MacDonald's son Ronald, newly engaged to artist Louise Blandy, sailed from England to America to teach school. The next summer he returned to England to marry Louise and bring her back to America. On August 27, 1890, Louise died leaving him with an infant daughter. Ronald once described losing a beloved spouse as "the near loss of everything". Dale Wayne Slusser unfolds this poignant story with unpublished letters and photos that give readers a glimpse into the close-knit MacDonald family. Also included is Ronald's essay about his father, *George MacDonald: A Personal Note*, plus a selection from Ronald's 1922 fable, *The Laughing Elf*, about the necessity of both sorrow and joy in life.

A Novel Pulpit: Sermons From George MacDonald's Fiction
David L. Neuhouser

Each of the sermons has an introduction giving some explanation of the setting of the sermon or of the plot, if that is necessary for understanding the sermon. "MacDonald's novels are both stimulating and thought-provoking. This collection of sermons from ten novels serve to bring out the 'freshness and brilliance' of MacDonald's message." from the author's introduction

Behind the Back of the North Wind: Essays on George MacDonald's Classic Book
Edited and with Introduction by John Pennington and Roderick McGillis

The unique blend of fairy tale atmosphere and social realism in this novel laid the groundwork for modern fantasy literature. Sixteen essays by various authors are accompanied by an instructive introduction, extensive index, and beautiful illustrations.

Through the Year with George MacDonald: 366 Daily Readings
Rolland Hein, editor

These page-length excerpts from sermons, novels and letters are given an appropriate theme/heading and a complementary Scripture passage for daily reading. An inspiring introduction to the artistic soul and Christian vision of George MacDonald.

Shadows and Chivalry:
C. S. Lewis and George MacDonald on Suffering, Evil, and Death
Jeff McInnis

Shadows and Chivalry studies the influence of George MacDonald, a nineteenth-century Scottish novelist and fantasy writer, upon one of the most influential writers of modern times, C. S. Lewis—the creator of Narnia, literary critic, and best-selling apologist. This study attempts to trace the overall affect of MacDonald's work on Lewis's thought and imagination. Without ever ceasing to be a story of one man's influence upon another, the study also serves as an exploration of each writer's thought on, and literary visions of, good and evil.

POETS AND POETRY

In the Eye of the Beholder: How to See the World Like a Romantic Poet
Louis Markos

Born out of the French Revolution and its radical faith that a nation could be shaped and altered by the dreams and visions of its people, British Romantic Poetry was founded on a belief that the objects and realities of our world, whether natural or human, are not fixed in stone but can be molded and transformed by the visionary eye of the poet. A separate bibliographical essay is provided for readers listing accessible biographies of each poet and critical studies of their work.

The Cat on the Catamaran: A Christmas Tale
John Martin

Here is a modern-day parable of a modern-day cat with modern-day attitudes. Riverboat Dan is a "cool" cat on a perpetual vacation from responsibility. He's *The Cat on the Catamaran* – sailing down the river of life. Dan keeps his guilty conscience from interfering with his fun until he runs into trouble. But will he have the courage to believe that it's never too late to change course? (For ages 10 to adult)

Pop Culture

To Love Another Person: A Spiritual Journey Through Les Miserables
John Morrison

The powerful story of Jean Valjean's redemption is beloved by readers and theater goers everywhere. In this companion and guide to Victor Hugo's masterpiece, author John Morrison unfolds the spiritual depth and breadth of this classic novel and broadway musical.

Through Common Things: Philosophical Reflections on Popular Culture
Adam Barkman

"Barkman presents us with an amazingly wide-ranging collection of philosophical reflections grounded in the everyday things of popular culture – past and present, eastern and western, factual and fictional. Throughout his encounters with often surprising subject-matter (the value of darkness?), he writes clearly and concisely, moving seamlessly between Aristotle and anime, Lord Buddha and Lord Voldemort... . This is an informative and entertaining book to read!"
 Doug Bloomberg, Professor of Philosophy, Institute for Christian Studies

Spotlight:
A Close-up Look at the Artistry and Meaning of Stephenie Meyer's Twilight Novels
John Granger

Stephenie Meyer's *Twilight* saga has taken the world by storm. But is there more to *Twilight* than a love story for teen girls crossed with a cheesy vampire-werewolf drama? *Spotlight* reveals the literary backdrop, themes, artistry, and meaning of the four Bella Swan adventures. *Spotlight* is the perfect gift for serious *Twilight* readers.

The Many Faces of Katniss Everdeen: Exploring the Heroine of The Hunger Games
Valerie Estelle Frankel

Katniss is the heroine who's changed the world. Like Harry Potter, she explodes across genres: She is a dystopian heroine, a warrior woman, a reality TV star, a rebellious adolescent. She's surrounded by the figures of Roman history, from Caesar and Cato to Cinna and Coriolanus Snow. She's also traveling the classic heroine's journey. As a child soldier, she faces trauma; as a growing teen, she battles through love triangles and the struggle to be good in a harsh world. This book explores all this and more, while taking a look at the series' symbolism, from food to storytelling, to show how Katniss becomes the greatest power of Panem, the girl on fire.

Myths and Motifs of The Mortal Instruments
Valerie Estelle Frankel

With vampires, fairies, angels, romance, steampunk, and modern New York all in one series of books, Cassandra Clare is exploding onto the scene. This book explores the deeper world of the Shadowhunters. There's something for everyone, as this book reveals unseen lore within the bestselling series.

Virtuous Worlds: The Video Gamer's Guide to Spiritual Truth
John Stanifer

Popular titles like *Halo 3* and *The Legend of Zelda: Twilight Princess* fly off shelves at a mind-blowing rate. John Stanifer, an avid gamer, shows readers specific parallels between Christian faith and the content of their favorite games. Written with wry humor (including a heckler who frequently pokes fun at the author) this book will appeal to gamers and non-gamers alike. Those unfamiliar with video games may be pleasantly surprised to find that many elements in those "virtual worlds" also qualify them as "virtuous worlds."

BIOGRAPHY

Sheldon Vanauken: The Man Who Received "A Severe Mercy"
Will Vaus

In this biography we discover: Vanauken the struggling student, the bon-vivant lover, the sailor who witnessed the bombing of Pearl Harbor, the seeker who returned to faith through C. S. Lewis, the beloved professor of English literature and history, the feminist and anti-war activist who participated in the March on the Pentagon, the bestselling author, and Vanauken the convert to Catholicism. What emerges is the portrait of a man relentlessly in search of beauty, love, and truth, a man who believed that, in the end, he found all three.

"This is a charming biography about a doubly charming man who wrote a triply charming book. It is a great way to meet the man behind A Severe Mercy."

Peter Kreeft, author of *Jacob's Ladder: 10 Steps to Truth*

Remembering Roy Campbell: The Memoirs of his Daughters, Anna and Tess
Introduction by Judith Lütge Coullie, Editor
Preface by Joseph Pearce

Anna and Teresa Campbell were the daughters of the handsome young South African poet and writer, Roy Campbell (1901-1957), and his beautiful English wife, Mary Garman. In their frank and moving memoirs, Anna and Tess recall the extraordinary, and often very difficult, lives they shared with their exceptional parents. Over 50 photos, 344 footnotes, timeline of Campbell's life, and complete index.

HARRY POTTER

The Order of Harry Potter: The Literary Skill of the Hogwarts Epic
Colin Manlove

Colin Manlove, a popular conference speaker and author of over a dozen books, has earned an international reputation as an expert on fantasy and children's literature. His book, *From Alice to Harry Potter*, is a survey of 400 English fantasy books. In *The Order of Harry Potter*, he compares and contrasts *Harry Potter* with works by "Inklings" writers J.R.R. Tolkien, C. S. Lewis and Charles Williams; he also examines Rowling's treatment of the topic of imagination; her skill in organization and the use of language; and the book's underlying motifs and themes.

Harry Potter & Imagination: The Way Between Two Worlds
Travis Prinzi

Imaginative literature places a reader between two worlds: the story world and the world of daily life, and challenges the reader to imagine and to act for a better world. Starting with discussion of Harry Potter's more important themes, *Harry Potter & Imagination* takes readers on a journey through the transformative power of those themes for both the individual and for culture by placing Rowling's series in its literary, historical, and cultural contexts.

Hog's Head Conversations: Essays on Harry Potter
Travis Prinzi, Editor

Ten fascinating essays on Harry Potter by popular Potter writers and speakers including John Granger, James W. Thomas, Colin Manlove, and Travis Prinzi.

Repotting Harry Potter: A Professor's Guide for the Serious Re-Reader
Rowling Revisited: Return Trips to Harry, Fantastic Beasts, Quidditch, & Beedle the Bard
Dr. James W. Thomas

In *Repotting Harry Potter* and his sequel book *Rowling Revisited*, Dr. James W. Thomas points out the humor, puns, foreshadowing and literary parallels in the Potter books. In *Rowling Revisted*, readers will especially find useful three extensive appendixes – "Fantastic Beasts and the Pages Where You'll Find Them," "Quidditch Through the Pages," and "The Books in the Potter Books." Dr. Thomas makes re-reading the Potter books even more rewarding and enjoyable.

Sociology and Harry Potter: 22 Enchanting Essays on the Wizarding World
Jenn Simms, Editor

Modeled on an Introduction to Sociology textbook, this book is not simply about the series, but also uses the series to facilitate the reader's understanding of the discipline of sociology and a develops a sociological approach to viewing social reality. It is a case of high quality academic scholarship written in a form and on a topic accessible to non-academics. As such, it is written to appeal to Harry Potter fans and the general reading public. Contributors include professional sociologists from eight countries.

Harry Potter, Still Recruiting: An Inner Look at Harry Potter Fandom
Valerie Frankel

The Harry Potter phenomenon has created a new world: one of Quidditch in the park, lightning earrings, endless parodies, a new genre of music, and fan conferences of epic proportions. This book attempts to document everything - exploring costuming, crafting, gaming, and more, with essays and interviews straight from the multitude of creators. From children to adults, fans are delighting the world with an explosion of captivating activities and experiences, all based on Rowling's delightful series.

www.ingramcontent.com/pod-product-compliance
Lightning Source LLC
Chambersburg PA
CBHW021426080526
44588CB00009B/444